W9-CLV-632
REAL ESTATE$ 9TH ED.$ CINCINNATI
3 3311 00045 323 5

REAL ESTATE

PRINCIPLES AND PRACTICES

9TH EDITION

GEORGE R. KARVEL
Professor and Holder of the
Minnesota Chair in Real Estate
St. Cloud State University

MAURICE A. UNGER
Professor Emeritus of Real Estate
University of Colorado

COLLEGE DIVISION South-Western Publishing Co.

CINCINNATI DALLAS LIVERMORE

FW761A

Sponsoring Editor: Jeanne R. Busemeyer
Production Editor: Rhonda Eversole
Production House: Bookman Productions
Cover Designer: Barbara Libby
Interior Designer: Elaine Lagenaur
Marketing Manager: David L. Shaut

Library of Congress Cataloging-in-Publication Data

Karvel, George R.
Real estate : principles and practices / George R. Karvel, Maurice A. Unger. — 9th ed.
p. cm.
Includes index.
Authors' names in reverse order on previous ed.
ISBN 0-538-80651-6 :
1. Real estate business. I. Unger, Maurice Albert, II. Title.
HD1375.K34 1991
333.33—dc20 90-42879
CIP

1 2 3 4 5 6 7 8 D 7 6 5 4 3 2 1 0

Printed in the United States of America

PREFACE

The purpose of the Ninth Edition of *Real Estate* is to provide, in a clear and understandable manner, a thorough discussion of the theories and practices of real estate in order to facilitate better real estate decisions. The "why" and "how" of buying, financing, owning, and selling real estate are emphasized.

Beyond clarity of writing, the authors have emphasized the language of real estate. Each chapter begins by identifying key terms to be understood. Each key term is defined and discussed in the chapter. For quick reference, key term definitions may be found in the glossary following each chapter.

The book has been written for undergraduate students, future real estate licensees, investors, practitioners, and other people simply wanting to know more about real estate. *Real Estate* is dynamic, incorporating knowledge of economics, social conditions, and problems within a legal framework. These broad concepts have been integrated with the practice of real estate appraisal, mortgage lending, investment, brokerage, development, and property management.

This edition is completely revised to reflect the most current developments in real estate. Some of the new topics are:

- Affordability and declining levels of home ownership
- Demographic change due to aging "baby boomers" and migration patterns
- Limitation on planning and zoning imposed by the First English and Nollan decisions
- Environmental hazard audits for appraisers and developers, including radon
- Essential locational factors for commercial and industrial site selection
- Residential leases and security deposit agreements
- Comparison of terms for various types of mortgages
- Savings and Loan crisis, Resolution Trust Corporation, and the evolving role of mortgage bankers as loan originators, underwriters, and servicers

- Current tax law and recent changes, as well as "tax-free" exchanges
- Net Present Value, Internal Rate of Return, and linear regression models
- Asset management
- Changing characteristics of the American home
- Community housing
- Schematic diagrams of the closing process
- The role of insurance in real estate

A significant complement to the Ninth Edition is a computer software package, which is provided free to users of this book. Beyond the fundamental tools of present value analysis, the software includes programs for loan amortization; buyer qualification for VA, FHA, and conventional mortgages; rent vs. buy analysis for residential property; and real estate investment analysis. These tools are fully integrated with the written material, and end-of-chapter exercises are provided for the appropriate chapters. Problems that can be solved by the software are designated by a disk icon.

We believe that the introduction of computer software facilitates computer literacy and makes learning easier and more fun. Consistent with our objectives in presenting *Real Estate* in an understandable manner, the computer software is user friendly. Readers will find that the software will help their real estate investing, financing, and home ownership decisions for years to come.

We would like to thank the many students, instructors, and practitioners whose suggestions have helped to make the Ninth Edition of *Real Estate* the best ever. We especially thank the following reviewers: Kenneth W. Beckerink, Alfred State College; Douglas S. Bible, Louisiana State University at Shreveport; Anthony B. Sanders, Ohio State University; Gala E. Waters, Southern Illinois University at Carbondale; and James R. Webb, Cleveland State University. We had fun writing the book. We hope you will enjoy reading and learning about real estate.

George R. Karvel
St. Cloud State University

Maurice A. Unger
Professor Emeritus
University of Colorado

BRIEF CONTENTS

PART ONE AN OVERVIEW OF REAL ESTATE

PART TWO THE BREADTH AND SCOPE OF REAL ESTATE

PART THREE PROPERTY RIGHTS

PART FOUR REAL ESTATE FINANCING, INVESTMENTS, AND TAXATION

PART FIVE PROPERTY VALUATION

PART SIX PROPERTY OWNERSHIP

PART SEVEN REAL ESTATE BROKERAGE

APPENDICES

CONTENTS

PART ONE AN OVERVIEW OF REAL ESTATE

PART TWO THE BREADTH AND SCOPE OF REAL ESTATE

PART THREE PROPERTY RIGHTS

PART FIVE PROPERTY VALUATION

PART SIX PROPERTY OWNERSHIP

PART ONE

AN OVERVIEW OF REAL ESTATE

1

THE ECONOMIC AND SOCIAL IMPACT OF REAL ESTATE

KEY TERMS

Appraisal
Commercial property
Consumer goods
Developers
Doubling up
Highest and best use
Industrial goods
Industrial property
Mortgage banker
NATIONAL ASSOCIATION OF REALTORS®
***Non*normal household**
Points
Property manager
Real estate broker
Real property mortgage
Rehabilitation
REIT
Shopping center
Standard Metropolitan Statistical Area
Subdividers
Urban planner

An aging population, homelessness, affordability of housing, falling levels of home ownership, and homes contaminated by the cancer-causing, invisible radon gas—these are the issues that will affect housing in the 1990s. Economic recovery in the last half of the 1980s was uneven and uncertain. The proportion of families owning homes declined each year beginning in 1980 (see Exhibit 1-1). Mortgage delinquencies and foreclosures were at their highest levels in 30 years. Nationally, vacancies in office buildings ranged from 8 percent in Cleveland to 40 percent in Houston. Agricultural land values fell 50 percent from 1981 to 1988, while construction costs continued to climb 4 to 5 percent per year. Notwithstanding continuing record federal budget deficits and a credit system damaged by poor lending practices and declining collateral values, never has the opportunity to succeed in all facets of real estate been better. In fact, the Japanese believed U.S. real estate provided a great opportunity: they invested $20 billion in U.S. property between 1985 and 1988.

Never before has an in-depth knowledge of real estate been more important to solving our nation's housing problems. The structure of future society is dependent on the effectiveness with which we use our real estate assets and understand and control the forces that affect them.

Exhibit 1-1 Homeownership Rate, 1970–1988

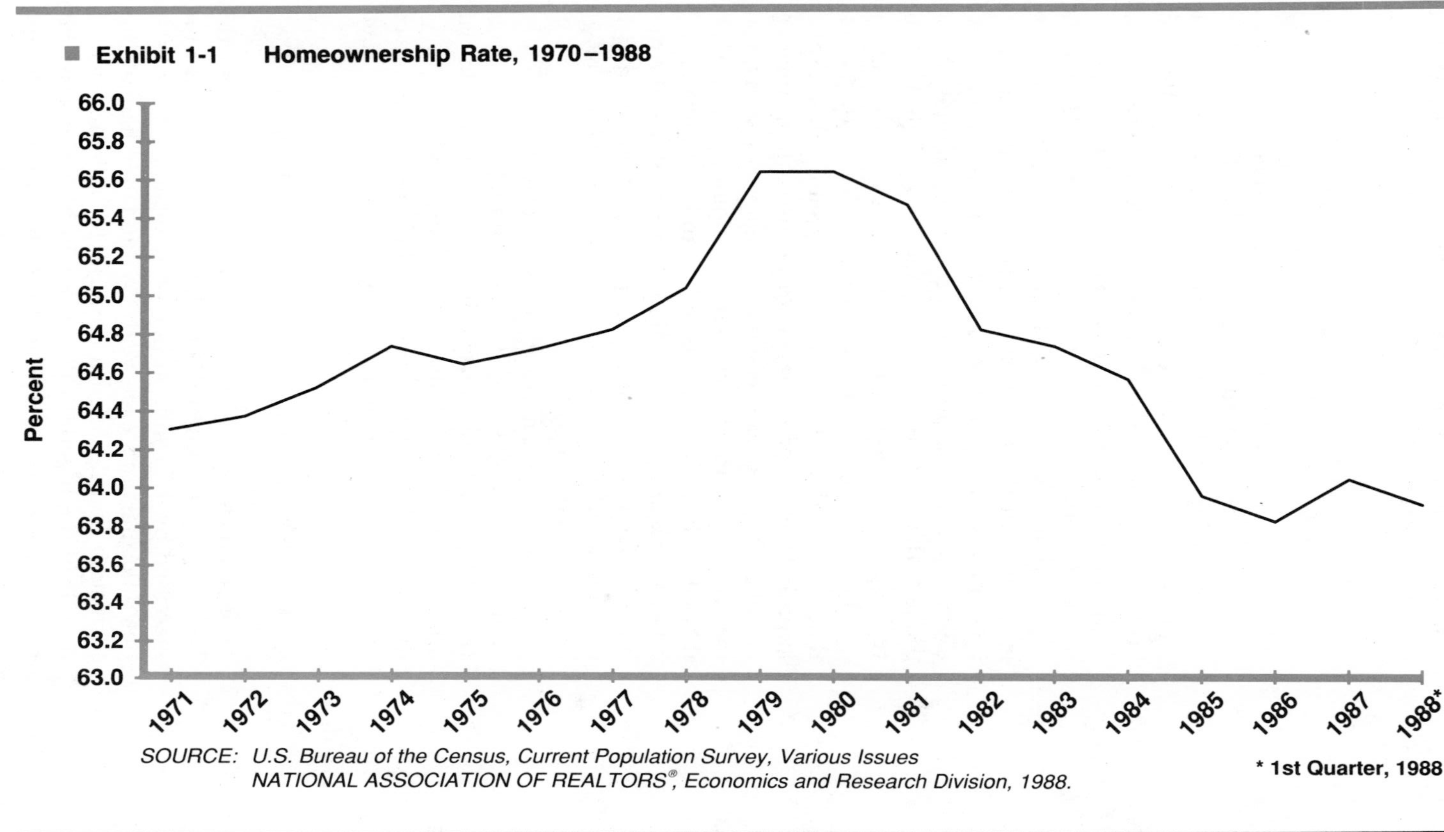

SOURCE: U.S. Bureau of the Census, Current Population Survey, Various Issues
NATIONAL ASSOCIATION OF REALTORS®, Economics and Research Division, 1988.

Adaptation, innovation, and change will characterize real estate throughout the 1990s.

WHAT IS REAL ESTATE?

Real estate is an integration of many specializations, an aggregation of disciplines resulting in a unique field of study. Real estate is the interrelationship of marketing, economics, finance, sociology, management, and law with the use of land and buildings. Real estate is more than breadth: it is the study of the specialized application of these disciplines to people and their use of real estate resources.

Therefore, real estate is the study of people, population, mobility, age distribution, divorce rates, shopping, leisure, apartments, income, profit, leverage, construction costs, highways, legal concepts, agriculture, value, investments, taxes, land use, zoning, industry, business cycles, sales, interest rates, inflation, and government regulations. Most importantly, real estate is the study of how these factors change, how these changes affect real estate, and how changes in real estate affect every individual.

The study of real estate also provides an introduction to information that may lead to a career in real estate sales, brokerage, investments, appraisal, property management, construction, finance, banking, or land use planning. As a consequence of real estate study, you will be better able to wisely purchase or sell your own home, to plan real estate investments that take advantage of tax benefits, and to understand the elements of real estate values and profits. Additionally, the study of real estate offers insight into the factors affecting property taxation, zoning, land use planning, environmental protection, urban redevelopment, and government assisted home financing programs.

Real estate is a massive industry. Private residential new construction alone contributes over $130 billion annually to our gross national product. In 1989, over 3 million existing homes were sold with a total value of approximately $270 billion. Over 16 percent of all U.S. employment is directly or indirectly related to real estate. Real estate constitutes over half our national wealth, and housing represents 27 percent of our real assets.

SOME SOCIAL IMPACTS OF REAL ESTATE

Population changes bring about needs and economic demand for housing. For example, during the latter half of the 1970s the number of households increased by 1.94 million per year, resulting in construction of 2 million new housing units each year. By the latter half of the 1980s, household formation had declined to around 1.5 million. Analysts forecast that the decade of the nineties will create new households at the rate of 1.1 million per year, with a corresponding decline in new housing construction.

The population pressures that created this need for housing may be attributed to (1) the post-World War II baby boom, (2) growing numbers of retired people living longer and independently, and (3) postponed marriages and increased divorce rates resulting in a booming "singles" home market. Table 1-1 illustrates the change in production of dwelling units over the previous decade.

When final figures are in, the population growth between 1980 and 1990 is expected to be 10 percent. The rate of growth over the past 20 years has been slower than in any period except during the 1930s. The numerical increase, however, of 22.8 million is the fourth largest growth recorded in any decade. Since 1980 our population has been growing by approximately 2.28 million people each year.

This yearly population increase is approximately equivalent to creating 11 cities, each containing 200,000 people. Each year in the present and foreseeable future, our country will experience a loss of over 1 million acres of prime agricultural land to strip mining, highways, power lines, and urban sprawl.

The phenomenal growth in residential, commercial, and industrial construction has taken place in and around **Standard Metropolitan Statistical Areas.** The Census Bureau defines an SMSA as "a county or group of contiguous counties (except in New England) which contains at least one central city of 50,000 inhabitants or more, or 'twin cities' with a combined

Table 1-1 Private Housing Starts (000s)

YEAR	SINGLE-FAMILY UNITS	FIVE UNITS OR MORE	MOBILE HOMES SHIPPED	TOTAL DWELLING UNITS
1976	1248	289	246	1783
1977	1573*	414	277	2264
1978	1558	462	276	2296*
1979	1316	429	277	2022
1980	962	331	222	1515
1981	797	288	241	1326
1982	743	319	240	1302
1983	1181	522	296*	1999
1984	1206	544	296*	2046
1985	1166	576*	284	2026
1986	1263	542	244	2049
1987	1212	409	233	1854
1988	1215	348	NA	***
1989	***	***	***	***

*Peak year

SOURCE: U.S. Department of Commerce, Bureau of the Census, Manufactured Housing Institute, and U.S. League of Savings Institutions.

population of at least 50,000." In these areas, comprising 1.7 percent of the total land area in the United States, lives over 70 percent of the population.

It becomes immediately obvious that most aspects of the real estate business, other than rural real estate, are concentrated about the 243 Standard Metropolitan Statistical Areas, constituting what is broadly classified as urban real estate.

With the growth of population, increasing demands are made on our water supply. The estimated industrial usage of water alone is well over 25 trillion gallons per year. Currently, over 55 percent of the nation is using water that has been used at least once before, and in some cities water is used as much as five times. Water is becoming more polluted, resulting in purification expenses, damage to fish and wildlife, recreation industry losses, and loss due to sickness amounting to an annual cost of untold millions of dollars. In addition, air pollution is making some cities dangerous places in which to live, and acid rain is killing lakes and forests.

Perhaps one of the greatest social costs of larger and larger cities has been pointed out in studies in the field of psychological ecology, the study of the number of people in a given space, their interrelationships, and their activities. These researchers have found that the larger the population, the less the involvement, the less the participation, the less the leadership opportunity. All persons—old and young—have more opportunity to serve in a small community. In growing metropolitan areas, people of all ages get less and less opportunity to become personally involved, with the result that more and more people feel useless and abandoned.

There has been much written concerning the "anti-growth" policies of some communities. To stabilize population, cities have imposed building moratoriums and slow growth policies and have refused to supply added municipal services. Additionally, minimum lot and home sizes have been set, and construction of multifamily dwellings have been prohibited or severely limited.

These constraints have been imposed in the name of preserving the character and quality of a community; e.g., growth is considered harmful. Although there is support for efficient optimal city size of 100,000 to 250,000, the character of a free society does not permit the massive centralized planning required to achieve this optimum.[1] The result of anti-growth policies is a restriction on individual property rights, which in effect contributes to exclusionary and discriminatory housing opportunities.

[1]George R. Karvel and Glenn H. Petry, *Optimal City Size,* Real Estate and Land Use Series, Monograph No. 72-5, Center for Real Estate and Land Use Studies, Business Research Division, Graduate School of Business Administration, University of Colorado, Boulder, Colorado.

RESIDENTIAL HOUSING

Four major factors involved in predicting the continuing need for residential dwelling units are population growth, mobility, household formation, and income levels.

Population Growth

Babies are being born at a slower pace than in the 1960s, but population is still growing. Every year, our population is raised by an amount approximating the population of metropolitan Minneapolis–St. Paul and its suburbs.

By the year 2000, some demographers estimate the total population of the United States will exceed 300 million persons. More conservative estimates place the expected population at approximately 265 million in the year 2000.

The actual population and demand for housing will be a function of how many children are born and annual immigration levels. The U.S. fertility rate and projection of the total population of the United States to the year 2080 are shown in Exhibit 1-2. Fertility rates have ranged from 1.8 to 1.84 since 1979.

Housing demand is also a function of population composition. As the baby boomers age, demand for products shifts with the population bulge they create. During the 1990s, baby boomers in their peak earning years are buying bigger homes with more amenities. Follow the baby boomers' impact on our real estate economy in Table 1-2. As the baby boomers reach age 65 in the year 2011, what is the likely impact on housing?

Mobility and the Rural-Urban-Suburban Migration

In the late 1770s when the United States was formed, 95 percent of our population was rural, living on farms and in small villages. Today, over 70 percent of our population lives in metropolitan areas. If those living in close proximity to our major cities are included, this figure jumps to 83 percent. Our nation's farm and rural population has declined substantially and approximately one-half of our 3,138 counties have lost population in the past ten years. By the year 2000, it is forecast that 75 percent of the U.S. population will live within 50 miles of the coast.

Population movement takes place in one of three ways: (1) within the same county, (2) within the same state but a different county, and (3) to a different state. When families move within the same state to a different county, they are likely moving to the city.

When movement is within the same county, it is most probable that the family is escaping city congestion for suburban space. One exception to this rule should be noted. Some families are moving to the city center and

Exhibit 1-2 U.S. Fertility Rate and U.S. Population

U.S. Fertility Rate
(Average number of births for each woman aged 15-49)

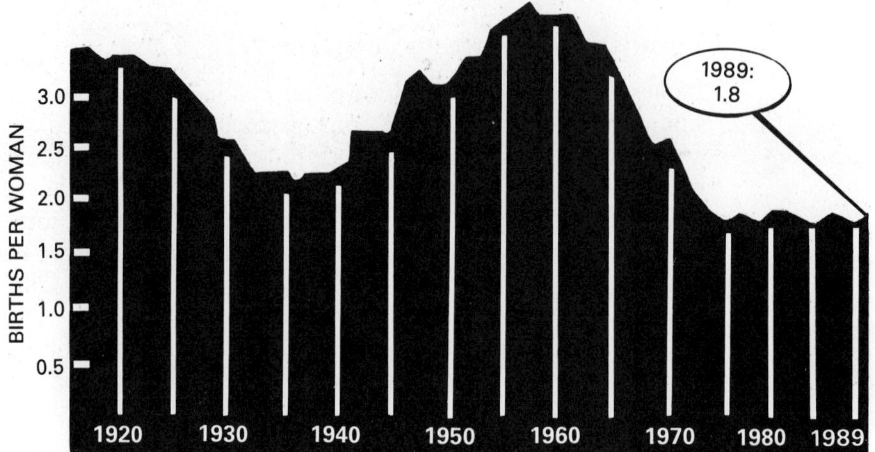

SOURCE: Population Reference Bureau and National Center for Health Statistics.

U.S. Population:
Three Possible Futures

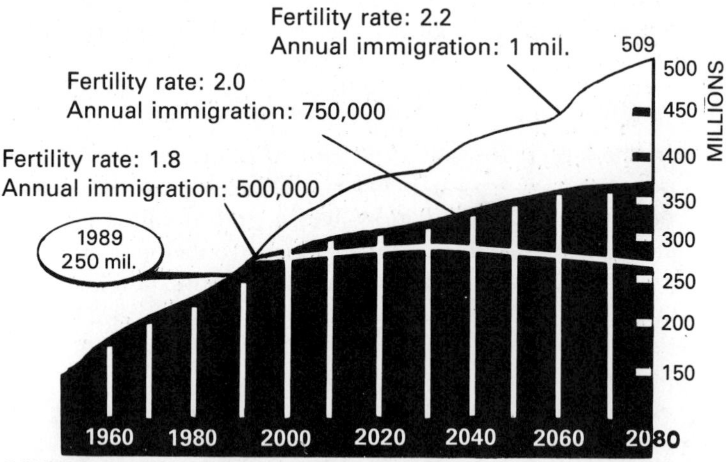

SOURCE: Population Reference Bureau and National Center for Health Statistics.

restoring turn-of-the-century homes in formerly blighted neighborhoods. This process of displacement of poor families by urban professionals is called "gentrification."

Table 1-2 Population Growth and Decline by Age Distribution—Percent of Total Growth

AGE	1949–59	1959–69	1969–79	1979–83	1983–87
Under 5	15.9*	<– 11.3>	<– 9.6>	18.7	6.6
5–15	40.2*	30.1*	<– 34.6>	<5.6>	.2
16–19	5.0	18.5*	11.4	<9.2>	<8.2>
20–24	<2.6>	22.2*	23.7*	2.9	<18.8>
25–44	7.9	3.5	67.6*	13.8*	86.9*
45–64	18.4	23.2	13.8	.3	6.9
65 and over	15.1	13.8	27.8	9.0	26.4*

*Baby boomers

SOURCE: U.S. Department of Commerce, Bureau of the Census, Population by Age Groups, 1929–1980. Table B-31, Economic Report of the President, January 1989, 343.

When families move to a different state, they are most likely leaving the populous East or Midwest to head for warm southern climates or the wide open spaces of the West or Pacific Coast.

Just as rural areas have lost population to large cities, our cities have lost population to adjoining suburban areas. Those cities that are experiencing growth are doing so at rates currently below rural areas and the suburban ring. Most notably, the growth of suburban areas during the 1950s and 1960s was greater than four times the growth of core cities and five to seven times greater than the growth of rural areas.

During the 1970s, rural areas and small towns experienced renewed population growth. The culture of the 1970s fled the city to avoid pollution, race conflict, school troubles, and the high cost of metropolitan housing.

Rural growth gave way to rural decline with the collapse of the agricultural economy in the 1980s. In fact since 1980, 86 percent of the nation's population growth has occurred in 282 metropolitan areas across the country.

The people in the United States are probably the most mobile the world has ever known. About one family in five moves each year. This means approximately 40 million people move every year, many of them to newly developed areas of the country.

The net effect of this migration is a decline in demand (hence value) for housing in those areas losing population. At the same time, there is an increasing demand (hence value) in those areas with increasing population. An analysis of the population growth of the 50 states from 1980 to 1986 is presented in Table 1-3. These growth patterns are expected to continue.

Out of 3,138 counties, 1,114, or 35 percent, lost population between 1980 and 1986. Exhibit 1-3 presents expected population changes, by state, during the 1990s.

Table 1-3 Changes in State Populations Since 1980

STATES ABOVE NATIONAL AVERAGE

	1986 Population	% Increase Since 1980
Alaska	534,000	33.3
Arizona	3,319,000	22.1
Nevada	963,000	20.5
Florida	11,675,000	19.9
Texas	16,685,000	17.3
California	26,981,000	14.8
Utah	1,665,000	14.0
New Mexico	1,479,000	13.8
Colorado	3,267,000	13.1
Georgia	6,104,000	11.7
New Hampshire	1,027,000	11.6
Hawaii	1,062,000	10.1
Oklahoma	3,305,000	9.2
South Carolina	3,377,000	8.3
Virginia	5,787,000	8.2
Washington	4,462,000	8.0
North Carolina	6,333,000	7.8
Wyoming	507,000	7.7
Louisiana	4,501,000	7.1
Delaware	633,000	6.3
Idaho	1,002,000	6.2
Maryland	4,463,000	5.8
Vermont	541,000	5.8
Tennessee	4,803,000	4.6
Maine	1,173,000	4.3
Alabama	4,052,000	4.2
Montana	819,000	4.1
Mississippi	2,625,000	4.1
Kansas	2,460,000	4.1
North Dakota	679,000	4.0
Arkansas	2,372,000	3.8
New Jersey	7,619,000	3.5
Minnesota	4,214,000	3.3
Missouri	5,066,000	3.0
Rhode Island	975,000	2.9
South Dakota	708,000	2.6
Connecticut	3,189,000	2.6
Oregon	2,698,000	2.5
Kentucky	3,729,000	1.8
Nebraska	1,598,000	1.8
Wisconsin	4,785,000	1.7
Massachusetts	5,832,000	1.7
Illinois	11,552,000	1.2
New York	17,772,000	1.2
Indiana	5,504,000	.3
Pennsylvania	11,888,000	.2

continued

Table 1-3 continued

STATES THAT LOST POPULATION

	1986 Population	% Increase Since 1980
Ohio	10,752,000	.4
Michigan	9,145,000	1.2
West Virginia	1,918,000	1.6
Iowa	2,851,000	2.1

SOURCE: Statistical Abstract of the United States, 1988.

Marriage, Divorce, and Household Formation

Much of the demand for dwelling units is derived from household formation. A household is an occupied dwelling unit. Households are divided into two distinct groups: households consisting of husband and wife, and households generally comprising single individuals, career people, divorced persons, widows, or widowers. Very often, two or more of these persons, whether related or not, will share the same household. One-person households have grown faster than normal households; 21.8 million singles now account for 28 percent of total U.S. households.

To a large extent, household formation determines the demand for dwelling space. Between 1800 and 1930, husband-wife households were about 80 percent of the total new annual household formation. Now, the new household formation consists of about 66 percent of husband-wife households and 34 percent of so-called ***non*normal households.**

During the recession that began in 1979 there was a significant collapse of many household units. By some estimates, the loss exceeded 1 million households. A high level of unemployment, coupled with high-cost housing, required many elderly people to move into the homes of their middle-aged children. Similarly, many young married couples and singles returned to live with their parents. This phenomenon, which occurs in periods of economic difficulty, is called **doubling up.** During periods of prosperity the process reverses itself. John Pfister, vice president and manager of market research for Chicago Title & Trust Co., has commented on this phenomenon with respect to "singles" age 20 to 34: "We have to remember that some of these households aren't fully formed." They can "double up and undouble, disappear and reappear."

Further details concerning "who buys what" are presented in Table 1-4. Homebuyer financial characteristics are found in Table 1-5.

■ **Exhibit 1-3 Changing Pattern of U.S. Population—Percent Change Expected 1990–2000**

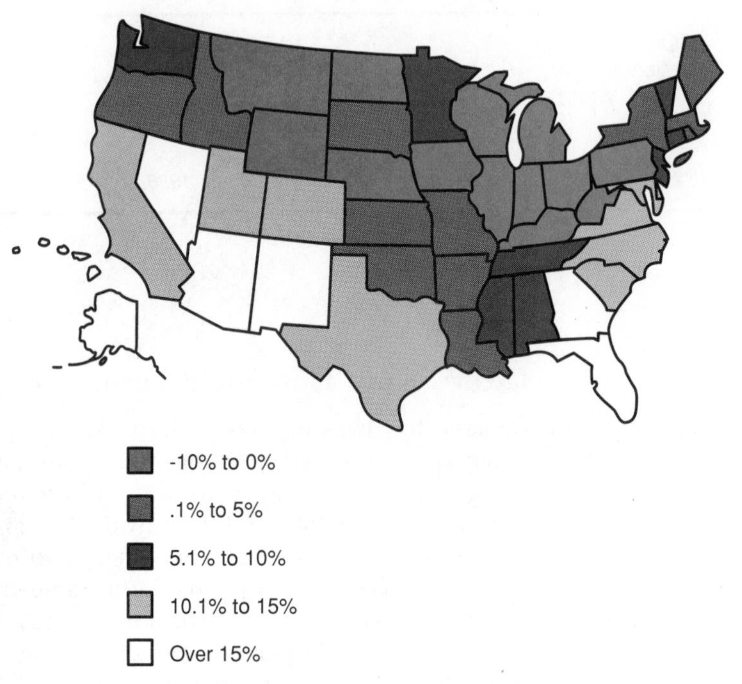

SOURCE: Statistical Abstract of the United States, 1989.

Income Levels

Disposable income is that amount left to individuals after taxes. The amount of disposable income of individuals has a direct effect on the demand for both used homes and new residential construction. Since 1950, disposable income has steadily increased. In the 1990s it is expected to be over 1250 percent greater than 1950 levels.

As a general rule, one might say that the proportion of homeowners in any income group varies directly with income. This means the more disposable income, the more home ownership, presuming, however, that the cost of home ownership has not increased more rapidly than income.

Other Factors Affecting Residential Housing

Costs. Within recent years, costs of housing have risen more dramatically than the costs of other goods and services. Since 1968, average conventional mortgage interest rates have increased from 6.9 percent to

Table 1-4 Homebuyers' Household Characteristics by Household Composition, 1984 and 1988

	SINGLES		MARRIED W/O CHILDREN		MARRIED W/ CHILDREN	
	1984	**1988**	**1984**	**1988**	**1984**	**1988**
Buyer Income						
Less than $25,000	29%	22%	11%	5%	7%	3%
$25,000–$34,999	30	26	26	18	23	14
$35,000–$44,999	16	28	26	20	25	26
$45,000–$59,999	9	13	19	26	21	22
$60,000 and over	16	11	18	32	24	35
Mean Income	$38,600	$39,700	$43,900	$50,000	$46,700	$51,300
Median Income	31,500	35,600	35,400	49,400	43,100	48,300
Buyer Age						
Less than 25 yrs.	8%	6%	7%	4%	3%	1%
25–34 years	58	54	54	45	62	39
35–44 years	22	24	23	22	28	51
45–54 years	10	7	6	12	6	8
55–64 years	1	7	9	14	1	1
65 or older	1	2	1	3	*	*
Median age	32.6 yrs.	32.8 yrs.	31.5 yrs.	35.3 yrs.	32.7 yrs.	36.5 yrs.
Buyers' Living Arrangements Prior to Purchase						
Rented	46%	51%	52%	40%	31%	33%
Owned	35	31	42	51	64	63
Lived w/parents	11	13	2	3	2	1
Unknown	8	5	5	6	3	3
Average number of children	NA	1.1	NA	NA	1.9	1.9
First-time buyers	45%	52%	42%	38%	23%	26%
Repeat buyers	55	48	58	62	77	74

*Less than one percent

Note: Components may not sum due to rounding.

SOURCE: NATIONAL ASSOCIATION OF REALTORS®, Real Estate Finance Division, "Residential Mortgage Finance Panel Survey" (Spring 1989).

approximately 10 percent, with fluctuations as high as 13 percent in the interim. The average price of existing homes in the same period increased steadily from $22,300 to $93,500. The combined effect has been to increase basic housing costs by approximately 550 percent since 1968. In the same time period, median family income increased from $28,199 to approximately $33,000.

Table 1-5 Homebuyers' Financial Characteristics by Household Composition, 1984 and 1988

MORTGAGE CHARACTERISTICS	SINGLES		MARRIED		MARRIED W/ CHILDREN	
(Averages)	**1984**	**1988**	**1984**	**1988**	**1984**	**1988**
Sales price	$60,000	$97,100	$88,500	$121,300	$106,300	$132,900
Down payment	18,300	21,300	18,600	33,200	25,800	23,500
1st mtg. amount	60,600	75,200	65,600	94,700	76,400	101,800
1st mtg. interest rate	11.86%	9.36%	11.84%	9.50%	11.87%	9.42%
Loan-to-value	78.6	81.4	81.2	81.9	79.1	81.9
Source of 1st Mortgage						
Assumption	17%	7	19%	6%	18%	5%
Commercial bank	8	15	9	15	8	15
Thrift institution	33	29	25	30	31	27
Mortgage banker	30	43	35	43	34	48
Private investor	2	—	1	2	1	1
Other	10	6	11	4	8	4

*Note: Components may not sum due to rounding.

SOURCE: NATIONAL ASSOCIATION OF REALTORS®, Real Estate Finance Division, "Residential Mortgage Finance Panel Survey" (Spring 1989).

Housing has become increasingly unaffordable. The relative cost of housing in 1968 and 1989 is compared in Table 1-6. Compounding the housing affordability issue, costs for property taxes, home insurance, repairs, and maintenance have increased at a more rapid rate than other expenses.

Regionally, the average price tends to be highest in the West and second highest in the Northeast, with southern and north central states ranking third and fourth, respectively.

One of the major social impacts of higher home costs is that new homes are becoming less and less available to lower income groups. At the same time, the prices of older homes have risen closely behind the prices of newer homes, suggesting that older homes are also not readily available to lower income groups. It is further suggested that a continued contraction in homes available for lower income groups might possibly increase political pressure for more direct government intervention in the housing industry through federal and state subsidized housing programs. Most certainly, high housing costs contribute to the homelessness problem.

Changes in the cost to construct a new home are presented in Exhibit 1-4. As a proportion of total home cost, the cost of building materials and labor have actually decreased, and builders' overhead and profit margins

Table 1-6 The Increased Cost of Housing 1968–1989

	AVERAGE CONVENTIONAL MORTGAGE INTEREST RATES	AVERAGE COST OF EXISTING HOMES*	PRINCIPAL & INTEREST 80% LOAN—30-Year AMORTIZATION
1968	7.0	$22,300	$118.69
1989	10.0	$93,500	$654.50
Increase	145%	419%	551%

SOURCE: NATIONAL ASSOCIATION OF REALTORS®, Economics & Research Division.

have remained stable. Besides inflation, the increased cost of new homes has been brought about by higher construction loan interest rates and increased land prices.

Government Housing Programs. Our national housing policy and the associated role of government have been to encourage and assist (1) the production of housing with sound standards of design, construction, livability, and size for adequate family life; (2) the reduction of costs of housing without sacrifice of such sound standards; (3) the use of new designs, materials, techniques, and methods in residential construction; (4) the use of standardized dimensions and methods of assembly of home-building materials and equipment; (5) the increase of efficiency in residential construction and maintenance; (6) the development of well-planned, integrated, residential neighborhoods and the development and redevelopment of communities; and (7) stabilization of the housing industry at a high volume of construction. These goals have been partially realized through government assisted financing of home purchases, regulation of interstate land sales, tax concessions, low-income housing subsidies, and urban redevelopment programs. The continued role of government in housing during this period of budget deficits is uncertain. What is certain, as illustrated in Exhibit 1-5, is that between 1970 and 1988 government-sponsored housing starts dried up.

Changes in Interest Rates. This area is discussed in detail in Chapter 14. The demand for residential housing is very sensitive to the level of interest rates. High interest rates reduce demand for two reasons: (1) high interest rates are associated with a shortage of money for home loans, and (2) high interest rates increase the cost of home ownership, causing marginal buyers to leave the home purchase market. High interest costs, coupled with record housing prices, require an annual income of over $30,000 to purchase an average priced home. The average wage earner presently cannot afford the average home in some areas of the United States.

■ **Exhibit 1-4 Cost to Construct a New Home**

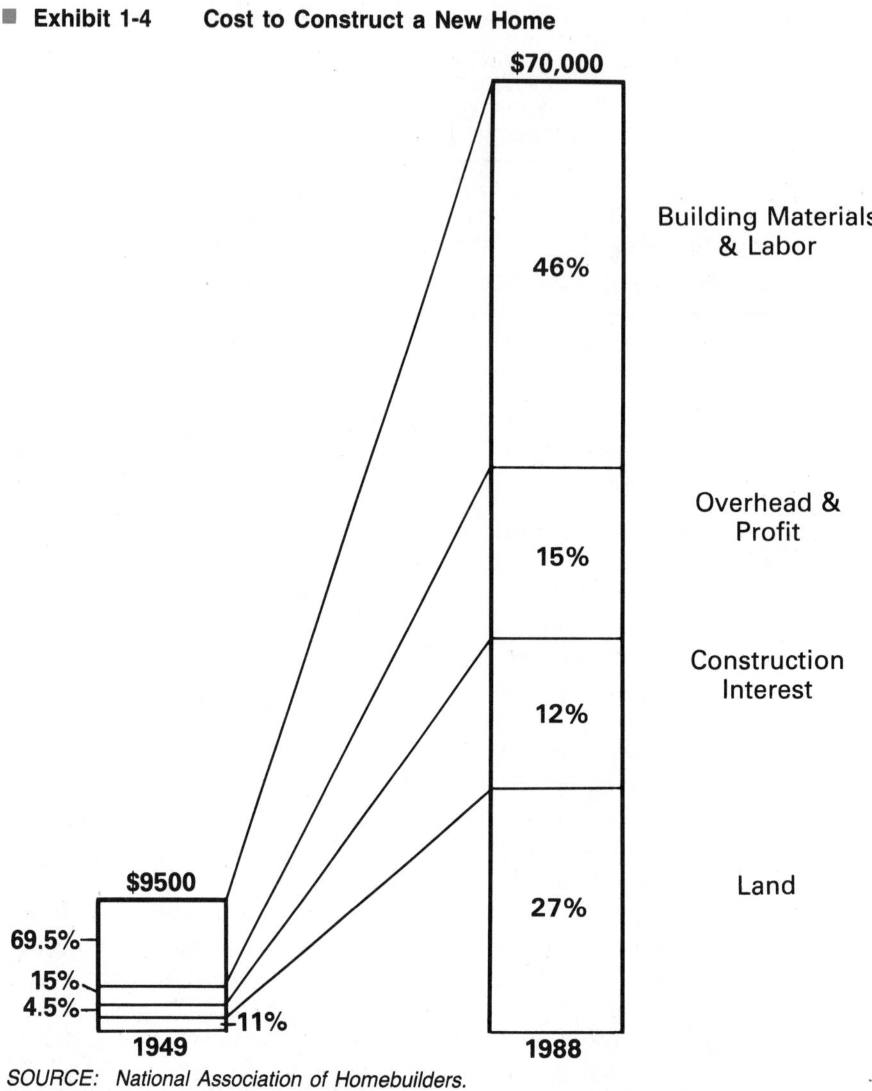

SOURCE: National Association of Homebuilders.

Technological Change. Power brownouts and the high costs of energy have brought about a revolution in the design and demand for homes. For example, Professor Thomas Bligh of MIT reports that when outside air temperatures are –25 degrees, an aboveground home with eight inches of glass wool insulation loses heat 6.5 times faster than an uninsulated underground home; with only four inches of glass wool insulation, the heat loss is ten times greater.[2] Homes lacking energy conserving insulation,

[2]Gregory King, "Getting Down to Earth," *Real Estate Today* (May 1981):16–20.

■ **Exhibit 1-5 The Decline of Subsidized Housing**

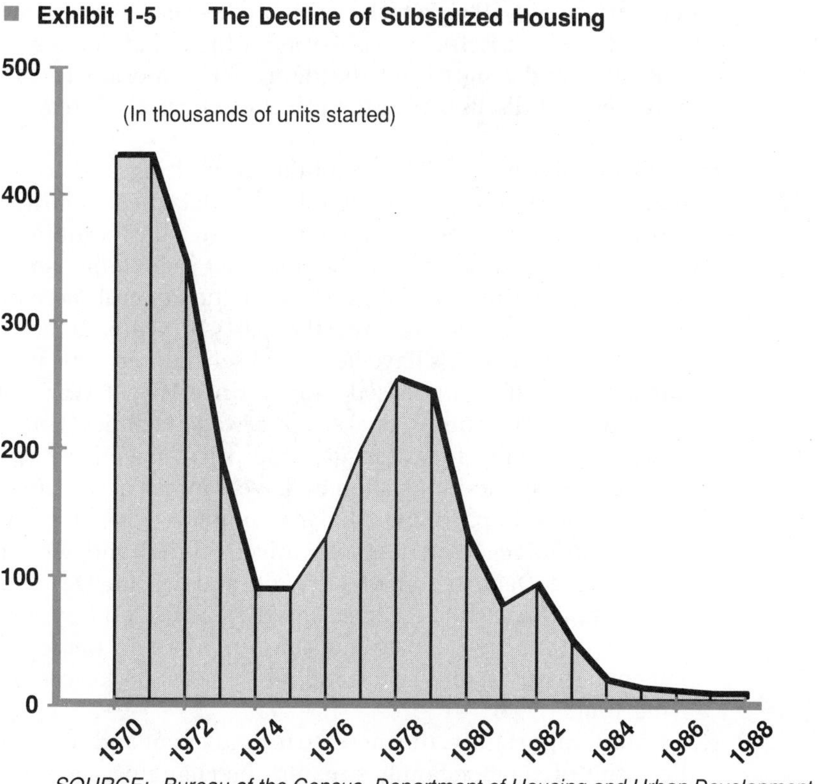

SOURCE: Bureau of the Census, Department of Housing and Urban Development.

thermopane windows, and solar heating systems are less in demand as high energy costs increase home heating, cooling, and operating costs.

MULTIFAMILY HOUSING

For statistical purposes, dwellings are classified as one-family or two or more family units. The latter classification (multifamily housing) includes rental units, townhouses, and apartment condominiums.

Until 1972, the trend had been toward construction of greater numbers of multifamily housing units. For example, in 1956 the total was 82,300 units; by 1964, this had increased 678 percent to 558,000 units; and by 1972, the figure jumped an additional 595 percent to 1.05 million multifamily units.

However, there has been a general decline in the construction of multifamily housing since 1972, with the exception of two bulges in construction occurring 1977–79 and 1983–86. The former was cut short by the recession of 1980. The latter was stimulated by the Economic Tax Recovery Act of 1981, which permitted 15-year depreciation, and was cut short by the Tax Reform Act of 1986, which limited tax-shelter benefits of real estate and lengthened the depreciation period to 27.5 years. For a more detailed discussion of the effect of taxation on real estate, see Chapter 15.

Generally, demand for multifamily housing and, consequently, construction increases when single-family detached housing becomes unaffordable. The cycles of single-family housing, multifamily housing, and mobile home shipments may be observed in Exhibit 1-6.

There are a number of reasons for the general increase in apartment and condominium living over the past 40 years. It appears that large numbers of individuals have become disenchanted with suburbia. Taxes in outlying areas have increased rapidly since World War II because of the demand for new schools, parks, and sewage facilities. Commutation fares, downtown parking fees, and gasoline prices have increased.

Costs of single-family homes have rapidly accelerated, making condominiums and apartments, having common walls and less land area per dwelling unit, relatively less expensive to build and sell. In 1974, a joint study by the Department of Housing and Urban Development, the Environmental Protection Agency, and the Council on Environmental Quality concluded that high density housing units use 44 percent less energy, 35 percent less water, and roads and utilities cost 55 percent less to build per living unit.

Most importantly, the increase in apartment and condominium living is the result of smaller family size and the changing age composition of the population. The median age in the United States is now 32.1, and newly formed households are typically demanders of small units, mainly apartments. Furthermore, among younger married people, the birth rate has declined substantially, leading to an increase in the demand for lower cost condominium units. These units require less down payment and less direct maintenance and have amenities such as swimming pools, tennis courts, and clubhouses that are unavailable to single-family homeowners.

In terms of numbers the second fastest growing age group is 65 and over. With their children having left home, these people seek the carefree living and smaller units found in apartment and condominium living. Examination of Table 1-7 reveals declining population growth and shifting age distribution through 1987.

COMMERCIAL PROPERTY

Commercial property has been defined as "real estate used for business purposes; e.g., office buildings, stores, banks, restaurants, service outlets."[3]

---

[3]American Institute of Real Estate Appraisers, *The Dictionary of Real Estate Appraisal,* 2d ed. (Chicago: American Institute of Real Estate Appraisers, 1989), 58.

Exhibit 1-6 **Housing Starts, 1976–1988 (000s)**

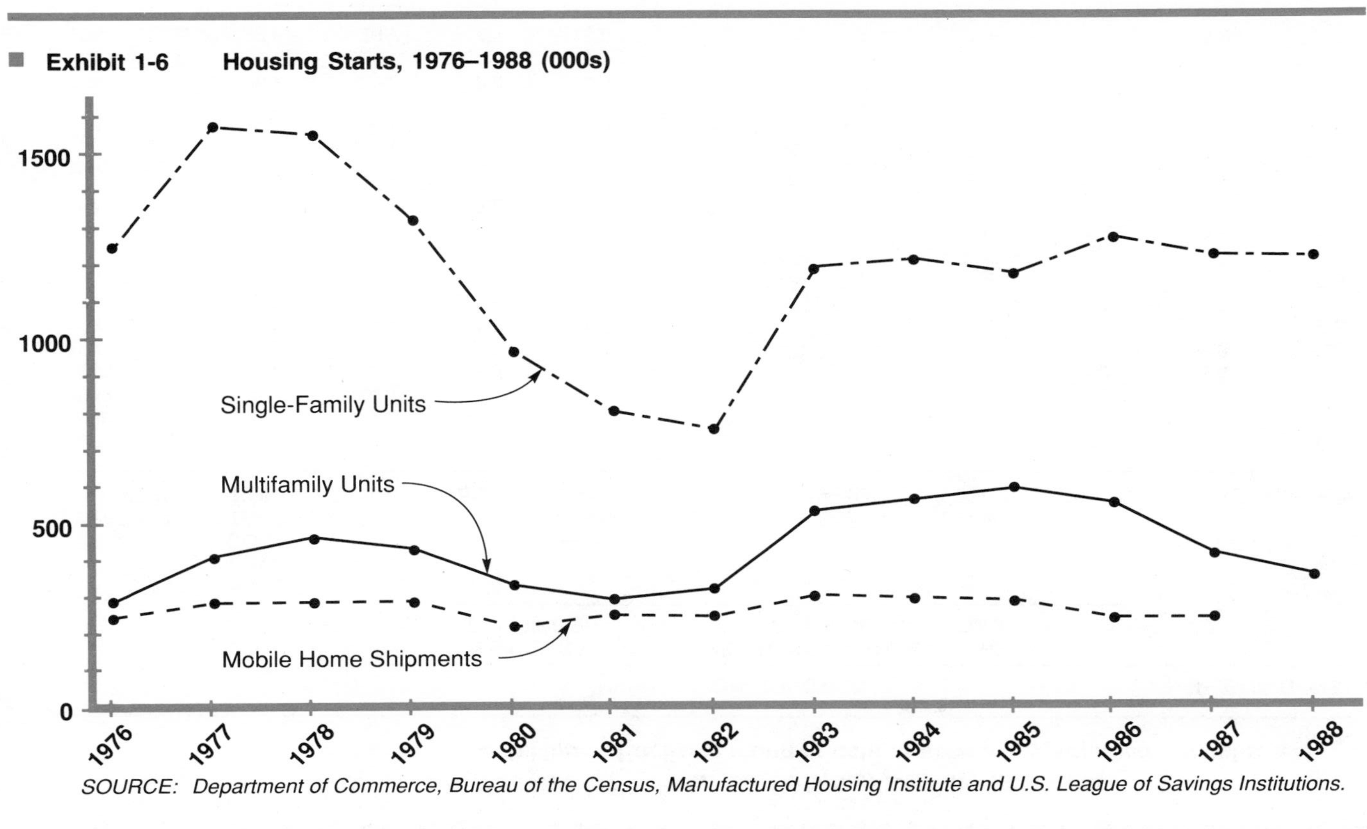

SOURCE: Department of Commerce, Bureau of the Census, Manufactured Housing Institute and U.S. League of Savings Institutions.

Table 1-7 New Construction Activity, 1929–1988

[Value put in place, billions of dollars; monthly data at seasonally adjusted annual rates]

		PRIVATE CONSTRUCTION							PUBLIC CONSTRUCTION		
			RESIDENTIAL BUILDINGS[1]		NONRESIDENTIAL BUILDINGS AND OTHER CONSTRUCTION[1]						
YEAR OR MONTH	TOTAL NEW CONSTRUCTION	TOTAL	Total[2]	New Housing Units	Total	Commercial[3]	Industrial	Other[4]	TOTAL	FEDERAL	STATE AND LOCAL[6]
1929	10.8	8.3	3.6	3.0	4.7	1.1	0.9	2.6	2.5	0.2	2.3
1933	2.9	1.2	.5	.3	.8	.1	.2	.5	1.6	.5	1.1
1939	8.2	4.4	2.7	2.3	1.7	.3	.3	1.2	3.8	.8	3.1
1940	8.7	5.1	3.0	2.6	2.1	.3	.4	1.3	3.6	1.2	2.4
1941	12.0	6.2	3.5	3.0	2.7	.4	.8	1.5	5.8	3.8	2.0
1942	14.1	3.4	1.7	1.4	1.7	.2	.3	1.2	10.7	9.3	1.3
1943	8.3	2.0	.9	.7	1.1	.0	.2	.9	6.3	5.6	.7
1944	5.3	2.2	.8	.6	1.4	.1	.2	1.1	3.1	2.5	.6
1945	5.8	3.4	1.3	.7	2.1	.2	.6	1.3	2.4	1.7	.7
1946	14.3	12.1	6.2	4.8	5.8	1.2	1.7	3.0	2.2	.9	1.4
New series											
1947	20.0	16.7	9.9	7.8	6.9	1.0	1.7	4.2	3.3	.8	2.5
1948	26.1	21.4	13.1	10.5	8.2	1.4	1.4	5.5	4.7	1.2	3.5
1949	26.7	20.5	12.4	10.0	8.0	1.2	1.0	5.9	6.3	1.5	4.8
1950	33.6	26.7	18.1	15.6	8.6	1.4	1.1	6.1	6.9	1.6	5.2
1951	35.4	26.2	15.9	13.2	10.3	1.5	2.1	6.7	9.3	3.0	6.3
1952	36.8	26.0	15.8	12.9	10.2	1.1	2.3	6.8	10.8	4.2	6.6
1953	39.1	27.9	16.6	13.4	11.3	1.8	2.2	7.3	11.2	4.1	7.1
1954	41.4	29.7	18.2	14.9	11.5	2.2	2.0	7.2	11.7	3.4	8.3
1955	46.5	34.8	21.9	18.2	12.9	3.2	2.4	7.3	11.7	2.8	8.9
1956	47.6	34.9	20.2	16.1	14.7	3.6	3.1	8.0	12.7	2.7	10.0
1957	49.1	35.1	19.0	14.7	16.1	3.6	3.6	9.0	14.1	3.0	11.1
1958	50.0	34.6	19.8	15.4	14.8	3.6	2.4	8.8	15.5	3.4	12.1
1959	55.4	39.3	24.3	19.2	15.1	3.9	2.1	9.0	16.1	3.7	12.3

1960	54.7	38.9	23.0	17.3	15.9	4.2	2.9	8.9	15.9	3.6	12.2
1961	56.4	39.3	23.1	17.1	16.2	4.7	2.8	8.7	17.1	3.9	13.3
1962	60.2	42.3	25.2	19.4	17.2	5.1	2.8	9.2	17.9	3.9	14.0
1963	64.8	45.5	27.9	21.7	17.6	5.0	2.9	9.7	19.4	4.0	15.4
New series											
1964	72.6	52.4	30.5	24.1	21.8	6.8	3.6	11.5	20.2	3.7	16.5
1965	78.5	56.6	30.2	23.8	26.3	8.1	5.1	13.1	21.9	3.9	18.0
1966	81.8	58.0	28.6	21.8	29.4	8.1	6.6	14.7	23.8	3.8	20.0
1967	83.5	58.1	28.7	21.5	29.4	8.0	6.0	15.4	25.4	3.3	22.1
1968	93.2	65.7	34.2	26.7	31.6	9.0	6.0	16.6	27.4	3.2	24.2
1969	100.5	72.7	37.2	29.2	35.5	10.7	6.8	17.9	27.8	3.2	24.6
1970	101.3	73.4	35.9	27.1	37.5	11.1	6.5	19.9	27.9	3.1	24.8
1971	117.9	88.2	48.5	38.7	39.7	13.0	5.4	21.3	29.7	3.8	25.9
1972	133.9	103.9	60.7	50.1	43.2	15.4	4.7	23.1	30.0	4.2	25.8
1973	147.4	115.0	65.1	54.6	49.9	17.7	6.2	26.0	32.3	4.7	27.6
1974	147.8	109.6	56.0	43.4	53.7	17.6	7.9	28.2	38.1	5.1	33.0
1975	144.3	102.6	51.6	36.3	51.0	13.9	8.0	29.1	41.7	6.1	35.6
1976	163.0	122.1	68.3	50.8	53.8	13.7	7.2	33.0	40.9	6.8	34.1
1977	188.0	148.6	92.0	72.2	56.6	15.7	7.7	33.2	39.4	7.1	32.4
1978	225.9	178.4	109.8	85.6	68.6	19.7	11.0	37.9	47.5	8.1	39.3
1979	252.4	200.7	116.4	89.3	84.3	27.1	15.0	42.3	51.7	8.6	43.1
1980	251.7	193.3	100.4	69.6	92.9	32.9	13.8	46.2	58.5	9.6	48.8
1981	260.2	203.6	99.2	69.4	104.4	38.0	17.0	49.4	56.5	10.4	46.1
1982	246.6	192.9	84.7	57.0	108.2	41.4	17.3	49.5	53.7	10.0	43.7
1983	281.3	227.5	125.5	94.6	102.0	41.0	12.9	48.1	53.8	10.6	43.2
1984	328.6	271.0	153.8	113.8	117.1	54.9	13.7	48.5	57.7	11.2	46.4
1985	355.7	291.7	158.5	114.7	133.2	66.9	15.8	50.5	64.1	12.0	52.1
1986	386.1	314.7	187.1	133.2	127.5	64.2	13.7	49.5	71.4	12.4	59.0
1987	398.9	323.8	194.8	139.9	129.0	62.8	13.7	52.5	75.0	14.1	61.0
1987: Jan ..	389.8	315.7	192.9	138.1	122.7	59.4	12.8	50.5	74.1	13.1	61.0
Feb ..	393.7	319.5	193.3	138.9	126.1	62.2	12.8	51.1	74.3	11.5	62.7
Mar ..	394.3	319.6	196.4	139.5	123.2	60.8	12.3	50.1	74.7	12.8	61.8
Apr ...	396.3	321.5	197.2	140.2	124.3	61.0	12.1	51.2	74.8	12.6	62.2
May .	397.9	322.6	195.8	139.3	126.9	62.5	13.6	50.8	75.2	14.9	60.3
June	392.6	319.5	193.5	138.6	126.0	61.2	13.8	51.0	73.0	14.1	59.0

continued

Table 1-7 continued

YEAR OR MONTH	TOTAL NEW CONSTRUCTION	PRIVATE CONSTRUCTION							PUBLIC CONSTRUCTION		
			RESIDENTIAL BUILDINGS[1]		NONRESIDENTIAL BUILDINGS AND OTHER CONSTRUCTION[1]						
		TOTAL	Total[2]	New Housing Units	Total	Commercial[3]	Industrial	Other[4]	TOTAL	FEDERAL	STATE AND LOCAL[6]
July ..	398.9	323.3	193.7	138.7	129.7	63.1	13.9	52.6	75.6	15.3	60.2
Aug ..	398.3	325.7	193.1	138.7	132.5	65.5	14.3	52.8	72.6	14.1	58.5
Sept .	405.4	327.1	194.8	140.0	132.3	63.7	15.3	53.3	78.2	17.2	61.1
Oct ...	400.8	325.9	194.5	140.7	131.4	63.9	14.0	53.5	74.9	13.0	61.9
Nov ..	407.1	331.5	195.6	142.3	135.9	66.5	14.5	54.9	75.6	14.3	61.2
Dec ..	410.9	331.6	195.8	142.8	135.8	63.3	14.1	58.4	79.2	15.8	63.5
1988: Jan ..	395.3	321.6	195.2	140.8	126.4	60.7	13.5	52.2	73.7	12.4	61.4
Feb ..	392.5	317.8	192.1	138.0	125.7	59.9	13.5	52.3	74.7	11.8	62.9
Mar ..	403.6	324.3	195.6	139.2	128.7	61.8	14.5	52.3	79.3	14.1	65.2
Apr ...	396.2	318.5	192.0	138.5	126.5	63.0	13.8	49.7	77.7	12.6	65.2
May .	398.5	320.2	190.4	137.7	129.8	64.2	13.9	51.8	78.3	12.3	65.9
June	395.7	317.7	188.1	136.8	129.6	63.8	13.7	52.2	78.0	14.0	64.0
July ..	401.8	322.5	192.8	136.4	129.7	63.1	13.2	53.4	79.3	13.2	66.1
Aug ..	402.8	326.2	195.8	137.2	130.4	62.6	12.9	54.9	76.7	13.5	63.2
Sept .	405.5	326.5	196.9	138.5	129.6	61.5	12.7	55.4	79.0	14.6	64.4
Oct ...	409.2	328.4	198.9	140.0	129.4	60.5	13.7	55.2	80.9	13.4	67.5

[1]Beginning 1960, farm residential buildings included in residential buildings; prior to 1960, included in nonresidential buildings and other construction.

[2]Includes residential improvements, not shown separately. Prior to 1964, also includes nonhousekeeping units (hotels, motels, etc.)

[3]Office building,s warehouses, stores, restaurants, garages, etc., and, beginning 1964, hotels and motels; prior to 1964, hotels and motels are included in total residential.

[4]Religious, educational, hospital and institutional, miscellaneous nonresidential, farm (see also footnote 1), public utilities, and all other private.

[5]Includes federal grants-in-aid for state and local projects.

SOURCE: U.S. Department of Commerce, Bureau of the Census and Economic Report of the President (January 1989), 366–367.

For the most part, commercial building follows the growth and movement of population. Trade is said to follow the customer. Shopping centers are a case in point. A **shopping center** is a tract of land, under individual or joint real estate ownership or control, improved with a coordinated group of retail buildings with a variety of stores and free parking.[4] Generally, there are four widely recognized types of shopping centers: community, neighborhood, regional, and super regional shopping centers.

With the flight to the suburbs, the universal use of the automobile, and congestion in the downtown areas of large cities, the shopping center became inevitable. The *Guinness Book of World Records* lists West Edmonton Mall, Edmonton, Alberta, Canada, as the world's largest shopping center. The mall cost approximately $900 million and covers 110 acres with approximately 700 stores and services, including entertainment and recreational facilities in addition to shopping.

In recent years, shopping facilities have shown an even more marked increase in suburban areas compared with the central city. The trend has been for a movement of amusement facilities—bowling alleys, drive-in theaters, swimming pools, and others—to follow the suburban pattern. Higher gas prices, however, have had an impact on traditional shopping patterns.[5]

Office space in central cities has been booming. Millions of square feet of space have been added. Not all growth has been in central cities, however. Various size office buildings and executive parks or complexes have also risen in suburban locations.

From 1962 to 1971, the growth in construction of commercial real estate was 216 percent. In the next decade, commercial construction activity had increased 637 percent over 1962 levels. In 1985, construction was a record $66.9 billion.

INDUSTRIAL PROPERTY

Industrial property is real estate used in connection with the manufacture of industrial and consumer goods. **Industrial goods** are goods used for further production, while **consumer goods** are purchased for immediate consumption. Industrial sites are particularly affected by business conditions in terms of the demand for both industrial and consumer goods.

In recent years, there has been a strong trend for industries to move from cities to the suburbs. Much of this movement has resulted from high taxes in the core of the metropolitan areas and lack of space for expansion. Some of this movement has slackened, however, as a result of increasing taxes in suburban areas brought about by the need for additional police

[4]*The Dictionary of Real Estate Appraisal,* 274.

[5]Rolf Christensen, "The Impact of Energy-Altered Shopping Habits on the Distribution of Retail Sales in Smaller SMSA's," *Proceedings of the Midwest Marketing Association* (March 1980).

and fire protection, sewage facilities, water mains, and gas and electric supplies needed to accommodate the new industries.

In no year since 1977 has industrial construction fallen below $10 billion per year and in several years it totaled over $15 billion. One of the current problems relating to industrial construction is the fact that industrial structures are rapidly becoming obsolete due to technological advances.

IMPACT OF CONSTRUCTION ON REAL ESTATE

The growth of commercial and industrial construction from 1976 through 1988 may be observed in Exhibit 1-7. New construction activity by sectors is reported for the period 1929 to 1987 in Table 1-7.

In a real sense, demand for commercial and industrial properties represents a secondary impact generally attributable to population increases and home purchases. But this impact is by no means limited to commercial and industrial properties.

Colean and Saulnier demonstrated this in their estimate that 100,000 new homes constructed at an average cost of ($119,000)[6] would cause the following direct economic impacts:

1. Site improvements, that is, sewage, streets, etc., at ($19,040) per home.
2. Other related buildings, that is, religious buildings and auxiliary streets at ($25,870) per home.
3. Service expenditures, that is, selling and closing costs at ($9,520) per home.
4. Special outlays, that is, furniture, shrubbery, etc., at ($25,900) per home.[7]

They further estimated that the construction of 100,000 new homes results in work to 95,000 on-site workers and 127,000 off-site workers.

SCOPE OF THE REAL ESTATE BUSINESS

Up to this point, our primary concern has been the economic and social impact of real property transactions with their many facets. We now turn our attention to a broad overview of the many ways in which individuals and business firms engage in the commercial aspects of these real property transactions.

---

[6]Data in parentheses added by authors. Figures represent an adjustment for price increases since 1961.

[7]M. L. Colean and R. J. Saulnier, *Economic Impact of the Construction of 100,000 New Homes* (a special study prepared for the U.S. Savings and Loan League, 1961), 3.

Exhibit 1-7 Commercial and Industrial Construction Activity, 1976–1988

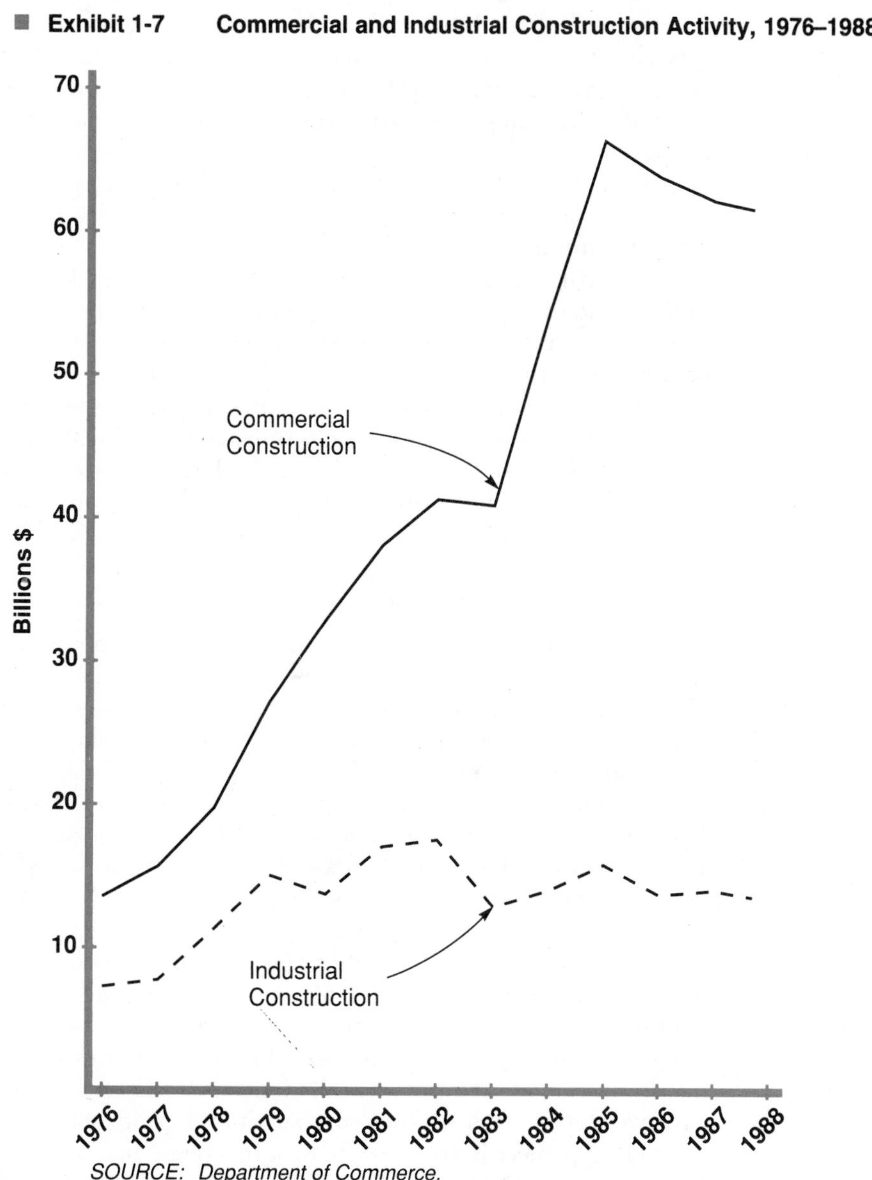

SOURCE: Department of Commerce.

Marketing Real Estate

When thinking of the real estate business, most people are apt to think of a local residential real estate broker whose signs are seen on the front lawns of homes. Of all the participants in the real estate industry, local salespersons and brokers who market residential real estate are most visible.

Commercial or income property brokers specialize in the marketing of apartments, office buildings, and shopping centers. Industrial brokers specialize in the marketing of land and buildings suitable for manufacturing, wholesaling, and warehousing. Their function includes the development of industrial parks. Farm brokers specialize in marketing agricultural property.

Legally, a **real estate broker** is defined as a person who, for a compensation, negotiates the purchase, sale, exchange, lease, or rental of real estate or any interest therein.

The broker is paid a commission, which may be a flat fee or a percent of the value of the lease, rent, or sales price of the property. Whatever the commission, it is negotiable and contingent upon the successful completion of the transaction.

Brokerage firms range in size from one- to two-person offices selling only existing homes, to huge monoliths specializing in all aspects of the real estate business. Annual sales volume for larger companies is in excess of $500 million. Commissions for individual salespersons range downward from over $150,000 per year.

Real Estate Finance

Purchasers of real estate rarely make down payments in excess of 30 percent of the sales price. Therefore, a major portion of the purchase price of each real estate transaction is paid for with borrowed money. The funds are supplied by federal agencies, life insurance companies, savings and loan associations, mutual savings banks, and commercial banks. Representing 11.3 percent of total mortgage funds supplied, credit unions, pension funds, real estate investment trusts (**REITs**), and individuals make substantial investments in real estate mortgages. The sources and uses of mortgage debt, which are presented in Exhibit 1-8, are discussed more fully in Chapter 14.

In practice, real estate finance takes two broad forms: mortgage investing and mortgage lending. A **real property mortgage** is an interest in real property as security for the payment of a debt or the fulfillment of an obligation. Mortgages are discussed in more detail in Chapter 9.

In mortgage investing, lenders lend with the expectation of profit on the investment. An insurance company purchasing a block of mortgages in a building project is an example of a mortgage investor. A company that lends money to the buyer of a property with the intention of retaining the loan in its portfolio is also a mortgage investor.

Mortgage banking has been defined as "the origination, sale, and servicing of mortgage loans by a firm or individual."[8] The **mortgage banker** earns an origination fee, paid by the borrower, for having obtained

[8]Marshall W. Dennis, *Mortgage Lending Fundamentals and Practices* (Reston, Virginia: Reston Publishing Co., 1981), 349.

Exhibit 1-8 Sources and Uses of Mortgage Funds, 1987

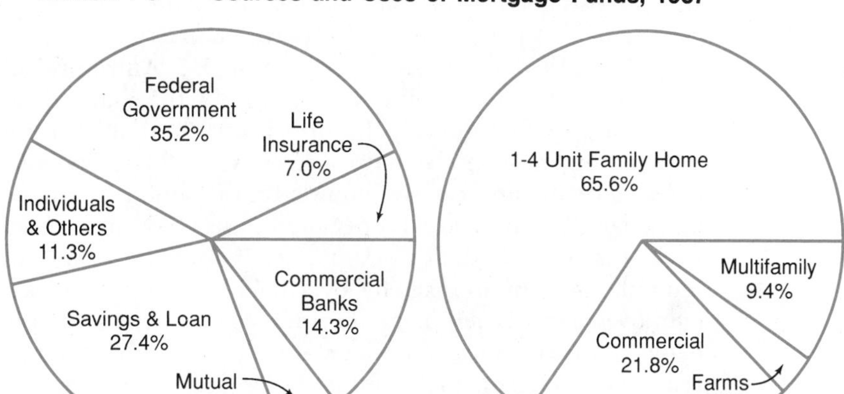

SOURCE: Data from Board of Governors of Federal Reserve System.

the money with which to buy. This fee is called **points.** One point equals 1 percent of the amount of the loan, two points equals 2 percent, etc.

After origination and sale of the mortgage to an investor, the mortgage banker collects the monthly payments from the borrower(s) and remits these sums to the mortgage investor. For this, the mortgage banker is paid a fee called a servicing fee.

There are some firms engaged in the business of mortgage brokerage. The function of these firms is to assist buyers and builders to obtain loans and negotiate the sale of mortgages to investors for individuals who wish to sell. Similar to the mortgage banker, the mortgage broker earns fee points for this service. A mortgage broker does not retain servicing.

To varying degrees, most commercial banks, savings and loan associations, and insurance companies act in the role of mortgage lender and mortgage investor. Mortgage bankers are primarily lenders while federal government agencies are principally mortgage investors.

Subdividing and Developing

Subdividers purchase raw acreage and, after having built roads, cut the land up into lots and sell the lots. **Developers** go a step further; they also build homes on the property.

Developing includes condominiums, apartments, shopping centers, and industrial parks. The developer acquires the property, obtains project approval from planning and zoning authorities, obtains financing, and supervises construction and project marketing. These topics are discussed in greater detail in Chapter 3.

Appraising

In appraising real estate an attempt is made to obtain a just and fair valuation of a parcel of real property. This is probably the most highly specialized field of the real estate business. An **appraisal** is the act or process of estimating value: an opinion of the nature, quality, value, or utility of specified interests in, or aspects of, identified real estate.[9]

The appraiser must have a keen sense of judgment, buttressed by experience and an extensive knowledge of economics, finance, and the real estate law. The individuals engaged in this work may be self-employed, in which case they do their work on a fee basis. Many others are employed by federal, state, or municipal governments or agencies. Most of those so employed are salaried. Large business firms, such as insurance companies, banks, oil companies, and chain stores, often employ appraisers in their real estate departments. Appraisals are used to support loan requests; to settle condemnation claims when governments exercise the right of eminent domain; and to facilitate the buying, selling, and leasing of real estate.

Property Management

A **property manager** acts as an agent for the owner by operating the property. The manager's major function is the operation of the property so that the owner is able to realize the maximum profit over the economic life of the property. Realization of maximum profit implies the preservation and maintenance of the property over a long period of time. Specific functions of the manager include renting apartments, collecting rents, maintaining the property, and making periodic financial reports to the property owner.

The most qualified property managers are those having training in the physical, economic, social, and esthetic elements of operation. Professional managers are able to handle the job of operating a building more efficiently than most owners, and their existence can be adequately justified because of their performance of this economic function. Those property managers meeting the training and experience requirements of the Institute of Real Estate Management of the **NATIONAL ASSOCIATION OF REALTORS®** may earn the designation CERTIFIED PROPERTY MANAGER®.

Consultation

With the increasing complexity resulting from rapid growth and taxation and the greater role of government in real estate, the job of consulting or acting in an advisory capacity is growing in importance. Real estate counselors determine and advise on alternative courses of action regarding a

[9] *The Dictionary of Real Estate Appraisal,* 14.

diversity of problems. For example, an individual lacking knowledge of the subtleties of real estate problems might be wise to seek counsel if desiring to develop property or buy an apartment building. Counsel might take the form of laying out the development or arranging for financing. Small insurance companies and other investment firms seek the advice of real estate counselors in arranging their mortgage investment portfolios. Industrial firms seeking advantageous sites and others desiring advice regarding the best types of lease arrangements might also seek counsel. Still others attempting to determine the highest and best use of land might use the real estate counselor. **Highest and best use** has been defined as that best possible and legal use or employment of land that will yield the greatest return per dollar of investment.

Real estate counselors meeting the training and experience requirements of the NATIONAL ASSOCIATION OF REALTORS® may be admitted to the Society of Real Estate Counselors and awarded the CRE (Counselor, Real Estate) designation.

Corporate Service

Many of the larger banks, insurance companies, railroads, oil companies, and chain stores have their own real estate departments offering employment in the real estate field. Banks and insurance companies tend to train mortgage loan people and appraisers. They develop, by this training, all-around real estate investment managers. Some insurance companies develop some of their employees into property managers to handle projects in which they have substantial investments. The chain stores are interested not only in capable appraisers but also, and more important, in people who are able to select the best sites for stores. All of these people must have a knowledge of basic economics, real estate principles, and real estate law.

Syndicate Operations and Limited Partnerships

A *syndicate* is a group of individuals or corporations who have agreed to undertake some common investment venture. The syndicate approach is used to purchase property when individual members have insufficient funds or when they desire to spread investment risk.

Very often, the legal structure of such a group is the limited partnership. The basis of the syndicate operation lies in the general partnership or syndicate agreement. This contract usually calls for a statement of the amount invested by the individual members, together with the disposition of the proceeds and capital on the death of an investor; a statement of the property purchased or about to be purchased, if that is the case; and a statement of the appointment of a general manager or partner. More often than not, the manager is a professional who is given full control of all matters pertaining to the purchase, management, and selling of the property.

Government

Much of the government activity in the field of real estate deals with aspects of financing that will be discussed in Chapter 14.

Employment may be found in the Federal Housing Administration, Veterans Administration, Bureau of Land Management, Department of Agriculture, Federal Home Loan Bank, Army Corps of Engineers, and many other federal agencies involved in the financing, ownership, regulation, and management of property. Similarly, city and county governments employ specialists to assist in the management of housing projects, land use planning, and zoning.

At the federal level, regulations are imposed to limit fraud and misrepresentation in interstate land sales. State and local government agencies are also heavily involved in enforcement of building and safety regulations.

Research and Education

The need for real estate research has increased proportionately with the complexity of financing, land use, planning and zoning, population movements, changing regional age distributions, resource shortages, increased costs, and the political-legal environment of government programs for subsidized housing, interest cost, and urban redevelopment.

Much research into the basic problems of the real estate business is done by various government agencies. For example, some work is being done involving the complexities of the housing market. This is just one of the many hundreds of problems being investigated. Much basic work is being done at universities and colleges. The NATIONAL ASSOCIATION OF REALTORS®, as well as state real estate associations and some of the real estate boards in the larger cities and counties, has, in recent years, become an ardent supporter of this research.

Real estate education is growing rapidly. Each state requires pre-license instruction and many require post-license and continuing education. Education requirements mandated by the states are presented in Appendix B. Appraisal licensing and education will be a nationwide requirement by 1990. Furthermore, some states are also considering legislation to require minimum education and licensing of mortgage bankers.

Universities and colleges have also expanded their real estate course offerings. Instructors with proper educational credentials and experience may find teaching a rewarding career.

Rehabilitation

Rehabilitation consists of remodeling basically sound older buildings with the purpose of making a profit from the resale of these properties. Many such rehabilitation projects are carried out by professional real property managers. However, individuals and practicing brokers also find this a profitable area of the real estate business.

Urban Planning

Urban planners may be employed by private firms or local government units. The **urban planner** aids the city or the developer to ensure a project complies with environmental standards and has adequate water, sewers, utilities, schools, parks, and streets. This is a rapidly growing speciality of growing importance to maintaining our quality of life.

The National Association

The National Association of Real Estate Boards, commonly known as NAREB, was founded in 1908. On November 14, 1972, the Board of Directors changed the name to the NATIONAL ASSOCIATION OF REALTORS®, effective January 1, 1974. By 1988, the association had reached an active membership list of approximately 700,000 members. The major purpose of this trade association is to encourage high standards of business conduct among its members. In 1913, NAREB drafted its first Code of Ethics, comprising three major parts: (1) the REALTOR®'s professional relations, (2) the REALTOR®'s relations to clients, and (3) the REALTOR®'s relations to customers and the public. The 1988 version of the complete Code of Ethics of the NATIONAL ASSOCIATION OF REALTORS® is given in Appendix A.[10]

The term "REALTOR" was coined by Charles N. Chadbourne, a member of the Minneapolis Real Estate Board. It was presented to and adopted by the National Association of Real Estate Boards in 1916. The term is now owned and controlled by the NATIONAL ASSOCIATION OF REALTORS® whose ownership has been decided by numerous court decisions, and anyone not duly authorized by the association is not entitled to be designated a REALTOR® in any manner.

An individual broker belonging to a local member board of the NATIONAL ASSOCIATION OF REALTORS® is also a member of the state real estate association in the state in which the local board is located, as

[10]The NATIONAL ASSOCIATION OF REALTORS® reserves exclusively unto itself the right to comment on and interpret the CODE and particular provisions thereof. For the NATIONAL ASSOCIATION's official interpretations of the CODE, see INTERPRETATIONS OF THE CODE OF ETHICS; NATIONAL ASSOCIATION OF REALTORS®.

In 1985, the Minnesota Real Estate Research Center was created to serve the research needs of government and industry. In 1988, executive development and professional certification programs were provided through the Minnesota Center for Real Estate and Housing Education.

well as a member of the NATIONAL ASSOCIATION OF REALTORS® itself.

As the NATIONAL ASSOCIATION OF REALTORS® grew with the passing years, it was recognized that specialization within the real estate business itself was growing. To fill the need for organizations of specialists, the NATIONAL ASSOCIATION OF REALTORS® began to sponsor specialized associations, or institutes. Membership in these associations now has, as a prerequisite, membership in the NATIONAL ASSOCIATION. However, the institutes themselves have set other prerequisites for membership. These prerequisites generally take the form of experience, special examinations, and recommendations by other members.

The institutes promote higher professional standards, educational facilities, publications, and, in general, the dissemination of new ideas for their members. The special institutes of the NATIONAL ASSOCIATION OF REALTORS® are:

1. REALTORS® National Marketing Institute
2. Institute of Real Estate Management
3. Society of Industrial and Office REALTORS®
4. REALTORS® Land Institute
5. American Society of Real Estate Counselors
6. Women's Council of REALTORS®
7. American Chapter/International Real Estate Federation

Except for the Society of Industrial and Office REALTORS®, which is headquartered in Washington, D.C., these institutes may be contacted by writing them at 430 North Michigan Avenue, Chicago, IL 60611-4087. The Society of Industrial and Office REALTORS® can be reached at 777 14th Street, N.W., Washington, D.C. 20005. Other real estate societies, institutes, and associations are listed in Table 1-8.

Actually, the main function of the institutes is to raise professional standards. Two of the institutes, for example, the American Institute of Real Estate Appraisers and the Institute of Real Estate Management, have very high educational, practical, and ethical requirements for entrance. The former, which now requires a college degree or an acceptable equivalent, carries an MAI (Member of the Appraisal Institute) designation, and the latter, CPM (Certified Property Manager). An analogy can be found in the CLU designation of the American College of Life Underwriters in insurance, or the CPA (Certified Public Accountant) certificate for accountants.

Table 1-8 Real Estate Societies, Institutes, and Associations

American Bankers Association
1120 Connecticut Avenue, NW
Washington, DC 20036

American Institute of Architects
1735 New York Avenue, NW
Washington, DC 20006

American Institute of Certified Planners (AICP)
1776 Massachusetts Avenue, NW
Washington, DC 20036

American Institute for Property and Liability Underwriters
720 Providence Road
Malvern, PA 19355

American Land Title Association (ALTA)
1828 L Street, NW, Suite 705
Washington, DC 20036

American Real Estate and Urban Economics Association
School of Business
Indiana University
Bloomington, IN 47405

American Society of Appraisers (ASA)
P. O. Box 17265
Washington, DC 20041

Associated General Contractors of America (AGCA)
1957 E Street, NW
Washington, DC 20006

Building Owners and Managers Association (BOMA)
1250 I Street, NW, Suite 200
Washington, DC 20005

International Association of Assessing Officers
1313 East 60th Street
Chicago, IL 60637

International Right of Way Association (IRWA)
9920 La Cienega Blvd., Suite 515
Inglewood, CA 90301

Mortgage Bankers Association of America (MBA)
1125 Fifteenth Street, NW
Washington, DC 20005

National Association of Home Builders of the U.S. (NAHB)
15th and M Streets, NW
Washington, DC 20005

National Council of Savings Institutions
1101 Fifteenth Street, NW
Washington, DC 20005

Society of Real Estate Appraisers (SREA)
225 N. Michigan Ave., Suite 724
Chicago, IL 60601

United States League of Savings Institutions (USLSI)
1709 New York Avenue, NW, Suite 801
Washington, DC 20006

Urban Land Institute (ULI)
1090 Vermont Avenue, NW
Washington, DC 20005

SOURCE: NATIONAL ASSOCIATION OF REALTORS®, Real Estate Finance Division, "Residential Mortgage Finance Panel Survey" (Spring 1989).

GLOSSARY

Appraisal An attempt to obtain a just and fair valuation of a parcel of real property

Commercial property Real property used for stores, restaurants, shopping centers, office buildings, hotels, and motels; retail property and office buildings

Consumer goods Goods purchased for immediate consumption

Developers Subdividers who build homes or other improvements on what was initially purchased as raw acreage

Doubling up The use of one housing unit by two or more families, which increases with a decline of general business activity

Highest and best use The reasonable and probable use that supports the highest present value as defined as of the date of the appraisal

Industrial goods Goods used for further production

Industrial property Real estate used in connection with the manufacture of industrial and consumer goods: storage buildings, warehouses, and loft buildings tenanted by manufacturers engaged in light industry

Mortgage banker Any person, firm, or corporation engaged in the business of lending money on the security of improved real estate in the United States and who publicly offers such securities, or certificates, bonds, or debentures based thereon, for sale as a dealer therein, or who is an investor in real estate securities, or is the recognized agent of an insurance company or other direct purchaser of first mortgage real estate securities for investment only

NATIONAL ASSOCIATION OF REALTORS® Trade association formed to encourage high standards of business conduct among its members. Only members of this group can be referred to as REALTORS®

***Non*normal household** A household consisting of singles, career people, divorced persons, widows, or widowers

Points An extra charge by the lender usually based on the amount of the loan

Property manager One who acts as an agent for the owner by operating the property

Real estate broker A person or corporation engaged primarily in the marketing of one or more of the various rights in real property

Real property mortgage An interest in real property as security for the payment of a debt or the fulfillment of an obligation

Rehabilitation Remodeling basically sound older buildings with the purpose of increasing their yield or making a profit from resale

Real Estate Investment Trusts (REITs) Corporations authorized to invest in real estate with exemption from federal corporate taxes, which may be passed on to the shareholders

Shopping center A tract of land improved with a coordinated group of retail buildings having a variety of types of stores, free parking, and under single real estate ownership or control

Standard Metropolitan Statistical Area A county or group of contiguous counties (except in New England) that contains at least one central city of 50,000 inhabitants or more or "twin cities" with a combined population of at least 50,000

Subdividers Persons who purchase raw acreage and, after building roads, cut the land up into lots and sell the parcels

Urban planner Person employed by a private firm or local government who aids the city or the developer in ensuring that a building project complies with environmental standards and provides adequate services such as water, sewers, utilities, schools, parks, and streets

QUESTIONS FOR REVIEW

1. What are the major factors involved in predicting the need for dwelling units?
2. Discuss how each of the above factors is changing and affecting the demand for housing.
3. Discuss the major reasons for declining homeownership in the United States since 1980.
4. How does the age distribution of population affect the demand for housing?
5. How did the recession of 1980, Economic Recovery Tax Act of 1981, and the Tax Reform Act of 1986 affect construction of multifamily housing?

PROBLEMS AND ACTIVITIES

1. In the light of the discussion on housing costs in the text and current economic conditions, discuss the following conclusions drawn by Richey and Clettenberg:

> There is a large gap between what millions of households can afford to pay for and the cost of providing ownership of what is regarded as adequate housing. Assuming that current zoning and building codes represent the minimums of adequate housing and that ownership is a part of the goal, fewer than one-half (32 percent) of the households have the income to meet these goals. This means that 68 percent of the households do not have the necessary income.[11]

2. Write to each real estate society, institute, or association (see Table 1-8) to obtain information on career opportunities, educational and membership requirements, and professional certification that may be earned. Discuss what you learn.

3. Using Decision Assistant Loan Amortization and the following information determine the increase in the cost of housing as measured by the monthly principal and interest payment. What does the change in the cost of housing tell you about affordability? Has the cost of housing increased more than the price of housing? Why?

YEAR	U.S. MEDIAN PRICES	DOWN PAYMENT	INTEREST RATE	AMORTIZATION PERIOD (YEARS)
1968	$20,100	20%	7.00%	30
1973	28,900	20%	8.00%	30
1978	48,700	20%	9.50%	30
1983	70,300	20%	12.50%	30
1988	89,300	20%	9.25%	30

[11]Clyde W. Richey and Karel J. Clettenberg, "Bankruptcy of Subsidized Housing" (Unpublished paper). With permission of the authors, 1978.

PART TWO

THE BREADTH AND SCOPE OF REAL ESTATE

2

CITY PLANNING AND ZONING

KEY TERMS

Building codes
Certificate of occupancy
Eminent domain
Enabling acts
Exclusionary zoning
Floor Area Ratio (FAR) zoning
Impact fees
Inclusionary zoning
In-fill development
Inverse condemnation
Master plan
Nonconforming use
Performance zoning
Planned Urban Development
Planning commission
Police power
Special Purpose Zoning and Planning
Special use permit
Transferable Development Rights
Variance
Zoning
Zoning board
Zoning ordinance

City planning and zoning, police power, eminent domain, condemnation . . . how dull and boring. Not so if your property is condemned (taken) for public purposes, or your land is downzoned, or it's your pet pig the neighbors want sent to the packing plant!

ORIGIN OF PLANNING AND ZONING

Zoning is the division of a municipality, county, or state into districts for the purpose of regulating the location and use of buildings, land, and building construction. Zoning was spawned by a need to separate gunpowder magazines from the residential and business areas of early Colonial towns. Similarly, frontier saloons, tanneries, and stables were relegated to the other side of the railroad tracks from churches, schools, and businesses.

Uniquely American, the theory of "police power" was conceived in 1827 by Chief Justice Marshall as an extension of the federal government's powers of taxation and eminent domain.[1] Twenty-four years later, the Massachusetts Supreme Court concluded that the right to establish all manner of wholesome and reasonable law for the welfare of society was

[1] *Brown v. Maryland,* 12 Wheaton 419 (1827).

residual and vested in state governments.[2] This inherent right was the "police power." Today, **police power** refers to the power of the government to regulate land use in the interest of the public welfare.

Zoning to regulate land use is an example of police power. In 1916, to regulate the height, bulk, and use of buildings in various areas of the city, New York City adopted the nation's first comprehensive zoning ordinance. The constitutionality of zoning ordinances, however, was questioned by many. The constitutional legitimacy of zoning was settled by the U.S. Supreme Court when it rendered an affirmative decision in *Village of Euclid v. Amber Realty Company*.[3]

Like other areas of real estate, zoning, planning, and eminent domain continue to reflect the changing needs of society. Issues range from litigation to permit a pig in a residential neighborhood (the family did convince the court that their pig was a pet and therefore permitted in a residential district: *Foster Village Community Association v. Hess,* 667 P.2d 850 [1983], to expanding standard zoning and subdivision regulations to include linkage fees, inclusionary zoning, inverse condemnation, building moratoriums, and impact fees. In Riverside County, near Los Angeles, new homeowners are being charged $1,950 per acre to build a preserve for Stephan's kangaroo rat. Declared endangered by the U.S. Fish and Wildlife Service, this little fellow will have his own 30 square miles of grassland costing $103 million.

Impact fees paid by the real estate developer compensate a city for costs of expanding water, sewer, and other city services to meet demand created by new developments. Linkage fees, in contrast, tie or link project approval to payments used by the city to provide for public housing, day care, or some other public benefit.

Eminent domain is the power of government, upon payment of just compensation, to take property for public use. In the exercise of this right of condemnation, the taker must use due process of law.

Inverse condemnation does not involve the condemnation and taking of land. It refers to the taking of rights associated with the land by actions such as changed zoning or building moratoriums (delays). Although these actions may be taking away rights, owners have, historically, not been compensated for the loss of value related to their loss of rights to use their land.

RECENT LIMITATIONS ON PLANNING AND ZONING

Land use planning, zoning, and inverse condemnation have been severely affected by three decisions of the 1987 Supreme Court: the First English,

---

[2]*Commonwealth v. Alger,* 7 Cushing (Mass.) 53, 85 (1851).

[3]*Village of Euclid v. Amber Realty Company,* 272 U.S. 365 (1926).

Nollan, and Keystone Coal cases.[4] The decisions resulted from communities pushing their police power beyond its constitutional limits. In the past, land use planners, zoning administrators, and regulators had justified their actions based on their perception of community needs. As long as the regulation was related to the safety, health, and welfare of the community, the presumption was the regulation could not be questioned.

First English invalidates this theory. Concern must be given for the property owner affected by the regulation. Actions such as downzoning, which change land use from high density multifamily housing to parkland or greenbelt areas, cannot be made without incurring the potential obligation to pay the property owner just compensation for the loss of value and use. Further, delaying tactics such as temporary moratoriums could result in the need to compensate a landowner for being temporarily deprived of the use of the property. Not all moratoriums will require compensation, but cities will not be able to act without considering whether compensation will be required. In Minnesota, Golden Valley Lutheran College, frustrated in attempts to sell its campus by a yearlong moratorium on development, sued the City of Golden Valley. In their suit, the college claimed the moratorium resulted in the "taking" of their property without due process of law. The moratorium, they claimed, was implemented to frustrate their efforts to sell or develop the property.

In *Nollan,* standards were set for community use of linkage fees. Essentially, the city must find that a significant relationship exists between the problems caused by the development and the purpose for which linkage or impact fees are used. Also at question is the requirement of having developers dedicate some of their land for a public purpose as a requirement for annexation or subdivision approval. Required dedication may, in fact, be nothing more than extortion.

In short, the courts concluded that in the name of public well-being, the rights of landowners have been ignored and this abuse of police power must stop. Interestingly, on March 15, 1988, a Presidential Executive Order required federal government agencies to evaluate the potential loss of value to property owners that may result from proposed regulations. In essence, federal, state, and local government actions may deprive property owners of the beneficial use of their land, for which compensation must be paid. The freedom with which regulators have acted to limit or delay land use has been significantly restricted. Only time will tell who will prevail in the battle between overregulation and some developers' wanton disregard of the public interest. Ideally, the pendulum will not swing from extreme to

[4]*First English Evangelical Lutheran Church v. County of Los Angeles,* 482 U.S. 304 (1987); *Nollan v. California Coastal Commission,* 483 U.S. 825 (1987); and *Keystone Bituminous Coal Association v. DeBenedictis,* 480 U.S. 470 (1987). For a case review and their implications, see Michael M. Berger, "Measuring Regulatory Hardship: A Different View of the Elephant," *Urban Land* (May 1989): 10–15.

extreme, but will stop at midpoint, which will protect the public interest, property rights, and facilitate rather than eliminate affordable housing.

DEVELOPMENT OF CITY PLANNING AND ZONING

Enabling Acts

Although zoning may be constitutionally permissible without enabling legislation, local zoning is an inappropriate exercise of the power vested in state government. To delegate to the cities the state's police power, enabling legislation is necessary.

Recognizing the need for state zoning enabling legislation, the Department of Commerce gathered a group of experts to develop model legislation. The Advisory Committee on Zoning completed its task in 1928. Quickly thereafter, **enabling acts** were passed in most states. Although the enabling acts vary from state to state, most of them follow the same general pattern.

Cities are conceived as having received their municipal police power through enabling legislation from the state. For example, under the laws of some states, an area with as little population as 125 may become a city. The citizens of the area, after voting on the issue, may seek to become an "incorporated" city. The municipality is granted a charter from the state much like a business corporation is granted a charter or certificate of incorporation. Like the incorporated business, the incorporated city must operate within the scope of the powers specifically granted by the charter. Cities cannot operate outside these delegated powers without subjecting themselves to legal action by citizens who might believe their constitutional rights have been invaded.

Once a city is incorporated and decides to proceed with enactment of a zoning ordinance, a zoning board or commission is appointed. The **zoning board** has responsibility for preparing a zoning ordinance and a map showing how each area of the city is to be zoned. The ordinance also describes how zoning regulations apply to each area of the city and its respective zoning classification.

A **zoning ordinance** is, in effect, a plan for the city. The responsibility for this plan is often delegated to professional planners or a planning commission.

Planning Commissions

Enabling acts provide for the establishment of a **planning commission.** Membership on the commission varies from state to state. Generally, there are from 5 to 15 members. The members are appointed by the mayor, city council, or the city manager with the consent of the city council.

The function of the planning commission is to prepare a plan or plans for the development or redevelopment of the community. The underlying theory is that proper planning will be the guide to the growth of the municipality and will protect citizens of the city from influences that would adversely affect both residential and investment properties.

Geographical Scope of Planning

The problem raised here is whether or not the city is limited by its boundaries with regard to planning. Usually, enabling acts recognize the impracticability of having planning stop at the city's edge. Some enabling acts give authority to the city planning commission as far as six miles from the edge of the city provided they do not extend into the boundaries of another city.

The model act provides for making plans for as far beyond the city limits as the commission thinks bears a close relationship to the planning of the city itself. In short, it recognizes that planning must be looked at as a whole unit and cannot be limited by arbitrary boundaries that might have come about as the result of historical accident. Conditions outside the city limits affect conditions within.

The Florida Legislature has required all cities and counties to adopt comprehensive plans. To begin integration of these plans to form a statewide master plan, the Florida State and Regional Planning Act of 1984 was enacted. The act requires the governor's office to prepare planning goals, policies, and infrastructure (water, sewer, electric) budgets on a statewide basis. Emphasis is to be placed on water resources, transportation systems, and orderly land use.

Capital Improvements

Only a few enabling acts carry with them a provision for capital improvement programming, although some states, notably New Jersey, are an exception: "In the preparation of the master plan the planning board shall give due consideration to the probable ability of the municipality to carry out, over a period of years, the various projects embraced in the plan without imposition of unreasonable financial burdens. . . ."

This suggests that the commissions make suggestions as to public improvements that are in keeping with such city plans as they are developed. It further suggests the necessity of planning commissions looking into the future and anticipating what public structures will be necessary to harmonize with their overall plan, and to implement these future plans by anticipating necessary financial requirements.

The Master Plan

Most enabling acts give much space to what is commonly referred to as the **master plan.** Section seven of the Standard City Planning Enabling Act of 1928 refers to the master plan as follows:

> The plan shall be made with the general purpose of guiding and accomplishing a coordinated, adjusted, and harmonious development of the municipality and its environs which will, in accordance with present and future needs, best promote health, safety, morals, order, convenience, property, and general welfare, as well as efficiency and economy in the process of development: including among other things adequate provisions for traffic, the promotion of safety from fire and other damages, adequate provision for light and air, the promotion of the healthful and convenient distribution of the population, the promotion of good civic design and arrangement, wise and efficient expenditure of public funds, and the adequate possession of public utilities and other public requirements.

One of the difficult problems with a master plan is that it is often obsolete as soon as it has been completed. City goals change over time, as demonstrated by recent emphasis on the environmental impact of growth and the demands of mass transit systems. Competent city planners see the master plan as dynamically changing over time to meet the needs and perceptions of the community.

The master plan is generally envisioned as a coordinated effort over a number of broad areas. Development of a master plan begins with a survey of the planning area in terms of present conditions and probable future growth. This type of analysis includes economic activity, population growth, composition of populations in terms of age groupings, breakdown of the labor force, etc. Transportation and traffic patterns are analyzed. Public facilities and physical resources and deficiencies are also considered. This facet of master planning is discussed in greater detail under the economic base analysis in Chapter 4.

One of the principal benefits of city master planning is stimulation of public interest and response to identification of city planning goals. For master planning to be effective, public support is necessary.

Through public participation in the planning effort, short- and long-range objectives may be identified. The master plan could contain provisions for meeting the stated objectives. For example, if parks are needed, the plan should contain a provision for establishing parks—perhaps in conjunction with a bikeway or an insulating greenbelt.

If the survey of the city reveals deficiencies in the nature of blighted areas, or fire and health hazards, a program of correction may be included in the master plan. This, for example, might include downzoning from commercial to residential use or demolition and construction of public housing. Master planning may even include protecting industrial areas from encroachment by commercial and residential developers. In Chicago, industrial land use planning led to creation of the city's first planned manufacturing district. Since prohibiting nonindustrial development, land values have stabilized and new industrial development has been attracted.

Master planning also facilitates coordination between various public agencies. It is always possible that the school board, parks and recreation department, and zoning commission are all looking at the same piece of land, each with different purposes in mind, e.g., a school, park, or residential use.

The master plan, ultimately, represents a compromise between differing interest groups, a plan of action based on expected growth, and a municipality's strengths and weaknesses. The master plan is a forecast of a city's future.

Implementing the Master Plan. One of the major problems met in practice by city planners is the need for obtaining public cooperation to implement the master plan. Some private interests will be injured and will object to the plan and, hence, resist adoption of the plan. One method of dealing with this problem, although often not necessarily the best method, is through the police power. The concept of the police power is broad and has been subject to much legal interpretation, which has increased the scope of the concept. "With the growth and development of the State, the police power necessarily develops, within reasonable bounds, to meet changing conditions."[5]

Common use of police power is found in zoning regulations, building codes, and the right of eminent domain. Zoning may be used to restrict some types of land use and encourage others. Building codes may place height or architectural constraints on potential construction. Eminent domain permits cities to employ condemnation as a final means of obtaining compliance with the master plan.

In the final analysis, the use of the police power involves a certain amount of control over the use of private property. It is recognized that more often than not the use of the police power is the only method by which private interests obstructing the implementation of the master plan can be dislodged. However, a better way, when possible, is to attempt to influence by sound reasoning and thus obtain the cooperation of those individuals opposing the city plan.

When the master plan is properly drawn, real estate investments are protected as a result of the long-term stability the plan provides. This often encourages opponents to support plans that promote desirable economic and social goals. Planning activity for future growth also identifies opportunities for residential, commercial, and industrial development. Successful investment and development help achieve the objectives of the plan.

Financing the Plan. Like many good things, city planning costs money. Therefore, another major problem in putting the city plan in operation is financing the plan. Although it can be easily demonstrated by planners that planning will pay off in the long run, many people, especially taxpayers, believe, as Lord Keynes, that in the long run we will all be dead. Often, immediate beneficial aspects of some of the phases of planning can be

[5]*City of Aurora v. Robert Burns,* 319 Ill. 93, 149 N.E. 784 at 788.

demonstrated in order to induce taxpayers to burden themselves with the costs. Other effects on increased earnings by business establishments, taxes, and assessments can readily be demonstrated. In addition, one can show how the anticipated benefits will increase the value of the land.

The need for financing the master plan has been intensified by federal cutbacks, loss of program subsidies, and limitations on industrial development and municipal mortgage bonds. As a result, cities have become innovative in their search for monies to meet community needs.

Office building developers in San Francisco are now required to help increase and preserve the city's housing stock. Developers of more than 50,000 square feet must provide aid to residential developers who in turn have constructed, rehabilitated, or financed 2,640 low- and moderate-income dwelling units. To preserve and enhance the downtown business district, Washington, D.C., now requires new buildings to devote 20 percent of their space to retail and service uses. East of San Francisco, in Contra Costa County, public transit, walking trails, and street maintenance are being financed by a one-half-cent sales tax for 20 years.

Although the amount of financial assistance to residential developers is negotiated on a case-by-case basis, the average cost is equivalent to a tax of $4 per square foot on new office space. The concept is now spreading to other metropolitan areas.

To make better use of existing water and sewer services and expand the supply of housing, communities have developed infill programs. **Infill development** is a system of incentives to encourage construction on overlooked or underutilized sites. Incentives include allowing second homes on existing sites, waiver of water and sewer connection fees, rezoning of underutilized commercial and industrial areas to permit residential housing, as well as requiring new developments to bear the full cost of extending water and sewer services.

The Future Scope of Planning

Christopher Tunnard pointed out in 1958 that the United States was on the way to creating a "man-made mess." He felt we could not afford to continue to have planning take place on a city or local basis without regard for the region. He cited power lines, clearings for gas pipelines, oil storage tanks, all cutting across the landscape in haphazard fashion; strings of houses cutting themselves off from the very landscape their owners moved out to enjoy; new roads being built without regard to topography or existing order, merely to solve the mounting traffic snarls or to take advantage of the least costly rights of way.

Tunnard outlined four major problems of urbanization as follows:

1. To see that the fringe housing is properly located and does not become a jerry-built slum.

2. To determine a rational use of land on a broad scale.

3. To design a highway network that makes industry, decentralized offices, and regional commercial centers accessible to more people.

4. To provide a vastly increased recreational system of parks and reservations.[6]

The implication for future planning was that it would be needed outside of city and county lines. Many students of regionalism felt that there was a need for some type of interstate planning, which suggested a new type of federalism across state lines.

The failure to heed Tunnard's warning and plan for the sprawling growth of cities has literally created the predicted "man-made mess." Getting to work has become more of a challenge. In Riverside, California, which provides relatively affordable housing, the commute to downtown Los Angeles takes two hours. In Los Angeles, a city committee fighting to eliminate gridlock has been considering the problem for two-and-one-half years. By 2010, Chicago's main beltway must carry double the current traffic load, and in 15 years, traffic delays and wasted gasoline will cost $50 billion, an increase of $38 billion.

Recognizing the need for intrastate planning and in the absence of federal land use legislation, 49 states have enacted, or are considering, state land use programs. The first such law, considered a comprehensive model for state land use planning, was enacted in Colorado in 1974. The legislation identified 13 areas of specific concern for which planning was desirable. They were: water projects, nuclear detonations, water and sewage facilities, solid waste sites, mass transit facilities, highways and interchanges, public utilities, airports, wildlife habitats, historical and archeological sites, natural hazard areas, mineral resource areas, and public utilities.

John Birmingham reported the scope of the four-point landmark legislation:

1. Local governments—counties and municipalities—were given money, encouragement, and direction to plan for, designate and regulate [these] certain specified land use matters. . . .

2. State power to intervene was no longer limited to narrowly defined emergency situations . . . the executive branch was given authority to force local governments to deal with these matters.

3. State agencies with experience in identifying and managing mineral, natural resource, and hazardous areas were brought into a coordinated program to make their information and expertise available to local governments.

4. Additional legislation enacted that year gave local governments the

---

[6]Christopher Tunnard, "America's Super Cities," *Harpers,* 217, no. 1299 (August 1958): 59–65.

> authority to regulate land use within the thirteen designated areas and to restrict usage on the basis of the effect on adjacent areas.[7]

One result of this effort to resolve traffic congestion through regional planning was a $950-million, 50-mile toll road in Denver. The road was expected to ease (not eliminate) traffic congestion in the city's eastern suburbs.

ZONING

Zoning means the division of a municipality, county, or state into districts for the purpose of regulating the location and use of buildings, land, and building construction and its regulation is brought about through rules that constitute the exercise of police power. These rules and regulations are uniform with respect to each class or kind of building or land within each district but may differ between districts. Land use or building use is enforced by the local government authority.

Generally, the zoning powers conferred by the state zoning laws on a municipality may be exercised within the municipality. Those zoning powers conferred upon a county may be exercised within the unincorporated areas of the county.

In addition, the zoning laws give authority to the proper local officials to bring action to prevent or restrain the construction, alteration, or repair of any building, or use or occupancy of any building or land in violation of the zoning regulations. For example, if an individual wishes to alter a large residence in a residential area to a small apartment house, the owner must first obtain permission of the proper zoning officials. If the owner proceeds without having first obtained permission, zoning officials may obtain a court order to restrain that individual from continuing with the alteration. Often, too, persons violating zoning regulations may be subject to fine and imprisonment.

Most zoning regulations actually predate the master plans now in effect, or they are used in many areas in the absence of a master plan. The initial zoning ordinance developed by the zoning board will typically include:

1. The purpose of the zoning ordinance.
2. A statement prohibiting construction, alteration, or use of land or buildings except in conformity with the zoning ordinance.
3. Recognition of property owner's right to continue the present use of the property although that use does not conform to the proposed zoning.

---

[7] John R. Birmingham, "1974 Land Use Legislation in Colorado," *Denver Law Journal* 51, no. 4 (Denver, Colorado: The University of Denver College of Law), 467–507.

4. Identification of each zoning classification and the area of the city to which that classification applies.
5. Detailed description of regulations that apply to each zoning classification.
6. Requirements for building permits and certificates of occupancy.
7. Procedures for zoning appeals, zoning enforcement, and penalties for violations of the zoning ordinance.
8. Procedures by which changes in the zoning ordinance may be made.

In places where the master plan is in effect, the zoning regulations are used in conjunction with a comprehensive plan and effectively aid the implementation of the plan.

Primary Zoning Purpose

Although zoning regulations provide control over land usage and generally take the form of designating land use districts, building size and height limitations, and density, the purposes for zoning controls are much broader. For example:

1. *Protection of aesthetic value.* Things that may constitute "eye sores" are to be avoided. In some municipalities, zoning regulations prohibit junkyards except in specifically designated areas. In many cases, zoning regulations go a step farther and provide that those engaged in the junk business must provide a fence of "at least eight feet in height" around the junkyard.

   Preservation of aesthetic value may also include restrictions on building near bluff lands or ridges so that a scenic attraction or historical site is preserved for all. Abuses of this purpose of zoning are found in regulations that restrict mobile home developments to the least desirable part of the city. Preservation of aesthetic value is alos used as justification for other discriminatory exclusionary zoning practices.[8]
2. *Protection of morals.* Zoning regulations may be used to protect the public from what may be considered adverse morality. For example, bars, dance halls, massage parlors, and poolrooms may be restricted to certain buildings in specified areas. It is on the grounds of both aesthetics and morality that a motel with a bar may be prohibited from building adjacent to a residential area.

[8]For an excellent discussion of discriminatory zoning practice, *Fair Housing and Exclusionary Land Use: Historical Overview, Summary of Litigation,* and a *Comment with Research Bibliography* may be obtained by writing the Urban Land Institute, 1090 Vermont Avenue, Washington, DC 20005.

3. *Protection from psychological nuisances.* Activities considered to be disturbing to the general public may be restricted to specified areas. Examples are funeral parlors, cemeteries, and crematoriums. A horse racing track with betting may be forced to locate in a rural area because it is unsightly, gambling is a corruptive force, and smells are psychologically disturbing.
4. *Protection against physical danger.* The public is protected against physical danger by zoning laws. For example, in some places special areas are allocated for necessary arsenals, fireworks factories, and other potentially dangerous industries that might endanger the public. Recently, some parts of the country have been quick to amend their zoning regulations to protect the public against accidents that might arise from atomic energy installations.
5. *Protection of the environment.* Protecting the environment includes preservation of light, air, and open space. This type of regulation leads to density and building height regulations. Building size, in this case, must conform to some stated relationship with lot size.

General Zoning Classification

Classic zoning is three-dimensional: residential, business or commercial, and industrial. However, modern zoning goes beyond the class form. New York City has 15 zoning districts and 18 different use groupings. The use groupings provide for four groups of areas for retail and commercial uses.

One of the major goals of zoning is an attempt to obtain a certain amount of homogeneity in each of the areas. Therefore, in all three categories, there is often a need for subdividing the categories. For example, a city may be zoned in terms of "A" Residential District, "B" Residential District, and so forth. There may be a minimum 100-front-foot lot required in the "A" zone, while the minimum for the "B" zone may be only 50 feet. Thus the homogeneity is achieved in each zone. This may continue in terms of height of homes, number of families to each home, and many other factors that limit the land use but are thought to be desirable.

Nonconforming Use

All zoning ordinances provide for what is commonly called a **nonconforming use,** a structure used in violation of a zoning regulation that was a lawful use at the time of the enactment of the zoning ordinance. In short, zoning regulations cannot be retroactive. For example, if an individual were using a large barn in the rear of a property for a truck garage at the time of the passage of the ordinance, the person may continue to use it as a truck garage even though the area has been classified as a residential district.

Generally, the regulations state if the nonconforming use is discontinued for a period of time (often three years), then any future use must be made in conformance with the rest of the zoned area. Often, too, the zoning ordinance will state that if the building is destroyed by fire or other causes to the extent of a certain percentage of its value, it cannot be repaired unless it conforms to the regulations.

Variances and Special Uses

A person seeking a change in the zoning regulations cannot do it easily. First, the person must submit a petition to the zoning board requesting the change. Next, a notice is published in a local newspaper, the time length varying from state to state. This notice calls for a public hearing on the proposed change. One of the major reasons for requiring a public hearing is to make it more difficult for politicians to impose pressure on the board. At the hearing, those favoring the change and those against the change may be heard. Finally, the board renders its decision. Certain minor variances can be made in some states without a public hearing.

In unique circumstances, the zoning board may issue a special use permit or grant a zoning variance. When need is demonstrated, a **special use permit** may be granted, which allows a nonconforming use in an area not zoned for that purpose. An example would be a special use permit allowing construction of a hotel facility in an industrial park.

A **variance** may be granted when the use conforms with the zoning classification, but slightly violates other provisions of that classification. The property owner, however, must demonstrate that strict compliance with zoning regulations results in undue hardship. For example, a variance may be granted that permits construction of a screened porch moderately violating set-back requirements.

Zoning Appeals

The zoning, or city planning, commission is an administrative body, and as such is governed in its actions by administrative law. In most areas, a board of appeals has jurisdiction over zoning cases brought before it *after* the appellants have been heard by the planning board or planning commission. A person who claims to have been aggrieved, and can so demonstrate, may appeal a decision of the planning board of appeals to the courts. An example of an improper action by the board might be in the case of the board arbitrarily prohibiting the admission of vital evidence in the hearing before the board. It should be noted that an individual appealing a decision of the board cannot appear before the courts before all administrative remedies have been exhausted. That is, the individual must first appear before the planning commission, then appeal to the board of appeals in those areas where it exists, and only after that go into court.

Current Developments

Over an extended period of time, traditional zoning is too rigid to cope with the dynamics of a rapidly changing urban environment. New concepts of land use and regulation have been developed to meet the need for flexibility.

Performance Zoning. Implementation of **performance zoning** allows multiple uses, regardless of type, as long as each use does not adversely affect other property owners. Performance zoning, however, does not mean that standards are not applied in evaluating the acceptability of the proposed use. Compatibility of the proposed use, with existing uses, is determined by evaluating the impact on traffic flow, density, appearance, environment, and property values.

Transferable Development Rights. **Transferable Development Rights** (TDRs) have been used to maintain the rural flavor of urban development yet permit high density multifamily housing. For example, 360 acres of farmland are zoned residential with a permitted density of one residence per acre. A developer wishes to build 240 apartment units on land zoned for 12 units. In effect, the developer needs to acquire the right to build 228 more units than presently permitted. When TDRs are recognized, the right to construct 228 housing units may be purchased from the landowner and transferred to the developer's site.

The 360-acre farm now has 120 development rights remaining. The developer has the right to erect 240 apartment units, the farm's owner has been compensated for the loss of rights to develop, and society benefits from the preservation of agricultural land and open space.

Traditionally the right to develop a site consistent with present zoning cannot be separated from the land. TDRs permit transference of the right to develop from one parcel to another. When one location is more intensely developed, the area from which TDRs were transferred remains undeveloped.

PUD Zoning. The **Planned Urban Development** (PUD) is a development incorporating a variety of uses planned and developed as a unit. Such development may be that of individual lots or may have common recreation or open space surrounding clustered buildings. Typically, common land is an essential element.[9]

To create a PUD, the owner must outline the development plan. If approved by the planning board (and/or city council, depending on the location) a *tentative* rezoning of the property is made following a public hearing. At this point, no building permit is issued. However, the owner must bind the property to those conditions listed in the final development plan. A final rezoning is then given. After this, subdivision regulations must be complied with (filing the plat, providing for streets, etc.) before building permits are issued.

---

[9]Many communities require that the functional open space, exclusive of parking or streets, be 25 percent of the total acreage.

The development plan referred to above includes maps showing enough of the area surrounding the proposed Planned Urban Development to show the relationship of the PUD to existing and proposed uses. They also must show existing natural and manufactured features and existing zoning of adjacent property. In addition, the applicant must show the types, locations, densities, and acreage consumed by all the land uses. A written statement is also required outlining the present ownership of all the land involved in the PUD, an expected schedule of beginning and completion, and a statement of intent concerning the provision of water, sewer, and highway improvements.

Floor Area Ratio Zoning. **Floor Area Ratio (FAR) zoning** is a formula approach to regulation of structural density. It may be used for multifamily and commercial structures to relate that portion of the total lot area covered by the building and building height.

For example, a FAR of 3.0 may permit (1) a 3-story building covering 90 percent of the lot, (2) a 6-story building covering 45 percent of the lot, or (3) a 12-story building covering 22.5 percent of the lot. Coverage ratios may be established to meet planning objectives and provide for off-street parking and open space. As illustrated, a single number describes a proportional relationship between building height and area of the parcel the building may occupy.

To provide incentives for the development of residences in the city center, some communities have offered developers density bonuses. In Hartford, Connecticut, for example, developers are permitted a floor area ratio (FAR) of more than 10 when providing downtown housing. Pittsburgh allows the FAR to increase from 7.5 to 10 if one-half the square footage constructed is for residential use. Miami gives developers two choices. They may either incorporate housing in their development or contribute to a housing fund; in turn, their FAR is doubled from 2.5 to 5.0 to permit greater density. These plans are seen as being essential to revitalization of downtown areas.

Exclusionary Zoning. **Exclusionary zoning,** sometimes called "snob zoning," is designed to keep out housing for low- or even moderate-income groups. To do this, minimum lot sizes, as well as minimum floor space specifications, have been mandated. For purposes of illustration, an exaggeration is used. Suppose a city or county passed a zoning ordinance stating that the minimum lot size should be 15 acres. In this case, land costs would be raised to the level that the general welfare would not be fostered or promoted and hence this ordinance would probably be unconstitutional as well as exclusionary.

Litigation against laws excluding the poor, that is, laws requiring large lots, swimming pools, tennis courts, etc., have generally been successful. In other words, the courts have held that laws excluding or prohibiting the type of housing needed by lower income families is discriminatory.

Inclusionary Zoning. Some communities have been sensitive to the need for lower income housing and practice **inclusionary zoning.** Through such practices as rezoning for multifamily units and establishing zoning variances and requirements to provide housing affordable to low- and middle-income families, discrimination through zoning is being reduced. Other tools being employed include providing low-cost tax-increment financing while requiring developers to provide 10 to 25 percent of new housing construction within an affordable size and price range. Deed restrictions are also used to limit resale prices and rents to prevent windfall profit to initial buyers and ensure that low-cost housing continues to remain affordable.

Critics have argued that inclusionary zoning is a response to excessive growth controls that created high prices for existing homes and land suitable for development. It would be far better, they argue, to relax limitations on lot sizes (density), availability of utility services, and the number of building permits.

Special Purpose Zoning and Planning. **Special purpose zoning and planning,** as the name implies, focuses on small areas with particular characteristics. These areas may be neighborhoods, central business districts, commercial corridors, industrial sites, scenic amenities, or areas in transition from one use to another. Rather than providing comprehensive area-wide planning, special purpose planning and/or zoning may include:

1. "A historic area of low income housing . . . designated a housing retention district . . .
2. Interim development control for a riverfront area . . .
3. An industrial area in transition to a more active part of the business district . . .
4. Conversion of an industrial corridor to commercial uses . . . (while) protecting scenic qualities adjacent to the parkway . . .
5. Urban conservation districts . . . in neighborhoods with special architectural qualities . . .
6. Residential historic districts to preserve housing . . .
7. Design analysis to preserve river views with view planes governing building height . . .
8. Experimental planned development (XPD) zoning category requiring review of island development proposals . . . and
9. New zoning classifications for research parks providing high standards for development and design review."[10]

A summary of communities making changes in local development regulations is presented in Table 2-1.

---

[10]Douglas Porter, "The Local Regulatory Scene: Overview and Outlook," *Development Review & Outlook 1984–1985* (Washington, D.C.: Urban Land Institute, 1985), 403–417.

Table 2-1 Local Development Regulations

	TOTAL	CENTRAL CITIES	SUBURBS	FAST GROWING CITIES	SLOW OR NO-GROWTH CITIES
Communities surveyed	62	29	33	36	26
Communities making changes: comprehensive or area plans	31	13	18	16	15
Zoning ordinances	44	25	19	22	22
Other programs	18	9	9	12	6
Communities having or considering in-fill programs	31	19	12	19	12
Communities having inclusionary housing programs	11	3	8	7	4
Communities having farmland preservation programs		3	4	7	–

SOURCE: Urban Land Institute.

BUILDING CODES

Although not strictly falling into the category of city planning and zoning, building codes should be mentioned because of their close relationship with planning and zoning. **Building codes** are municipal ordinances limiting private property rights by regulating the construction and occupancy of buildings. There are usually variances in the codes from city to city, although there is now a movement to somewhat standardize the building codes by geographical area; for example, the Southern Building Code. Most of the codes relate to sanitary requirements, structural safety, number of windows required per room, fireproofing, and the like. In most areas having building codes, a builder is first required to obtain a building permit before proceeding with new construction or certain alterations. In these areas of the country, there are regularly appointed, and sometimes elected, building inspectors who determine whether the codes have been complied with. Generally, an application for a certificate of occupancy is filed simultaneously with the issuance of the building permit. The **certificate of occupancy** is a statement issued by the building inspector stating that the building code and/or zoning regulations have been complied with. In this manner, the zoning boards are able to exercise greater control over the enforcement of the regulations. In the event that the building code and/or zoning regulations are not complied with, the building inspector will not issue the certificate. The real estate practitioner should be aware of the importance of the certificate of occupancy, because often financial institutions require a certified copy of the certificate before they will close a mortgage loan.

GLOSSARY

Building codes Municipal ordinances limiting private property rights by regulating the construction and occupancy of buildings

Certificate of occupancy A statement issued by the building inspector stating that the building code and/or zoning regulations have been complied with

Eminent domain The power of the government to take property for public use after making just compensation; to authorize such taking by a corporation or individual engaged in a quasi-public operation

Enabling acts Legislation that permits municipalities to establish planning agencies if they desire

Exclusionary zoning "Snob zoning," designed to keep out housing for low- or even moderate-income groups

Floor Area Ratio (FAR) zoning A formula approach to regulation of structural density

Impact fees Fees paid by the real estate developer that compensate a city for costs of expanding water, sewer, and other city services to meet demand created by the new development

Inclusionary zoning Rezoning for multifamily units and establishing zoning variances and requirements to provide housing affordable to low- and middle-income families

In-fill development A system of incentives to encourage construction on overlooked or underutilized sites

Inverse condemnation Refers to the taking of rights associated with land when, for example, zoning changes or building delays occur

Master plan A plan for guiding and accomplishing a coordinated, adjusted, and harmonious development of a municipality and its environs in accordance with present and future needs, best promoting health, safety, morals, order, convenience, property, and general welfare, as well as efficiency and economy in the process of development; the forecast of a city's future

Nonconforming use A structure used in violation of a zoning regulation that was a lawful use when the zoning ordinance was enacted

Performance zoning Zoning that allows multiple uses, regardless of type, as long as each use does not adversely affect other property owners

Planned Urban Development The incorporation of a variety of uses planned and developed as a unit

Planning commission A body appointed by the mayor, city council, or city manager that prepares a plan for the development or redevelopment of the community

Police power The power of the government to regulate land use in the interest of the public welfare

Special purpose zoning and planning Zoning that focuses on small areas with particular characteristics

Special use permit Permission granted by a zoning board allowing a nonconforming use in an area not zoned for that purpose

Transferable Development Rights Transference of zoning rights from one parcel to another

Variance A special concession made when the use of property conforms with the zoning classification but slightly violates other provisions of that classification

Zoning The division of a municipality, county, or state into districts for the purpose of regulating the location and use of buildings, land, and building construction

Zoning board The board or commission that regulates zoning

Zoning ordinance A plan for the city

QUESTIONS FOR REVIEW

1. What is an *enabling act?*
2. How may zoning changes result in inverse condemnation?
3. Compare impact fees with linkage fees.
4. What is a *master plan?*
5. What is the concept of the police power, and how is it related to city planning?
6. How is zoning related to city planning?
7. Name at least five points that should be addressed in an initial zoning ordinance.

8. How are building codes related to city planning?

9. Discuss Transferable Development Rights.

PROBLEMS AND ACTIVITIES

1. One of the many surveys that must be done in connection with city planning is on the parking problem. Using the following five headings, attempt to make a checklist of items for a parking survey:

   a. Street parking facilities and their use.
   b. Present off-street parking facilities and their use.
   c. Potential off-street parking sites.
   d. Demand for street and off-street parking facilities.
   e. Economics of off-street parking facilities of different types; for example, parking lots, wall-less garages, underground garages, etc.

   One example in the checklist under item (a) above might be "relation to business"; another, "interference with moving traffic"; and so on.

2. A report for the city of Worcester, Massachusetts, suggests that the planners turn the heart of the city's central business district into an exclusive pedestrian area, prohibiting all vehicular traffic on downtown Main Street and streets abutting it. The common vehicles would have access to the central business district by way of a high-speed distribution loop. The elevated loop would permit uninterrupted movement of pedestrians along the Main Street Mall. Opening off the loop would be one of a series of garages planned for the downtown area.

   a. Comment in detail.
   b. Suppose an individual objected to the overhead loop. What action might the city take?

3. The Worcester plan calls for a high expenditure of funds. If the major objective is to increase sales and fight off the encroachment of the outlying shopping center, what may be a major problem even if the project is completed?

3

SUBDIVISIONS AND DEVELOPMENTS

KEY TERMS

Developer
Environmental Impact Statement
Interstate Land Sales Full Disclosure Act
Metes and bounds
Nonalienation clause
Option
Partial Release clause
Plat
Property Report
Restrictive covenants
Rolling option
Statement of Record
Subdivider
Subordination agreement
Zoning Laws

Decisions regarding subdivision and development are no longer simple. Financing has become complex. Locational patterns have changed significantly. Internationalization of the U.S. economy increased the difficulty of forecasting demand for space. This chapter presents some of the basic concepts associated with subdivision and development.

Although the terms *subdivider* and *developer* are frequently used interchangeably, each has a distinct meaning. A **subdivider** acquires undeveloped acreage, divides the tract into smaller parcels in accordance with government regulations, installs streets and utilities, and sells the parcels to investors or builders.

A **developer,** by combining land with a completed structure, advances the process a step farther. Developments may include industrial parks, shopping centers, multifamily housing, or single-family residences. The developer is also responsible for financing, marketing, and sale to the ultimate user.

However, in the complicated world of the 1990s, the lines between developer, property manager, and retailer often become blurred. Developers now provide property rental and management services for their projects. One developer, Hoover Corporation, has even gone so far as to acquire retail store chains and put these stores, as tenants, in their newly developed shopping centers.

PRELIMINARY PROBLEMS

Any sound marketing plan, whether from the point of view of the manufacturer or the middleman, begins with the customer. The business stands or falls on the ability to satisfy the needs of the consumer. If the real estate subdivider or developer is able to satisfy customer needs, the result will be not only great personal satisfaction but also increased profits.

Analyzing the Market

Before beginning a subdivision or development, the subdivider or developer should analyze the market and study consumers to determine their needs and whether the time is ripe for a subdivision. There are many cases when ideas that are fundamentally sound fail because the time for their promulgation is premature. For example, Suffolk County, Long Island, is dotted with subdivisions that failed during the 1920s; yet, after World War II, these same areas sold rapidly. After World War II, credit was easily available and there was a pent-up demand for housing caused by increasing marriages, increasing population, high income, and improved transportation. To determine whether the time is appropriate for a development, it is necessary to analyze the market as shown in Chapter 4.

Builders, investors, and speculators often purchase and hold inventories of land in the path of growth. Their purpose is to buy before development is feasible. In many instances, land is acquired five to ten years in advance of actual subdivision. In other words, feasibility is often determined by the willingness to buy and hold land until growth and economic conditions permit maximum profits.

Selecting a Site

Sites upon which to create a development or subdivision must be selected with the greatest possible care. Many and varied factors have to be considered. As far as possible, the site selected should be in the natural path of the city's growth. As a general rule, cities move outward from their original point along main arteries of traffic in a pattern influenced by natural and artificial barriers. Although this is a general rule, sometimes a developer can change the direction of the natural growth of a city; in order to do this, however, a considerable expenditure for promotion must be made.

The specific problems of site selection divide into two major parts: prepurchase analysis and post-purchase operation. The purpose of the former, of course, is to select the proper site *before* investing substantial sums and to check items that may spell the difference between profit or loss. The purpose of post-purchase operation is to carry the subdivision plan to a point of profit maximization.

PREPURCHASE PROCEDURES

Land Cost

This is discovered, of course, through discussion with the landowner, who will give a price on the raw land. Many subdividers begin with a simple rule of thumb. A five-to-one ratio of selling price to cost is expected to be necessary to yield a profit. That is, the subdivider asks the question If I pay $3,000 per acre for the raw land, can I expect a return of $15,000 when this land is cut up?

Experienced developers use this guide to ensure sufficient margin for a profit equal to 10 percent of sales. This is necessary. Although profits account for 10 percent of sales and raw land costs are equal to 20 percent of sales, the remaining revenue can be expected to be consumed bringing the project to completion. In other words, other cost factors will account for 70 percent of the final sales price of each lot.

Of course, these rules of thumb are guides, which can be, and often are, changed to conform to local conditions.

Road Costs

The cost of building roads in the project must be estimated and divided among the estimated number of lots in order to determine the cost per lot. Because the problem of roads is so great in any development, it will be discussed at length later in this chapter.

Other Cost Factors

The next logical step is to prepare, either alone or with the help of a qualified surveyor and land planner, a tentative **plat** or layout to determine the number of lots. The major reason for this is that one may, in this manner, estimate the lot price of the improvements.

Typically, improvements requiring cost estimation include site grading, water mains, sewage systems, street grading and surfacing, curbing, and costs for bringing gas, electric, and telephone services to the site. Other necessary costs to be considered include surveying, legal fees, advertising, sales commissions, and miscellaneous expenditures associated with maintaining a land sales office.

In short, once these costs have been estimated, they should then be allocated to each of the lots available for sale. The more lots, the lower the cost of improvements per lot.

Drainage, Soil Tests, and Topography

The property should be examined for drainage. Without proper drainage, the cost of developing a satisfactory solution for the drainage of street and storm waters may be prohibitive.

Soil tests are important in areas where septic tanks are expected to be used. In those areas, the county public health departments have percolation maps indicating where septic tanks may be used. In the event tests have not been run on land the developer has in mind, the health department will run them.

Topography is important in any development. The site should be adaptable to its proposed use. If the land is rough and hilly, thought must be given to the manner in which the roads and lots will be laid out.

Existing Utilities

The location of utilities may govern the design of the subdivisions. In some cases, the absence of gas, sewers, water, and electricity may cause the project to be abandoned. When the utility lines are reasonably near the proposed project, it is necessary to contact the utility companies to determine the cost of installing new utilities in the project. This is done with the idea of allocating the cost of the utilities on a per lot basis.

Environmental Audit

Hidden environmental contamination can turn a profitable real estate development into a fiscal nightmare. A complete and thorough environmental site evaluation is necessary to comply with state laws and limit liability and financial risk. New Jersey, Connecticut, Iowa, Illinois, California, and Oregon now have requirements for environmental audits and reporting of findings. Legislation is pending in 13 other states.

With passage of the Comprehensive Environmental Response Compensation Liability Act (Superfund Act) in 1980, liability for site cleanup is assigned to any party who owns, operates, or takes temporary title to property. This means developers and subdividers should watch out: environmental cleanup is expensive and may cost more than the value of the property purchased. To assess the environmental condition of a site, the following steps are suggested:

1. Evaluate the site's history, including past use and any potential for environment accidents.
2. Evaluate the condition of above- and below-ground storage tanks, piping, and storage areas for potential environmental hazards and contamination.
3. Evaluate buildings for asbestos insulation and building materials that may require removal.
4. Evaluate ground and surface water quality by testing.
5. Evaluate adjoining land uses for sources of potential contamination.

The services of an environmental evaluation and engineering firm should be used to identify existing or potential site contamination. Although a 1986 amendment to the Superfund Act incorporates an "innocent landowner defense" clause, subdividers and developers should not count on it to protect them from loss and the responsibility for cleanup.

Transportation, Schools, and Shopping Districts

Easily available transportation can often make or break a development or subdivision. Therefore, it should be determined if any freeways are nearby or proposed for the near future. What about bus and railroad transportation? Nearness of schools should be determined as well as shopping districts. Availability of these facilities often makes the task of the subdividers easier. In addition, subdividers might think in terms of creating space for nearby schools and building their own shopping center. This has been done in the larger subdivisions.

Subdivision Restrictions

Zoning. **Zoning laws** are restrictions imposed by municipalities on the use of property. Every prospective subdivider or developer should obtain a copy of the local zoning regulations as soon as possible. All land prior to purchase must be thought of in terms of existing zoning laws. The land examined might be zoned for industry or business rather than for residential purposes. Although the developer had planned a controlled shopping center and a housing development, the land might be zoned for residential purposes only. Rather than make plans and then be forced to change them, the developer or subdivider should determine beforehand what restrictions must be observed or if zoning may be changed to conform with the intended property use.

The lot sizes must be carefully examined in the light of existing zoning laws. For example, the divider might be thinking in terms of lots with a 40-foot frontage when the zoning ordinances for the city require the minimum to be 50 by 100 feet.

Not only the size of the lot may be restricted by zoning ordinances, but also the height and the area of the building on the lot. For example, a typical ordinance may state the following requirements:

> HEIGHT—In the "A" Residential District, no building, hereafter erected or altered, shall exceed thirty-five (35) feet or three (3) stories. . . .
>
> "A" Building Area—In the "A" Residential District, the total building area shall not exceed twenty-five (25) percent of the total lot area.

Regulations. Subdivision regulations establish:

1. Size of lots and blocks.
2. Specifications for alignment, grading, surfacing, and width of rights-of-way and streets.
3. Building set-back lines, building heights, and land/building ratios.
4. Easements for public utilities.
5. Areas to be dedicated for use as parks or schools.
6. Standards for installation of water, sewer, and electric service.

The developer or subdivider must be familiar with zoning requirements and subdivision regulations. Only by working closely with the local planning board and meeting local standards is final approval assured.

Restrictive Covenants. The *Underwriting Manual* of the FHA offers the following recommendations regarding restrictive covenants:

> The protection afforded by suitable covenants is of primary importance in areas which lack the benefit of adequate and effective zoning. In properly zoned areas protective covenants are an important supplementary aid in maintaining neighborhood character and values. The extent of zoning protection is limited to governmental exercises of the police powers of maintaining and promoting public health, safety, and welfare. Protective covenants, being agreements between private parties, can go much further in meeting the needs of a particular development and in providing maximum possible protection.[1]

Private restrictions limiting land use are usually conceived by the subdivider or developer at the time a project is planned. The **restrictive covenants** are drawn, recorded, and are a matter of public record. Subsequent sale and use of the land are subject to these limitations. Typical restrictive covenants are as follows:

1. Set-back lines shall be a minimum of 35 feet from the road frontage and 25 feet from the side lines.
2. On each parcel of land there shall be erected only one one-family residence not exceeding two stories in height.
3. Each dwelling unit shall contain not less than 1,500 square feet of finished living space and valued at not less than $60,000.
4. No parcel of land shall be resubdivided except as directed by public authorities.
5. The keeping, breeding, or raising of pigs, swine, or other livestock shall be specifically prohibited.
6. No unsightly exterior storage is permitted. Boats, campers, or recreational trailers may be parked only in a location shielded from public view.
7. Enforcement of these covenants may be initiated by any owner through appropriate legal channels.
8. These covenants may be amended by a two-thirds vote of the owners of parcels within the tract.
9. Only one vote per parcel is permitted.

Enforcement of restrictive covenants is the responsibility of each property owner. If lot owners stand idly by while the violation is being committed, they may lose their right to a court order enforcing the covenants and preventing the violation. The loss of the right to enforce restrictive covenants occurs when property owners do not assert their claim or there is substantial undue delay in seeking enforcement. This right is said to be lost through *laches*. Restrictive covenants will be discussed in more detail in Chapter 8.

---

[1]FHA, *Underwriting Manual,* Sec. 1354, Art. 4.

Financing

The problem of financing a subdivision or development is a difficult one. Almost always, money must be borrowed to bring the project to fruition. The subdivider or developer typically employs one of the following five methods:

The *FIRST* and simplest method is for the purchase cost to be financed from personal funds.

The *SECOND* method involves partial financing by the seller. The purchase of the raw land may be partially financed by the seller, using a purchase money mortgage; e.g., the down payment is paid by the purchaser and the seller takes back a mortgage. Depending on the bargaining position of the parties, the mortgage may contain a **subordination agreement, partial release clause,** and some form of the **rolling option.** If possible, the subdivider will wish to exclude the nonalienation clause from the mortgage.

Subordination Agreement. To facilitate homesite sales and encourage immediate building, the mortgagee's security interest may be subordinated (given a second position) to a building loan. This encourages the bank to lend a builder construction funds and may relieve the subdivider from the cash requirements of a partial release. Typically, the subordinated interest and construction loan are paid off when the home is sold and a permanent mortgage obtained.

Partial Release Clause. The partial release clause permits the subdivider to sell property and, on making a specified principal payment, have the lot released from the terms of the mortgage. The homesite is "free and clear" and may be used by the purchaser as collateral for a building loan. A partial release is valuable when the subdivider plans to make cash sales or has sufficient capital to make necessary principal payments as the land is sold.

The Rolling Option. Many of the larger developers and subdividers use "the rolling option." The rolling option is simply a device to free capital and minimize risk. For example, a subdivider may intend to subdivide 150 acres. If desired, the subdivider may choose to purchase the 150 acres and subdivide it all at one time. However, this ties up a large amount of capital and creates a risk of loss in the event the project fails. Consequently, to avoid this risk the subdivider simply enters into an option agreement with the seller of the land that could be substantially as follows: (1) purchase 50 acres outright, (2) take an option to buy the second 50 acres within a stated time, (3) take a further option to buy the third 50-acre tract within a stated time. Thus, if the subdivider fails on the first 50-acre project, no obligation exists to buy the second 50-acre tract. If things go well, the whole tract will be subdivided, with options being exercised step-by-step.

For small developers, this plan may be applied equally well to 5-acre units in a 25-acre development. For the builder purchasing lots from a subdivider, the rolling option may be applied to release a lot at a time from a 5- to 10-lot purchase.

Nonalienation Clause. The presence of the **nonalienation clause** may prohibit the sale of property without payment to the mortgagee. Its absence permits the subdivider to sell lots and provide financing on contract or wraparound the existing mortgage. For purchasers who don't plan to build immediately, subdivider financing can be quite helpful. Coincidentally, the subdivider benefits from increased sales.

The *THIRD* method of financing, which depends upon the bargaining position of the subdivider, is to purchase an **option** on the property. The reason for a purchase option is to "buy time" to obtain tentative project approval from the local planning commission and FHA or to obtain other financing.

The length and cost of the option is negotiable. Basically, the subdivider enters into a purchase agreement contingent upon fulfillment of express conditions; e.g., obtaining financing, planning commission approval, proper zoning, etc.

When unable to fulfill the conditions within the specified time period, the subdivider is released from the obligation to purchase, minus the option money. The importance of the option is that the subdivider can determine the practicability of the subdivision without risking a great deal of money.

FOURTH, the development funds may be obtained from local banks or a Real Estate Investment Trust (REIT). This can be accomplished only after the plat has been filed and has met the standards set by the FHA, Environmental Protection Agency, and local planning boards, and is in compliance with the requirements of the Land Sales Full Disclosure Act. These loans are usually for one to three years and may be used to finance site improvements such as clearing and grading of land, installation of utilities, construction of roads, and placement of curbs and gutters. The mortgage may contain provisions for partial release and subordination. Sophisticated financial institutions are unlikely to consider rolling options or elimination of the nonalienation clause in their best interest.

In the *FIFTH* and final method of financing, the subdivider or developer may form a limited partnership, syndicate, or corporation in which stock is sold. Each of these organizations embraces a number of persons who put up part of the cash and share in the profits.

The subdivider, when selling lots to builders or developers, more often than not will be asked to accept a subordinated interest or permit a rolling option purchase with partial release of each individual lot. The techniques by which land is purchased and financed are often the way it must be sold.[2]

---

[2]See discussions in subsequent chapters as follows: Options (Chapter 7); Partial release clause (Chapter 11); Subordination agreement (Chapter 11); Nonalienation (Chapter 13).

THE NEED FOR PLANNING

Some developers are distressed by what they regard as insufferable delays of planning "red tape." Others feel that communities are placing undue cost burdens upon them. Yet, one developer built a large development, and then it was discovered that not a single foot of space had been left for schools, whereupon five acres of brand new homes had to be knocked down for the invasion of suburbia's children. In suburban Rochester, New York, a builder built a 640-home development without a sewer system. Almost immediately the inhabitants were engulfed by septic tank effluent. Subsequently, the health officials stepped in and ordered the installation of a sewage system—at a cost. Because of lack of planning, the taxpayers were forced to carry an additional burden. These are but two instances of hundreds that demonstrate both social and money costs of poor planning.

Does good planning pay? More often than not it does, for both the developer and the taxpayer. A study of a square mile of Trenton, New Jersey, has shown that under proper planning $450,000 could have been saved in street improvement costs and 65 acres set aside for recreation and other purposes—this, without a cent's loss to landowners and developers.

The U.S. Savings and Loan League suggests that land planning pays because:

1. It cuts development costs by requiring less lineal feet of streets, less curbing, less cutting and grading (by respecting the contours of the land).
2. It secures investment for generations and preserves the tax base through protection of property values and property rights.
3. It eliminates the misuse of property, thus preventing damage to the health, safety, and convenience of the community as a whole.
4. It eliminates hazardous or other unsatisfactory conditions that depress property values.
5. It saves municipal government unnecessary expense by providing suitable sites for schools and parks at a time when land values are low.
6. Its total effect is to take speculating out of subdividing.

In further support of sound planning, HUD has estimated potential cost savings for installing residential utilities. This information is presented in Table 3-1.

PLANNING THE SUBDIVISION

People buy property in subdivisions near cities because they want to get out of the city. They want to build in the "country." For that reason, successful subdividers attempt to retain as much of the country in the subdivision as possible. Where possible, wide streets and winding roads, coupled with

Table 3-1 Cost Saving Innovations for Installing Residential Utilities

Utility	INNOVATIVE/ALTERNATIVE PRACTICES Practices	Potential Savings
Sewer	Curvilinear sewers	19 percent
	Reduced minimum slopes for gravity sewer lines	$200 per acre
	Common sanitary sewer service laterals	$250–$300 per sewer connection
	Small diameter gravity sewer lines	$100 per residential unit
	Cleanouts on sanitary sewer lines	$800–$1000 per substituted manhole
	Increased spacing between manholes	$1000–$1500 per manhole
Water	Multiple water services from a common tap	$200 + per service tap
	Reduced size water mains	$100 + per residential unit
	Two water meters in one meter box	$200 per eliminated connection
	Common trenching of water and electric lines	$3.50 per linear foot
	No service saddles on home service connections with ductile iron pipe	$20–$30 per service tap
	Plastic tubing for home service lines	$0.71–$0.87 per linear foot
	Blow-offs versus hydrants	$600–$800 per hydrant
	Eliminate curb stops	$60 per connection
Water and/or sewer	Polyvinyl chloride pipe (PVC)	$0.50–$3 per linear foot
	Reduced horizontal separation distance between water and sewer lines	less land required
	Common trenching of water and sewer lines	$2–$5 per linear foot

SOURCE: Innovative Site Utility Installations, U.S. Department of Housing and Urban Development (November 1983).

trees and foliage, make the subdivision attractive to people who have been reared in the cities. Lots must be laid out as attractively as possible, both in size and physical appearance. Some subdivisions have parks and playgrounds to make them more attractive to the buyer with children.

To make a subdivision or city attractive to families, the following guidelines are suggested to provide a child-friendly and stimulating environment:

1. A network of safe, low-traffic or traffic-free places and streets that encourage children to explore neighborhoods.
2. Periodic access during the day to one or both parents, made possible by bringing living and working places closer together, or providing safe and inexpensive transportation between them.

3. The opportunity to observe people of all ages and backgrounds engaged in a variety of activities.
4. A visually interesting environment, containing a variety of textures, colors, materials, shapes, and forms.
5. A variety of public events open to children that generate surprise and delight.
6. Occasions that provide a sense of community history and traditions.
7. The opportunity to observe many forms of nature.
8. Easily accessible (and participatory) public art.
9. Protected public places where children's safety is guaranteed by the presence of trusted adults.[3]

In planning subdivisions these principles should be observed:[4]

1. Street intersections should be at right angles to minimize traffic hazards. Lots with double frontage are uneconomical and undesirable and should be avoided.

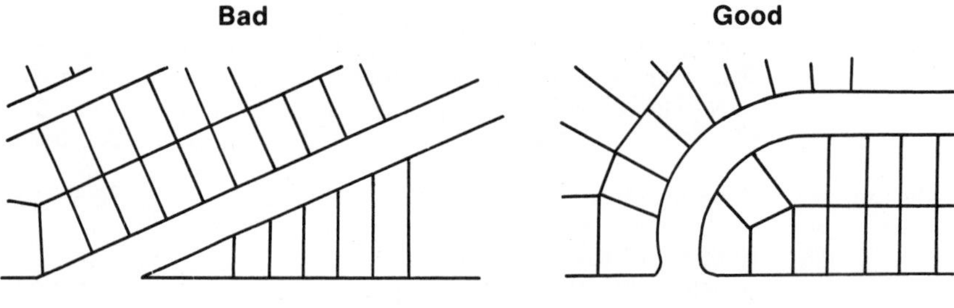

2. Intersections of minor streets with arterial or collector streets should be held to a minimum to avoid hazard and delay.

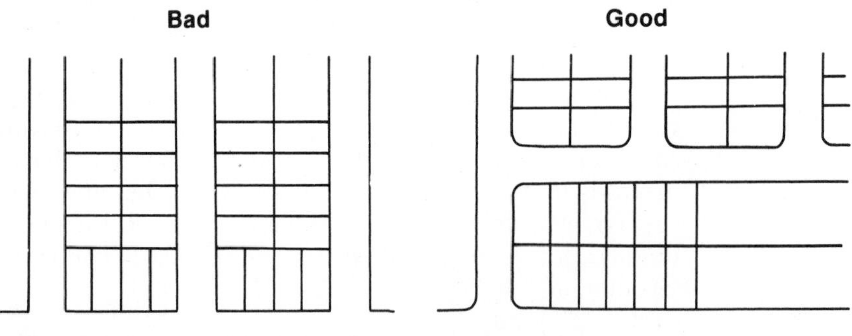

[3]Suzanne Crowhust Lennard and Henry Lennard, "Making Cities Better for Children," *Urban Land* (June 1989): 26.

[4]Designs from "Control of Land Subdivisions," State of New York, Department of Commerce.

3. Dead-end streets should be avoided.

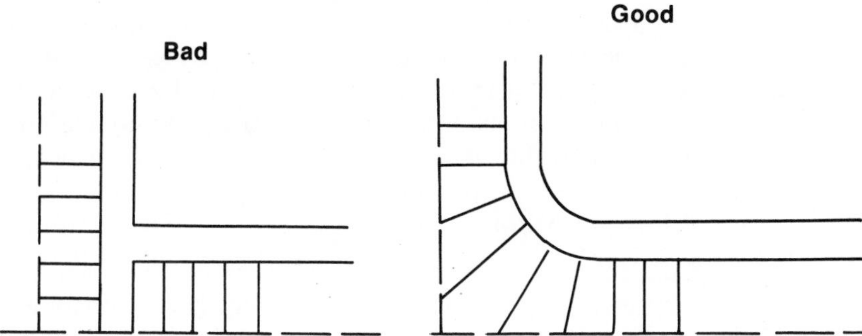

4. Street jogs with center-line offsets of less than 125 feet should be avoided.

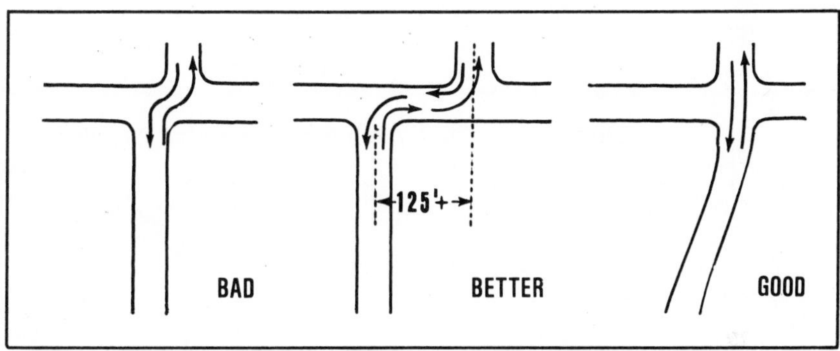

5. Corner lots require greater widths than interior lots in order to provide proper setback of the dwellings from the side street.

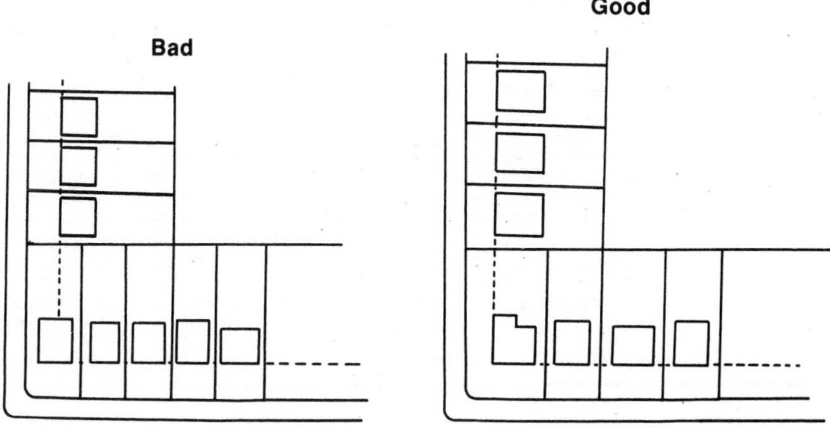

Exhibit 3-1 shows good and bad planning and includes some of the principles illustrated above.

It is interesting to note, when analyzing the above recommendations, that nearly every suggestion either provides the subdivider with a good selling point or tends to save money. At the same time, the community is benefited. For example, a properly planned subdivision will have no heavy through traffic, an important factor in selling to people with children.

Filing the Plat

As a result of the actions of some incompetent and unscrupulous subdividers, most states have enacted stringent laws regulating the subdividing of real property.

A map must be filed designating lots, blocks, streets, and their dimensions. The map also specifies utility easements and land dedicated for public use. The first problem is to have a map made by a competent, licensed surveyor. In most cases this map, or plat as it is called, must first be

Exhibit 3-1 Good and Poor Subdivision Planning

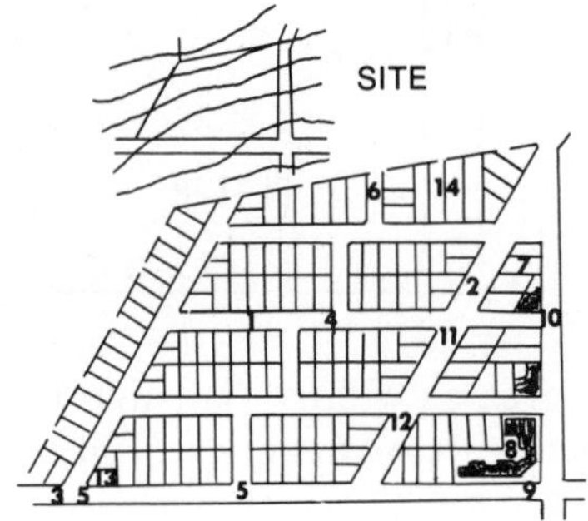

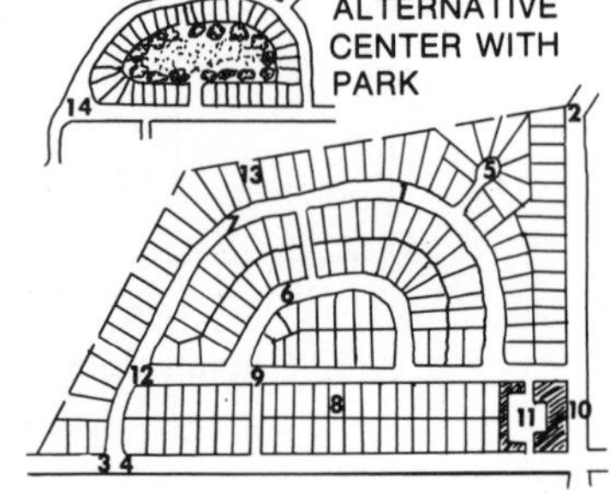

POOR PLANNING and what is wrong with it:

1 Gridiron street pattern without purpose.
2 Heavy traffic within subdivision.
3 Angular intersections.
4 Non-abutting cross streets.
5 Numerous subdivision entrance streets.
6 Dead-end streets.
7 Small, uneconomical blocks.
8 Ribbon shopping districts.
9 No off-street parking space.
10 Stores amid residences.
11 Lots not perpendicular to streets.
12 Angular lots.
13 Small corner lots.
14 Deep lots.

GOOD PLANNING and what is good about it:

1 Curved street pattern adds subdivision appeal.
2 Heavy traffic diverted.
3 Safe, perpendicular intersections.
4 Few subdivision entrance streets.
5 Quiet street.
6 Local streets for local traffic only.
7 Streets fit topography.
8 Long, economical blocks.
9 Cross walks in long blocks.
10 Organized shopping center.
11 Off-street parking space.
12 Wide corner lots.
13 Lots perpendicular to streets.
14 Provision for interior park.

SOURCE: "Control of Land Subdivisions," State of New York, Department of Commerce.

approved by the town, county, or city planning board, or sometimes by the city commissioners. It is suggested that the name of a surveyor to do the job be obtained from the planning consultant, city commissioner, or whoever first approves the plat. In this manner, much trouble regarding the acceptance of the plat can be avoided.

If the owner of a parcel of raw land has a map made and sells from an unrecorded map by a lot and block description, most states provide that each lot sold or conveyed in that manner shall result in a fine to the person selling. This does not, however, preclude an owner from having a map made and selling parcels by a **metes and bounds** description.

The most complicated situation in filing a plat is the number of bodies that must approve the filing. Sometimes when a map is being filed, it must have approval not only from county officials but also from the township officials.

Before acquiring raw land, the subdivider should inquire about the requirements of the town planning board. Although the requirements vary, in general they have to do with building the road to proper specifications. For example, some townships require that the road-cut be made to a width of 50 feet, and oiled to a width of at least 40 feet. These requirements vary from township to township, but in any event there will be some road-building specifications that have to be followed. The specifications not only will call for the road to be cut to a specified width, but they will also specify the method of applying the oil, asphalt, or cement; for example, the number of gallons of a specified grade per square yard, the number of coats of oil, and the amount of the "blotter coat" of sand that must be applied. Similar requirements are set for other types of pavements. In some areas it is necessary to place a bond with the town board to insure that the road will be built in accordance with the specifications set down by the board. The bond is usually two-thirds of the cost of building the road and is posted in cash or "the equivalent thereof." As the road is built, it is inspected by the town supervisor of highways; and if it is not built according to specifications, the bond money is used by the township to properly complete the building of the road.

In other areas, planning board approval may be dependent on dedication of land for public use. Most commonly, such dedication is for parks, bikeways, schools, or boulevards.

When the plat is approved by the town board and a bond is furnished to insure the proper building of the road, the map is filed with the proper county official, generally the county clerk. In most states an abstract covering at least 20 years must be filed with the map. In addition, most places require that a certificate be obtained from the county treasurer showing that all of the taxes due and payable on the land have been paid as of the date of filing. Some counties specify the size of the map to be filed. In some areas of the country, especially those areas where there is no city water or sewage system, approval must be obtained from the local board of health for sewage disposal and water supply systems. For example, when it is necessary for a well to be drilled on the property, the health department often requires that the cesspool or septic tank for sewage disposal be built at least 75 feet from the well. This, too, will vary from county to county, but generally a minimum distance of 75 feet is required from the water system to the sewage disposal system. These requirements for filing the plat are general throughout the United States, although there are local variations that must be checked.

Government Involvement

The significance of the government's role in subdividing and development should not be underestimated. The FHA, to ensure minimum standards, may withhold mortgage insurance from homes built in subdivisions failing to assure the health and safety of future occupants.

The reason for these standards is to promote harmony in the neighborhood, reduce the likelihood of blight, and protect against the creation of slums. Subdividers and developers providing a maximum of privacy; protection from excessive noise, dust, and traffic; reasonable access to schools, shopping, and public transportation; and necessary utilities, generally meet the minimum requirements. In addition, sound, attractive developments make property sales easier while simultaneously enhancing the subdivider's or developer's reputation.

Due to declining federal and state investment in community development, some communities have implemented development fees to help defray costs. The use of development fees to pay for plan processing, water taps, water treatment expansion, parks, storm drainage, building permits, and electrical fees has been successful in Ft. Collins, Colorado. Development fees help cover costs for expansion of public utility services not directly related to the subdivision or development.

The most direct impact of government on subdivisions and developments has been through regulations designed to protect the environment and consumers from past mistakes of subdividers and developers. The major acts affecting real estate land development and providing a measure of protection for our natural resources are enumerated below.

1. The *Coastal Zone Management Act* provides for federal aid to encourage states to establish standards for public and private development of salt and fresh water coastline.
2. The *Clean Air Act* provides that states and communities have primary responsibility for developing national air quality standards and implementing programs of local enforcement.
3. The *Solid Waste Disposal Act, Resource Recovery Act,* and *Resource Conservation and Recovery Act* combine to promote development of improved means for processing, storage, and disposal of solid and hazardous waste materials.

4. The *Energy Supply and Environmental Coordination Act* requires review, before construction, of facilities creating new sources of air pollution.
5. The *Clean Water Act, Water Quality Improvement Act, Water Pollution Control Act,* and amendments have strengthened water pollution standards, created objectives for cleaning navigable streams and lakes of pollutants, provided quality minimum for suppliers of water, and updated identification of dangerous water pollutants.

Interstate Land Sales Full Disclosure Act

As a result of fraudulent land sales, Congress passed the **Interstate Land Sales Full Disclosure Act** in 1969. Basically, the act requires the seller of subdivided property to make a full, complete, and accurate disclosure of all relevant information about the property prior to the consummation of the sale to the buyer of the land. The act protects the buyer against fraudulent and deceptive sales practices by providing civil and criminal remedies against the land developer and the sales agent for willful violations of the act.

Land developers are required to file a Statement of Record with the Office of Interstate Land Sales Registration (OILSR), Department of Housing and Urban Development. The **Statement of Record** details information summarized in a document called the **Property Report,** which must be given to the prospective purchaser prior to a sale. It contains such things as name and location of developer and subdivision; effective date of the report; road distances to nearby communities; financial terms and refund policies, if any; mortgages and liens; protection, if any, afforded the buyer in case of financial default of the developer; leasing arrangements; taxes and special assessments to be paid by the buyer; escrow and title arrangements, plus any restrictions, easements, and covenants and their effects on the buyer; recreational facilities available and expected dates of completion of proposed ones; availability or lack of utilities and services, such as trash collection, sewers, water supply; any need for drainage and fill before the land can be used for building; presence of schools, medical facilities, shopping, and transportation or proposed dates of availability of such services; number of homes now occupied; accessibility of lots by roads. Developers' financial statements are also required, as well as any other data HUD may require.

The rights of purchasers of lots and the responsibility and liability of developers were expanded by a comprehensive revision of regulations and congressional amendments to the act in 1979.

Significant elements of current rights, obligations, and liability are presented below.

1. Property reports must be furnished to purchasers 48 hours prior to sale.

2. Reports may not contain untrue statements or omission of material fact that, when disclosed to the buyer, would likely result in a decision not to purchase; e.g., lakeshore lot is located adjacent to a sewage disposal pipe for a chemical plant.
3. Lots may not be sold by fraudulent or deceptive advertising or misrepresentation that was relied on by the purchaser.
4. Sales contracts must contain purchasers' Notice of Rescission Right. Purchasers may rescind within seven days after signing the contract. Contracts must also include all promises to provide or complete water, sewer, gas or electric services, roads, and recreational facilities.
5. Purchasers may seek redress for violations of the act against the developer, developer's agents, brokers, advertising agents, and mass marketing firms that offer or sell subdivision lots.
6. Purchasers of lots have three years after discovery of violations of anti-fraud provisions of the act to bring suit. For violations of other provisions of the act, purchasers have three years from the date of purchase.

Not all subdividers or developers are required to comply with provisions of the act. Exemptions and partial exemptions may be granted when certain conditions are met. Partial exemptions are exempt from registration requirements but not anti-fraud provisions of the act.

Exemptions

1. Sale of land restricted or zoned for industrial or commercial purposes.
2. Lots sold for later resale or sold to contractors and builders.
3. Sales of cemetery lots, mortgages, deeds of trust, securities sold by REITs, and sales by government agencies.
4. Sales from subdivisions with less than 25 lots.
5. Sales of lots on which a residential, commercial, or industrial structure will be erected within two years or on which such a structure is already present.

Partial Exemptions

1. Single-family subdivisions that comply with specified local subdivision standards, whose lots are on paved, maintained streets, and are provided with water, sewer, and electric service at the time of closing, may earn partial exemption status. The developers, however, must provide a title insurance policy showing they held good title prior to sale, allow on-the-lot inspections, and deliver a deed within 180 days of purchase. Developers may not use direct mail, telephone solicitation, offers of gifts, trips, dinners, or similar inducements to sell lots.

2. Subdivisions having sales of less than 13 lots per year may also earn partial exemption. Sale of the thirteenth lot and subsequent sales will require registration.
3. Sales from noncontiguous parcels, each of which contain less than 20 lots, are partially exempt. For this provision to apply, purchasers must make on-site inspections.
4. Sales from subdivisions in which no lot is smaller than 20 acres. On-site inspection, however, is required.
5. Intrastate sales of lots that are free and clear of encumbrance.
6. Sale of lots, free and clear, to purchasers who all live within the same SMSA.
7. Lots sold by developers who provide or promise that a mobile home will be placed on the site within two years. Qualification for partial exemption under this provision, however, requires that the lot be served by water, sewer, and electricity within two years. Also, proceeds of sale must be held in escrow until these obligations are fulfilled.

Federal regulations set minimum standards of disclosure for interstate land sales. The sale of subdivided land within a particular state may be subject to more stringent requirements. These requirements must be met by those selling land located out of the state to residents within the state. In-state subdividers, selling land to local residents, are exempt from federal regulations but must comply with state land use regulations.

State Land Use Regulations

Many states have, and most states will move into the area of, land use regulations because of full disclosure and environmental considerations.

For example, in 1963 California revised its subdivision laws based on the principle of full disclosure. In that year, the legislature gave the California Real Estate Department power to withhold public reports of subdivisions unless subdividers gave certain detailed information. The real estate commission required proof of title; interest contracted for; satisfactory demonstration that adequate financial arrangements had been made for off-site improvements and community facilities; and specific information indicating that parcels of land could, indeed, be used in the way in which they were intended.

As soon as California strengthened its laws, some unscrupulous developers moved to neighboring states. In 1964, California added an additional law that gave the Real Estate Department power to refuse out-of-state advertising if it felt that such advertising constituted an investment danger to its citizens. In that year Nevada, New Mexico, and Oregon passed laws patterned after California.

To sell subdivided lands in Minnesota, the following disclosures are required for registration and approval:

1. Legal description verified by affidavit of an independent professional surveyor.
2. Topographical map.
3. Plat map showing dimensions of individual lots.
4. Statement of condition of title, all encumbrances, restrictions, and covenants.
5. Copies of instruments to be delivered to purchasers:
   a. Evidences of ownership.
   b. Contracts and other agreements required to agree or sign.
   c. Range of selling prices.
   d. Rents.
   e. Mandatory fees for memberships.
6. Copies of instruments by which interest in the subdivided lands was acquired.
7. Legal description of all liens and encumbrances:
   a. Steps taken to clear title.
   b. Steps taken to protect purchaser in event of failure to discharge liens and encumbrances.
8. Copies of instruments creating, altering, or removing easements, restrictions, or encumbrances.
9. A statement of and evidence showing compliance with zoning, other governmental laws, ordinances, and regulations including:
   a. Dates of zoning changes.
   b. Existing taxes.
   c. Proposed taxes, special taxes and assessments affecting the subdivided lands.
10. Statement of the existing provisions for access.
11. Availability of sewage disposal and other public utilities.
12. Proximity of the subdivision to nearby communities.
13. Scope of police and fire protection.
14. Location of public schools.
15. Statement of improvements to be installed, and who will install and maintain these facilities.
16. Assurance of completion of improvements by filing a bond, letter of credit, or depositing funds in escrow.
17. Narrative description of the promotional plan with copies of all advertising material.
18. Proposed public offering statement.
19. Financial statement of the subdivider audited by an independent CPA.
20. Description of the land as it existed in its natural state prior to development and any changes that occurred due to actions by the subdivider.
21. Statement of compliance with federal, state, and local environmental quality standards.

22. Statement of required federal, state, and local permits noting those received, applied for, and refused.
23. Statement indicating whether the subdivider or any of its officers, directors, or partners have been convicted of crimes involving land sales or subject to administrative orders or injunctions.

Minnesota also sets more stringent requirements for exemption from registration and permits less leeway in the buyer's right to rescind than federal statutes. Sellers of less than ten separate lots in any 12-month period are exempt from registration. The right to rescind is limited to five days from receipt of a legible copy of the binding agreements.

Environmental Impact Statements (EIS)

An awareness that uncontrolled development has had a shattering impact on the environment has led to environmental impact laws—and more to come in the future. For example, California's Environmental Quality Act of 1970 required state agencies to publish detailed reports on the environmental impact of their projects. However, in *Friends of Mammoth Mountain v. Mono County,* a California court ruled the act also applied to private developers, saying that to limit the operation of the E.Q.A. solely to what were essentially public works projects would frustrate the effectiveness of the act.

At this time most states have enacted legislation providing some degree of environmental control over private development projects. Many of the remaining states are considering legislation to require an **Environmental Impact Statement** before licensing subdivisions and building projects.

The demand for an Environmental Impact Statement (EIS) is considered by many to be the most significant new development affecting real estate in the past decade. The advent of EIS assures that developments preserve the environmental quality of life.

In the most general sense, when speaking of environment, reference is made to cultural, physical, and natural elements affected by a proposed development. An EIS, therefore, is a document identifying, analyzing, and discussing a development's impact on the economic, social, and physical environment. As a practical matter, the EIS has become as necessary for obtaining planning board approval as the plat map or proper zoning. Based on experience, Storm Allman has identified ten essential elements of an EIS. (See Exhibit 3-2.)

Controversy often surrounds major developments and portions of the EIS are singled out for special attention. Daniel Luttenegger, a member of the Environmental Services Group of Barton-Aschman Associates, Inc., has found special attention most often directed toward one of the environmental areas in Exhibit 3-3.

Hopefully, the use of environmental impact statements will aid in the planning, preservation, and ultimately the liveability of our cities and

Exhibit 3-2 Elements of the Environmental Impact Study

I. Description of project
II. Environmental description
III. The environmental impact of the proposed action
   A. Impact of the land form
   B. Impact of noise
   C. Impact of water quality on hydrology
   D. Impact on air quality
   E. Impact on the natural systems (landscape, vegetation, and wildlife)
   F. Impact on open space system (parks and recreation systems)
   G. Impact on historical/scientific resources
   H. Impact on other environmental features
IV. Any adverse environmental effects which cannot be avoided if the proposed project is implemented
V. Mitigation measures proposed to minimize the impact
VI. The alternatives to the proposed action
VII. Relationship between local short-term uses of man's environment and the maintenance or enhancement of long-term productivity
VIII. Any irreversible changes if the proposed action is implemented
IX. The growth-inducing impact of the proposed action
X. Summary and conclusion of the report

SOURCE: Storm A. Allman, "Environmental Impact Studies: Their Need and Components," Journal of Property Management *(May/June 1973): 105–109.*

environment. At the present, many developers see the EIS only as an obstacle to be overcome: a costly, time-consuming, bureaucratic hassle that adds significantly to the cost of homes already high priced. In response to this criticism, to reduce the cost of environmental impact reviews (EIRs), and to speed development approval, many California communities now use "mitigated negative declarations." Cooperating cities have granted approval to projects that have substantial environmental impact on the condition that project plans are revised to minimize detrimental effects. Regardless of viewpoint, rest assured the EIS is here to stay; and environmental controls, approvals, permits, and licensing will become more extensive in the future.

GLOSSARY

Developers Subdividers who build homes or other improvements on what was initially purchased as raw acreage

Environmental Impact Statement A statement of the impact of a proposed project on the cultural, physical, and natural elements of the area

Exhibit 3-3 Environmental Issue Identification

Built Environment
1. Traffic congestion
2. Visual blight
3. Conformity with plans and plan implementation
4. Flood control

Socioeconomic Environment
1. Fiscal revenues
2. Public services
3. Jobs
4. Utilities
5. Energy
6. Health and welfare

Physical Environment
1. Air quality
2. Water quality
3. Noise

Natural Environment
1. Rare or endangered species
2. Sensitive ecosystems

SOURCE: Daniel J. Luttenegger, "Preparing an Environmental Impact Statement," Real Estate Today *(August 1976): 15.*

Interstate Land Sales Full Disclosure Act Federal act passed in 1969 requiring subdividers of certain real property to make a full disclosure of relevant information to buyers prior to a sale

Metes and bounds Measures and direction; a method of defining property boundaries

Nonassumption (nonalienation) clause A clause stating that the mortgagor cannot sell the property and have the buyer assume the mortgage without the consent of the lender

Option A contract to keep an offer open

Partial release clause A clause inserted in a purchase money mortgage stating that upon partial payment of the mortgage, the mortgagee will issue a partial satisfaction piece releasing a particular parcel or lot from the terms of the mortgage

Plat A map designating lots, blocks, streets, and their dimensions

Property Report Information on subdivision lots subject to the Interstate Lane Sales Full Disclosure Act

Restrictive covenants A type of covenant running with the land that imposes certain restrictions upon the purchaser involving use of the property

Rolling option An option designed to permit a developer to free capital and minimize risk

Statement of record A statement that must be filed with the Department of Housing and Urban Development for lots subject to the Interstate Land Sales Full Disclosure Act

Subdividers Persons who purchase raw acreage and, after building roads, cut the land up into lots and sell the parcels

Subordination agreement A device by which those with superior rights subordinate those rights in favor of inferior rights

Zoning laws The statutes giving municipalities the authority to regulate land use

QUESTIONS FOR REVIEW

1. When selecting a site for a subdivision, what pertinent points must the subdivider examine?
2. Explain the rule of thumb used by subdividers in estimating the necessary return per dollar of outlay for acreage.
3. Why is zoning important to a developer?
4. What is the rolling option and how is it used?
5. Subdivision planning benefits both the subdivider and the community. Discuss.
6. Explain in detail the legal requirements of filing a map or plat.
7. Describe and discuss the essential features of the Interstate Land Sales Full Disclosure Act.
8. What prompted the federal government to enact the Interstate Land Sales Full Disclosure Act?
9. Discuss the need for Environmental Impact Statements.

PROBLEMS AND ACTIVITIES

1. You are given the opportunity to purchase a parcel of land 2,000 feet deep with a 290-foot frontage on main highway. The only approach to the property is from the main highway because there is wooded area on either side of the parcel. The owner tells you the purchase price is

$48,000. The parcel is located five miles from the outskirts of a small but growing city. From previous investigations, you feel there is a need for more housing in the area. There is no water or sewage, but in that section of the country most people drill their own wells and build their own septic tanks anyway, so that doesn't bother you too much. Electricity is available. You speak to the town engineer who recommends an old friend as a surveyor. The surveyor to whom you speak about the project states that if you decide to go through with the idea, the Town Planning Board would be happier if you cut a road parallel to the main highway, 1,000 feet back from the main highway. In addition, the surveyor tells you that the planning board will refuse to accept the plat unless you have a "50-foot turnaround" at the far end of any proposed road. You are told that this means a circle with a 50-foot radius.

Studying the zoning ordinance, you find that the property is located in what is called the "C" Residence District. You discover on further reading that it states:

> "C" Size of Lot-Area—In the "C" Residential District, no building shall be erected or altered on a lot of any area less than five thousand (5,000) square feet, or upon a lot having a frontage of less than fifty (50) feet.
>
> In the "C" Residence District, the total building area shall not exceed thirty-five (35) percent of the total lot area.
>
> In the "C" Residence District, the required front yard shall be at least twenty-five (25) feet.
>
> In the "C" Residence District, there shall be two (2) side yards, one (1) on each side of the building, the total aggregate of both sides to be eighteen (18) feet and no one (1) side to be less then eight (8) feet wide.

After examining the ordinance, you decide that if you do go through with the deal, you should sell some of the lots. Then if things go well, you might try building houses. After all, your finances are limited—you have only $20,000 in cash. The zoning ordinance also reveals to you that you must have a minimum of a 50-foot cut for a road. A road-building contractor tells you that when you begin to build your road, you must deposit two-thirds of the cost with the Town Planning Board to insure that the road will be built according to their standards. This deposit must be in cash. The road-building contractor assures you that the cost of the road will be $6 per lineal foot.

You approach the owner, who agrees to sell you the property for $48,000; $10,000 cash will be required and the owner will take back a purchase money mortgage in the amount of $38,000. It will be a blanket mortgage with a partial release clause calling for the payment of $400 per lot toward the purchase price on the first ten lots sold. The mortgage is for three years at 12 percent.

a. Draw a diagram showing the maximum number of lots, size of lots roads, and turnaround.

b. Determine the price of the lots at four times the average cost of the land and the cost of the road. Each lot is priced the same. You call the subdivision Greenacres.
c. Prepare a classified advertisement to be inserted in the local papers. You have decided to sell the lots for cash.
d. You sell ten lots and then decide to build homes on the remainder of the property. What do you obtain from the mortgagee at this point?
e. An architect submits plans to you for a house having dimensions of 42 feet by 30 feet. It is a popular ranch-type house, but you reject the drawings. Why?
f. You finally select a house that you believe will sell for $82,000. You go to your banker and arrange to finance the building. What does the banker ask you to give as security for a proposed loan?
g. The cost to you of the house including the lot is $70,000. You find a buyer and the two of you go to a bank that agrees to give the buyer a loan of $64,000. What takes place at the closing?
h. List any restrictions you might want in the deeds given by you to the lot purchasers and to the home purchasers.

4

REAL ESTATE MARKET ANALYSIS

KEY TERMS

Acceleration principle
Base ratio or location quotient
Contraction
Economic base
Economic base analysis
Expansion
Feasibility report
Major business cycles
Market analysis
Minor business cycles
Primary employment
Recession
Revival
Seasonal variations
Secondary employment
Secular trend

The 1980s were a period of record losses on real estate investments. Office vacancy rates exceeded 20 percent, substantial overbuilding of multifamily housing occurred in the sunbelt, and the value of agricultural property dropped, in some instances, to 50 percent of peak prices.

These factors contributed to record failures of commercial banks and savings and loans and threatened the solvency of the Farm Credit System and Federal Savings and Loan Insurance Corporation (FSLIC). These problems were attributed to asset-based lending and poor preconstruction investigation of market demand, economic conditions, and project illiquidity; in other words, bad lending practices.

THE NEED FOR MARKET ANALYSIS

The net result of the problems of the 1980s was tighter lending/investment standards and recognition of the need for thorough real estate market analysis. Much of the demand for market studies, feasibility reports, and project documentation came from financial institutions. When large sums are involved, the institutions simply will not finance on the assurance by developers that a proposed project is sound. Lenders want much more.

The **feasibility report** begins with discussion of the national economy, then proceeds to focus more sharply on the specific proposal, and closes with emphasis on the credit, character, and capacity of the principal investors. It consists of three essential elements: (1) analysis of the economic bases, (2) analysis of the target market, and (3) data specific to the proposed project.

Economic base analysis includes forecasting regional and national economic conditions When the analysis is related to local industry, employment, growth, and income, the analyst is not only able to forecast changes in local economic conditions but to relate these changes to demand for specific types of real estate.

Market analysis combines the demand for real estate with a survey of competitive projects and the economic, social, and environmental impact of the proposed project. The market analysis emphasizes discovery of neglected or increasing demand for specific types of real estate.

Once demand has been established, specific data relevant to the proposed project may be formulated, such as rental or sales prices, unit design, and size mix. Assembled with pro forma income statements, personal financial statements, investor biographies, blueprints, and plat, the feasibility report may be prepared.

The reason for preparation of such a project package is to assure lenders that all the factors have been considered that may affect a proposed project. Real estate can be a volatile and highly cyclical business. It is unwise to assume that, because real estate generally is prospering, a particular undertaking will also prosper. General market conditions do not always apply to specific submarkets.

The importance of understanding the real estate market and the business cycle should not be underestimated. Properly presented to the investing financial institution, total market analysis accompanying the project package is the key to obtaining project financing.

THE BUSINESS CYCLE

For purposes of analysis, the business cycle has been divided into four distinct phases. The first of these phases is called the period of **expansion.** It is here that business activities are on the upswing. Characteristically, more and more durable goods are being manufactured. Demand is increasing. Business people who formerly needed only three machines now need and order ten machines, or may order larger and more complex machines. Employment is increasing, and national income and savings are up; and more and more money is being poured into new investment, generating a multiplying effect on national income. The future looks bright, and business looks toward further expansion.

But business conditions do not level off and remain at a high point. When the peak is reached, some factor or factors precipitate the second phase, the **recession.** A downswing is now perceptible. Following the recession, the third phase of the cycle, the period of **contraction,** begins. This is the opposite of the expansion period of the cycle. Fewer and few durable goods are purchased. Businesspeople who, in the expansion period, bought more machinery, now begin to take their machines out of production and do not order new ones. Fewer goods are manufactured, unemployment grows by leaps and bounds; wages drop and with them the national income; savings and new investments are small. Conditions become darker and darker.

The length of the stay at the bottom of the trough varies until a **revival** period begins (after machines have become worn and inventory has declined). This is the fourth and last phase of the cycle. Then it begins all over again.

The example presented in Table 4-1 illustrates the phases of the business investment cycle. Note that small changes in demand have had a much greater impact on investment. In other words, while consumption has increased steadily, business investment has gone through a complete cycle of expansion, recession, contraction, and revival. The investment phases of the business cycle and related consumption demand are presented in Exhibit 4-1.

Cycle Movements

Time-series movements exist in business cycles. These time-series movements or patterns are observable and can be measured statistically. Although there have been measurements made of numerous movements, the most important for our brief analysis are (1) secular, (2) major and minor business cycles, and (3) seasonal variations.

Secular Trend

The **secular trend** is a long-run movement (generally thought of as 20 years or more) resulting from forces such as population growth, capital accumulation, new markets, and technological improvements. For example, the Gross National Product (GNP) of the United States has in-

Table 4-1 Investment Phases of the Business Cycle

YEAR	UNITS OF CONSUMPTION	CONSUMPTION % CHANGE	REQUIRED EQUIPMENT	WORN-OUT EQUIPMENT	PURCHASES OF REQUIRED EQUIPMENT	INVESTMENT % CHANGE
1	50,000	—	10	1	1	—
2	55,000	10	11	1	2	100
3	65,000	18.2	13	1	3	50
4	75,000	15.4	15	1	3	0
5	80,000	6.7	16	1	2	−33
6	80,000	0	16	1	1	−50
7	85,000	6.3	17	1	2	+100
8	95,000	11.8	19	1	3	50

Assumptions: Each machine can produce 5000 units; machine life is ten years; one machine wears out each year.

■ **Exhibit 4-1 Investment Phases of the Business Cycle**

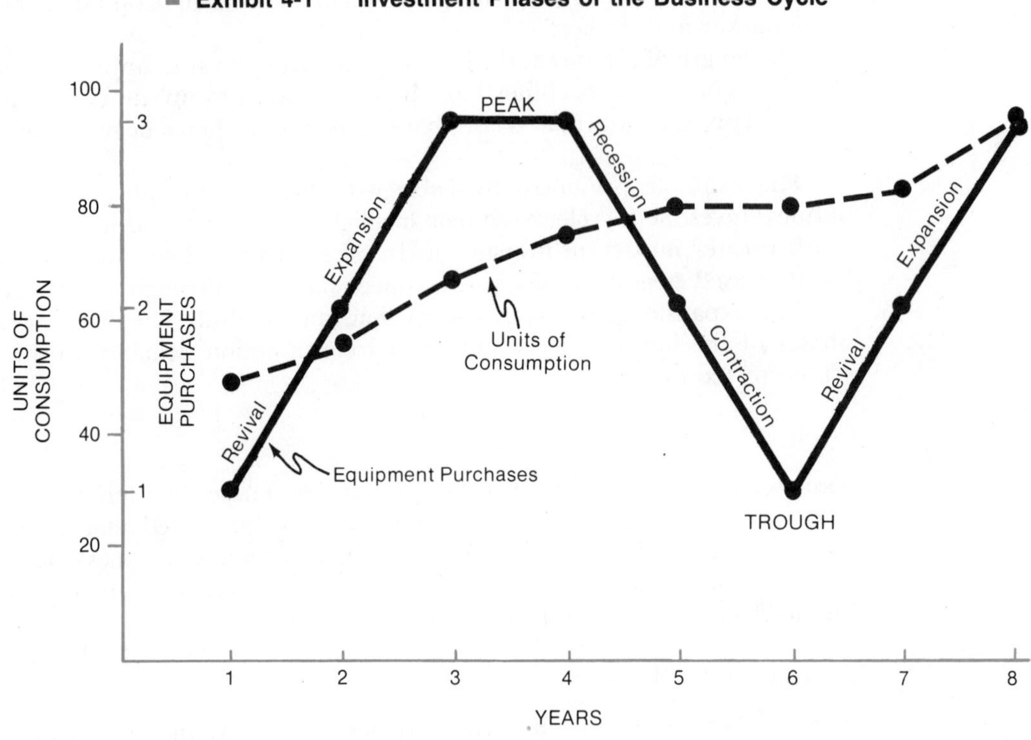

creased 3 to 4 percent per year for the past 45 years, which is an average and represents the secular trend. However, in the period that growth averaged 3 to 4 percent, some years showed a decline in GNP, while other years showed growth substantially in excess of 4 percent.

Major and Minor Cycles

Major business cycles are characterized by the relatively long length of the expansion and contraction phases. **Minor business cycles** are of shorter duration. Minor or major, cycles may last no longer than a year or up to 13 years.

Unhappily for the real estate analyst, each cycle is unique. The combination of factors creating the current cycle are different from any preceding cycle and are unlikely to be repeated in the future. In other words, the lengths of expansion and contraction phases seem to have no relationship and are essentially impossible to predict with any accuracy. However, there are certain elements essential to real estate ventures, components of the real estate cycle, that will be discussed in more detail later in this chapter. Generally, some of the factors are inventory adjustments, employment and income levels, local population growth, and government monetary policies.

Seasonal Variations

Monthly, quarterly, and weekly data suggest that there exists a regular recurrence of seasonal fluctuations. For example, the construction industry is more active during summer months; hence, residential sales peak in August and September.

These repetitive intra-annual changes, or **seasonal variations,** are thought for the most part to be related to climate, holidays, vacation periods, and even differences in the number of working days in a month. These patterns frequently are repetitive because they are entrenched in custom. For example, school begins in September; therefore, families buy a home so the children can be enrolled. September can be a hectic time for residential sales. Seasonal sales of existing single-family homes from January 1986 through April 1989 may be observed in Exhibit 4-2.

THE REAL ESTATE CYCLE

Although comparatively few studies have been made of the real estate cycle, it is generally agreed that building activity somewhat follows the business cycle in a wave-like movement. It is further indicated that the volume of real estate activity does not necessarily advance with the increases in general business, and declines in real estate activity generally precede general business declines. It appears that the troughs and peaks of the real estate cycle go deeper and higher than those of the business cycle. Needless to say, improper timing of real estate projects could lead to disaster because of the cyclical nature of the industry. Recent real estate and recession cycles may be observed as shaded areas on Exhibit 4-2.

In a sense, real property is unique; it is different from most consumer goods that are produced. This uniqueness results from the fact that the supply of real estate cannot be as rapidly adjusted to demand as can other consumer products. For example, if the demand for refrigerators declines, the factory producing the refrigerators may immediately shut down or curtail production, thus affecting the supply of refrigerators. Such an adjustment, however, cannot be made so readily in the real estate business because of the length of time that it takes to produce a dwelling unit, which can be as long as six months for a custom-built home. Once begun, a large apartment project may take well over a year to complete; commercial and industrial projects, longer.

In the real estate cycle, if a decrease in demand takes place, supply cannot be adjusted and will actually continue to increase as units under construction are completed. Also, the sharing of dwellings by families, or doubling up, acts to increase the available supply of housing. This phenom-

Exhibit 4-2 **Existing Single-Family Home Sales for the United States, Monthly, 1986–1989**

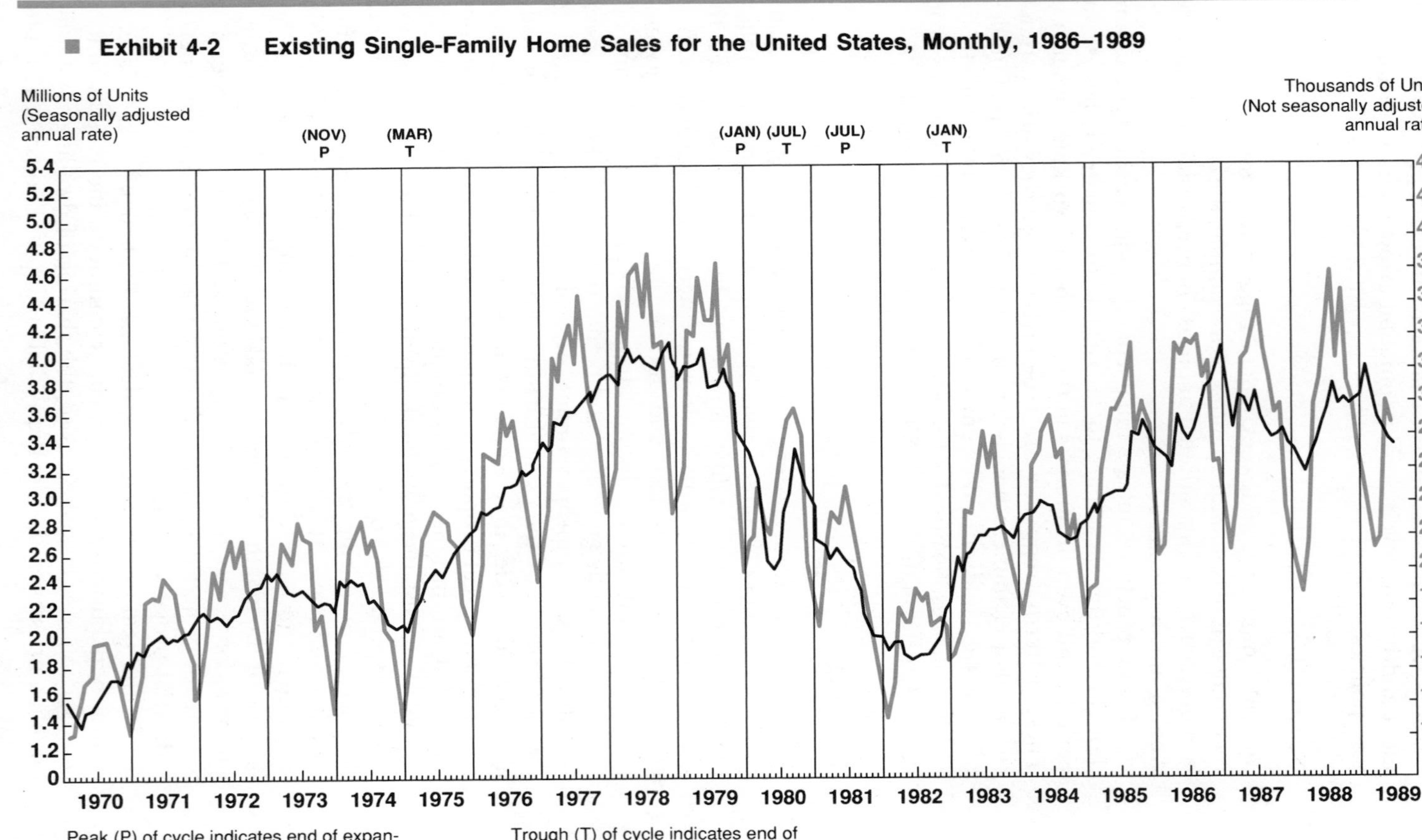

SOURCE: NATIONAL ASSOCIATION OF REALTORS®, Economics & Research Division.

enon is most apparent during periods of general economic recession. These increases in the available supply of housing, together with a reduction in demand, cause the amplitudes of the real estate cycle to be even greater than those of the business cycle.

Recovery from the "trough" of the real estate cycle is dependent on increasing employment levels, adequate money being available to finance home purchases, and substantial reduction in the oversupply of dwelling units. For example, to reduce the available supply of housing and facilitate the recovery of the housing industry from the 1974–75 recession, Congress gave a special tax incentive to individuals purchasing new homes. Specifically, a purchaser of new housing constructed, or under construction, before March 26, 1975, qualified for an income tax credit of 5 percent of the purchase price, up to a maximum of $2,000. No special effort was made to relieve the real estate industry of the burden of the 1979–83 recession.

The real estate cycle is predominantly a function of many scattered and local markets, the local markets showing greater degrees of variation than the aggregate, both in amplitude and frequency. In other words, conditions of prosperity or depression in local real estate markets may be more or less than similar conditions for real estate nationally. It is also possible that local conditions are diametrically opposed to those that exist nationally. For example, real estate is booming in Southern California and depressed in the oilbelt. "Know Your Market!" is an axiom to remember.

THE REAL ESTATE MARKET

It is generally agreed that the real estate market consists of a series of highly stratified submarkets and operates relatively efficiently. However, it also performs certain economic and social functions. Most important among these is the dissemination of information, particularly through local multiple listing services.

Although we find many isolated markets that tend to be connected with and affected by the overall real estate cycle and the business cycle as previously described, we do find in these isolated markets a competitive force at work, tending to bring about a uniform price for similar properties. That force is information and the elements of supply and demand.

The NATIONAL ASSOCIATION OF REALTORS®, local Boards of REALTORS®, and MLS (Multiple Listing Service) are sources of local, regional, and national real estate information for associated real estate brokers and salespersons. Coupled with a knowledge of local real estate transactions, real estate professionals act as a clearinghose for information between buyers and sellers. In that sense, it is your local real estate professional who creates the real estate market. The information we refer to is knowledge of recent prices, financing, and available properties for sale or rent.

Real estate professionals act as sources of information and as a result of their knowledge iron out the imperfections of the real estate market. Their services make it possible to buy, sell, finance, or rent property as advantageously as current market conditions permit.

Another function of the real estate market is to determine the use of land. Accordingly, in the long run, land has a strong influence on city growth. Since real estate owners are constantly striving to secure the highest return on their investment, they determine how land will be used. Furthermore, returns from land are generally maximized if land is put to its highest and best use. This means the property is utilized to its greatest economic advantage or the largest return of income over a given period of time. Thus, in the real estate market, knowledge tends to force land to be put to its highest and best use to ensure investors the highest returns. Therefore, it may be said that the real estate market determines how land will be used within the limits imposed by zoning and other governmental and private restrictions. Additionally, one other major function performed by the real estate market is the adjustment of space to demand. This adjustment is done on either a long-run or a short-run basis.

To be aware of the condition of the real estate market is important. However, it is equally important to understand the forces that cause a change in prices and to be able to analyze these factors.

THE ECONOMIC BASE

Although this discussion relates primarily to the city as an economic base, remember that the principles and techniques discussed may be applied to any defined geographic area. Remember also that, whatever conclusions are reached with regard to a specific base, they must be related logically to conditions and trends existing at the regional and national level. Exceptions must be carefully explained in the body of the feasibility report.

Whether planning for a land subdivision, residential development, apartment, shopping center, or industrial park, the decision to proceed, as well as necessary financing and ultimate profitability, is dependent on the thoroughness with which the feasibility package has been prepared.

Definition

There have been numerous definitions of the so-called economic base. Often the definitions depend on the objective of those studying the economic base of cities and regions. Marketing people, for example, are interested in sales potentials within an area; city planners are interested in terms of predicting future land use. One of the most useful concepts, however, seems to be that an **economic base** is a specific area (base) in relation to the United States as a whole. We can also say that it is a city or sharply defined area studied from the point of view of money inflows versus money outflows. For purposes of illustration, one can think of a city into which no money flows and in which all necessities of life have to be purchased from outside the city. In such a case, it can be safely concluded that over a given period of time (the time at which all of the inhabitants run out of funds), the city will slowly die.

Another way of thinking of money inflow versus outflow is in terms of the mercantilist concept of foreign trade with regard to a nation. The mercantilist writers of the seventeenth and eighteenth centuries considered that a nation in order to prosper needed what they called a favorable balance of trade. This meant that a nation's exports had to exceed its imports. This also meant that as a result of the excess of exports over imports, a nation's gold supply increased. In a sense it might be said that a city with a favorable economic base is a city in which its exports exceed its imports. This cannot be thought of only in terms of exports of goods but also in terms of exports of services.

The base must be sharply defined, whether it be the city itself or a metropolitan area; after all, the area under study can encompass the entire United States. The Census Bureau recognizes this problem and provides population and other statistical data by defining the city in three ways:

1. The corporate city proper.
2. The urbanized area; that is, the area determined by cutting off the "city" at the point where urban characteristics stop and rural characteristics begin.
3. The Standard Metropolitan Statistical Area.

Purposes of Base Studies

Different groups prepare base studies for different reasons. Yet, in spite of an announced objective by any particular group, one basic purpose of the study is an attempt to forecast the future economic growth of the community in terms of population, employment, and income. There has recently been an increasing awareness on the part of responsibile community executives and business people of the growing competitive struggle between communities. Implicit in this is the recognition that growth in terms of increased employment and population depends on exporting more than is imported.

The practical significance of a base study to the real estate practitioner can be found in the effects of all this on property values and project feasibility. The practitioner is interested in the economic base because in a dying city values naturally decline; and in a growing area, with increased demand for real property, values will almost universally increase. These factors in turn determine the potential success of real estate projects.

Those Interested in Economic Base Studies

There are many governmental and business groups that may have an interest in forecasting population and economic growth. Among these are appraisers and real estate brokers.

One of the fundamentals of the appraisal process is the prediction of economic conditions for the nation, region, and the community. Thus, base studies are of prime importance for appraisers. It has been suggested that since it is necessary for the appraiser to forecast future incomes for industrial, commercial, and residential property, the appraiser must understand the structure of that economy. It appears that an analysis of the community's economic base is more important when the capitalization of income method of appraisal is employed.

Brokers, particularly those interested in industrial real estate, often find economic base studies a must. Before an industry goes into a new area, management will raise questions as to the availability of skilled and unskilled labor, labor rates, transportation, taxes, availability of sufficient industrial water supply, availability and cost of energy, and sometimes climate.

Brokers considering the development of a residential subdivision or the construction of an apartment building find that the demand for housing is dependent on the growth in employment and income within the base. Similarly, the design or type of shopping centers and dwellings constructed is dependent upon the economic, hence social, status of the base.

EMPLOYMENT AND INCOME WITHIN THE BASE

Types of Employment Within the Base

The two major types of employment within a community are called primary and secondary, or service, employment. **Primary employment** is that employment that brings purchasing power into the base from outside. **Secondary employment** refers to those employment opportunities supported by those engaged in primary employment.

In essence, it is from primary employment that money flows into the base area. The service, or secondary, employment activities feed off those engaged in primary employment; for example, retail trade within the defined base, local construction, and the like. It follows then that secondary employment is contingent on the amount and composition of primary employment.

As a result of primary employment, a ratio is created between primary employment and secondary employment. For example, a study might show a ratio of primary employment to secondary employment of 1:1.54 in Denver, which means that for every 100 persons employed in primary employment there are 154 employed in secondary employment, or a total of 254 employed. For purposes of predicting future population growth and economic activity within a community, the general rule is that if primary employment grows, secondary employment will grow in a ratio to it. Finally, the question now remains: What is the projected total population, including women, children, and unemployed? Here, too, a ratio is employed. This ratio is based on figures obtained from the last available census data. Suppose that for every person employed there are three individuals in the community. The ratio would then be one employed to each three unemployed persons. In this case the *total population* of the base for 1992 might be projected as four times the total expected employment.

As a word of caution, one cannot assume that in all instances secondary employment will be completely dependent on primary employment. For example, primary employment will often fail to grow as expected because of lags in secondary employment. If a community fails to provide proper facilities, industrial expansion will be slowed because labor forces will refuse to migrate to this area. It should also be noted that ratios between primary and secondary employment do not necessarily remain constant.

Form of Income

Income in the base may be in wages, salaries, dividends, royalties, pensions, rents, insurance, interest, and profits. Of course, individual income may be received in one or any combination of these forms.

Sources of Income

The Bureau of the Census breaks employment in industry studies into different categories. Table 4-2 shows the results of a Chamber of Commerce study in Las Cruces, New Mexico. Included therein is the number employed in ten categories and the percent of the total in each of the categories.

Table 4-2 Results of New Mexico Study

SOURCE OF EMPLOYMENT	NUMBER EMPLOYED	PERCENT OF TOTAL
All other	1,850	15
Manufacturing	800	6
Mining	1,600	13
Contract construction	725	5
Trans., comm., elec., gas, & S.S.	850	7
Wholesale & retail trade	2,550	21
Finance, ins., & real estate	275	2
Service	1,225	10
Government	1,150	9
Agriculture	1,450	12
Total	12,475	100

There are several reasons for this sort of breakdown, the major one being the ability to determine more strongly a position with regard to establishing primary and secondary employment as the result of a particular industry. In addition, as will be discussed, diversification of industry within the base might prove important in the event of a recession or depression. What is suggested, then, is that all the sources of income within the base must be identified, first in terms of numbers employed in the various categories and, second, in terms of percentages of these to the total. It is also helpful when establishing employment growth trends by industry to use ten years of historical data.

Primary and Secondary Sources of Employment and Income

In wholesale and retail trade, some of the income flows into the base as the result of the base having a trading area outside the immediate confines of the area. It is entirely conceivable, for example, that most of the business done by retail stores comes from outside the base. Thus, part of the employment in the retail stores would constitute primary employment and some would constitute service employment. As was suggested above, it is important to break the figures into primary employment and secondary employment in order to determine the ratios and, consequently, to make population projections based on employment growth. One question remains: If total employment in wholesaling and retailing is x numbers, how much of x is attributable to primary employment, and how much is attributable to secondary employment?

The most accurate method of determining whether sales in wholesaling and retailing come from within or without the base is to analyze each side. This, of course, would prove nearly impossible. Hence, compromise is in order. This is done in the following manner. Data are obtained as to the number of workers per 1,000 of population in the United States engaged in wholesaling and retailing. For example, assume the ratio in the United States is 100 persons engaged in wholesaling and retailing to every 1,000 of population. Suppose in the base under study there are 150 persons per 1,000 population engaged in wholesaling and retailing. In this case, one assumes that 100 persons per 1,000 receive income from service employment within the community, while 50 persons per 1,000 population receive their incomes from primary employment due to sales outside the economic base.

The same sort of problem arises with regard to manufacturing, except it is even more complex. One of the problems is that some of the manufactured products are consumed within the area. If so, then it follows that no money flows into the base from the outside. In practical operation, however, it is almost impossible to determine the exact number of products manufactured and sold during the year within the base.

Therefore, a formula is used to estimate the proportion of total primary local employment in a particular industry employed in a secondary or service context. This formula has been called the **base-ratio,** or **location quotient,** technique. Reduced to a formula, that is:

$$\frac{x}{\text{total local employment}} = \frac{\text{national employment in industry I}}{\text{total national employment}}$$

When one solves for x, one finds the numbers necessary in industry I to supply the base needs. To summarize, assume x is 3,000, the amount necessary for the locality (really based on the rest of the nation). If there are 5,000 employed in industry I in the base, then it is assumed that the surplus employees (2,000) are engaged in an export or primary employment activity.

LOCAL ECONOMIC STABILITY

In a base analysis, one of the major questions that needs to be raised is: To what extent is the primary employment within the base tied to fluctuations in national income and employment? For example, as a general rule the automobile industry is seriously affected when the demand for new cars decreases during a recession. Thus, when primary employment is hurt, secondary employment is likewise hurt. It has been said that the primary industries thus become the local area's link to the national economy.

The question is, of course, How closely is primary employment within a base tied to the nation as a whole? The answer depends mainly on two things: (1) the nature of the goods and services produced and (2) the diversification of production in the local area.

Goods and Services Produced

A fact long recognized by economists is that different types of products have widely different ranges of fluctuations. Luxury versus necessity and heavy industrial machinery versus light consumer goods are examples of this. In the former, during a depression, an individual may be forced into a diet of fatback and hominy grits and away from beef and milk. During a depression or recession, a woman might be forced into temporary contentment with the purchase of a less costly perfume though she would prefer an expensive scent. The point is that a base engaged in the manufacture of expensive perfume for the outside world can expect to be more seriously hurt economically during a recession than an area manufacturing a lower quality perfume, which sells at a much lower price.

In an economic base engaged in manufacturing basic and heavy industrial machinery, fluctuations during downswings in the cycle are even more vicious and injurious. Part of this phenomenon in the heavy industrial goods industry is explained by the **acceleration principle.** This means that a given change in the demand for consumer goods causes a greater change in the demand for capital goods. For an example, refer to the prior discussion of the business cycle.

Some sensitivity relationships are suggested in Table 4-3, which was adapted from a similar table prepared by the U.S. Department of Commerce. It shows the percent change in expenditures of disposable income, with the effect of the trend held constant.

Table 4-3 Changes in Expenditures of Disposable Income

	COEFFICIENT OF SENSITIVITY
ABOVE-AVERAGE SENSITIVITY	
Durable Goods	
Boats and pleasure craft	3.1
Luggage	1.9
Furniture	1.4
Nondurable Goods	
Flower seeds and potted plants	1.6
Stationery and writing supplies	1.4
Services	
Admissions: legitimate theater and opera	1.9
Fur storage and repairs	1.6
AVERAGE SENSITIVITY	
Durable Goods	
Ophthalmic products and orthopedic appliances	.8
Nondurable Goods	
Toys and sport supplies	1.0
Services	
Admissions professional baseball	.9
Beauty parlor service	.8
BELOW-AVERAGE SENSITIVITY	
Durable Goods	
China, glassware, tableware, and utensils	.7
Nondurable Goods	
Drug preparations and sundries	.6
Gasoline and oil	.5
Services	
Funeral and burial services	.6
Water	.2
Electricity	.2

This table suggests, among other things, that if disposable income goes down one percent, the expenditures for boats go down 3.1 percent. Also, with a one percent decline in disposable income, expenditures for electricity go down only .2 percent.

Diversification of Production in the Local Area

This deals with the effect on the local economy of diversification in industries giving rise to primary employment. For example, at one time the little town of Mauch Chunk (now Jim Thorpe), Pennsylvania, depended for its existence on one industry, namely, repair yards for the Lehigh Valley Coal and Navigation Company. When the railroad moved its repair yards, the entire economy of the community collapsed. With the breakdown of the local economy, real estate values rapidly decreased, contrary to the national trend. The question raised is If that same community had had many diversified primary industries bringing in the same total revenue, would the economy have suffered as greatly?

There appears to be a relationship between instability of local areas and the degree of concentration of industry within the area. In the recession of 1974–75, for example, Detroit suffered greatly as a result of depressed conditions in the automotive industry. At the same time, other areas whose source of primary employment was diversified seemed relatively isolated from depressed business conditions. As a general rule, but only as a general rule, one can conclude that the larger the number of products produced in an area, the more stable the local economy is likely to be. However, this generalization is also governed by the type of product produced within the base. Again, an area may be heavily diversified, but if it is highly diversified in the production of heavy industrial goods, the mere diversification will not necessarily lead to greater stability.

FURTHER AREAS OF INVESTIGATION

In addition to analyzing types of employment within the base, sources of income, and local economic stability, it is also necessary to analyze a more complete inventory of local economic resources. This inventory consists of a number of general areas with appropriate subdivisions. Five of the most important of these are discussed below.

Population and the Labor Force

A long-term population trend of the base under study should be obtained to determine whether there have been population increases, decreases, or if it has been static. These figures must be compared with long-term trends of the United States and should also be compared with trends of cities of similar size and composition. The sex and age of the local population should be analyzed against national figures to determine if an area might be extremely deficient in male or female population of the age suitable for the work force. The population figures of the area should be further analyzed in terms of socioeconomic characteristics and age to ascertain the demand for various types of housing. The education of the population should be examined for numbers of school years completed since highly complex modern production methods call for a literate work force.

The labor force itself must be scrutinized as to its relative size (compared with the rest of the United States), and sex examined in terms of relationship of female to male workers, from which one might conclude that some part of the labor force is not being utilized to its fullest capacity. It is important in determining the training and skills of the work force to examine the various occupations of the labor force. Finally, figures must be obtained for the professional and technical workers of the community—teachers, lawyers, and nurses, for instance. Remember that all of these figures should be compared with those of cities of similar size and with the United States as a whole.

Transportation, Power, and Natural Resources

Any transportation facilities available to the community should be studied. A major question that must be answered concerns freight rates. Studies must be made of the rates of all types of transportation facilities, with particular emphasis on rates of raw materials and semifabricated goods shipped into the community. These costs must be compared with those of communities engaged in the manufacture of similar products. This is particularly relevant to brokers considering an industrial development.

Future highway plans should also be examined to determine the impact on industry and housing. Off-street parking facilities for downtown areas should be studied, too, to determine the impact of lack of facilities on retail trade. For example, one might determine that a certain amount of retail trade comes from outside the urban area, but an off-street parking study might show that the retail trade area is losing part of its potential as the result of lack of parking space. Hence, an opportunity for building a parking ramp may be discovered.

Power resources must be studied and analyzed. For example, industries requiring a great deal of electric power will have a tendency to move to areas where that type of power is the cheapest. An example is the growth of the aluminum industry in the so-called Inland Empire (that area surrounding Spokane, Washington). Hence, it is important to obtain comparative rates on electricity and gas. If there are foreseeable plans for the increase of power in the area, they should be noted also.

Natural resources have a tremendous effect on the growth potential of a base area. Industrial water supplies should be noted and compared with similar cities. Generally, as a city grows, water requirements also tend to rise. In some areas, it is vital that conservation methods be studied in order to avoid inhibiting the growth of the area. Minerals in the area of the base should be studied and broken down by type with estimates of the amounts and ease of extraction. Where relevant, agriculture in the area surrounding the base must be studied. There are many cities in the United States that serve as a service center for an agricultural area. Often the fortunes of the base community are tied to the agricultural economic conditions of the surrounding area. It is important, therefore, to note farm employment, crop values, specific crops and their long-term potentials, and farm purchases within the base.

Financial Resources

Here one attempts to determine the status of local financial institutions. Have savings in the community been increasing or decreasing over a period of the past ten years? What sort of loan funds are available: short-term, intermediate, or long-term loans? An inquiry should also be made as to the interest rates paid by both business and individuals for the use of these funds. If possible, it should be determined whether any local funds are available for more speculative ventures, either from special institutions or individuals.

Local Taxation and Expenditures

The local tax structure must be determined and compared with similar cities. Often this structure will lead an industry to locate in the area under study. Some people maintain that industry is being driven out in some states because of high property taxes. What are the expenditures in the area for schools, fire protection, and other municipal facilities? All figure obtained should be compared with those of similar cities.

Sources of Information

In order to obtain data for the inventory suggested, a great deal of work must be done. Help is available from census reports, local newspapers, Chambers of Commerce, civic organization, planning officials, and tax offices. Useful private publications such as *Sales Management* and *Standard Rate and Data Guide* are also available. These publications, which are published annually, contain much of the information necessary for the area. The most important resource for obtaining information, though, is plenty of legwork. With a little luck, the base analyst may receive aid from civic organizations for this work.

ANALYZING THE REAL ESTATE MARKET

Completion of an economic base analysis permits forecasting of expected growth in primary and secondary employment. This, of course, is dependent on the economic stability and future of the primary industries located within the base. Most importantly, base analysis gives a preliminary indication of the demand for housing, retail, and industrial space. This, then, must be related to available real estate inventories, and specific needs must be identified. For this purpose, a market analysis is conducted.

The real estate market is analyzed by weighing certain supply and demand factors and drawing conclusions from them. The first problem in any market analysis is to determine the primary objective of the analyses. For example, an analysis of the condominium market is quite different from an analysis of the single-family residential market. By the same token, an analysis of the market for one-bedroom apartments is quite different from an analysis of the market for three-bedrom apartments. However, several factors are important to all markets and these will be explored first.

Government Policies

The government has entered the picture of the real estate market in an attempt to even out business cycles. The tremendous impact of the monetary policies of the Federal Reserve System on the real estate market will be discussed in detail in Chapter 14. There, it will be shown how the Federal Reserve raises and lowers interest rates and thus affects the supply of money for real estate financing and consequently the market for real estate. Federal income tax provisions for real estate will be discussed in Chapter 15.

Analysis of the role of government in real estate generally takes the form of determining whether present and future policies are likely to cause business expansion or contraction. This should be coupled with a judgment of the availability of financing for the purchase or development of real property.

State and Local Conditions

Usually the economies of the individual states tend to move in the same direction as the national economy. However, this is not always the case. For example, a state whose economy is predominantly agricultural may, at certain times, be more seriously affected by adverse business conditions that a state whose economy is more diversified. Information with regard to state business conditions can be obtained from the *Federal Reserve Bulletin*, the monthly review of the federal reserve bank in the district in which the state is located, and from bureaus of business research of state universities.

As previously indicated, the real estate cycle tends to rise and fall with general national and state business conditions. Yet there are times when local booms and depressions occur that do not follow the pattern of general business activity.

Demand Factors

What are the demand factors in the real estate market that may sometimes be converted into sales?

Population. The first thing to determine about a community or an area where a study is being made is population trends. Is population rising, static, or falling? Frequently, these figures are obtained from the Bureau of the Census, a county or state planning board, *Sales Management's* "Survey of Buying Power," or a local Chamber of Commerce.

Age Distribution. Once having obtained gross population figures, it is important to determine the composition of the population. For example, how many are in the 25- to 34-, 35- to 44-year-old age group, and so forth? This is important for an analysis of the market. For purposes of illustration, suppose you are trying to determine if there is a market for tri-level homes. If it turns out that a large portion of the population is over 65, as in Tucson, Arizona, then the project might as well be forgotten. On the other hand, such a discovery might lead to building a condominium-apartment retirement community.

Family Size. Family size is another market factor. For example, it has been determined that condominium owners generally have three or fewer household members. On the other hand, if it is determined that each household in the market area has more than three members, it is probably a bad market for condominiums and a better market for three-bedroom homes.

Income, Employment, and Wages. The determination of the average income of a population is important for analyzing the possible price of the real estate product. For example, suppose you are analyzing a potential market for $90,000 homes. Obviously, the persons who might buy at this price must have sufficient incomes.

Employment is assuredly a dynamic factor regarding the conversion of latent demand into effective demand; that is, the ability of the individual to convert desires to purchases. Employment rarely becomes fixed at a constant figure, but is in a constant state of flux. The important thing for the builder-developer to keep in mind is the trend of employment and average income in the area for which the subdivision is planned. This is determined by examining the figures over a period of time. From a positive viewpoint, increasing or steady employment in a particular area is indicative of chances for success for a subdivision when weighed against other factors. Negatively, decreasing employment in an area over a period of time increases the chances for failure, for demand for housing will slacken with decreasing employment.

Marriage and Divorce Rates. Increasing marriages can generally be interpreted as a sign of an increased future demand for detached single-family housing. By the same token, an increased divorce rate often, but not necessarily, is indicative of a decline in the demand for detached single-family housing units. However, divorced couples may create a demand for apartments or condominium units, whereas previous demand was for single residences. Information concerning the number of marriages and divorces can be obtained from the office of the county clerk in the county in which the market is being analyzed.

Doubling Up. The use of one housing unit by two or more families is usually referred to as doubling up. In general, doubling up increases with a decline in general business activity.

Supply Factors

Demand factors, taken by themselves, are insufficient to analyze the real estate market. These factors must be considered together with the supply factors. If the demand is high and the supply is even greater, then the time is probably not right for developing or subdividing.

Vacant Units. The normal rate of vacancy for an area is considered to be about 5 percent of the available units. If demand factors are high and vacancies are at a normal level, then it would probably be an indication that a development is warranted. If vacancies are abnormal, for example, 15 percent, it might be indicative that sales in a development would lag until surplus housing units are sold or rented. However, a distinction should be made between apartment rental vacancies and single-home vacancies. It is possible for a surplus of single-family homes to exist side by side with a shortage of apartments.

Construction Costs. As costs affect the supply of all consumer goods, so do costs affect the supply of housing. As costs mount, supply has a tendency to fall until there is an adjustment upward in selling prices. Construction cost is a factor, then, that must be weighed before beginning a development.

Here, too, local real estate boards and qualified appraisers should be contacted to determine construction costs. Many boards have compiled accurate records of costs. The building department of the city should also be contacted in order to obtain cost data.

Labor Supply. Another factor to be taken into consideration is skilled labor. A shortage of skilled labor in an area will have a tendency to affect the supply of housing that can be built.

Indicators of Market Activity

Two of the best indexes of market activity are mortgage foreclosures and deed transfer series.

Mortgage Foreclosures. The rate of mortgage foreclosures is a good indication of the status of the local real estate market, as well as the national real estate market. Increasing numbers of foreclosures are usually an indication of a decline in the real estate activity. Some students of real estate cycles draw a fairly close parallel between the number of foreclosures and the rise and fall in the real estate cycle.

Information regarding mortgage foreclosures can be obtained in the office of the county clerk of the county where the information is being sought.

Deed Transfer Series. Deed transfer series are indications of what may be expected in the real estate market in the immediate future. The procedure is generally to obtain from the county recorder's office the number of deeds recorded by month and year for at least two prior real estate cycles. From these statistics, relationships can be drawn between transfer activity, income, and foreclosures. In addition, turning points in the transfer series may point to turning points in the foreclosure series and thus be a basis for forecasting.

Other indicators of building activity include building permits issued, water and electric meters installed, and new telephone installations. Information on the latter items may be obtained from the water department, local electric utility, and telephone company, respectively.

Information on building permits may be obtained from the county or city building department in the area being analyzed. Each permit should list the number, value, and type of unit being constructed.

Weighing the Factors

After having obtained data concerning the various supply and demand factors, it is necessary to weigh these factors. For example, ordinarily, an upward pressure on rents indicates a strong possible demand for housing units. This factor considered by itself is insufficient and should be weighed against construction costs. If costs are rising, the question is whether they are rising more rapidly than rents. If rents are rising more rapidly than costs, wages are rising, and employment is steady, it would indicate housing units should sell in spite of rising costs of construction. Similarly, all the data in an analysis should be weighed, and consideration should be given to their relative merits.

Forecasting Housing Supply and Demand

Three pieces of information are essential for estimating housing demand: (1) historical and projected population growth, (2) historical housing inventory, and (3) historical building starts. This information should be obtained, if possible, for the previous ten-year period.

An Illustration

For purposes of illustration, Table 4-4 presents data that has been gathered for Hypothetical, Arizona. From the three data series presented, a simple supply-and-demand analysis can be prepared.

Table 4-4 Population and Building Series for Hypothetical, Arizona 1980–1990

		HOUSING INVENTORY			BUILDING STARTS		
	Population	**Single-Family Units**	**Multi-Family Units**	**Total**	**Single-Family Units**	**Multi-Family Units**	**Total**
1980 Actual	43,736	10,668	2,185	12,853	1,353	364	1,717
1986 Estimate	48,200	12,021	2,549	14,570	1,704	464	2,168
1987	54,100	13,725	3,013	16,738	1,750	618	2,375
1988	60,300	15,482	3,631	19,113	1,260	322	1,582
1989	63,700	16,742	3,953	20,695	2,575	579	3,155
1990 Actual	71,689	19,318	4,532	23,850	1,029	453	1,482
1991 Estimate	76,500	20,347	4,985	25,332	972	777	1,749
1992	78,875	21,319	5,762	27,081	1,526	1,187	2,713
1993	84,500	22,845	6,949	29,794	1,526	1,187	2,713
1994	92,300	24,371	8,136	32,507			
1995	98,000						
1996	101,500						
1997	104,000						
1998	108,500						
1999	113,000						
2000	118,500						

After the basic data have been gathered, it is possible to calculate the occupancy ratio, determine the extent of under- or overbuilding, and project the future demand for housing.

Occupancy Ratio

Based on the 1980 and 1990 Census, a comparison of the change in number of occupants per dwelling unit may be made. The general formula is

$$\frac{\left(\dfrac{\text{1990 population}}{\text{1990 housing inventory}}\right) - \left(\dfrac{\text{1980 population}}{\text{1980 housing inventory}}\right)}{\text{10 years}} = \text{average change in the number of occupants per dwelling unit per year}$$

Once the change in the number of occupants per dwelling unit has been calculated, it should be divided by ten to provide the average change from 1980 to 1990. Using the data given, the average change in the occupancy ratio from 1980 to 1990 represents a decline of .0397 occupants per unit per year. This figure represents the continued expected decline in the occupancy ratio to the year 2000.

The occupancy ratio is used first to estimate housing demand by dividing the projected population for a particular year by the forecast ratio. Over- or underbuilding may then be determined by subtracting housing demand from housing inventory. This analysis is presented in Table 4-5.

Analysis of Table 4-5 indicates entering the 1994 year with an oversupply of 87 dwelling units. With continued population increases for 1994, this oversupply will be absorbed quickly.

A major shortcoming of the analysis so far is that the relationship of single- and multifamily units is unknown. For example, an oversupply of 87 housing units could conceivably consist of a shortage of 300 homes and an excess of 387 apartments. Refinement of the data to reflect demand for single- and multifamily housing is the next step.

Single-Family and Multifamily Housing

This is perhaps the most difficult step in the supply-demand analysis. The demand for apartment units is a function of the growth in the numbers of divorced, single, and elderly people. The best manner to determine the supply of apartment units is through an extensive survey of existing build-

Table 4-5 Supply and Demand for Housing in Hypothetical, Arizona, 1994

POPULATION		HOUSING INVENTORY[1]	OCCUPANCY RATIO[2]	HOUSING DEMAND[3]	OVER- (OR UNDER-) BUILDING[4]
1990 Census	71,689	23,850	3.0058	23,850	—
1991 Estimate	76,500	25,332	2.9661	25,791	(459)
1992	78,875	27,081	2.9264	26,953	128
1993	84,500	29,794	2.8867	29,272	522
1994	92,300	32,507	2.8470	32,420	87
1995	98,000	—	2.8073	34,909	—
1996	101,500	—	2.7676	36,674	—
1997	104,000	—	2.7279	38,125	—
1998	108,500	—	2.6882	40,362	—
1999	113,000	—	2.6485	42,666	—
2000	118,500	—	2.6088	45,423	—

[1]Based on 1990 census of housing plus total building starts for current year.
[2]Based on decline in occupancy ratio at historical rate of .0397 persons.
[3]Population divided by occupancy ratio.
[4]Housing inventory less housing demand.

ings and their vacancy rates. Five percent apartment vacancy is considered normal; vacancies greater or less than this amount are indicative of over-supply or undersupply of apartment units.

Growth patterns for those demanding apartment units may be estimated through examination of census data, specifically of growth in numbers of individuals under 30 and over 65 in proportion to total population growth. This proportion multiplied by total expected housing demand will give an approximation of the demand for multifamily units.

Rental Housing Projects

There are essentially five major questions that must be answered to test the feasibility of producing a rental housing project.

1. *What type and size of family unit is in greatest demand?* This requires a close examination of the local market in terms of competitive projects. This also includes a determination of the number of vacancies in the local market, a determination of proposed projects, and a determination of the unit size demanded.

2. *Where are the particular locations in which these units will command and continue to command the maximum rentals?* There is a tendency for the market to pay for the size and type unit it desires according to the desirability and popularity of the location. In short, higher rentals are obtainable in the choice locations, and lower rentals are obtainable in those areas that are considered less desirable.

3. *How much does it cost to acquire the land and build the property?* The figures can be obtained from an architect; and, of course, if the costs in terms of the estimated returns are too great, then the project is not practical.

4. *How much will it cost to operate the property?* This can be determined from a comparison with properties of similar nature. It is customary in rental properties to think of effective net income, which is the income the property will return at the proposed rentals, assuming the property is 100 percent rented, less an allowance for vacancy and collection losses.

5. *What rate of return on capital does the market demand?* One must determine the return necessary to induce intelligent investors to invest in this type of property. As a practical matter, if the rate is 6 percent and the effective net income is $5,000 on a proposed structure that will cost $100,000 to build, then investors will not invest because 6 percent of $100,000 is $6,000. This suggests that intelligent investors are more likely to invest in an alternative investment opportunity where they will be able to receive a 6-percent return on their investment.

Future Demands

From Table 4-5, it can be seen that total population is anticipated to increase to 98,000 by the beginning of 1995. When divided by the occupancy ratio, demand for 34,909 dwelling units may be forecast: an increase of 2,489 during the 1994 year.

A sample survey of apartment units, however, has revealed an average vacancy rate of 9 percent for 8,136 multifamily units. In other words, approximately 732 vacant units, or 325 units in excess of a normal 5 percent vacancy of 407 units.

Further comparison of 1980 and 1990 census data reveals substantial increases in the population group demanding apartment units. For Hypothetical Arizona, assume 40 percent of the total population; therefore, demand will be for multifamily units. A summary of this information is contained in Table 4-6.

The last step is to check with the local building department, planning board, and zoning commission. The purpose is to ascertain the number of dwelling units presently under construction, units for which permits have been issued, and the units associated with any forthcoming development. Further adjustment of 1995 housing needs must be made to reflect current and planned construction to finally determine the extent of any unfilled demand or overbuilding.

Environmental Impact Study

Often, the environmental impact is significant when obtaining necessary planning board approval and building permits and therefore should be

Table 4-6 Demand for Single- and Multifamily Dwellings in Hypothetical, Arizona, 1994

		SINGLE-FAMILY	MULTIFAMILY
Demand for housing	2,489[1]	1,493[2]	996[2]
Current over- (under-) supply of housing	87[3]	(238)	325[4]
Total 1995 housing needs	2,402	1,731	671

[1]1995 demand less 1994 demand (Table 4-5).

[2]60 percent single-family and 40 percent multifamily based on analysis of Bureau of the Census Data and projected population growth.

[3]1994 housing inventory less 1994 demand (Table 4-5).

[4]Based on survey of apartments. Vacancies in excess of 5 percent.

included as part of the feasibility report. Chapter 3 contained a discussion of the elements to be included in the Environmental Impact Statement.

THE FEASIBILITY REPORT

The feasibility report is used to persuade investors and a mortgage lender of the forethought, planning, ultimate completion, and profitability of the proposed project. In essence, the feasibility report sells the project proposal.

Not only is all the previously discussed data and analysis included, but also included is all specific information relevant to the undertaking, as well as personal information about the promoters. Specific project data include complete site analysis, e.g., evaluation, drainage, vegetation, soil types, and proposed roads. These data are included on the plat map showing the location of the development relative to major highways, shopping centers, schools, and churches. An aerial photograph is recommended to aid in the study of traffic patterns and proximity to service facilities. Chapter 3 contained a thorough discussion of the steps required for subdivision and development, and these should be considered as important to the feasibility report.

Blueprints for each model house or apartment building are also included in the feasibility report. Each set of blueprints contains a specification sheet discussing the details of amenities such as fireplaces, landscaping, lighting, and other special features.

Complete financial statements of the corporation or partnership, as well as individual investors, are included with projected sales, expenses, profits, and a cash flow statement for the project. Accompanying individual financial statements is a biographical sketch indicating the qualification and expertise of the development's management team.

GLOSSARY

Acceleration principle A given change in the demand for consumer goods causes a greater change in the demand for capital goods

Base ratio, or location quotient A formula used to estimate the proportion of total primary local employment in a particular industry employed in a secondary or service context

Contraction The third phase of the business cycle; the opposite of the expansion period, during which fewer durable goods are purchased, fewer goods are manufactured, unemployment increases, and wages drop

Economic base The export activities of a community that bring in its net earnings and enable it to continue as an independent entity; a specific area (base) in relation to the United States as a whole

Economic base analysis Part of a feasibility report

Expansion The first of the four distinct phases of the business cycle, where business activities are on the upswing

Feasibility report A discussion of the national economy coupled with an analysis of a specific proposal and the capacity of principal investors

Major business cycles Periods of time characterized by the relatively long length of the expansion and contraction phase (duration 6 to 13 years)

Market analysis The demand for real estate combined with a survey of competitive projects and the economic, social, and environmental impact of the proposed project

Minor business cycles Periods of time of shorter duration than major business cycles, generally superimposed on a major cycle (average duration 3½ years)

Primary employment Employment that brings purchasing power into the base from the outside

Recession The second phase of the business cycle, which occurs after the peak has been reached and is manifested in a downswing

Revival Fourth period of business cycle, which begins after machines have become worn and inventory has declined; precursor of expansion phase and beginning of new cycle

Seasonal variations Variations in the activity of certain industries corresponding with particular periods of the year, e.g., swim wear, construction

Secondary employment Those employment opportunities supported by those engaged in primary employment

Secular trend The long-run movement in a business cycle, generally thought of as 20 years or more, resulting from forces such as population growth, capital accumulation, new markets, and technological improvements

QUESTIONS FOR REVIEW

1. What observations may be made about the real estate cycle from an analysis of Exhibit 4-3?
2. Why is "Know Your Market!" an important axiom to remember?
3. Define *highest and best use.*

4. Why should real estate practitioners be interested in economic base studies?
5. What is meant by the ratio of primary employment to secondary employment?
6. How does the acceleration principle affect local economic stability?
7. What has product diversification to do with local economic stability?
8. List the major elements to be considered in preparing a real estate market analysis.
9. What is meant by the occupancy ratio? What factors are likely to make the ratio increase? Decrease?

PROBLEMS AND ACTIVITIES

1. Prepare a market analysis of your town, your county, and your state, using as a guide the information given in the text.
2. You are given the following figures on an economic base: primary employment, 15,550; secondary employment, 33,280.
   a. Determine the ratio.
   b. A new factory engaged in primary employment is moving into the base and intends to employ 350 persons. What can you say about the possible future population growth in town, the demand for labor, and the demand for real estate?
3. Prepare a supply-and-demand analysis for total dwelling units in your community for the current year. Also, prepare an estimate of the demand for multifamily units.

5

INDUSTRIAL AND COMMERCIAL PROPERTY

KEY TERMS

Derived demand
Factor evaluation
Factor weight
Fully packaged estate
Industrial park
Industrial subdivision
Industrial tract
Industrial zone
Locational analysis
Office condominium
Production-cost orientation
Retail property
Strip shopping center
Transport-cost orientation

Commercial property (which includes stores, restaurants, shopping centers, office buildings, hotels and motels) and industrial property (which includes factories, warehouses, manufacturing facilities, and industrial sites) grew rapidly in the early 1980s. This growth slowed in the mid-1980s due to deflation and competition from imports, overbuilding, and the Tax Reform Act of 1986.

THE DEMAND FOR INDUSTRIAL AND COMMERCIAL PROPERTY

The demand for land and for industrial and commercial property is said to be **derived demand.** The thought underlying this is that there are four things which a producer has to employ in combination to produce a good. These four items are land, labor, capital, and enterprise or management. In combination, these items are called the production function.

The demand by profit-seeking firms for these factors arises because consumers are willing to pay for the produced good now or in the future. Consequently, the demand for the factors is ultimately derived from effective consumer demand. Thus, if there is a demand for men's shirts, there will then be a demand for land upon which to construct the factories to produce men's shirts. Similarly, if there is a population (consumer) movement from the central city to outlying areas, there will be a derived demand for retail space to serve these customers.

LOCATION OF INDUSTRIAL ACTIVITY

Industry and manufacturing follow the growth of trade. However, there are additional factors affecting the location of industry. Most important is the availability of adequate and economical transportation. Historically, the most economical transportation was both water and rail.

Heavy industry locates close to sources of raw materials so that the hauls will be relatively short and transportation charges will be relatively low. Conversely, location of industries near the markets assures shorter hauls and lower transportation charges on the finished products.

There are a number of patterns of industry location relating to transportation. The petroleum refining industry frequently locates close to the source of crude oil from which refined oil can be economically transported by pipeline. Forest product processing, which results in reduction of weights, is frequently located near areas producing timber because of transportation charges. Mineral smelting is conducted near industrial cities to which ore can be economically transported from the mines. In short, freight rates are used as a device for promoting or concentrating industry or for its dispersion. The importance of transporation facilities and rates cannot be overemphasized in the location of industry. Other principal factors in the location of industry include:

1. Available labor supply, number of skills represented, wage rates, degree of unionization, history of labor-management relations.
2. Location of markets to be served.
3. Accessibility to raw materials used in the industrial process.
4. Community acceptance of the industry, degree of cooperation to be expected from governmental officials in granting permits, equitable tax rates, and similar terms.
5. Costs of operation in the location, including utilities, labor, and materials.
6. Living conditions for employees.
7. Existence of competing and supplementary industries.

Analysis of a number of studies evaluating industrial location factors bears out these basic assumptions and reveals ten major factors determining location selection:

1. Raw Materials (accessibility of).
2. Markets (proximity to sale outlets).
3. Physical Site (level, sloping, sandy, etc.).
4. Transportation and Shipping (accessibility and costs).
5. Labor (availability, skills, prevailing wage rate).
6. Energy (gas, fuel oil, electricity: availability and cost of).
7. Utilities (availability of).
8. Community (quality of life, recreation, schools, services).

9. Taxes (rates for property, sales, income, and inventory).
10. Financial Inducements (tax subsidy, prepared site, financing).

Of these ten factors, five are significant, regardless of the type of industry: labor, markets, raw materials, transportation, and energy. In the future, it is possible that energy will emerge as the predominant factor affecting the choice of industrial location.

A recent survey of 385 chief executive officers (CEOs) of America's largest corporations reported the essential factors for the location of office facilities and industrial sites. Table 5-1 lists the locational criteria in rank order.

Location From the Viewpoint of the Firm

Whether a manufacturer of steel or assembler of electronic components, industrial **locational analysis** is based predominantly on the ten factors previously listed. Although each factor is not equally important, some weight is given to each factor when evaluating alternative locations.

Factor Weight. Some firms approach site location mathematically; beginning with the ten factors listed and a careful analysis of company needs, the importance of each factor may be quantified. For example, a highly automated firm will not feel that labor is as significant a factor as a firm

Table 5-1 Essential Locational Factors (in Rank Order of Importance)

	OFFICE FACILITIES	MANUFACTURING AND WAREHOUSE DISTRIBUTION FACILITIES
Easy access to domestic markets	1	1
Cost and availability of labor	2	3
Cost of office space	3	NA
Cost of sites	NA	2
Climate created by state and local government	4	5
Easy access to raw materials	NA	4
Quality of life	5	7
Easy access to international markets	6	8
Economic development incentives	7	6

SOURCE: Business America Real-Estate Monitor, *Cushman and Wakefield, Inc., 1166 Avenue of the Americas, New York, NY 10036.*

needing 1,000 assembly-line workers. Similarly, for industries using bulky, perishable, or costly to ship raw materials, location near the supply is more important than for a firm producing micro-miniaturized circuits.

After analysis of company needs, a **factor weight** signifying degree of importance in selecting a location may be assigned to each factor. Table 5-2 presents weighting of major factors for a typical manufacturer.

Factor Evaluation. Each individual factor may be further reduced to the elements affecting its evaluation. For example, analysis of shipping and transportation will reveal those elements essential to the **factor evaluation.** Table 5-3 presents the elements and probable weights of significant importance to the evaluation of shipping and transportation. Also included in Table 5-3 are scores for each identified element, the weighted element score, and total factor score, which also appears in Table 5-2. This process should be applied to each of the other factors for each location being considered. Thus, each element for each factor and for each location ultimately permits comparison and an optimal selection.

The government climate and taxes factor (Table 5-2) may be evaluated using the specific elements presented in Table 5-4. In the CEO survey conducted by Cushman and Wakefield, they reported that the CEO's absolutely essential criterion for locating new office, warehouse, distribut-

Table 5-2 Location Analysis

FACTOR	FACTOR WEIGHT	FACTOR EVALUATION (1–100)[1]	WEIGHTED FACTOR SCORE[2]
Raw materials	.12		
Markets	.11		
Physical site	.05		
Shipping and transportation	.16	67.35[3]	10.776
Labor	.20		
Energy	.10		
Utilities	.05		
Community	.10		
Government climate and taxes	.08		———
Financial inducements	.03		
Total	1.00		[4]

[1]Maximum total score for any location is 100 points.

[2]Weighted factor score is obtained by multiplying the factor weight by the factor evaluation.

[3]From Table 5-3.

[4]Maximum of 100 points.

Table 5-3 Location Analysis of Shipping and Transportation Factor

ELEMENT	ELEMENT WEIGHT	ELEMENT EVALUATION (1–100)[1]	WEIGHTED ELEMENTS SCORE[2]
Freight in and out (costs)	.33	75	24.75
Railroad service	.18	40	7.20
Airport service	.11	70	7.70
Trucking service	.25	85	21.25
Postal service	.04	20	.80
Travel distance from			
corp headquarters	.02	50	1.00
main highway system	.04	90	3.60
water transportation	.03	35	1.05
Total	1.00		67.35[3]

[1]Maximum total score for each element is 100 points.
[2]Weighted element score is obtained by multiplying the element weight by the element evaluation; maximum element evaluation is 100 points.
[3]To Table 5-2.

ing, or manufacturing facilities was government responsiveness to (business) needs.

Industrial Orientation. It should be remembered that different industries have different locational needs. Table 5-5 illustrates how various business characteristics or orientations help determine the most desirable location. Factors are broadly defined as having **transportation-cost** or **production-cost orientation.** In most cases, however, it is not one factor but a combination of factors that determines the final choice.

Table 5-4 Evaluating the Climate Created by State and Local Government (in Rank Order of Importance)

Government responsiveness to needs
Cutting red tape
Flexible zoning
Tax considerations
Improved infrastructure
Low cost land leasing
Subsidized financing and site preparation
Employee training
Enterprise zones

SOURCE: Business America Real Estate Monitor.

Table 5-5 Types of Locational Orientation of Industry

ORIENTATION	DECISIVE CHARACTERISTIC	OPTIMUM LOCATION	EXAMPLES
TRANSPORT-COST ORIENTED	High bulk-to-value ratio, hence transport inputs relatively important		
Materials oriented	Weight-, or perishability-, losing process	Close to materials sources	Ore refining, steel, fruit and vegetable canning
Market oriented	Weight-, perishability-, or fragility-gaining process	Close to market	Brewing, baking, automobile assembly
PRODUCTION-COST ORIENTED	Low bulk-to-value ratio, hence transport inputs relatively unimportant		
Labor oriented	Labor-intensive process	Low wage area[1]	Textiles
Power oriented (Energy)	Power-intensive process	Cheap power area	Auminum refining
Amenity oriented	Employs high proportion of specialized, highly paid personnel	Attractive physical and social environment	Research and development
Communication oriented	Need for face-to-face contact with customers or suppliers	Close to customers or suppliers	Corporate head offices, advertising, law, investment banking
External-economy oriented	Need for specialized ancillary services	A city of appropriate size or specialized character	Apparel manufacturing, broadcasting

[1]For labor of the required skill level.

SOURCE: James Heilbrun, Urban Economics and Public Policy *(New York: St. Martin's Press, 1974), 72.*

State-of-the-art assistance in industrial site selection is provided by the Business Resource Center in Oklahoma City. Funded by Oklahoma Gas and Electric Company, the center allows prospective employers to look for possible locations throughout the state in a video display center. Candidates control what they see, select from a variety of topics such as local recreational and housing facilities, population demographics, transportation, and local government. If a potential site is vacant, computer graphics are used to impose a building on the site. The computer removes potholes, adds shrubbery, and even adds the client's name to the building. Similar systems are in operation in Florida. The Georgia center is credited with bringing $1 billion of new investment to the state since 1986.

Location From the Viewpoint of the Community

Most communities feel that industry is an asset to the community. Some specific reasons were given in Chapter 4. Basically, the reason for the desire for additional industry in an area is economic.

In smaller cities, young people frequently leave the community because of lack of employment opportunities. Having invested much money in the education of youth, their leaving is an economic waste. Their leaving also reduces the pool of industrial labor resulting in possible demands for increased wages by remaining labor. This, in turn, may force local industry into other areas.

Another argument for having industry in the community has been termed the tax-profit aspect of manufacturing. Briefly, this means that industrial and commercial property on a per property basis have a high value; and community services, for example, fire protection, are less expensive to the community as a result. For example, it is cheaper to protect one $2 million industrial building than 50 homes of $40,000 each that are spread out over a relatively large area. Hence, the idea of tax profits. Of course, from a community viewpoint, it behooves city fathers to tax industry equitably rather than make it the "tax goat" as some cities have done.

When industry is treated as a tax goat, an increasingly larger share of the property tax burden is shifted to industry in order to keep residential property taxes low. This situation is illustrated in Exhibit 5-1. Why is this allowed to happen? In politics people vote, buildings don't.

When trying to attract industry, many communities seek industry that is considered "clean." In short some community leaders argue that industry must not be offensive to sight, sound, or smell. This implies "light" manufacturing in most cases. As a general rule, this attitude is reduced in proportion to city growth. The idea of "clean" versus "unclean" industry is highly controversial and will continue to be for some time to come. It might be well for some of the city's leaders to recognize that as a general rule clean industry is light industry, frequently renting space rather than purchasing space. This implies, of course, that light industry can move its operations to another community more readily than "heavy" industry.

INDUSTRIAL ZONING

Although zoning was discussed in detail in Chapter 2, it seems appropriate to mention industrial zoning here. As the name falsely implies, an **industrial zone** is an area set aside for industrial use. The false implication, which breeds trouble, arises as a result of what some regard as an improper

Exhibit 5-1 Commercial/Industrial Percent of Net Property Taxes, 1974–1990

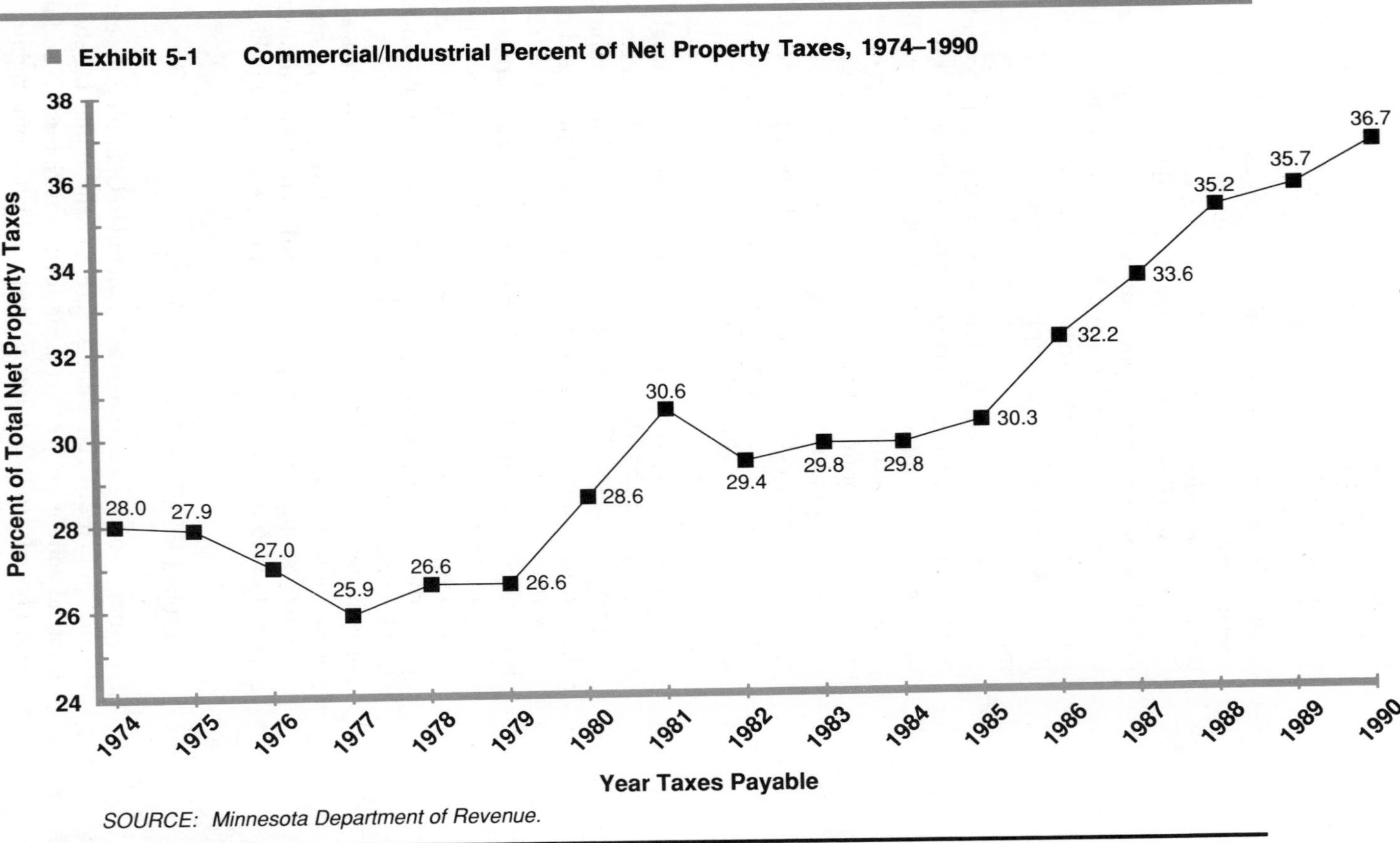

SOURCE: Minnesota Department of Revenue.

approach to industrial zoning—that frequently residences are permitted in industrial areas.

Historically, the industrial zone was not highly regarded by planners. Land was set aside for industry, but residences were permitted to encroach on the industrial zone. No thought was given to the *detrimental* effects residences might have on the industrial zone, such as a loss in efficiency of operation, a loss of tax profits, or even complaints by homeowners in the industrial area.

More and more citizens and city planners have come to realize that manufacturing is an asset to a community. Not only are residences being excluded from industrial zones, but in many areas the industrial park, both privately and community owned, has grown. In both cases, the zoning regulations frequently prohibit more than 50 percent of the land being covered by buildings. Urban industry in dingy buildings generally downgrades the quality of adjoining residential zones. Living near an industrial park surrounded by acres of woods and meadow often proves the reverse.

INDUSTRIAL PARKS

In recent years, there has been a rapid growth of the so-called modern industrial park. It has been said that the industrial park is the twin of the residential subdivision. In most cases, industrial parks are located in suburban areas and are spacious and beautifully landscaped, and as such are very attractive. It has even been noted that urban dwellers lacking sufficient city park space often are observed on a Sunday afternoon driving around industrial parks just to get out into the wide-open spaces.

What Is an Industrial Park?

One of the best definitions of the **industrial park** is that of the California State Chamber of Commerce: "a planned industrial park in a special or exclusive type of industrial subdivision developed according to a comprehensive plan to provide serviced sites for a community of compatible industries." The industrial park, under continuing management, provides for adequate control of the tract and buildings through restrictive covenants and/or adequate zoning, with a view to maintaining aesthetic value throughout the development.

Types of Industrial Parks

There are basically three types of industrial parks classified according to improvements and facilities:

1. The **industrial tract,** which is simply an improved tract of land including provisions for streets, access roads, and utilities. There are no buildings provided.
2. The **industrial subdivision,** which includes an improved tract

of land with industrial buildings. No special services or facilities are provided.

3. The **fully packaged estate,** which is an improved tract with buildings and a large enough area to provide sufficient economies of scale and to offer special facilities to industrial occupants.

Types of Industrial Park Tenants

Who are the tenants and buyers of industrial property? To bring a product from concept to consumer, it is convenient to think of five classes of industrial property:

1. Research and development facilities.
2. Manufacturing, including fabricating.
3. Assembly plants.
4. Distribution warehouses.
5. Wholesale showrooms.

Benefits to Industry

The following are a few of a number of reasons why it may be desirable for industry to locate in an industrial park:

1. Site development costs are reduced. As a rule of thumb, industrial development costs, such as putting in streets, sewers, railroad spurs, etc., will run from three to eight times the cost of the raw land. In the park, the economies of scale by the developer permit cheaper per acre development costs.

2. Smaller plants may have the advantages of large-scale operations (e.g., a common sewer plant).

3. The site is ready. The time lag between the decision to locate and the beginning of production is reduced.

4. Package plans are often available. In short, industry does not need to get involved in local negotiations for such things as a zoning change. Furthermore, many industrial parks can offer engineering services and, often, financing of both the land and proposed buildings.

5. Investment protection. Industry doesn't have to buy excess land to insulate itself from deterioration of nearby properties if the industrial park is well conceived.

Benefits to the Community

The community may gain from:

1. Diversification of industry. In short, the economic base of the com-

munity may be broadened by diversification and become economically more stable than a one-industry town.

2. Increased payroll and hence income to the community as a whole.
3. Lower community costs. Duplication of streets, utilities, etc., are often avoided.
4. Compatibility and sound relationship of land use.

Limitations of the Industrial Park

Like most ideas, the industrial park does have limitations.

1. Industrial parks are not suitable for all industries; for example, operations with large land and utility requirements, such as a steel plant.
2. Industry expansion problems. A firm will have difficulty expanding if no more land is available within the park.
3. Developmental restrictions. Times change and restrictions that once seemed reasonable may become burdensome as production processes change with the introduction of such things as new product lines.
4. A young firm may not be able to afford to locate in the park.

Financing Industrial Parks

Although many industrial parks are sponsored by private community groups (generally a group of interested business people, railroads, joint municipal government and private community groups, or by government), many are sponsored by private real estate developers. When a private real estate developer is involved, the development is generally financed with the assistance of a financial institution. This is done in two ways: the mortgage plan and the purchase-lease plan.

Under the mortgage plan:

1. The developer erects the buildings, leases the property, and then applies for a mortgage loan.
2. The developer sells the site; the purchaser applies for a loan and erects the buildings.

Under the purchase-lease plan:

1. The developer can erect a building, lease the property, and then offer it for sale to an institutional investor.
2. The developer sells the site; the purchaser erects a building. The purchaser sells the property to an institutional investor and leases it back, or sells the property to a private investor and leases it back.

OPPORTUNITIES IN INDUSTRIAL REAL ESTATE

Industries are moving from central business districts and more will probably move in the future. The main reason for this is the decay and obsolescence in the central city. In spite of the higher cost of moving, there has been a shift in industrial employment from the traditional concentrations in the Northeastern and North Central United States, to the South, Southwest, South Central, and Pacific regions. This has required many new industrial sites in the expanding areas. Consequently, this should suggest two business opportunities for the real estate practitioner: (1) a marketing opportunity, and (2) an opportunity for rehabilitation.

It is suggested that practitioners may conduct their own surveys to discover firms desiring new plant locations and attempt to fit their listings to their needs.

As older properties in the central business district become available, possibilities of rehabilitation exist. Typically, the older buildings are located in a mixed area of industrial, commercial, and residential zones. Typically, too, these buildings are multistory buildings. The nearness to residences enables some industries to locate in rehabilitated space because of the proximity of a good labor supply for apparel manufacturing, for assembly of electrical components, and for clerical work. The central location has also encouraged rehabilitation for discount houses, warehouses oriented to central business districts. Thus, the location poorly situated for intensive industries is often adaptable to other industries.

All floors are rented, frequently to different smaller firms. To do this, it is suggested that the purchase price must be low enough, the property tax assessments must not be discriminatory, and the physical features must be such as to encourage rents high enough to justify rehabilitation. This includes such things as on-site parking and building accessibility.

LOCATION OF COMMERCIAL ACTIVITY

It would seem desirable for analytical purposes to examine commercial space in terms of retail space and other commercial property.

Retail Space

Like the demand for industrial property, the demand for **retail property** is said to be a derived demand. Put more succinctly, retail trade follows the consumer. As a general rule, retail trade, hence the demand for retail space, has been moving along with suburbia to areas outside the central business district.

With the movement of population to suburban areas, shopping centers have developed. A shopping center is an area in which a large number of stores and shops of various types are located and in which the large majority of consumer wants may be satisfied.

There are five commonly identified retail areas: (1) central shopping districts, (2) secondary shopping centers, (3) local neighborhood shopping areas, (4) ribbon-type business developments along streets zoned for commercial use, and (5) modern, planned, integrated centers.

Central Shopping Districts. Historically the central retail district contained large department stores, clothing, jewelry, and variety stores, all within walking distance of one another. The financial district, including banks, brokerage houses, and office buildings, was also part of the so-called downtown central business district. Entertainment and cultural activities were concentrated in the city center.

Public transportation was generally available, roads converged, and use of the automobile was relatively minimal; hence, available parking was adequate. Increased use of the automobile after World War II resulted in a demand for shopping space that would accommodate the automobiles by providing adequate free parking.

Movement of population to suburban areas and construction of shopping centers brought decline and decay to the central city core. Revitalization of the central cities in the 1980s has been stimulated by historic preservation, gentrification, and energy-related modifications of shopping patterns. The automobile, which contributed to decentralization of commercial and industrial space, is likely, due to higher cost gasoline, to contribute to its rehabilitation. As people move back to the city, so will retail establishments and industry.

To encourage retail shopping in the central business district, city planners in Washington, D.C., working with the zoning commission, require developers of office facilities to provide retail space in each new office building. Specifically, new buildings are required to allocate 20 percent of their rentable space to retail and service uses.

Shopping Centers. Centers are divided into seven main categories.

1. The *superregional shopping center* or malls consisting of two, three, or four major department stores with an aggregate store area of 500,000 square feet; specialty apparel stores with 200,000 square feet; and other stores with 300,000 square feet. There must be a minimum of 100 acres, with additional space for office buildings and apartment buildings adjacent to or in the center. There must be at least 100,000 families with an estimated annual income of at least $1 billion to support such a center.

2. The *regional shopping center* with a major department store of 100,000 square feet and a total area of 250,000 to 1 million square feet on a 50- to 100-acre tract. This type center can be supported only in a trade area with a population of 200,000 persons or more.

3. A *community center* with a junior department store of 25,000 to 90,000 square feet, and a total store area of 100,000 to 400,000

square feet on a site of 15 to 40 acres, supported by a population of 100,000 or less.

4. A *large neighborhood center* with a variety or clothing store of 10,000 to 20,000 square feet as the largest unit with a total store area of 50,000 to 100,000 square feet on a site of 10 to 20 acres.
5. *Small neighborhood centers* with a supermarket of 20,000 to 30,000 square feet as the largest unit and a total of not over 50,000 square feet including a drugstore, hardware store, and other local convenience shops on a site of 5 to 10 acres. These centers need a population of about 5,000 to 10,000 people.
6. The **strip shopping center,** which is "street-oriented," is a group of retail and/or service shops, with space ranging from 15,000 to 20,000 square feet. In recent years, these centers have grown rapidly. Los Angeles–based La Mancha Development Company has built over 300 strip centers in California, Arizona, Nevada, Illinois, and Missouri. There are two major reasons for their fast growth: (1) retailers have been shifting to smaller centers to obtain lower rents; and (2) according to a Coldwell Banker study of 12 cities, strip centers have been able to increase their rental rates by a higher percentage than community centers or malls. As a result, builder-developers have moved into this area for higher profits, and retailers are still able to realize rent savings over larger centers.
7. The *convenience center,* which is a rapidly increasing variation of the strip center, consists of five or six stores and a small parking area. Most commonly, these include a convenience store, a video store, and possibly a hairdressing salon.

The important point here is that all of these retail structures are the result of a demand derived from population. In the development of a shopping center, both prospective tenants and financial institutions demand an economic feasibility study to determine whether or not a shopping center is likely to succeed. These studies usually consist of six parts: (1) population; (2) income of the population; (3) buying power (attempting to break down dollars available to population in relation to expenditures by proposed store types and price lines); (4) competitive facilities; (5) accessibility of the proposed site; and (6) other related considerations, for example, shoppers' buying habits.

Other Commercial Property

Other commercial property includes, for example, office buildings, wholesale buying and selling offices, warehouses, and loft-type buildings housing light industry. Office buildings are typically located in the central city core. Warehouses and light industry are frequently located on the periphery of the central business district.

Central Business Districts. Central business districts have been primarily left to office buildings devoted to financial institutions, lawyers, and others rendering service to other businesspeople and industrialists. Satellites, such as stationers or supply houses for office equipment, would fall into this category. Two major factors seem to have prevented offices engaged in financial activities from fleeing as rapidly to suburbia: (1) information is the stock-in-trade of security dealers and bankers, i.e., information on credit standings; and (2) face-to-face negotiations are often crucial in financial transactions.

The Office Space Glut. A period of rapidly expanding office space occurred between 1981 and 1986. Construction was stimulated by enormous tax advantages given by the federal and state governments, which encouraged investing in real estate via the limited partnership. Additionally, the shift in national employment from manufacturing to service industries, particularly financial services, resulted in increased demand for office space.

The supply of office space constitutes the number of square feet of available rental space placed on the market. Construction begun in 1981, 1982, and 1983 was "delivered" to market in 1984, 1985, and 1986. Although the total number of office workers increased rapidly during that period, the supply of office space grew at an even faster pace; by early 1986, the national vacancy rate reached 18 percent due to the mismatch between supply and demand. The oversupply of office buildings has been so great that vacancy rates as high as 35 percent have continued through 1990.

More importantly, like the market for real estate in general, the market for office space is segmented. Cities in which the demand for office workers, and hence office space, depends primarily on one industry have been particularly hard hit. In these cities, office buildings have been referred to as "see through" buildings. Houston, heavily dependent on oil, is an example. When the price of oil fell, the office buildings delivered to market in that city were unrented. According to Robert A. Frank, Baltimore real estate analyst:

> I was in Houston not too long ago. The downtown area has a weird feeling like somebody dropped a neutron bomb, killed all the people, and left the buildings standing (*Barron's,* January 20, 1986).

Hopefully at some future time, these problems will be resolved. By mid-1986, construction of commercial buildings reached a standstill in many markets. Many office properties have fallen in value, with investors turning heavily mortgaged properties back to lenders. It has been estimated that it will take at least five years for demand to catch up with supply.

Occupancy can be optimized, in part, by successful design. The Institute of Urban Studies at the University of Texas in Arlington analyzed

Table 5-6 Variables Affecting Office Occupancy Rates

	CORRELATION WITH OCCUPANCY
1. Open space—percent landscaped	.73
2. Arterial road access	.70
3. Pedestrian amenities	.68
4. Nonoffice land use	.63
5. Public amenities	.45
6. Concrete buildings	− .53
7. L-shaped building	− .44
8. Square building	− .43
9. Age of building	− .26
10. Mixed pattern of windows	− .23

SOURCE: University of Texas at Arlington, Institute of Urban Studies, 1988.

the design characteristics that contribute to an office building's occupancy or vacancy. The five characteristics with greatest positive and negative correlation with occupancy are presented in Table 5-6.

FUTURE TRENDS

As of this writing, one factor, more than any other, will affect future trends in the location and design of industrial and commercial property. That factor, whose impact is presently unassessed, is energy.

Available electric and natural gas supplies are destined to become increasingly important in relocation and expansion decisions. State industrial development commissions, local Chambers of Commerce, and private developers recruiting new industry will need to provide evidence of adequate energy supplies, if their efforts are to be successful.

It is important to realize that the full impact of the energy shortage is yet unknown. Speculatively, some possible consequences include the following:

1. Movement of industries to warmer climates where energy demands are minimized.
2. Renewed industrial preference for locating near railroad and water transport centers.
3. Lessened need for employee parking and a desire to be near transportation will encourage industrial and commercial relocation in cities' central core.
4. Industrial relocation to states where energy supplies are deemed adequate.

5. Resurgence of downtown shopping areas serviced by public transportation.
6. Redevelopment of neighborhood shopping centers within walking distance for customers.

All factors presently significant in site selection will continue to remain important. Each factor adversely affected by the energy shortage, however, will become increasingly important in the future.

Another recent development experiencing increased popularity is extension of the condominium concept to office buildings and shopping centers. Ownership of the **office condominium** or store provides the advantage of:

1. Tax deductions for interest, depreciation, taxes, and other operating expenses.
2. Equity buildup through loan amortization and inflationary appreciation.
3. Security of knowing the lease won't be cancelled or the rent increased.
4. Cost savings through shared ownership of land, physical plant, and common areas.

Operation of the condominium office building or shopping center is governed by the declaration and by-laws of the owners' association. Similar precautions apply to the office or retail space as to a condominium residence. An area of critical concern is assessments for maintenance, financing, and insurance. Buyers must remember that office condominiums are owner-directed and professionally managed. Some attention to operations is required by owners to ensure that management acts in the owners' interest.

Also new to the scene is the "modular concept," which has been innovatively applied to the design of office buildings. Recent construction has employed only a minimum of permanent dividing walls. Instead, whereever possible, modular or portable walls have been employed to permit a maximum of freedom and flexibility in creating an office layout. The concept has been well received, particularly in medical office buildings where tenant needs are diverse.

GLOSSARY

Derived demand The demand for industrial and commercial property as a result of product demand by consumers

Factor evaluation The process of analyzing various factors in site location of industry

Factor weight The mathematical importance of ten location factors for industry

Fully packaged estate An industrial park improved with buildings and large enough to provide economies of scale and to offer special facilities to occupants

Industrial park An exclusive subdivision developed according to a comprehensive plan to provide serviced sites for a community of compatible industries

Industrial subdivision An improved tract of land with buildings to be used for industry

Industrial tract An improved tract of land with no buildings, including provisions for streets, access roads, and utilities

Industrial zone An area set aside for industrial use

Locational analysis In-depth study of the importance of location on the success of industrial and commercial ventures

Office condominium A condominium restricted to office space

Production-cost orientation Low bulk-to-value ratio; hence, transport inputs relatively unimportant

Retail property Buildings one or two stories high, with retail establishments on the first floor and office space on the second floor

Strip shopping center A group of smaller, street-oriented retail and/or service shops

Transport-cost orientation High bulk-to-value ratio; hence, transport imports are important

QUESTIONS FOR REVIEW

1. The demand for industrial property is a derived demand. Explain.
2. List the ten principal factors in the location of industry.
3. Discuss the impact of energy as a factor in industrial location.
4. Why is "government climate" an essential factor in site selection?
5. In recent years, the concept of industrial zoning has changed. Comment.
6. List and discuss the limitations of the industrial park.
7. Why has retail trade been moving from the central business district in recent years?

8. What are the five commonly identified retail areas?

9. What types of offices are located primarily in central business districts and why?

PROBLEMS AND ACTIVITIES

1. Tax discrimination is frequent against industrial property by some communities. Too often assessors have failed to realize that older buildings have become functionally obsolete. Assume you wish to prepare a study for purposes of pointing out this form of tax discrimination. You search the county clerk's records and find 15 sales of industrial property at a total of $17 million. You also find 32 sales of commercial properties with total sales prices of $22 million were consummated during the same period. All property sales of 38,500 parcels during that time period totaled an even $516 million. An examination of records in the assessor's office shows that (a) the 15 industrial sales were assessed at $5.61 million, (b) the commercial properties were assessed at $8.36 million, and (c) all properties were assessed at $154 million.

   From this information, prepare an argument for reassessment of the industrial properties.

PART THREE

PROPERTY RIGHTS

6

THE NATURE AND CLASSIFICATION OF PROPERTY RIGHTS

KEY TERMS

Accretion
Adverse possession
Community property
Concurrent ownership
Condominium
Confiscation
Constructive annexation
Contingent remainder
Curtesy
Dedication
Deed
Derivative title
Devise
Dominant tenement
Dower
Easement
Easement by grant
Easement by implied grant
Easement by necessity
Easement by prescription
Easement by reservation
Emblements
Eminent domain
Encroachment
Escheat
Estate
Estate of inheritance
Estate of less than freehold
Estate on condition
Estate on condition precedent
Estate on condition subsequent
Estover
Fee simple conditional
Fee simple determinable
Fee simple or fee simple absolute
Fixtures
Forfeiture
Freehold estate
Grantee
Grantor
Joint tenancy
License
Life estate
Life estate *pur autre vie*
Original title
Personal property
Prescription
Public grant
Real property
Reliction or dereliction
Remainder
Reversion
Right of survivorship
Servient tenement
Severalty
Tenancy by the entireties
Tenancy in common
Title
Title by cession
Title by conquest
Title by descent
Title by occupancy
Title by purchase

Trade fixture
Unity of interest
Unity of possession
Unity of time
Unity of title
Vested remainder
Waste

Before one can understand real estate principles or the real estate profession with any degree of completeness, it is necessary to have some understanding of the various means and degrees by which title to real property may be held.

LAND, REALTY, REAL ESTATE, AND REAL PROPERTY

The major physical characteristic of land is its fixed location. From this springs a second characteristic, namely, heterogeneity. Land is unique; there are no two parcels exactly alike. It is not fungible; that is, no two parcels can be mixed as can two measures of wheat or two barrels of oil. This factor has led to important special legal treatment of land, as will be pointed out in subsequent chapters. Land is also indestructible. Land does not wear out, except through erosion and depletion. This may affect the value of the land for farming purposes and perhaps somewhat for residential purposes, but as a general rule land remains the same, physically, year after year.

In addition to the physical characteristics of land, there are certain economic characteristics. Land is relatively scarce. The improvements on the land are relatively long-lasting. This suggests that demand has a tremendous effect on both price and intensity of land use, demand being particularly important when the commodity demanded is relatively scarce. Location is a third economic characteristic of land. Location, coupled with population and standards of living, tends to produce greater values in one parcel of land as opposed to another. The word *realty* was used historically to connote the land. It is now used in practice as a synonym for real property (which means, strictly speaking, the interest in land) or anything that partakes of the nature of real property. *Real estate* is basically a term that has come about as the result of commercial usage. It has two meanings. In common usage, it is often employed interchangeably with "realty" and "real property" in the sense that it is the thing itself. In the second sense of its meaning, it is the term used to designate those persons concerned with commercial transactions in realty or real property.

Real property is defined as the land and, generally, whatever is erected, growing upon, or affixed to the land. Crops requiring annual cultivation are not usually included in this definition.

The idea of property has had a long and complicated history. Philosophers, economists, and lawyers have all had a hand in the development of the idea of property. Some regard *property* as the rights and interests of an individual in anything subject to ownership. Some regard property as anything having value in exchange. In any event, the right of property can exist only when it is protected by society from encroachment by others. For our purposes here, we may look on the first definition as a working tool.

CLASSIFICATION OF PROPERTY

Property is divided into sets of rights involving land and personal things *(chattels)*. Historically, these rights or proprietary interests were classified as analogous to things of a physical nature; namely, (1) land or those things annexed to the land so as to be considered a part of it, and (2) articles of a movable character that were neither annexed as a part of the land nor annexed in the view of the law as a part thereof.

After the middle of the seventeenth century, these two classifications were commonly referred to as *real property* and *personal property*. The names were derived from two types of legal actions: one called real actions and the other personal actions. The first was an action brought by persons who were deprived of freehold interests (interests of indefinite duration) in land, or incorporeal things, such as the rights to the use of another's land. The second, personal action, was brought to obtain restitution from deprivation of movable goods. The first action was said to "sound in realty" and the second to "sound in personalty."

Real Property

One classification of rights or interests referred to above became known as real property interests. The land, in legal theory, is conceived of as being not only the lot or tract referred to in a deed, but as extending upward over the land to the sky and downward from the lot to the center of the earth. Most attachments to the house or building become a part of the real property and are dealt with under the heading of fixtures.

Personal Property

Just as the first class of rights became known as real property, so the second classification of rights became known as personal property interests. **Personal property** is defined as everything that is subject to ownership and not coming under the domination of real estate; hence, anything that is not attached to the land or any buildings thereon. These articles, that is to say *things* themselves, are called *personalty*. Thus, the interests or ownership of an automobile is a personal property interest. The thing itself, the automobile, is personalty. In practice, personal property is used as a synonym for personalty.

Some property interests in land are treated as personal property. Often these interests are called leasehold interests, for they are created by leases. Leasehold interests are discussed more fully in Chapter 10.

Sometimes an article of real property may change in character from real property to personal property. For example, trees when growing are to be considered a part of the real property; and the ownership therein is a real property interest. However, when the trees are cut, they are considered personalty, even though they may be lying on the particular parcel of real property on which they grew. The interest in the cut trees becomes a personal property interest and is no longer a real property interest.

Fixtures

Just as trees or other real property may change in character from real property to personal property, so may personal property change to real property. Articles that have changed from personalty to real property are commonly known as **fixtures.** Confusion sometimes exists as to when personal property becomes real property. For example, an oil burner displayed in the window of a store is an item of personal property. However, once the oil burner is removed from the store and installed in a permanent manner and has become an inherent part of a building, it is then classified as real property. When permanently attached to the building it is commonly called a fixture.

The Tests of a Fixture

In determining whether or not an article in a building is a fixture, the courts will look into the intent of the parties, the method of annexation, the relation of the parties, and the adaptation of the article.

Intent of the Parties. The courts, on raising the question of the intent of the parties when an article is placed in a building, ask whether or not the item was attached with the idea (or intent) of making it a permanent part of the building. Refrigerators in apartment houses have been held to be a part of the real estate.[1] The reasoning has been that the refrigerators were installed and were *intended* to remain permanently because their presence increased the rental value of the apartments.

Method of Annexation. The courts consider the method of annexation of an article to real property and raise the question of whether there would be substantial injury to the real property if the article were removed.

The plumbing in a house must be regarded as a fixture, for substantial injury to the property would result from its removal. There exists, too, what is known as **constructive annexation** in the case of those articles that are not fastened to the realty but are made for use in connection with real property. A key is an example.

Relation of the Parties. Suppose a landlord rents a building to a tenant for the purpose of operating a restaurant, and the tenant installs a counter.

---

[1]*Guardian Life Insurance Companay v. Swanson,* 286 Ill. App. 278, 3 N.E. (2d) 324.

Could the landlord claim that it was a permanent fixture and that its title had therefore passed to the landlord? No, for the courts encourage tenants to equip themselves with the necessary tools of their trade. The tenant, however, must remove the counter, called a **trade fixture,** before the expiration of the lease; otherwise, it would become a fixture. If it became a fixture, it would be regarded as real property, and title would pass to the landlord.

Adaptation of the Article. This test also tends to show the intention of the annexing party. When an article is essential to the purpose for which the building was intended, it is presumed to be a fixture. This presumption holds true even though the article can be severed from the building.

TITLES TO REAL PROPERTY

A **title** is a legal right referring to the ownership of property. One may hold titles to personal property and real property.

Titles may be divided into original titles and derivative titles. **Original titles** include those acquired by discovery, occupancy, conquest, or cession. **Derivative titles** are subdivided into titles by descent and titles by purchase.

Derivative titles are titles that are not original titles. An individual can hold only by a derivative title. Derivative titles are obtained either by purchase or by descent. **Title by descent** arises when a person obtains land from a relative who dies intestate (without a will). **Title by purchase** includes all methods of acquiring title other than by descent. Technically, the word *purchase* includes transfers by will, voluntary transfers, and involuntary transfers.

Original title to real property can never be in an individual, but is acquired by a nation. It may be acquired by discovery. At one time the mere discovery of land, not subject to any civilized nation, vested title in the nation whose subject made the discovery. However, at the present time, discovery gives only the first right of occupancy to the nation.

Title by occupancy occurs when the first nation to occupy a territory not previously owned by any civilized nation acquires title thereto. **Title by conquest** arises when one country takes territory from another by force of arms. In such cases, only the title to public lands is affected; private land titles usually are recognized. The last method is **title by cession,** which includes all titles derived by grant from one country to another.

Private Grant

Most grants or transfers of property are between individuals. The transfer is effected by means of a deed. A **deed** is an instrument conveying (transferring) the lands of one individual to another. A deed may be voluntary or involuntary. A voluntary deed is made pursuant to an agreement between the parties, and an involuntary deed is made pursuant to an order of the court. Deeds are discussed in greater detail in Chapter 8.

Dedication. A transfer of property by an individual to the public is called a **dedication.** For example, when *A* desires to grant a parcel of realty to the public for a road, the grant is by means of a dedication. There must be an intent on the part of the grantor to surrender it to the public, and the public (government) must accept the grant.

Devise. The **devise,** a will or clause in a will conveying property, is a form of private conveyance. Wills disposing of real estate must be in writing and must comply with the statutes of the various states. A more thorough treatment of wills is presented in Chapter 8.

Public Grant

A **public grant** refers to the granting of title to public lands by a governmental body. The authority to grant title to such lands is given by the U.S. Congress, or a state legislature, either by a special act expressly transferring certain lands to certain parties, or by a general act expressing the means by which individuals may acquire title to public lands. In the first instance, the special legislative act serves as evidence of title. In the second instance, persons acquiring title under a general legislative act receive a patent from the government. A *patent,* in this sense, is a complete appropriation of the land it describes and a conveyance of all interests in that land to the grantee. In the exercise of this right, the state must exercise due process of law.

Title From Nature

Title from nature arises from either accretion or reliction. **Accretion** is the increase of land caused by gradual and imperceptible additions thereto caused by the washing of a body of water. **Reliction** (or **dereliction**) is the gradual recession of waters leaving dry land where there had formerly been water.

Title From Civil or Political Acts

Under certain circumstances, title to property may be taken by governments against the wishes of the owners of the property. Details of the circumstances are explained in the following paragraphs.

Eminent Domain. **Eminent domain** is the power of the government, on payment of just compensation, to take property for public use, or to authorize such taking by a corporation or individual engaged in a quasi-public operation. In the exercise of this right, the taker must exercise due process of law.

Escheat. **Escheat** is a second method of acquiring title from civil or political acts. This is the right of the government to take the property of an intestate (a person dying without a will) who dies without leaving any heirs.

Confiscation. **Confiscation** is the right of government to take the property of its enemies in time of war. Generally this right is confined to personal property, but it may extend to real property.

Forfeiture. For many years it had been thought that property of an individual could be subject to **forfeiture** to the state for only two reasons: failure to pay taxes and commission of a treasonous act. There now appears to be a third reason: the violation of anti-drug laws. A boat or plane clearly used to smuggle cocaine into the United States is, for example, subject to forfeiture. The same thing holds true for real property; for instance, if an individual's home is used for the manufacture of illicit drugs, it, too, is subject to forfeiture. Furthermore, land may be lost as the result of growing marijuana.

Titles From Public Policy

Under certain circumstances, an individual may take title or use the property contrary to the wishes of the owner of the property. Details of the circumstances are given in the following paragraphs.

Adverse Possession. **Adverse possession** is the right of an occupant of land to acquire title against the real owner, when the possession has been actual, continuous, hostile, visible, and exclusive for the legal period. More detailed information is given about this method of acquiring title in Chapter 8.

Prescription. **Prescription** is the right of an adverse user of another's land who continues the use of this land for the legal period.[2] This use results in an *easement,* which will be discussed later in this chapter.

ESTATES AND INTERESTS IN LAND

Estates

An **estate** is the interest that a person holds in land. Estates are divided into several types according to the degree of interest held. Estates according to their quantity or duration of interest are divided into **freehold estates** and **estates of less than freehold.** The endurance of an estate of freehold is of indeterminate length. It is distinguished from the estate of less than freehold because the length of the latter is capable of accurate determination. The estates of freehold are generally treated in the legal sense as real property; the estates of less than freehold are generally treated as personal property in the nature of leasehold interests. Estates of the latter type are discussed in Chapter 10.

---

[2]In most states, statutes prescribe the time period; a minority of the states still follow the common law.

Estates of freehold are further subdivided into estates of inheritance and life estates. The **estate of inheritance** is one which upon the death of the holder still continues and descends to the heirs, while the *life estate* extends for the life of an individual.

Fee Simple

The **fee simple** or the **fee simple absolute,** as it is sometimes called, is an absolute estate. It is the largest estate and most prevalent interest in land; it is the entire property in land—the complete ownership of land. During one's lifetime, the owner of a fee simple title may do anything one wishes with the land, provided it is not used as a nuisance. Thus, having the complete ownership of the land, the owner may dispose of it entirely by sale or by gift while living. At death, the owner may dispose of the property by will. If no will is left, it will pass to the owner's issue, if any, or to collateral relatives in the event there are no heirs of the body.

Creation During Owner's Life. Because the fee simple is the absolute ownership in land, the owner may dispose of the land in any manner desired while living. This type of ownership, being the more common, is thus most often subject to transaction. For a valid transfer of real property to exist, there must be a competent grantor and a grantee capable of taking title. The **grantor** is the person who makes a grant (transfer); the **grantee** is the person to whom a grant is made. A competent grantor is usually a person of legal age and sound mind. A grantee capable of taking real property is any person natural or artificial (a corporation), unless excluded by state statute. The deed creating the fee simple will either read "from *A* to *B* and his or her heirs" or "*A* bargains, grants, and conveys into *B*," depending upon the state statutes.

Creation by Will or Descent. A fee simple may be created either by will (devise) or by descent. If *A* dies and by the will leaves property to *B*, then in due time *B* will receive from the executor of *A*'s estate a deed called an executor's deed. In the event *A* dies without a will, then an administrator (administratrix, if female) of the estate will be appointed and *A*'s heirs will receive an administrator's deed.[3] Both these forms of deed can effect a conveyance of a fee simple.

Since fee simple is the absolute ownership of real property, it follows that all other estates in real property must be held in terms of quantity of ownership or time of holding that are less than a fee simple.

Fee Simple Determinable

The **fee simple determinable** is a freehold estate of indefinite duration, but less than a freehold estate of inheritance. The determinable fee, sometimes called a qualified fee or a base fee, is an estate fee that is to continue

[3] Although title actually passes upon death, the administrator makes out the deed.

until the happening of a certain event. For example, *A* conveys property to a church, so long as the realty is used for a church; in the event the property is not used for a church, the property is to revert to *A* or her or his heirs. This is a fee simple determinable, and the church will have the fee so long as the property is used for a church. *A* and her or his heirs are spoken of as having a possibility of *reverter.* If the property ceases to be used for a church, *A* or her or his heirs get title to the property.

Because one of the essential characteristics of a fee is that it may endure forever, the named event creating the determinable estate must be a contingency, not a certainty.[4]

Fee Simple Conditional

The **fee simple conditional** has been defined as "an estate restrained to some particular heirs, exclusive of others, as to the heirs of a man's body, by which only his lineal descendants were admitted in exclusion of collateral; or to the heirs male of his body, in exclusion of heirs female, whether lineal or collateral."[5] It is called a conditional fee by reason of the condition expressed or implied in the donation of it that if the donee died without such particular heirs, the land should revert to the donor. In short, a limitation was made on a transfer of real property with the implication that if the donee did not produce the particular heirs named, then the title would revert to the donor. If he did produce those heirs, then the donee took the property in fee simple.

Estate on Condition

An **estate on condition** is one that, by the terms of the instrument by which it is created, is subject to a contingency not forming a part of the limitation of the estate. If the estate is to begin on the happening of a contingency, it is called an **estate on condition precedent;** if it is to terminate on the happening of a contingency, it is called an **estate on condition subsequent.** Most states have abolished the estate on condition precedent.

The normal estate on condition subsequent is created as follows: *A* gives land by will to his widow for life, provided she does not remarry. The nonmarriage is the condition subsequent. If she does marry, *A*'s heirs may *reenter,* or make a claim for the estate. If they do not make this claim within a reasonable time, the widow may retain the estate. This is the big distinction between the fee simple determinable discussed above and the estate on condition. In the fee simple determinable, the estate is terminated by the mere happening of the event. In the example above, by the mere fact that the widow remarried while in the estate on condition, the heirs, or whoever

---

[4]Herbert Thorndike Tiffany, *A Treatise on the Modern Law of Real Property and Other Interests in Land* (Chicago: Callaghan and Company, 1912), Sec. 81.

[5]*Willis v. Mutual Loan & Trust Co.,* 183 N.C. 267, 111 S.E. 163, 165.

else has an interest in the property, must take some action to terminate the estate.[6]

This is not an ancient history concept. In 1980, a Texas court upheld the concept. In 1920, a residential lot was sold with a restriction stating that if any store or shop selling merchandise or other commodities were to be erected on Lot *A*, the land would "revert to the Grantors herein, should they so elect." An art gallery was built on the property in 1973 and sold in 1975. The grantor asserted an interest in 1976, and the court upheld the re-entry.[7]

Life Estate

The **life estate** is an estate one may receive either for the duration of his or her life or the life of another. This latter estate is known technically as a **life estate** *pur autre vie.* The recipient of the estate for life may receive it either by deed or by will, or in some states by law where estates are granted to either a widow or a widower as the result of marriage. For example, *A* may by deed convey to *B* for life, and on the death of *B,* to *C* and his or her heirs. The grantee of a life estate is generally referred to as the *life tenant.* As life tenant, the grantee may do with the estate almost as much as could be done with a fee simple, subject, however, to a number of exceptions.

1. The life tenant may sell. The grantee of a life estate will receive an estate that will terminate on the death of the life tenant. As a practical matter, on the sale of the life estate, the life tenant will not be paid nearly so much as the real value of the property because the purchaser will be aware that possession may be lost at any time.

2. The life tenant has a right to receive any rents or profits from the land, but cannot injure the land to such an extent as to commit waste upon the land.

3. The life tenant is entitled to what is technically known as **estovers,** which is the right of the life tenant to take a reasonable amount of wood from the land for fuel and for repairs to any buildings on the land.

4. Like any other tenant, in the absence of any agreement to the contrary, the life tenant is bound to make reasonable repairs, but need not make any improvements. If improvements are made, the cost cannot be recovered from the owner of the inheritance.

5. The tenant must pay interest on encumbrances and taxes.

---

[6]The possibility of reverter was made assignable by a New York statute effective September 1, 1962. New Jersey and Connecticut adopted a similar statute over 100 years ago.

[7]*Humphrey v. the C.G. Jung Educ. Center of Houston,* 624 F2d 637 Tex. 1980.

A life tenant may mortgage a life estate, but the mortgage terminates at death. On the death of the life tenant, the mortgage would no longer constitute a lien upon the property.

The life estate, as outlined, is an example of what is commonly called fee splitting. The absolute ownership of the land is divided, part of the estate going to someone for life and part being more or less held in abeyance during the lifetime of the grantee or the lifetime of another. The problem then arises as to how these interests in real property are dealt with. Commonly, they are called remainders and reversions.

Remainders and Reversions

If *A* conveys to *B* for life and upon *B*'s death to *C* and his or her heirs, *B* has received from *A* a life estate. What, then, has *C* received? *C* has received an interest in the estate called a **remainder,** and *C* is called the *remainderman.* Remainders are either vested remainders or contingent remainders. If the remainderman can be determined at the time of the grant, then the estate is called a **vested remainder.** *C,* in the example, can be determined; hence, the interest *C* has in the estate is that of a vested remainder. On the death of *B, C* or his or her heirs will be entitled to the fee simple.

Contingent Remainders. A **contingent remainder** exists when the remainderman cannot be ascertained at the time of the transfer. For example, *B* conveys to *A* for life with a remainder to *A*'s eldest son. This is contingent until a son is born, at which point it becomes vested. If the transfer reads to *A* for life and the remainder to the eldest son at the time of *A*'s death, then the remainder would still remain contingent until *A*'s death, because only at that time can it be determined who is the eldest living son.

Reversions. If, in the examples above, the grant had read "*B* to *A* for life and on the death of *A* to *B* and his or her heirs," then, a **reversion** would exist, and it would be said that *B* had a reversionary interest (revert meaning to come back).

Waste

Although the persons having a life estate may use the land and receive the profits from it, they still may not appropriate or injure any part of what is regarded as a permanent part of the land. For example, a life tenant may not take minerals and the like from the land without having committed waste, unless such life tenant was expressly permitted to do so by the terms of the grant. The removal or the destruction of a building that is upon the land has been held by the courts to constitute **waste.** In either case, the life tenant is liable for damages if it is held that waste has been committed. A person having a reversionary interest in the land can bring the action against the life tenant, and the person who has a vested remainder in the land may also bring the action. The contingent remainderman may not bring the action because his or her interest is a mere possibility and does not ripen until the death of the life tenant.

There is often a possibility of merging the reversionary or remainder interests with the life estate to create a fee. For example, *A* is a life tenant and *B* has a vested remainder. A sale of the fee simple may be made to *X*, if a grant of the life estate is obtained from *A* and a proper deed obtained from *B* of the vested remainder, which will merge the life estate with the vested remainder to transfer the fee simple to *X*.

CONCURRENT OWNERSHIP

Concurrent ownership of property simply means that title to the same piece of property is in two or more persons at one and the same time. This type of ownership is distinguishable from an estate in **severalty,** which is an estate held by one in one's own right only, without any other person being joined or connected.

The most prevalent type of concurrent ownership is called a joint tenancy.

Joint Tenancy

A **joint tenancy** exists when two or more persons own the same land and have the same unity of interest, time, title, and possession together with the right of survivorship. This latter factor has often been called the "grand incident" of the joint tenancy.

The two or more parties concerned with the joint tenancy are considered as having but one estate in the land. Each is considered to be the owner of the whole. In order for there to be a joint tenancy, the four unities (interest, time, title, and possession) must exist.

1. **Unity of interest** means that the interest of the owners must be of the same duration. For example, if the conveyance were made by the same instrument, to *A* in fee and to *B* for life, there could exist no joint tenancy because one of the four unities would be lacking.

2. **Unity of time** has been construed to mean that the title to the property must vest in the tenants at the same time. One tenant cannot hold the property in possession while another holds it in remainder.

3. **Unity of title** means that both or all of the tenants must have one and the same interest arising out of one and the same conveyance.

4. **Unity of possession** means that each of the tenants must have undivided or equal rights of possession.

The so-called grand incident of the joint tenancy is the **right of survivorship.**[8] This means that when a joint tenancy exists, title passes to the survivor on the death of one of the parties. For example, if *A* and *B* hold property as joint tenants and *A* dies, the title in fee to the entire property passes to *B*. It is for this reason that many of the states have passed specific statutes requiring that the joint tenancy be spelled out in a deed. In Idaho, the law (55-508 ICA) states:

> Every interest in real estate granted or devised to two or more persons other than executors or trustees, as such, constitutes a tenancy in common, unless expressly declared in the grant or devise to be otherwise.[9]

To create the joint tenancy the deed should read "to *A* and *B* as joint tenants," or, to be on the safe side, "to *A* and *B* as joint tenants and not as tenants in common."

The joint tenancy, and, of course, the right of survivorship, will be destroyed by a conveyance by one of the tenants to a stranger. For example, if *A* and *B* are joint tenants and *B* conveys to *C*, then *A* and *C* hold as tenants in common, without the right of survivorship. If there are four joint tenants, *A*, *B*, *C* and *D*, and *D* conveys to *X*, then *A*, *B*, and *C* hold as joint tenants as to each other and as tenants in common with *X*. If *A* were to die, *B* and *C* would get *A*'s share by survivorship and remain tenants in common with *X*.[10]

Tenancy by the Entireties

Tenancy by the entireties exists generally only in real property and exists only between husband and wife. When a husband and wife take title together, they are said to hold title as tenants by the entireties because of the common-law concept that a husband and wife are one person.[11] The

---

[8]In Alabama, Arizona, Florida, Georgia, Kansas, Kentucky, Maine, North Carolina, Ohio, Oregon, Pennsylvania, South Carolina, Tennessee, Texas, Virginia, and West Virginia the right of survivorship in a joint tenancy has been abolished. Thus at death, the joint tenant's share passes to the heirs as if it were a tenancy in common, unless the deed expressly states that the property shall go to the surviving grantees.

[9]New York State expresses the same thing thus: "Every estate granted or devised to two or more persons in their own right shall be a tenancy in common, unless expressly declared to be a joint tenancy; but every estate, vested in executors or trustees as such, shall be held by them in joint tenancy . . ." (Sec. 66. Real Property Law).

[10]Sometimes the question regarding simultaneous deaths of the joint tenants arises. The Uniform Simultaneous Death Act, adopted in all states except Louisiana and Georgia, provides in effect that the property passes to the heirs of each joint tenant. For example, if there are two joint tenants, half goes to the heirs of each. If there are four joint tenants, a quarter goes to the heirs of each, and so on.

result is a fifth unity added to those discussed under joint tenancy; namely unity of person. This is the reason a tenancy by the entireties can exist *only* between husband and wife. The deed must be made out to them both at the same time while they are married. If it is made out to them prior to their marriage, no tenancy by the entireties exists. The so-called grand incident of the tenancy by the entireties is that the surviving spouse gets title to the entire parcel on the death of the other. For example, if a couple holds a parcel as tenants by the entireties and the husband dies, then the wife receives a fee simple title to the parcel. As tenants by the entireties, neither can sell the property without first obtaining the signature of the other spouse on the deed, and neither can force a partition of the property.

If the husband and wife divorce, they are then said to hold the property as tenants in common. The reason for this is that the tenancy by the entireties is based on the common-law theory of the husband and wife being one; after the divorce, there is no longer a unity and there can be no tenancy by the entireties; it must become a tenancy in common.

Tenancy by the Entireties vs. Joint Tenancy

As a result of the feminist movement, it appears that there is a shift in most states regarding the holding of real property between husband and wife from a tenancy by the entireties to a joint tenancy provided there is an intention clearly expressed that they shall take as joint tenants. This is due to the fifth unity in the tenancy by the entireties—namely, that husband and wife are considered as one and therefore cannot act individually to sell his or her share of the property.

Worthy of mention here is what might be termed the "joint tenancy trap." In a joint tenancy between husband and wife, any liens against the husband alone pass with the title on his death. In a tenancy by the entireties, title passes to the surviving wife *unencumbered.*

For example, assume a situation in which a wife is completely uninvolved. The husband gets into a brawl, and a judgment is obtained against him for $10,000. Later he dies, and one of the following situations exists:

1. Husband and wife hold as joint tenants. On the husband's death, title passes to the wife. The judgment creditor can force the sale of the property and collect $10,000 from the proceeds.

---

[11]This is recognized in the states of Alaska, Arkansas, Delaware, Florida, Indiana, Kentucky, Massachusetts, Michigan, Mississippi, Missouri, New Jersey, New York, North Carolina, Ohio, Oklahoma, Oregon, Pennsylvania, Rhode Island, Tennessee, Utah, Virginia, Washington, and West Virginia and in the District of Columbia. In Arkansas, New Jersey, New York, and Oregon, either spouse can transfer his or her right to possession together with his or her contingent right of survivorship.

2. Husband and wife hold as tenants by the entireties. On the husband's death, title passes to the wife, but because of the fifth unity, title passes to the wife unencumbered. The judgment creditor gets nothing.[12]

Tenancy in Common

A **tenancy in common** exists when two or more persons own the same land with undivided interests. Their interests may exist under different titles, or under the same title if it contains words of limitation importing that the grantees are to own undivided shares. There is not right of survivorship in the tenancy in common, distinguishing it from the joint tenancy and the tenancy by the entireties. Also, the tenants do not have to own equal shares. For example, *A*'s interest may be in one-third of the property and *B*'s in two-thirds.

Condominium

An ancient concept of co-ownership given a modern dress by the Housing Act of 1961 is the condominium. A **condominium** is a form of ownership of real property characterized by the fee ownership of individual units, commonly apartments, coupled with an undivided interest in common with the remainder of the property. Basically, the idea is for an individual to own the apartment in which he or she lives. It is paid for either in cash or by a mortgage plus a proportionate annual sum for maintenance and management of the building.

Prior to the Housing Act of 1961, which permitted FHA insurance on condominiums for the first time, there were a number of cooperative apartments—a concept that must be distinguished from the idea of condominium. Cooperative apartments are corporations that sell shares of stock to the "tenants." In a cooperative setup, if the corporation fails to pay taxes the owner could lose the apartment. In addition, the owner could become liable for the tenant's failure to make payments to the co-op. The owner of the condominium can pay off the mortgage, and cannot be foreclosed upon even if the other owners have not paid. Furthermore, the owner of the condominium can sell without permission of the other owners; but in cooperative apartments, each owner must have permission of the other owners. The condominium concept is spreading from apartment buildings to shopping centers and business offices in downtown areas.

For the condominium to exist, individual states had to pass legislation permitting city assessors to assess each apartment individually as a prerequisite for FHA insurance. All 50 states have now done this. The first condominium was completed in Hallandale, Florida, in April 1962.

---

[12]In Massachusetts most residences are held by husband and wife to avoid state inheritance taxes.

DOWER AND CURTESY

Dower

In common law, **dower** is the right of the wife to a life estate in one-third of all of the lands of inheritance owned by the husband during the period of the coverture (marriage). Under some state statutes, Oregon, for example, the one-third interest provided by the common law has been raised to a one-half interest. This is an example of acquiring title to real property as a result of marriage, and also an example of the acquisition of title by law. Dower has been abolished in many states.[13] In some states a property settlement has been substituted in its place. Where dower has been abolished, the wife need no longer join with her husband on a deed conveying the property, unless she holds as a tenant by the entireties or by community property, or as joint tenant.[14,15]

Curtesy

In common law, **curtesy** is an estate for life given by law to the husband in *all* the real property owned by his wife. For curtesy to exist, certain conditions must be met. There must be a valid marriage from which there was issue born alive. The husband will then have a one-third interest in all land owned by the wife during the marriage.[16]

Community Property

Community property is a joint interest between husband and wife, existing for the most part in the Western United States; namely, the states of Idaho, Washington, California, Arizona, New Mexico, Texas, Nevada, and Louisiana. The law of community property is somewhat technical, but the underlying theory (of Spanish origin) is that the husband and the wife should share equally in property acquired by them through their joint efforts during the marriage. Each has a half interest in the real property. Community property states also recognize the existence of separate property in each of the spouses; for example, that property that may have been owned by one of the parties at the time of the marriage, acquired later by

---

[13]Alaska, Colorado, Connecticut, Illinois, Indiana, Iowa, Maine, Minnesota, Mississippi, Missouri, Nebraska, New York, North Dakota, South Dakota, Utah, Wyoming, and the community property states.

[14]In Georgia, Tennessee, and Vermont, dower is limited to land owned by the husband at the time of his death.

[15]During the life of the husband, the wife is said to have "inchoate dower." This expectancy cannot be defeated by the husband. Upon his death prior to hers, it is said to be the wife's inchoate right of dower.

[16]Curtesy continues only in the states of Alabama, Arkansas, Delaware, Hawaii, Maryland, Massachusetts, New Hampshire, New Jersey, North Carolina, Ohio, Oregon, Rhode Island, Tennessee, Virginia, West Virginia, and Wisconsin.

gift or inheritance, or property purchased exclusively by one of the spouses from separate funds.[17] In the community property states, it is extremely important for the practitioner to recognize the need for obtaining the signature of both parties on an instrument of conveyance, or on any other instrument that might affect the title to real property.

MISCELLANEOUS INTERESTS

Encroachments

An **encroachment** may be best thought of as an overlapping. For example, the most common encroachment is that of the eaves of a garage overlapping a property line and extending over the land and property of another. Branches from trees that extend over a neighbor's property are also classified as an encroachment. When these circumstances exist, the title to the property might be considered unmarketable; hence, under the general terms of the real property contract when the seller has agreed to deliver marketable title to the buyer, the buyer may be relieved from the terms of the agreement if the seller is unable, because of an encroachment, to deliver marketable title to the buyer.

Emblements

Emblements are rights in growing crops that a person possesses when the person has an estate in land of uncertain duration. For example, an individual is granted permission to enter upon a parcel of farm property and plant a crop and he or she takes advantage of the opportunity. The owner of the land may not evict the person and take possession of the growing crops. This so-called tenant at will who has planted the crops still has the right to go upon the land to reap the harvest.

Easements

An **easement** is a right in the owner of one parcel of land to use, by reason of such ownership, the land of another for a special purpose not inconsistent with a general property right in the owner.

An example of an easement is a right-of-way over another's property, a party wall, or the right of ingress and egress (entering and leaving) over the land of another. It is, in the final analysis, a nonpossessory right in the use of another's land.

Easements may be acquired or created in a number of ways: by grant, reservation, implied grant, prescription, necessity, or condemnation.

To create an **easement by grant,** an agreement is drawn between the parties and duly signed and acknowledged. It should be recorded in the office of the county clerk of the county in which the property is located in the same manner as any other conveyance.

[17]Sec. 31-903, Idaho Code Annotated.

An **easement by reservation** is generally created in favor of a grantor in a deed. For example, if *A* conveys property to *B*, and *A* desires to retain a right-of-way over the land after the transfer has been completed, the right-of-way can be retained by including in the deed express words that will create the easement in *A*'s favor.

A third way is through an **easement by implied grant.** Technically, easements of this type are called quasi-easements, but they are usually referred to simply as easements. They may come about in this way: *A* has a house on each of two adjoining lots. On one of them a sewage drain is maintained for the benefit of the other parcel. *A* sells one of the houses to *B* and then refuses to allow *B* drainage through the existing pipe. The courts under these circumstances generally hold that *B* has a right to such drainage, an easement, as a result of an implied grant.

An **easement by prescription** may also be created. For example, *A* uses the land of *B* for a shortcut and continues to use the land for the period of time prescribed by the state statute for adverse possession. As a result, *A* will usually be said to have an easement over the land of *B*. This type of easement is said to arise by prescription.

Another type of easement is one created by necessity. When *A* has a parcel of land and sells the rear part to *B*, and the only way open for *B* to reach a highway is over the land of *A*, then *B* is said to have an **easement by necessity.** There must be an actual necessity, however, or the easement will not exist. But *B* need not use unreasonable means, such as climbing over a mountain, to avoid crossing *A*'s land.

In what way, then, are easements extinguished? In the case of the easement by necessity, the easement will be extinguished when the necessity no longer exists. In the hypothetical case given above, if a road is built so *B* can have a means of egress that is not unreasonable, then the easement will be extinguished and *B* will no longer have the right to cross the land of *A* to leave the property.

An easement may be extinguished by an express release or by the acquisition by the holder of the easement of the fee. *B*, the holder of the easement (technically, the **dominant tenement**), may release the easement or may purchase the property from the owner, *A* (technically, the **servient tenement**), in fee simple.

An easement may also be extinguished by abandonment. This is brought about when the dominant tenement no longer uses the easement and indicates by nonuse an intention to abandon the easement.

License

License is the permission given by an owner of a parcel of real property to perform a particular act or series of acts upon the land. The recipient of the permission receives no interest in the real property. Generally, the permission may be revoked at any time by the owner of the property.

GLOSSARY

Accretion The increase of land caused by gradual and imperceptible additions thereto caused by the washing of a body of water

Adverse possession The right of an occupant of land to acquire title against the real owner, when the possession has been actual, continuous, hostile, visible, and exclusive, for the legal period

Community property A joint property system between husband and wife prevailing in Idaho, Washington, California, Arizona, New Mexico, Texas, Nevada, and Louisiana (the underlying theory is that husband and wife should share equally in property acquired by them through their joint efforts during the marriage)

Concurrent ownership A situation in which title to the same piece of property is in two or more persons' names at one and the same time

Condominium A form of ownership of real property characterized by the fee ownership of individual units, coupled with an undivided interest in common with the remainder of the property

Confiscation The right of the government to take the property (generally confined to personal property) of its enemies in time of war

Constructive annexation Articles not fastened to the realty but which are made for use in connection with the real property and are therefore regarded as fixtures (e.g., key)

Contingent remainder A condition that exists when the remainderman cannot be ascertained at the time of the transfer

Curtesy An estate for life given by law to the husband in all real property owned by his wife

Dedication A transfer of property by an individual to the public

Deed A written instrument that conveys an interest in real property to another

Derivative title Title to the property gained by descent or by purchase; all titles that are not original titles

Devise A private conveyance or real property by will

Dominant tenement The holder of the easement

Dower The common law right of the wife to a life estate in one-third of all the lands of inheritance that were owned by her husband during the period of coverture (marriage)

Easement The right in the owner of one parcel of land to use, by reason of such ownership, the land of another for a special purpose not inconsistent with a general property right in the owner

Easement by grant An agreement involving an easement drawn between the parties and duly signed and acknowledged

Easement by implied grant A right implied by law (e.g., property owner of adjoining property entitled to drainage through existing pipe and sewage drain maintained on neighbor's property)

Easement by necessity A situation in which one must, by necessity, use part of the property of another in order to use one's own property

Easement by prescription The creation of an easement because an individual "adversely possesses" or continues to use part of the land of another over the prescribed legal period (e.g., continuously taking a short-cut over another's land)

Easement by reservation An easement generally created in favor of a grantor in a deed

Emblements Rights in growing crops that a person possesses when the person has an estate in land of uncertain duration

Eminent domain The power of the government to take property for public use after making just compensation; to authorize such taking by a corporation or individual engaged in a quasi-public operation

Encroachment An overlapping of one person's property onto the property of another (e.g., tree branches)

Escheat The right of the government to take the property of an intestate (person dying without a will) who dies without leaving any heirs

Estate The interest a person holds in land

Estate of inheritance An estate that on the death of the holder, still continues and descends to the heirs

Estate of less than freehold An estate of a definite duration treated as personal property

Estate on condition An estate that, by the terms of the instrument by which it is created, is subject to a contingency not forming a part of the limitation of the estate

Estate on condition precedent An estate that begins on the happening of a contingency

Estate on condition subsequent An estate that terminates on the happening of a contingency

Estover The right of the life tenant to take a reasonable amount of wood from the land for fuel and for repairs to any buildings on the land

Fee simple conditional An estate limited to certain specified heirs, exclusive of others, e.g., the heirs of a man's body, by which only his lineal descendants are admitted in exclusion of collateral descendants

Fee simple determinable An estate of indefinite duration that will revert to the grantor or grantor's heirs when a specified event occurs

Fee simple or fee simple absolute The greatest and most complete ownership of land; ownership subject to no limitations on inheritance

Fixtures Articles that have changed from personalty to real property

Forfeiture A process by which the property of an individual inures to the state either because of failure to pay taxes or treason

Freehold estate A holding of indeterminate length, generally treated in the legal sense as real property

Grantee The person to whom the interest in the property is being transferred

Grantor The person who is transferring the interest in the property

Joint tenancy A type of concurrent ownership whereby two or more persons own the same land and have the same unity of time, title, interest, and possession, as well as the right to survivorship

License The permission given by an owner of a parcel of real property to perform a particular act, or series of acts, on the owner's land

Life estate An estate that one may receive either for the duration of his or her life or the life of another

Life estate *pur autre vie* An estate measured by the life of one other than the holder

Original titles Includes those titles acquired by discovery, occupancy, conquest, or cession

Personal property Everything that is subject to ownership that does not come under the domination of real estate

Prescription The right of an adverse user of another's land who continues the use of this land for the legal period

Public grant The granting of title to public lands by a governmental body

Real property The land and, generally, whatever is erected, growing upon, or affixed to the land

Reliction or dereliction The gradual recession of waters leaving dry land where there had formerly been water

Remainder A future interest created in the same conveyance as is a present possessory estate

Reversion When *B* conveys to *A* for life and on *A*'s death to *B* and his or her heirs, the interest conveyed is said to be a reversionary interest

Right of survivorship When a joint tenancy exists, title passes to the survivor(s) upon the death of one of the parties

Servient tenement The owner of the property upon which another has an easement

Severalty An estate held in one's own right, without any other person joined or connected

Tenancy by the entireties A type of concurrent ownership held only by a husband and wife (based on common law concept that a husband and wife are one person)

Tenancy in common A type of concurrent ownership that exists when two or more persons own the same land with undivided interests

Title A legal right referring to the ownership of property

Title by cession All titles derived by grant from one country to another

Title by conquest Title obtained when one country takes territory from another by force of arms and usually affecting only title to public lands

Title by descent Title acquired by an individual whose relative died intestate

Title by occupancy Title obtained when the first nation to occupy a territory not before owned by any civilized nation acquires title thereto

Title by purchase All methods of acquiring title other than by descent

Trade fixtures Those articles of personal property that the tenant annexes to the real estate for the furtherance of a trade

Unity of interest The interest of the owners (joint tenants) must be of the same duration

Unity of possession Each of the tenants must have undivided or equal rights of possession

Unity of time The title to the property must vest in the tenants at the same time

Unity of title Both or all of the joint tenants must have one and the same interest arising out of one and the same conveyance

Vested remainder A remainder to an ascertained person which is subject to no conditions precedent

Waste Appropriation or injury to any part of what is regarded as a permanent part of the land; any improper use of the premises by the tenant that does injure or diminish the value of the landlord's reversion

QUESTIONS FOR REVIEW

1. How does real property differ from personal property?
2. Distinguish between *title* to real property and an *estate* in land.
3. How does escheat come about?
4. What is the difference between an estate of freehold and an estate of less than freehold?
5. Distinguish between a reversion and a remainder interest in real property.
6. What is the so-called grand incident of the joint tenancy?
7. A joint tenancy is said to have four unities and a tenancy by the entireties has five. Name the extra unity the tenancy by the entireties has and explain the effect this unity might have on a married woman.

PROBLEMS AND ACTIVITIES

1. Winston Pabst conveys Lot 1, Block 16, of Security Acres to "Alfred A. Leon and his heirs." At the time, Alfred has a wife, Susan. Alfred dies without leaving a will. What, if anything, does Susan receive?
2. Frank Brown, by deed, conveys Lot 1, Block 15, of Security Acres to "Jill Battestone and her heirs for so long as the property is used as a church." What estate did Jill get?
3. Joan Schmidt, by deed, conveys Lot 1, Block 16, of Security Acres, to her father, "Ralph Snyder, for the term of his natural life and upon his death to Joan Schmidt or her heirs."
   a. What does Ralph Snyder get?
   b. What are the characteristics of the estate?
   c. What, if anything, do Joan Schmidt and her heirs have at the time of the conveyance?
   d. What, if anything, will Joan Schmidt or her heirs get on the death of Ralph Snyder?

7

CONTRACTS

KEY TERMS

Acceptance
Apportionments
Appurtenant
Consideration
Contingencies
Contract
Contract for the exchange of real property
Contractual ability
Disaffirmance
Escrow
Executed contract
Executory contract
Liquidated damages
Marketable title
Meeting of the minds
Mortgagee's Certificate of Reduction
Offer
Offeree
Offeror
Option
Property under contract
Purchase money mortgage
Receipt and agreement to purchase
Regulation Z
Specific performance
Status quo ante
Statute of Frauds
Truth in Lending Act
Valid contract
Voidable contract
Void contract

The contract for the sale of real property is the basic legal instrument with which all real estate brokers and their clients eventually become involved. It is the fundamental instrument of the real estate business. Therefore, it is important for the real estate broker, as well as buyers and sellers of real estate, to have some basic knowledge of contracts and the manner in which they are specifically applied to real property transactions.

Generally, a **contract** is an exchange of promises or assents by two or more persons, resulting from an obligation to do or refrain from doing a particular act, which obligation is recognized or enforced by law. A contract may be formed when a promise is made by one person in exchange for an act or the refraining from the doing of an act by another. The substance of the definition of a contract is that by mutual agreement or assent the parties have created legally enforceable duties or obligations that did not exist before.

If all the terms of a contract have been fulfilled, it is said to be an **executed contract.** If something in the contract remains to be done, it is said to be an **executory contract.**

In terms of their validity, contracts are valid, voidable, and void. A contract that is binding and enforceable against both parties is a **valid contract.** A **void contract** is neither binding nor enforceable against either party.

A **voidable contract** is an agreement that may or may not be binding and enforceable. In this type of contract, one person usually has an option to avoid or a power to validate the contract. In real property transactions, the question of voidable contracts arises most frequently in contracts with minors—generally under 18 to 21 years of age. As a rule, in a minor's contract—or more accurately, agreement—as long as the contract is executory, the minor is under no enforceable duty; no act of avoidance is necessary. However, if the minor receives a part performance and still retains the contract, it must be given up, for its continued retention after the minor becomes of age operates as a ratification. This means that the agreement will become binding and enforceable.

ESSENTIALS OF A CONTRACT

For a binding and enforceable contract to exist, certain specific requirements must be met.

Parties to the Contract

There are always two or more parties to a contract; in real property, the parties are the seller and the purchaser. The parties who enter into a contract may be individuals, partnerships, corporations, or governments. The contract need not be between two individuals, but may exist between any combination of persons or entities having contractual ability. Parties with **contractual ability** are competent to enter into a valid agreement. The first class of individuals whose competency to contract is in question is minors. To some degree, the relative validity of a minor's contract depends on whether the contract concerns real property or personal property.

Minors' Real Property Contracts. Minors' real property contracts differ from the general rule of law. In general, a minor may disaffirm a contract either before or within a reasonable time after reaching majority. **Disaffirmance** is an indication by word or act not be bound by the contract. The general rule is different, however, in a real estate sale. In this case, minor cannot disaffirm the sale of real estate until he or she reaches majority. However, in some jurisdictions possession of the property may be recovered while the person is still a minor; in other jurisdictions the court will require the adult to account to the minor for the use of the property during the term of the latter's minority.

Minors' Personal Property Contracts. In general, when a minor has entered into a personal property contract, it may be disaffirmed at the minor's election either before reaching majority or within a reasonable time thereafter. The contract is said to be voidable. If, after having reached majority, the person does not avoid the contract within a reasonable time, the contract is ratified and is therefore binding. This suggests that great care should be taken in real property contracts to ascertain whether or not the party being dealt with is still a minor.

Insane Persons. The contracts of mental incompetents are generally voidable. As a general rule, the test of mental incompetency is whether or not the individual's mental faculties are so impaired as to render that person incapable of understanding the nature or the consequences of whatever acts are necessary in the transaction in question.

If an insane person becomes sane, the person may ratify or disaffirm a contract. If a proper court has declared a person to be insane and has appointed a guardian for the insane person, any contracts entered into thereafter by the insane person are void. A guardian (called a conservator in some states) would have to make contracts for the insane person.

Intoxicated Persons. If an intoxicated person knew that a contract was being made, the validity of the contract is not affected by the fact of intoxification. If, however, it can be shown that a person was deliberately made drunk in order to induce that person to make the contract, then the contract may be invalidated.

If the person executing the contract was too drunk to know what was happening, then the contract may be voidable. It may be either affirmed or disaffirmed within a reasonable time after the person becomes sober.

Offer

Not only must the parties to the contract possess contractual ability, but there must also be an offer and an acceptance of this offer. An **offer** is a statement made by one person, referred to as the **offeror,** of what that person will give in return for some act or promise of a second person, referred to as the **offeree.** An offer may end at an express time, by death of the offeror, or by revocation of the offer by the offeror prior to the time acceptance is attempted. An offer consists of two parts: the promise and the communication of the promise. Thus, if an offer is not communicated to an offeree, there is no offer, and hence no contract.

In real estate transactions, a property is listed with the real estate broker at a proposed sale price, for example, $200,000. Often the offer is communciated through the broker to a prospective purchaser. Assume that the purchaser signs an earnest money agreement and in it states a willingness to pay $180,000 for the property. This action is a counteroffer by the prospect, rather than an acceptance of the original offer, and constitutes an offer to the seller, which may be accepted or rejected. If the seller states a willingness to take $190,000, then this is another counteroffer; and the broker communicates that offer to the prospect, who may in turn either accept or reject it.

Acceptance

In order to complete the agreement, there must be an **acceptance** of the offer by the offeree. In a real property contract, the normal transaction contemplates an offer by the seller to deliver possession and title of realty to the purchaser for a price, and an acceptance by the purchaser of this offer and the purchaser's promise to pay the price. If both parties are thinking of the same thing and there is an offer and acceptance, there is said to be a **meeting of the minds.**

Consideration

The fourth requirement of a contract is the **consideration** for the contract. The payment of money in return for the conveyance of property is said to be sufficient consideration for a contract. Mutual promises—that is, a promise for a promise or the forbearance by a person of something that could lawfully be done in return for a promise by the offeror—are also sufficient considerations for a contract.

In the absence of fraud, the courts will not normally inquire into the adequacy of consideration for a contract. Thus, if a real estate operator purchases a building from *A* for $200,000 and later sells it for $250,000, *A* will not be allowed to say there was insufficient consideration for the contract.

Legality of Object

In addition to parties to the contract, an offer, an acceptance, and consideration, there must be a legal objective on the part of the contracting parties. In short, the contract must not be in violation of some law or against public policy. If it violates either, then the contract may not be enforceable. A contract, for example, between *A* and *B* whereby *A*, for a consideration, agrees to burn *C*'s property is obviously illegal and hence unenforceable.

Real estate contracts ordinarily deal with objectives and objects that are neither illegal nor against public policy and ordinarily are not set aside on this ground.

Statute of Frauds

The **Statute of Frauds** involves contracts that must be in writing to be enforceable. One section of the statute requires that contracts relating to real property be in writing in order to be enforceable. If *A* agrees with *B* to purchase a lead pencil for the price of $1 and *A* agrees orally to deliver the pencil and then fails to do so, *B* may bring an action against *A* for any damages that may have been suffered. If the same situation takes place, except the oral agreement contemplates the transfer of real property rather than personal property and *A* fails to keep the bargain, *B* will be unable to bring a successful action against *A*, for oral contracts concerning many real estate transactions are void under the Statute of Frauds. It is stated, for example, in Section 259 of the New York Real Property Law as follows:

> A contract for the leasing for a longer period than one year, or for the sale of any real property or an interest therein, is void unless the contract, or some note or memorandum thereof, expressing the consideration, is in writing, subscribed by the party to be charged, or by his lawful agent, thereunto authorized in writing.

Similarly, other state statutes make substantially the same declaration.

Of what then must this memorandum in writing consist to render a contract for the sale of real property enforceable? Four things must be done to bring the contract for the sale of real property into compliance with the Statute of Frauds. The memorandum must have a date, terms of payment, and a description of the property and it must bear the signature of the party to be charged.[1]

In one case, a prospective purchaser gave a check to a seller as earnest money and on the reverse side of the check wrote a statement briefly describing the property and the method by which the balance was to be paid. The seller endorsed the check and deposited it. It was held that this was a memorandum sufficient to bring the contract within the Statute of Frauds. This procedure is not recommended, however.

CONTRACT FOR THE SALE OF REAL PROPERTY

The elements of the contract are described and illustrated in some detail in the following pages.

Date

The contract begins by stating, "This agreement made this . . . day of . . ., 19 . . ." The date has importance when time limits are set for executing the provisions of the contract or for executing the contract itself.

Parties

The parties to the contract are generally referred to as the seller and the purchaser. Their names and addresses are spelled out in full. If John Smith is the seller and he is a married man, his wife should join with him on the contract, especially in those states having community property laws, homestead rights, and dower rights. When there is a tenancy by the entireties, the wife must join on the contract as one of the sellers. It is only

---

[1]The *party to be charged* is the person against whom the suit is brought, but good practice dictates that both parties sign.

when the co-owners sign the contract that they can be forced to convey the real property by specific performance in the manner described later in the chapter.

When property is being sold by a corporation, the president or other officer of the corporation is generally authorized by the board of directors to execute the contract of sale. Under the officer's signature on the contract, the corporate seal is impressed. Usually the board of directors has obtained, by a vote of the common stockholders, the authority to sell the property.

Description

The methods of describing real property are discussed in detail in Chapter 8. After the names of the parties to the contract, there generally follows this statement:

> The seller agrees to sell and convey, and the purchaser agrees to purchase, all that lot or parcel of land, with the buildings and improvements therein, in the. . . . [Here might follow the city or the township or even the county; and then a complete description by metes and bounds, by lot and block number, or by government survey.]

Personal Property

To avoid any misunderstanding at the title closing that might result from not knowing what personal property items are included with the house, a statement substantially as follows might be inserted:

> All fixtures and articles of personal property attached or appurtenant to, or used in connection with said premises, are represented to be owned by the seller, free and clear from all liens and encumbrances except as herein stated, and are included in this sale. Without limiting the generality of the foregoing, such fixtures and articles of personal property include . . . [a list of the personal property].

Real estate brokers know that sometimes it is the personal property that can give them the most trouble at a closing; therefore, salespeople should be especially careful when obtaining their listings to know exactly what items of personal property are included.

Purchase Price

The purchase price is a most important feature of the contract and should be spelled out in detail for all of the parties concerned. Generally, the method of payment is broken into its component parts after a statement is made of the total purchase price. For example, if the price of the property is $300,000 and $5,000 was paid on the signing of the contract, the balance of $20,000 to be paid at the closing of title, and the purchaser is to take the property subject to a $275,000 mortgage, then the statement as to the price in the contract would read substantially as follows:

The price is Three Hundred Thousand and 00/100 ($300,000) Dollars, payable as follows:

a. Five Thousand and 00/100 ($5,000) Dollars, paid as a deposit on the . . . day of . . . , 19 . . . , receipt of which has heretofore been acknowledged.

b. Twenty Thousand and 00/100 ($20,000) Dollars in cash or good certified check upon the delivery of the deed as hereinafter provided.

c. Two Hundred Seventy-five Thousand and 00/100 ($275,000) Dollars by taking subject to a first mortgage now a lien upon said premises in that amount and bearing interest at . . . percent per annum, the principal being due and payable. . . .

Encumbrances and Restrictions

The contract contains a statement that premises are sold and are to be conveyed subject to:

1. Zoning restrictions and ordinances adopted by any municipal, town, village, or other governmental authority.

Although strictly speaking a zoning regulation is not an encumbrance, it is included in the contract as a restriction for the protection of the seller because under certain circumstances the existence of a zoning restriction will prevent the owner from obtaining specific performance. (Specific performance is discussed in detail later in this chapter.)

2. Encroachments of stoops, areas, cellar steps, trim and cornices, if any, upon any street or highway.

The insertion of the preceding clause ordinarily is interpreted to mean that the purchaser must take title even though these encroachments would render the title unmarketable.

3. Consents by the seller or any former owner of premises for the erection of any structure or structures on, under, or above any street or streets on which said premises may abut.
4. Any state of facts that an accurate survey might show.

This clause is a good one from the seller's viewpoint, especially where no survey has been made on the property or if a survey has not been made recently. However, the purchaser should, if possible, seek to have the clause read: "Any state of facts that an accurate survey might show, provided the title is not thereby rendered unmarketable."

5. Covenants and restrictions of record, if any.

This is an important clause of the contract; without it, there is a possibility of the purchaser's avoiding the contract after having discovered restrictions in the abstract or report of title.

Rights to Road

The contract also contains this clause:

> This sale includes all right, title, and interest, if any, of the seller in and to any land lying in the bed of any street, road or avenue opened or proposed, in front of or adjoining said premises, to the center line thereof, and all right, title, and interest of the seller in and to any award made or to be made in lieu thereof and in any unpaid award for damage to said premises by reason of change of grade of any street; and the seller will execute and deliver to the purchaser, on closing of title, or thereafter, on demand, all proper instruments for the conveyance of such title and the assignment and collection of any such award.

Certificate of Reduction

If there is a mortgage on a parcel of property the purchaser is either "assuming" or "taking subject to," the purchaser should make certain of the balance due at the time of closing of title. Therefore, a provision is made in the contract that the seller will deliver to the purchaser a certificate stating the amount due on the mortgage at the time of the closing of title. This is commonly called the **Mortgagee's Certificate of Reduction.**

The contract will then state:

> If there be a mortgage on the premises, the seller agrees to deliver to the purchaser at the time of the delivery of the deed a proper certificate executed and acknowledged by the holder of such mortgage and in form for recording, certifying as to the amount of the unpaid principal and interest thereon, date of maturity thereof and rate of interest thereon, and the seller shall pay the fees for recording such certificate.

A further discussion of this instrument appears in Chapter 11.

Violations

In most states, when the contract is silent in regard to violations of law or municipal ordinances, the purchaser will be required to accept the property subject to any existing violations. Therefore, to avoid this, the purchaser will require a clause in the contract to this effect:

> All notes or notices of violation of law or municipal ordinances against or affecting the premises at the date hereof shall be complied with by the seller and the premises shall be conveyed free and clear of the same, and this provision of this contract shall survive delivery of the deed hereunder. The seller shall furnish the purchaser with an authorization to make the necessary searches therefor.

Thus, if it is discovered after the date of closing that violations were in existence on the date of the contract and the purchaser has to pay for such violations, the seller will then be liable to the purchaser for such damages because the clause provides that the covenant will survive the delivery of the deed.

Apportionments

The mechanics of **apportionments** are explained fully in Chapter 22; however, it is here in the contract that the bases for such apportionments are laid. This is done by the statement:

> The following are to be apportioned to the day of taking title:
> 1. Rents as and when collected.
> 2. Interest on mortgages.
> 3. Premiums on transferable insurance policies or renewals of those expiring prior to the closing.
> 4. Taxes and sewer rents, if any, on the basis of the fiscal year for which assessed.
> 5. Water rates on the basis of the calendar year.
> 6. Fuel, if any.
>
> If the closing of the title shall occur before the tax rate is fixed, the apportionment of taxes shall be upon the basis of the tax rate for the next preceding year applied to the latest assessed valuation.
>
> If there be a water meter on the premises, the seller shall furnish a reading to a date not more than 30 days prior to the time herein set for closing of title, and the unfixed meter charge and the unfixed sewer rent, if any, based thereon for the intervening time shall be apportioned on the basis of such last reading.

Marketable and Insurable Title

Often the contract contains a clause requiring the vendor to deliver either a marketable title or an insurable title. When there is no such clause, the seller is required to deliver marketable title.[2] **Marketable title** is title that is clearly so good that the courts will order its acceptance by a purchaser.

One should be aware of the distinction between marketable title and insurable title. They are not necessarily the same thing. Often, although marketable, a title is not insurable, for the title companies sometimes refuse to insure the title for fear of incurring the expense of defending a lawsuit. Often, too, a title company will insure a title even though it may be strictly speaking, unmarketable. The instance of the insertion of either marketable or insurable title in a real property contract depends to a large extent on the bargaining position of the respective parties to the contract. In the last analysis, a title is insurable if a title company says it is. One company may say a title is uninsurable; another may state it is insurable.

Deed

The specifications of the deed follow:

> The deed shall be the usual . . . [the type of deed to be delivered] deed in the proper statutory form for record and shall be duly executed and

---

[2] In the Midwest, "merchantable" is often used synonymously with "marketable."

acknowledged so as to convey to the purchaser the fee simple of said premises free and clear of all encumbrances, except as herein stated.

Delivery of Deed

The contract contains a clause providing for the delivery of the deed and the payment of the balance of the purchase price at a certain place at a certain time and date. It may also contain a clause stating "time is of the essence." In the absence of this latter statement, the seller has a reasonable time within which to cure defects of title; and the purchaser can, for good reason, seek to have the closing adjourned. However, when the contract does contain the statement "time is of the essence," this has been held to mean, in effect, that delivery of the deed has to be made at the time stated in the contract. Great care should be taken with this statement. If, for example, *A* enters into a contract with *B* for the purchase of a parcel of property on September 1, and at the same time *A* enters into a contract with *C* for the sale of the same premises on September 2, then *A* must insist that the statement "time is of the essence" be included in the contract with *B* to avoid any possible damage for failure to deliver the property to *C* at the time stated in the contract with C.

Risk of Loss

In many states if the premises are destroyed between the execution of the sales contract and the date of closing, the purchaser bears the risk of loss. Some states[3] have adopted the Uniform Vendor and Purchaser Risk Act. This act places the risk of loss on the seller when neither title nor possession of the property has passed to the purchaser.

In any event, no chances of risk of loss until closing should be borne by the purchaser. The purchaser should insist on a clause in the contract stating, in effect, "The risk of loss or damage to said premises until the delivery of the deed is hereby assumed by the seller." The risk may be borne by the purchaser if desired; however, insurance may be used for protection.

Liquidated Damages

With the statement concerning the time of closing of title, there may be inserted in the contract a statement about **liquidated damages,** which is the amount the parties of the contract may stipulate to be paid in case of default. The inclusion of a clause of this type is particularly apropos where rent control is in effect, or if there is a suspicion on the part of the

[3]California, Connecticut, Hawaii, Illinois, Kentucky, Louisiana, Maine, Massachusetts, Michigan, New Hampshire, Oregon, Rhode Island, South Carolina, Texas, and Wisconsin.

purchaser that the seller will not or will be unable to deliver possession of the premises on the date of the closing of title.

The clause may be inserted substantially as follows:

> In the event that the seller fails to deliver possession of the premises herein at the time of delivery of the deed as called for by these presents, then it is hereby agreed by and between the seller and the purchaser that the seller shall pay to the purchaser the sum of Ten and 00/100 ($10) Dollars for each and every day that he or she shall remain in possession of the premises described herein on and after the date of closing of the title called for herein, the sums so paid to be construed as liquidated damages and not as a penalty.

A statement of this type will usually ensure delivery of possession at the time of closing. Care must be taken not to make the sum for the liquidated damages unreasonable.

RECEIPT AND AGREEMENT TO PURCHASE

In many sections of the United States, real estate brokers use a contract called the **receipt and agreement to purchase.**[4] The broker fills in the spaces on the contract, and an attorney is usually not involved.

After receiving an offer, the broker prepares a receipt and an agreement to purchase. The instrument is dated and states:

> Received from . . . (hereinafter referred to as the Purchaser) the sum of . . . ($ . . .) Dollars as a deposit and earnest money in part payment of the purchase price of the following described real property situated in . . . (a description of the property).

The contract contains a number of clauses described above and in addition a statement:

> If Seller does not approve this sale within . . . days hereafter, or if the Seller's title is not merchantable or insurable and cannot be made so within a reasonable time after written notice containing statement of defects is delivered to the Seller, then said earnest money herein receipted for shall be returned to the purchaser on demand. . . .

After the purchaser signs the receipt and agreement to purchase, the broker submits it to the seller for signature. If the seller signs the agreement, then a contract for the sale of the property is in effect. Copies are made for the seller and the purchaser and for the broker. Exhibit 7-1 shows a contract used in Minnesota.

---

[4]The title and form of these contracts differ from state to state. In Michigan, for example, substantially the same agreement is used, but is called the Purchase Agreement. In Florida, it is called the Receipt for Deposit—Offer to Purchase and Contract for Sale.

Exhibit 7-1 Purchase Agreement

Edina Realty Inc.

PURCHASE AGREEMENT

This form approved by the Minnesota Association of REALTORS®: Minnesota Association of REALTORS® disclaims any liability arising out of use or misuse of this form.

1. Date ______
2. Page 1 of ______ Pages

3. **RECEIVED OF** ______
4. the sum of ______ Dollars ($______)
5. by **CHECK-CASH-NOTE** (circle one) **as earnest money to be deposited upon acceptance of Purchase Agreement by all parties, on or**
6. **before the next business day after acceptance, in a trust account of listing broker but to be returned to Buyer if Purchase**
7. **Agreement is not accepted by Seller.** Said earnest money is part payment for the purchase of the property located at:
8. Street Address: ______
9. City of ______, County of ______, State of Minnesota,
10. Legally described as: ______
11. ______
12. including the following property, if any, owned by Seller and used and located on said property: garden bulbs, plants, shrubs, and
13. trees; storm sash, storm doors, screens and awnings; window shades, blinds, traverse and curtain and drapery rods; attached lighting
14. fixtures and bulbs; plumbing fixtures, water heater, heating plants (with any burners, tanks, stokers and other equipment used in
15. connection therewith), central air conditioning equipment, electronic air filter, **Water Softener OWNED / RENTED / NONE,** (circle one) built-in humidifier
16. and dehumidifier, liquid gas tank and controls (if the property of Seller), sump pump; attached television antenna, cable TV jacks
17. and wiring; **BUILT-INS:** dishwashers, garbage disposals, trash compactors, ovens, cook top stoves, microwave ovens, hood fans,
18. intercoms; **ATTACHED: carpeting; mirrors; garage door openers and all controls; smoke detectors; fireplace screens, doors and**
19. **heatolators; AND: the following personal property:** ______
20. ______
21. ______
22. all of which property Seller has this day agreed to sell to Buyer for sum of: ($______)
23. ______ Dollars.
24. which Buyer agrees to pay in the following manner: Earnest money of $______
25. and $______ cash on or before ______, the date of closing, and
26. the balance of $______ by financing in accordance with the attached addendum:
27. **Conventional FHA VA Assumption Contract for Deed Other:** ______ (circle all that apply)
28. This Purchase Agreement **IS / IS NOT** (circle one) contingent upon the sale of another property. (If answer is **IS**, see attached addendum.)
29. Attached are other addenda which are made a part of this Purchase Agreement. (Enter page or pages on line 2)
30. **DEED/MARKETABLE TITLE:** Upon performance by Buyer, Seller shall deliver a ______ Warranty Deed
31. joined in by spouse, if any, conveying marketable title, subject to:
32. (A) Building and zoning laws, ordinances, state and federal regulations; (B) Restrictions relating to use or improvement of the property without
33. effective forfeiture provisions; (C) Reservation of any mineral rights by the State of Minnesota; (D) Utility and drainage easements which do not
34. interfere with existing improvements; (E) **Rights of tenants as follows** (unless specified, not subject to tenancies): ______
35. ______
36. (F) Others (Must be specified in writing): ______
37. **TITLE & EXAMINATION:** Seller shall, within a reasonable time after acceptance of this agreement, furnish an abstract of title, or a registered
38. property abstract, certified to date to include proper searches covering bankruptcies, state and federal judgments and liens, and levied and
39. pending special assessments. Buyer shall be allowed 10 business days after receipt of abstract for examination of title and making any objections
40. which shall be made in writing or deemed waived. If any objection is so made, Seller shall have 10 business days from receipt of Buyer's written
41. title objections to notify Buyer of Seller's intention to make title marketable within 120 days from Seller's receipt of such written objection. If notice
42. is given, payments hereunder required shall be postponed pending correction of title, but upon correction of title and within 10 days after written
43. notice to Buyer the parties shall perform this Purchase Agreement according to its terms. If no such notice is given or if notice is given but
44. title is not corrected within the time provided for, this Purchase Agreement shall be null and void, at option of Buyer; neither party shall be liable
45. for damages hereunder to the other and earnest money shall be refunded to Buyer; Buyer and Seller agree to sign cancellation of Purchase
46. Agreement. Buyer agrees to accept an owner's title policy in the full amount of the purchase price in lieu of an abstract of title if the property
47. is subject to a master abstract or if no abstract of title is in Seller's possession or control. If Buyer is to receive such policy (1) the title examination
48. period shall commence upon Buyer's receipt of a current title insurance commitment and (2) Seller shall pay the entire premium for such policy
49. if no lender's policy is obtained, and only the additional cost of obtaining a simultaneously issued owner's policy if a lender's policy is obtained
50. (Buyer shall pay the premium for the lender's policy).
51. **REAL ESTATE TAXES** shall be paid as follows:
52. Buyer shall pay, **prorated from day of closing, ____12ths, all, none** (circle one) real estate taxes due and payable in the year 19______.
53. Seller shall pay, **prorated to day of closing, ____12ths, all, none** (circle one) real estate taxes due and payable in the year 19______. In the event
54. the closing date is changed, the real estate taxes paid shall, if prorated, be adjusted to the new closing date. Seller warrants
55. taxes due and payable in the year 19______ will be **FULL-PART-NON** (circle one) -homestead classification. In the event 19______ real estate
56. taxes are part or non-homestead classification, Seller agrees to pay Buyer at closing $______ toward the non-homestead
57. portion of the real estate taxes. Buyer agrees to pay any remaining balance of non-homestead taxes when they become due and payable.
58. Neither Seller nor Agent(s) make any representation concerning the amount of subsequent real estate taxes.
59. **SPECIAL ASSESSMENTS** shall be paid as follows:
60. **BUYER AND SELLER SHALL PRORATE AS OF THE DATE OF CLOSING / SELLER SHALL PAY ON DATE OF CLOSING** (circle one) all installments of
61. special assessments certified for payment with the real estate taxes due and payable in the year of closing.
62. **BUYER SHALL ASSUME / SELLER SHALL PAY** (circle one) on date of closing all other special assessments levied as of the date of closing.
63. **BUYER SHALL ASSUME / SELLER SHALL PROVIDE FOR PAYMENT OF** (circle one) special assessments pending as of the date of closing for
64. improvements that have been ordered by the City Council or other assessing authorities. (Seller's provision for payment shall be by payment into
65. escrow of 2 times the estimated amount of the assessments, or less as required by Buyer's lender.)
66. **BUYER SHALL ASSUME / SELLER SHALL PAY** (circle one) on date of closing any deferred real estate taxes or special assessments payment of which is
67. required as a result of the closing of this sale. Buyer shall pay real estate taxes due and payable in the year following closing and thereafter and any
68. unpaid special assessments payable therewith and thereafter, the payment of which is not otherwise provided.
69. **POSSESSION:** Seller shall deliver possession of the property not later than ______ after closing.
70. All interest, homeowner association dues, rents, fuel oil, liquid petroleum gas and all charges for city water, city sewer, electricity, and natural
71. gas shall be prorated between the parties as of ______.
72. Seller agrees to remove ALL DEBRIS AND ALL PERSONAL PROPERTY NOT INCLUDED HEREIN from the property by possession date.

■ Exhibit 7-1 (continued)

PURCHASE AGREEMENT

Date____________________________

Page 2 of______________________Pages

SUBDIVISION OF LAND: If this sale constitutes or requires a subdivision of land owned by Seller, Seller shall pay all subdivision expenses and obtain all necessary governmental approvals. Seller warrants the legal description of the real property to be conveyed has been or will be approved for recording as of the date of closing.

GENERAL WARRANTIES: SELLER WARRANTS THAT THE BUILDINGS, IF ANY, ARE ENTIRELY WITHIN THE BOUNDARY LINES OF THE PROPERTY. SELLER WARRANTS THAT THERE IS A RIGHT OF ACCESS TO THE PROPERTY FROM A PUBLIC RIGHT OF WAY. THESE WARRANTIES SHALL SURVIVE THE DELIVERY OF THE DEED OR CONTRACT FOR DEED.

SELLER WARRANTS THAT PRIOR TO THE CLOSING PAYMENT IN FULL WILL HAVE BEEN MADE FOR ALL LABOR, MATERIALS, MACHINERY, FIXTURES OR TOOLS FURNISHED WITHIN THE 120 DAYS IMMEDIATELY PRECEDING THE CLOSING DATE IN CONNECTION WITH CONSTRUCTION, ALTERATION OR REPAIR OF ANY STRUCTURE ON OR IMPROVEMENT TO THE PROPERTY.

SELLER WARRANTS THAT SELLER HAS NOT RECEIVED ANY NOTICE FROM ANY GOVERNMENTAL AUTHORITY AS TO VIOLATION OF ANY LAW, ORDINANCE OR REGULATION. IF THE PROPERTY IS SUBJECT TO RESTRICTIVE COVENANTS, SELLER WARRANTS THAT SELLER HAS NOT RECEIVED ANY NOTICE FROM ANY PERSON OR AUTHORITY AS TO A BREACH OF THE COVENANTS. ANY NOTICES RECEIVED BY SELLER WILL BE PROVIDED TO BUYER IMMEDIATELY.

SPECIAL WARRANTIES EXCEPT AS NOTED ON REAL ESTATE TRANSFER DISCLOSURE STATEMENT:
SELLER WARRANTS THAT THE PROPERTY IS **DIRECTLY** CONNECTED TO: **CITY SEWER** ☐**YES** ☐**NO CITY WATER** ☐**YES** ☐**NO.**
SELLER WARRANTS THAT ALL APPLIANCES, HEATING, AIR CONDITIONING, WIRING AND PLUMBING SYSTEMS USED AND LOCATED ON SAID PROPERTY WILL BE IN PROPER WORKING ORDER ON THE DATE OF CLOSING. BUYER HAS THE RIGHT TO INSPECT PROPERTY PRIOR TO CLOSING. BUYER ACKNOWLEDGES THAT NO ORAL REPRESENTATIONS HAVE BEEN MADE BY EITHER SELLER OR AGENT(S) REGARDING POSSIBLE PROBLEMS OF WATER IN BASEMENT, OR DAMAGE CAUSED BY WATER OR ICE BUILD-UP ON THE ROOF OF THE PROPERTY AND BUYER RELIES SOLELY IN THAT REGARD ON THE FOLLOWING STATEMENT BY SELLER: SELLER **HAS / HAS NOT** (circle one) HAD A WET BASEMENT, AND **HAS / HAS NOT** (circle one) HAD ROOF, WALL OR CEILING DAMAGE CAUSED BY WATER OR ICE BUILD-UP. (If answer is **HAS**, see Seller's explanation on the real estate transfer disclosure statement, if applicable.) Buyer **HAS/HAS NOT** (circle one) received and accepted a real estate transfer disclosure statement. **(If answer is HAS NOT, Buyer relies solely on Buyer's own inspection of the property and the warranties of Seller expressly set forth in this agreement.) BUYER HAS RECEIVED THE TRUTH IN HOUSING INSPECTION REPORT, IF REQUIRED BY MUNICIPALITY.**
BUYER & SELLER INITIAL: Buyer(s)________________ Seller(s)________________

RISK OF LOSS: If there is any loss or damage to the property between the date hereof and the date of closing, for any reason including fire, vandalism, flood, earthquake or act of God, the risk of loss shall be on Seller. If the property is destroyed or substantially damaged before the closing date, this Purchase Agreement shall become null and void, at Buyer's option, and earnest money shall be refunded to Buyer; Buyer and Seller agree to sign cancellation of Purchase Agreement.

BUYER/SELLER ARBITRATION SYSTEM:
ANY CLAIM OR DEMAND OF SELLER(S), BUYER(S), BROKER(S) OR AGENT(S), OR ANY OF THEM, ARISING OUT OF OR RELATING TO THE PHYSICAL CONDITION OF THE PROPERTY COVERED BY THIS PURCHASE AGREEMENT (INCLUDING WITHOUT LIMITATION CLAIMS OF FRAUD, MISREPRESENTATION, WARRANTY AND NEGLIGENCE), SHALL BE SETTLED BY ARBITRATION IN ACCORDANCE WITH THE RULES, THEN IN EFFECT, ADOPTED BY THE AMERICAN ARBITRATION ASSOCIATION AND THE MINNESOTA ASSOCIATION OF REALTORS®. THIS IS A SEPARATE VOLUNTARY AGREEMENT BETWEEN THE PARTIES AND BROKERS/AGENTS. FAILURE TO AGREE TO ARBITRATE DOES NOT AFFECT THE VALIDITY OF THIS PURCHASE AGREEMENT. THIS DISPUTE RESOLUTION SYSTEM IS ONLY ENFORCEABLE IF ALL PARTIES AND BROKERS/AGENTS HAVE AGREED TO ARBITRATE AS ACKNOWLEDGED BY INITIALS BELOW.
BUYER(S)______ SELLER(S)______ LISTING BROKER/AGENT______ SELLING BROKER/AGENT______

TIME OF ESSENCE: Time is of the essence in this Purchase Agreement.

ENTIRE AGREEMENT: This Purchase Agreement, any attached exhibits and any addenda or amendments signed by the parties, shall constitute the entire agreement between Seller and Buyer, and supercedes any other written or oral agreements between Seller and Buyer. This Purchase Agreement can be modified only in writing signed by Seller and Buyer.

ACCEPTANCE: Buyer understands and agrees that this Purchase Agreement is subject to acceptance by Seller in writing. Agents are not liable or responsible for any covenants, obligations or warranties made in this Purchase Agreement, except the agents are liable to return or account for the earnest money and to arbitrate, if so agreed. The delivery of all papers and monies shall be made at the listing broker's office.

DEFAULT: If title is marketable or is corrected as provided herein, and Buyer defaults in any of the agreements herein, Seller may terminate this Purchase Agreement and payments made hereunder may be retained by Seller and Agent, as their respective interests may appear. This provision shall not deprive either Buyer or Seller of the right to recover damages for a breach of this agreement or of the right of specific performance of this agreement, provided this Purchase Agreement is not terminated, and further provided, as to specific performance, such action is commenced within six months after such right of action arises.

AGENCY DISCLOSURE: ________________ (selling agent) **STIPULATES HE OR SHE IS REPRESENTING THE** ____________ **IN THIS TRANSACTION. THE LISTING AGENT OR BROKER STIPULATES HE OR SHE IS REPRESENTING THE SELLER IN THIS TRANSACTION. BUYER & SELLER INITIAL:** Buyer(s) ______ Seller(s) ______

I, the owner of the property, accept this agreement and authorize the listing broker to withdraw said property from the market, unless instructed otherwise in writing.

I agree to purchase the property for the price and on the terms and conditions set forth above.

(Seller's Signature)	(Date)	(Buyer's Signature)	(Date)
(Seller's Printed Name)	(Marital Status)	(Buyer's Printed Name)	(Marital Status)
(Seller's Signature)	(Date)	(Buyer's Signature)	(Date)
(Seller's Printed Name)	(Marital Status)	(Buyer's Printed Name)	(Marital Status)

DATE OF FINAL ACCEPTANCE ____________ SELLING AGENT ____________

THIS IS A LEGALLY BINDING CONTRACT BETWEEN BUYERS AND SELLERS.

MN:PA (8/88)
ER 170-2 (8/88)

IF YOU DESIRE LEGAL OR TAX ADVICE, CONSULT AN APPROPRIATE PROFESSIONAL.

■ Exhibit 7-1 (concluded)

Edina Realty Inc.

CONTINGENCY ADDENDUM

This form approved by the Minnesota Association of REALTORS®: Minnesota Association of REALTORS® disclaims any liability arising out of use or misuse of this form.

Date ____________

Page ________ of ________ Pages

Addendum to Purchase Agreement dated ____________, 19____ pertaining to the purchase and sale of the property at ____________

_____ HOUR CONTINGENCY

This agreement is contingent upon the Buyer entering into a valid purchase agreement for the sale of Buyer's property located at ____________ on or before ____________, 19_____, which is listed or will immediately be listed with ____________ broker. In the event a valid purchase agreement is not signed by the date mentioned, this agreement is null and void and the earnest money will be refunded to Buyer. The Seller and the Seller's agents shall have the right to continue to offer the property for sale unless this contingency is removed. Seller may demand removal of this contingency at any time by service of a written notice in the form as shown on the Request For Removal Of Contingency (form MN:RFR). If Buyer does not remove this contingency as specified herein within _______ hours of service of the written notice, this agreement shall be null and void and the earnest money shall be refunded to Buyer. The _______ hours shall start when the request for removal of contingency is served upon the selling agent or any agent in the selling agent's office. The agent upon whom the written notice is served shall accept, date and time the notice. It is the selling company's responsibility to deliver the papers to the Buyer for the Buyer's immediate consideration. **IN COMPUTING THE _______ HOURS, THE PERIOD FROM 12:01 A.M. SATURDAY THROUGH 12:01 A.M. MONDAY AND THE 24 HOUR PERIOD OF ANY NATIONAL HOLIDAY SHALL BE EXCLUDED.** Both Buyer and Seller agree to sign cancellation papers in the event the contingency is not removed.

To remove the contingency, Buyer shall serve upon the listing agent or any agent in the listing agent's office a notice of intent to remove contingency, in the form as shown on the Request For Removal Of Contingency (form MN:RFR), within the _______ hours. The agent upon whom the notice is served shall accept, date and time the notice. It is the listing company's responsibility to deliver the notice and accompanying documents to the Seller for the Seller's immediate consideration. The notice of intent to remove contingency must be accompanied by a true copy of a valid purchase agreement for the sale of the Buyer's property.

To be valid, the purchase agreement must not be contingent upon anything other than financing and must have a closing date not later than the closing date in this Purchase Agreement. In the alternative, the notice of intent to remove contingency may be accompanied by written proof of the Buyer's ability to consummate this transaction without the sale of the Buyer's property. The decision whether such written proof is acceptable shall be solely that of the Seller. If the notice of intent to remove contingency is accompanied by a valid purchase agreement, as specified above, the Seller shall accept the removal of this contingency. If the notice of intent to remove contingency is accompanied by anything other than the valid purchase agreement, Seller shall have _______ hours, from the time noted on the notice of intent to remove contingency, within which to review the documentation and accept or reject the attempted removal of this contingency. Unless the Seller specifically rejects, by so indicating on the form and delivering same to the listing agent within the _______ hour period, the contingency shall be deemed removed and the transaction shall proceed accordingly.

In the event there is more than one Buyer or Seller, the parties agree that any one Buyer or Seller may sign the Request for Removal of Contingency or the Notice of Intent to Remove Contingency.

OTHER:

(Seller)	(Date)	(Buyer)	(Date)
(Seller)	(Date)	(Buyer)	(Date)
(Listing Agent)	(Date)	(Selling Agent)	(Date)

THIS IS A LEGALLY BINDING CONTRACT BETWEEN BUYERS AND SELLERS.
IF YOU DESIRE LEGAL OR TAX ADVICE, CONSULT AN APPROPRIATE PROFESSIONAL.

MN:CNTG (5/88)
ER 107 (6/88)

More often than not, transactions do not proceed this smoothly. Typically, the buyer makes an offer lower than the listed price, the seller makes a counterproposal, and it is then up to the buyer to either accept or reject. Often this sort of negotiation takes place four or five times until the final terms are agreed upon and a deal is struck.

CONTRACT FOR THE EXCHANGE OF REAL PROPERTY

Frequently, a broker effects an exchange of real property; it is at this time that the **contract for the exchange of real property** is used. Basically, this contract is the same as the contract for the sale of real property, with only two major changes. In the exchange contract, the parties are not described as the purchaser and the seller, but as the party of the first part and the party of the second part. The contract then states:

> The party of the first part, in consideration of Ten Dollars, the receipt of which is hereby acknowledged, and of the conveyance by the party of the second part hereinafter agreed to be made, hereby agrees to sell, grant, and convey to the party of the second part, at a valuation, for the purpose of this contract, of . . . Dollars.

A description of the property of the party of the first part and a list of any encumbrances that might exist thereon follow. A statement is made by the party of the second part in the same manner as the party of the first part has made above, together with the valuation of the property. The property is described and followed by this statement:

> The difference between the values of the respective premises, over and above encumbrances, for the purpose of this contract, shall be deemed to be . . . Dollars, and the sum shall be due and payable as follows, by the party of the. . . .

Thus, if the property of the party of the first part is valued at $80,000 and the property of the party of the second part is valued at $72,000, then $8,000 is due to the party of the first part.

The balance of the contract for the exchange then follows the terms of the contract for the sale of real property, along with any special agreement that might be reached.

MISCELLANEOUS PROVISIONS IN REAL ESTATE CONTRACTS

Contingencies

In any contract, whether it be the receipt and agreement to purchase, the contract for the sale, or the contract for the exchange of property, any **contingencies** must be carefully spelled out. If the transaction is to be subject to obtaining FHA approval for a loan in the amount of $30,000, then the contract should state this categorically, not "subject to obtaining an FHA loan," but "subject to obtaining an FHA loan in the amount of $30,000," or whatever the amount may be. If a man is to purchase the property and does not know whether or not his wife will approve the transaction, he might even go so far as to insist on the statement "subject to the approval of my wife, Mary" in the contract.

Provision for Purchase Money Mortgage

Although the purchase money mortgage is discussed in detail in Chapter 13, it merits some mention here. A **purchase money mortgage** is a mortgage given by the buyer to the seller as part of the consideration. The seller "takes back" a mortgage as a part of the purchase price. If the seller agrees to do this, the contract should contain a clause stating this willingness.

Assume that the purchase price of a parcel of property is $270,000, $10,000 on the signing of the contract, $40,000 at the closing of title, and a purchase money mortgage in the amount of $220,000. The clause spelling out the method of payment in the contract would read:

> The price is Two Hundred Seventy Thousand and 00/100 ($270,000) Dollars, payable as follows:
>
> Ten Thousand and 00/100 ($10,000) Dollars on the signing of this contract, receipt of which is hereby acknowledged; Forty Thousand and 00/100 ($40,000) Dollars on the delivery of the deed as hereinafter provided, and the balance of Two Hundred Twenty Thousand and 00/100 ($220,000) Dollars, by the purchaser or her or his assigns executing, acknowledging, and delivering to the seller, her or his note secured by a purchase money mortgage on the above premises, in that amount payable in monthly installments of $2,000 or more at the option of the owner of the premises, together with interest at the rate of 13.5 percent per annum payable with said installments, until four years after the date of the mortgage when the balance shall be due and payable.

Water Rights

Water rights are construed as being appurtenant to real property. **Appurtenant** means incidental to the land when it is a thing used by right with the land for its benefit. Generally, a contract for the sale of real property includes those things that are appurtenant to the land. Because water rights are generally considered to be appurtenances, they are included in a conveyance of the land. However, in many sections of the country, water rights consist of stock held in irrigation companies. If this is the case, special mention should be made of this in the contract. At the closing of title, the stock in the water companies will be assigned to the purchaser. This method of disposition of water rights should be spelled out in detail rather than left to be interpreted.[5]

[5]This is particularly important in certain areas of Arizona, California, Colorado, Idaho, Montana, Nevada, New Mexico, Oregon, Utah, Washington, and Wyoming.

Acquisition of Plottage

Often a real estate operator will attempt to assemble many small plots of land with the idea of constructing one large building on the entire piece. For example, two contiguous parcels of property, owned separately, each have a frontage of 50 feet. *A* decides to construct a building, but needs a frontage of 100 feet. *A* cannot, without adequate protection, enter into a contract with *X* to purchase *X*'s 50-foot frontage without knowing that *Z*'s property can be obtained at the same time. For *A* to be protected in the event both parcels cannot be acquired, *A* will insert a clause into the contract with *X* to the effect that if it is not possible to obtain good and marketable title to both parcels of property, the contract may be cancelled at *A*'s option.

Property Under Contract

Property under contract is a special clause used in real property contracts under certain circumstances. For example, *A* enters into a real property contract with *B* to purchase *B*'s property. Several days later, prior to obtaining title to the property from *B*, *A* has the opportunity to sell the property to *X* for a profit. Ordinarily, the contract will be assigned from *B* to *X*. However, in some circumstances, the contract may be unassignable. In that case, *A* will insert in the contract with *X* a clause to the effect that *A* now has the property under contract. The clause will be as follows:

> The seller is not the owner of said premises but represents that she or he has an interest therein as purchaser under contract dated . . . , 19 . . . with . . . , which contract the seller herein believes to be valid and binding and which contract was exhibited and read in its entirety by the purchaser herein.

Termite Clause

In those parts of the country where termites exist, it is customary to include a termite clause in the real property contract. This is generally worded: "The seller, at her or his own expense, shall have the premises inspected for termite damage, and if any be found, it is to be repaired at the seller's expense."

Radon Clause

Radon is a naturally occurring, colorless, odorless gas coming from elements found in soil and rocks. When it has accumulated in a building in sufficient quantities, it may result in lung cancer or present other health risks to persons who are exposed to it over time.

Because of soil differences, radon gas can be found in one house and not in any other home in the immediate neighborhood. There are methods available for reducing the levels of gas present in a home. In general, the cost will run between $1,000 and $4,000 per home.

As a result of the recent attention qiven to the hazard of radon gas, a number of states[6] have passed laws requiring that a clause be inserted in contracts for the sale of real property whereby the seller is held financially responsible for removing the radon hazard prior to sale.

ESCROW AND HOW IT IS USED

Escrow is a scroll, writing, or deed delivered by the grantor into the hands of a third person to be held by the latter until the happening of a contingency or the performance of a condition, and then delivered by the third person to the grantee.

Like many words, *escrow* has come to have many meanings. Closings of title are sometimes said to be in escrow, as outlined in Chapter 22. Funds belonging to others must be held by brokers, attorneys, and other persons operating in a fiduciary capacity and must be held in a separate checking account and not commingled with their own money.

To understand one use of escrow, it must be recognized that in many parts of the country sales are made "on contract," as it is commonly called. Thus, when the seller desires to do the financing, instead of taking a purchase money mortgage back as part of the consideration, delivering the deed, and recording the mortgage as a lien against the property, the deal may be financed "on contract," or "on a land contract." The seller receives part of the purchase price in cash and the balance of the purchase price later, according to the terms of a contract signed by the seller and the purchaser. This contract names the parties, describes the property, and states the purchase price and details of payment. The purchaser is required to insure the premises in favor of the seller as is done under a mortgage. The purchaser is entitled to possession as of a time stated in the contract. No deed is delivered to the purchaser; however, for the protection of the purchaser, the contract often will state as follows:

> The seller within . . . days from the date of this contract will deposit in escrow with . . . [the name of the escrowee] a good and sufficient deed together with an executed copy of this contract and such other documents including abstract of title or title insurance policy and fire insurance policies, which shall pertain to this contract, to be by such escrow agent held in escrow until the terms of this contract shall be completely executed, or until default is made under the same. The terms of such deposit in escrow shall be given by separate escrow agreement to be at the said time executed.

---

[6]Florida and New Jersey have such laws. Effective August 1, 1989, sellers in Minnesota must disclose status and location of all known wells on the property prior to signing a purchase agreement. Failure to disclose a well's existence makes the seller liable to buyer for costs of sealing the well plus attorneys' fees.

In California, Colorado, Idaho, Minnesota, Nevada, North Dakota, Oregon, South Dakota, Washington, and Wyoming, escrow is used quite extensively. In those states, when the real estate broker has a purchase agreement signed between buyer and seller, the entire transaction is delivered to an escrow agent. The escrow agent orders a title search made and then proceeds to close the entire transaction, making the apportionments and performing all the other details performed by lawyers and brokers in the other states, in much the same manner as described in Chapter 22.

The escrow agent—usually a bank, the escrow department of a brokerage firm or title insurance firm, or a separate escrow firm—is paid a fee for holding the instrument in escrow; the agent then collects the monthly, semiannual, or annual payments on the contract from the purchaser and turns the receipts over to the seller. Escrow agents are often used when the property being purchased is financed by an installment contract.

In the event of default under the terms of the contract, the seller has a right to foreclose in much the same manner as a mortgagee will foreclose on a mortgage.

OPTIONS

An **option** is a contract to keep an offer open. In Chapter 3 it was explained that an offer may be withdrawn at any time before it is accepted. The option is a device to prevent the seller from withdrawing the offer for a specified time. It has all of the elements of a contract, including a consideration that is paid to the seller for keeping the offer open. When an option is drawn, the practice is usually to prepare a contract for the sale of the property that is complete except for execution. The contract is, by custom, attached to the option.

Often a builder will request an option on a number of lots. This will be done when it is not certain whether the houses will sell readily and when the builder wishes to remain financially liquid. For example, if there are ten lots in which the builder is interested, one may be purchased outright and an option obtained from the seller on the other nine. After the first house is sold, the builder may, if the first house was profitable, exercise the option on the other nine lots.

In this situation, the seller should, depending on the bargaining position held, insist that the builder exercise the option on at least two lots at a time. If the lots vary in their price because some are more valuable than others, the owner might examine the possibility of the optionee's exercising the option on a high-priced lot and a low-priced lot at the same time. Otherwise, a builder might just exercise the option on the choice lots and leave the seller with the poorer lots. This is particularly applicable in a situation where there is a flat price per lot. If the purchaser exercised the option only on the choice lots, the seller would be left in an unprofitable position.

ASSIGNMENT OF CONTRACTS

Although a contract may specifically prohibit the assignment of the instrument, most contracts are freely assignable. Suppose *A* enters into a contract with *B* for the sale of real property. *B*, the purchaser, may arrange to sell the property to *X*. *B* will then assign the contract and thus avoid the possibility of two title closings. If *B* does assign the contract, instructions for drawing the need and other instruments should be given to *A*, the seller, as long in advance of the closing date as possible.

The option is also freely assignable. After an assignment has been made, the assignee may exercise the same rights that had been held by the assignor.

The procedure for making an assignment is quite simple. Generally, the following statment is endorsed on the contract:

> For value received, the within contract and all the rights, title, and interest of the purchaser hereunder are hereby assigned, transferred, and set over unto . . . and said assignee hereby assumes all of the obligations of the purchaser hereunder.

The assignment is dated and executed by the parties concerned.

SPECIFIC PERFORMANCE

Specific performance deals with the methods of enforcing the terms of the real property contract. When a contract has been breached by the seller, the buyer may do one of two things: (1) rescind the contract, that is, declare it terminated, recover the deposit, and in effect be in **status quo ante;** or (2) sue for damages and, if successful, obtain a personal judgment against the seller for the difference between the contract price and the market price at the time of the breach. The seller may also rescind or sue for damages in the event of a breach of the contract.

As another alternative, the buyer or the seller may bring an action for **specific performance,** an action to compel a party to a contract to perform the contract. This action is brought in a court of equity and generally allowed to be brought in equity by virtue of the fact that real property is unique—there is only one such parcel in existence and a suit for damages will not result in an adequate remedy. If a seller brings an action for specific performance, this will, in effect, compel the buyer to go through with the deal. If the buyer refuses in the face of the court order to tender the purchase price and receive the deed, the buyer stands in contempt of court.

The buyer, too, may bring this remedy; and this alternative will be chosen more often than not in a period of rising real estate values.

RIGHT TO RESCIND TRANSACTIONS INVOLVING REAL PROPERTY

Under the Consumer Credit Protection Act of 1968 and **Regulation Z** (the **Truth in Lending Act**), it is sometimes possible to rescind a real estate contract. The right to rescind, however, does not apply where a purchase money security interest in real property is involved, in which the creditor retains or will acquire or retain a security interest in real property that is the principal residence of the customer. The customer has the right to rescind the transaction until midnight of the third business day following the date of consummation of the transaction or delivery of the disclosures required under Regulation Z, whichever is later.

The purchase money mortgage will be discussed at length in Chapter 13. Regulation Z, which was adopted by the Board of Governors of the Federal Reserve Board on February 10, 1969, spells out not only the disclosures, including finance charges and annual percentage rates that must be made by creditors, but also the manner in which they must be made.

> The Act does not apply to business loans or commercial loans such as a construction loan to builders, but it will apply when the construction loan is converted to a consumer loan made to the purchaser of the house. The Act will apply only if payment of the loan is made in more than four installments or if a finance charge is or may be made.[7]

Thus, if *A* signs a contract for a residence and financing is arranged through a financial institution, the transaction may be rescinded. The creditor may be notified of intent to do so by mail, telegram, or other writing. A creditor is defined by Regulation Z (Sec. 226.2(m)) as "a person who in the ordinary course of business regularly extends or arranges for the extension of consumer credit."

If the customer elects to rescind, said customer is not liable for any fnance or other charge and any security interest becomes void. Within ten days after receipt of the notice of rescission, the creditor must return to the customer any money or property given as earnest money or as a down payment.

The customer may modify or waive the right to rescind if:

1. The extension of credit is needed in order to meet a good faith, immediate personal financial emergency of the customer.
2. The customer has determined that a delay of three days will jeopardize the welfare, health, or safety of natural persons, or endanger property that belongs to the customer or for which the customer is responsible.

---

[7]Keith T. Koskie, Commissioner of Real Estate, State of Colorado, "Truth in Lending" (unpublished paper), 1967.

3. The customer furnishes the creditor with a separate dated and signed personal statement describing the situation and in which the customer modifies or waives the right of rescission.

Printed forms may not be used for this purpose. Any waiver must be signed by all joint owners.

GLOSSARY

Acceptance To complete a contract, the offeree accepts the offer made by the offeror

Apportionments The dividing of such things as interest, taxes, etc., upon taking of title

Appurtenant Something that passes with land, commonly a right of way or other easement

Consideration That which is bargained for and exchanged in a contract (i.e., money, promises, forbearances)

Contingencies Conditions stipulated in a contract that must be satisfied in order for the contractual obligations to be fulfilled

Contract An exchange of promises or assents by two or more persons, resulting from an obligation to do or refrain from doing a particular act, which obligation is recognized or enforced by law

Contract for the exchange of real property A contract used when a broker arranges an exchange or trade of real property

Contractual ability The qualities possessed by a party to a contract that make the party competent—as determined by law—to enter into a valid agreement (age, sobriety, mental competence)

Disaffirmance An act or word by a minor indicating minor's intention not to be bound by a contract

Escrow A scroll, writing, or deed delivered by the grantor into the hands of a third person to be held by the latter until the happening of a contingency or the performance of a condition, and then delivered by third person to grantee

Executed contract A contract the terms of which have been fulfilled

Executory contract A contract with some term(s) remaining to be fulfilled

Liquidated damages The amount of parties to a contract stipulate are to be paid in case of default

Marketable title A title that is clearly so good that the courts will order its acceptance by a purchaser

Meeting of the minds Both parties are (or appear to be) thinking of the same thing, and there is an offer and acceptance; mutual assent

Mortgagee's Certificate of Reduction An instrument executed by a mortgagee stating the balance due on a mortgage

Offer A statement made by one person of what that person will give in return for some act or promise of a second person

Offeree The one to whom the offer is made

Offeror The person making the offer

Option A contract to keep an offer open

Property under contract A special clause employed in real property contracts when the contract itself is unassignable

Purchase money mortgage A mortgage given by the buyer to the seller as part of the consideration for the sale of real property

Receipt and agreement to purchase A type of real property contract used in some sections of the United States which combines the features of the binder and the formal contract used elsewhere

Regulation Z A regulation of the Federal Reserve System that establishes maximum interest rates paid by commercial banks on deposits

Specific performance An action brought to compel a party to a contract to perform the contract

Status quo ante In the same position as if there had been no contract

Statute of Frauds Statutes which involve contracts that must be written to be enforceable

Truth in Lending Act An act to encourage competition among financial institutions by informing consumers of the cost of credit and permitting consumers to compare various credit terms available

Valid contract A contract that is binding and enforceable against both parties

Voidable contract An agreement that may or may not be enforceable; generally, one party has the option to avoid or the power to validate the contract

Void contract A contract that is neither binding nor enforceable against either party

QUESTIONS FOR REVIEW

1. Distinguish between executory contract and executed contract. Into which category does a real estate contract normally fall?

2. What is the difference between marketable title, insurable title, and merchantable title?
3. What are liquidated damages? Why ought a purchaser insist that a sum for liquidated damages be inserted in a contract for the sale of real property?
4. If a parcel of land is sold on contract (or a contract for deed, as it is sometimes called), why should the contract and deed be placed in escrow?
5. What is an option and how is it used?
6. Explain what an individual must do under Regulation Z to keep from being bound under a contract for sale of real property or a receipt and agreement of purchase.

PROBLEMS AND ACTIVITIES

1. Margaret English (seller) and Dennis Black (purchaser) discussed the purchase of a parcel of real property by Black from English. Black gave English $2,000, and the following agreement was entered into:

   Jan. 15, 1985

   For the sum of $70,000, I, the undersigned, agree to sell my property, located at the corner of Ocean Avenue and Thomas Street, known as 281 Thomas Street. Received as earnest money, $2,000.
   /s/ MARGARET ENGLISH

   On February 15, 1989, Dennis Black tendered $70,000 to Margaret English and requested a deed. English refused and offered to return Black's $2,000, which Black in turn refused. Black then sued for specific performance. The defense of English was that the memorandum failed to comply with the Statute of Frauds. Who wins and why?
2. Gerald Williams has a house for sale at $200,000. Elaine Logan approaches you, a broker, and states that she is willing to purchase the house at that price, but she has only $20,000 for a down payment. From your past experience as a broker, you realize most banks would be reluctant to lend Logan $180,000 on a mortgage, even though she is a stable person with a fairly good job. You learn from Logan that she is presently living in an apartment and is paying $1,375 a month rent without any undue financial strain.

   You believe a bank would readily lend $160,000 on Williams's property; but, of course, a loan of that amount is impossible.

   You approach your client, Williams, and explain the situation to him. To your surprise (you should have known this when you listed the property), Williams states that he would be willing to help finance the sale himself, but doesn't know how to go about it.

   a. Give a step-by-step explanation of how this can be done.

b. When you have finished your explanation, Williams says, "That's all very well, but I'd like to get the balance paid off as soon as possible. I can't wait forever for my money." Explain two possible ways Williams might obtain the balance of the money due him within four years.

3. Obtain a blank form of binder or receipt and agreement form that is used by brokers in your state. If you are unable to find one, follow the form given in the text. Fill in the blanks from the following:

   On December 16, 1989, Howard L. Olsen and his wife, Marie, gave a listing to Dorothy M. Thomas, a registered (in some states called a licensed) broker of Gainesville, Florida. The property listed was lot #26 and the east half of lot #25 of the Highland Acres tract recorded July 10, 1966, otherwise described as 1111 N.W. 12th Ave., Gainesville, Florida. Commission is 7 percent; listing price, $275,000. The sellers stated they need at least $50,000 in cash and would be willing to accept a note (or bond as used in some states) secured by a first mortgage for the remainder, to be amortized over 15 years in equal semiannual installments, which would include interest at 14 percent on the unpaid balance. The first installment is to become due six months after the closing of title. Possession is to be on or after April 1, 1990. Policy of title insurance is to be paid for by the sellers.

   Thomas received an offer from Cecil Holmes and his wife, Kathy, residing in Gainesville, subject to the following conditions: occupancy by February 1, 1990; deposit to be returned if the sellers do not agree to the terms and conditions within seven days from the tender of the offer.

   On December 26, 1989, Dorothy Thomas, broker, agreed to submit the Holmes's offer of $10,000 less than the listing price and she accepted a $5,000 deposit to bind the offer on the following financial terms: $80,000 cash down including the deposit, remainder by note (or bond) and a first mortgage to be amortized by monthly payments on the unpaid balance at 13.5 percent; title policy to be paid for by the sellers.

4. Smith offers Brown a parcel of land for $25,000. The offer is in writing and contains a clause: "This offer is to remain open until January 15, 1989." The offer is dated December 1, 1988. On January 2, 1989, Smith notifies Brown that the offer is withdrawn. On January 8, 1989, Brown writes Smith accepting the offer. Is there a contract for the sale of land?

5. A contract for the sale of real property provided that the seller would convey "subject to any state of facts that an accurate survey would show provided that the same did not render the title unmarketable." The contract also provided that the seller "shall give and the purchaser shall accept a title" such as a named title company "or any reputable title company will approve and insure." The report of the title company excepted from the coverage an encroachment of 2.79 feet uncovered by a survey. The purchaser rejected title at the closing as being unmarketable and uninsurable and sued for the $6,500 down payment. Who wins and why?

8

DEEDS AND CONVEYANCES

KEY TERMS

Administration
Administrator's deed
Air lot
Base line
Bench mark
Bequest or legacy
Checks
Cloud on title
Collateral heirs
Covenant
Covenant against emcumbrances
Covenant of further assurance
Covenant of quiet enjoyment
Covenant of seizin
Covenants running with the land
Datum
Devisee
Executor's deed
Government survey
Habendum
Inter vivos
Intestate
Intestate succession
Legatee
Letters of administration
Lineals or lineal descendents
Meridians
Operative words of conveyance or granting clause
Parallels
Premises
Principal meridians
Quitclaim deed
Range
Seal
Sections
Special warranty deed
Statute of limitations
Tacking
Testate
Testator
Testatrix
Township
Warranty deed
Warrant of title
Will

Because in the Middle Ages the ability to write was a scarce commodity, a person conveyed his interest in the land "in the name of seizin of the land" symbolically: a piece of turf or twig was delivered to a grantee simultaneously with a statement to effect the transfer. (Or, as one wag put it: "The grantor got to throw a clod in the face of the grantee.")

Later, a writing accompanied the livery of seizin. In a further development, the twig or turf was done away with and the written instrument alone was delivered to the grantee. This writing became what is presently known as the deed.

A *deed* is an instrument in writing conveying an interest in real property. In a strict sense, to *convey* is to transfer an interest in land. A deed must be signed, sealed (in some states), and delivered. Because it is a contract, the deed must satisfy the requirements of the contract as outlined in Chapter 7.

PARTS OF A DEED

Parties

Like all instruments, a deed contains the names of the parties to the transaction. The parties in a deed are called the grantor and the grantee. The *grantor* is the person who is transferring interest in the property, and the *grantee* is the person to whom the interest is being transferred. In the normal transaction handled by the broker, the seller is commonly the grantor and the purchaser the grantee.

Some state statutes require that the full addresses of both the grantor and the grantee be given in the deed, and it is strongly recommended that they be included in the instrument even when not specifically required by statute. The full address includes the street address, the city or village, the township (in the Eastern United States), the county, and the state.

Consideration

In all valid contracts a consideration is mentioned. Thus, a deed may contain the statement that the grantor "in consideration of Ten and 00/100 Dollars, lawful money of the United States, paid by the grantee. . . ."

The consideration named in the example above is a nominal consideration.[1] Naming the actual or an obviously nominal consideration in a deed avoids the possibility of the REALTOR®'s becoming an innocent party to misleading others about the purchase price of a parcel of property.

Operative Words of Conveyance

Following the statement of the consideration are the so-called **operative words of conveyance** or **granting clause.** The words *grant and release, grant and convey,* or *grant, bargain, and sell* are operative words of conveyance. These words show the intent on the part of the grantor to transfer the property. Following the words of grant are words of limitation denoting the quantum of the estate granted. In many states the granting clause will read:

> WITNESSETH, that the party of the first part, in consideration of Ten and 00/100 ($10) Dollars lawful money of the United States and other good and valuable consideration paid by the party of the second part, does

[1]A few states, Nebraska, for example, require that the actual consideration be named in the deed. See Neb. Rev. Stat—Sect. 76-214 (1950). However, where a deed is executed by a grantor acting as a fiduciary, such as guardian or executor, a statement as to the actual purchase price is necessary in *all* states.

hereby *grant and release unto the party of the second part, his or her heirs or successors and assigns forever.* [A description of the premises follows.]

In the statement above, the words *heirs or successors and assigns forever* are considered the words denoting the quantum of the estate to be conveyed. In most states, the words *heirs or successors and assigns* create the fee simple. In such states the absence of these words creates a life estate in the grantee.

To create a fee simple in a corporation that has no heirs, the deed would read substantially as follows: "To the ABC Corporation, its successors and assigns."

Some states have done away with the necessity of stating "and his or her heirs" in the deed from *A* to *B* in order to convey a fee simple. Notably, Idaho (55-506 I.C.A.) states briefly: "Words of inheritance or succession are not requisite to transfer a fee in real property." Other states having similar statutes are Ohio, Pennsylvania, Tennessee, and Illinois. In such states the deed would read:

> Know All Men by These Presents: That Richard Roe, residing at 801 "B" Street, City of Boise, County of Ada, State of Idaho, in consideration of Ten Dollars, does hereby grant, bargain, sell, and convey unto Jane Doe, the following property in Latah County, State of Idaho, to wit: [the description of the property]. (If it is a life estate, "for life" will appear after "Jane Doe.")

Property Description

Following the words of conveyance in a deed, the property to be conveyed is described. The description should be a formal, legal one. The property is described by lot and block number, by metes and bounds, or by government survey.[2]

Lot and Block Number. Every map, or plat, filed by a subdivider or developer with the clerk of the county in which the property is located contains lot and block numbers. Although a street on a map so filed my contain only a name, the law generally requires that these streets be given block numbers and that each lot be given a lot number. Sometimes, only lot numbers are required. After the acceptance of the plat by the proper authorities, the owner of the subdivision may from that time forth describe by lot and block number the property in any conveyance made. For example, if a map is filed under the title "The Map of Smith Acres Development Company," the description may read:

> Lot 3, Block 19, of the Map of Smith Acres Development Company, surveyed by James Ramirez, Patchogue, July 17, 19 . . . as recorded on page . . . in Book . . . of the county of. . . .

---

[2]Metes and bounds descriptions are used in all 50 states. The government survey method is applicable in all states except the original 13 states where government surveys were not employed.

Anyone desiring to know the exact size of the lot can get the information in the office of the county clerk where the plat is filed.

Metes and Bounds. A description by metes (measures) and bounds (direction) is a second method of defining boundaries of a property. It is often called an irregular description. The property is described by beginning at a certain point and measuring and indicating the direction and length of the boundaries of the property until the point of beginning is again reached.

For example, a metes and bounds description of the property on Long Island Avenue as shown in Exhibit 8-1 would be as follows:

> All that tract or parcel of land, together with the buildings and improvements thereon, situate, lying and being at Medford, in the Town of Brookhaven, County of Suffolk, State of New York, bounded and described as follows:
>
> COMMENCING at a concrete monument set for a bound on the northerly side of Long Island Avenue, distant Two Hundred and Fifty (250) feet westerly from the point of intersection of the Bellport Road; thence running N. 83° 25′ 40″ W. by and with the northerly line of Long Island Avenue, One Hundred Ten (110) feet to a certain point; thence running N. 7° 56′ 50″ E. by and with other land now or formerly of Michael Weiner, One Hundred Seventy (170) feet to a certain point; thence running S. 83° 25′ 40″ E., by and with other land now or formerly of said Michael Weiner, One Hundred Ten (110) feet to land now or formerly of one Parisi, thence by and with the land now or formerly of one Parisi S. 7° 56′ 50″ W. One Hundred Seventy (170) feet to the point of beginning.

Exhibit 8-1 Map of Parcel of Land

In the event the land had not been surveyed, the property could still be described by metes and bounds; however, the description would probably not be as accurate.

Government Survey. The **government survey,** or rectangular survey as it is sometimes called, was adopted early in our history by Congress and is used largely outside the original 13 states. The system refers to a grid of north and south lines and east and west lines that are established in the Land Office in Washington (see Exhibit 8-2A).

The north and south lines are called **meridians,** and the east and west lines are called **parallels.** The distances between those parallels and meridians are 24 miles in each direction and are called **checks.**

Division of the Check. Each check of 24 miles square is divided into 16 townships of 6 miles square as shown in Exhibit 8-2B.

Base Line. Certain of the parallels are designated as **base lines,** running east and west. These base lines, running along the parallels, vary among the states; for example, Wisconsin employs a base line that is the southern boundary of the state. Oklahoma, on the other hand, uses a line passing

■ **Exhibit 8-2 Government Survey and Division of a Check**

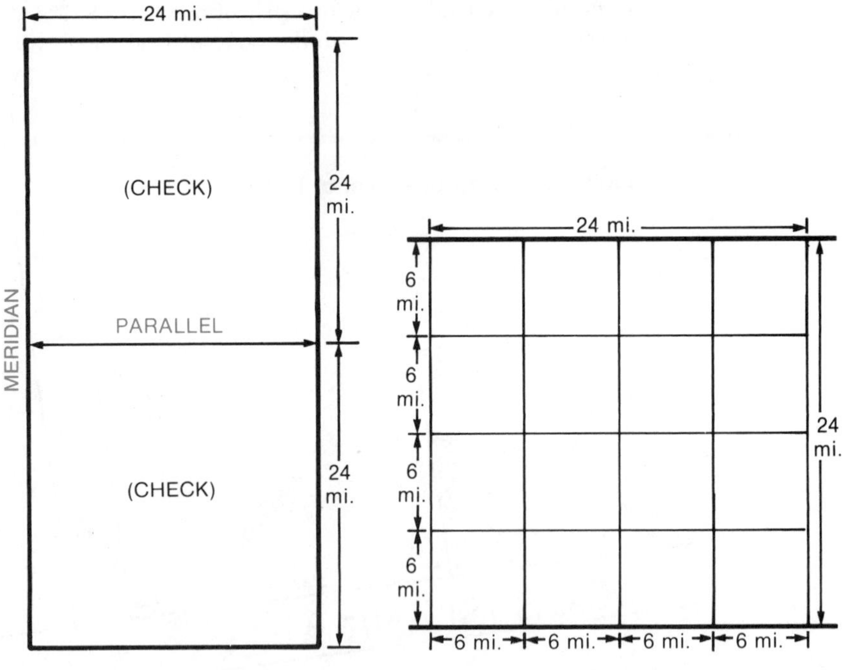

A. The Government Survey

B. Division of a Check into 16 Townships

through two towns, Duncan and Sulphur; however, in the Panhandle section, the base line is the boundary between the Texas and Oklahoma "panhandles."

Townships, or tiers as they are often called, are numbered and designated as being either north or south of the base line.

In Exhibit 8-3, the upper right-hand part of the figure is designated T.4N., which means this particular township is four tiers or four townships north of the base line. All townships or tiers the same distance north of the base line are numbered the same, that is, T.4N. This designation is also applicable to townships or tiers south of the base line.

The description T.4N. is meaningless by itself. What pinpoints the exact township or tier north or south of the base line is the range east or west of a principal meridian along which a particular township or tier is located.

Exhibit 8-3 Townships or Tiers North and South of the Base Line

24 mi.
PARALLEL

T. 4 N.	T. 4 N.	T. 4 N.	T. 4 N.
T. 3 N.	T. 3 N.	T. 3 N.	T. 3 N.
T. 2 N.	T. 2 N.	T. 2 N.	T. 2 N.
T. 1 N.	T. 1 N.	T. 1 N.	T. 1 N.
T. 1 S.	T. 1 S.	T. 1 S.	T. 1 S.
T. 2 S.	T. 2 S.	T. 2 S.	T. 2 S.
T. 3 S.	T. 3 S.	T. 3 S.	T. 3 S.
T. 4 S.	T. 4 S.	T. 4 S.	T. 4 S.

24 mi.
24 mi.
MERIDIAN
MERIDIAN
Townships North of Base Line
BASE LINE
Townships South of Base Line
PARALLEL

Principal Meridians. Just as certain parallels are designated as base lines, so certain of the meridians are designated as **principal meridians.** Nebraska, Kansas, and Colorado, for example, use the sixth principal meridian, which passes about one mile west of Solomon, Kansas. Washington and Oregon use the Willamette meridian, and Idaho uses the Boise meridian. Information regarding the principal meridians can be obtained from any local surveyor or abstractor.

Just as the tiers or townships are numbered north or south of the base line, they are also numbered east or west of a principal meridian. The township rows east or west of the principal meridian are called **ranges.** Each range in either an easterly or westerly direction from the principal meridian is identified with a number. Thus, a township may be described as T.1N., R.1W., which means it is in the first tier north of the base line and in the first range west of the principal meridian. A diagram of the townships of two checks is shown in Exhibit 8-4.

A frequent and often puzzling question arises with regard to two base lines, one directly above the other. If one begins counting townships north from the southernmost base line, when does one begin to run into townships counted south from the northernmost base line? The answer given by many is that the place where one stops counting south or north is determined by local custom. However, what is behind the local custom? For example, the New Mexico principal meridian runs north and south through that state and is intersected by a base line. Directly north of this New Mexico base line is a base line in Colorado, which runs east and west from the border of Missouri to the Utah border and intersects the sixth

Exhibit 8-4 The Townships of Two Checks

24 mi. | 24 mi. (widths); 24 mi. (height)

T. 4 N. R. 4 W.	T. 4 N. R. 3 W.	T. 4 N. R. 2 W.	T. 4 N. R. 1 W.	T. 4 N. R. 1 E.	T. 4 N. R. 2 E.	T. 4 N. R. 3 E.	T. 4 N. R. 4 E.
T. 3 N. R. 4 W.	T. 3 N. R. 3 W.	T. 3 N. R. 2 W.	T. 3 N. R. 1 W.	T. 3 N. R. 1 E.	T. 3 N. R. 2 E.	T. 3 N. R. 3E.	T. 3 N. R. 4 E.
T. 2 N. R. 4 W.	T. 2 N. R. 3 W.	T. 2 N. R. 2 W.	T. 2 N. R. 1 W.	T. 2 N. R. 1 E.	T. 2 N. R. 2 E.	T. 2 N. R. 3 E.	T. 2 N. R. 4 E.
T. 1 N. R. 4 W.	T. 1 N. R. 3 W.	T. 1 N. R. 2 W.	T. 1 N. R. 1 W.	T. 1 N. R. 1 E.	T. 1 N. R. 2 E.	T. 1 N. R. 3 E.	T. 1 N. R. 4 E.

BASE LINE

North Tiers and West Ranges — PRINCIPAL MERIDIAN — North Tiers and East Ranges principal meridian running north from the northern border of Oklahoma through Kansas and Nebraska to the southern border of South Dakota (see Exhibit 8-5).

Assuming one is counting north from the base line in New Mexico, when does one meet southern tiers from the base line in Colorado? The answer is that the original surveys laid out sharply defined areas in blocks. These defined areas point out in the meeting places of the extreme southern tiers and the extreme northern tiers extending from any base line.

Township. The **township** or tier north or south of the base line is numbered in the manner previously shown. If it is the sixth township north of the base line and the first township east of the principal meridian, it will be designated as T.6N., R.1E. or Twp.6N., R.1E. Either T. or Twp. is correct for use in a description. A township consists of an area of 36 square miles, each of which is divided into square-mile tracts. These tracts are called **sections,** and each section is numbered. Thus, T.6N., R.1E., when divided into sections, would appear as shown in Exhibit 8-6.

Section. To summarize, the check, an area 24 miles by 24 miles, is broken into 16 townships, each 6 miles by 6 miles; they in turn are each broken into 36 sections, 1 mile by 1 mile. These sections, containing 640 acres, are each numbered as shown in Exhibit 8-4. Thus, if a description referred to Section 8 of Township 6N., R.1E., it would be designated Sec. 8, T.6N., R.1E.

The question now arises as to how the section is reduced for descriptive purposes when a parcel of land less than 640 acres is being described. The answer is that the section is halved and then quartered as shown in Exhibit 8-7A on page 194. As an example, examine the lower left quarter of the exhibit. It is designated as SW¼ Sec. 8, T.6N., R.1E. The interpretation of this designation is as follows: The SW quarter of a section consists of 160 acres, that is, 640 acres divided by 4; Section 8 is of the Township 6N., which means a township six tiers or six townships north of a base line; and R.1E. means that this sixth township north of a base line is one range east of a principal meridian.

The quarter sections of 160 acres can be further broken down as shown in Exhibit 8-7B. Assume that it is Section 8, Township 6 North, Range 1 East. The upper left-hand quarter, the northwest quarter, is divided into three parts. The bottom part has been halved, and the upper half has been divided into two equal parts. The south half has been designated as the S½ of the NW¼, an area of 80 acres that is the south half of the northwest quarter of the section. It would be described as the S½ of the NW¼ of Sec. 8, T.6N., R.1E.

Looking at the north half of the quarter, we find that it has been divided down the middle into two areas: the west one-half of the north half of the northwest quarter, and the east one-half of the north half of the northwest quarter. The first is designated as W½ of the N½ of the NW¼, and the second as the E½ of the N½ of the NW¼. The westerly half is

■ **Exhibit 8-5 Principal Meridians of the Government Rectangular Survey System**

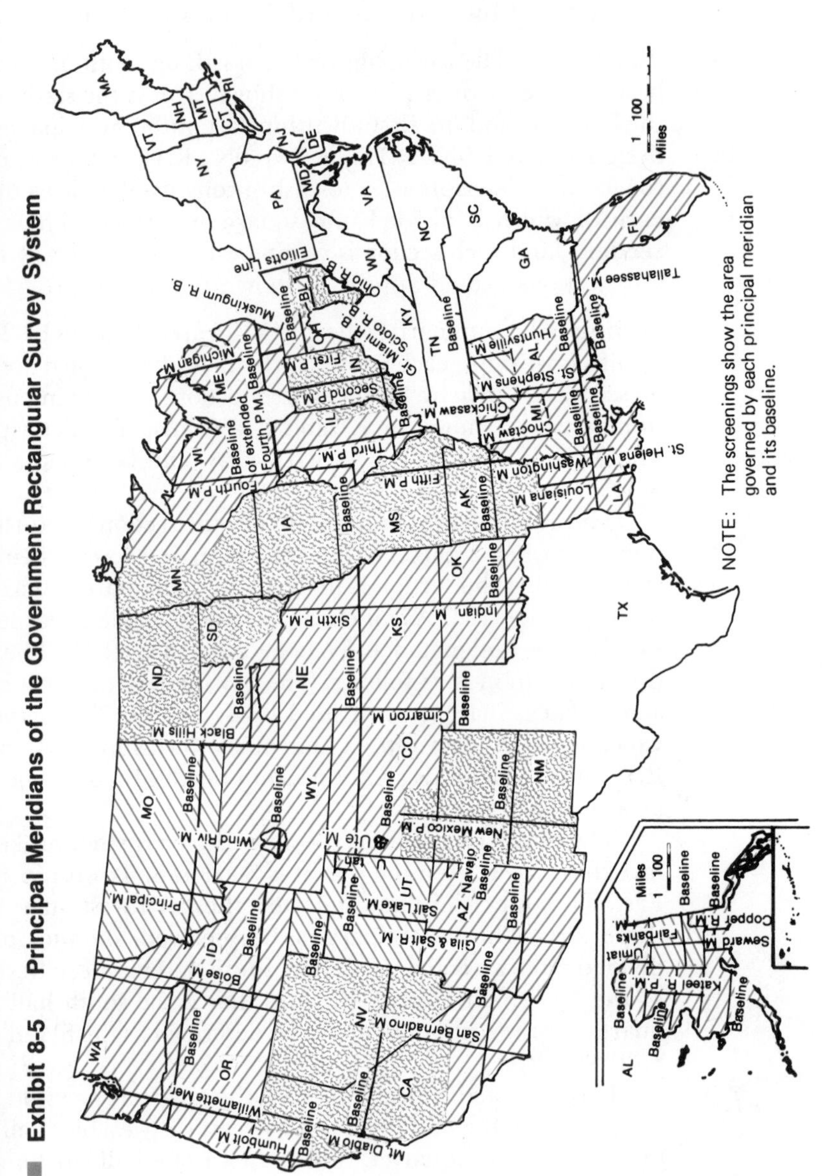

NOTE: The screenings show the area governed by each principal meridian and its baseline.

Exhibit 8-6 Division of Township into Sections. (Each township is divided into 36 sections of 1 square mile each. All townships are numbered in the same manner.)

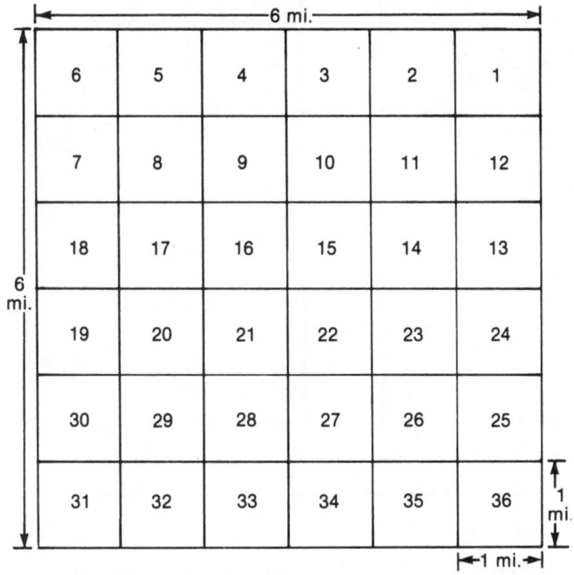

6 mi.

6	5	4	3	2	1
7	8	9	10	11	12
18	17	16	15	14	13
19	20	21	22	23	24
30	29	28	27	26	25
31	32	33	34	35	36

6 mi.

1 mi.

1 mi.

described as the W½ of the N½ of the NW¼ of Sec. 8, T.6N., R.1E., while the easterly half is described as the E½ of the N½ of the NW¼ of Sec. 8, T.6N., R.1E.

Datum. **Datum** is a thing given as a basis for reasoning. In surveying, it is defined as a point, line, or surface from which elevations are measured or indicated. The U.S. Geological Survey regards datum as the mean sea level in New York harbor.

Most cities use a local official datum to measure elevation rather than the USGS datum. This means the elevation will differ from a survey based on the USGS, but, when necessary, the figures are changed to conform with the USGS.

Bench Marks. To facilitate surveying, permanent reference points have been established throughout the United States. In addition, cities with a local datum have established permanent reference points. These are called **bench marks.**

Air Lots. An **air lot** is a space above a given parcel of land. It is described by describing the parcel of land underneath and the elevation of the air lot above the parcel.

It is most used in describing condominiums and, most recently, in describing commercial condominiums. Most commercial users prefer to

■ **Exhibit 8-7 Division of 640-Acre Section**

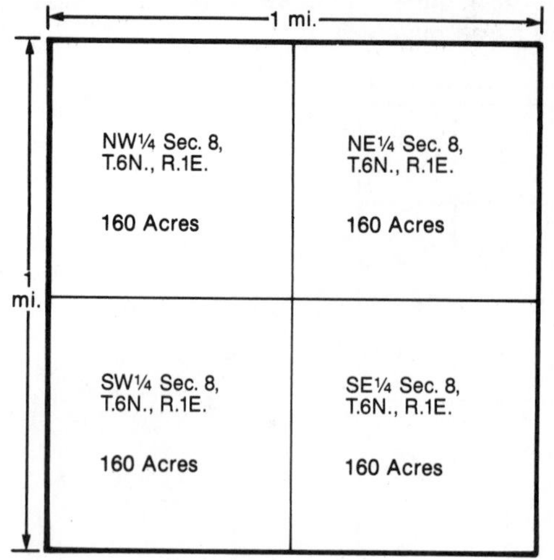

A. Section of 640 Acres Divided into Four Quarters B. Section Divided into Smaller Parcels

buy open space and then install walls to meet their requirements. However, at the moment, most state condominium statutes require units to be described in terms of space bounded by walls, floors, and ceilings. Illinois and California now have statutes permitting developers to sell large units of space (an entire floor) and the purchaser can divide the space to suit its needs. The majority of states have enacted similar statutes.

Appurtenances

After the description of the property there is a clause stating:

> . . . together with the appurtenances and all the estate and rights of the party of the first part in and to said premises.

An *appurtenance* is something that passes with the land, commonly, a right of way or other type of easement. In those areas where water rights

■ **Table 8-1 Table of Land Measure**

LINEAR MEASURE	SQUARE MEASURE
1 link = 7.92 inches	1 acre = 160 sq. rods; 10 sq. chains
1 rod = 25 links; 16½ feet; 5½ yards	1 section = 640 acres
1 chain = 100 links; 66 feet; 4 rods	1 square mile = 640 acres
1 mile = 5,280 feet; 320 rods; 80 chains	1 township = 36 square miles

for irrigation purposes are important, these water rights are generally held to be appurtenant to the land except when the rights are in a stock company. The broker or attorney handling such a transaction should investigate the exact nature of the water rights.

Premises

All the essential parts of the deed as outlined thus far—the names of the parties, the consideration, the operative words of conveyance, the property description, and the appurtenance provisions—are called the **premises.**

Habendum

The **habendum** follows the premises and states:

> To have and to hold the premises herein granted unto the party of the second part . . . [limits the estate to be taken by the grantee].

Any reservation or declaration of trust is made at this point in the deed.

There is a possibility of conflict between the limitation of the estate as expressed in the habendum and the limitation of the estate as expressed by the operative words of conveyance in the premises of the deed. Every attempt should be made to draw a habendum that is consistent with the premises. The general rule is that in the event of a conflict between the habendum and the premises, the premises are construed to indicate the intent of the deed and the habendum is ignored.

Execution and Acknowledgment

Customarily, the deed is executed or signed only by the grantor or grantors. It is only when the grantee is assuming a mortgage, as outlined in Chapter 13, that both the grantor and the grantee sign the deed. In the event the grantor is unable to write, his properly witnessed mark is acceptable in lieu of a written signature.

When the grantor is a corporation, an officer is authorized to sign and seal the deed. These words will precede the signature of the officer authorized to sign the instrument:

> In witness whereof, the party of the first part has caused its corporate seal to be hereunto affixed, and these presents to be signed by its duly authorized officer the day and year first above written.

Generally, the signature is attested to by another person.[3]

In order for a deed to be recordable, it must be acknowledged. This has been defined as the act by which a party who has executed an instru-

---

[3]Some states, notably Alaska, Arkansas, Connecticut, Florida, Georgia, Louisiana, Maryland, Michigan, Ohio, South Carolina, and Texas, require that the deed be executed in the presence of, and subscribed by, one, and sometimes two or more, credible witnesses. The reason for this is to prevent forged deeds.

ment of conveyance as grantor goes before a competent officer and declares or acknowledges the same as her or his genuine and voluntary act or deed. The competent officer referred to is generally a notary public. The reason for this is to prevent forged instruments from being recorded. The notary will require identification of those who sign and will require that the instruments be executed in her or his presence.[4]

The Seal

In some states, the deed must be sealed in order for there to be a valid conveyance. The **seal** is a formality and is sometimes defined as a particular sign, made to attest in the most formal manner the execution of an instrument. Where legally required, the seal is affixed on the line containing the grantor's signature, with the letters "L.S." (*locus sigilli,* the place of the seal). In many states, however, the seal is not required by law.

Delivery

For the conveyance to be complete, there must not only be a deed drawn and executed in the proper form, but there must also be an actual delivery of the deed. The delivery must be made directly to the grantee, or it may be made in escrow, that is, to a third person for ultimate delivery to the grantee upon the happening of certain stated events.

Between the grantor and the grantee, the conveyance is effected at the time of the delivery of the deed; however, when a deed is delivered in escrow, the time of the conveyance generally refers to the date of delivery to the escrow agent. For example, on July 1, 1989, a deed is delivered to an escrow agent to be delivered to the grantee upon the final payment of the purchase price on August 14, 1995. When the price has been paid and physical transfer of the deed given to the grantee, the date of the conveyance will usually relate back to the day of delivery to the escrow agent, in this case, July 1, 1989.

Recording

Although the delivery of a proper deed from the grantor to the grantee is valid between the grantor and the grantee, it would not ordinarily be valid to third parties. The recording of the deed with the proper official, usually the clerk of the county[5] in which the property is located, gives notice to the world of the conveyance. If there are two successive grantees for value of the same parcel of property, the person recording the property first, in the absence of fraud, has the good title. This is discussed in detail in Chapter 21.

---

[4]In some states, the instrument does not have to be executed in the presence of the notary if the grantor acknowledges her or his signature. In Arizona and Ohio, the deed must be acknowledged to be *valid.*

[5]In Connecticut, deeds and other instruments are recorded in the office of the town clerk.

TYPES OF DEEDS

Quitclaim Deed

The simplest form of deed is the **quitclaim deed.** This deed states, in effect, that the grantor transfers to the grantee her or his rights, if any, in the property described. When it is used to convey property, there is no implication that the grantor has good title or any title at all. If the grantor has nothing, then nothing is conveyed. If the grantor has good title, then the grantee can obtain a fee simple by means of the quitclaim deed; however, a transfer by quitclaim deed does not carry with it any implication that the grantee will receive any after acquired title rights.[6]

In general, the quitclaim deed is used when the grantee has, or claims to have, incomplete or partial title to the premises and the grantor or another person has a possible interest that would otherwise constitute a **cloud on title.** Often when there is an heir who might have a right to the property, the quitclaim deed is used.

A very practical use of the quitclaim deed exists when a person, for example, has purchased a tax deed from a county. In some states this individual may go through a "Torrens" proceeding and register the title, but often it is simpler to obtain a quitclaim deed from the person who formerly owned the property.

A quitclaim deed is shown in Exhibit 8-8.

Bargain and Sale Deed

There are two types of bargain and sale deeds in general use: the bargain and sale deed *without* covenant and the bargain and sale deed *with covenant.* A **covenant** may be best described as any agreement or promise. In a deed, it is a promise reduced to writing and contained within the deed.

The operative words in the quitclaim deed state:

> The party of the first part [the grantor] does hereby remise, release and quitclaim unto the party of the second part . . .

In the bargain and sale deed, either with or without covenant, the operative words are:

> The party of the first part [the grantor] does hereby grant and release unto the party of the second part . . .

Exhibit 8-9 is an example of a bargain and sale deed without covenant.

The distinction, then, is that in either the bargain and sale deed with covenant or the bargain and sale deed without covenant, the grantor asserts by implication that said grantor has the possession of a claim to or

---

[6]If the sales contract fails to specify that the seller is to convey by warranty deed or a quitclaim deed, the general rule is that it will be a compliance of the contract for the seller to convey by quitclaim deed.

Exhibit 8-8 Quitclaim Deed Form

QUITCLAIM DEED--Individual or Corporation

THIS INDENTURE, made the 28th day of March , nineteen hundred and --
BETWEEN David P. Rush, residing at 425 Mareposa Street, East Meadow, County of Nassau, State of New York,

party of the first part, and Eugene Koprowski, residing at 2080 Pine Street, East Meadow, County of Nassau, State of New York,

party of the second part,

WITNESSETH, that the party of the first part, in consideration of ten dollars paid by the party of the second part, does hereby remise, release and quitclaim unto the party of the second part, the heirs or successors and assigns of the party of the second part forever,

ALL that certain plot, piece or parcel of land, with the buildings and improvements thereon erected, situate, lying and being in the

[here follows a complete legal description of the property]

TOGETHER with all right, title and interest, if any, of the party of the first part in and to any streets and roads abutting the above described premises to the center lines thereof; TOGETHER with the appurtenances and all the estate and rights of the party of the first part in and to said premises; TO HAVE AND TO HOLD the premises herein granted unto the party of the second part, the heirs or successors and assigns of the party of the second part forever.

[1]AND the party of the first part, in compliance with Section 13 of the Lien Law, hereby covenants that the party of the first part will receive the consideration for this conveyance and will hold the right to receive such consideration as a trust fund to be applied first for the purpose of paying the cost of the improvement and will apply the same first to the payment of the cost of the improvement before using any part of the total of the same for any other purpose.

The word "party" shall be construed as if it read "parties" whenever the sense of this indenture so requires.

IN WITNESS WHEREOF, the party of the first part has duly executed this deed the day and year first above written.

IN PRESENCE OF: /s/ David P. Rush

/s/ Judith J. DeFore

[Acknowledgment]

Standard Form of New York Board of Title Underwriters

[1] In those states in which there is no trust created by statute, this clause is omitted.

■ Exhibit 8-9 Bargain and Sale Deed Farm

BARGAIN AND SALE DEED, WITHOUT COVENANT AGAINST GRANTOR'S ACTS--Individual of Corporation

THIS INDENTURE, made the 14th day of May , nineteen hundred and--

BETWEEN Herbert Senkoff, residing at 143 Walnut Street, Patchogue, County of Suffolk, State of New York,

party of the first part, and Donna Schneider, residing at 18 Beach Street, Patchogue, County of Suffolk, State of New York,

party of the second part,

WITNESSETH, that the party of the first part, in consideration of ten dollars and other valuable consideration paid by the party of the second part, does hereby grant and release unto the party of the second part, the heirs or successors and assigns of the party of the second part forever,

ALL that certain plot, piece or parcel of land, with the buildings and improvements thereon erected, situate, lying and being in the

[here follows a complete legal description of the property]

TOGETHER with all right, title and interest, if any, of the party of the first part in and to any streets and roads abutting the above described premises to the center lines thereof; TOGETHER with the appurtenances and all the estate and rights of the party of the first part in and to said premises; TO HAVE AND TO HOLD the premises herein granted unto the party of the second part, the heirs or successors and assigns of the party of the second part forever.

[1]AND the party of the first part, in compliance with Section 13 of the Lien Law, covenants that the party of the first part will receive the consideration for this conveyance and will hold the right to receive such consideration as a trust fund to be applied first for the purpose of paying the cost of the improvement and will apply the same first to the payment of the cost of the improvement before using any part of the total of the same for any other purpose.

The word "party" shall be construed as if it read "parties" whenever the sense of this indenture so requires.

IN WITNESS WHEREOF, the party of the first part has duly executed this deed the day and year first above written.

IN PRESENCE OF:

/s/ Herbert Senkoff

/s/ Judith J. DeFore

[Acknowledgment]

Standard Form of New York Board of Title Underwriters

[1] In those states in which there is no trust created by statute, this clause is omitted.

interest in the property. This implication is not present in the quitclaim deed.

The bargain and sale deed with covenant, goes one step farther. There is one covenant inserted in the instrument by the grantor that reads:

> That the party of the first part [the grantor] has not done or suffered anything whereby the said premises have been encumbered in any way.

This means the grantor has not done anything during ownership to encumber the land; in short, the grantor has not allowed any liens to be placed against the property.

Warranty Deed

A **warranty deed** is a deed in which the owner of property warrants that she or he has good and merchantable title to the property being conveyed. It may specify just what interest the owner is conveying and include covenants to protect the grantee in the event the title should not be as represented. Because the warranty deed gives the grantee the greatest guarantee, it is the best deed that can be received.

There are five so-called common covenants in a full covenant and warranty deed: (1) seizin, (2) quiet enjoyment, (3) further assurance, (4) encumbrance, and (5) warrant of title. New York and several other states include a sixth covenant, the trust covenant.[7] Exhibit 8-10 is an example of a warranty deed with full covenants.

Seizin. The first covenant in the full covenant and warranty deed is the **covenant of seizin.** This covenant, made by the grantor, is that the grantor is seized or has full possession of the premises in fee simple or any other quantum of estate that the grantor purports to convey. If, for example, the grantor states that he or she is seized of the premises in fee simple, then that statement amounts to a covenant that he or she has a fee simple to convey.

The covenant is not broken if there is a lien on the land, but it is broken if the title is in a third person, or if the grantor does not possess the extent of the estate that is purported to be conveyed.

Quiet Enjoyment. The **covenant of quiet enjoyment** states that the grantee shall ". . . quietly enjoy the said premises."

This covenant means that if the grantee is evicted either by the grantor or a third person having a better title than the grantee, then the grantee has a cause of action against the grantor. The meaning goes further than

[7]California uses a grant deed that contains fewer covenants than the warranty deed. The grantor impliedly warrants that she or he has not conveyed the same estate, or any right, title, or interest therein, to any person other than the grantee and that at the time of the execution the estate is free from any encumbrances due by the grantor or any person claiming under her or him.

Exhibit 8-10 Warranty Deed Form

WARRANTY DEED WITH FULL COVENANTS—Individual or Corporation

THIS INDENTURE, made the 1st day of June , nineteen hundred and – –

BETWEEN John Di Silva, a single man, residing at 20 Water Street, Babylon, County of Suffolk, State of New York

party of the first part, and Susan McKenna, a single woman, residing at 1492 Columbus Avenue, Middle Village, County of Queens, State of New York

party of the second part,

WITNESSETH, that the party of the first part, in consideration of Ten and 00/100 ($10.00)---

-- dollars,

lawful money of the United States, and other valuable consideration paid

by the party of the second part, does hereby grant and release unto the party of the second part, their heirs or successors and assigns of the party of the second part forever,

ALL that certain plot, piece or parcel of land, with the buildings and improvements thereon erected, situate, lying and being in the

[here follows a complete legal description of the property]

TOGETHER with all right, title and interest, if any, of the party of the first part in and to any streets and roads abutting the above described premises to the center lines thereof,

TOGETHER with the appurtenances and all the estate and rights of the party of the first part in and to said premises,

TO HAVE AND TO HOLD the premises herein granted unto the party of the second part, the heirs or successors and assigns of the party of the second part forever.

AND the party of the first part, in compliance with Section 13 of the Lien Law, covenants that the party of the first part will receive the consideration for this conveyance and will hold the right to receive such consideration as a trust fund to be applied first for the purpose of paying the costs of the improvement and will apply the same first to the payment of the cost of the improvement before using any part of the total of the same for any other purpose.

AND the party of the first part covenants as follows:

FIRST.——That said party of the first part is seized of the said premises in fee simple, and has good right to convey the same;

SECOND.—That the party of the second part shall quietly enjoy the said premises;

THIRD.——That the said premises are free from incumbrances, except as aforesaid;

FOURTH.—That the party of the first part will execute or procure any further necessary assurance of the title to said premises;

FIFTH.——That said party of the first part will forever warrant the title to said premises.

The word "party" shall be construed as if it read "parties" whenever the sense of this indenture so requires.

IN WITNESS WHEREOF, the party of the first part has duly executed this deed the day and year first above written.

IN PRESENCE OF:

[Acknowledgment]

Standard Form of New York Board of Title Underwriters

this. In the event the grantee sells the property and the subsequent grantee is evicted by a third person, the grantee may also bring an action against the grantor. For example, *A* conveys to *B,* and in the conveyance there is a covenant of quiet enjoyment made by *A. B* then conceys to *C.* Then *X,* who has a paramount title, evicts *C. C,* in the absence of fraud, may sue *A* for the damages sustained.

The reason *C* may bring the action is that the covenant of quiet enjoyment is a covenant running with the land, which is explained later in this chapter.

Further Assurance. This covenant states that ". . . the party of the first part will execute or procure any further necessary assurance of the title to said premises."

The **covenant of further assurance,** although omitted in some states from the full covenant and warranty deed, is important. By virtue of this covenant, the grantor may be required to perform such acts as are necessary to perfect title in the grantee. For example, *A* conveys to *B,* and it is later discovered that the description on the deed is incorrect. The covenant of further assurance then requires *A* to give *B* a correction deed.

This covenant is enforceable by an equity suit for specific performance and not ordinarily by a suit for damages.

Encumbrance. The **covenant against encumbrances** states that the ". . . premises are free from encumbrances except as aforesaid."

If, for example, there is an encumbrance against the property such as a mortgage, this will have been stated previously in the deed. If, however, any encumbrances do exist against the property and are not expected, the covenant is violated and the grantee has a cause of action against the grantor.[8]

Warrant of Title. This covenant states that the grantor ". . . will forever warrant the title to said premises."

The **warrant of title** is important because it guarantees both possession and title to the premises. In the event this covenant is broken by virtue of a third person having a better title, then the grantor will be liable to the grantee for damages sustained by the grantee.

Trust. In New York and several other states, a statutory covenant has been created that is placed in all types of deeds. The need for this covenant arose because of fraudulent sellers. Suppose, for example, that *A* desires to sell a piece of real property. To obtain a better price, a painter is hired to redecorate. *A* does not pay the painter, but immediately sells the property to *B*. The painter then obtains a mechanic's lien against the property as will

[8]"Encumbrance" covers mortgages, tax liens, judgment liens, restrictions, easements, and outstanding dower rights. In California, the term includes taxes, assessments, and all liens upon real property (Cal. Civil Code, Sec. 1114).

be explained in Chapter 12. *B,* the new owner, is then placed in a position where there is a lien on the property and thus *B* will become involved in legal process. In order to avoid this, the following is inserted in a deed:

> That in compliance with Section 13 of the Lien Law, the party of the first part will receive the consideration for the conveyance and will hold the right to receive such consideration as a trust fund to be first applied for the purpose of paying the cost of improvement and that the party of the first part [the grantor] will apply the same first to the payment of the cost of improvement before using any part of the total of the same for any other purpose.

This clause then makes the seller in effect the trustee of the funds received from the sale of the property for the benefit of any potential mechanic's lienors. If the seller, after having received the purchase price, does not pay for the improvements on the property, the seller is guilty of a breach and may be held liable under the penal statutes.

Special Warranty Deed

Some states use what is commonly called a **special warranty deed** in which the grantor warrants only against claims asserted by, through, or under him or her. In brief, the grantor warrants the title against defects arising after the property has been acquired and not against defects arising before that time. In the final analysis, it is much like the bargain and sale deed with covenant.

Other Deeds

There are several other special-purpose deeds. These are explained in Appendix E.

COVENANTS RUNNING WITH THE LAND

Covenants running with the land refer to those covenants within a deed that pass certain rights and duties to subsequent grantees of the land, for example, the covenant of quiet enjoyment mentioned previously.

Restrictive covenants are another type of covenant running with the land. If the owner of a subdivision restricts the size of the buildings on the land, limiting them to two stories, the covenant would be said to be a restrictive covenant and would run with the land. A person buying land in the subdivision would be subject to legal action if constructing a three-story building on it.

These restrictions are enforceable in a court of equity unless they are against public policy. The person seeking to enforce a restriction or covenant running with the land can attempt to obtain an injunction against the person violating the covenant.

When a property is subdivided and the deeds from the common grantor contain a statement to the effect that all buildings must be built 25 feet back from the street, and if the restriction is commensurate with the quality and character of the land, then it is enforceable by the people whom it was intended to benefit.

The possible existence of covenants running with the land is one of the compelling reasons for making a title search. For example, if *A* conveys property to *B* with the type of restriction that runs with the land, and *B* conveys to *C* without mention of the restriction in the deed, the covenant still runs with the land on the theory that *C*, or any other subsequent grantee for that matter, has constructive notice of the existence of the covenant.

Covenants running with the land generally are limited to a period of time. In any event, a covenant may be ineffective if the neighborhood has changed sufficiently. When this change does take place, a legal action may be necessary to remove the covenant from record.

FRAUDULENT CONVEYANCES

Generally speaking, the courts will not inquire into the consideration in a real property transaction. However, there are some instances when they will. If a grantor conveys property to another without sufficient consideration, and if it can be proved that the conveyance was made with the intent to defraud creditors, then the courts will compel the grantee to reconvey the property to the grantor to satisfy the claims of the creditors.

The situation often arises when property is conveyed to a family member for a nominal consideration. If there is an indebtedness to other parties in existence at the time of the conveyance, the conveyance is generally held to be presumptively fraudulent. If the conveyance is made before indebtedness is incurred, however, it becomes necessary to show fraudulent intent to set the conveyance aside.

CONVEYANCE BY WILL

Conveyances of real property described in the previous sections of this chapter are generally called transfers ***inter vivos*** (among the living). On the average of once every 25 years, however, all real property is transferred either by wills or by reason of persons dying without wills.

Wills

A **will** is ordinarily a writing that provides for the distribution of property on the death of the writer, but that confers no rights prior to that time. Prior to death, the writer may destroy or cancel the will. The person making the will is known as the **testator,** if male; **testatrix,** if female. When a person dies leaving a will, it is said that the person died **testate;** a person dying without a will is said to have died **intestate.**

A gift of land by will is known as a devise, and the person receiving the gift is called a **devisee.** A **bequest** or a **legacy** is a gift of personal property, generally money, under a will and the person receiving the gift is called a **legatee.**

Executor's Deed

The **executor's deed** is used to convey real property that was owned by a person who died testate. Basically, it is the same as any other deed except that it contains a covenant against grantor's acts, the grantor being the executor or executors. If there is more than one executor, they must all join on the deed to effect a valid conveyance. If the property is sold, the deed recites the full consideration being paid for the property. If the property is being distributed, then it will recite that fact.

TRANSFER BY INTESTACY

If a person does not effectively dispose of his or her property by will or does not leave a will, the property will be distributed to certain relatives. Since such persons acquire or succeed to the rights of the decedent and since the circumstances under which they do so are in the absence of an effective will, they acquire title by **intestate succession.** The right of intestate succession is not an inherent right, but exists only because the legislature so provides. The legislatures of the individual states have the right to change, modify, or destroy the right to inherit property.

Plan of Intestate Distribution

Actual plans of intestate distribution (called *per stirpes,* out of the stock) vary from state to state, but in general they exhibit the following pattern:

Spouses. The surviving spouse, whether husband or wife, will share in the estate. The extent of the share generally depends on the number of children and other heirs. In the absence of surviving blood relations, the surviving spouse generally takes the entire estate.

Lineals. **Lineals** or **lineal descendants** are blood descendants of the decedent. The portion not distributed to the surviving spouse is generally distributed to lineals.

Parents. If the estate has not been exhausted, the remainder is commonly distributed to the decedent's parents.

Collateral Heirs. These are persons who are not descendants of the decedent but who are related through a common ancestor. Generally, **collateral heirs** include brothers and sisters of the decedent.

Administration of Estates

Administration is the means of distributing property of a decedent who has died intestate. When no will is left by the decedent, the court or an officer designated by law appoints one or more persons who are then entitled to administer the estate of the decedent. Generally, the close relatives of the deceased are entitled to **letters of administration** issued by the probate court authorizing the distribution of the assets of the estate. The letters are usually issued to the first relative who applies. When there are creditors of the deceased and no previous application for letters of administration has been made, the letters may be granted to the creditors. In the absence of creditors or known relatives, letters may be issued by the court to a public administrator or administratrix. In any event, once the letters have been granted to the administrator, the job becomes much the same as the executor's; that is, gathering the assets of the deceased and distributing them in accordance with the pattern of intestate succession established in the state. If there is real property to be sold, the administrator does this by means of an administrator's deed.

Administrator's Deed

The **administrator's deed** is similar in many respects to the executor's deed. To make a valid conveyance by an administrator's deed, however, an administrator must in all cases obtain specific permission from the court to convey the property. The deed is executed by the administrator and specifically recites the authorization of the court for the sale.

TRANSFER BY ADVERSE POSSESSION

All states have a **statute of limitations.** When a cause of action exists, the person having the cause of action has a certain time limit within which to proceed with the proper legal action. For example, in many states the statute of limitations bars a lawsuit on a debt after six years. In the final analysis, the law concerning adverse possession of real property is in the nature of a statute of limitations. Thus, a true owner may be unable to assert true ownership of a parcel of real property against another after a period of years outlined by the statutes or common law.

To obtain title to real property by adverse possession, certain requisites must be met. If *A* goes on *B*'s property and the statutory period for adverse possession is 15 years,[9] *A*'s possession during the 15-year period must be continuous or uninterrupted in order to ripen into ownership. The possession must also be actual, visible, exclusive, and it must be hostile (holding under a claim inconsistent with the rights of the owner) to the owner. In the situation above, when *A* claims the adverse possession of the property, the statement is made that *A*'s possession must be continuous and uninterrupted. This is necessary for *A* to claim the property by adverse

[9]The time varies from 2 years in Arizona (under certain circumstances) to 30 years in Louisiana (under some circumstances). In Colorado, it is basically 18 years but only 7 years if the occupant has paid the real property taxes.

possession. But suppose *A* dies and *X*, the son and heir, acquires possession at the end of the seventh year of *A*'s possession; and suppose *X* then holds the property continuously and without interruption for another eight years. This succession of possession whereby the time of possession of *A*, the first claimant, is added or tacked to the time of possession of *X*, the second claimant, is called **tacking.** When there is a privity between the persons successively in possession and those persons hold the property for the requisite period, it is generally held that *X*, the second claimant in adverse possession, will have good title to the property and *B* will be barred from asserting any claim to the property. In some states it is necessary to go into possession of the property under some *color of title;* that is, claiming under what appears to be a muniment of title. Often the payment of taxes by the person in possession is considered evidence of color of title, and sometimes evidence of being "hostile."

GLOSSARY

Administration The means of distributing property of a decedent who has died intestate

Administrator's deed An instrument used in conveying property of a person who has died intestate

Air lot Space above a parcel of land

Base line The east-west line associated with each principal meridian

Bench marks Permanent reference points to facilitate surveying

Bequest (or legacy) A gift of personal property, often money

Checks Distances between parallels and meridians

Cloud on title An outstanding claim or encumbrance that might affect the title to a property

Collateral heirs Persons who are not descendants of the decedent but who are related to the deceased through a common ancestor

Covenant Any agreement or promise

Covenant against encumbrances An agreement whereby a grantor states that the premises are free from encumbrances except as aforementioned

Covenant of further assurance A clause in a deed stating that the grantor will perform such acts as are necessary to perfect title in the grantee

Covenant of quiet enjoyment A clause stating that the grantee shall quietly enjoy the said premises; if the grantee is evicted either by the grantor or a third person having a better title than the grantee, the grantee has a cause of action against the grantor

Covenant of seizin A clause in a warranty deed in which the grantor promises to be seized or in full possession of the premises in fee simple or any other quantum of estate that grantor purports to convey

Covenants running with the land Clauses within a deed that pass certain rights and duties to subsequent grantees of the land

Datum A point, line, or surface from which elevations are measured

Devisee Person receiving a devise

Executor's deed A deed used to convey real property that was owned by a person who died testate

Government survey A rectangular survey; a boundary-defining descriptive system that refers to a grid of north, south, east, and west lines established in the Land Office in Washington, D.C.

Habendum A portion of a deed beginning with the words *to have and to hold;* part of a deed that determines what estate or interest is granted by the deed

Inter vivos Among the living

Intestate Dying without leaving a will

Intestate succession The means by which certain persons related to the intestate decedent acquire title to decedent's properties

Legatee A person who receives a gift of personal property under will

Letters of administration Close relatives of the intestate deceased are generally entitled to these papers issued by the probate court that authorize distribution of the assets of the estate

Lineals (or lineal descendants) Blood descendants of the decedent

Meridians North and south lines used to define boundaries

Operative words of conveyance (granting clause) The words in a contract showing the grantor's intent to transfer the property

Parallels East and west line used to describe boundaries

Premises The essential parts of a deed, including the names of the parties, consideration, operative words of conveyance, property description, and appurtenance provisions

Principal meridians Designated survey lines running north and south that govern legal descriptions in 30 states

Quitclaim deed The simplest form of deed, whereby the grantor transfers to the grantee any rights grantor holds in described property

Ranges The township rows east or west of the principal meridian

Seal A formality: a particular sign used to attest, in the most formal manner, the execution of an instrument

Sections The square mile tracts that comprise the township

Special warranty deed A deed in which the grantor warrants only against claims asserted by, through, or under him or her

Statute of limitations Law setting a time limit within which one must proceed with the proper legal action, if ever

Tacking Where the time period of possession of one adverse possessor is added or tacked to the possession of another

Testate When a person dies leaving a will the person is said to die testate

Testator A male individual who makes a will

Testatrix A female individual who makes a will

Township Consists of an area of 36 square miles; the tier north or south of the base line

Warrant of title A clause wherein the mortgagor warrants or guarantees title to the premises

Warranty deed A deed in which the owner warrants that she or he has good and merchantable title to the property being conveyed

Will A writing that provides for the distribution upon the death of the writer but which confers no rights prior to that time

QUESTIONS FOR REVIEW

1. Villains in Westerns often show a paper before the hearing, shouting: "Sign the bill of sale and then the ranch will be mine." Aside from duress, what, if anything, is wrong with this?

2. Every type of deed contains language known as "operative words of conveyance." What does this mean?

3. Almost any instrument involving real property must contain a legal description of the property. What ways may property be described?

4. What is the meaning of *appurtenance*? Give an illustration.

5. A deed is delivered to an escrow agent today with the final payoff on the contract to be 10 years from today. If final payoff is actually made 4 years from today, what is the effective delivery date of the deed?

PROBLEMS AND ACTIVITIES

1. Bob Ralston signs a deed over to Joe Gregg. In the premises is written: "I hereby convey Lot 1, Block 16, of Security Acres to Joe Gregg and his heirs forever." In the habendum is written: "I hereby convey Lot 1, Block 16, of Security Acres to Joe Gregg and his heirs forever, to have and to hold forever, provided that should Joe Gregg die without issue before Dorothy Donovan then Lot 1, Block 16, of Security Acres is to revert to Dorothy Donovan." What estate is given to Joe Gregg under the deed?
2. Frank LePage owned a piece of land in fee simple. He sold it to Mary Palmer, who paid cash for it. LePage signed a full covenant and warranty deed to Mary Palmer, describing the property as follows: "I hereby grant to Mary Palmer and her heirs that certain Lot 10, Block 5, of Security Acres addition to the City of Durham, State of North Carolina, according to that certain map on page 100 of Book 15 of Maps and Plats filed in the Office of the County Recorder of Durham County, State of North Carolina." Mary Palmer promptly recorded the deed.

   Later, Frank LePage borrowed money on a mortgage from the Fast Bank. This mortgage was secured by several pieces of property, including the property he sold to Mary Palmer. The Fast Bank then started to foreclose and Mary Palmer defended. The Fast Bank stated the description was insufficient to convey title. At the trial, Palmer sought to introduce into evidence the map and plat as it appeared on page 100 of Book 15 of Maps and Plats. Is this evidence admissible?
3. In the material at the end of Chapter 7, you were to prepare a contract for the sale of real property. From this contract, prepare a full covenant and warranty deed using the material from the contract.
4. The diagram on page 211 shows a section. Assume it is Sec. 8, T.4N., R.23W., Cedar County, Kansas.

   a. Describe the area marked *A* and determine the number of acres it contains.
   b. Describe the area marked *B* and determine the number of acres it contains.
   c. Describe the area marked *C* and determine the number of acres it contains.
   d. Describe the area marked *D* and determine the number of acres it contains.
   e. Describe the area marked *E* and determine the number of acres it contains.

f. Describe the area marked *F* and determine the number of acres it contains.

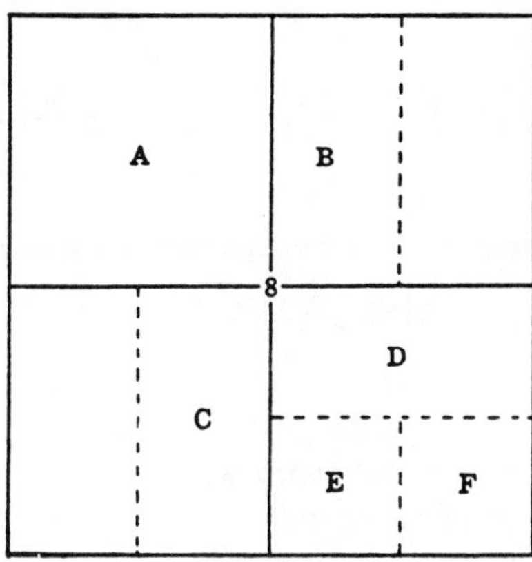

5. Draw a sketch from the following property description. How many acres does the parcel contain?

> Commencing at the South quarter corner of Section 36, a distance of 1593.79 feet on a bearing of North 0° 09' 50" East to the REAL POINT OF BEGINNING; thence South 66° 01' 12" East 699.49 feet; thence North 0° 03' 37" East, 1311.74 feet; thence North 89° 26' 08" West, 637.57 feet, thence South 0° 09' 50" West, 1033.74 feet, to the REAL POINT OF BEGINNING.

(Courtesy of Robie Real Estate, Salmon, Idaho)

9

MORTGAGES AND DEEDS OF TRUST

KEY TERMS

Abstract of title
Acceleration clause
Covenant against removal
Covenant of insurance
Covenant to pay attorney's fees
Covenant to pay indebtedness
Covenant to pay taxes
Deed of trust
Default in prior mortgage clause
Estoppel clause
Foreclosure
Foreclosure by advertisement
Good repair clause
Goodwill
Intermediate theory of mortgages
Junior mortgage
Lien theory of mortgages
Lis pendens
Mortgage
Mortgagee
Mortgage foreclosure
Mortgagor
Owner rent clause
Prepayment clause
Promissory note
Receiver
Receiver clause
Reconveyance
Sale in one parcel clause
Subordination clause
Title theory of mortgage
Trust clause
Trustee
Warrant of title

In the ancient Anglo-Saxon language, *mort* meant "death" and *gage* meant "pledge." Thus, the word *mortgage* meant a "dead pledge," because when a property was mortgaged it was considered dead during the term of the mortgage. In fact, very little could be done with the land in terms of conveyancing as long as the mortgage was still in effect. This, of course, is no longer true.

It is extremely rare today that real property is sold without a mortgage. Only 50 years ago, mortgages from financial institutions were unobtainable unless at least 50 percent of the purchase price was paid in cash by a purchaser.

The mortgage and deed of trust are tantamount to giving the property as security for a debt.

In all transactions where land is given as security for a debt, there are two instruments involved. Sometimes these instruments are, for brevity's sake, combined into one form; but in the final analysis, they remain two separate and distinct instruments. These instruments are the promissory note and the mortgage. The mortgage, which will be more fully discussed later, is the creation of an interest in property as security for the payment of a debt or the fulfillment of some obligation.

The deed of trust, which will be discussed later in the chapter, is a deed absolute to secure the payment of a debt. In the following discussion of the mortgage, one should be aware that much of the information relative to the real property mortgage is also applicable to the deed of trust.

THE NOTE

A promissory note is evidence of the debt with the land being used as collateral security for the note. A **promissory note** is a written promise by one person to pay money to another.

There are two major corporations engaged in the business of purchasing notes and mortgages or notes and deeds of trust. These are the Federal National Mortgage Association and the Federal Home Loan Mortgage Corporation (these will be fully discussed in Chapter 14). For example, if a savings and loan association lends a home buyer money on a mortgage, it will probably use the standard forms, hoping perhaps one day to sell the mortgage to FNMA or FHLMC.

A standard promissory note is shown in Exhibit 9-1. It is used in *every* state of the Union, and is the same in every state with the exception of the last sentence, which is modified as follows:

1. In states using the Mortgage, the last sentence begins: "The indebtedness evidenced by this Note is secured by a Mortgage dated. . . ."
2. In states using the Deed of Trust, the last sentence begins: "The indebtedness evidenced by this Note is secured by a Deed of Trust, dated. . . ."

THE MORTGAGE

A **mortgage** is the creation of an interest in property as security for the payment of a debt or the fulfillment of an obligation. Property, as was discussed in Chapter 6, is divided into real property and personal property. By implication, our brief definition of the mortgage suggests that real property and personal property may be mortgaged, and so they can. Both types of mortgages are made by an agreement or contract. Thus, an agreement that creates an interest in personal property as security for the payment of a debt or the fulfillment of an obligation might be said to be a *chattel* (personal property) *mortgage,* and an agreement that creates an interest in real property for the payment of a debt or the fulfillment of an obligation might be said to be a *real property mortgage.* Of course, we are primarily interested in the latter.

Exhibit 9-1 Promissory Note

NOTE

US $ 42,500.00 .... Denver, ..., Colorado
City
June 18, ..., 19--

FOR VALUE RECEIVED, the undersigned ("Borrower") promise(s) to pay MIDLAND FEDERAL SAVINGS AND LOAN ASSOCIATION, or order, the principal sum of Forty-Two Thousand Five Hundred---- Dollars, with interest on the unpaid principal balance from the date of this Note, until paid, at the rate of Thirteen (13) ..... percent per annum. Principal and interest shall be payable at 1418 - 17th Street, Denver, Colorado ...., or such other place as the Note holder may designate, in consecutive monthly installments of Eight Hundred Sixteen and 00/100 -------------- Dollars (US $816.00 ....), on the 5th .... day of each month beginning July 5, ..., 19--... Such monthly installments shall continue until the entire indebtedness evidenced by this Note is fully paid, except that any remaining indebtedness, if not sooner paid, shall be due and payable on July 5, 20-- ....

If any monthly installment under this Note is not paid when due and remains unpaid after a date specified by a notice to Borrower, the entire principal amount outstanding and accrued interest thereon shall at once become due and payable at the option of the Note holder. The date specified shall not be less than thirty days from the date such notice is mailed. The Note holder may exercise this option to accelerate during any default by Borrower regardless of any prior forbearance. If suit is brought to collect this Note, the Note holder shall be entitled to collect all reasonable costs and expenses of suit, including, but not limited to, reasonable attorney's fees.

Borrower shall pay to the Note holder a late charge of five (5) percent of the principal and interest of any monthly installments not received by the Note holder within fifteen (15) days after the installment is due.

Borrower may prepay the principal amount outstanding in whole or in part. The Note holder may require that any partial prepayments (i) be made on the date monthly installments are due and (ii) be in the amount of that part of one or more monthly installments which would be applicable to principal. Any partial prepayment shall be applied against the principal amount outstanding and shall not postpone the due date of any subsequent monthly installments or change the amount of such installments, unless the Note holder shall otherwise agree in writing. If, within five years from the date of this Note, Borrower make(s) any prepayments in any twelve month period beginning with the date of this Note or anniversary dates thereof ("loan year") with money lent to Borrower by a lender other than the Note holder, Borrower shall pay the Note holder (a) during each of the first three loan years ...... Four .... percent of the amount by which the sum of prepayments made in any such loan year exceeds twenty percent of the original principal amount of this Note and (b) during the fourth and fifth loan years ..... Six .... percent of the amount by which the sum of prepayments made in any such loan year exceeds twenty percent of the original principal amount of this Note.

Presentment, notice of dishonor, and protest are hereby waived by all makers, sureties, guarantors and endorsers hereof. This Note shall be the joint and several obligation of all makers, sureties, guarantors and endorsers, and shall be binding upon them and their successors and assigns.

Any notice to Borrower provided for in this Note shall be given by mailing such notice by certified mail addressed to Borrower at the Property Address stated below, or to such other address as Borrower may designate by notice to the Note holder. Any notice to the Note holder shall be given by mailing such notice by certified mail, return receipt requested, to the Note holder at the address stated in the first paragraph of this Note, or at such other address as may have been designated by notice to Borrower.

The indebtedness evidenced by this Note is secured by a Deed of Trust, dated June 18, 19-- ...., and reference is made to the Deed of Trust for rights as to acceleration of the indebtedness evidenced by this Note.

/s/ Marvin J. Miller

368 Stout Street — /s/ Cynthia Miller

Denver, Colorado

Property Address — *(Execute Original Only)*

COLORADO—1 to 4 Family—6/75—FNMA/FHLMC UNIFORM INSTRUMENT

M-501

Essentials of the Mortgage

A mortgage is a contract. Therefore, the instrument creating the mortgage must embrace the elements of a contract, namely:

1. Competent parties.
2. Offer and acceptance.
3. Consideration.
4. Legality of object.
5. Because it is real property and subject to the Statute of Frauds, it must be in writing and signed.

These elements were discussed in Chapter 7.

The Parties

In general there are two parties to a mortgage: the mortgagor and the mortgagee. The **mortgagor** is the party pledging the property. This person is the borrower on the note. The **mortgagee** is the party to whom the pledge of the property is made. Therefore, the mortgagee is the lender on the note.

Theories of Mortgages

There are three theories of mortgages used in the United States: the title theory, the lien theory, and the intermediate theory.

Title Theory.[1] The basic concept of the **title theory of mortgages** is that upon making the mortgage, the mortgagor passes title to the property, the subject of the mortgage, to the mortgagee, subject to a condition subsequent. This condition subsequent is the payment of the debt. Upon fulfillment of the condition, title to the property divests (reverts to) to the mortgagor.

For example, *A* (the mortgagor) mortgages real property to *B* (the mortgagee) in a title state. Under the terms of the instrument, title passes to *B*. However, the instrument will state that if *A* complies with the condition (makes payment), then the instrument will be void.[2]

During the period of the mortgage, by virtue of a provision in the mortgage, *A* is generally entitled to remain in possession of the property even though title is passed to the mortgagee.

---

[1]States using the title theory are Alabama, Arkansas, Connecticut, Maine, Maryland, Massachusetts, New Hampshire, Pennsylvania, Rhode Island, Tennessee, Vermont, Virginia, and West Virginia and the District of Columbia.

[2]In the strict sense of the word, *void,* based on the maxim *ex nihilo nihil fit,* meaning "out of nothing comes nothing," *B* never actually holds title if *A* fulfills the condition.

Lien Theory.[3] The majority of the states use the **lien theory of mortgages.** Under this theory, title remains with the mortgagor, and the mortgage that is placed on the property is a charge on the title. The mortgage instrument says nothing about title, but states: "The mortgagor does hereby mortgage to. . . ." After the recording of the instrument, it becomes a lien on the property described in the mortgage.

The rule regarding the priority of mortgages whether in *title* or *lien* states is substantially the same rule as that regarding the priority of deeds: the instrument recorded first, in the absence of fraud, is the operative one. For example, *A* mortgages property to *B* on October 15 with the instrument bearing that date. On the following day, *A* mortgages the same property to *C*. *C* records the mortgage before *B*. In the absence of fraud, *C* has a valid enforceable mortgage. To avoid such circumstances, mortgages should be recorded immediately.

From this idea of having the first lien against the property, the term *first mortgage* was derived. The term *first mortgage* simply means the party holding such instrument has recorded that instrument first in point of time and thus has priority over any subsequently recorded mortgages. Second mortgage, third mortgage, and so on, indicates the order of the recording and the priority in case of foreclosure for the private creditors. It should be remembered that in some states, notably California, tax liens, judgment liens, and mechanic's liens can have priority over the first mortgage. This will be discussed more fully in Chapter 12 dealing with liens.

Intermediate Theory.[4] The **intermediate theory of mortgages** involves a combination of title and lien theory. In short, title does not pass to the lender when the loan is made. It stays with the borrower, as in the lien theory, but if the borrower defaults, then title automatically passes to the lender.

FNMA/FHLMC Mortgage

The mortgage shown in Exhibit 9-2 is another example of an FNMA/FHLMC Uniform Instrument. In every state using the mortgage rather than the deed of trust, the first 17 clauses are *exactly* the same. Any differences between the states are contained from clause 18 on. As a practical matter, FNMA and FHLMC do not care what individual lenders might add after clause 18.

---

[3]States using the lien theory are Alaska, Arizona, California, Colorado, Delaware, Florida, Georgia, Hawaii, Idaho, Indiana, Iowa, Kansas, Kentucky, Louisiana, Michigan, Minnesota, Missouri, Montana, Nebraska, Nevada, New Mexico, New York, North Dakota, Oklahoma, Oregon, South Carolina, South Dakota, Texas, Utah, Washington, Wisconsin, and Wyoming.

[4]The states using the intermediate theory are Illinois, Mississippi, New Jersey, North Carolina, and Ohio.

Exhibit 9-2 Open-End Mortgage

OPEN-END MORTGAGE

THIS MORTGAGE is made this........16th................day of.....June.................., 19--.., between the Mortgagors. John M. Wilks and Elizabeth S. Wilks..(herein "Borrower"), and the Mortgagee,...The First......Savings and Loan Association.........................., a corporation organized and existing under the laws of.......Ohio..........................., whose address is. 203 Indianola Avenue, Columbus, Ohio...(herein "Lender").

WHEREAS, Borrower is indebted to Lender in the principal sum of. Forty-Seven Thousand and 00/100 ....($47,000.00). ---------------------- Dollars, which indebtedness is evidenced by Borrower's note dated. June 16, 19--..............(herein "Note"), providing for monthly installments of principal and interest, with the balance of the indebtedness, if not sooner paid, due and payable on....July 1, 20--.............................;

TO SECURE to Lender (a) the repayment of the indebtedness evidenced by the Note, with interest thereon, the payment of all other sums, with interest thereon, advanced in accordance herewith to protect the security of this Mortgage, and the performance of the covenants and agreements of Borrower herein contained, and (b) the repayment of any future advances, with interest thereon, made to Borrower by Lender pursuant to paragraph 21 hereof (herein "Future Advances"), Borrower does hereby mortgage, grant and convey to Lender the following described property located in the County of..........Franklin....................., State of Ohio:

[here follows a complete legal description of the property]

which has the address of. 14 "E" Avenue, Columbus,..............., ...,
[Street] [City]

....Ohio 43207..............(herein "Property Address");
[State and Zip Code]

TOGETHER with all the improvements now or hereafter erected on the property, and all easements, rights, appurtenances, rents, royalties, mineral, oil and gas rights and profits, water, water rights, and water stock, and all fixtures now or hereafter attached to the property, all of which, including replacements and additions thereto, shall be deemed to be and remain a part of the property covered by this Mortgage; and all of the foregoing, together with said property (or the leasehold estate if this Mortgage is on a leasehold) are herein referred to as the "Property".

Borrower covenants that Borrower is lawfully seised of the estate hereby conveyed and has the right to mortgage, grant and convey the Property, that the Property is unencumbered, and that Borrower will warrant and defend generally the title to the Property against all claims and demands, subject to any declarations, easements or restrictions listed in a schedule of exceptions to coverage in any title insurance policy insuring Lender's interest in the Property.

OHIO—1 to 4 Family—6/75—FNMA/FHLMC UNIFORM INSTRUMENT

Exhibit 9-2 (continued)

UNIFORM COVENANTS. Borrower and Lender covenant and agree as follows:

1. **Payment of Principal and Interest.** Borrower shall promptly pay when due the principal of and interest on the indebtedness evidenced by the Note, prepayment and late charges as provided in the Note, and the principal of and interest on any Future Advances secured by this Mortgage.

2. **Funds for Taxes and Insurance.** Subject to applicable law or to a written waiver by Lender, Borrower shall pay to Lender on the day monthly installments of principal and interest are payable under the Note, until the Note is paid in full, a sum (herein "Funds") equal to one-twelfth of the yearly taxes and assessments which may attain priority over this Mortgage, and ground rents on the Property, if any, plus one-twelfth of yearly premium installments for hazard insurance, plus one-twelfth of yearly premium installments for mortgage insurance, if any, all as reasonably estimated initially and from time to time by Lender on the basis of assessments and bills and reasonable estimates thereof.

The Funds shall be held in an institution the deposits or accounts of which are insured or guaranteed by a Federal or state agency (including Lender if Lender is such an institution). Lender shall apply the Funds to pay said taxes, assessments, insurance premiums and ground rents. Lender may not charge for so holding and applying the Funds, analyzing said account, or verifying and compiling said assessments and bills, unless Lender pays Borrower interest on the Funds and applicable law permits Lender to make such a charge. Borrower and Lender may agree in writing at the time of execution of this Mortgage that interest on the Funds shall be paid to Borrower, and unless such agreement is made or applicable law requires such interest to be paid, Lender shall not be required to pay Borrower any interest or earnings on the Funds. Lender shall give to Borrower, without charge, an annual accounting of the Funds showing credits and debits to the Funds and the purpose for which each debit to the Funds was made. The Funds are pledged as additional security for the sums secured by this Mortgage.

If the amount of the Funds held by Lender, together with the future monthly installments of Funds payable prior to the due dates of taxes, assessments, insurance premiums and ground rents, shall exceed the amount required to pay said taxes, assessments, insurance premiums and ground rents as they fall due, such excess shall be, at Borrower's option, either promptly repaid to Borrower or credited to Borrower on monthly installments of Funds. If the amount of the Funds held by Lender shall not be sufficient to pay taxes, assessments, insurance premiums and ground rents as they fall due, Borrower shall pay to Lender any amount necessary to make up the deficiency within 30 days from the date notice is mailed by Lender to Borrower requesting payment thereof.

Upon payment in full of all sums secu ed by this Mortgage, Lender shall promptly refund to Borrower any Funds held by Lender. If under paragraph 18 hereof the Property is sold or the Property is otherwise acquired by Lender, Lender shall apply, no later than immediately prior to the sale of the Property or its acquisition by Lender, any Funds held by Lender at the time of application as a credit against the sums secured by this Mortgage.

3. **Application of Payments.** Unless applicable law provides otherwise, all payments received by Lender under the Note and paragraphs 1 and 2 hereof shall be applied by Lender first in payment of amounts payable to Lender by Borrower under paragraph 2 hereof, then to interest payable on the Note, then to the principal of the Note, and then to interest and principal on any Future Advances.

4. **Charges; Liens.** Borrower shall pay all taxes, assessments and other charges, fines and impositions attributable to the Property which may attain a priority over this Mortgage, and leasehold payments or ground rents, if any, in the manner provided under paragraph 2 hereof or, if not paid in such manner, by Borrower making payment, when due, directly to the payee thereof. Borrower shall promptly furnish to Lender all notices of amounts due under this paragraph, and in the event Borrower shall make payment directly, Borrower shall promptly furnish to Lender receipts evidencing such payments. Borrower shall promptly discharge any lien which has priority over this Mortgage; provided, that Borrower shall not be required to discharge any such lien so long as Borrower shall agree in writing to the payment of the obligation secured by such lien in a manner acceptable to Lender, or shall in good faith contest such lien by, or defend enforcement of such lien in, legal proceedings which operate to prevent the enforcement of the lien or forfeiture of the Property or any part thereof.

5. **Hazard Insurance.** Borrower shall keep the improvements now existing or hereafter erected on the Property insured against loss by fire, hazards included within the term "extended coverage", and such other hazards as Lender may require and in such amounts and for such periods as Lender may require; provided, that Lender shall not require that the amount of such coverage exceed that amount of coverage required to pay the sums secured by this Mortgage.

The insurance carrier providing the insurance shall be chosen by Borrower subject to approval by Lender; provided, that such approval shall not be unreasonably withheld. All premiums on insurance policies shall be paid in the manner provided under paragraph 2 hereof or, if not paid in such manner, by Borrower making payment, when due, directly to the insurance carrier.

All insurance policies and renewals thereof shall be in form acceptable to Lender and shall include a standard mortgage clause in favor of and in form acceptable to Lender. Lender shall have the right to hold the policies and renewals thereof, and Borrower shall promptly furnish to Lender all renewal notices and all receipts of paid premiums. In the event of loss, Borrower shall give prompt notice to the insurance carrier and Lender. Lender may make proof of loss if not made promptly by Borrower.

Unless Lender and Borrower otherwise agree in writing, insurance proceeds shall be applied to restoration or repair of the Property damaged, provided such restoration or repair is economically feasible and the security of this Mortgage is not thereby impaired. If such restoration or repair is not economically feasible or if the security of this Mortgage would be impaired, the insurance proceeds shall be applied to the sums secured by this Mortgage, with the excess, if any, paid to Borrower. If the Property is abandoned by Borrower, or if Borrower fails to respond to Lender within 30 days from the date notice is mailed by Lender to Borrower that the insurance carrier offers to settle a claim for insurance benefits, Lender is authorized to collect and apply the insurance proceeds at Lender's option either to restoration or repair of the Property or to the sums secured by this Mortgage.

Unless Lender and Borrower otherwise agree in writing, any such application of proceeds to principal shall not extend or postpone the due date of the monthly installments referred to in paragraphs 1 and 2 hereof or change the amount of such installments. If under paragraph 18 hereof the Property is acquired by Lender, all right, title and interest of Borrower in and to any insurance policies and in and to the proceeds thereof resulting from damage to the Property prior to the sale or acquisition shall pass to Lender to the extent of the sums secured by this Mortgage immediately prior to such sale or acquisition.

6. **Preservation and Maintenance of Property; Leaseholds; Condominiums; Planned Unit Developments.** Borrower shall keep the Property in good repair and shall not commit waste or permit impairment or deterioration of the Property and shall comply with the provisions of any lease if this Mortgage is on a leasehold. If this Mortgage is on a unit in a condominium or a planned unit development, Borrower shall perform all of Borrower's obligations under the declaration or covenants creating or governing the condominium or planned unit development, the by-laws and regulations of the condominium or planned unit development, and constituent documents. If a condominium or planned unit development rider is executed by Borrower and recorded together with this Mortgage, the covenants and agreements of such rider

■ Exhibit 9-2 (continued)

shall be incorporated into and shall amend and supplement the covenants and agreements of this Mortgage as if the rider were a part hereof.

7. Protection of Lender's Security. If Borrower fails to perform the covenants and agreements contained in this Mortgage, or if any action or proceeding is commenced which materially affects Lender's interest in the Property, including, but not limited to, eminent domain, insolvency, code enforcement, or arrangements or proceedings involving a bankrupt or decedent, then Lender at Lender's option, upon notice to Borrower, may make such appearances, disburse such sums and take such action as is necessary to protect Lender's interest, including, but not limited to, disbursement of reasonable attorney's fees and entry upon the Property to make repairs. If Lender required mortgage insurance as a condition of making the loan secured by this Mortgage, Borrower shall pay the premiums required to maintain such insurance in effect until such time as the requirement for such insurance terminates in accordance with Borrower's and Lender's written agreement or applicable law. Borrower shall pay the amount of all mortgage insurance premiums in the manner provided under paragraph 2 hereof.

Any amounts disbursed by Lender pursuant to this paragraph 7, with interest thereon, shall become additional indebtedness of Borrower secured by this Mortgage. Unless Borrower and Lender agree to other terms of payment, such amounts shall be payable upon notice from Lender to Borrower requesting payment thereof, and shall bear interest from the date of disbursement at the rate payable from time to time on outstanding principal under the Note unless payment of interest at such rate would be contrary to applicable law, in which event such amounts shall bear interest at the highest rate permissible under applicable law. Nothing contained in this paragraph 7 shall require Lender to incur any expense or take any action hereunder.

8. Inspection. Lender may make or cause to be made reasonable entries upon and inspections of the Property, provided that Lender shall give Borrower notice prior to any such inspection specifying reasonable cause therefor related to Lender's interest in the Property.

9. Condemnation. The proceeds of any award or claim for damages, direct or consequential, in connection with any condemnation or other taking of the Property, or part thereof, or for conveyance in lieu of condemnation, are hereby assigned and shall be paid to Lender.

In the event of a total taking of the Property, the proceeds shall be applied to the sums secured by this Mortgage, with the excess, if any, paid to Borrower. In the event of a partial taking of the Property, unless Borrower and Lender otherwise agree in writing, there shall be applied to the sums secured by this Mortgage such proportion of the proceeds as is equal to that proportion which the amount of the sums secured by this Mortgage immediately prior to the date of taking bears to the fair market value of the Property immediately prior to the date of taking, with the balance of the proceeds paid to Borrower.

If the Property is abandoned by Borrower, or if, after notice by Lender to Borrower that the condemnor offers to make an award or settle a claim for damages, Borrower fails to respond to Lender within 30 days after the date such notice is mailed, Lender is authorized to collect and apply the proceeds, at Lender's option, either to restoration or repair of the Property or to the sums secured by this Mortgage.

Unless Lender and Borrower otherwise agree in writing, any such application of proceeds to principal shall not extend or postpone the due date of the monthly installments referred to in paragraphs 1 and 2 hereof or change the amount of such installments.

10. Borrower Not Released. Extension of the time for payment or modification of amortization of the sums secured by this Mortgage granted by Lender to any successor in interest of Borrower shall not operate to release, in any manner, the liability of the original Borrower and Borrower's successors in interest. Lender shall not be required to commence proceedings against such successor or refuse to extend time for payment or otherwise modify amortization of the sums secured by this Mortgage by reason of any demand made by the original Borrower and Borrower's successors in interest.

11. Forbearance by Lender Not a Waiver. Any forbearance by Lender in exercising any right or remedy hereunder, or otherwise afforded by applicable law, shall not be a waiver of or preclude the exercise of any such right or remedy. The procurement of insurance or the payment of taxes or other liens or charges by Lender shall not be a waiver of Lender's right to accelerate the maturity of the indebtedness secured by this Mortgage.

12. Remedies Cumulative. All remedies provided in this Mortgage are distinct and cumulative to any other right or remedy under this Mortgage or afforded by law or equity, and may be exercised concurrently, independently or successively.

13. Successors and Assigns Bound; Joint and Several Liability; Captions. The covenants and agreements herein contained shall bind, and the rights hereunder shall inure to, the respective successors and assigns of Lender and Borrower, subject to the provisions of paragraph 17 hereof. All covenants and agreements of Borrower shall be joint and several. The captions and headings of the paragraphs of this Mortgage are for convenience only and are not to be used to interpret or define the provisions hereof.

14. Notice. Except for any notice required under applicable law to be given in another manner, (a) any notice to Borrower provided for in this Mortgage shall be given by mailing such notice by certified mail addressed to Borrower at the Property Address or at such other address as Borrower may designate by notice to Lender as provided herein, and (b) any notice to Lender shall be given by certified mail, return receipt requested, to Lender's address stated herein or to such other address as Lender may designate by notice to Borrower as provided herein. Any notice provided for in this Mortgage shall be deemed to have been given to Borrower or Lender when given in the manner designated herein.

15. Uniform Mortgage; Governing Law; Severability. This form of mortgage combines uniform covenants for national use and non-uniform covenants with limited variations by jurisdiction to constitute a uniform security instrument covering real property. This Mortgage shall be governed by the law of the jurisdiction in which the Property is located. In the event that any provision or clause of this Mortgage or the Note conflicts with applicable law, such conflict shall not affect other provisions of this Mortgage or the Note which can be given effect without the conflicting provision, and to this end the provisions of the Mortgage and the Note are declared to be severable.

16. Borrower's Copy. Borrower shall be furnished a conformed copy of the Note and of this Mortgage at the time of execution or after recordation hereof.

17. Transfer of the Property; Assumption. If all or any part of the Property or an interest therein is sold or transferred by Borrower without Lender's prior written consent, excluding (a) the creation of a lien or encumbrance subordinate to this Mortgage, (b) the creation of a purchase money security interest for household appliances, (c) a transfer by devise, descent or by operation of law upon the death of a joint tenant or (d) the grant of any leasehold interest of three years or less not containing an option to purchase, Lender may, at Lender's option, declare all the sums secured by this Mortgage to be immediately due and payable. Lender shall have waived such option to accelerate if, prior to the sale or transfer, Lender and the person to whom the Property is to be sold or transferred reach agreement in writing that the credit of such person is satisfactory to Lender and that the interest payable on the sums secured by this Mortgage shall be at such rate as Lender shall request. If Lender has waived the option to accelerate provided in this paragraph 17, and if Borrower's successor in interest has executed a written assumption agreement accepted in writing by Lender, Lender shall release Borrower from all obligations under this Mortgage and the Note.

Exhibit 9-2 (concluded)

If Lender exercises such option to accelerate, Lender shall mail Borrower notice of acceleration in accordance with paragraph 14 hereof. Such notice shall provide a period of not less than 30 days from the date the notice is mailed within which Borrower may pay the sums declared due. If Borrower fails to pay such sums prior to the expiration of such period, Lender may, without further notice or demand on Borrower, invoke any remedies permitted by paragraph 18 hereof.

NON-UNIFORM COVENANTS. Borrower and Lender further covenant and agree as follows:

18. Acceleration; Remedies. Except as provided in paragraph 17 hereof, upon Borrower's breach of any covenant or agreement of Borrower in this Mortgage, including the covenants to pay when due any sums secured by this Mortgage, Lender prior to acceleration shall mail notice to Borrower as provided in paragraph 14 hereof specifying: (1) the breach; (2) the action required to cure such breach; (3) a date, not less than 30 days from the date the notice is mailed to Borrower, by which such breach must be cured; and (4) that failure to cure such breach on or before the date specified in the notice may result in acceleration of the sums secured by this Mortgage, foreclosure by judicial proceeding and sale of the Property. The notice shall further inform Borrower of the right to reinstate after acceleration and the right to assert in the foreclosure proceeding the non-existence of a default or any other defense of Borrower to acceleration and foreclosure. If the breach is not cured on or before the date specified in the notice, Lender at Lender's option may declare all of the sums secured by this Mortgage to be immediately due and payable without further demand and may foreclose this Mortgage by judicial proceeding. Lender shall be entitled to collect in such proceeding all expenses of foreclosure, including, but not limited to, costs of documentary evidence, abstracts and title reports.

19. Borrower's Right to Reinstate. Notwithstanding Lender's acceleration of the sums secured by this Mortgage, Borrower shall have the right to have any proceedings begun by Lender to enforce this Mortgage discontinued at any time prior to entry of a judgment enforcing this Mortgage if: (a) Borrower pays Lender all sums which would be then due under this Mortgage, the Note and notes securing Future Advances, if any, had no acceleration occurred; (b) Borrower cures all breaches of any other covenants or agreements of Borrower contained in this Mortgage; (c) Borrower pays all reasonable expenses incurred by Lender in enforcing the covenants and agreements of Borrower contained in this Mortgage and in enforcing Lender's remedies as provided in paragraph 18 hereof, including, but not limited to, reasonable attorney's fees; and (d) Borrower takes such action as Lender may reasonably require to assure that the lien of this Mortgage, Lender's interest in the Property and Borrower's obligation to pay the sums secured by this Mortgage shall continue unimpaired. Upon such payment and cure by Borrower, this Mortgage and the obligations secured hereby shall remain in full force and effect as if no acceleration had occurred.

20. Assignment of Rents; Appointment of Receiver. As additional security hereunder, Borrower hereby assigns to Lender the rents of the Property, provided that Borrower shall, prior to acceleration under paragraph 18 hereof or abandonment of the Property, have the right to collect and retain such rents as they become due and payable.

Upon acceleration under paragraph 18 hereof or abandonment of the Property, Lender shall be entitled to have a receiver appointed by a court to enter upon, take possession of and manage the Property and to collect the rents of the Property, including those past due. All rents collected by the receiver shall be applied first to payment of the costs of management of the Property and collection of rents, including, but not limited to, receiver's fees, premiums on receiver's bonds and reasonable attorney's fees, and then to the sums secured by this Mortgage. The receiver shall be liable to account only for those rents actually received.

21. Future Advances. Upon request of Borrower, Lender, at Lender's option prior to release of this Mortgage, may make Future Advances to Borrower. Such Future Advances, with interest thereon, shall be secured by this Mortgage when evidenced by promissory notes stating that said notes are secured hereby. At no time shall the principal amount of the indebtedness secured by this Mortgage, not including sums advanced in accordance herewith to protect the security of this Mortgage, exceed the original amount of the Note plus US $............................

22. Release. Upon payment of all sums secured by this Mortgage, Lender shall discharge this Mortgage, without charge to Borrower. Borrower shall pay all costs of recordation, if any.

IN WITNESS WHEREOF, Borrower has executed this Mortgage.

Witnesses:

/s/Bonita C. Greene .... /s/John M. Wilks .... —Borrower

.... /s/Elizabeth S. Wilks .... —Borrower

STATE OF OHIO, ...Franklin.........County ss:

On this....16th....day of.....June.................19--., before me, a Notary Public in and for said County and State, personally appeared John M. Wilks and Elizabeth S. Wilks ...., the individual(s) who executed the foregoing instrument and acknowledged that they did examine and read the same and did sign the foregoing instrument, and that the same is..their..... free act and deed.

IN WITNESS WHEREOF, I have hereunto set my hand and official seal.

[Seal]

My Commission expires: /s/Leroy P. Starkey .... Notary Public

(Space Below This Line Reserved For Lender and Recorder)

MORTGAGE CLAUSES AND THEIR MEANINGS

In general, most of the statutory forms of the mortgage require: (1) a date, (2) the names of the parties, (3) the amount of the debt, and (4) a statement that the "mortgagor hereby mortgages to the mortgagee" certain described property. These elements of a mortgage are discussed in detail on the following pages. It should be noted that many of these clauses are also standard in the deed of trust.

General Clauses

Following the description of property, the statutory form of mortgage states: "And the mortgagor covenants with the mortgagee as follows:. . . ."

The six general clauses or covenants found in the statutory mortgages in most states are described below. They vary slightly among the states, but in general they are used in nearly every type of simple mortgage.

Covenant to Pay Indebtedness. The **covenant to pay indebtedness** states, "The mortgagor will pay the indebtedness as hereinbefore provided." This is self-explanatory.

Covenant of Insurance. The **covenant of insurance** is a promise that the premises shall be covered by fire insurance in a stated amount for the benefit of the mortgagee and that the mortgagor will assign and deliver the policies to the mortgagee. Depending on the location of the property, a statement should be added to the mortgage regarding an extended coverage endorsement, because the standard fire policy specifically exempts damage from wind and rain. In hurricane or frequent storm areas, the mortgagee has insufficient protection with the fire policy alone because of the possibility that damage might be done by wind and rain.

Covenant Against Removal. The **covenant against removal** is often included in the statutory form of mortgage and states that the mortgagor will not remove or demolish any building without the consent of the mortgagee. This clause is necessary because the amount generally loaned is based on an appraisal that includes both land and buildings. One case involving this clause arose when a mortgage was given on a farm. The mortgagor, anticipating that default on the mortgage was possible and having heard that real property consisted of land and things that were attached to the land, built all of the outbuildings on skids. After the mortgagor defaulted on the mortgage, the buildings on the skids were hauled off the land. The court held that despite the fact that the buildings were not physically attached to the land, they were still under the terms of the mortgage. Thus, the mortgagee was entitled to foreclosure on those buildings.

Covenant to Pay Taxes. The **covenant to pay taxes** is a promise by the mortgagor that all taxes and assessments that might be levied against the property will be paid. There is generally an acceleration clause with this covenant stating that if the taxes or assessments are not paid after a certain time elapses, the mortgagee, at mortgagee's option, may declare the entire amount of principal and interest due. This clause, in effect, gives the mortgagee the right to foreclose after a stated period if the taxes or assessments are not paid.

Acceleration Clause. The mortgage form contains an **acceleration clause.** This clause specifies that, if the mortgagor fails to keep the covenants or has a defective title, the entire debt will become due and collectible at the option of the mortgagee.

Warrant of Title. Most statutory forms of mortgage contain a **warrant of title** clause stating that the mortgagor warrants title to the premises, which means, in effect, that the mortgagor guarantees the title to the property.

Special Clauses

In addition to the general clauses, there are many other clauses that can be and are inserted in the mortgage agreement to cover special situations. The most common ones are discussed in the following paragraphs.

Covenant to Pay Attorney's Fees. In some states, the mortgagor promises under the terms of the mortgage to pay reasonable attorney's fees together with costs and disbursements if the mortgagee finds it necessary to foreclose. Some states do not require a **covenant to pay attorney's fees** inasmuch as the mortgagee may demand reasonable fees in the event of foreclosure without the statement being included in the instrument.

Receiver Clause. The **receiver clause** states that in any action to foreclose a mortgage the holder of the mortgage shall be entitled to the appointment of a receiver. The **receiver** is one who will collect any rents and profits from the property and maintain the property. This clause is intended to protect the mortgagee during the interval between the commencement of the foreclosure action and the final court order. If the receiver, after having satisfied the mortgagee's claim, has a net balance, the mortgagor is credited with that balance.

This clause is especially important when the sale concerns a parcel of real property on which there is a business. For example, suppose *A* sells *B* real property on which there is a shoe store. *B* is really purchasing three things: the land and building, the stock in the store, and the goodwill of the store, which is often regarded by business people as having the greatest value. The **goodwill,** or the reputation a business enjoys, is referred to by business people as "the key." Suppose *A* is going to finance the purchase in part by actually becoming the mortgagee for part of the purchase price. Commonly, it is said that *A* "takes back" a mortgage. When a person takes back a mortgage as part of the purchase price, the person is said to have a purchase money mortgage, as will be discussed in Chapter 13.

Assume *B* defaults on the payments. *A* has security for the value of the land in the land itself and has probably been paid for the stock, but what about the goodwill or key? This may have given the sale its greatest value. Between the time of default and the time of termination of foreclosure action, *B* might operate the business in such a way as to destroy the value of the goodwill.

With a receiver clause in the mortgage, *A* can readily have a receiver appointed who will run the business in a satisfactory manner and thus preserve the value of the goodwill.

Estoppel Clause. The **estoppel clause** states that on the request of the mortgagee (lender), the mortgagor (borrower) will furnish a written statement "duly acknowledged of the amount due on this mortgage and whether any offsets or defenses exist against the mortgage debt." In some states this is known as a *certificate of no defense.*

Although it might appear strange for the mortgagee to make a request of the mortgagor of how much the mortgagor owes on the mortgage, the inclusion of this is extremely important to the mortgagee in the event the mortgagee desires to sell the mortgage. If the mortgagee decides to sell the mortgage to raise capital for a further investment, when the mortgagee approaches a third party to sell the mortgage, the third party will want to know the current value of the mortgage. The third party can demand to see the mortgage, but this will not tell the current value because part of the face value may have been paid. If the mortgage contains an estoppel clause, the mortgagee can demand an estoppel certificate from the mortgagor indicating the unpaid balance of the mortgage. In addition, the mortgagor will certify that there are no defenses to date in the event of a foreclosure action. After having certified that there are no defenses to a foreclosure, the mortgagor cannot later assert in court that mortgagor had a defense as of that time. Technically, mortgagor is said to be "estopped."

Good Repair Clause. The **good repair clause** states that if the mortgagor does not keep the premises in "reasonably good repair" or if the owner fails to comply with the requirements of any governmental department within three months, then the mortgagee, at mortgagee's option, may foreclose. The test of what is reasonably good repair is that the mortgagee is entitled to foreclose if mortgagee's security is being impaired.

The inclusion of this clause resulted from the condemnation of buildings by municipalities as being unfit for human habitation. For example, *A* is the mortgagee on an apartment building and *B* the owner and mortgagor. *B* has tenants in the building and allows the building to deteriorate to such a state of disrepair that the municipality feels it necessary to take action by condemning the property as unfit for human habitation. *B* then abandons the building, leaving *A* with a worthless, in the sense of untenantable, building. With a good repair clause inserted in the mortgage, *A* could foreclose on the mortgage prior to the time that the municipality takes action and thus protect the security for the debt.

Sale in One Parcel Clause. The **sale in one parcel clause** is generally written as follows: "In case of a sale, said premises, or as much thereof as may be affected by this mortgage, may be sold in one parcel." This clause is applicable when more than one lot is covered by the terms of the mortgage. In the event of a foreclosure, the mortgagee must offer the lots for sale one at a time until the amount due under the mortgage is paid. If the mortgagor has sold any of the lots "subject to the mortgage," the mortgagee must sell those lots in inverse order of their sale. In short, mortgagee must sell those still owned by the mortgagor and then sell those that the mortgagor has already sold, but in inverse order of their sale, last ones first. After they are sold, if this does not bring in enough money, they may be sold in bulk. The sale of the individual lots is tentative until it is ascertained that they have brought sufficient funds to cover the debt.

Owner Rent Clause. The **owner rent clause** creates a landlord-tenant relationship between the mortgagee and the mortgagor in the event of a foreclosure. By means of this clause, the owner agrees to pay a reasonable rent for the premises during the time in which owner is in possession of the building after the commencement of the foreclosure action. In some states, even if a receiver under the terms of the mortgage has been appointed, the receiver cannot collect any money except that due on property contracts that the owner had. The owner rent clause enables the receiver to collect rent from the owner of the property.

Trust Clause. A **trust clause** is inserted in the deed in some states. In New York State, for example, this clause states:

> The mortgagor will, in compliance with Section 13 of the Lien law, receive the advances secured hereby and will receive the right to such advances as a trust fund to be applied first for the purpose of paying the cost of the improvement and will apply the same, first to the payment of the cost of the improvement before using any part of the total of the same for any other purpose.

The purpose of the trust clause is to prevent the owner from improving the property before applying for a loan and not paying the cost of the improvement. If an owner, for example, hires a painter to paint the house and then obtains a loan without paying the painter, the painter may file a mechanic's lien against the property. A *mechanic's lien* is a species of lien or charge created by statute that exists in favor of persons who have performed work or furnished materials in the erection or repair of a building.

The placing of the lien on the property will involve the mortgagee in legal action. When this clause is included in a mortgage, it puts the burden on the mortgagor to pay for these improvements. If mortgagor does not pay, mortgagor has breached what amounts to a trust agreement for the benefit of those persons who have improved the property, and the mortgagor will, in case of breaching the agreement, become liable under the penal code.

Prepayment Clause. The **prepayment clause** is inserted in the mortgage at the request of the mortgagor. It generally states that the mortgagor may pay the entire or stated amounts on the mortgage principal at any time mortgagor chooses prior to the due date. The mortgagor could not do this without the insertion of the prepayment clause. Some of the prepayment clauses call for the payment of a penalty by the mortgagor for the privilege of prepayment. This penalty may be inserted in the prepayment clause by stating that the entire amount due on the mortgage may be paid on 90 days' written notice to the mortgagee and on "the payment of two months' interest." The two months' interest then is the penalty, which is in addition to the interest paid between the time of giving of notice and the prepayment. If a bank is the mortgagee, this penalty helps defray some of the bank's costs of making the mortgage.

With FHA loans, there are no prepayment penalties to borrowers who pay off their loans before the first ten years of the amortization period have passed. Under VA loans, no prepayment charges are imposed.

JUNIOR MORTGAGE

A **junior mortgage** is a mortgage that is subordinate to any other mortgage of record. This type of mortgage is drawn in the same manner as a first mortgage, with the exception that it should contain the following two additional appropriate clauses.

Default in Prior Mortgage Clause

The **default in prior mortgage clause** states that if the mortgagor defaults in the payment of interest on a prior mortgage, the junior mortgagee may pay the amount, add it to the loan, and immediately institute a foreclosure action.

Subordination clause

The **subordination clause** states that in the event a prior mortgage is removed, the junior mortgage will not automatically become a first mortgage but will be content to remain in a junior position in case the mortgagor seeks a new mortgage. The clause states also that if the mortgagee receives a new mortgage in a greater amount than is on the premises at the time of execution of the instrument, the excess over the present mortgage will be paid to reduce the principal of the junior mortgage.

THE DEED OF TRUST

There are a number of states that use a **deed of trust,** a trust deed, or a trust indenture, as it is sometimes called, in the nature of a mortgage.[5] In many of these states the lender is given a choice of using either a mortgage or a deed of trust as the security for a real property loan.

In the ordinary mortgage transaction, as was shown above, there are usually only two parties, the mortgagor and the mortgagee. In the deed of trust, however, there are three parties to the transaction. The borrower executes the deed of trust, which conveys the property to a third person known as the **trustee** who receives from the conveyance sufficient title to carry out the trust. This trustee holds for the benefit of the owner of the note executed by the borrower at the time of the transaction. The note is the evidence of the debt. If the borrower defaults, the property is either transferred to the lender, after proper legal proceedings have been completed, or disposed of at a public sale at which the trustee transfers title to the purchaser.

Depending upon state law, the trustee is either a *private trustee* whose only qualification is contractual capacity, or the trustee is a public trustee. Generally speaking, the *public trustee* is either the county clerk or an individual appointed by the governor of the state; in some states, title companies or attorneys can act as trustee. The public trustee in these states is bonded and handles all of the trust deeds recorded in the particular county.

The deed of trust is also used as security for some corporate bond issues. A corporation, for example, will sell bonds and at the same time deliver a deed of trust to a third person as security for the payment of the money due on the bonds. If the corporation defaults on its payments, the trustee, after proper legal proceedings, will sell the property and pay the proceeds to the bondholders up to the extent of the indebtedness.

Action on Payment of the Indebtedness

Depending on the laws of a particular state, one of two things happens on the payment of the indebtedness under the terms of the trust deed. In one case, it is done by means of an instrument called a **reconveyance** that releases the security (the land and improvements) from the trust. There are two types of reconveyance. One is a *full reconveyance,* which is made by the trustee and evidences satisfaction in full and release of the security. Second, there is a *partial reconveyance,* which is made by the trustee and

---

[5]Alabama, Alaska, California, Colorado, Delaware, Illinois, Mississippi, Missouri, Nevada, New Mexico, Oregon, Tennessee, Texas, Utah, Virginia, and West Virginia and the District of Columbia. The Small Tract Financing Act (Sec. 52-401 et seq. Revised Code of Montana) provides for a deed of trust, but "only for parcels not exceeding three (3) acres." In Idaho, the deed of trust can be used on parcels of 20 acres or less.

evidences satisfaction in part and the release of a portion of the security.[6] Both full and partial reconveyances must describe the deed of trust accurately and in detail, and a partial reconveyance must contain the legal description of the security being released.

Another way the deed of trust is handled on payment of the indebtedness is as follows. The beneficiary under the trust deed signs an instrument known as a *Request for Release of Deed of Trust,* which is presented either to the private, or in most cases, to the public, trustee together with the canceled note and the deed of trust. The trustee then signs a Release of Deed of Trust and it is then recorded in the office of the county clerk or recorder of the county in which the property is located. As in the case of the mortgage, the release may be complete or partial.

Standard Deed of Trust

Like the standard mortgage, the FNMA/FHLMC deed of trust has been standardized. Again, in every state using the deed of trust, the first 17 clauses are *exactly* alike. Any variations among the states and the District of Columbia begin with clause 18.

The standardized form is shown in Exhibit 9-3.

MORTGAGE FORECLOSURE

In the event of default in the payment of principal, interest, or a breach of any of the covenants of the mortgage, the mortgagee may foreclose on the mortgage. A **mortgage foreclosure** means that the mortgagee may institute proceedings to force a sale of the mortgaged property.

Title Search

One of the first things the mortgagee does in pursuing a foreclosure action is to have a title search or an abstract of title prepared. The **abstract of title** is a brief history of the particular property with which the action is concerned. The reason for having the abstract prepared is that presumably the mortgagee has the first lien on the property; second, it is necessary to bring in all other parties in interest, who generally are lienors junior to mortgagee's lien. There may be good possibility of the action cutting off the rights of the other lienors, and, consequently, they should have notice of the action. In the event any surplus monies result from a foreclosure sale, the junior lienors then have the requisite notice to commence a surplus money proceeding in order to establish their rights to whatever surplus monies exist.

[6]Some states, Tennessee and Maryland, for example, use a "marginal release." A marginal entry is made on the record in the office where the mortgage is recorded, or a release of mortgage is written on the original and then filed in the office where the mortgage is recorded (cf. Maryland Code, Art. 21, Secs. 38–44).

Exhibit 9-3 Deed of Trust

DEED OF TRUST

THIS DEED OF TRUST is made this........18th..................day of...June........................, 19--.., among the Grantor, Marvin J. Miller and Cynthia Miller.. (herein "Borrower"), the Public Trustee of ....Denver..County (herein "Trustee"), and the Beneficiary, MIDLAND FEDERAL SAVINGS AND LOAN ASSOCIATION, whose address is 444 17th Street, Denver, Colorado 80202 (herein "Lender").

BORROWER, in consideration of the indebtedness herein recited and the trust herein created, irrevocably grants and conveys to Trustee, in trust, with power of sale, the following described property located in the County of ....Denver.................................., State of Colorado:

Lot 6, Block 8, of the Map of Security Acres Subdivision recorded in the office of the Recorder of the County of Denver, May 1, 1953.

which has the address of..318 Stout Street............................, ...Denver............
[Street] [City]

Colorado 80208 ....(herein "Property Address");
[State and Zip Code]

TOGETHER with all the improvements now or hereafter erected on the property, and all easements, rights, appurtenances, rents (subject however to the rights and authorities given herein to Lender to collect and apply such rents), royalties, mineral, oil and gas rights and profits, water, water rights, and water stock, and all fixtures now or hereafter attached to the property, all of which, including replacements and additions thereto, shall be deemed to be and remain a part of the property covered by this Deed of Trust; and all of the foregoing, together with said property (or the leasehold estate if this Deed of Trust is on a leasehold) are herein referred to as the "Property";

TO SECURE to Lender (a) the repayment of the indebtedness evidenced by Borrower's note dated. June 18, ..19--....................(herein "Note"), in the principal sum of. Forty-Two Thousand Five Hundred and 00/100 ($42,500.00)-------------- Dollars, with interest thereon, providing for monthly installments of principal and interest, with the balance of the indebtedness, if not sooner paid, due and payable on ....July 5, 20--..........................; the payment of all other sums, with interest thereon, advanced in accordance herewith to protect the security of this Deed of Trust; and the performance of the covenants and agreements of Borrower herein contained; and (b) the repayment of any future advances, with interest thereon, made to Borrower by Lender pursuant to paragraph 21 hereof (herein "Future Advances").

Borrower covenants that Borrower is lawfully seised of the estate hereby conveyed and has the right to grant and convey the Property, that the Property is unencumbered, and that Borrower will warrant and defend generally the title to the Property against all claims and demands, subject to any declarations, easements or restrictions listed in a schedule of exceptions to coverage in any title insurance policy insuring Lender's interest in the Property.

COLORADO—1 to 4 Family—6/75—**FNMA/FHLMC UNIFORM INSTRUMENT**

M-504 L

Exhibit 9-3 (continued)

UNIFORM COVENANTS. Borrower and Lender covenant and agree as follows:

1. Payment of Principal and Interest. Borrower shall promptly pay when due the principal of and interest on the indebtedness evidenced by the Note, prepayment and late charges as provided in the Note, and the principal of and interest on any Future Advances secured by this Deed of Trust.

2. Funds for Taxes and Insurance. Subject to applicable law or to a written waiver by Lender, Borrower shall pay to Lender on the day monthly installments of principal and interest are payable under the Note, until the Note is paid in full, a sum (herein "Funds") equal to one-twelfth of the yearly taxes and assessments which may attain priority over this Deed of Trust, and ground rents on the Property, if any, plus one-twelfth of yearly premium installments for hazard insurance, plus one-twelfth of yearly premium installments for mortgage insurance, if any, all as reasonably estimated initially and from time to time by Lender on the basis of assessments and bills and reasonable estimates thereof.

The Funds shall be held in an institution the deposits or accounts of which are insured or guaranteed by a Federal or state agency (including Lender if Lender is such an institution). Lender shall apply the Funds to pay said taxes, assessments, insurance premiums and ground rents. Lender may not charge for so holding and applying the Funds, analyzing said account or verifying and compiling said assessments and bills, unless Lender pays Borrower interest on the Funds and applicable law permits Lender to make such a charge. Borrower and Lender may agree in writing at the time of execution of this Deed of Trust that interest on the Funds shall be paid to Borrower, and unless such agreement is made or applicable law requires such interest to be paid, Lender shall not be required to pay Borrower any interest or earnings on the Funds. Lender shall give to Borrower, without charge, an annual accounting of the Funds showing credits and debits to the Funds and the purpose for which each debit to the Funds was made. The Funds are pledged as additional security for the sums secured by this Deed of Trust.

If the amount of the Funds held by Lender, together with the future monthly installments of Funds payable prior to the due dates of taxes, assessments, insurance premiums and ground rents, shall exceed the amount required to pay said taxes, assessments, insurance premiums and ground rents as they fall due, such excess shall be, at Borrower's option, either promptly repaid to Borrower or credited to Borrower on monthly installments of Funds. If the amount of the Funds held by Lender shall not be sufficient to pay taxes, assessments, insurance premiums and ground rents as they fall due, Borrower shall pay to Lender any amount necessary to make up the deficiency within 30 days from the date notice is mailed by Lender to Borrower requesting payment thereof.

Upon payment in full of all sums secured by this Deed of Trust, Lender shall promptly refund to Borrower any Funds held by Lender. If under paragraph 18 hereof the Property is sold or the Property is otherwise acquired by Lender, Lender shall apply, no later than immediately prior to the sale of the Property or its acquisition by Lender, any Funds held by Lender at the time of application as a credit against the sums secured by this Deed of Trust.

3. Application of Payments. Unless applicable law provides otherwise, all payments received by Lender under the Note and paragraphs 1 and 2 hereof shall be applied by Lender first in payment of amounts payable to Lender by Borrower under paragraph 2 hereof, then to interest payable on the Note, then to the principal of the Note, and then to interest and principal on any Future Advances.

4. Charges; Liens. Borrower shall pay all taxes, assessments and other charges, fines and impositions attributable to the Property which may attain a priority over this Deed of Trust, and leasehold payments or ground rents, if any, in the manner provided under paragraph 2 hereof or, if not paid in such manner, by Borrower making payment, when due, directly to the payee thereof. Borrower shall promptly furnish to Lender all notices of amounts due under this paragraph, and in the event Borrower shall make payment directly, Borrower shall promptly furnish to Lender receipts evidencing such payments. Borrower shall promptly discharge any lien which has priority over this Deed of Trust; provided, that Borrower shall not be required to discharge any such lien so long as Borrower shall agree in writing to the payment of the obligation secured by such lien in a manner acceptable to Lender, or shall in good faith contest such lien by, or defend enforcement of such lien in, legal proceedings which operate to prevent the enforcement of the lien or forfeiture of the Property or any part thereof.

5. Hazard Insurance. Borrower shall keep the improvements now existing or hereafter erected on the Property insured against loss by fire, hazards included within the term "extended coverage", and such other hazards as Lender may require and in such amounts and for such periods as Lender may require; provided, that Lender shall not require that the amount of such coverage exceed that amount of coverage required to pay the sums secured by this Deed of Trust.

The insurance carrier providing the insurance shall be chosen by Borrower subject to approval by Lender; provided, that such approval shall not be unreasonably withheld. All premiums on insurance policies shall be paid in the manner provided under paragraph 2 hereof or, if not paid in such manner, by Borrower making payment, when due, directly to the insurance carrier.

All insurance policies and renewals thereof shall be in form acceptable to Lender and shall include a standard mortgage clause in favor of and in form acceptable to Lender. Lender shall have the right to hold the policies and renewals thereof, and Borrower shall promptly furnish to Lender all renewal notices and all receipts of paid premiums. In the event of loss, Borrower shall give prompt notice to the insurance carrier and Lender. Lender may make proof of loss if not made promptly by Borrower.

Unless Lender and Borrower otherwise agree in writing, insurance proceeds shall be applied to restoration or repair of the Property damaged, provided such restoration or repair is economically feasible and the security of this Deed of Trust is not thereby impaired. If such restoration or repair is not economically feasible or if the security of this Deed of Trust would be impaired, the insurance proceeds shall be applied to the sums secured by this Deed of Trust, with the excess, if any, paid to Borrower. If the Property is abandoned by Borrower, or if Borrower fails to respond to Lender within 30 days from the date notice is mailed by Lender to Borrower that the insurance carrier offers to settle a claim for insurance benefits, Lender is authorized to collect and apply the insurance proceeds at Lender's option either to restoration or repair of the Property or to the sums secured by this Deed of Trust.

Unless Lender and Borrower otherwise agree in writing, any such application of proceeds to principal shall not extend or postpone the due date of the monthly installments referred to in paragraphs 1 and 2 hereof or change the amount of such installments. If under paragraph 18 hereof the Property is acquired by Lender, all right, title and interest of Borrower in and to any insurance policies and in and to the proceeds thereof resulting from damage to the Property prior to the sale or acquisition shall pass to Lender to the extent of the sums secured by this Deed of Trust immediately prior to such sale or acquisition.

6. Preservation and Maintenance of Property; Leaseholds; Condominiums; Planned Unit Developments. Borrower shall keep the Property in good repair and shall not commit waste or permit impairment or deterioration of the Property and shall comply with the provisions of any lease if this Deed of Trust is on a leasehold. If this Deed of Trust is on a unit in a condominium or a planned unit development, Borrower shall perform all of Borrower's obligations under the declaration or covenants creating or governing the condominium or planned unit development, the by-laws and regulations of the condominium or planned unit development, and constituent documents. If a condominium or planned unit development rider is executed by Borrower and recorded together with this Deed of Trust, the covenants and agreements of such rider shall be incorporated into and shall amend and supplement the covenants and agreements of this Deed of Trust as if the rider were a part hereof.

7. Protection of Lender's Security. If Borrower fails to perform the covenants and agreements contained in this Deed of Trust, or if any action or proceeding is commenced which materially affects Lender's interest in the Property, including, but not limited to, eminent domain, insolvency, code enforcement, or arrangements or proceedings involving a bankrupt or decedent, then Lender at Lender's option, upon notice to Borrower, may make such appearances, disburse such sums and take such action as is necessary to protect Lender's interest, including, but not limited to, disbursement of reasonable attorney's fees and entry upon the Property to make repairs. If Lender required mortgage insurance as a condition of making the loan secured by this Deed of Trust, Borrower shall pay the premiums required to maintain such insurance in effect until such time as the requirement for such insurance terminates in accordance with Borrower's and

Exhibit 9-3 (continued)

Lender's written agreement or applicable law. Borrower shall pay the amount of all mortgage insurance premiums in the manner provided under paragraph 2 hereof.

Any amounts disbursed by Lender pursuant to this paragraph 7, with interest thereon, shall become additional indebtedness of Borrower secured by this Deed of Trust. Unless Borrower and Lender agree to other terms of payment, such amounts shall be payable upon notice from Lender to Borrower requesting payment thereof, and shall bear interest from the date of disbursement at the rate payable from time to time on outstanding principal under the Note unless payment of interest at such rate would be contrary to applicable law, in which event such amounts shall bear interest at the highest rate permissible under applicable law. Nothing contained in this paragraph 7 shall require Lender to incur any expense or take any action hereunder.

8. Inspection. Lender may make or cause to be made reasonable entries upon and inspections of the Property, provided that Lender shall give Borrower notice prior to any such inspection specifying reasonable cause therefor related to Lender's interest in the Property.

9. Condemnation. The proceeds of any award or claim for damages, direct or consequential, in connection with any condemnation or other taking of the Property, or part thereof, or for conveyance in lieu of condemnation, are hereby assigned and shall be paid to Lender.

In the event of a total taking of the Property, the proceeds shall be applied to the sums secured by this Deed of Trust, with the excess, if any, paid to Borrower. In the event of a partial taking of the Property, unless Borrower and Lender otherwise agree in writing, there shall be applied to the sums secured by this Deed of Trust such proportion of the proceeds as is equal to that proportion which the amount of the sums secured by this Deed of Trust immediately prior to the date of taking bears to the fair market value of the Property immediately prior to the date of taking, with the balance of the proceeds paid to Borrower.

If the Property is abandoned by Borrower, or if, after notice by Lender to Borrower that the condemnor offers to make an award or settle a claim for damages, Borrower fails to respond to Lender within 30 days after the date such notice is mailed, Lender is authorized to collect and apply the proceeds, at Lender's option, either to restoration or repair of the Property or to the sums secured by this Deed of Trust.

Unless Lender and Borrower otherwise agree in writing, any such application of proceeds to principal shall not extend or postpone the due date of the monthly installments referred to in paragraphs 1 and 2 hereof or change the amount of such installments.

10. Borrower Not Released. Extension of the time for payment or modification of amortization of the sums secured by this Deed of Trust granted by Lender to any successor in interest of Borrower shall not operate to release, in any manner, the liability of the original Borrower and Borrower's successors in interest. Lender shall not be required to commence proceedings against such successor or refuse to extend time for payment or otherwise modify amortization of the sums secured by this Deed of Trust by reason of any demand made by the original Borrower and Borrower's successors in interest.

11. Forbearance by Lender Not a Waiver. Any forbearance by Lender in exercising any right or remedy hereunder, or otherwise afforded by applicable law, shall not be a waiver of or preclude the exercise of any such right or remedy. The procurement of insurance or the payment of taxes or other liens or charges by Lender shall not be a waiver of Lender's right to accelerate the maturity of the indebtedness secured by this Deed of Trust.

12. Remedies Cumulative. All remedies provided in this Deed of Trust are distinct and cumulative to any other right or remedy under this Deed of Trust or afforded by law or equity, and may be exercised concurrently, independently or successively.

13. Successors and Assigns Bound; Joint and Several Liability; Captions. The covenants and agreements herein contained shall bind, and the rights hereunder shall inure to, the respective successors and assigns of Lender and Borrower, subject to the provisions of paragraph 17 hereof. All covenants and agreements of Borrower shall be joint and several. The captions and headings of the paragraphs of this Deed of Trust are for convenience only and are not to be used to interpret or define the provisions hereof.

14. Notice. Except for any notice required under applicable law to be given in another manner, (a) any notice to Borrower provided for in this Deed of Trust shall be given by mailing such notice by certified mail addressed to Borrower at the Property Address or at such other address as Borrower may designate by notice to Lender as provided herein, and (b) any notice to Lender shall be given by certified mail, return receipt requested, to Lender's address stated herein or to such other address as Lender may designate by notice to Borrower as provided herein. Any notice provided for in this Deed of Trust shall be deemed to have been given to Borrower or Lender when given in the manner designated herein.

15. Uniform Deed of Trust; Governing Law; Severability. This form of deed of trust combines uniform covenants for national use and non-uniform covenants with limited variations by jurisdiction to constitute a uniform security instrument covering real property. This Deed of Trust shall be governed by the law of the jurisdiction in which the Property is located. In the event that any provision or clause of this Deed of Trust or the Note conflicts with applicable law, such conflict shall not affect other provisions of this Deed of Trust or the Note which can be given effect without the conflicting provision, and to this end the provisions of the Deed of Trust and the Note are declared to be severable.

16. Borrower's Copy. Borrower shall be furnished a conformed copy of the Note and of this Deed of Trust at the time of execution or after recordation hereof.

17. Transfer of the Property; Assumption. If all or any part of the Property or an interest therein is sold or transferred by Borrower without Lender's prior written consent, excluding (a) the creation of a lien or encumbrance subordinate to this Deed of Trust, (b) the creation of a purchase money security interest for household appliances, (c) a transfer by devise, descent or by operation of law upon the death of a joint tenant or (d) the grant of any leasehold interest of three years or less not containing an option to purchase, Lender may, at Lender's option, declare all the sums secured by this Deed of Trust to be immediately due and payable. Lender shall have waived such option to accelerate if, prior to the sale or transfer, Lender and the person to whom the Property is to be sold or transferred reach agreement in writing that the credit of such person is satisfactory to Lender and that the interest payable on the sums secured by this Deed of Trust shall be at such rate as Lender shall request. If Lender has waived the option to accelerate provided in this paragraph 17, and if Borrower's successor in interest has executed a written assumption agreement accepted in writing by Lender, Lender shall release Borrower from all obligations under this Deed of Trust and the Note.

If Lender exercises such option to accelerate, Lender shall mail Borrower notice of acceleration in accordance with paragraph 14 hereof. Such notice shall provide a period of not less than 30 days from the date the notice is mailed within which Borrower may pay the sums declared due. If Borrower fails to pay such sums prior to the expiration of such period, Lender may, without further notice or demand on Borrower, invoke any remedies permitted by paragraph 18 hereof.

NON-UNIFORM COVENANTS. Borrower and Lender further covenant and agree as follows:

18. Acceleration; Remedies. Except as provided in paragraph 17 hereof, upon Borrower's breach of any covenant or agreement of Borrower in this Deed of Trust, including the covenants to pay when due any sums secured by this Deed of Trust, Lender prior to acceleration shall mail notice to Borrower as provided in paragraph 14 hereof specifying: (1) the breach; (2) the action required to cure such breach; (3) a date, not less than 30 days from the date the notice is mailed to Borrower, by which such breach must be cured; and (4) that failure to cure such breach on or before the date specified in the notice may result in acceleration of the sums secured by this Deed of Trust and sale of the Property. The notice shall further inform Borrower of the right to reinstate after acceleration and the right to assert in the foreclosure proceeding the non-existence of a default or any other defense of Borrower to acceleration and sale. If the breach is not cured on or before the date specified in the notice, Lender at Lender's option may declare all of the sums secured by this Deed of Trust to be immediately due and payable without further demand and may invoke the power of sale and any other remedies permitted by applicable law. Lender shall be entitled to collect all reasonable costs and expenses incurred in pursuing the remedies provided in this paragraph 18, including, but not limited to, reasonable attorney's fees.

■ Exhibit 9-3 (concluded)

If Lender invokes the power of sale, Lender shall give written notice to Trustee of the occurrence of an event of default and of Lender's election to cause the Property to be sold. Lender shall mail a copy of such notice to Borrower as provided in paragraph 14 hereof. Trustee shall record a copy of such notice in the county in which the Property is located. Trustee shall publish a notice of sale for the time and in the manner provided by applicable law and shall mail copies of such notice of sale in the manner prescribed by applicable law to Borrower and to the other persons prescribed by applicable law. After the lapse of such time as may be required by applicable law, Trustee, without demand on Borrower, shall sell the Property at public auction to the highest bidder for cash at the time and place and under the terms designated in the notice of sale in one or more parcels and in such order as Trustee may determine. Trustee may postpone sale of all or any parcel of the Property by public announcement at the time and place of any previously scheduled sale. Lender or Lender's designee may purchase the Property at any sale.

Trustee shall deliver to the purchaser Trustee's certificate describing the Property and the time when the purchaser will be entitled to Trustee's deed thereto. The recitals in Trustee's deed shall be prima facie evidence of the truth of the statements made therein. Trustee shall apply the proceeds of the sale in the following order: (a) to all reasonable costs and expenses of the sale, including, but not limited to, reasonable Trustee's and attorney's fees and costs of title evidence; (b) to all sums secured by this Deed of Trust; and (c) the excess, if any, to the person or persons legally entitled thereto.

19. Borrower's Right to Reinstate. Notwithstanding Lender's acceleration of the sums secured by this Deed of Trust, Borrower shall have the right to have any proceedings begun by Lender to enforce this Deed of Trust discontinued at any time prior to the earlier to occur of (i) the fifth day before sale of the Property pursuant to the power of sale contained in this Deed of Trust or (ii) entry of a judgment enforcing this Deed of Trust if: (a) Borrower pays Lender all sums which would be then due under this Deed of Trust, the Note and notes securing Future Advances, if any, had no acceleration occurred; (b) Borrower cures all breaches of any other covenants or agreements of Borrower contained in this Deed of Trust; (c) Borrower pays all reasonable expenses incurred by Lender and Trustee in enforcing the covenants and agreements of Borrower contained in this Deed of Trust and in enforcing Lender's and Trustee's remedies as provided in paragraph 18 hereof, including, but not limited to, reasonable attorney's fees and Trustee's expenses and withdrawal fee; and (d) Borrower takes such action as Lender may reasonably require to assure that the lien of this Deed of Trust, Lender's interest in the Property and Borrower's obligation to pay the sums secured by this Deed of Trust shall continue unimpaired. Upon such payment and cure by Borrower, this Deed of Trust and the obligations secured hereby shall remain in full force and effect as if no acceleration had occurred.

20. Assignment of Rents; Appointment of Receiver; Lender in Possession. As additional security hereunder, Borrower hereby assigns to Lender the rents of the Property, provided that Borrower shall, prior to acceleration under paragraph 18 hereof or abandonment of the Property, have the right to collect and retain such rents as they become due and payable.

Upon acceleration under paragraph 18 hereof or abandonment of the Property, Lender, in person, by agent or by judicially appointed receiver, shall be entitled to enter upon, take possession of and manage the Property and to collect the rents of the Property including those past due. All rents collected by Lender or the receiver shall be applied first to payment of the costs of management of the Property and collection of rents, including, but not limited to, receiver's fees, premiums on receiver's bonds and reasonable attorney's fees, and then to the sums secured by this Deed of Trust. Lender and the receiver shall be liable to account only for those rents actually received.

21. Future Advances. Upon request of Borrower, Lender, at Lender's option prior to release of this Deed of Trust, may make Future Advances to Borrower. Such Future Advances, with interest thereon, shall be secured by this Deed of Trust when evidenced by promissory notes stating that said notes are secured hereby.

22. Release. Upon payment of all sums secured by this Deed of Trust, Lender shall request Trustee to release this Deed of Trust and shall produce for Trustee duly cancelled all notes evidencing indebtedness secured by this Deed of Trust. Trustee shall release this Deed of Trust without further inquiry or liability. Borrower shall pay all costs of recordation, if any, and shall pay the statutory Trustee's fees.

23. Waiver of Homestead. Borrower hereby waives all right of homestead exemption in the Property.

IN WITNESS WHEREOF, Borrower has executed this Deed of Trust.

/s/ Marvin J. Miller
—Borrower

/s/ Cynthia Miller
—Borrower

[Acknowledgment]

Commencing the Action

The summons and the complaint begin the foreclosure action.[7] A copy of the summons and a copy of the complaint are served on the mortgagor and

[7]In Arizona, California, Florida, Idaho, Illinois, Iowa, Kansas, Montana, New Jersey, New Mexico, North Dakota, Oklahoma, and Oregon, a foreclosure suit is the only method of foreclosure on a mortgage.

on any of the lienors that were determined from the title search. If the mortgagor has a defense against the foreclosure action, the complaint is answered, raising an issue that is triable by jury. In some states a "master in chancery" hears the matter without a jury. In the event the mortgagor defaults, then the foreclosure proceeds to its conclusion. At the time of the filing of the summons and the complaint, a *lis pendens* (notice of pendency of action) is filed with the clerk of the county in which the property is located. The ***lis pendens*** is a warning to anyone concerned with or about to be concerned with the mortgaged property that there is an action pending on it. It is discussed further in Chapter 12.

Completing the Action

After the mortgagor defaults, the mortgagee is entitled to a judgment decree, which is obtained and filed with the court. This judgment directs that the property be sold at public auction, either by a referee appointed by the court or by the sheriff. Notice of the sale is given to all defendants, and it is published in such newspapers as the judge directs and is published for the number of times required by law. At the sale, bids are made on the property; but if the mortgagee does not think the bids are high enough, mortgagee may also bid on the property.

If there is a surplus of monies resulting from the sale, the other defendants in the foreclosure divide it according to the outcome of a surplus money action that establishes their priorities. If there is a deficiency, the mortgagee obtains a judgment for the deficiency on the note against the mortgagor and seeks to collect that amount. In some states, Oregon and California, for example, it is not possible to obtain a deficiency judgment on a purchase money mortgage. Deficiency judgments have been abolished in California, Maine, Nebraska, and North Dakota.

Most states have a statutory right of redemption, the right given mortgagors, judgment creditors, etc., to redeem the land from the foreclosure sale within a certain time by paying the foreclosure sale price.[8] The time limitation varies among the states from two months to two years after the sale.

Foreclosure is a long and involved proceeding. As a practical matter in order to avoid additional expenses, especially when the prices of real property are deflated, it may be more suitable for all concerned if the mortgagee seeks and obtains a quitclaim deed from the mortgagor.

OTHER REMEDIES OF THE MORTGAGE

Foreclosure by Advertisement

The **foreclosure by advertisement** is a rarely used means of foreclosing a mortgage. It is employed in some states, however. Under this procedure,

[8]In some states, Alabama, for example, the entire indebtedness must be paid.

upon the default of the mortgagor notice is given to the owner, public sale of the property is advertised, and the property is sold at such public sale. The purchaser at the public sale is not given possession of the property. To gain possession, purchaser may bring an action in ejectment, which is long and costly; therefore, the foreclosure by advertisement is seldom used.[9]

Foreclosure by Entry and Possession

In several states (Maine, Massachusetts, New Hampshire, and Rhode Island), the mortgagee may foreclose by taking peaceful possession of the mortgaged premises and by remaining in possession for a specified time. The entry is made in the presence of witnesses, and a certificate of that fact is filed. The mortgagor has a period in which to redeem the property. If mortgagor does not redeem, then the mortgagee receives good title to the premises.

Foreclosure by Writ of Entry

In some states (Maine, Massachusetts, and New Hampshire), a court proceeding is brought and a writ of entry issued stating the amount due on the mortgage and specifying a time in which the mortgagor has to redeem the property. If no redemption is made within this time, the mortgagee receives good title.

Foreclosure on Deed of Trust

If there is a default on a deed of trust, the trustee is officially notified of the default by the lender. The trustee then commences the action as outlined above. The property is advertised and the trustee conducts the sale. The owner has a period of redemption varying between 90 and 180 days.

Foreclosure and Bankruptcy

Under the Bankruptcy Act, there is an automatic stay of foreclosure proceeding or any action to obtain possession of the property on the borrower's filing of a bankruptcy petition. The stay, however, does not apply to an action by the Secretary of Housing and Urban Development to foreclose on an FHA-insured property or to a property consisting of five or more living units.

GLOSSARY

Abstract of title A condensed history of the title of land

Acceleration clause Entire mortgage debt becomes due and collectible

[9]Tennessee, North Dakota, and South Dakota do not require an action in ejectment.

Covenant against removal A clause in a mortgage stating that the mortgagor will not remove or demolish any building without the consent of the mortgagee

Covenant of insurance A clause in mortgage promising that the premises shall be covered by fire insurance in a stated amount for the benefit of the mortgagee and that the mortgagor will assign and deliver the policies to the mortgagee

Covenant to pay attorney's fees The mortgagor promises to pay reasonable attorney's fees under terms of the mortgage

Covenant to pay indebtedness A clause in a mortgage whereby a mortgagor promises to pay a debt

Covenant to pay taxes A promise by the mortgagor to pay the taxes and assessments that might be levied against the property

Deed of trust A deed absolute to secure the payment of a debt

Default in prior mortgage clause If mortgagor defaults in interest payments on a prior mortgage, junior mortgagee may pay amount due, add it to the loan, and immediately institute foreclosure

Estoppel clause A section of a mortgage stating that, upon the request of the mortgagee, the mortgagor will furnish a written statement, duly acknowledged, of the amount due on the mortgage and whether any offsets or defenses exist against the mortgage debt

Foreclosure A decree whereby the right to redeem property is cut off unless the debt is paid by the time named in the decree

Foreclosure by advertisement A rarely used means of foreclosing a mortgage in which a public sale is advertised and property is sold at a public sale

Good repair clause A statement that if the mortgagor does not keep the premises in "reasonably good repair" or if the owner fails to comply with the requirements of any governmental department within three months, then the mortgagee may foreclose

Goodwill The reputation a business enjoys

Intermediate theory of mortgages A system whereby title to the property remains with the borrower, but automatically passes to the lender on default

Junior mortgage A mortgage subordinate to any other mortgage of record

Lien theory of mortgages Concept wherein title remains with the mortgagor, and the mortgage that is placed on the property is a charge on the title

Lis pendens A notice of pendency of action

Mortgage The creation of an interest in property as security for the payment of a debt or the fulfillment of some obligation

Mortgage foreclosure If mortgagor defaults, the mortgagee may institute proceedings to force a sale of the mortgaged property

Mortgagee The party to whom the pledge of property is made

Mortgagor The party pledging the property

Owner rent clause A statement that creates a landlord-tenant relationship between mortgagee and mortgagor in event of foreclosure

Prepayment clause A statement that the mortgagor may pay the entire (or stated) amount(s) on the mortgage principal at any time the mortgagor chooses prior to the due date

Promissory note A written promise by one person to pay money to another

Receiver One who, in the event of a foreclosure, will collect any rents and profits from the property and will maintain the property

Receiver clause Clause in a mortgage stating that in any action to foreclose a mortgage, the holder of the mortgage shall be entitled to the appointment of a receiver

Reconveyance Upon the payment of the indebtedness, an instrument that releases the security (the land and improvements) from the trust

Sale in one parcel clause Clause in a mortgage stating that "in case of a sale, said premises, or as much thereof as may be affected by this mortgage, may be sold in one parcel"

Subordination clause A clause stating that in the event a prior mortgage is removed, the junior mortgage will not automatically become a first mortgage but will be content to remain in a junior position in case the mortgagor seeks a new mortgage

Title theory of mortgages A concept wherein, upon making the mortgage, the mortgagor passes title to the property, the subject of the mortgage, to the mortgagee, subject to a condition subsequent

Trust clause A clause in a mortgage used to prevent the owner from improving the property before applying for a loan, and not paying the cost of the improvement

Trustee A third party who receives from the deed of trust sufficient title to carry out the trust and holds for the benefit of the owner of the note or bond executed by the borrower at the time of the transaction

Warrant of title A clause wherein the mortgagor warrants or guarantees title to the premises

QUESTIONS FOR REVIEW

1. If *A*, as a mortgagor, makes a mortgage to *B* and one to *C* dated one year later on the same property and *C* records the mortgage first, which mortgage, in the absence of fraud, is valid? Why?
2. What is the difference between the lien theory, the title theory, and the intermediate theory of mortgages?
3. How and when is an estoppel certificate used?
4. What is a prepayment clause in a mortgage?
5. What are the advantages, if any, of a deed of trust over a mortgage?
6. How does a deed of trust differ from a mortgage? In what respects is it the same?
7. Why must a title search be made in a mortgage foreclosure?

PROBLEMS AND ACTIVITIES

1. *A* agrees to purchase Lot 6 of the map of Moore's Addition from *B* for $14,000 subject to a mortgage of $6,500 and interest to date. Draw a deed and insert the proper clause.
2. Martha Nolan, a mortgagor, signed a check to make a payment on her mortgage on which there was an unpaid balance of $31,000. Her bookkeeper put the check for the payment in an envelope, then promptly misplaced it. She had a ten-day grace period. One month and eight days after it was due, the holder of the mortgage notified her that the money had not been received and started foreclosure proceedings. Prior to the foreclosure, the mortgagor was never late on a single payment and furthermore had spent $300,000 on improvements on the property. If you were the presiding judge of this matter, how would you rule and why?
3. David Marks, a mortgagor, had paid down a mortgage to a balance of only $6,000. He contacted the mortgagee of record and said that he was ready to pay it off. Susan Stegman, the mortgagee of record, said she couldn't satisfy the mortgage because the note and the mortgage were in the possession of her brother. Marks then contacted Stegman's brother who said that he did have the mortgage papers, but that he had had a fight with his sister and that she became angry and refused to sign a satisfaction piece even though she was the mortgagee of record. He said he was sorry, but there was nothing he could do. The mortgage incidentally contained a prepayment clause. Can anything be done?

10

LEASES AND LEASING

KEY TERMS

Assignment of lease
Automatic renewal clause
Condemnation proceeding
Constructive eviction
Distraint
Estate for years
Eviction
Farm lease
Gross lease
Habitability statute or repair and deduct statute
Holdover tenant
Indexed lease
Lease
Lessee
Lessor
Net lease
Oil and gas lease
Option to purchase
Option to renew
Percentage lease
Recapture clause
Rent
Security deposit
Sewage tax
Subletting of lease
Surrender
Tenancy at sufferance
Tenancy at will
Tenancy from year to year or periodic tenancy
Water charges

A **lease** is a contract creating what is commonly known as a landlord-tenant relationship. The landlord is called the **lessor,** and the tenant, the **lessee.** The contract between the two parties conveys the right of possession of the leased premises to the tenant in return for which the tenant pays the landlord rent. **Rent** is the compensation, whether money, provisions, chattels, or labor, received by the owner of the soil or buildings from the occupant thereof.

In addition to the promise of the landlord agreeing to transfer possession, the agreement contains numerous other covenants defining and limiting the rights of the parties in the leased premises. These covenants are discussed later in this chapter.

A lease may be thought of primarily as a contract; as a general rule, the parties to a contract may agree to almost anything in a lease.[1] As in any other contract, however, they cannot agree to things against public policy.

[1]Actually, the lease is *both* a contract and a conveyance.

For example, two people enter into an apartment lease. The lease contains a clause stating that the landlord shall not be liable for negligence regarding that apartment. The landlord hires an incompetent painter who negligently paints the windows in such a manner that they stick. The tenant, in attempting to open the window, slips and pushes one hand through the pane and is seriously injured. The landlord is sued on the ground that the injury was caused by reason of the negligence of the landlord. The landlord in defense states that the tenant agreed in the lease to waive any claim of negligence against the landlord; and since the lease is a contract, it is binding on the parties. In a case such as this, the courts will hold that although it is true that a lease is a contract, it is against public policy to allow landlords to contract out of liability for their own negligence.

As in all contracts, a lease must be entered into by persons having contractual ability. There must be consideration, a delivery, and an acceptance. In addition, to validate a lease, there must be a description that locates the premises with reasonable certainty. A lease should contain the term or the duration of the lease and must also have a definite beginning and a certain ending. Study the following example. A written lease stating that the tenant's occupation was for the term of "one year, two years, three years" was sent to the landlord, who was to strike out all except one of the terms mentioned and execute the lease. The landlord, however, executed the lease without striking out any of its terms. The court held there was no meeting of the minds.[2]

A lease must also contain an agreement, technically called "an agreement to let and take," although the words *let and take* rarely appear in the lease. The lease will generally state that the lessor "grants, demises and lets unto the lessee." This is considered to be the agreement to let and take. These words give the tenant the right of possession, and also, in the event that someone appears later who has a better title to the premises than the landlord, give the tenant the right to proceed against the landlord for damages.

Finally, the lease must be executed in accordance with the statute. Some statutes state that the lease must be acknowledged, while others do not contain this provision. As a practical matter, it is a good procedure to have the lease acknowledged in order to enable the lease to be recorded, if the occasion arises.

STATUTE OF FRAUDS

The Statute of Frauds is designed to prevent the use of the law courts for the purpose of enforcing certain oral agreements or alleged oral agreements. It specifies which contracts must be in writing in order to be

[2]*Sayles v. Lienhardt,* 119 Misc. 851, 198 N.Y. Supp. 337.

enforced. The fourth section of the English statute on which the states base their statutes provides that "no action shall be brought unless the agreement upon such action shall be brought, or some memorandum or note thereof, shall be in writing, and signed by the party to be charged therewith, or some person thereunto by him lawfully authorized."

The Statute of Frauds enters the picture regarding leases much in the same manner as it does in other types of real property contracts. An owner may lease property for as long a period as is wished, but in many states only a lease for less than one year's duration may be oral. Under the Statute of Frauds, leases for over one year must be in writing and must contain the requisites described.

If the state law requires a lease to be in writing and the parties have failed to comply with this, or if the lease fails for any reason to meet the statutory requirements, then the lease cannot be enforced. If the lease cannot be enforced and the tenant has not yet gone into possession, the landlord may refuse such possession. If the tenant is already in possession under a lease that should have been written but was not, the lease may be terminated at any time by the landlord. On the other hand, the tenant may refuse to take possession, without any liability, under an enforceable lease. If possession has been taken, however, the tenant will be liable for "use and occupancy" during the period the tenant has occupancy of the premises.

RECORDING

Under some circumstances, depending on the term of the lease, the lease may be recorded. In New York, for example, a lease for more than three years may be recorded. This is not to imply that a lease must be recorded; it is merely better practice to record long-term leases. The recording gives notice to the world of the rights of the tenant in the property, although in many cases actual possession of the premises is sufficient to give such notice.

TENANCIES

It will be recalled that in Chapter 6 estates in land were classified as freehold estates (estates of indefinite duration) and estates of less than freehold (estates of definite duration). The tenancies with which we are now concerned may be considered as being estates of less than freehold.

Types of Tenancies

There are four kinds of tenancies or leasehold estates: (1) estate for years, (2) tenancy from year to year, or periodic tenancy, (3) tenancy at will, and (4) tenancy at sufferance.

Estate for Years. An **estate for years** conveys the land for a definite, stated period. It has a time of beginning and a certain end. This period is called the *term.* The estate may terminate before the time period by agreement of the parties, under conditions stated in the lease, by application of law,[3] or by merger.[4]

Tenancy From Year to Year. The **tenancy from year to year** or **periodic tenancy** is a tenancy that never exists for more than a year and is commonly from month to month. This lease may be either oral or written. It may be terminated by agreement of the parties at the end of any period and by giving proper notice to quit. In most states, notice to terminate the tenancy of less than a year requires a notice of equal length to the period of letting.

Tenancy at Will. A **tenancy at will** is a tenancy that may be terminated by either party at any time. It is distinguishable from the tenancy from month to month by the fact that the term is indefinite. In short, it may be terminated "at the will" of either party. The relationship between the landlord and tenant may be created here either expressly or by implication. Although under the common law no notice was necessary to terminate the landlord-tenant relationship, most states require that notice be given.

Problems arise when there are tenancies at will existing on farm properties. For example, a tenant at will on a farm plants a crop; the crop is about ready to be harvested, and the landlord attempts to terminate the tenancy. In these cases, the tenant has a right to go on the property to harvest the crops.

Tenancy at Sufferance. A **tenancy at sufferance** is the lowest estate known to law. It exists when a tenant rightfully in possession continues to occupy the property after the expiration of the term. The tenant holds the property merely at the sufferance of the landlord and under the common law is not entitled to notice to quit; however, by statute many states require that even the tenant by sufferance be given notice to quit.

Holding Over

When a tenant stays on at the expiration of the term of the lease, the tenant is said to be a **holdover tenant,** even though actually a tenant at sufferance. Tenants often "hold over" in either a month-to-month tenancy or a tenancy for years.

If no agreement is made extending the term of the lease, the landlord may bring dispossess proceedings against the tenant; that is, proceedings to oust the tenant from possession and to recover the reasonable value for the use and occupancy of the premises during the time the tenant held over. As an alternative, the landlord may elect to treat the tenancy as renewed for another term on the same terms and conditions as those of the original lease.

---

[3]For example, a lease calls for a property to be used as a furniture store and the lessee uses it for a garage.

[4]The fee simple is conveyed to the lessee.

Thus, when a year-to-year tenancy exists, if the tenant pays rent and the landlord accepts the rent, the tenancy generally continues for a period of another year. During this continuation period, both parties are bound as if a new lease had been drawn and signed.

When the original lease is for a period longer than a year, the holding over is limited to one year. For example, if a tenant holds over at the expiration of a three-year lease, the tenant may remain on the premises for the following year only; in some states, on a month-to-month basis.

LEASES

Long-Term Leases

Leases can range in duration from the tenancy at will to 99 or 999 years. Generally, long-term leases provide for erection of a new building by the lessee and the demolition of the structures on the leased premises at the time of the execution of the lease. Often, too, these long-term leases provide that the tenant shall pay taxes, assessments, and all operating expenses. This provision creates what is sometimes called a net lease.

Net Lease

The **net lease** is a lease in which the tenant pays the taxes, assessments, and all operating expenses in connection with the use of the premises. The landlord receives a net figure.

Most long-term leases are net leases. The net lease has become increasingly popular with owners of investment properties. Many owners do not want to sell the property, but wish to obtain a steady income from the property without incurring any of the headaches of supervising the premises. The owner may lease the property and receive a flat rental from the lessee. The lease will provide that the lessee pay all of the expenses of maintaining and managing the property. In a net lease, the lessee hopes to make a profit out of the rents received from the building.

Gross Lease

The **gross lease,** or sometimes known as the *absolute gross lease,* is a lease in which the premises are rented at a fixed rate. The tenant pays rent to the landlord, and the landlord, in turn, agrees to pay the taxes, insurance, and any other expenses that might be incurred in the operation of the premises. The possible exception to this is that the tenant would pay extraordinary repairs if they were called for under the terms of the lease.

Percentage Lease

The **percentage lease** is a lease in which the rental is based either on a flat fee plus a percentage of the gross or on the net income received by a tenant doing business on the premises.

There are several factors of importance that must be considered in the percentage lease. Suppose, for example, the rental is based on a small flat rent plus a percentage of the gross. *A* goes into possession as the tenant and does a gross business that by far exceeds expectations; consequently, the rent is high. Across the street from *A* is a vacant property that may be rented at a flat or gross rental. *A* then proceeds to open another store across the street from the first store. In effect, *A* enters into competition with the original store by drawing away some of the patronage. This results in a reduction of gross receipts in the store where the percentage base is in effect. To guard against such a situation, the landlord should insert in the percentage lease a clause to the effect that the tenant may not enter into competition with the leased premises either in the city, if it is a small city, or within a stated number of blocks of the leased premises, if it is a large city.

The lease should contain a clause giving the lessor the right at any time during the demised term to examine all the books and other records that might reflect the operations of the business.

The parties also might consider the feasibility of inserting a **recapture clause.** This clause gives the landlord the right to take back the demised premises in the event the tenant's business does not reach a certain gross. The clause may also give the tenant the right to surrender the premises in the event business does not reach a stated gross.

In the final analysis, the percentages paid will be a matter of bargaining between the parties. This is especially true with shopping centers. Frequently, a shopping center developer will lease to a few large chain operations at an extremely low percentage and on very favorable terms. These large stores attract the smaller ones, which do not always receive favorable treatment. There are a number of cases where the smaller operations have received three-year leases with two-year options, often at a much higher percentage. At the end of the five years, the rates are apt to be raised a great deal for the smaller stores. In one case, a nut stand on the mall of a shopping center, occupying very little space, netted $40,000 per year during the first five years and paid a reasonable percentage in rent. At the end of the five-year period, the operator of the stand was given a choice to vacate or sign another five-year lease at 50 percent of net.

It should be added, perhaps, that developers of shopping centers use the lease as a financing device. In brief, leases are obtained from nationally known chains prior to completion of, or even starting, the center. Armed with these leases, the developer approaches a financial institution who loans on the basis of the leases. Financing is often obtained in this manner.

The percentage lease is a device that is beneficial to the landlord and the tenant both during inflationary periods as well as during periods of deflation or depression.

Oil and Gas Lease

In many sections of the United States, real estate brokers are becoming more and more involved in dealings concerning oil and gas properties. Oil companies lease property that they believe contains oil and/or gas by executing an **oil and gas lease.** Generally, the lessee proposes a flat sum for the rental of the land for the purpose of drilling for oil and gas for a stated period of years. The leasing company usually agrees that if oil is discovered, they will pay a stated royalty, often one-eighth of a barrel from each barrel of oil, and one-eight of the proceeds from the sale of gas. If drilling operations are not started within one year, the lease generally calls for a flat sum to be paid to the lessor. This payment gives the lessee another year in which to commence drilling operation.

The lease also calls for the right of either party to assign the lease with all of the covenants of the lease binding on the heirs, assigns, or successors of the parties to the lease. The right is given to the lessee, in the event drilling operations have commenced, to continue the drilling operation; and the term of the lease is extended and continued as long as the lessee continues drilling or continues the production operation.

Oil and gas leases are often obtained by individuals who later sell their rights in them to oil companies. Sometimes the leases are assigned to individuals who, in turn, sell them to oil-producing companies.

Farm Lease

In rural areas, real estate brokers are often called upon to deal in farm leases. **Farm leases** are drawn for a flat sum of money to be paid to the landlord, or are drawn so that a share of the crops is paid to the landlord in lieu of a flat rent.

Indexed Lease

With the growth of inflation and innovative mortgage financing, such as adjustable rate mortgages, or any other form of rollover mortgage, **indexed leases** are becoming common (see Chapter 13). To accomplish this, an escalation clause is inserted in the lease to provide for periodic rental increases based on a well-defined index or a set of rules. For example, if the lessor has a rollover mortgage, the rate increase may be based on the lessor's increase in interest payments. The most common index, however, is the *Consumer Price Index* (CPI), a statistical measure of the change in price over time of a "market basket" of goods and services typically purchased by urban consumers. The market basket includes such expenditure groups as food, housing, transportation, apparel, health, and recreation.

FORM OF THE LEASE

A lease need not be in any particular form of language, provided it is clear and definite, showing an intention to transfer possession by way of lease. The written lease usually contains (1) an execution date; (2) an identification of the parties; (3) a designation of the term for which the tenancy is to exist; (4) a description of the premises; (5) a statement of the amount of rent to be paid by the tenant, the manner of payment, and any other obligations of the parties; and (6) the signatures of the parties.

Exhibit 10-1 is an example of a residential lease agreement and security deposit receipt.

COMMON LEASE COVENANTS

Rent

The term *rent* has been previously defined as the compensation in money, provisions, chattels, or labor received by the owner of the soil or buildings from the occupant. Under common law, rents were due and payable at the end of the term. The concept was that the rent was to be paid out of the profits derived from the use of the premises and that the profits could not be determined until the end of the term. However, most modern leases provide that the rent shall be paid at stated periods, usually the first of each month.

In the discussion of the gross, net, and percentage leases, it was seen that the leases vary mainly in the method of determining the amount of the rent to be paid by the lessee.

The most common residential rent is based on a flat scale, or at a stated amount per month. Some rentals are based on a sliding scale with an increase over the term of the lease. Recently, there have been some attempts to base rentals on the Consumer Price Index. Hence, if the cost of living during a certain period rises 5 percent, then the rent is increased proportionately. On the other hand, if the cost of living decreases, then the rental paid is decreased proportionately. The percentage lease, however, is much more common for business properties and is becoming increasingly more common.

Use of the Premises

When a property is leased, the landlord receives the right to the rent, and the tenant receives the right of possession. In a sense, the tenant is the owner of the premises during the period of the lease. The tenant may use the possession in any legal manner, in the absence of any covenants to the contrary, and the landlord may not prevent the tenant from so doing. There is, however, one restriction by implication on all tenants; that is, that the tenant cannot do anything that will injure or diminish the value of the landlord's interest. Any improper use of the premises by the tenant that does injure or diminish the value of the landlord's reversion is waste.

The tenant injures the value of the reversion, the landlord may bring an action for damages, or an injunction resulting in a court order restraining the tenant from committing waste, or both. The lease may also provide that such breach by the tenant gives the landlord the right to terminate the lease.

Exhibit 10-1 Residential Lease Agreement and Security Deposit Receipt

RESIDENTIAL LEASE AGREEMENT
AND SECURITY DEPOSIT RECEIPT

THIS INDENTURE, made this 3rd day of April, 19--, between Ruth Sloane, hereinafter designated the Lessor or Landlord, and Celeste O'Brien, hereinafter designated the Lessee,

WITNESSETH: That the said Lessor/Landlord does by these presents lease and demise the residence situated at 13 Water Street in Pullman City, Whitman County, Washington State,

of which the real estate is described as follows:

13 Water Street, Pullman, Washington,

upon the following terms and conditions:

1. **Term:** The premises are leased for a term of one (1) years, commencing the 5th day of April, 19--, and terminating the 4th day of April, 19--.

2. **Rent:** The Lessee shall pay rent in the amount of $300.00 per month for the above premises on the 5th day of each month in advance to Landlord.

3. **Utilities:** Lessee shall pay for service and utilities supplied to the premises, except None which will be furnished by Landlord.

4. **Sublet:** The Lessee agrees not to sublet said premises nor assign this agreement nor any part thereof without the prior written consent of Landlord.

5. **Inspection of Premises:** Lessee agrees that he has made inspection of the premises and accepts the condition of the premises in its present state, and that there are no repairs, changes, or modifications to said premises to be made by the Landlord other than as listed herein.

6. **Lessee Agrees:**
   (1) To keep said premises in a clean and sanitary condition;
   (2) To properly dispose of rubbish, garbage and waste in a clean and sanitary manner at reasonable and regular intervals and to assume all costs of extermination and fumigation for infestation caused by Lessee;
   (3) To properly use and operate all electrical, gas, heating, plumbing facilities, fixtures and appliances;
   (4) To not intentionally or negligently destroy, deface, damage, impair or remove any part of the premises,their appurtenances,facilities, equipment, furniture, furnishings, and appliances, nor to permit any member of his family, invitee, licensee or other person acting under his control to do so;
   (5) Not to permit a nuisance or common waste.

7. **Maintenance of Premises:** Lessee agrees to mow and water the grass and lawn, and keep the grass, lawn, flowers and shrubbery thereon in good order and condition, and to keep the sidewalk surrounding said premises free and clear of all obstructions; to replace in a neat and workmanlike manner all glass and doors broken during occupancy thereof; to use due precaution against freezing of water or waste pipes and stoppage of same in and about said premises and that in case water or waste pipes are frozen or become clogged by reason of neglect of Lessee, the Lessee shall repair the same at his own expense as well as all damage caused thereby.

8. **Alterations:** Lessee agrees not to make alterations or do or cause to be done any painting or wallpapering to said premises without the prior written consent of Landlord.

9. **Use of Premises:** Lessee shall not use said premises for any purpose other than that of a residence and shall not use said premises or any part thereof for any illegal purpose. Lessee agrees to conform to municipal, county and state codes, statutes, ordinances and regulations concerning the use and occupation of said premises.

10. **Pets and Animals:** Lessee shall not maintain any pets or animals upon the premises without the prior written consent of Landlord.

11. **Access:** Landlord shall have the right to place and maintain "for rent" signs in a conspicuous place on said premises for thirty days prior to the vacation of said premises. Landlord reserves the right of access to the premises for the purpose of:
   (a) Inspection;
   (b) Repairs, alterations or improvements;
   (c) To supply services; or
   (d) To exhibit or display the premises to prospective or actual purchasers, mortgagees, tenants, workmen, or contractors.
Access shall be at reasonable times except in case of emergency or abandonment.

12. **Surrender of Premises:** In the event of default in payment of any installation of rent or at the expiration of said term of this lease, Lessee will quit and surrender the said premises to Landlord.

13. **Security Deposit:** The Lessee has deposited the sum of $ 350.00, receipt of which is hereby acknowledged, which sum shall be deposited by Landlord in a trust account with Lincoln ~~bank,~~ savings and loan association ~~or licensed escrow~~, Pullman branch, whose address is One Depot Street, Pullman, Washington.

All or a portion of such deposit may be retained by Landlord and a refund of any portion of such deposit is conditioned as follows:
   (1) Lessee shall fully perform obligations hereunder and those pursuant to Chapter 207, Laws of 1973, 1st Ex Session or as may be subsequently amended;
   (2) Lessee shall occupy said premises for one (1) months or longer from date hereof;
   (3) Lessee shall clean and restore said residence and return the same to Landlord in its initial condition, except for reasonable wear and tear, upon the termination of this tenancy and vacation of apartment;
   (4) Lessee shall have remedied or repaired any damage to apartment premises;
   (5) Lessee shall surrender to Landlord the keys to premises;
Any refund from security deposit, as by itemized statement shown to be due to Lessee, shall be returned to Lessee within fourteen (14) days after termination of this tenancy and vacation of the premises.

IN WITNESS WHEREOF, the Lessee has hereunto set ~~his~~ her hand and seal the day and year first above written.

/s/ Ruth Sloane — LANDLORD

/s/ Celeste O'Brien — LESSEE

20 Water Street
Pullman, Washington
ADDRESS

[Acknowledgment]

It is customary in modern leases to limit the use of the premises by inserting a covenant in the lease stating what the premises are to be used for and including the words *only* or *no other*. For example, the lease may state: "For use as a grocery store and no other (or only)." The words *only* or *no other* limit the use of the premises to that specifically stated.

In many states, the use of the premises will not be effectively limited in the absence of these words. In addition, there are statutes in many states providing that a lease may be terminated if the lessee makes *illegal use of the premises*. The lease under these statutes is declared void.

Covenant to Make Repairs

In the absence of any specific covenant in the lease or of custom or agreement on the point, it is the tenant's duty to make only such repairs as are necessary to prevent any damage that might diminish the value of the landlord's interest in the premises.[5]

Commonly, it is stated in the lease that "the tenant shall keep the premises in good repair." Under this provision, the tenant is required to repair the damage done to the premises, regardless of whether the damage is the tenant's fault or not. However, where damages to the premises require rebuilding of the premises or extensive structural changes, the courts generally hold that large expenditures are not within the contemplation of the parties when the lease is drawn.

The terms of some leases limit the amount of money the tenant is required to pay for repairs. Often, too, a clause will be inserted in the lease requiring the tenant to make all "inside repairs" or "all repairs not requiring structural changes." Phrases of this type are construed in accordance with the ordinary meaning of the words used, taking into consideration the magnitude of the required expenditure in proportion to the rental paid, the length of the term, and all other circumstances to determine whether it was reasonably within the contemplation of the parties that the burden of repair should be put on the tenant.

Generally, the lease not only requires the premises to be kept in good repair, but also the landlord may elect to terminate the lease if the tenant does not maintain the premises in good repair. In the absence of a provision giving the landlord the option to terminate the lease if the tenant fails to make repairs, the landlord's only recourse is to bring a suit for damages for breach of contract.

Ordinarily, when a tenant leases an entire building, the landlord is liable for repairs only if expressly agreed to by the parties in the lease. However, most states and many cities have statutes or ordinances requiring landlords to repair their property. These statutes are particularly applicable to multiple dwellings.

---

[5]Alabama, California, Connecticut, Georgia, Indiana, Iowa, Kentucky, Louisiana, Massachusetts, Michigan, Montana, New Jersey, New York, North Dakota, Oklahoma, Pennsylvania, South Dakota, and Wisconsin have enacted statutes requiring the landlord to keep the rented housing premises in good repair.

Covenant Not to Sublet or Assign

Difference Between Subletting and Assigning. In the absence of a provision to the contrary, a tenant has a right to assign the lease or to sublet the premises. An **assignment of lease** is the transfer of the entire term of the lease by the tenant; a **subletting of lease** is, in effect, the making of a new lease in which the original tenant is the lessor and the subtenant the lessee. In the former, the assignee steps into the shoes of the tenant and is generally liable for the payment of the rent to the original landlord. In the latter, the subtenant is generally not liable for the rent or other obligations to the original landlord. However, the assignor may also be held for failure of assignee to live up to terms and conditions of the lease.

One distinction between a sublet and an assignment lies in the period of time involved. For example, if a lease was drawn for a term running from January 1 to July 15 and the tenant delivered the premises to another person until July 14, this would be a sublease. However, if the premises were occupied by another person from January 1 to July 15, which is the end of the term, then this would be construed as an assignment regardless of what the transaction was called. A second distinction is that a sublease may convey only a portion of the premises.

Wording of the Covenant. To prevent the subletting or assignment of leased property, the landlord will usually insist that the lease contain a covenant in which the tenant agrees not to sublet or assign without the written consent of the landlord. The covenant will generally provide that the lease may be terminated if the tenant violates this covenant. Many landlords specifically insert a clause both to keep out undesirable tenants and to receive a bonus from the tenant in the event a tenant desires to sell a business opportunity.

At the time of the drawing of the lease, the tenant should ask to have inserted after the clause preventing assignment these words: ". . . and the landlord shall not unreasonably withhold his consent."

The effect of the insertion of these words is that the landlord must grant permission to assign or sublet unless the prospective assignee or sublessee is not financially responsible.[6]

Uncommon Use of the Sublease. In some parts of the Western United States (notably California), a large number of subdivisions have been built on land belonging to various Native American tribes. The tribes themselves are not permitted to sell the land to developers. With the consent of the Bureau of Indian Affairs, a master lease is drawn between the tribe and the builder-developer. As the homes are built and sold, a sublease for a particular lot is given, with the approval of the Bureau of Indian Affairs, to the

---

[6]Recently, a minority rule has developed to the effect that a landlord must act reasonably in deciding to consent to an assignment or sublease "unless a freely negotiated provision in the lease gives the landlord an absolute right to withhold consent" (Restatement (2d) of Property Sec. 15.2(2) cf. *Kendall v. Ernest Pestana, Inc.,* 220 Cal. Rptr. 818 (1985)).

home purchaser and the purchaser takes possession under the lease instead of receiving a deed.

Generally the term of the lease is 65 years, with the rent being adjusted every 5 years. For example, if the initial rent is $20 per month for the first 5 years, it may be raised, say 10 percent, for the second 5-year period and so forth. In addition, the rent may be tied to the Consumer Price Index so it will rise with the inflation rate during an inflationary period.

Covenant to Pay Water Charges

Most leases of business properties contain a covenant by the lessee to pay for the **water charges.** Often the right is given the lessor to install a meter to measure the amount of water used by the lessee in order to determine lessee's charge.

Recently, some cities have instituted a special tax commonly called a **sewage tax.** The tax is based on the amount of water entering the premises. The municipality figures that an equal amount would flow from the building in the form of sewage. Thus, the higher the water charge, the higher the sewage tax. Generally speaking, the covenant for payment of the water rates by the lessee does not mention any charge for sewage tax to be paid by the lessee because, at present, it is imposed by only a few municipalities. However, this form of taxation will probably become more and more common as time goes on. In anticipation of such a tax, the lessor, for protection, should include in the covenant to pay water charges a statement that the lessee will pay any sewage taxes if and when the municipality imposes and assesses such taxes against the property.

Fixtures

In the discussion of fixtures in Chapter 6, it was stated that ordinarily trade fixtures—for example, shelving, counters, and similar fixtures—are removable by the lessee when the term of the lease expires. There are instances, however, when fixtures may become the property of the landlord if so expressed in the lease. There are also instances in which some misunderstanding might arise as to whether or not a particular item installed by a tenant was a trade fixture or became a part of the real property. For example, if the tenant were to install heating equipment in a building, there would be a question of the right of the tenant to remove the equipment on expiration of the lease.

To prevent misunderstanding concerning the disposition of fixtures, a clause should be inserted in the lease describing the method of disposition of fixtures.

Option to Renew

An **option to renew** a lease usually must be exercised within a stated time prior to the expiration of the lease. The right to renew may be either for a definite renewal period or for an automatic renewal. The option to renew a different amount to be paid as rent for the renewal term may be included in this covenant.

In the first instance, the option gives a right to the lessee to notify the lessor within a stated time, prior to the end of the term of the lease, that lessee desires to renew the lease for a stated period under the same terms and conditions as the old lease. The option to renew in the original lease states further that the old lease will be renewed as is, except for the deletion of the clause granting the option to renew. This suggests, then, that the lease may not be renewed under the option a second time.

The **automatic renewal clause** is slightly different in that it gives *either* party the right to notify the other within a stated period that she or he does not choose to renew. In the ordinary option to renew, the right is given only to the lessee, but here both parties have the right to refuse to renew. It is different, too, from the option to renew for a definite period in that the option states that the renewal shall be in accordance with all of the provisions of the old lease "including this covenant." This suggests, then, that after the first renewal of the lease, the lease may again be renewed at the option of both parties to the original lease.

Option to Purchase

Usually, when a tenant erects a building upon the premises of the landlord, the lease contains an **option to purchase** giving the tenant the right to purchase the improvement and the land at the end of the term. The option may state a price to be paid for the property, or the option may provide that if the lessor and the lessee are unable to negotiate a price, then the lessor and the lessee shall each appoint an appraiser, who shall then appoint an umpire. Each of the appraisers and the umpire appraise the property. In general, the lease states that the decision of any two appraisers (one of whom is the umpire) as to the price shall be binding on the parties. In the event the third party refuses to accept the decision of the other two, most states hold that the proper remedy for the enforcement of the option to purchase at an appraised valuation is by specific performance.[7] This is done in substantially the same manner as was discussed in Chapter 7. When such a clause exists, the proper procedure for its enforcement is by a suit for specific performance in a court of equity.

Distraint

Many leases contain a covenant giving the landlord the right "to distrain for the rent due" or declare the lease terminated if the tenant fails to pay the rent. **Distraint** is the right of the landlord to levy on the tenant's goods

[7] *Rae Company v. Courtney,* 250 N.Y. 71, 165 N.E. 289 (1929).

and chattels for rent in arrears. This remedy is not available for the collection of any other claim.

Quiet Enjoyment

Ordinarily, a lease contains a covenant of *quiet enjoyment.* It states that if the tenant pays the rent and performs the other conditions of the lease, the tenant "shall and may peaceably and quietly have, hold, and enjoy the leased premises for the term herein mentioned."

Although this covenant may not be written into the lease, the tenant by implication has a right to quiet enjoyment. This covenant, whether it is written into the lease or whether it is by implication, means the tenant will not lose possession by any act of the landlord, by failure of the landlord's title, or by the enforcement of any lien superior to the landlord's title. Any breach of the covenant of quiet enjoyment is known technically as an *eviction.*

TERMINATION OF LEASES

Breach of Condition

All of the lease covenants are generally made conditions of the lease. A breach of any of the covenants is ground for termination of the lease. One of the conditions of the lease is that the tenant shall pay rent to the landlord. If tenant fails to pay the rent, the lease is breached, and the landlord may then evict the tenant for nonpayment of rent.

Eviction. **Eviction** is the dispossession of the tenant by the landlord. The eviction may be actual (by law or wrongful), constructive, or retaliatory.

Actual Eviction by Law. Lawful eviction may be by what is commonly called a "summary proceeding" or "dispossess proceeding." A summary or dispossess proceeding may be brought by a landlord against a tenant for failure to pay rent, or where necessary, for any breach of the covenants of the lease.

In a dispossess proceeding, a statutory notice and the necessary papers are served on the tenant. The tenant is given a time limit in which to appear in court and present a defense. If the tenant fails to appear or if defense fails, a warrant is issued to a constable or other proper official directing that official to dispossess or evict the tenant from the premises. Generally, at the time of issuing the warrant, the court will grant a judgment against the tenant for any rent that may be in arrears.

When the tenant is dispossessed, the lease is terminated, and ordinarily tenant's obligation to pay rent is terminated. However, most written leases contain a provision that the landlord may retain the right to hold the tenant in damages, measured by the amount thereafter occurring less any amounts the tenant received from reletting the premises.

Actual Eviction (Wrongful). This situation generally occurs when a landlord wrongfully evicts a tenant from part of the premises. In this case the tenant is generally not liable for the rent.

Constructive Eviction. **Constructive eviction** includes acts done by the landlord that so disturb or impair the tenant's possession he or she is justified in moving from the premises. If the tenant moves because of constructive eviction by the landlord, tenant is not liable for any monies due under the terms of the lease. The premises must be rendered uninhabitable because of some act or omission by the landlord, and the tenant must have actually moved out. For example, when an apartment is vermin-infested to such a degree as to make it uninhabitable, and when the tenant has notified the landlord and has actually moved from the premises, the tenant is said to be constructively evicted. Therefore, the tenant is not liable to the landlord for the unexpired term of the lease.

Retaliatory Eviction. The consumer movement has forced many states, either by statute or judicial decision, to prohibit evictions by the landlord in retaliation for the tenant's assertion of rights created by habitability statutes or implied warranty.

A **habitability statute** (or a **repair and deduct statute**) requires a landlord of rental property to keep the premises in tenantable condition. The tenant is usually limited to making repairs and deducting up to one month's rent.

Some courts, in conjunction with this thinking, have held that there is an implied warranty of habitability in every residential lease; namely, that it is warranted that the premises do and will comply with local building codes. If there is a breach of warranty, these courts have held that the tenant's rent be reduced by as much as the rental value of the premises is decreased by code violations.[8]

Basically, the suit starts when the tenant withholds rent. The landlord seeks to dispossess, and the tenant defends on the basis of building code violations. During the trial, the rents are deposited with the court until final decision is reached.

The retaliatory eviction is an outcome in the following example. The tenant withholds rent under a repair and deduct statute, and the landlord seeks to terminate the tenancy. If it can be shown that the attempt to terminate the tenancy arose because of tenant's assertion of rights, the right to terminate will be denied. This right is usually denied for between six months and one year following the repair.

Surrender and Acceptance

Technically, a **surrender** is the reconveying of the unexpired portion of the lease from the tenant to the landlord. In some cases, a surrender may be in

---

[8] *Sans v. Century Kreist Apartments,* 507 S.W. 2d 526 (Tex. Civ. App. 1978).

writing to conform with the Statute of Frauds. If the surrender is accepted by the landlord, no rent accrues thereafter. If a tenant abandons the leased property, the landlord need not take possession of the property nor find another tenant for the unexpired portion of the term. The tenant under these conditions is still liable for the rent because the landlord did not under this situation accept the surrender.

However, the situation may arise when the tenant abandons the property and the landlord, in order to protect the property, might inhabit it. This might be construed as an acceptance on the part of the landlord and therefore relieve the tenant for liability of rent for the balance of the term. In order to avoid this, there is generally inserted in the lease a clause to this effect: "If the demised premises are abandoned during the term, the lessor at his or her option may repossess them as agent of the lessee and relet the premises for the account of the lessee, charging the lessee with any expense, commission, or fee occasioned by such releasing."

In this way the landlord is able properly to care for the property and may proceed to recover from the tenant, if the tenant fails to release the property to the landlord, any rents due and remaining on the lease.

Eminent Domain

Eminent domain is the right of the government to take private property for public use after making just compensation. The legal proceeding to take property under eminent domain is called a **condemnation proceeding.**

Ordinarily when a leased property is condemned, the tenant has no right to recover any damages that may have been suffered from the landlord.[9] To avoid any possible legal entanglements that might arise because of this, the lease will contain a clause that in the event of condemnation ". . . the lessee shall not be entitled to any part of the award as damages, or otherwise for such condemnation, and the lessor is to receive the full amount of such award. . . ."

Suppose, for example, *A* rents space in a building for a garage. Over a period of time, goodwill is built up that gives value to the business over and above the fixtures and equipment. Assume the equipment is worth $3,000, but because of the goodwill, the business is worth $15,000. *A* sells the business to *B* in return for which *A* receives $15,000. If the property is then condemned, the landlord will receive compensation for the property, but *B* will be forced to move from the premises; and all that *B* will be able to take will be the $3,000 worth of equipment. *B* will thus suffer the loss of $12,000 paid to *A* for the goodwill of the business. If *A* had not sold the business, the value of the goodwill developed by *A* would have never been recovered.

It is therefore important, from the viewpoint of the lessee, to insist on a clause in the lease stipulating payment to lessee in the event of condemna-

[9]Sometimes in extremely rare cases the tenant may seek damages from the firm or political subdivision that condemned the property.

tion. This clause generally states, in effect, that if the property is condemned before a certain date, the lessee is to receive a stated sum. Other dates are generally inserted with other sums stated, and the clause also contains a final date after which the tenant is not entitled to any part of the condemnation award.

For example, in the event of condemnation, the clause will state:

> The lessee shall receive the following amounts and none other as his or her agreed share of the award for such condemnation when, as and if it is paid.
>
> If such final order of condemnation is entered before April 1, 1989, the sum of $6,000; if between April 1, 1989, and April 1, 1992, the sum of $4,000; if between April 1, 1992, and April 1, 1994, the sum of $2,000; if thereafter, no award or share whatsoever.

Destruction of the Premises

Under the common law, the tenant was held liable for rent in the event the premises were destroyed. By statute in several states, however, a complete destruction of the premises terminates the lease and relieves the tenant from any liability for further rents.[10]

Miscellaneous Terminations

Expiration of the term causes a lease to be terminated. In certain cases, a lease may terminate by mortgage foreclosure.

Ordinarily, it is the duty of the landlord to keep up the payments on a mortgage, comply with the other obligations under the mortgage, and protect the tenant. If this is not done and the tenant is dispossessed by a mortgagee, the landlord will be liable to the tenant for any damages that might have been sustained. However, if the lease is subordinate to the mortgage and the tenant has been properly served with the necessary papers by the mortgagee, the tenant may be forced out when the foreclosure sale takes place. A lease is subordinate to a mortgage if it has been recorded prior to the making of the lease.

In addition to the above means of termination, most leases will contain a clause that if the lessee becomes bankrupt, the lease will be terminated.

SECURITY FURNISHED THE LANDLORD

Deposits

Very often the tenant is required to give a **security deposit** to the landlord to ensure faithful performance of the covenants of the lease. Many states, notably New York, provide by statute that a deposit continues to be the

[10]These states are Arizona, Connecticut, Kentucky, Maryland, Michigan, Minnesota, Mississippi, New Jersey, New York, North Carolina, Ohio, Virginia, West Virginia, and Wisconsin.

money of the lessee and is to be held in trust by the lessor. The lessor is thus prevented from mingling these funds. The statutes further provide that the parties cannot waive the provisions of the statute requiring that deposits be placed in a trust fund. Ordinarily, the tenant is not entitled to interest on deposits unless there is an expressed agreement to that effect in the lease.

The landlord should place a provision in the lease stating that, in the event the property is sold, landlord has the right to transfer the deposits to the purchaser after notice to the tenant. If this provision is not written into the lease, the landlord remains personally liable to the tenant even after the property has been sold.

In early 1973, the Pennsylvania Legislature amended the Landlord-Tenant Act of 1951 regarding residential property basically as follows: After the *second* year, security deposits of more than $100, which cannot amount to more than two months' rent held by a landlord, must:

1. Be deposited in an interest-bearing account in an institution regulated by the Federal Reserve Board, the Federal Home Loan Bank Board, the Comptroller of the Currency, or the Pennsylvania Department of Banking.
2. The tenant must be paid interest earned on the deposit every year.
3. The landlord must deduct a percent of the deposit from the tenant's interest payments for administration of the account.
4. The security deposit may not be increased when the rent has been increased after a tenant has been in possession for five years or more.[11]

With increased interest in consumerism in recent years, more states have adopted similar pro-tenant legislation.

Guarantors

Sometimes the landlord will insist that the rents due under the lease shall be guaranteed by someone other than the contracting parties. This situation most often arises when the lease is being signed by a newly formed corporation, and the landlord may have some doubt about its ability to pay rent. In this event, either a separate agreement is entered into between the lessor and a third party, who guarantees payment of the rent, or an endorsement is made on the lease between the lessor and the third party wherein payment is guaranteed by the third party.

[11]Effective July 1, 1989, Minnesota law provides that tenants can deposit rents in district court when their building is in violation of county codes. This action by tenants will trigger a hearing on the code violation.

GLOSSARY

Assignment of lease The transfer to another by a tenant of the entire term of a lease

Automatic renewal clause A clause in a lease that gives both landlord and tenant the right to notify the other that he or she does not wish to renew the lease

Condemnation proceedings Legal proceedings by which property is taken by eminent domain

Constructive eviction Acts done by the landlord that so disturb or impair the tenant's possession that tenant is justified in moving from the premises

Distraint The right of the landlord to levy upon the tenant's goods and chattels for rent in arrears

Estate for years A tenancy that conveys the land for a definite stated period

Eviction Dispossession of tenant by landlord

Farm lease A lease drawn for a flat sum of money to be paid to the landlord, or allowing a share of the crops be paid to the landlord in lieu of a flat rent

Gross lease A lease in which the premises are rented at a fixed rate

Habitability statute (or repair and deduct statute) A law requiring the landlord of rental property to keep the premises in tenantable condition

Holdover tenant A tenant who stays on at the expiration of the term of a lease

Indexed lease A lease with a clause providing for periodic rental increases based on a well-defined index

Lease A contract creating a landlord-tenant relationship that conveys the right of possession of the leased premises to the tenant in return for which the tenant pays the landlord rent

Lessee A tenant

Lessor The landlord

Net lease A lease in which the tenant pays the taxes, assessments, and all operating expenses connected with the use of the premises and the landlord receives a net figure

Oil and gas lease A lease of land giving the lessee the option within a stated period of years to drill for oil or gas

Option to purchase The right given a tenant to purchase leased property

Option to renew An option that must usually be exercised within a stated time prior to the expiration of the lease

Percentage lease A lease in which the rental is based either on a flat fee plus a percentage of the gross or on the net income of a tenant doing business on the premises

Recapture clause In a percentage lease, a clause giving the landlord the right to take back the demised premises in the event that the tenant's business does not reach a certain gross

Rent The compensation, whether money, provisions, chattels, or labor, received by the owner of the soil or buildings from the occupant thereof

Security deposit A deposit given by a tenant to the landlord to insure performance of the covenants of the lease

Sewage tax A special tax levied in some cities, figured on the basis of the amount of water entering the premises

Subletting of lease The transfer of a lease by a tenant to another for a part of the balance of the term of the lease, in effect making a new lease in which the original tenant is the lessor and the subtenant the lessee

Surrender The reconveying of the unexpired portion of the lease from tenant to landlord

Tenancy at sufferance A tenancy existing when a tenant rightfully in possession continues to occupy the property after expiration of the term

Tenancy at will A tenancy that may be terminated by either party at any time

Tenancy from year to year (or periodic tenancy) A tenancy of indefinite duration of specified rental periods never exceeding a year

Water charges Right of the lessor to meter the amount of water use by the lessee

QUESTIONS FOR REVIEW

1. What is the difference between a gross lease, a net lease, and a percentage lease?
2. Name and explain two important clauses that should be inserted in a percentage lease.

3. What are the causes of the increased use of indexed leases?
4. How may one limit the use of certain demised premises?
5. When a lease contains a covenant of repair, what amount of repairs must be made by a tenant?
6. What is an option to purchase and when is it generally inserted in a lease?
7. List four ways in which a tenancy may be terminated.
8. What is the difference between constructive eviction and retaliatory eviction?
9. What should be inserted in a lease to protect a tenant in the event of a condemnation proceeding?
10. Who is a guarantor of a lease?

PROBLEMS AND ACTIVITIES

1. Arnold Brown, landlord, and Nancy Allen, tenant, draw up a three-year lease, which is unsigned. It should have been signed under the Statute of Frauds.

   a. At this point, what sort of tenant is Allen?
   b. Allen, after two months, pays rent but still fails to sign the lease. What sort of tenant is Allen now?

2. Arnold Brown, landlord, had Nancy Allen for a tenant under a lease that expired June 1. To the landlord's surprise, Allen is still in possession on June 3, but has paid no rent. What sort of tenant is Allen?

3. Arnold Brown, landlord, has Nancy Allen for a tenant under a signed one-year lease. Allen moves in, but is unhappy. The premises are overrun by roaches, so much so that, to her horror, she even finds a number of them merrily munching on her toothpaste! She notifies Brown, but he does nothing. At the end of a week, she packs up and leaves. Brown is unable to re-rent the premises and, at the end of the term, sues Allen for rent. What defense, if any, does Allen have?

4. Nancy Allen, the tenant, sublets her apartment for the summer to her good friend, John Leach. Unfortunately, Leach has a habit of throwing wild parties. One night, things really get out of hand and the walls are severely damaged. The damages are so severe that not only must gaping holes be repaired, but an entire paint job is necessary.

   Brown, the landlord, sues Allen, citing the covenant to repair in the lease. Allen declares that it is a covenant that runs with the estate and, consequently, Leach is liable. Is Leach liable? Why or why not?

11

SUPPLEMENTARY REAL ESTATE INSTRUMENTS

KEY TERMS

Affidavit of title
Assemblage
Assignee
Assignment of mortgage
Assignor
Assumption statement
Building loan agreement
Consolidation agreement
Consolidation and extension agreement
Declaration of homestead
Estoppel certificate
Extension agreement
Partial release
Participation agreement
Power of attorney
Release of easement
Restriction agreement
Satisfaction of mortgage
Subordination agreement

In previous chapters the basic real estate instruments were discussed. This chapter deals with what are called "supplementary real estate instruments." In a real sense these documents complement the basic real estate instruments. For example: What instrument is used when a mortgage or deed of trust is paid? How is a mortgage transferred from one person to another? What instrument is used to secure the loan of a lender when a building is under construction?

The legal papers discussed in this chapter are often used along with the basic real estate instruments or complete the transaction initiated by them.

INSTRUMENTS RELATIVE TO MORTGAGES

Assignment of Mortgage

The **assignment of mortgage** is an instrument used by a mortgagee to transfer the mortgagee's interest in a mortgage to a third party. Since the mortgagee is the maker of the assignment, such person is called the **assignor.** The person to whom the assignment is made is called the **assignee.** The instrument names the parties and the consideration and states that the assignor "hereby assigns unto the assignee" his or her interest in the mortgage being transferred. The mortgage is identified by giving, among other things, the book and the page number in which the mortgage is recorded in the county clerk's office. In some states, the assignment makes provision for the description of the property assigned, which should be verified against the premises described in the recorded mortgage. Some assignments may contain a convenant by the assignor stating there are no defenses to the mortgage in case it becomes necessary to foreclose, and the assignor verifies the amount due on the mortgage at the time of the assignment (see Exhibit 11-1).

The signature of the assignor is acknowledged, and the assignment is sent to be recorded to the office of the county clerk in the county in which the property is located. There, the assignment is given a book number and a page number, is entered in the book, and a photostatic copy is made. At the same time, the county clerk makes a notation on the margin of the photostat of the assigned mortgage indicating the book and page where the assignment has been entered. Instruments are then indexed on *microfiche.* The microfiche refers to a film number on which there is a copy of the instrument that can be enlarged for examination. This enables anyone later searching the records to have notice of the assignment.

A prospective purchaser of a mortgage should have the records searched to determine whether or not a mortgage has been satisfied, has been previously assigned, or whether there are any actions pending on the property described in the mortgage being considered.

Estoppel Certificate

An **estoppel certificate** is an instrument executed by a mortgagor showing the amount of the unpaid balance due on a mortgage and stating that the mortgagor has no defenses or offsets at the time of the execution of the certificate, in the event of foreclosure of the mortgage (see Exhibit 11-2). This is sometimes called a *certificate of no defense* and is used in conjunction with the assignment of the mortgage.

One of the clauses of the mortgage usually states:

> The mortgagor within . . . days upon request in person or within . . . days upon request by mail will furnish a statement of the amount due on this mortgage and whether any offsets or defenses exist against the mortgage debt.

It is this covenant that gives the mortgagee the right to demand that an estoppel certificate be made by mortgagor.

This instrument, which is signed by the mortgagor, is acknowledged. It states the amount due on the mortgage at the time of the execution of the instrument and whether or not the mortgagor has a defense in the event of a foreclosure action. Its purpose is to enable the prospective assignee of the mortgage to learn from the mortgagor the balance due under the mortgage and also whether the mortgagor has a defense in the event of foreclosure. After having signed and delivered the estoppel certificate, the mortgagor is barred from later asserting that the mortgage was in a lesser amount, or that there was a defense to a foreclosure action. Thus, the

■ Exhibit 11-1 Assignment of Mortgage with Covenant Form

ASSIGNMENT OF MORTGAGE WITH COVENANT

KNOW THAT Pauline Rich, residing at 220 Tulip Lane, Borough of Brooklyn, County of Kings, State of New York,

, assignor,

in consideration of Eighty Thousand and 00/100 ($80,000.00)

dollars,

paid by Richard W. Tracy, residing at 2200 Ocean Avenue, Sayville, County of Suffolk, State of New York,

, assignee,

hereby assigns unto the assignee,

Mortgage dated the 8th day of June , 19-- made by Ronald W. Stanton

to Pauline Rich

in the principal sum of $ 80,000.00 and recorded on the 19th day of June 19-- , in ~~(Liber) (Record Liber)~~ (Reel) 1492 of Section 8 of Mortgages, page , in the office of the Clerk of the County of Suffolk covering premises

(here follows complete legal description of the property)

TOGETHER with the bond ~~or note or obligation~~ described in said mortgage , and the moneys due and to grow due thereon with the interest,

TO HAVE AND TO HOLD the same unto the assignee and to the successors, legal representatives and assigns of the assignee forever.

AND the assignor covenants that there is now owing upon said mortgage , without offset or defense of any kind, the principal sum of Eighty Thousand and 00/100 ($80,000.00) dollars,

with interest thereon at 13-3/4 per centum per annum from the 3rd day of March , nineteen hundred — —

The word "assignor" or "assignee" shall be construed as if it read "assignors" or "assignees" whenever the sense of this instrument so requires.

IN WITNESS WHEREOF, the assignor has duly executed this assignment the 4th day of January , 19— —.

IN PRESENCE OF:

/s/ Rosemary Roe /s/ Pauline Rich

(Acknowledgment)

Standard Form of New York Board of Title Underwriters

Exhibit 11-2 Owner's Estoppel Certificate Form

OWNER'S ESTOPPEL CERTIFICATE

THE UNDERSIGNED, owning premises situate in the Village of Rye, County of Westchester, State of New York, known as 63 Wheat Street, Rye, New York

covered by the following mortgage :

Mortgage for $ 80,500 dated the 18th day of June 19-- and recorded in ~~(liber) (record liber)~~ (reel) 2080 of section 6 of mortgages, page in the office of the Clerk of the County of Westchester

which mortgage is about to be assigned by the holder thereof to Franklin Donovan

DOES **HEREBY CERTIFY,** in consideration of the sum of One Dollar paid, the receipt whereof is hereby acknowledged, and to enable said assignment to be made and accepted, that said mortgage is a valid lien on said premises for the full amount of principal and interest now owing thereon, namely, Sixty-Eight Thousand, Two Hundred Fifty-Two and 58/100 ($68,252.58) ---
Dollars, and interest thereon at 11-3/4 per centum from the 4th day of June , 19--

and that there are no defenses or offsets to said mortgage or to the bond or note secured thereby, and that all the other provisions of said bond or note and mortgage are in force and effect.

DATED the 5th day of July 19--

IN PRESENCE OF:

/s/ Judith J. DeFore /s/ Bryan P. Goldstein

[Acknowledgment]

Standard Form of New York Board of Title Underwriters

courts will not later allow the mortgagor (who is estopped) to assert in court that the amount stated in the certificate was not owed.

In practice, mortgages are sometimes sold at a discount (less than the balance due and unpaid). For example, *A* is the mortgagee and may desire to liquidate a mortgage. At the time the mortgage was made, the amount was $66,000. At the time *A* wishes to sell, the amount has been reduced to $14,500. *B* is the mortgagor. *A*, the owner of the $14,500 mortgage, tells *X* that *X* may have it for $12,000. If *X* examines the record, it will be discovered that the mortgage states it is for $66,000. Therefore, in order to determine the balance, a request is made by *A* of *B* for an estoppel certificate, which can then be shown to *X* verifying *A*'s statement that the mortgage is really worth $14,500.

Satisfaction of Mortgage

The **satisfaction of mortgage,** or what is called the release of mortgage in some states, is a receipt signed by the mortgagee stating that the amount due under the mortgage has been paid and may be discharged of record (see Exhibit 11-3). This means that on recording, the county clerk will stamp the photostat or typewritten copy of the mortgage as being paid. This instrument is acknowledged and recorded. The effect on recording is to clear the record of the mortgage.

Many states have statutes imposing criminal penalties on mortgagees who refuse to deliver the satisfaction when the debt has been paid.

Too much emphasis cannot be placed on the desirability of immediately recording the satisfaction of mortgage. Without the satisfaction being placed on record, the opportunity presents itself for a fraudulent assignment of the mortgage because a prospective assignee, on examining the record, will be led to believe the mortgage has not been paid and satisfied. Further difficulties are apt to arise if the mortgagor, after having paid a mortgage, fails to record the satisfaction, then attempts to sell the property or obtain a new mortgage. The record will show the mortgage as not having been paid. In addition, failure to record a satisfaction of mortgage may cause difficulties in case of death of the mortgagor.

To avoid this and to prevent fraudulent assignments, some states require that the mortgage be delivered to the county clerk together with the satisfaction piece in order for the mortgage to be properly discharged of record. The clerk will then efface the original mortgage to prevent fraudulent negotiation of mortgages that have been paid. To efface the mortgage, the clerk stamps either "discharged" or "satisfied" in the margin of a copy of the mortgage filed in the office and gives also the book and page number where a copy of the satisfaction piece is kept.

Some states, notably New York, prohibit more than one mortgage being discharged by a single satisfaction piece. In New York, if the mortgage has been assigned, the assignment must be stated in the satisfaction together with the date of each assignment in the chain of title of the

■ **Exhibit 11-3 Satisfaction of Real Estate Mortgage Form**

SATISFACTION OF REAL ESTATE MORTGAGE
(INDIVIDUAL)

Know all Men by these Presents:

That Gardner Jones, residing at 23 Elm Street, City of Pullman, County of Whitman, State of Washington,

*do*es *hereby certif*y *that a certain real estate mortgage bearing date* June 18, 19--, *in volume* 142 *page* 18 *of mortgage records of* Whitman *County, State of Washington made and executed by* Mawa Keyes and John Keyes *as Mortgagor* *to* Gardner Jones *as Mortgagee has been fully paid, and is hereby satisfied, released and discharged, and the real estate covered thereby is hereby released from the lien thereof.*

IN WITNESS WHEREOF I *ha*ve *hereunto set* my *hand* *and seal* *said* 18th *day of* December, *19*--.

/s/ Gardner Jones

STATE OF WASHINGTON } ss. (INDIVIDUAL ACKNOWLEDGMENT)
County of Whitman

I, Jane Ott, Notary Public in and for the State of Washington, do hereby certify that on this 18th day of December, 19--, personally appeared before me ~~Gardner Jones~~ to me known to be the individual described in and who executed the within instrument and acknowledged that be signed and sealed the same as his free and voluntary act and deed for the uses and purposes herein mentioned.

GIVEN UNDER MY HAND AND OFFICIAL SEAL this 18th day of December, 19--.

/s/ Jane Ott

Notary Public in and for the State of Washington, residing at Pullman in said County.

persons signing the instrument. The interest assigned and the book and page where each assignment is recorded must be stated. In the event the mortgage has not been assigned, this fact must be stated in the satisfaction piece.

In those states using a deed of trust, the same thing is accomplished by a release of deed of trust. The public trustee is notified by a lender that the loan has been paid. The public trustee then releases the lien of the deed of trust, which is then recorded, effectively removing the loan from the record.

Partial Release

The **partial release** is an instrument that releases part of the mortgaged premises from the terms of the mortgage. It simply recites the mortgage, the amount paid for the release, and a description of the part of the mortgaged premises that has been released. The instrument is acknowledged and recorded in the office of the county clerk in the county in which the property is located. The effect of this instrument is that part of the property so released is no longer subject to the mortgage. The owner may then, if desired, obtain a new mortgage on the released parcel (see Exhibit 11-4).

Participation (Ownership or Share) Agreement

The **participation agreement**[1] is the instrument used to define the ownership or shares that two or more persons may have in the same mortgage. It states the terms on which the parties to the instrument agree to share in the mortgage. Generally, if both parties share equally in a single mortgage, they appear as co-owners on the face of the original mortgage. If they do not share equally, one of the parties will be junior to the other. The participation agreement indicates the extent to which one party is to hold a prior interest and the extent to which the other party is to hold a junior interest in the existing mortgage. It authorizes one of the parties to collect the interest and defines the method of distribution of principal and interest. It also recites the respective rights of the parties if there is a need to foreclose the mortgage.

This instrument is acknowledged but is generally not recorded. It may, however, be recorded if it is subsequently necessary to bring any action under the terms of the instrument.

The participation agreement can sometimes be employed rather effectively in complicated deals involving assemblage. **Assemblage** is the act of bringing together two or more parcels of real estate to form an aggregate whole.[2]

Subordination Agreement

The **subordination agreement** is a device by which those with superior rights subordinate those rights in favor of inferior rights. The following is an example of a situation requiring its use.

A building, on which *A* held a first mortgage for many years, is now worth $125,000. *A* still owns a first mortgage on the building, but the mortgage has been reduced to $12,000. As far as *A* is concerned, it is a good investment. There is ample security, and the mortgage does not contain a prepayment clause, which means the owner cannot pay off the indebtedness before the maturity date of the mortgage. *A*, however, wishes to sell the property to *B*, and *B* goes to a bank and receives a commitment for a $90,000 loan. The bank or any other lender will discover the existing first mortgage in the amount of $12,000. By law, the bank cannot, nor probably can anyone else, lend $90,000 behind an existing first mortgage.

---

[1]There are several other "participations," which will be discussed later in the text.

[2]In a few areas, "assemblage" is synonymous with "plottage."

Exhibit 11-4 Release of Part of Mortgaged Premises Form

RELEASE OF PART OF MORTGAGED PREMISES

THIS INDENTURE, made the 18th day of June , nineteen hundred and — —

BETWEEN Jenny C. Foster, residing at 361 First Street, Amityville, County of Suffolk, State of New York,

party of the first part, and Denise Plant, residing at 1492 North 115th Street, Amityville, County of Suffolk, State of New York,

party of the second part,

WHEREAS, the party of the first part is the holder of the following mortgage and of the ~~bond---or~~ note secured thereby:

Mortgage dated the 14th day of July , 19-- , made by Denise Plant

to Jenny C. Foster

in the principal sum of $ 30,000 and recorded in (~~Liber) (Record Liber~~) (Reel) 16 of section 8 of mortgages, ~~page~~ in the office of the Clerk of the County of Suffolk

covering certain lands and tenements, of which the lands hereinafter described are part, and

WHEREAS, the party of the first part, at the request of the party of the second part, has agreed to give up and surrender the lands hereinafter described unto the party of the second part, and to hold and retain the residue of the mortgaged lands as security for the money remaining due on said mortgage ,

NOW THIS INDENTURE WITNESSETH, that the party of the first part, in pursuance of said agreement and in consideration of Fifteen Thousand and 00/100 ($15,000.00) ------------- -- Dollars, lawful money of the United States,

paid by the party of the second part, does grant, release and quitclaim unto the party of the second part, all that part of said mortgaged lands described as follows:

Lots numbers 1 and 16 of the Map of Security Acres Development Company, surveyed by Rebecca Johnson, April 1, 19-- and recorded in the office of the Clerk of the County of Suffolk, August 7, 19--.

TOGETHER with all right, title and interest, if any, of the party of the first part in and to any streets and roads abutting the above described premises to the center lines thereof and in and to any fixtures and articles of personal property which are now contained in said premises and which may be covered by said mortgage.

TOGETHER with the hereditaments and appurtenances thereunto belonging, and all right, title and interest of the party of the first part, in and to the same, to the intent that the lands hereby released may be discharged from said mortgage , and that the rest of the lands in said mortgage specified may remain mortgaged to the party of the first part as heretofore.

TO HAVE AND TO HOLD the lands and premises hereby released and quitclaimed to the party of the second part, and to the heirs, successors and assigns of the party of the second part forever, free, clear and discharged of and from all lien and claim under and by virtue of said mortgage aforesaid.

IN WITNESS WHEREOF, the party of the first part has executed this release the day and year first above written.

IN PRESENCE OF:

/s/ Richard Roe /s/ Jenny C. Foster

[Acknowledgment]

Standard Form of New York Board of Title Underwriters

The subordination agreement is then put into play. The bank and *A*, the first mortgagee, agree to place the first mortgage in a secondary position.[3]

The subordination agreement recites the parties, who, in the above case, are *A* and the bank. The subordination agreement recites the existing mortgage by book and page number and describes the premises. It also recites the fact that the present owner is about to deliver to the second party (the bank) a mortgage in the amount of a sum certain. The agreement continues with the statement that the second party refuses to give a mortgage on the property under the circumstances unless the first party (*A*) agrees to become subordinated to any mortgage to be granted. This statement is followed by a covenant binding on the heirs and assigns of the parties to the effect that the present holder of the first mortgage agrees to become subordinated to the mortgage given by the bank.

This instrument is acknowledged and recorded in the county in which the property is located.

Mortgagee's Certificate of Reduction

The mortgagee's certificate of reduction is an instrument executed by a mortgagee stating the balance due on a mortgage. In a sense, it is the counterpart of an estoppel certificate. An estoppel certificate is signed by the mortgagor in order to inform a prospective assignee of the balance remaining due under a mortgage, and also to indicate whether the mortgagor has a defense in the event of a foreclosure. The reduction certificate is used to inform a prospective real property purchaser, who is either assuming the mortgage or taking the property subject to the mortgage, of the amount due on the mortgage. The logical person to certify the amount still due on the mortgage is, of course, the mortgagee.

The demand for a reduction certificate usually comes about in this manner. *A* lists with a broker a property having a purchase price of $300,000 on which there is a $250,000 mortgage. *A* is willing to sell the property for $50,000 over and above the existing mortgage. This means the buyer must either "assume" or take "subject to" the $250,000 mortgage. The only way the purchaser can make certain there is only $250,000 due under the mortgage, not a greater sum, is to obtain a reduction certificate from the mortgagee.

After the contract for the sale of the property is entered into and prior to the closing date, the owner (who is the mortgagor) requests the reduction certificate from the mortgagee. In the event the mortgage has been assigned, the certificate is obtained from the assignee of the mortgage.

The instrument is acknowledged, but it need not be recorded. The certificate is delivered to the purchaser at the time of closing. In this way

---

[3]The first mortgagee, as a practical matter, usually agrees to this for a slight consideration.

the purchaser is certain that the amount of the mortgage being assumed or taken subject to is the bona fide amount.

Depending on the state, this is handled in one of two ways; this is only safe, however, when a financial institution is the mortgagee rather than an individual.

The amount being assumed is sometimes determined by requesting a letter from the institution stating the amount due and the monthly payments. In some states, the institution prepares a simple form called an **assumption statement** wherein the amount due the institution on the loan and the monthly payments are so stated.

Consolidation/Extension Agreement

The *consolidation/extension agreement* is another attempt by FNMA and FHLMC to create uniform instruments. The same form is used in all states.

This particular uniform agreement can actually be used as three separate agreements depending on what is, or is not, deleted from the form. These three agreements are a (1) consolidation agreement, (2) an extension agreement, and (3) a consolidation and extension agreement.

1. The **consolidation agreement** can arise in several ways:
   a. Assume a lender has a first and second mortgage on a piece of property. The consolidation agreement combines both loans into a first mortgage.
   b. More commonly, a lender has an old first mortgage on, say, a home. The home has increased in value. The borrower approaches the lender and wants to borrow using the appreciated value of the home as security. The lender will place a new mortgage on the home but it will be a second mortgage. To avoid this, the borrower simply signs the consolidation agreement, which makes the old and new mortgage into "but one first mortgage and a single lien on the property."

2. The **extension agreement** is a device extending the due date of the mortgage, consequently modifying the original mortgage and note. The modification may take the form of a different rate of interest, different method of amortization, or both.

   The situation arises when the mortgage is soon to come due and the mortgagor cannot or does not want to make the payment. If the payment is not made, the mortgage will either be foreclosed or remain open. In the latter case, the mortgagee has the right to foreclose at any time. The mortgagee may, however, be willing to extend the time in which the mortgagor must pay off the mortgage indebtedness. The other effect is simply that the monthly payments are reduced when the time is extended.

3. The **consolidation and extension agreement** is the most common use of the form.

For example, *A* has a first mortgage with Ace-High Savings and Loan. *A*'s property has appreciated. *A* wants to borrow money. Ace-High places the second mortgage against the property, and it is consolidated with a first. Usually the time payment, for all practical purposes, has to be extended in order to make the monthly payments fit the budget of the borrower.

Building Loan Agreement

The **building loan agreement** is an agreement entered into between a builder and a lender who agrees to lend a builder construction money while building. The lender agrees to advance the money to the builder at various stages of construction.

The building loan agreement recites the names of the parties, referring to the builder as the borrower, and the lending institution as the lender. The agreement provides that the borrower will build according to the plans and specifications that have been submitted to the lender, will file the plans and specifications with the proper government authorities, and will obtain the necessary building permits.

An affidavit showing all the expenses outside of the actual cost of construction and stating the amount available for improvements is generally included in the building loan agreement. Two of the expenses are architect's fees and broker's commissions.

Before the builder enters into negotiations for the land, a commitment is received from the lender for the building loan. Often the lender is not willing to be committed in writing on this, but it should be understood between the builder and the lender that the lender will give the loan.[4]

Often when the builder reaches the proper stage of construction, a purchase money mortgagee will be paid the amount due on the particular lot and the builder will receive a partial release of mortgage from the purchase money mortgagee.

When the building has been completed and the money, under the terms of the building loan, completely transferred to the builder, the builder may deliver to the lender a "permanent" mortgage on the premises.

The builder will generally place the house on the market when it reaches an advanced stage of construction or completion. When a purchaser is found, a contract of sale is entered into with that purchaser. The purchaser will ordinarily be financed by the same lending institution as was the builder. The lender will then lend money to the purchaser and obtain a note and a mortgage on the premises. The builder will pay off the building loan, and the difference between that and the purchase price will be the builder's profit.

---

[4]Sometimes written commitments are given to facilitate the purchase of materials by the builder, but only when the builder has an outstanding credit rating.

OTHER REAL ESTATE INSTRUMENTS

Affidavit of Title

The **affidavit of title** is a sworn statement made by the owner of a parcel of real property stating that the owner actually is the owner of the property in question (see Exhibit 11-5). It states further that the owner's possession has never been disturbed, the owner's title is free and clear of encumbrances, and no repairs, alterations, or improvements, which have been completed for no longer than the period of filing a mechanic's lien prior to the date of the instrument, have been made to the premises.

A further statement is made to the effect that the affidavit was made to induce the buyer to accept a deed or to induce the mortgagee to give a mortgage on the premises. This statement is inserted in the instrument in order to allow the admission of the affidavit in evidence to establish proof of fraud in the event that the affiant (one who makes an affidavit) has made false statements.

The instrument establishes the identity of the person offering the deed at a closing to be the same person as appears from the record. For example, suppose the judgment roll shows John Smith has a judgment entered against him. John Smith, the grantor, states that the judgment is against another John Smith and that he is willing to sign the affidavit because it is, in fact, another John Smith against whom the judgment is recorded. In this case, the affidavit of title will state:

> That there are no judgments against me unpaid or unsatisfied of record entered in any court of this state or of the United States. . . .

This instrument might be used effectively in those states where the lien laws are lax, or where there is a fear the seller might have unpaid bills for improvements on the premises. As previously mentioned, in New York State the warranty deed provides that the seller of a parcel of real property is required to hold the proceeds from the sale as a trust fund to apply toward the cost of any improvements that were made to the property, and that the seller will do so before using any part of the monies for any other purpose. Most states do not have such a provision either in the statutes or in the warranty deed. The occasion arises often in those states when the broker or attorney checking title is suspicious of the seller. For example, the broker or attorney may believe the seller has caused improvements to be made on the premises without having paid for them. In this case, the broker or attorney might obtain an affidavit of title from the seller at the closing. This affidavit should contain the statement:

> That there are no actions pending affecting said premises. That no repairs, alterations, or improvements have been made to said premises, which have not been completed more than [the time limit for the filing of a mechanic's lien in the state] prior to the date hereof.

Exhibit 11-5 Affidavit of Title Form

Affidavit of Title

State of New York } ss.:
County of Suffolk }

Title No. ....

Brandon Ward , being duly sworn, says:
I reside at No. 23 Thomas Street, Village of Patchogue, State of New York,
I am the * [1]
owner in fee simple of premises known as 23 Thomas Street, Patchogue, New York
and am the grantee described in a certain deed of said premises recorded in the Register's Office of Suffolk County in ~~(Liber)~~ ~~(Record Liber)~~ (Reel) 42 of Conveyances, ~~page~~ .

Said premises have been in my/its possession since 19-- ; that my/its possession thereof has been peaceable and undisturbed, and the title thereto has never been disputed, questioned or rejected, nor insurance thereof refused, as far as I know. I know of no facts by reason of which said possession or title might be called in question, or by reason of which any claim to any part of said premises or any interest therein adverse to me/it might be set up. There are no federal tax claims or liens assessed or filed against me/~~it~~ . There are no judgments against me/~~it~~ unpaid or unsatisfied of record entered in any court of this state, or of the United States, and said premises are, as far as I know, free from all leases, mortgages, taxes, assessments, water charges, sewer rents and other liens and encumbrances, except

None

Said premises are now occupied by your deponent

No proceedings in bankruptcy have ever been instituted by or against me/~~it~~ in any court or before any officer of any state, or of the United States, nor have I/~~has it~~ at any time made an assignment for the benefit of creditors, nor an assignment, now in effect, of the rents of said premises or any part thereof.

[2] *I am a citizen of the United States, and am more than 18 years old. I am by occupation a commercial photographer . I am married to Barbara Ward who is over the age of 18 years and is competent to convey or mortgage real estate. I was married to her on the 3rd day of January 19-- . I have never been married to any other person now living. I have not been known by any other name during the past ten years.

[3] *That the charter of said corporation is in full force and effect and no proceeding is pending for its dissolution or annulment. That all license and franchise taxes due and payable by said corporation have been paid in full.

There are no actions pending affecting said premises. That no repairs, alterations or improvements have been made to said premises which have not been completed more than four months prior to the date hereof; nor have any obligations been incurred which have become or will become liens on the above premises.

There are no facts known to me relating to the title to said premises which have not been set forth in this affidavit.

This affidavit is made to induce Oscar Davenport
to accept a conveyance of/~~on~~ said premises, and to induce The Title Guarantee Company and Pioneer National Title Insurance Company hereinafter called "The Company" to issue its policy of title insurance covering said premises knowing that they will rely on the statements herein made.

Sworn to before me this 5th
day of February , 19 -- /s/ Brandon Ward

/s/Rosemary Roe

Notary Public, County of Suffolk, N.Y.
Suffolk County Clerk's No. 3030 My Commission Expires March 31, 19--

Standard Form of New York Board of Title Underwriters

[1] If owner is a corporation, fill in office held by deponent and name of corporation.
[2] This paragraph to be omitted if owner is a corporation.
[3] This paragraph to be omitted if owner is not a corporation.

Power of Attorney

A **power of attorney** authorizes an agent to perform certain acts in the place and stead of a principal (see Exhibit 11-6). For the purposes of real estate, it enables the agent to convey property, mortgage the property of the principal, or perform other acts concerning real property if the principal were present. The power of attorney is acknowledged and recorded in the county in which the real property in question is located.

For example, if someone is leaving a state and turns real property over to a broker to be sold, the proper form of power of attorney will be executed and recorded in favor of the broker. If the broker makes a sale, she or he is empowered to sign the deed. The broker signs it in the name of the owner, and under the owner's signature signs the broker's own name as attorney-in-fact. If the owner has died or is abjudicated incompetent prior to the time of the signing of the deed, then the transaction is invalid because the death or incompetency of the principal terminates the agency.

The general rule that an agency may be terminated by the principal at any time applies here, too. If the owner wishes to terminate the agency when a power of attorney has been given and recorded, the owner must, in most states, prepare a revocation and record it in the office of the clerk of the county in which the original power of attorney was recorded.

More than one person may be named to act as attorney-in-fact for a principal. In this case, it is necessary to name the parties in the power of attorney and to state that they have been authorized to act jointly.

Restriction Agreement

A **restriction agreement** is an agreement between property owners limiting the use of occupancy of real estate. Restrictions are placed on land by a restrictive covenant in a deed.

These restrictive covenants are usually placed in the deed by a subdivider or developer. For example, when a large tract of land is divided into lots, the subdivider may feel it will be advantageous to place restrictive covenants in the deed. The subdivider may therefore provide that all houses placed on the property be of a certain size, of a certain value, or a certain distance from the street. In a sense, these restrictive covenants are an attempt by an individual through private agreement to accomplish much the same ends as is done by municipalities through the enactment of zoning ordinances (which are limitations placed upon the land by municipalities).

The courts will generally uphold only those restrictions that are reasonable and will not enforce them if the character of a neighborhood has so changed that the original beneficial purpose for which the restrictions were imposed can no longer be achieved.

■ Exhibit 11-6 General Power of Attorney Form

GENERAL POWER OF ATTORNEY

Notice: The powers granted by this document are broad and sweeping. They are defined in New York General Obligations Law, Article 5, Title 15, sections 5-1502A through 5-1503, which expressly permits the use of any other or different form of power of attorney desired by the parties concerned.

KNOW ALL MEN BY THESE PRESENTS, which are intended to constitute a **GENERAL POWER OF ATTORNEY** pursuant to Article 5, Title 15 of the New York General Obligations Law:

That I, Myra P. Smith

residing at No. 35 Ocean Avenue, Village of Patchogue, Town of Brookhaven, County of Suffolk, State of New York,

do hereby appoint Mary Beth Bronson

residing at No. 16 Jennings Avenue, Village of Patchogue, Town of Brookhaven, County of Suffolk, State of New York,

my attorney(~~s~~)-in-fact TO ACT[a]

(a) If more than one agent is designated and the principal wishes each agent alone to be able to execute the power conferred, insert in this blank the word "severally". Failure to make any insertion or the insertion of the word "jointly" will require the agents to act jointly.

FIRST: in my name, place and stead in any way which I myself could do, if I were personally present, with respect to the following matters as each of them is defined in Title 15 of Article 5 of the New York General Obligations Law to the extent that I am permitted by law to act through an agent:

[Strike out and initial in the opposite box any one or more of the subdivisions as to which the principal does NOT desire to give the agent authority. Such elimination of any one or more of subdivisions (A) to (K), inclusive, shall automatically constitute an elimination also of subdivision (L).]

To strike out any subdivision the principal must draw a line through the text of that subdivision AND write his initials in the box opposite.

(A) real estate transactions; [ ]
(B) chattel and goods transactions; [ ]
(C) bond, share and commodity transactions; [ ]
(D) banking transactions; [ ]
(E) business operating transactions; [ ]
(F) insurance transactions; [ ]
(G) estate transactions; [ ]
(H) claims and litigation; [ ]
(I) personal relationships and affairs; [ ]
(J) benefits from military service; [ ]
(K) records, reports and statements; [ ]
(L) all other matters; [ ]

[Special provisions and limitations may be included in the statutory short form power of attorney only if they conform to the requirements of section 5-1503 of the New York General Obligations Law.]

The powers granted under (A) or (B) above are enlarged so that all fixtures and articles of personal property which at the time of such transaction are or which may thereafter be attached to or used in connection with the real property may be included in the deeds, mortgages, agreements and any other instruments to be executed and delivered in connection with real estate transactions and which may be described in said instruments with more particularity.

I will not question the sufficiency of any instrument executed by my said attorney(s)-in-fact pursuant to this power notwithstanding that the instrument fails to recite the consideration therefor or recites merely a nominal consideration; any person dealing with the subject matter of such instrument may do so as if full consideration therefor had been expressed therein.

SECOND: with full and unqualified authority to delegate any or all of the foregoing powers to any person or persons whom my attorney(~~s~~)-in-fact shall select.

THIRD: this power of attorney shall not be affected by the subsequent disability or incompetence of the principal.

IN WITNESS WHEREOF I have hereunto signed my name and affixed my seal this 12th day of March, 19--.

/s/Myra P. Smith ....(Seal)
(Signature of Principal)

[Acknowledgment]

Standard Form of New York Board of Title Underwriters

A typical restrictive covenant in a deed might be worded as follows:

> This conveyance is made upon the express condition that the party of the second part covenants that the premises shall be used for residential purposes only, and the premises are to be used for no other purpose than those herein specified.

These restrictive covenants are covenants running with the land and are binding on the heirs and assigns of the parties.

Release of Easement

A **release of easement** is an agreement between the dominant tenement and servient tenement removing an easement.

The release of the easement recites the instrument, if any, by which the dominant tenement received the easement, the names of the parties, and a statement substantially as follows:

> . . . in consideration of Ten and 00/100 ($10) Dollars and other good and valuable considerations, I do hereby release, remit, and quitclaim to the said John Doe, his heirs and assigns forever, the said right-of-way and easement described as follows. . . .

Then follows the description of the easement as contained in the original grant. The instrument should be recorded in the office of clerk of the county in which the property is located.

Declaration of Homestead

The **declaration of homestead** is used in the states having homestead laws. In those states, the declaration of homestead may be filed by the family that owns and occupies a tract of land as their home. This instrument is normally filed by the husband, although there has been a shift toward permitting the head of a family to file.[5] It states the filer's marital status, briefly describes the land, and declares an estimated value of the homestead. After it is acknowledged, it is filed in the office of the clerk of the county in which the property is located.

In some states, homestead rights attach only to a certain area; in others, homestead rights attach only in terms of a limited value. In most states, homestead rights do not attach unless the declaration is completed and properly filed.

Once the homestead has been created, it cannot be sold at a forced sale for the payment of debts. It cannot be mortgaged during the lifetime of the husband and the wife without the consent of both. At the death of the husband, the property may be occupied by the widow and the children during the life of the widow and the minority of the children. The latter is a special provision not generally applicable to all homesteads.

---

[5]In California and some other states, the declaration may be filed by a head of a family as well as a husband. In Florida, the effect of a homestead declaration by the head of the family will exempt the first $25,000 of the property's assessed value from the real property tax.

GLOSSARY

Affidavit of title A sworn statement made by the owner of a parcel of real property stating that the owner actually is the owner of the property in question

Assemblage Bringing together two or more real estate parcels to form an aggregate whole

Assignee Person to whom the assignment is made

Assignment of mortgage An instrument used by a mortgagee to transfer mortgagee's interest in a mortgage to a third party

Assignor Person who makes the assignment

Assumption statement A statement issued by a lender when a mortgage is assumed showing the unpaid principal, interest, rate of interest, and date of maturity of the mortgage

Building loan agreement An agreement entered into between a builder and a lender whereby lender agrees to lend the builder money to build on certain described property

Consolidation agreement An agreement by a lender and a borrower to create a single first mortgage on a property when a lender has both a first and second mortgage on the property

Consolidation and extension agreement A device used by a mortgagee who has either a first and second mortgage on a single piece of property or who has purchased two mortgages on one piece of property to create a single mortgage out of the two, which then becomes a first mortgage

Declaration of homestead A device used in some states to protect one's home from being sold at a forced sale in the event of bankruptcy or insolvency

Estoppel certificate An instrument executed by a mortgagor showing the amount of the unpaid balance due on a mortgage and stating that the mortgagor has no defenses or offsets at the time of the execution of the certificate, in the event of foreclosure

Extension agreement A device employed to extend the due date of the mortgage and, in some cases, to modify the original note and mortgage

Partial release An instrument used to release part of the mortgaged premises from the terms of the mortgage

Participation agreement An instrument used to define the ownership or shares two or more persons may have in the same mortgage

Power of attorney Legal authorization for an agent to perform certain acts in the place and stead of a principal

Release of easement An agreement between the dominant tenement and servient tenement removing an easement

Restriction agreement An agreement between property owners limiting the use or occupancy of real estate

Satisfaction of mortgage A receipt signed by the mortgagee stating that the amount due under the mortgage has been paid and may be discharged of record

Subordination agreement A device by which those with superior rights subordinate those rights in favor of inferior rights

QUESTIONS FOR REVIEW

1. After many years, you have finally paid off your mortgage (or deed of trust). What does the lender give you to indicate it has been paid?
2. When is a subordination agreement used?
3. You decide to buy a home and assume an existing mortgage, which the seller states in the contract for sale is approximately $60,000. What must be given you at the closing of title to ensure that the loan to be assumed is really $60,000 and not more than that?
4. What situation may develop that might bring about the use of a consolidation and extension agreement?
5. Suppose you, as the broker, have a seller with a common name, say, Mary Jones. The title company finds a judgment in the amount of $50,000 against a Mary Jones. This judgment would, of course, constitute a lien against the property of a Mary Jones. Your client, Mary Jones, denies she ever had any judgments against her. What should your Mary Jones be required to sign to reassure both the title company and a prospective buyer of the property?

PROBLEMS AND ACTIVITIES

1. Assume you are the mortgagee on Lot 9 of the map of the Security Acres Development Company located in your city and state. Ralph Shepherd, who also lives in your city and state, is the mortgagor. He pays you the full amount of the mortgage. Prepare the necessary papers for him.
2. Assume you are a builder and a bank in your city and state agrees to lend you $100,000 while you are building on Lot 56 of the map of Security Acres Development Company located in your city and state.

You have purchased Lots 1–60 on a purchase money mortgage from Robert Slater, and he has agreed to release them to you on the payment of $15,000 on each lot. You begin to build and finally complete the building and enter into a contract for $150,000 for the sale of the property with Patricia Maxwell, also of your city and state. The bank that gave you the building loan agrees to give Maxwell a 20-year, self-amortizing mortgage in the amount of $120,000. Make a list of the instruments that need to be drawn.

3. Some brokers spend part of their time in what is sometimes called mortgage brokerage, which means they negotiate the sale of mortgages for a commission. Frequently, these mortgages with which they deal are second mortgages. They are frequently sold at a percentage of face value called a discount (discussed in Chapter 14). Assume, then, a second mortgage with a face value of $22,500 and a discount of 23 percent. The broker's commission is 2.5 percent. An investor is willing to buy the mortgage.
   a. How much cash does the investor pay?
   b. What is the net to the seller?
   c. What should the investor do for protection against possible fraud on the part of the seller?
   d. What instrument(s) should the investor require?
   e. If the mortgage is due in two years and calls for 12.5 percent interest, what is the effective rate of return.

12

LIENS

KEY TERMS

Assignment of lien
Bail bond lien
Completion bond
Corporation franchise tax
Defendant
Equitable liens
Federal tax lien
General lien
Holding funds
Improvement
Lien
Lienee
Lienor
Mechanic's lien
Plaintiff
Prime contractor
Priority of liens
Satisfaction of lien
Specific lien
State inheritance tax
Statutory liens
Subcontractor
Vendee
Vendee's lien
Vendor
Vendor's lien
Waiver of lien

A **lien** is a hold or claim that one person has on the property of another as security for a debt or charge against the property of another. There are two parties involved in the lien, the lienor and the lienee. The **lienor** is the person who owns or holds a lien, and the **lienee** is the person whose property is subject to a lien.

The ownership of a lien is capable of being transferred by means of an assignment. For example, a mortgage may be a lien; and the ownership of the mortgage (lien) is transferred by an assignment of mortgage, as we saw in Chapter 11.

There are many different kinds of liens that exist as the result of a statute or by virtue of the common law.

There are two types of real property liens: statutory and equitable liens. **Statutory liens** are created by statute. **Equitable liens** are not rights in the land itself but personal obligations or rights against the owner or the grantor of the land, which the courts will enforce under their equitable jurisdiction. An equitable lien arises when the owner makes a written agreement that the land shall be security for some obligation (a mortgage, for example). In the final analysis, the courts will declare the existence of equitable liens mainly because considerations of right and justice under the circumstances seem to require such action. All the liens with which we are concerned are statutory liens, with the possible exception of the vendor's and vendee's lien. In most states this, too, is a statutory lien, but in some jurisdictions it is an equitable lien by means of which the unpaid vendor has an equitable lien on the land for the remainder of the purchase price.

The liens against real property with which we are concerned may be further classified as specific liens and general liens. The **specific lien** affects only a specified piece or pieces of real property; the **general lien** affects all the property of a debtor.

THE MECHANIC'S LIEN

The **mechanic's lien,** created solely by statute, gives the right of lien to those persons who have furnished work or materials for the improvement of real property (see Exhibit 12-1). The persons who are entitled to the lien include contractors, subcontractors, laborers, material suppliers, engineers, and architects.

The underlying basis of the right of lien lies in the fact that as a result of the work done, or materials furnished a property, the property is improved. **Improvement** is generally the erection, alteration, or repair of any structure upon, connected with, or beneath the surface of any real property. Some state laws define improvement as follows:

> [Improvement] . . . shall also include any work done or materials furnished for its [the structure's] permanent improvement, and shall also include any work done or materials furnished in equipping any such structure with any chandeliers, brackets, or other fixtures or apparatus for supplying gas or electric light, and shall also include the drawing by any architect or engineer or surveyor of any plans or specifications or survey, which are prepared for or used in connection with such improvements, and shall also include the value of materials manufactured for but not delivered to the property.[1]

Because the lien is based on the idea of improvement, it can be placed against only the improved property. For example, *A* owns two parcels of property. *B* works on one of them and is not paid. *B*'s right to a lien exists against only the property on which work has actually been done. The right of lien does not exist against both parcels of property.

Because the mechanic's lien is created by statute, all the requirements must be strictly complied with. If they are not, the lien may prove ineffective.

Consent or Contract of Owner to Improvement

Although the lien laws are different among the states, they may be generally classified as either contract statutes or consent statutes. In states having

[1]New York Lien Law (Section 2).

Exhibit 12-1 Notice of Mechanic's Lien Form

NOTICE OF MECHANIC'S LIEN (New York Form)

To the clerk of the County of Westchester and to all others whom it may concern:
PLEASE TAKE NOTICE THAT [1] Lawrence Lienor
residing at [2] 2675 East Hardy Way
City of Jamaica County of Westchester
has and claims a lien for principal and interest for the value and the agreed price of the labor and materials hereinafter mentioned upon the real property hereinafter described and upon the improvements, pursuant to the provisions of the Lien Law of the State of New York and all the acts and laws amendatory thereof, as follows:

1. The name of the owner of the real property against whose interest therein a lien is claimed and the interest of the owner, as far as known to the lienor, is as follows:

[3] Barbara Owner
and her interest in the said property is that of the owner in fee.

2. The name of the person by whom the lienor was employed and to whom he furnished materials is [4] Jerry Contractor

3. The labor performed and the materials furnished and the agreed price thereof are as follows: All of the electrical work including wiring, electrical fixtures and all other articles necessary to complete the building on the premises hereinafter described and all the work and labor in installing said materials in said building, and the agreed price and the value of such materials was Two Thousand Five Hundred and 00/100 ($2,500)--- dollars and the reasonable value of certain extra work, included in the materials and labor above enumerated, was the sum of Two Hundred and 00/100 ($200) ------- dollars, which work and materials were directed to be performed and furnished by the person with whom the lienor made the contract above stated.

4. The amount unpaid to the lienor for such labor and material is the sum of One Thousand and 00/100 ($1,000) ---------------------------- dollars.

5. The time when the first item of said work was performed was the [5] 12th day of April , 19-- , and the first item of materials was furnished on the [5] 12th day of April , 19-- , and the time when the last item or work was performed was the 31 day of May , 19-- .

6. The property subject to this lien is known as [6] [legal description]
dated the 28th day of July , 19-- .

/s/ Lawrence Lienor

[Acknowledgment]

The filing of the above notice with the county clerk creates the mechanic's lien against the property therein described.

1 The name of the lienor.
2 The address of the lienor.
3 The name of the owner.
4 If the lienor is a contractor or subcontractor, the name of the person with whom the contract was made is inserted here.
5 The reason for inserting these dates is to ascertain that the lien is filed within the statutory period.
6 Here is inserted a description of the property; the more complete, the better.

contract statutes, the lienor must show that the improvement was made at the *request* of the owner or the owner's agent. This prevents the owner from having a lien placed on property when the improvement has not been requested. For example, when a tenant orders work done on the landlord's house without the request of the landlord, the person ordinarily entitled to the lien cannot place a lien on the landlord's property. In other states it is enough to show that the owner or owner's agent *consented* to the improvement. These statutes are called *consent statutes.*

Notice of Mechanic's Lien

The first step in the establishment of the mechanic's lien is the filing of a notice of mechanic's lien. After the notice has been prepared, the original is generally filed with the clerk of the county in which the property is located, and a copy of the notice is sent by registered mail to the owner of the property against which the lien is being placed. In some states, a mailed notice is not required.

Because the lien is created by statute, there must be strict compliance with the statute. Therefore, the notice of lien must be properly drawn. The notice gives the name of the lienor, the name of the party with whom the lienor entered into the contract, a description of the labor performed, and the materials furnished for the job. In addition, the notice states the contract price, the amount paid under the contract, and the balance remaining due and unpaid. The notice states, too, the dates when the work was begun, when the first items of materials were furnished, and when the work was completed, or the last items of materials were furnished. The property is also described, and the description must sufficiently identify the property. The notice is verified by the lienor or the lienor's agent.

Time in Which to File

In most states, the notice of lien also contains a statement regarding the time in which to file. Generally, it states:

> . . . that four months have not elapsed dating from the last item of work performed, and dating from the last items of materials furnished. . . .

The purpose of this statement is to show compliance with the statute when, for example, the statute states that the notice must be filed within four months after the last work was completed or last items of materials were furnished. Although most state statutes require that the lien be filed within four months, other states vary. The time in which the material supplier and the laborer have a right to file may also vary. For example, in Idaho and Oregon, the material supplier must file within 60 days after the last items of materials are furnished; the laborer must file within 90 days after performing the last work. In Colorado, a laborer has only 30 days within which to file, while contractors and subcontractors have 90 days within which to file. To be on the safe side, one should examine the laws of each state.

Priority

The problem concerning the **priority of liens** may be divided into two parts: first, between various mechanic's liens; second, between the mechanic's lien and the mortgage.

The priority that establishes the rights between the various mechanic's liens that may be placed against a property is fixed by the time of recording. When the notice of lien reaches the county clerk's office, the date and time of the recording are stamped on the notice of lien, and a note indicating the time of recording is entered in the proper index, which establishes the priority. The first notice of mechanic's lien filed has the prior right over subsequently filed notices of liens.

In some states, the lien of the mechanic is attached when work is begun. The date of priority is not dependent on the actual filing of the notice; although if the lien is not filed within the requisite period, it may be lost. In these states, a number of situations can arise. For example, the owner has a mortgage on the property, and *A* commences work. In this case, the rights of the mortgagee are superior to *A*. But if *A* begins work and then the owner mortgages the property, *A*'s lien will be superior to the mortgage even though the notice has not yet been filed. The third situation that can arise occurs when there is no mortgage and *A* commences work. The owner then mortgages the property and hires *B*. In this case, the right of *A* is superior to the mortgagee, but the right of the mortgagee is superior to that of *B*, who began working after the mortgage was recorded.

The situation varies among the states as to the rights of the mechanic's lien over the rights of a mortgagee. In New York, for example, if the mechanic's lien is filed before the mortgage is recorded, the rights of the lienor are superior to the rights of the mortgagee. On the other hand, if the mortgage is recorded prior to the filing of the lien, the mortgagee's rights are superior. The reason for this is that the lien does not attach until it is actually filed. The states following this rule are said to operate under the New York System of mechanic's liens.

In some states, the lien will date back to the day of the beginning of the job by the prime contractor. For example, a prime contractor begins a job on July 1. On August 1, the owner obtains a mortgage on the premises. On August 15, the prime contractor hires a painter as a subcontractor to finish the job. In these states, the painter will have a lien against the premises superior to that of the mortgagee, the time relating back to the commencement of the job by the prime contractor, which was July 1.[2]

---

[2]These states are Alabama, Alaska, Colorado, Illinois, Indiana, Maine, Michigan, Missouri, Montana, Oregon, Texas, Virginia, and Wyoming

In still other states, it is the date of the contract that controls, even though work has not commenced. For example, on July 1 a contract is entered into between an owner and a prime contractor; a mortgage is placed on the property on August 1; and work is actually commenced on August 15. The lien in this case relates back to the agreement between the owner and the prime contractor. Therefore, the lien takes priority over the mortgage.[3]

Length of Lien

The mere filing of the lien does not in itself entitle the lienor to payment. The lienor may have one to three years to commence an action to enforce the lien.[4] The enforcement of the lien is by a foreclosure action handled in much the same manner as the foreclosure of a mortgage that has been defaulted.

Lis Pendens

Lis pendens is a notice of pendency of action (see Exhibit 12–2). It is, in effect, constructive notice to a prospective purchaser, or any party in interest, that an action is pending involving a particular parcel of property. Because of the time limits set by the several states for the commencement of an action to foreclose a mechanic's lien, the *lis pendens* takes on an additional importance. The filing of the *lis pendens* prevents the lapsing of the lien within the time limit after the filing of the notice of mechanic's lien. In other words, when the time limit of the lien is one year, and a *lis pendens* or notice of action to foreclose the mechanic's lien is filed, then the mere passage of one year does not in itself cause the lien to lapse.[5]

Contractors and Subcontractors

In regard to *contractors* and *subcontractors,* the laws of the states divide themselves generally into one of two classes: those using the New York System and those using the Pennsylvania System.

In defining the rights of lienors, it is necessary to distinguish between the contractor and the subcontractor: A **prime contractor** is a person who is hired directly by the owner; a **subcontractor** is hired by the contractor.

---

[3]In Arizona, Arkansas, California, Connecticut, Delaware, Georgia, Idaho, Iowa, Kansas, Louisiana, Minnesota, Nebraska, Nevada, New Hampshire, New Mexico, Ohio, Oklahoma, Rhode Island, Tennessee, Utah, Washington, West Virginia, Wisconsin, and the District of Columbia, mechanic's liens growing out of a particular job relate back to the beginning of the job. In Illinois and Maine, a mechanic's lien attaches to the land on the date on which the owner contracted for improvements.

[4]In Colorado and Oregon, the lienor must begin an action within six months.

[5]In the few remaining common law states, a *lis pendens* need not be filed. In those states the suit itself is notice.

Exhibit 12-2 Notice of Pendency of Action Form

[1]NOTICE OF PENDENCY OF ACTION

Supreme Court of the State of New York,
County of Suffolk

Charles W. Brown

Plaintiff

—against—

John Jones, HoHum Construction Co., Inc.,
and Olivia Ware

[2] Defendants

NOTICE IS HEREBY GIVEN that an action has been commenced and is pending in this Court upon the complaint of the above-named plaintiff against the above-named defendants for foreclosure of a certain mortgage bearing date the 15th day of June, , 19-- executed by the defendant John Jones to the plaintiff to secure the payment of the sum of Four Thousand and 00/100 ($4,000.00) -----------Dollars

with interest which mortgage was recorded in the Office of the Clerk of the County of Suffolk on the 16th day of June, 19-- , in Liber 2350 of Mortgages, page 342 .AND NOTICE IS FURTHER GIVEN that the premises affected by said foreclosure action are, at the time of of the filing of this notice, situated in the Town of Brookhaven , County of Suffolk , State of New York and are described in the said mortgage as follows:

[3][here follows a complete legal description]

Date the 20th day of July , 19 --.

/s/ Joan Apple
Attorney for the Plaintiff
(P.O. Box Address)

The Clerk of the County of Suffolk is hereby directed to index this notice to the names of all the defendants.

/s/ Joan Apple
Attorney for the Plaintiff
(P.O. Box Address)

[1] The Notice of Pendency of Action is the lis pendens referred to in the text. It is filed in a mortgage foreclosure as shown here; a partition action to foreclose a mechanic's lien, and a tax lien, to mention only some. It is usually filed at the time of filing a verified summons and complaint with the county clerk.

[2] The fact that there are a number of defendants here indicates that they are parties in interest to the action.Conceivably, HoHum Construction Co., Inc., may have a mechanic's lien against the property. They are all made parties to the action.

[3] The exact description of the property as it appears on the mortgage is entered here.

New York System. Under the New York System, a subcontractor is limited in the amount that can be collected by the amount due the contractor from the owner. For example, an owner enters into a contract with a builder for $50,000, and the contractor hires a subcontractor to do work in the amount of $10,000. If the subcontractor gives the owner notice as to the amount of monies that will become due on the subcontractor's contract with the contractor, then the owner is entitled to withhold that sum from any payments to the contractor. Notice to the owner is imperative. If the subcontractor has not given notice to the owner and the owner pays the entire contract price of $50,000 to the contractor, the subcontractor cannot collect the $10,000 from the owner but must look to the contractor.

In many states following the New York System, the law contains very strict provisions governing the actions of the contractor. For example, a prime contractor makes a contract with an owner for $45,000 and then hires a subcontractor. The owner pays the contractor in full, but the prime contractor fails to pay the subcontractor; the subcontractor may then make a demand on the contractor for the books and records concerning that particular job. If the contractor fails to produce such books and records within a specified time, there is a presumption of grand larceny by the contractor. In the event the contractor produces books and they show that any part of the $45,000 received under the contract has been diverted, the contractor may also be held for grand larceny. The term *diverting funds* means either that the contractor employed the monies for personal use or used the money for another job. For example, if the contractor was working two jobs at one time and used part of the $45,000 to pay a lumber bill on the second job, then the contractor is guilty of diverting funds; and there is a subsequent presumption of grand larceny.

Pennsylvania System. Under the Pennsylvania system, the subcontractor has the right to file a mechanic's lien for labor performed even though the entire contract price has been paid by the owner to the contractor. In short, there is no indebtedness from the owner to the contractor. Under this system, a hardship is often placed on the owner because the subcontractor is entitled to collect from the owner even though the owner has honestly and in good faith paid the entire contract price to the contractor.

Protection Against Liens

Most states are concerned with a serious question that is continually being raised by prospective mortgagees and owners about the methods by which they might have protection against liens that are placed against their properties. In some states, New York, for example, there is no serious question as far as mortgagees are concerned. As was stated above, if the mortgage is filed prior to a lien, then it has priority over the lien. However, what can be done in the other states? In some states, there is the so-called no lien contract. This is a contract between the owner and the prime contractor wherein the prime contractor agrees that no liens can be placed against the property. This contract is then recorded. By virtue of the recording, there is constructive notice to the world. Therefore, subcontractors become bound by the terms of the contract and cannot file effective liens against the property.

Waiver of Lien. When the **waiver of lien** is signed by the contractor, the right of the contractor to file any liens against the premises of the owner is relinquished. Sometimes this is signed when final payment is made and sometimes the instrument is executed prior to beginning work on the premises. In the event the contractor enters into this type of agreement, the contractor is bound by its terms not to file liens. However, in some states, although the contractor cannot file a lien if payment has not been made, a personal judgment may still be obtained against the owner.

Completion Bond. Another means of protection against liens is to have the contractor obtain a **completion bond,** a type of surety bond, prior to commencing a job. If any parties remain unpaid, they will be taken care of under the terms of the bond, and no liens will be attached to the property of the owner.

Holding Funds. Often when a business opportunity is sold, the purchaser will hold part of the purchase price for payment to possible creditors. **Holding funds** can be utilized effectively to thwart mechanic's liens. The owner merely holds back part of the contract price until the period for the filing of the mechanic's liens has passed. After this period, the balance due the contractor is paid.

In those states where the lien relates back to the commencement of the job, another method of holding back funds is employed. A mortgage is executed by the owner and mortgagee of the property, who records it. After the recording, the contractor starts the job. In this case, no actual cash is delivered to the mortgagor at the time of execution of the mortgage, but it is turned over to the mortgagor for payment to the contractor as the job progresses. The mortgage is recorded prior to the beginning of the job and, therefore, is prior in right to any subsequent mechanic's liens. This method is used mainly on new construction.

Payment by Lender. Because most construction is immediately financed with a construction loan, as previously outlined, financial institutions may insist on paying the bills directly. As each step in the construction is completed, the prime contractor submits the subcontractors' and/or material suppliers' bills to the lender who draws checks against the prime contractor's funds. In this way, the lender has reasonable assurance that liens will not be filed.

Disputes Between Contractor and Subcontractor

Disputes often arise between the contractor and the subcontractor. For example, a general contractor enters into a contract with a masonry subcontractor to erect the foundation for a building. When the foundation is completed, the general contractor refuses to pay the subcontractor because the foundation was not built according to specifications. In all probability, the subcontractor will attempt to file a mechanic's lien. If so, the contractor should deposit the amount in dispute with the county clerk for distribution after final decision by the court.

The great temptation for contractors is the feeling that they are justified in refusing to pay the subcontractors and, therefore, the money is not deposited. Instead, they use the money for other jobs and, in many states, face being charged with diversion of funds, a possible criminal offense.

Assignment of Lien

A lien is a cause of action and an asset. It may be assigned, therefore, much like any other cause of action. In an **assignment of lien,** the lienor creates an irrevocable power of attorney in the assignee, giving the assignee the right to act in the assignor's place and stead. The assignment, in addition to giving the assignee the right to act in the place of the lienor, contains a statement that assignor has done nothing to encumber or to impair the lien in any way. Armed with this, the assignee may then proceed to foreclose on the lien.

Satisfaction of Lien

When a lien has been paid, the lienor signs and acknowledges the **satisfaction of lien.** This instrument is then recorded and effectively discharges the lien of record. It is illustrated in Exhibit 12–3.

Liens Discharged by Court

After the time for the prosecution of the lien has passed, the lien appears open on the records of the county clerk. This may be objectionable to a title company from whom title insurance is being sought, or it may be objectionable to an attorney who is passing on the abstract of title. In any event, the lien should be removed from the record by obtaining a court order to vacate or cancel the lien for failure to prosecute. In this case, the court will issue an order discharging the lien. It is filed with the county clerk and has the effect of removing the lien from the record. On the record of the lien is written "Discharged by Order of the Court."

Partial Release of Lien

Just as there may be a partial release of mortgaged premises, so there may be a *partial release of a mechanic's lien.* For example, a contractor obtains a lien against two adjoining lots. If the owner pays a sufficient amount on account, the contractor may, if desired, partially release the lien. The important thing to remember here is that the description must be accurate and describe *only* that part of the premises to be released from the mechanic's lien.

■ **Exhibit 12-3 Satisfaction of Mechanic's Lien Form**

SATISFACTION OF MECHANIC'S LIEN

State of New York
County of Suffolk } ss.:

I, Lawrence Lienor, residing at number 14 Maiden Lane, in the Village of Bellport, Town of Brookhaven, County of Suffolk, State of New York, DO HEREBY CERTIFY, that a certain Mechanic's Lien, filed in the office of the Clerk of the County of Suffolk, on the 12th day of April 19, at 10 o'clock in the forenoon, in favor of Lawrence Lienor, claimant, against the building and lot with the improvements thereon situated on the northerly side of Main Street, being more particularly described as follows:

[here follows a complete legal description of property]

for the sum of One Thousand Eight Hundred and 00/100($1,800.00)Dollars, claimed against Laura Lienee as owner, is paid and satisfied, and I hereby consent that the same be discharged of record.

Witness my hand this 29thday of September ,19--

/s/Lawrence Lienor

State of New York
County of Suffolk } ss.:

On this 29th day of September ,19-- , personally appeared before me Lawrence Lienor, known to me, and to me known to be the person described in and who executed the foregoing instrument and he acknowledged to me that he executed the same.

/s/Elizabeth Roe
Notary Public, Suffolk County, N.Y.

OTHER SPECIFIC LIENS

Vendors' and Vendees' Liens

In any real property contract, the seller is commonly known as the **vendor** and the purchaser as the **vendee.** Under certain curcumstances, each of them may obtain a lien against the property involved in the contract of sale. The **vendor's lien** happens when title has been conveyed to a parcel of real property, but the entire purchase price has not been received. The vendor then has a lien to the extent of the unpaid balance and may foreclose against the property much in the nature of a mortgage foreclosure.

The real significance of the vendor's lien occurs when there is a contract for deed. In that case, legal title is in the vendor. Upon failure of the vendee to pay the balance or comply with the terms of the contract, the vendor may elect to foreclose on the contract.

The **vendee's lien** comes about when the purchaser has placed a deposit on a parcel of property and seeks the return of the down payment when the seller has defaulted. For example, a purchaser places a deposit on a parcel of property and the seller is unable to deliver marketable title and refuses to return the down payment. In this case, the vendee impresses a vendee's lien against the property.

A vendee's lien does not ordinarily extend to damages for loss of bargain, or to attorneys' fees or cost of title examination. However, if the contract of sale provides that the seller is to pay attorneys' fees in any legal action and the cost of title examination, the vendee may impress a lien for attorneys' fees and cost of title examination in addition to the amount of the down payment.

Both vendor's and the vendee's liens are equitable liens and enforceable by foreclosure. The equitable liens in general may be said to be liens so declared by the courts to prevent injustice, or an unjust enrichment of a party at fault.

Bail Bond Lien

Usually when a person is arrested on a criminal charge, bail is set for that person. The bail may be arranged either by placing an equal amount in cash, by a bond placed with the court by a professional bondsman, or by offering real property in lieu of cash or bond. Ordinarily, when real property is used for bail, the equity of the owner must be at least twice the amount of bail. Thus, **bail bond lien** is established against the real property. The lien is discharged by a certificate of discharge obtained from the district attorney and recorded after the person held on bail is discharged from bail.

Real Property Taxes and Assessments

Municipal and county governments generally raise the money necessary for their operation by means of *real property taxes.* The property is assessed and the amount of the tax entered on the tax rolls. If the tax is not paid within a stated time, the property is sold for taxes. A tax certificate is delivered to the purchaser, and the owner has the right to redeem the property, usually within three years; that is, if the taxpayer pays the purchaser of the tax certificate the back taxes, together with interest on the money (in some localities, 18 percent), the taxpayer then has a right to the property. If the taxpayer does not redeem within the period, the county will give the purchaser a quitclaim deed; or the county may foreclose and deliver marketable title to the purchaser.

GENERAL LIENS

Judgments

When an action at law is commenced, there are two or more parties to the action: the **plaintiff,** the party who brings the action, and the **defendant,** the party against whom the action is brought. At the conclusion of the action, the plaintiff, if successful, is more often than not awarded a money judgment. The *judgment* is then recorded in the office of the clerk of the county in which the judgment has been rendered. The clerk indexes the judgment alphabetically, with the name of the defendant as the judgment debtor and the name of the plaintiff as the judgment creditor. At this point, the judgment creditor may levy against the goods and chattels of the judgment debtor. However, prior to levying against the property of the judgment debtor, the judgment creditor must determine whether or not the judgment debtor has any assets. This determination is usually done by a supplementary proceeding whereby a *subpoena duces tecum* ("thou shalt bring with thee") is served upon the judgment debtor. The *subpoena duces tecum* orders the judgment debtor into court to be examined, and it further orders that books and records of account of the judgment debtor be brought to court. The judgment debtor is examined to determine what assets are possessed. If any are found, an order is made to the sheriff to seize them and sell them for the account of the judgment creditor. If the assets sold cover the amount of the judgment, the county clerk is notified to mark the judgment as satisfied. In some states, tax liens and judgments have priority over other liens, but not as a general rule.

As soon as the judgment is entered, it becomes a lien against the real property of the judgment debtor. The duration of the lien usually varies according to the statutes of the individual states; for example, from 1 year in Tennessee to 5 years in Idaho to 10 years in California, Colorado, New York, and most other states. In the third instance, although the judgment may be good for 20 years, it is a lien against real property for a period of only 10 years unless renewed.

In the event that *A* owns a parcel of property with a judgment filed against it and sells the property to *B* without satisfying the judgment, the lien follows the property. That is, the new owner will have a cloud on the title. If a judgment is entered in Suffolk county and the judgment debtor has property in Nassau County, the judgment may also be filed in Nassau County, and it becomes a lien against the property in Nassau County.

Federal Court Judgments

Title 28, Section 812, of the U.S. Code provides that a judgment rendered in a federal court in any state shall become a lien on property in the state in the same manner as if it were rendered in a state court of general jurisdiction. Thus, if a judgment is obtained in a federal court and is docketed in the proper county clerk's office, it becomes a lien on the debtor's property. If the state fails to provide a statute for the docketing of federal judgments, the federal judgment is automatically made a lien on the debtor's property in the state.

Federal Tax Liens

Federal tax liens attach either because of transfer of the property on death or because of violation of the income tax laws. In the first instance, the inheritance tax, if not paid, becomes a lien on the estate of the decedent. In the second case, if a person is delinquent in paying income tax, the government may issue a tax warrant, which is filed in the county in which property of the delinquent taxpayer is located, and it becomes a lien on that property.

State Inheritance Tax Liens

The **state inheritance tax** is a tax imposed by most states on the property of deceased persons. The amount of the tax becomes a lien against the estate. The discovery of this lien is an important step in the search and examination of title.

Corporation Franchise Tax Liens

Most states impose a **corporation franchise tax** on the right of the corporation to do business within the state. There is generally a minimum tax, for instance $25 per year, and graduated rates, depending on the amount of net income. If this tax is not paid by the corporation, the state may file a lien against the property belonging to the corporation.

Liens for Debts of Decedent

When a person dies, the property passes either to heirs or devisees. Creditors' rights are superior to the rights of heirs or devisees and the latter, therefore, take the property subject to the debts of the deceased. Debts are first paid out of the personal property of the estate, using, first, the property not specifically bequeathed, and second, the property disposed of by legacies. If there are still debts outstanding after this, the real property may be sold. When real property is being sold, it is therefore necessary to ascertain that there are no liens outstanding in favor of creditors of the decendent.

GLOSSARY

Assignment of lien An action in which the lienor creates an irrevocable power of attorney in the assignee

Bail bond lien Real property given in lieu of cash to cover an individual's bail

Completion bond An owner's means of protection against liens that is obtained prior to commencing the job; a type of surety bond

Corporation franchise tax A tax imposed by most states on the right of the corporation to do business within the state

Defendant The party against whom a court action is brought

Equitable liens Personal obligations or rights against the owner or the grantor of the land, which the courts will enforce under their equitable jurisdiction

Federal tax liens Liens attached either because of transfer of property upon death or because of violation of the income tax laws

General lien A claim against all of a person's assets

Holding funds When buying a business opportunity, a purchaser will often hold back part of the purchase price for payment to any possible creditors, and thus thwart mechanic's liens

Improvement Generally, the erection, alteration, or repair of any structure upon, connected with, or beneath the surface of the property

Lien A hold or claim that one person has on the property of another as security for a debt or charge against the property of another

Lienee The person whose property is subject to a lien

Lienor The person who holds or owns a lien

Mechanic's lien The right of claim given to those persons who have furnished work or materials for the improvement of real property (created solely by statute)

Plaintiff The party who brings an action at law

Prime contractor A person who is hired directly by the owner

Priority of liens The establishment of rights among the various liens placed against a property

Satisfaction of lien An instrument acknowledging that a lien has been paid, which, when recorded, discharges a lien of record

Specific lien A lien that affects only a specified piece or pieces of real property

State inheritance tax A tax imposed by most states upon the property of deceased persons

Statutory liens Liens created by statute

Subcontractor A person hired by the contractor

Vendee The purchaser

Vendee's lien A lien given to a vendee when the seller defaults on a contract to insure that the vendee receives his earnest money

Vendor The seller

Vendor's lien The lien given to a vendor after conveying title when the vendor has not received the full purchase price called for by the contract

Waiver of lien A written agreement signed by a contractor waiving the contractor's right to file a lien

QUESTIONS FOR REVIEW

1. Distinguish between a statutory lien, an equitable lien, a general lien, and a specific lien.
2. Regarding the order of priority of liens, what is the general rule under the New York System?
3. What is a *lis pendens*?
4. In a state using the Pennsylvania System of mechanic's liens, how can a prospective lender be protected against liens on new construction?
5. You own a home and have a savings account. Unhappily, a judgment is filed against you for $20,000. Simultaneously, you sell your home, empty your savings account, and flee to another state. What recourse does the judgment creditor have?

PROBLEMS AND ACTIVITIES

1. Assume you are a builder and have constructed a home valued at $75,000 on which the owner, Richard Randall, still owes you $25,000.

The house is on Lot 9 of the map of Security Acres in your city, your state. Within 79 days after completion of the job, you decide to file a mechanic's lien. Prepare the notice. After you file the notice, what is the next step?

2. Suppose you file a notice of mechanic's lien in the above situation but do nothing for four years. To your horror, you discover you are too late to foreclose on the lien. Is there anything you can do?

PART FOUR

REAL ESTATE FINANCING, INVESTMENTS, AND TAXATION

13

MORTGAGE FINANCING

KEY TERMS

Adjustable-rate mortgage
Assumable mortgage
Balloon note
Budget mortgage
Conventional-insured mortgage
Conventional mortgage
Convertible loan
Equity lending
FHA mortgage
Fixed-rate mortgage
Grannie Mae
Ground lease
Growing equity mortgage
Installment contract or contract for deed
Loan-to-value ratio
Nonassumption or nonalienation clause
Open-end mortgage
Package mortgage
Quick-pay mortgage
Sale and leaseback
Split-constant mortgage
VA mortgage
Wraparound mortgage

Mortgages, notes, and deeds of trust as legal documents and their provisions were discussed at length in Chapter 9. Now we turn to the many types of financing available to borrowers and the continued expansion of alternatives to enable more buyers to qualify for home ownership.

From the lenders' point of view, the dramatic rise of interest rates in the early 1980s left them caught with portfolios of low, fixed-rate mortgages while new loanable funds were paying higher rates. To alleviate this problem, mortgage lenders developed some new mortgage instruments; however, many of these had, in fact, originated in instruments used prior to the Great Depression.

Prior to the 1930s, for instance, a person might borrow $10,000 at 4 percent interest for ten years. Each year, the interest was paid; and at the end of the term, the principal was paid. Today, this would be called an interest-only loan. Next came the fixed-payment loan, in which part of the principal and interest was paid monthly.

TYPES OF MORTGAGES

There are basically three types of mortgages: the FHA-insured, the VA-guaranteed, and the conventional mortgage. Most others are variations of these types.

FHA-Insured Mortgage

The primary feature of the **FHA mortgage,** as far as the lender is concerned, is that the loan is insured. A loss as a result of failure of mortgagor to meet payments will be met by the Federal Housing Administration, which was instituted under the National Housing Act of 1934. It is now under the jurisdiction of the Department of Housing and Urban Development. This insurance feature enables lending institutions to lend a higher percent of value than they would have under ordinary circumstances.

FHA loans are calculated on a sliding scale as a percentage of the loan (the **loan-to-value ratio**). The maximum loan currently is $101,250 on one-family dwellings, $114,000 for two-family dwellings, $138,000 for three-family dwellings, $160,500 for four-family dwellings, and $90,000 on condominiums. These maximums change from time to time and differ in the various states. They also may vary within a state; for example, the maximum loan in an area with low median prices is likely to be less than the maximum loan in a prosperous city with more expensive homes.

The ratios are on a sliding scale:

97 percent of the first $25,000 of appraised value
95 percent of the excess

For example, if a single-family home is appraised at $90,000, the maximum loan is

.97 × $25,000 =	$24,250	
.95 × $65,000 =	61,750	
	$86,000	amount of loan
	$90,000	appraised value
	− 4,000	down
	$86,000	amount of loan

Because the FHA is an insured mortgage, premiums are paid by the borrower. The FHA mortgage insurance premimums (M.I.P.) are presented in Table 13-1.

Table 13-1 FHA One-Time M.I.P. Factor Table*

THE M.I.P. INSURANCE MUST BE PAID IN CASH AT CLOSING OR ADDED TO THE MORTGAGE

	15-Year	20-Year	25-Year	30-Year
Financed	.024	.030	.036	.038
Cash	.02344	.02913	.03475	−.03661

________ × ________ = ________

Mortgage Amount M.I.P. Factor Total M.I.P

*This does not apply to condominiums.

VA-Guaranteed Mortgage

The **VA mortgage**, the so-called GI mortgage, is a part of the Servicemen's Readjustment Act of 1944 (as amended). The crux of the law pertaining to real property is that the Veterans Administration will guarantee a certain percentage of a mortgage loan to a veteran up to a maximum amount to qualified lenders who lend money on homes purchased by veterans. The amount of the maximum guarantee, the rate of interest, and the length of the loan can be changed by an act of Congress. They have varied in the past and will probably be changed again.

Currently, the maximum amount of a VA loan is $144,000 with no down payment for one to four units. For loans of less than $45,000, 50 percent of the loan is guaranteed. For loans greater than $45,000, the guarantee is never less than $22,500. Otherwise, the amount the VA guarantees the lender is $36,000 or 40 percent of the loan, whichever is the lesser.

Conventional Mortgage

A **conventional mortgage,** as it is presently used, refers to a mortgage that is neither FHA-insured nor VA-guaranteed. In general, the down payment on a conventional mortgage is more than either the FHA or VA mortgages.

Mortgage Insurance. A conventional mortgage insured by a private mortgage insurance company is referred to as a **conventional-insured mortgage.** Although there were some private mortgage insurance companies forced into bankruptcy in the depression of the 1930s, the modern conventional-insured mortgage company came into being in 1956 with the formation of the Mortgage Guaranty Insurance Corporation (MGIC).

The premiums paid vary with the down payment. The greater the down payment, the lesser the rate. Although the rates are generally state-regulated, they are about the same from company to company, as shown by Table 13-2.

Assume a 95 percent loan with 25 percent insurance coverage and 5 percent down. Diagrammatically, it would appear like this:

100% purchase price = 5% down payment + 95% loan
95% loan = 25% insurance coverage + 70% at risk by lender
5% down payment +
25% insurance coverage = 30% "cushion" to lender

In short, the 5 percent down payment plus the 25 percent insurance coverage amounts to a 30 percent down payment by the borrower.

In most cases, particularly in a risky market, the lender stands to lose very little. Furthermore, on the higher-priced homes, the total amount of the loan is greater than the permissable FHA-insured loan and the premiums are lower than the FHA premiums. The result is that the private

Table 13-2 Private Mortgage Insurance Premiums

Insurance Coverage	Loan-to-Value Ratio	Annual Premium Plan	INSURANCE COST AS A PERCENT OF THE LOAN — Single-Premium Plans by Years of Coverage: 4	5	7	10	15
25%	91–95%	1% first year ¼% annually	—	1¾%	2%	2½%	2¾%
	80–90%	¾% first year ¼% annually	1¼%	—	—	2¼%	2½%
20%	91–95%	¾% first year ¼% annually	—	1½%	1¾%	2¼%	2½%
	80–90%	½% first year ¼% annually	1%	—	—	2%	2¼%
	80% and under	¼% first year ¼% annually	—	¾%	1%	1½%	—
10%	80% and under	0.15% first year .15% annually	—	0.6%	0.8%	1%	—

SOURCE: Mortgage Guarantee Insurance Corporation.

insurers have had to become highly competitive with FHA-insured loans and, therefore, have contributed to the decline in volume of the FHA loan.

New Rules Established in 1985. The Federal National Mortgage Association ("Fannie Mae") laid down guidelines effective October 15, 1985. Fannie Mae, which is more fully described in Chapter 14, is the nation's largest single buyer of mortgages from lenders such as savings and loan associations.

In an attempt to prevent losses, the 1985 rules call for refusal to buy mortgages unless the buyer pays 10 percent down or shows that she or he can qualify for the loan as a result of having a greater amount of income. They further stipulate that if the buyer pays less than 10 percent down, the buyer's *payment-to-income ratio* must be between 25 percent and 33 percent. Thus, the cost of buying the home (principal, interest, taxes, and insurance payments) plus monthly installment payments cannot exceed 33 percent of gross income.

Because Fannie Mae buys 10 percent of all home mortgages, these guidelines result in other lenders also adopting a toughened stance and following the rules to the letter (FHA and VA programs are not affected).

Unless FHA and VA loans can take up the slack, many marginal buyers will be forced out of the market. For example, prior to the effective date of the ruling, a buyer of a $76,500 home could put 5 percent down, secure a mortgage of 12.2 percent with monthly payments of $859, and qualify for the loan with an annual income of $36,814. Under the new guidelines, it takes an annual income of $41,232 to qualify.

Guidelines for Mortgage Loans

When a mortgage loan is retained as part of the lender's portfolio, the lender may use whatever guidelines are acceptable to its board of directors. General guidelines are presented in Chapter 20.

After receiving a loan application, the lender evaluates the borrower's credit history and capacity or financial ability to repay the mortgage loan as agreed. A significant determining factor is the borrower's gross monthly income. Essentially, the mortgage loan will not be made if housing expenses, which include mortgage principal and interest payments, home insurance, property taxes, and long-term-debt payments, exceed 25–41 percent of gross monthly income. Long-term debt generally consists of monthly payments extending six to ten months into the future; for example, automobile loans. Gross monthly income includes income of the husband and wife, alimony, child support payments, and any public assistance program.

When a FHA, VA, or conventional mortgage loan does not meet the requirements, the loan is denied. Although lenders may set whatever guidelines they wish for "retained" loans, the guidelines for VA-guaranteed, FHA-insured, or conventional mortgage loans sold to the secondary market are specific. These guidelines are summarized in Exhibit 13-1.

State Housing Finance Programs

In addition to the above mortgages, most states have various housing finance programs that provide mortgage money to qualified borrowers. Some states have many programs and some have only a few. These are summarized in Exhibit 13-2.

FIXED-RATE MORTGAGES

A **fixed-rate mortgage** is a mortgage on which a fixed rate of interest is charged during the life of the loan. From the end of World War II until the beginning of 1980, the fixed-rate mortgage was the most common loan offered by lenders to home buyers.

Generally, mortgage payments are made monthly; part is interest and part is principal. As payment is made in each period, the amount paid as interest declines and the amount paid as principal increases.

There are three types of fixed-rate mortgages: the 30-year fixed, the 15-year fixed, and the bi-weekly fixed. Assuming the same amount of loan, monthly payments rise as they progress from the 30-year fixed to the 15-year fixed to the bi-weekly (twice a month) fixed-rate mortgage. Over the life of the loan, the total amount of interest paid declines as it moves from the 30-year fixed to the bi-weekly mortgage (see Table 13-3).

Exhibit 13-1 Qualifying Buyers for a Mortgage Loan

FEDERAL HOUSING ADMINISTRATION (FHA) & CONVENTIONAL INCOME QUALIFYING

I. HOUSING RATIO

Gross Monthly Income	$ ________	
Times[1]	× ________ %	
Maximum P.I.T.I.[2]	= $ ________	
Less: Monthly Est. for:		
Real Estate Taxes	– ________	
Home-owners Ins.	– ________	
Mortgage Ins. (see chart below)	– ________	
Equals: Maximum P & I	= ________	(A)

II. FIXED PAYMENT RATIO

Gross Monthly Income	$ ________	
Times[3]	× ________ %	
Maximum P.I.T.I.[2] & Long Term Debt	= ________	
Less: Monthly Est. For:		
Real Estate Taxes	– ________	
Homeowners Ins.	– ________	
Mortgage Ins. (see chart below)	– ________	
Long-Term Monthly Debt[4]	– ________	
Equals: Maximum P & I	= $ ________	(B)

MAXIMUM MORTGAGE

For FHA or Conventional Loan, use lower of P & I Figure from A and B above	$ ________
Principal & Interest Factor [5]	= ________
Maximum Mortgage Loan	$ ________

VA INCOME QUALIFYING

I. RESIDUAL INCOME QUALIFYING

Gross Monthly Income	$ ________	
Less:		
Federal Taxes	– ________	
State Taxes	– ________	
Social Security (.0751) Max. $282	– ________	
Real Estate Taxes (monthly est)	– ________	
Home-owner's Insurance (monthly est)	– ________	
Long Term Monthly Debt (LTC) (credit cards, all loans, child care/support, etc.)	– ________	
Income Required for Family Support (see chart below)	– ________	
Equals: Maximum P & I	= $ ________	(A)

II. RATIO QUALIFYING

Gross Monthly Income	$ ________	
Times:	× .41*	
Equals: Maximum Housing Expense + LTD	= ________	
Less:		
Real Estate Taxes (monthly est)	– ________	
Home-owner's Insurance (monthly est)	– ________	
Long Term Monthly Debt[4]	– ________	
Home-owners Assoc. Dues/ Special Assess.	– ________	
Equals: Maximum P & I	= $ ________	(B)
Maximum P & I (Lower of A or B above)	________	
Principal & Interest Factors	± ________	
Equals: Maximum Mortgage	= $ ________	

MINIMUM REQUIREMENT FOR FAMILY SUPPORT
LOAN AMOUNTS OF $69,999 AND BELOW

LIVING AREA SQ. FT.	FAMILY SIZE 1	2	3	4	5	6	7
1–1100	463	710	840	936	974	1,050	1,128
1101–1500	478	726	857	954	984	1,071	1,149
1501–up	493	742	875	973	1,013	1,092	1,170
LOAN AMOUNTS OF $70,000 AND ABOVE							
1–1100	516	798	945	1,056	1,096	1,177	1,260
1101–1500	531	814	962	1,074	1,116	1,198	1,281
1501–up	546	830	980	1,093	1,135	1,219	1,302

ADD $75.00 FOR EACH ADDITIONAL PERSON

If source of heat is other than gas add $40.00

*May go to .46 with compensating factors.

NOTE: It is important to take into account the veteran's credit history, job stability, proposed mortgage payment in relation to previous housing expenses, liquid assets after closing, etc.

ANNUAL MORTGAGE INSURANCE FACTORS

LTV	30 Yr. Fixed Pay. 1st Year*	30 Yr. Fixed Pay. Renewal**	30 Yr Non-fixed Pay. 1st Year*	30 Yr Non-fixed Pay. Renewal**	15 Yr. Fixed Pay. 1st Year*	15 Yr. Fixed Pay. Renewal**
91%-95%	1.00%	.49%	1.20%	.54%	.90%	.25%
86%-90%	.40%	.34%	.50%	.44%	.40%	.20%
81%-85%	.30%	.29%	.35%	.34%	.25%	.20%

*Use 1st year factor to determine premium to be paid at closing.
**Use Renewal factor to determine monthly premium for income qualifying.
These factors are subject to frequent change.

[1] For a conventional loan, use 28 percent; for FHA loan use 29 percent.
[2] Principal, interest, taxes and insurance.
[3] For a conventional loan with 10 percent or larger down payment, use 36 percent; with a down payment less than 10 percent, use 33 percent. For an FHA loan, use 41 percent.
[4] For a conventional loan, total of monthly payments to be made each of ten or more months in the future; for VA or FHA loan, total of monthly payments to be made six or more months in the future.
[5] Same as Appendix C, Column 6, installment to amortize.

■ Exhibit 13-2 State Housing Finance Programs

	Single-Family			Multi-Family			Special Projects										
	Mortgage Purchase	Direct Construction	Direct Permanent	Mortgage Purchase	Direct Construction	Direct Permanent	Home Improvement Loan/Grant	Mobile Home Loan	Modular Housing	Housing for the Elderly	Seed Money Loans	Section 8	Public Housing	Housing for the Disabled	Energy Conservation	Other	Federal Program Participation
Alabama	✓	–	–	–	–	–	–	–	–	–	–	–	–	–	–	–	–
Alaska	✓	–	–	–	–	–	✓	✓	–	–	–	–	–	–	–	✓	–
Arizona	–	–	–	–	–	–	–	–	–	–	–	–	–	–	–	–	–
Arkansas	✓	–	✓	–	✓	✓	✓	–	–	–	–	–	–	–	–	–	✓
California	–	–	–	–	✓	✓	–	–	–	–	–	–	–	–	–	–	–
Colorado	–	–	–	–	✓	✓	✓	–	–	–	–	✓	–	–	–	✓	✓
Connecticut	✓	–	–	–	✓	✓	✓	–	–	–	–	✓	–	–	✓	✓	✓
Delaware	✓	–	–	–	✓	✓	–	–	✓	✓	✓	✓	–	–	–	–	✓
Washington, D.C.	–	–	–	–	–	–	–	–	–	–	–	–	–	–	–	–	–
Florida	–	–	–	–	✓	–	–	–	–	–	–	–	✓	–	–	–	–
Georgia	–	–	–	–	–	–	–	✓	✓	✓	✓	✓	✓	–	–	–	–
Hawaii	✓	–	–	–	–	–	–	–	–	✓	–	✓	✓	–	–	–	–
Idaho	✓	–	–	–	✓	✓	✓	–	–	✓	–	✓	✓	✓	–	✓	✓
Illinois	–	–	–	–	✓	✓	–	–	–	✓	–	✓	–	✓	–	–	✓
Indiana	✓	–	–	–	–	–	–	–	–	–	–	–	–	–	–	–	–
Iowa	✓	–	–	–	–	–	–	–	–	–	–	–	–	–	–	–	–
Kansas	–	–	–	–	–	–	–	–	–	–	–	–	–	–	–	–	–
Kentucky	✓	✓	–	–	✓	–	✓	–	–	–	✓	✓	–	–	✓	✓	✓
Louisiana	–	–	✓	–	✓	–	–	–	–	–	–	–	–	–	–	–	✓
Maine	–	–	–	✓	–	–	–	–	✓	✓	✓	✓	–	✓	✓	✓	✓
Maryland	✓	–	✓	–	✓	✓	✓	–	–	✓	✓	✓	✓	✓	✓	✓	✓
Massachusetts	✓	–	–	–	✓	✓	–	–	–	✓	–	✓	–	✓	✓	✓	✓
Michigan	–	–	✓	–	✓	✓	✓	–	✓	✓	✓	✓	✓	✓	✓	✓	✓
Minnesota	✓	–	–	–	✓	✓	✓	–	–	–	–	✓	–	✓	✓	✓	✓
Mississippi	✓	–	–	–	–	–	–	–	–	–	–	–	–	–	–	–	–
Missouri	–	✓	✓	–	✓	✓	–	–	–	✓	–	✓	✓	–	–	✓	✓
Montana	✓	–	–	–	✓	✓	–	–	–	–	–	–	–	–	–	–	✓
Nebraska	✓	–	–	–	–	–	–	–	–	–	–	–	–	–	–	–	–
Nevada	–	–	–	✓	–	–	–	✓	✓	–	–	–	–	–	–	–	✓
New Hampshire	✓	–	–	✓	–	–	–	–	–	–	–	✓	–	✓	–	–	✓
New Jersey	✓	–	–	–	✓	✓	–	–	–	–	–	✓	–	–	✓	–	✓
New Mexico	–	–	–	–	–	–	–	–	–	–	–	–	–	–	–	–	–
New York	✓	–	–	–	✓	✓	–	–	–	✓	–	✓	–	–	–	✓	✓
North Carolina	✓	–	–	✓	–	–	–	–	–	–	–	–	–	–	–	–	✓
North Dakota	–	–	–	–	–	–	–	–	–	–	–	✓	–	–	–	–	✓
Ohio	–	–	–	–	–	–	–	–	–	✓	–	✓	–	–	–	–	✓
Oklahoma	✓	–	–	–	✓	–	–	–	–	–	–	✓	–	–	–	–	✓
Oregon	–	–	–	–	✓	✓	–	✓	✓	✓	–	✓	–	–	–	✓	✓
Pennsylvania	✓	–	–	–	✓	✓	–	–	–	–	–	✓	✓	–	–	✓	✓
Rhode Island	✓	–	–	–	✓	✓	–	–	–	–	–	–	–	–	–	–	✓
South Carolina	–	–	–	–	–	–	–	–	–	–	–	✓	–	–	–	–	✓
South Dakota	✓	–	–	–	✓	✓	–	–	–	–	–	✓	–	✓	–	–	✓
Tennessee	–	–	✓	–	✓	✓	–	–	–	✓	✓	✓	–	–	–	–	✓
Texas	✓	–	–	–	–	–	–	–	–	–	–	–	–	–	–	–	–
Utah	✓	–	–	–	✓	✓	–	✓	–	✓	–	✓	–	–	–	–	✓
Vermont	✓	–	–	–	✓	✓	–	–	–	✓	✓	✓	–	–	–	✓	✓
Virginia	–	✓	✓	–	✓	✓	–	–	–	–	–	✓	–	✓	✓	✓	✓
Washington	–	–	–	–	–	–	–	–	–	–	–	–	–	–	–	–	–
West Virginia	✓	–	–	–	✓	✓	✓	–	–	–	✓	–	–	–	✓	✓	✓
Wisconsin	–	–	–	–	✓	✓	✓	–	–	–	–	–	–	–	–	–	✓
Wyoming	✓	–	–	–	✓	✓	–	–	–	–	–	–	–	–	–	–	✓

SOURCE: Urban Land Institute, Development Review and Outlook 1983–1984.

Table 13-3 Comparison of Monthly Payments on Various Fixed-Rate Mortgages

$75,000 MORTGAGE

	30-YEAR FIXED-RATE AT 10%	15-YEAR FIXED-RATE AT 10%	BI-WEEKLY MORTGAGE AT 10%	GROWING EQUITY MORTGAGE (GEM) AT 9.625%	ARM AT 9% w/5% CAP*
Monthly Payment	$ 658	$ 806	$ 658 ($329 × 2)	$637 Years 1–6 Years 7–16 increases 7% per year	$603 Year 1 713 Year 2 883 Years 3–30
Interest cost first year	7,481	7,398	7,434	7,199	6,729
Interest cost fourth year	7,336	6,606	7,061	7,049	10,327
Mortgage balance first year	74,583	72,726	74,476	74,549	74,488
Mortgage balance fourth year	73,052	64,372	69,817	72,907	73,619
Interest cost life	$161,942	70,062	104,331	97,017	237,330
Difference from 30-year fixed-rate		−$91,880	−$ 57,611	−$64,925	+$ 75,388

*For the sake of comparison, the interest rate on the ARM used in this example increased 2 percent in the second year and 3 percent in the third year, bringing it up to the 5 percent lifetime cap. This is a hypothetical situation. Not all ARMs will behave in this manner; some will increase (or decrease) more slowly, some more rapidly. In each case, the monthly payments and interest costs will differ.

SOURCE: Mortgage Bankers Association of America.

Budget Mortgage

The **budget mortgage** is a further development of the self-amortizing mortgage, which provides for monthly payments of part interest and part principal. The budget mortgage includes in the monthly payments one-twelfth of the year's taxes, a proportionate amount of the yearly fire insurance premiums, and any other charges that might, if left unpaid, constitute a basis for foreclosure of the mortgage.

Generally, this is referred to as a PITI mortgage, meaning part of the monthly payment goes to principal, part to interest, part to taxes and insurance.

Package Mortgage

The **package mortgage** goes a step farther than the budget mortgage. Usually, it incorporates all the features of the budget mortgage plus payments for certain mechanical equipment put in the home. In this manner, all charges are met in one payment.

Open-End Mortgage

The **open-end mortgage** is a mortgage in which the borrower is given a limit that may be borrowed. For example, the loan may be authorized up to $20,000, and the borrower may initially borrow only $15,000; but at a later date borrower may increase the loan to the maximum authorized, in this case $20,000, without changing the terms of the original agreement.[1]

Quick-Pay Mortgage

The **quick-pay mortgage** is a 15-year fixed-rate mortgage. The monthly payments are higher than for a 30-year fixed-rate loan. The down payment is also greater than for a 30-year fixed-rate mortgage; therefore, fewer people can qualify for the loans.

One of the advantages of the quick-pay mortgage is that interest payments over the life of the loan are reduced. Another is that equity in the home builds at a faster rate, which may enable the homeowner with this increased equity to trade up sooner. The other side of the coin is that paying less interest on the mortgage means losing the tax benefits of higher mortgage interest deductions.

GEMs

GEMs **(growing equity mortgages),** give the borrower the right to increase payments at a set amount each year. Generally, these increases are between

[1]Connecticut, Florida, Kentucky, Louisiana, Maryland, Massachusetts, Missouri, Montana, Nebraska, New Hampshire, New Jersey, North Dakota, Rhode Island, South Dakota, and Vermont have statutes limiting the amount of future advances that can be included in a single mortgage.

2 and 7 percent. The increases are applied to principal and stop after the tenth year of the loan with payments remaining constant thereafter. The term of the mortgage ranges from 15 to 30 years.

Borrowers, however, must be confident that their incomes will keep pace with the payment increases because although interest rates are fixed, monthly payments change.

From about 1981 to early 1985, due to high interest rates, the emphasis shifted to adjustable-rate mortgages and other alternative mortgage forms. During this period, nearly 75 percent of all new loans were in this category. However, by March 1986, due to lower interest rates, there was a return to the fixed-rate mortgage. About 80 percent of all new mortgages were fixed-rate and 20 percent were adjustable-rate and other forms. As a general rule, when rates rise there is an increase in adjustable-rate mortgages; conversely, when rates decline the number of fixed-rate mortgages increases.

In periods of inflation, lending institutions are locked in to interest payments from borrowers that are less than their cost of capital (interest paid on savings deposits). Consequently, alternative mortgage forms have been examined, experimented with, and used in recent years, with the major objective of providing an escape for institutions from fixed-interest rates of return on their loans.

ADJUSTABLE-RATE MORTGAGES

The **adjustable-rate mortgage** (ARM) is a variation of the variable-rate mortgage (VRM). In both cases, a home buyer agrees to a mortgage that incorporates a flexible rate of interest—one in which the rate of interest can fluctuate up or down based on some predetermined index of interest rates. The ARM interest rate can be adjusted up or down as often as every 90 days or as seldom as every five years. Most ARMs, however, are adjusted every six months, each year, or every three years on 30-days notice given by the lender to the borrower.

The reason for the widespread use of the ARM is that most residential loans are made by savings and loan associations who borrow short-term from depositors and lend on long-term mortgages. In the past, they often had loaned out funds at a fixed rate of interest, and when interest rates rose they lost money because their cost of funds rose to a level higher than the rates they were receiving from their mortgage loans.

Borrower Should Be Wary of the ARM

In some cases borrowers have taken out loans that limit interest rate rises to no more than .25 percent every 6 months, *but it doesn't work out that way.* It is written somewhere in small type that if the rate goes up 1 percent in that period, the lender can save the unused .75 percent and apply it in future adjustment periods. Thus, even if rates fall, the borrower's rate can continue to rise. Borrowers must be cautious and ask a number of questions before agreeing to an ARM mortgage.

1. *Index.* What is the barometer of interest rates to which the ARM is tied? Most are tied to interest rates on U.S. Treasury securities. Those securities have interest rates that change with general economic conditions. A borrower should try to avoid an ARM tied to a bank's or a savings and loan's cost of funds, which does not necessarily change in the same direction and amount as do the general interest rates.
2. *Interest rate caps.* How much and how often can the interest rate change in each adjustment period? Is there a maximum level beyond which the interest rate cannot be changed? If interest rates drop, how far and how fast is the interest rate adjusted downward? Is there a limit below which the interest payment cannot decline?
3. *Initial interest rate.* How low is the initial interest rate compared with the market rate and how soon will the rate be changed? The borrower should be wary of interest rates more than 2 percent below the current market rate. A larger discount may be reflected in the price of the home. Borrowers should also be sure they can afford the payments when the new higher rate of interest takes effect.
4. *Payment caps.* When there is an interest rate cap, there is an automatic limit on the maximum payment. The borrower, however, may have a payment cap without an interest rate cap. If this happens, negative amortization results, which means the unpaid interest will be added to the principal of the loan.
5. *Adjustment period.* What is the adjustment period—3, 6, or 12 months, every three years or every five years? The more frequent the adjustment period, the lower the initial interest rate. However, frequent adjustment is riskier when rates are rising.
6. *Assumability.* Can the home be sold to another individual and can that individual assume the ARM without a change in terms, conditions, or a transfer penalty?

The FHA ARM

On July 30, 1984, after congressional approval, the FHA ARM was introduced by HUD. FHA insurance is available on these loans for up to 30 years on owner-occupied one- to four-family structures.

Interest rate adjustments are limited to a 1 percent increase or decrease per year and no more than a 5 percent increase or decrease will be permitted over the life of the loan. The index used in calculating the annual rate adjustments (up or down) is the weekly yield on U.S. Treasury securities adjusted to a one-year constant maturity. The index is published weekly in the *Federal Reserve Bulletin Statistical Release H15* and in the *Wall Street Journal.*

When the borrower applies for the loan, the lender must make a full disclosure of the terms and conditions of the loan and a copy of such terms and conditions must be received and signed by the borrower. This disclosure statement must also show a worst-case scenario, designed to show the borrower what the monthly payments would be if the interest rate increased 1 percent for each of the first five years of the loan (thus reaching the legal cap) with no decrease in the interest for the remaining life of the loan.

Furthermore, the loan must be assumable and it may be converted to a fixed-rate loan. Most importantly *no* negative amortization is permitted.

The Reverse ARM

The reverse ARM is an adjustable-rate mortgage designed for older Americans. A lender makes a loan based on a percentage of appriased value of the borrower's home. The borrower buys an annuity payable monthly to the lender in an amount equal to the monthly payments. The term of the loan can be for life or until the house is sold.

In effect, the older person is receiving cash for monthly living expenses from a lender based on the equity in the home that is either paid for or almost paid for. This sum is greater than the cost of the annuity. Therefore, the main advantage to the borrower is that equity built up by the older person in the home is unlocked.

There are also disadvantages. If the borrower wants to move and sell the home in order to buy a new one, there may not be enough equity left to enable the borrower to do so. There also may be very little or no equity remaining for the borrower's heirs.[2]

EQUITY LENDING

When the lender participates in the equity, **equity lending,** another form of lending, takes place.

Equity Funding or Participation

Used for many years in commercial financing, equity funding or participation generally takes one of two forms, or both. The lender lends at a relatively low rate in return for which the lender receives a percentage of the rents, or, upon sale, the lender receives a percentage of the profits. Usually, the lender shares in both.

---

[2]This may also occur with a fixed-rate mortgage.

Convertible Loan

A variation of equity funding, the **convertible loan,** is used in large loans for commercial projects. It is a debt instrument that converts to equity after a period of time. For example, assume a $500,000 loan by an institution on a $1 million project. An agreement is made that the $500,000 loan will convert to a 50 percent ownership position after a fixed term, say five years. The borrower is given a lower-than-market rate of interest during that five-year period plus 100 percent of ownership tax benefits. At the end of the five years, the lender is given 50 percent of the ownership at the first year's price, but he or she has also realized 50 percent of the capital appreciation of the project. In addition, the lender has had fixed earnings during that five-year period.

SELLER FINANCING

Because of the increasing difficulty of obtaining loans, sellers are finding themselves in a position where they must finance all or part of the selling price. This can be handled in various ways.

Purchase Money Mortgage

The purchase money mortgage is a mortgage given as part of the consideration for the sale of real property. This type of mortgage typically arises when the seller agrees to "take back" (as it is commonly said) a mortgage as part of the purchase price in a transaction. The seller is really financing, or partially financing, the transaction. For example, *A* wants to sell to *B* a piece of property for $50,000, and *B* has only $10,000 in cash and is without recourse to any other type of mortgage. In such a case, *A* might take the $10,000 from *B* and take back a mortgage in the amount of $40,000. It should be remembered that a purchase money mortgage is created by spelling it out in the mortgage instrument. In short, a statement that it is a purchase money mortgage, is written into the instrument (sometimes called, colloquially, a PM mortgage).

Although some builders use the option as was outlined in Chapter 7, a combination blanket mortage (covering more than one parcel) containing a partial release clause (releasing one parcel under the blanket) is perhaps a more favored instrument of the builder who is operating with little cash and who does not want capital tied up in real property. For example, *A* is a builder and *B* has 100 lots for sale. *A* arranges a transaction with *B* that requires very little cash. After *A* has received a tentative commitment from a bank for a building loan, *A* approaches *B* and offers him $1,000 per lot. *A* proposes to pay $100 cash for each of the lots and gives *B* a blanket purchase money mortgage covering $900 per lot for the balance of the consideration of the transaction. This is accepted by *B*, and *A* insists that the mortgage contain a partial release clause to the effect that, on payment of $900, *B* will release from the terms of the mortgage any one of the lots that *A* desires. *B* agrees to all of this, and *A* pays only 10 percent cash at this point, begins building, obtains a commitment from the bank when enough of the house has been build to satisfy the bank appraiser, pays *B* for one lot, receives cash from the bank, finishes the building, and sells it for a profit.

This hypothetical problem is, of course, an oversimplification, but not completely. The only variations on the figures given would depend on the bargaining position of the parties. *A,* the builder, might have to put down more than 10 percent cash; but, in the final analysis, this can be done with very little money.

The practitioner will recognize at once that there are "two sides to every coin." If the seller and the builder do make a deal as far as a price is concerned, should the seller draw up the partial release clause releasing one lot for the payment of the balance due on that one lot? It is thought that it might offer more protection to the seller to have *A,* the builder and mortgagee, pay off, perhaps $1,000 dollars on each lot released, the extra $100 to be applied toward the payment of the principal on the balance of the mortgage.

It might be stated here that the seller should take other precautionary measures in the transaction outlined above. Seller should insist upon substantially the same protection as that discussed under "Options" in Chapter 7. As all practitioners know, different lots in a block usually have a different value; hence, the partial release clause should be drawn in terms of at least two lots being paid for in full by the purchaser and released at the same time. One lot will be considered to be of greater value than the other. This will effectively avoid the seller's being left with the poorer lots if the builder defaults before the mortgage has been completely paid.

Conveyance of Mortgaged Premises

If there is an existing mortgage on the property when a buyer and seller enter into a contract for the sale of real property, the purchaser may take the property subject to the mortgage, or may assume the mortgage if it is an **assumable mortgage.**

Subject to Versus Assuming. When a parcel of property is purchased subject to a mortgage, there is inserted in the deed the statement:

> This deed is made subject to the following: a certain first mortgage in the amount of $10,000 and interest to date, made by Arlene Jones to Arthur Brown on January 2, 1987, recorded January 3, 1987, in the office of the Clerk of the County of Nassau, State of New York, in Liber 2159 of Mortgages at page 5.

This statement means that the purchaser recognizes the existence of a mortgage on the property. For example, a buyer moves into a house and makes the payments that are due on the property mortgage. At this point things run smoothly; however, what happens if buyer fails to meet the payments? The seller, who had the mortgage placed on the property originally, signed either a note or bond along with the original mortgage. If payments are not met, the mortgagee will commence foreclosure proceedings. The property will be sold and buyer will be evicted. Suppose, however, there is a deficiency of $2,000 due the mortgagee after the foreclosure sale has been completed. The question now is Who is liable for the deficiency, the seller, who is the mortgagor, or the buyer, who took the property "subject to" the mortgage? Buyer promised nothing when taking the property subject to the mortgage. In effect, buyer merely recognized the existence of the mortgage. Seller, however, promised to pay the mortgagee when signing either the note or the bond. Therefore, the mortgagee will have recourse to the seller for the $2,000 deficiency, except in those states where deficiency judgments are prohibited by law.

When the seller sells the property subject to a mortgage, the seller may be liable for any deficiency. On the other hand, when the purchaser buys subject to the mortgage, the purchaser is not liable for any deficiency; and the most that the purchaser can lose in the event of foreclosure is any equity that may have been built up in the property.

A quite different situation arises when property is sold on which there is a mortgage and the purchaser "assumes" the mortgage.

When a mortgage is assumed, the purchaser covenants and promises to pay the deficiency. In other words, a contract has been entered into with the seller for the benefit of a third party, the mortgagee. Thus, the mortgagee may collect the deficiency from the purchaser. If the purchaser cannot pay, then the mortgagee seeks payment from the mortgagor on the note. However, in view of the fact that there is a contract between the mortgagor and the purchaser, the seller (mortgagor) may seek the amount of the deficiency from the purchaser.

In practice, when there is an assumption clause in a deed, both the purchaser and the seller sign the deed as contrasted to the normal situation when the grantor alone signs the deed, because by virtue of the assumption clause the parties are entering into what amounts to a written contract in addition to a deed conveying title to the property.

In about half the states, purchasers customarily buy subject to the mortgage; and in the other half, they assume the mortgage.

Nonassumption or Due-On-Sale Clause. In recent years, financial institutions have adopted the practice of inserting a **nonassumption clause** (or **nonalienation clause**) in conventional mortgages. In essence, this clause states that the mortgagor cannot sell the property and have the buyer assume the mortgage without the consent of the lender. From the point of view of the institutional lenders, the reason is quite simple. For example, suppose a mortgage carries 8 percent interest and that the interest rate drops to 7 percent. In this case, the institution will readily give permission to the mortgagor to sell the property and have the buyer assume the mortgage (carrying 8 percent instead of the new rate of 7 percent). However, if the rate jumps from 8 percent to, say, 13 percent, then the institution will refuse permission to the borrower to sell and have the buyer assume at the old rate. They hope, of course, the property will be refinanced and a new mortgage issued at 13 percent.

In October 1982, legislation making the due-on-sale clause in conventional mortgages enforceable was signed into law. It should be noted that the nonassumption clause applies only to conventional mortgages, not to FHA or VA mortgages.

Wraparound Mortgage

In states using a deed of trust, the **wraparound mortgage** is referred to as an all-inclusive deed of trust. It developed many years ago in New York where usury laws pertaining to individuals were strictly held at 6 percent. In addition, it was used as a sweetener, or "kicker" as it was called.

Suppose, for example, an owner offered a property at $100,000 on which there was an assumable mortgage of $60,000 at 4 percent. A buyer has $20,000 cash. Thus, the $60,000 mortgage assumed, plus the $20,000 cash, is $80,000. The seller could take back a purchase money mortgage (second) of $20,000 at 6 percent. However, if the $80,000 balance was "wrapped around," the seller could legally earn greater than 4 percent and thus "beat" the usury law.

In this case, the buyer assumes the $60,000 mortgage at 4 percent, but agrees to pay to the seller 6 percent on the entire $80,000. Therefore, the buyer pays $20,000 cash and makes payments to the seller on the $80,000 at 6 percent. The seller than makes the payments on the $60,000 at 4 percent to the lender. Thus, the seller has $20,000 at risk earning 6 percent plus the extra 2 percent on the lender's $60,000, giving the seller a greater yield on the $20,000 at risk. The effective yield in this example is approximately 12 percent.

When the financial institutions introduced the nonassumption or due-on-sale clause in mortgages, the wraparound (or Magic Wrap as some call it) was re-created, not to beat usury but to beat the nonassumption clause. Here, the buyer wraps around the nonassumable mortgage, and the seller continues to pay the institution with monies received from the buyer and retains the rest. There is some question, however, as to the legality of this; namely, if the institution discovers violation of the nonassumption clause, can it still foreclose? This method can be legally employed if the original mortgage instrument fails to contain a due-on-sale clause.

In both cases, the seller has, in effect, a second mortgage.

Land Contract

Installment Contract. The **installment contract** (or **contract for deed)** is a device used in the sale of property for which financing is not available. A contract is entered into between the seller and the buyer after the buyer has paid a deposit for the property. The buyer agrees to pay a certain sum monthly on the balance due under the contract and also agrees to pay the taxes and insurance. The seller retains title to the property under such an agreement. However, seller agrees to deliver clear title when the balance has been completely paid. In addition, there is generally a provision that, in the event the purchaser defaults, the sums paid are to be construed as rent and forfeited to the seller.

If the buyer has built up a large equity (30 percent in Ohio, by statute; in most states, by court decision), then forfeiture is precluded and the contract must be foreclosed and any amount received on the sale over the indebtedness goes to the purchaser. This need to foreclose and the precluding of forfeiture are now being challenged in the courts resulting from a rising real estate market. It is likely to be a question raised more and more in the future (cf. *Curry v. Tucker,* 616 P2d 8 [Alaska, 1980]).

In some areas, the installment contract has been used to finance houses. For example, *A* desires to purchase a home and has insufficient funds for the down payment. The builder or owner may enter into an installment contract with *A* provided that, when enough has been paid on the contract to satisfy lending institutions, the balance of the purchase price will be financed by an FHA loan or other suitable financing. In some cases, the buyer is permitted to pay the entire amount in installments, the deed being withheld until full payment has been made.

An installment contract is illustrated in Exhibit 13-3.

Second Mortgage as a Junior Financing Device. The second mortgage is very often used as a *junior financing* device. For example, when the purchase price of a property is $60,000, there exists a first mortgage in the amount of $50,000, and the broker has a prospect with only $4,000 cash, a contract may be used for financing the balance of $6,000 instead of a second purchase money mortgage. The seller then receives the $4,000 cash, the parties to the transaction enter into a contract for $6,000, and the purchaser will either assume or take the property subject to the $50,000 mortgage. This is done where refinancing is not possible.

Balloon Note or Balloon Mortgage

Used in conjunction with any form of financing, this instrument generally provides for periodic payments that *do not* amortize the loan by its termination date, leaving the balance due to be paid in a lump sum.

Generally the **balloon note** takes one of two forms:

1. *Interest-only note.* For example, you borrow $100,000 at 12 percent and agree to pay interest only for ten years and at the end of the ten years to pay the $100,000 in a lump sum.

2. *Straight note with periodic payments of principal and interest.* For example, you borrow $100,000 at 12 percent and agree to pay $1,300

■ **Exhibit 13-3 Real Estate Installment Contract Form**

REAL ESTATE INSTALMENT CONTRACT

(Sick or Unemployment Clause

IT IS HEREBY AGREED by and between Maureen T. Jensen

of Colfax *State of* Washington

the vendor *and* Martin Claxton

of Seattle *County of* King*, State of Washington, the vendee*, *that the vendor* *will sell and the vendee* *will buy the following described real estate, situate in the County of* King *and State of Washington, to-wit:*

[here follows complete legal description of the property]

upon the following terms and conditions: The purchase price of said property is Forty-Five Thousand and 00/100 ($45,000.00) *DOLLARS, of which the sum of* $15,000.00 *Dollars has been paid in cash, receipt whereof is hereby acknowledged and the balance of the purchase price amounting to* Thirty Thousand and 00/100 ($30,000.00)

Dollars is to be paid in monthly *instalments of* Six Hundred Eighty-Five and 00/100 ($685.00)

Dollars each, beginning on the 18th *day of* June *19*-- *, each and every month thereafter until the balance of* Thirty Thousand and 00/100 *Dollars has been fully paid, with interest on the unpaid instalments from date at the rate of* 13% *per cent. per annum, payable* *annually. All of said payments to be made at* Washington Mutual Savings Bank, Colfax, *Washington, or at such other place as may be mutually agreed upon.*

The vendee *agree*s *to pay all taxes and asse ments that shall become due on this property after this date.*

When the vendee *ha*s *fulfilled all of the conditions of this contract a good and sufficient Warranty Deed shall be executed by the vendor*, h*er* *heirs, executors, or administrators to the vendee*, his *heirs or assigns, and a complete abstract of title or title insurance, at seller's option, to said property will be furnished.*

Time is of the essence of this contract; and in case of the failure of the vendee *to make the payments at the time specified, all payments made hereunder shall be forfeited to the vendor as and for liquidated damages and this agreement shall be null and void at the option of the vendor*, *and* S*he* *shall have the right to re-enter and take possession of said land and premises, and every part thereof.*

In case the vendee *should become seriously sick, or out of employment, and unable to meet any of the payments hereunder the vendor will grant a reasonable extension upon application in writing therefor.*

EXECUTED in duplicate, this 18th *day of* May *A.D. 19*--.

/s/ Maureen T. Jensen *(SEAL)*

(SEAL)

(SEAL)

(SEAL)

STATE OF WASHINGTON,

County of Whitman

This is to certify that on this 18th *day of* May *A.D. 19*--

before me, a Notary Public in and for the State of Washington, duly commissioned and sworn, personally came Maureen T. Jensen and Martin Claxton

to me known to be the individuals in and who executed the foregoing instrument, and acknowledged to me that they signed and sealed the same as their free and voluntary act and deed, for the uses and purposes therein mentioned.

Witness my hand and official seal the day and year in this certificate first above written.

/s/ Lillian Stefferino

Notary Public in and for the State of Washington, residing at Colfax per month principal and interest for ten years and the balance at the end of that time period.

Contract for Deed as a Wraparound

The contract for deed, as previously discussed, can also be wrapped around a mortgage. For example, *A* has a mortgage with a financial institution in the amount of $20,000 at 10 percent. *A* sells to *B*, who owes *A* $30,000. A contract is drawn whereby total payments toward the $20,000 owed by *A* to the institution plus payments on the $10,000 owed to *A* by *B* are paid by *B* to *A*. Then *A* pays the amount due to the institution and retains the amount due to *A*.

Sale and Leaseback

Sale of a fixed asset, which is then leased back to the original owner, is a **sale and leaseback.** The buyer then becomes the lessor, and the seller becomes the lessee. In essence, it is a form of financing.

Although historians have traced this device back to Asia Minor in 200 B.C. and to England, in 1882, substantial growth of the sale-leaseback did not develop in the United States until shortly after World War II.

Generally, the initial term of the lease is determined by the economic life of the building with a time period left so that the buyer-lessor will have some residual. For example, the estimated economic life of the improvement may be 40 years with an initial lease period of 30 years. The residual is then 10 years. In practice, most of the leases run from 20 to 25 years.

Frequently, the lease contains an option to renew and sometimes a purchase option. Periodic rental payments are always included in the lease. The payments are set so that the original investment plus a predetermined rate of return will go to the original investor over the initial term of the lease.

Pros and Cons of the Sale-Leaseback to the Buyer-Lessor. Both parties to a transaction of this nature must always analyze the deal in terms of real advantages.

The advantages to the buyer-lessor are

1. The rate of return should be higher than on a mortgage investment because the buyer-lessor's risk is greater than the risk of a mortgage investor.

2. The buyer-lessor has direct control over the investment as compared with the purchaser of a mortgage whose control is indirect.

3. If the lease is renewed, the buyer-lessor's rate of return will be very high because the cost of the property (under a properly drawn lease) will have been returned over the initial period of the lease.

4. Taxable income is reduced. As the owner of what is now a rental property, the lessor may depreciate the building and thus lower taxable income.

5. Even if the lease is not renewed, there is a potential remainder value. Thus the value will, at a sale, probably exceed the equity.

The disadvantages to the buyer-lessor are

1. The risk is greater than, say, an investment in a mortgage because the loan is only a percentage of the property value rather than the whole value.

2. The buyer-lessor is tied into the credit rating and business management ability of the seller-lessee.

3. The buyer-lessor's income taxes may be high depending on his or her tax position.

Pros and Cons of the Sale-Leaseback to the Seller-Lessee. The advantages to the seller-lessee are

1. Cash position is improved. For example, instead of tying up $100,000 in a building, the seller-lessee now has the right of possession plus the $100,000, which presumably will be used for working capital purposes.

2. If the seller-lessee had originally sold the property at a profit, it would probably be subject to capital gains tax savings.

3. If the seller-lessee were making mortgage payments, they would not be deductible from income tax; but the rental payments are. The rental payments are commonly greater than the depreciation allowances the seller would realize by retaining ownership of the property because one can depreciate only the value of the improvements, not the value of the land. Also, the monthly payments by the lessee include a sum for the use of the improvement as well as an additional sum for the use of the land.

The disadvantages to the seller-lessee are

1. If business declines, the seller-lessee may be in serious financial difficulty resulting from the high fixed rentals.

2. The property will be lost to the seller-lessee at the termination of the lease, which may be undesirable.

3. The costs may be high. Generally, leasebacks run .25 to 1 percent higher than other types of financing.

4. The mobility of the seller-lessee is restricted under the terms of what amounts to a long-term lease. For example, what is now a good

business location may decline as the result of decline of the business area. Yet the seller-lessee is obligated under the terms of the lease to remain in a location or pay the rent without using the premises.[3]

OTHER FINANCING

There are several other forms of recently developed financing that should be given consideration.

Ground Lease Plus Mortgage

When King Charles I gave a grant of the territory now comprising Maryland to the first Lord Baltimore and his heirs, there were two conditions: (1) the king was to get 20 percent of all the gold and silver in the territory, and (2) the king was to be rendered a yearly "rent service." To accomplish the latter, Lord Baltimore granted tracts of land to settlers under 99-year leases.

Presently, among the states, **ground leases** are most common in Hawaii. However, mainland developers are increasing the use of the ground lease for several reasons.

First, they enable more home buyers to qualify for loans. For example, assume land plus home valued at $100,000, land at $20,000, and a loan-to-value ratio of 80 percent. The loan application, if the land is leased, will be for $64,000 ($80,000 × .80), as opposed to $80,000 if the fee is transferred, with a down payment of $16,000 versus $20,000. Of course, the lease will be subordinate to the mortgage or deed of trust.

Second, some developers favor the ground lease because the income from the lease will be spread over time and consequently reduce their taxes in the year the structure is sold.

Connecticut Reverse Annuity

The Connecticut Reverse Annuity is a method of obtaining income from a house already owned by the borrowers. It is used by older people who have a large equity in their home. The choice is to sell the house or to borrow funds, secured by the equity in the house, and purchase an annuity.

The Connecticut Legislature defined the *reverse annuity mortgage loan* in its statute as one in which:

> . . . loan proceeds are advanced to the mortgagors either directly or indirectly, in installments, and which, together with unpaid interest, if any, are to be repaid upon sale of the property securing such loan or the demise of the mortgagors, whichever occurs first.

---

[3]There are numerous forms of sale leasebacks. See Maurice A. Unger and Ronald W. Melicher, *Real Estate Finance*, 2d ed. (Cincinnati: South-Western Publishing Co., 1984), 215–220.

For example, a single man age 75 borrows $50,000, an amount representing 80 percent of his equity. He buys an annuity that pays $7,566 annually. Of this amount, $4,500 pays interest on his loan and the balance of $3,066 supplements social security and other income.

Grannie Mae

Grannie Mae (Golden Age Retirement Annuity Mortgage Association) is a private corporation established to aid those 65 or older to cash in on their equity and it carries the Connecticut Reverse Annuity a step further in that the property is actually sold.

The way this method works is that a person 65 or older makes application and pays $200 to cover an appraisal of the property and an investment and tax analysis. The property is then sold to an investor, which may be the children of the retiree. The net proceeds from the sale are then invested in an income annuity payable forever.

The distinction between this and the reverse annuity is that in the reverse annuity the payments received by the retiree can run out. In the case of Grannie Mae they cannot. If the retiree wishes to continue to live in the property, it can be rented from the investor at its fair market value.

SMILE

The Family-Backed Mortgage Association, which first offered the Grannie Mae, has developed the SMILE program. Its name is an adaptation of "Seller-Move." In this case, older homeowners sell their principal residence, usually tax free due to the $125,000 capital gains exclusion for homeowners over the age of 55. Their children purchase a new smaller home, which is rented to the parents. The cash from the sale of the older home is invested in an annuity that pays the rent for life and provides additional monthly income. The children receive the monthly rent, but can deduct the depreciation, maintenance, taxes, and insurance from their income taxes, thus providing a tax shelter for the children and possible capital appreciation when the home is sold at a later time.

Split-Constant Mortgage

The **split-constant mortgage** is in reality a combination of an interest-only mortgage and a standard fixed-rate mortgage. It is used to finance shopping centers and large apartment complexes.

For example, assume a $1 million loan at 10.5 percent for 25 years. The mortgage calls for interest only for 10 years and fixed payments for the next 15 years. Annual payments for 25 years on a fixed-payment mortgage would be $114,430 per year. However, under the transaction outlined above payments would be as follows:

1. First 10 years, interest only $105,000
2. Second 15 years, interest and principal $135,250

GLOSSARY

Adjustable-rate mortgage A mortgage whereby lenders can adjust the rate of interest up or down based on a predetermined index of interest rates

Assumable mortgage A situation in which the purchaser takes over, or covenants to pay, the mortgage debt

Balloon note A note providing for periodic payments that do not amortize the note by its termination date, leaving the balance due to be paid in a lump sum

Budget mortgage A self-amortizing mortgage that includes monthly payments of one-twelfth of the year's taxes, a proportionate amount of the yearly fire insurance premiums, and any other charges that might, if left unpaid, constitute a basis for foreclosure of the mortgage

Conventional-insured mortgage A conventional mortgage insured by a private insurance company

Conventional mortgage A mortgage that is neither FHA-insured nor VA-guaranteed and that generally requires a higher down payment

Convertible loan A debt instrument that converts to equity funding over time

Equity lending A loan whereby the lender participates in the equity of the property

FHA mortgage A type of mortgage whereby the federal government insures the payment of the loan to the lender

Fixed-rate mortgage A mortgage on which a fixed rate of interest is charged during the life of the loan

Grannie Mae (Golden Age Retirement Annuity Mortgage Association) A private corporation established to aid those 65 or older to obtain cash from their home equity

Ground lease The leasing of land to enable more home buyers to qualify for loans and to spread the income from the lease over time

Growing equity mortgage (GEM) A mortgage in which the borrower can increase payments at a set amount each year

Installment contract (or contract for deed) An agreement in which the seller promises to deliver title when the installment payments are completed if the buyer has observed other purchase terms

Loan-to-value ratio The amount of the mortgage loan divided by the purchase price

Nonassumption (nonalienation) clause A clause stating that the mortgagor cannot sell the property and have the buyer assume the mortgage without the consent of the lender

Open-end mortgage A mortgage in which the borrower is given a limit that may be borrowed

Package mortgage A mortgage that incorporates all the features of the budget mortgage plus payments for certain mechanical equipment put in the home

Quick-pay mortgage A 15-year fixed-rate mortgage

Sale and leaseback The sale of a fixed asset which is then leased back to original owner

Split-constant mortgage Combination of interest-only and fixed-rate mortgage used mainly to finance shopping centers and large apartment complexes

VA mortgage A guaranteed loan, wherein a part of a mortgage is guaranteed by the Veterans Administration

Wraparound mortgage A covenant contained within a mortgage used as a "sweetener" to entice a seller of commercial-type property to sell to a buyer with a relatively small down payment and used during periods of high interest rates

QUESTIONS FOR REVIEW

1. What is meant by a budget mortgage?
2. Distinguish between a variable-rate mortgage and an adjustable-rate mortgage.
3. What are the major disadvantages of an ARM?
4. Why are some developers using a combination of a lease and a mortgage?
5. What are the disadvantages of a sale-leaseback?
6. Differentiate between SMILE and Grannie Mae.

PROBLEMS AND ACTIVITIES

1. Much is heard these days of seller financing. Assume that *X* has an assumable mortgage of $75,000 at 8 percent and decides to sell at

$125,000. *X* is approached by *B* who has $25,000 cash and is willing to pay the $125,000, but refuses to finance through an institution whose current interest rate is 15 percent. *X* is willing to engage in seller financing at 13 percent.

a. Detail three ways in which this can be done.
b. In one of these three ways, it is conceivable that *X*, the seller, can increase effective yield to more than 13 percent. Explain how this can be done.

2. Using the procedures outlined in Exhibit 13-1 or Decision Assistant Buyer Qualification, determine the conventional mortgage amount that Mr. and Mrs. Newhome may borrow. The Newhomes have two children and cash for a down payment of $25,000, and both work. Mr. Newhome earns $30,000 as a school teacher, and Mrs. Newhome is a C.P.A. earning $47,000 per year. They would like to buy a home that costs $135,000 with over 2,000 square feet of living space. Monthly payments for their new cars are $450 for three years; other monthly payments total $175. Homeowners insurance will cost $480 per year, property taxes $2,400. The current mortgage interest rate is 10 percent.

a. How expensive a home are Mr. and Mrs. Newhome qualified to buy?
b. Assume all of the prior conditions except: Mr. Newhome is a qualified veteran earning $55,000 per year and Mrs. Newhome is not employed outside the home. Can the family afford to buy the home without a down payment? Assume the federal tax rate is 15 percent and state taxes are 3 percent.
c. All conditions in (b) apply except: Mr. Newhome is not a veteran and only $10,000 is available for a down payment. How much down payment do the Newhome's need to purchase and obtain an FHA insured loan?

14

INTEREST RATES AND THE SECONDARY MORTGAGE MARKET

KEY TERMS

Commercial banks
Credit union
Deflation
Discount point
Discount rate
Disintermediation
Farmers Home Administration
Federal Agriculture Mortgage Corporation (Farmer Mac)
Federal Home Loan Mortgage Corporation (Freddie Mac)
Federal National Mortgage Association (Fannie Mae)
Fractional reserve system
Government National Mortgage Association (Ginnie Mae)
Inflation
Interest rate
Moral suasion
Mortgage company
Mutual savings banks
Pension funds
Reintermediation
Reserve requirements
Restrictive open market policy
Savings and loan associations
Secondary mortgage market
Selective controls
Tandem plan

In the early 1980s, mortgage money almost completely dried up. Interest rates on mortgages rose to 18 percent, and some financial institutions stopped lending on mortgages altogether. By 1985, the situation had reversed itself; and in 1986, some rates had declined to as low as 8.75 percent.

What causes mortgage money to become scarce of plentiful? The answer is tied directly to the efforts of the Federal Reserve System to combat inflation or to stimulate the economy.

THE FEDERAL RESERVE SYSTEM AND THE INTEREST RATE

The Federal Reserve System

In 1913, the Federal Reserve Act was passed by Congress and signed by President Wilson. The act divided the country into 12 federal reserve districts, with a federal reserve bank in each district. The initial capital was obtained by stock subscriptions of commercial banks within the districts. The subscribers are the member banks. Technically, the federal reserve banks are owned by the member banks although, in practice, the Federal Reserve works closely with the president and the U.S. Treasury. They work so closely that the Federal Reserve is in reality a central banking authority. One of the functions of this central bank is to influence the cost, the availability, and the supply of money and, consequently, the rate of interest. By making money scarce, interest rates rise—often called a tight money policy.

The Interest Rate

The **interest rate** is thought of as being the price paid for the use of money. Some define it as *rent* paid for the use of money. Money is a commodity like other goods in the sense that the price, or interest rate, tends to fluctuate with shifts in the supply and demand. For example, if the supply of money becomes scarce and the demand for money is high, the price, or interest rate, rises. This suggests that if the interest rate is allowed to move up and down according to the law of supply and demand, those persons willing to pay the higher interest rates will be the ones who will receive the mortgage loans. Suppose the interest rate rises to 20 percent, as it did in the early 1980s. Those persons willing to pay 20 percent for mortgage money could get the money; those unwilling to pay would be unable to borrow money.

In real life, however, there are legal restrictions on the amount persons can pay for the use of money. Most states stipulate a maximum contract rate of interest, which is the highest legal rate that can be charged in that state. Consequently, if the rate goes up to 20 percent, investors faced with alternative investment opportunities tend to move away from mortgages and into other investments to take advantage of the higher rate. The net result of this shift is a shrinkage of funds available for mortgage financing.

Why Interest Rates Are Controlled

The interest rate is raised and lowered by the Federal Reserve because it is thought to have a direct effect on inflation and deflation. **Inflation** occurs when there is an increase in the volume of money or in the rate of money turnover in relation to the supply of goods and services for sale. In short, when an excess in the supply of money begins chasing scarce goods and services, the prices of the goods and services will rise.

Deflation arises from an increase in the supply of goods and services in relation to the money available for buying them. For example, if production were suddenly to double throughout the nation and people did not have the money or credit with which to purchase this increased production, prices would drop and deflation would result.

Briefly, the thinking of the Federal Reserve in raising the interest rates to avoid or reduce inflationary pressures goes something like this. Suppose a businessperson desires to build an irrigation ditch to furnish water to farmers in an arid area of the West. It is estimated that the return will be 20 percent per year; consequently, the project will pay for itself in five years. The cost of borrowing money is 18 percent. It would, therefore, pay the person to proceed with the project because a 2 percent profit will be made. This person's actions, combined with the actions of many others working on similar projects, will put inflationary pressures on the price of cement, machinery, and other commodities that might be relatively scarce.

The Federal Reserve thinks that when it raises the interest rate to 19 percent, businesspeople will not proceed with their projects. They will figure they cannot earn enough money. The net result will be no inflationary pressure on cement, machinery, and the other commodities.

If the Federal Reserve is worried about the possibility of deflation, it will reverse the process. In short, it will reduce the interest rate to make the building of projects more profitable. For example, it might reduce the interest rate as low as 16 percent to make proposed projects more profitable.

How Interest Rates Are Shifted

The Federal Reserve System can raise interest rates and fight inflation in five ways: (1) adopt a restrictive open market policy; (2) increase the discount rate; (3) increase reserve requirements, thereby reducing the reserve base for credit expansion; (4) when authorized by Congress, impose selective controls; (5) moral suasion.

Restrictive Open Market Policy. The Federal Reserve has the right, through its open market committee, to buy and sell government bonds. By making the interest rate attractive, government bonds are sold to banks. As the banks purchase these bonds, dollars are exchanged for them, which reduces the amount of dollars available in banks for loans. Money is now scarce. Bankers are more selective regarding individuals to whom they are willing to lend money; and, because they are faced with the opportunity of buying more government bonds with no risk and little handling cost, they will begin raising the rate of interest on the money they have left. This is known as **restrictive open market policy.**

Increase Discount Rate. The **discount rate** is the rate of interest a bank must pay when it borrows from its federal reserve bank. Member banks may take certain promissory notes they have received from customers and discount these notes with the Federal Reserve. In short, they discount notes to their district federal reserve bank and with the funds received make further loans. To do this, they must pay the Federal Reserve a sum of money. When this rate is raised, it sometimes no longer pays to discount the notes. More often, however, it exerts a significant influence on credit psychology, inducing the banking system to re-examine its lending policies, and other lenders to reappraise credit conditions.

The result, of course, leads to a scarcity in the money supply. Money is no longer borrowed from the Federal Reserve. This scarcity leads to the raising of the interest rate.

Increase Reserve Requirements. The banking system in the United States operates as a **fractional reserve system,** legally prohibiting banks from lending 100 percent of their deposits. For example, if a bank receives a deposit of $1,000, it can lend only part of this sum. The balance must be deposited in the federal reserve bank in its district. This deposit is called a legal minimum-reserve balance and must be equal to a stipulated percentage of demand deposits (checking accounts) and a smaller, but stipulated, percentage of time deposits (savings accounts). The percentages that must be held in reserve are set by Congress, which, from time to time, sets a minimum and a maximum reserve requirement. The Board of Governors of the Federal Reserve System is permitted to change the reserve requirements of member banks within this set minimum and maximum.

For example, suppose $1,000 is deposited with a member bank and suppose the reserve requirement is 20 percent. The member bank must deposit 20 percent of the $1,000 with the Federal Reserve, which leaves only $800 available for loans. If the Board of Governors decides to raise the reserve requirement to 25 percent, then a member bank will be permitted to lend $750, the balance of $250 being deposited with the federal reserve bank.

It can readily be seen that if the Federal Reserve wishes to raise interest rates by making the money available for loans scarce, it can do so by raising the minimum **reserve requirements,** thereby taking additional sums out of circulation.

Selective Controls. **Selective controls** are authorized from time to time by Congress and provide specific terms under which credit may be used. One example of this was Regulation X of the Defense Production Act of 1950. It empowered the president to regulate certain aspects of real estate financing. Under this act, the Federal Reserve Board from time to time increased down payments on homes and reduced the time of maturity on mortgages. The authority for this act ceased in 1953, but the act is an example of a selective control.

Increased down payments under this act, coupled with reduced maturity mortgages, forced certain buyers from the market. This, too, tended to reduce inflationary pressure.

Moral Suasion. **Moral suasion** is sometimes called jawbone policy. In an inflationary period, the federal reserve banks sometimes try to discourage banks from extending undue amounts of credit for speculative purposes that are inconsistent with the maintenance of sound credit conditions. Their influence may cause bankers to restrict credit.

SECONDARY EFFECTS OF A TIGHT MONEY POLICY

Higher Interest Rates and the Bond Market

Increased interest rates affect the bond market. This, in turn, is a disruptive influence on the mortgage money market. For example, suppose there is an existing government bond with a face value of $100 that pays 8 percent or $8 per year. If the Federal Reserve desires to raise interest rates, it may issue a $100 bond at 16 percent paying $16 per year. The net result will be that the value of existing bonds begins to drop. Theoretically, the 8 percent bond will decline in price from $100 to $50 because those individuals holding the 8 percent bonds would sell them for $100 and buy a $100 bond of the new issue that will earn them 16 percent on the same investment. In real life, however, the investors in bonds are fully aware of what is taking place; therefore, if a prospective investor has $100 to invest in bonds, the investor is certainly not going to pay $100 for a bond paying only $8 when the same amount of principal will buy a $100 bond of the new issue, and earn $16 per year. Thus, when old bondholders offer bonds for sale, they are offered only $50 earning $8 per year, or 16 percent, the equivalent of the new issue, i.e., $100 × .16 = $16.

In practice, the old bond will not drop $50 unless the date of maturity approximates the new issue. The drop is related to the date of maturity on the old bond. Obviously, if the due date on the old bond is next year, no one will sell it for $50 if in only one year the government will pay $100 or the full face value of the bond.

Thus, with the increase in interest rates, federal, state, local, and corporate bonds begin to drop. This has a serious effect on institutional lenders. These institutions often hold government bonds because they are highly liquid. They may intend to sell some of their bonds and invest that money in real estate mortgages. When the bond market drops, they cannot afford to sell and thereby take a capital loss. They must hold onto those bonds. As a direct result of this they are unable to liquidate, thereby adding to the scarcity of mortgage money.

Effect on Existing Mortgages

In addition to the effects of a tight money policy on institutional investors, there are also repercussions in the secondary market for existing mortgages. Existing mortgages are purchased on the secondary market, as will be detailed later in this chapter. For example, a mortgage in Dallas, Texas, may be purchased by a savings and loan association in Springfield, Massachusetts. The money moves from Springfield to Dallas. The effect of this is to release more money for mortgages in Dallas. However, mortgages fluctuate in price like anything else. A mortgage may sell at a premium or at a discount, *again depending on the interest rate.* When the rate goes up, mortgage prices go down.

Suppose the interest rate rises to 12 percent and a mortgage is yielding 7 percent. If an investor has $10,000 to invest, the investor would be unwise to invest in a mortgage yielding 7 percent when the money could be earning 12 percent, assuming the risks are equivalent. Therefore, the secondary market purchasers of mortgages will not pay $10,000 for a mortgage bearing a face value of $10,000. They will purchase the mortgage only if it can be had at a discount to yield 12 percent.

Discount Points. A loan discount is a one-time charge used to adjust the yield to what market conditions demand. The discount may be either on conventional loans, FHA, or VA loans. In the latter case, it must be paid by the seller.

The discount is expressed in points. Each **discount point** is equal to one percent of the amount of the mortgage. For example, if the mortgage is for $80,000 and the discount is two points, then the discount is $1,600. The amount loaned by the institution is only $78,400 but the amount to be paid back will be $80,000. Consequently, this increases the yield to the lender.

Disintermediation. In periods of tight money, **disintermediation** takes place when the public is buying stocks and bonds rather than placing its funds in financial institutions (the mortgage lenders). When rates go up, households divert funds directly into credit and equity instruments, because they can make more than when leaving the money with the institutions. This leaves the institutions short on money available for mortgage loans.

The reverse takes place when rates decline. Households deposit funds with institutions, thus increasing the funds available for mortgage loans. This process is called **reintermediation.**

Effects of Tight Money on Junior Financing Devices

A tight money policy affects junior financing devices in several ways. First, it has a tendency to increase the numbers of second mortgages and contracts in use. In some parts of the country, where new construction is heavy, bank refinancing of older homes comes to a virtual standstill. If a seller desires to sell a home for $100,000, a prospective buyer is unable to obtain a new mortgage from a bank. Assume there is a $50,000 mortgage on the property and a prospective buyer has only $30,000 cash. Without new bank financing, the seller has little choice but to do the financing of the remaining $20,000. The seller will receive $30,000 cash, and the buyer will either assume or take the property subject to the $50,000 mortgage, and give the seller a contract or a second mortgage for the remaining $20,000. Either a contract or second mortgage will be used depending on the section of the country where the transaction takes place.

A second effect on junior financing takes place in the market for contracts and second mortgages. Investors trade in second mortgages and in junior contracts. During times when mortgage money is relatively plentiful, these junior liens sell at discounts between 10 and 25 percent. A $20,000 second mortgage, for example, sold to an investor at a 20 percent discount will bring the seller $16,000. However, when money is tight, the number of junior liens increases. This makes investors more selective. Coupled with an increase in the supply of junior liens *and* the higher interest rate, the discount rate for junior liens may jump as high as 30 percent in some instances. Therefore, a seller who takes back a junior lien for $20,000 can get only $14,000 for it instead of $17,000 when it is discounted at 15 percent.

When sellers are aware of this, they sometimes attempt to pass all or part of this increased discount on to the buyer. If the buyer in the case above lacks $20,000 on a $100,000 purchase price, sellers will try to raise the purchase price. For example, they might point out to the buyer that they will have to discount the junior lien 30 percent and may insist the buyer sign the second mortgage or contract for roughly $26,000 instead of $20,000.

HYPERSENSITIVITY OF MORTGAGE FUNDS TO MONETARY MANAGEMENT

The two classes of borrowers for residential construction funds are home purchasers and home builders.

Table 14-1 Some General Effects of Monetary Management

TIGHT MONEY	EASY MONEY
1. Marginal borrowers are forced out of credit market.	1. Converse true—more marginal borrowers.
2. Some potential borrowers will defer projects, expecting rates to decline.	2. Converse true—less deferment of projects.
3. Bond prices decline, reducing the supply of loan money. Institutions holding bonds are reluctant to sell and take capital losses in order to make other loans.	3. Converse true—institutions will sell bonds at capital gain to make other loans.
4. Credit standards are raised by financial institutions.	4. Converse true—credit standards slackened.
5. Attempts are made to liquidate marginal credit.	5. Converse true—little attempt to liquidate marginal credit.
6. Disintermediation takes place, reducing the supply of mortgage funds.	6. Reintermediation takes place, increasing the supply of mortgage funds.

Home Purchasers

Prior to 1974, there were two primary reasons home purchaser borrowers were relatively unaffected by higher or lower interest rates.

1. Since down payments were smaller with a higher ratio of mortgage loans to property value, smaller down payments were required. This brought marginal purchasers into the market.
2. Extended maturities, for example, increasing maturity time of FHA loans from 25 to 30 years, required smaller monthly payments over longer periods of time. Because of this, more lower income groups were able to become purchasers.

Since 1974, borrowers have been whipsawed by volatile interest rates, which have continued to the present. As rates increased, many homeowners simply could not afford to purchase property and make the monthly mortgage payments. Additionally, due to record levels of foreclosures, higher income standards, tougher appraisal requirements, and lower loan-to-value ratios, it became more difficult for many marginal buyers to buy homes. The new, tougher lending standards of FNMA were outlined in Chapter 13.

Builder Borrowers

With rising interest rates, builder borrowers are adversely affected. The question is not whether the higher rates per se affect them adversely, but they are affected because available mortgage money declines.

It has been suggested that demands for mortgage funds are apt to be more sensitive to interest rate changes than, for example, consumer installment loans. There are a number of reasons for this extreme sensitivity, as indicated previously. To these might be added the fact that mortgage borrowers have a distinct disadvantage in the competition for funds with corporate borrowers.

Mortgage borrowers, in the final analysis, seek financial institutions as lenders. These are savings and loan associations, life insurance companies, commercial banks, and mutual savings banks, as will be discussed later. Once these funds are exhausted in a tight money situation, mortgage borrowers, for all practical purposes, have no place to go. Corporate borrowers not only go to the institutions for money but can turn to individual investors as purchasers of bonds. This group is relatively untapped and is generally unavailable as a source of funds to mortgage borrowers.

Additionally, alternative investment opportunities pose a continuing threat to the availability of mortgage money, particularly during periods of rising rates. Money market funds are an example.

SAVINGS AND THE AVAILABILITY OF MORTGAGE MONEY

Homes are durable goods. Home building plays a significant role in the nation's economy because it adds to the nation's stock of real capital resources. And any investment in capital assets, whether it be by groups or individuals, is very closely related to savings, for mortgage money comes from savings.

Savings and Investment Process

The savings and investment processes are often independent acts made by different groups or individuals. It is obvious that saving—that is, not consuming all of one's current income—is necessary to permit someone else to invest in any excess of that individual's current resources. For example, *A* may save by depositing $10,000 in a savings and loan association, and that same $10,000 may be loaned to *B* on a mortgage for the construction of a home. More often than not, however, it takes many savers depositing a total of $100,000 to provide money that would be loaned to finance *B*'s investment in a home.

In some cases, the savings and investment process takes place with the same person. For example, one may decide to invest the $10,000 in one's own home, in which case the person is both saving and investing.

Competition for Savings

Savings constitutes part of the pool of money for which builders, home buyers, and other users of funds compete. It should be understood that annual savings is only part of the pool of funds. The balance consists of paybacks from outstanding mortgages and other types of past savings.

One type of competition for funds that must be met by builders and home buyers comes from local authorities selling tax exempt bonds. Corporations also need additional funds and often go to the market to obtain these. The U.S. Treasury is one of the largest users of borrowed funds and is very active in the money market. Consumers, too, are demanders of part of the nation's savings with which to finance installment purchases. Farmers and small unincorporated businesses also dip into the pool of savings for necessary funds.

INSTITUTIONAL LENDERS AS SOURCES OF FUNDS

There are four major financial institutions currently active in the home mortgage market: (1) savings and loan associations, which have had enormous problems in the 1980s; (2) commercial banks, which are taking an expanding role in the latter half of the 1980s; (3) insurance companies, some of whom are following the lead of commercial banks; and (4) mutual savings banks.

There are also a number of other sources of mortgage funds, which are discussed in subsequent sections of this chapter.

SAVINGS AND LOAN ASSOCIATIONS

Savings and loan associations are state or federally chartered and either mutual or stock-type operations. In Massachusetts, they are called cooperative banks, and in Louisiana, homestead associations.

Historically, the first savings and loan association began in 1831 with 40 members who founded the Oxford Provident Building Association in Frankford, Pennsylvania, now a part of Philadelphia. Each member was to save a certain sum each week; and, as soon as the accumulated sums were large enough, the money would be loaned to one of the members of the group for home-building. Because savings were limited, some members had to postpone home purchases; thus, they began inviting savings accounts from others.

Most of the savings and loan association mortgage loans were conventional mortgages, both privately insured and noninsured, which yielded a higher rate of interest than either the FHA-insured or VA-guaranteed mortgages. The savings and loan associations were permitted to lend up to 90 percent of the appraised valuation of the property on a conventional mortgage provided it was insured by a private mortgage company.

From the beginning, savings and loan associations specialized in home financing. However, as a result of the Monetary Control Act of 1980, discussed below, this has changed.

The Savings and Loan Crisis

In early 1988, the Federal Savings and Loan Insurance Corporation was forced to close a number of insolvent savings and loans. There were many more that should have been closed, but the Federal Savings and Loan Insurance Corporation (FSLIC) was unable to so do because it had exhausted its funds. When the plight of the savings and loans was discovered by the press, headlines read: "Lending and Looting: The S&L Debacle," "Uncle Sam Fat from Foreclosure," "Savings Crisis Laid to Crime."

To illustrate the extent of the crime involved, one savings and loan president bought a Rolls Royce, $5 million in art, trips to Europe, a California beach home, and $110 bottles of perfume for his wife. And the vice president of that same savings and loan admitted hiring prostitutes to entertain during meetings of the board of directors. To put the problem into perspective: the cost of the later bailout of the Vernon, Texas, savings and loan was $1.3 billion, a figure for this one S&L that is greater than the bailout of the Chrysler Corporation. For the record, Chrysler has long since repaid its debt; the savings and loans never will.

Causes of the S&L Debacle

Prior to 1980, the amount of interest savings and loans could pay to passbook depositors was regulated by Federal Reserve Board Regulation Q. The rates paid to depositors ranged between 5 and 5.5 percent. Mortgage loans were made at fixed rates from 6.25 to 7.5 percent. Then rates on alternative securities began to rise rapidly. As a result, depositors withdrew their money (disintermediation) and invested in these alternative investments paying a higher interest rate.

Congress reacted to the above by passing the Monetary Control Act of 1980. Interest rate limitations were phased out. In essence, the savings and loans were given the characteristics of a commercial bank. They were permitted to offer checking services (NOW accounts), and remote service units, and to issue credit cards. They were also given the following powers:

1. To make secured or unsecured loans (not to exceed 20 percent of the association's assets) for personal or household purposes.
2. To invest in, sell, or hold commercial paper and corporate debt securities (not to exceed 20 percent of the association's assets).
3. To make business and agricultural loans.
4. To act as trustees.
5. To have access to the Fed discount window on the same terms as member banks.

Regarding mortgages on single-family and multifamily dwellings, the act specifically provided that associations could:

1. Make mortgage loans without dollar limitations, substituting a 90 percent loan-to-value ratio.
2. Make mortgage loans without geographical limitations.
3. Authorize second mortgages and deeds of trust.

Additionally, the federal deposit insurance was raised from $40,000 to $100,000 per account for both savings and loans and banks.

As anticipated, money flowed back into the S&Ls when depositors were offered higher rates, but the new deposits required the S&Ls to pay more interest than they were earning on the old mortgages they had issued at rates between 6.5 and 7.5 percent. In fact, some of the loans made during the early 1970s were as low as 5 percent. As a result, many S&Ls lost billions of dollars and failed in this first wave of trouble.

In 1982, Congress reacted again by passing the Garn-St. Germain Depository Institutions Act. Because interest rate ceilings were still in effect on the NOW accounts, all depositories were permitted to issue new money market accounts that did not have an interest rate ceiling. Furthermore, S&Ls were permitted to issue adjustable-rate mortgages, commercial loans, and nonresidential loans of *all* types.

For all practical purposes, by the mid-1980s the Garn-St. Germain Act had left the savings and loans completely unregulated. They could do anything—and they did! Billions of dollars, attracted by higher rates, poured into the booming Southwest, Florida, and California for any and all projects whether worthy or not. Many institutions were trying to make up for profits lost as the result of holding the old 30-year, fixed-rate mortgages. New savings and loans were created or bought by "fast-buck" operators. The Federal Savings and Loan Insurance Corporation insured deposits up to $100,000, so many of the unethical operators capitalized on this and high certificate of deposit rates to entice depositors. Some of these deposits found their way into the pockets of the operators, thence to Swiss bank accounts, or completely disappeared. This is not an exaggeration! By mid-1989, 12,000 civil suits were filed against these operators by the federal government with an additional 75,000 planned. There are other claims that are not being pursued because the money simply cannot be found. Only a few criminal charges have been filed.[1]

During this time, the Reagan administration cut the funds available for regulators to audit the books of the S&Ls. When some of the institutions were finally closed, it was discovered that they had not been audited for over three years. Nevertheless, some of the S&Ls *were* closed.

In 1986, international oil prices plunged, adding to the S&L crisis. This, in turn, caused a collapse primarily in the economies of Texas, Louisiana, and Oklahoma. The lending that had taken place in those states, especially Texas, with little or no regard for the future, caused overbuilding of office buildings, apartment houses, and many high-priced homes. Developers were forced to default on their loans. The lenders (S&Ls) foreclosed, but the market was so depressed that the foreclosed property was worth only a fraction of the cost of construction. As a result, many more savings and loans were technically insolvent and should have been closed. However, the FSLIC no longer had the funds to pay off depositors, and the insolvent institutions were permitted to remain open. S&Ls nationwide were posting losses amounting to $20 million a day.

By early 1989, Congress reacted and created the Resolution Trust Corporation. The savings and loan bailout began August 14, 1989.

The Essence of the Bailout

The Financial Institutions Reform, Recovery and Enforcement Act, referred to as the Savings and Loan Bailout Bill, is lengthy (1,000 pages) and complex. The Bush administration estimates that it will cost $166 billion. Some experts have estimated the cost to be closer to $198 billion. Senator Donald Riegle (D-Mich.) of the Senate Banking Committee has declared that the result would be "the most massive financial restructuring since the 1930s" and Representative Jim Leach (R-Iowa) stated, "We're looking at

[1] *USA Today,* August 16, 1989, 1B.

the biggest bailout in American history—the biggest fraud story—and the taxpayer is on the line."[2]

The important features of the bill are

1. The Federal Home Loan Bank Board was abolished. The Federal Home Loan Bank Board, which was established in 1932, served the same purpose with respect to savings and loan associations as the Federal Reserve System was intended to perform for commercial banks. The functions of the FHLBB are to be handled by the Office of Thrift Supervision under the control of the Federal Deposit Insurance Corporation (FDIC).

2. The Federal Savings and Loan Insurance Corporation (FSLIC) has been abolished. Its functions have been taken over by the Resolution Trust Corporation, which is under the Treasury Department and managed by the head of the Federal Deposit Insurance Corporation. A new fund, the Savings Association Insurance Fund, has been created that is designed to handle the bailouts after 1992 and build a reserve to protect future depositors. The insurance on deposits remains at $100,000 per account; for the first time, however, there is an explicit declaration to the depositors that deposits are backed by the full faith and credit of the U.S. government.

3. The Resolution Trust Corporation is to sell the assets of closed S&Ls, consisting of real estate, automobiles, executive cars, and the good loans. A great fear is that real property might be "dumped" on the market, further depressing real estate prices in areas where prices are already low. Consequently, Congress imposed restrictions on the Resolution Trust Corporation with regard to the sale of real estate:

   a. Arkansas, Colorado, Louisiana, Oklahoma, New Mexico, and Texas have been labeled distressed markets. In these states, the RTC must demand a minimum disposition price: a price no lower than what the RTC decides is 95 percent of fair market value.
   b. Another clause in the bill, which is difficult to comprehend, basically warns the RTC that under some circumstances market prices will not be acceptable.

      Some experts feel these restrictions may result in some property being held for as long as 20 years. Some feel it will eventually bring as little as 50 cents on the dollar. Others feel that, over time, the property will deteriorate and won't sell at any price. Then the buildings will have to be torn down.
   c. In the future, S&Ls will have to keep 70 percent of their assets in housing-related activities. Whether this will allow the remaining

[2] *USA Today,* August 15, 1989, 28.

S&Ls to be financially healthy is questionable. Again, they will be taking short-term deposits and lending long term, as long as 30 years on mortgages. Even with adjustable-rate mortgages, there may be some financial danger if short-term rates fluctuate wildly.

Currently, it is estimated that of the 3,000 S&Ls, 1,000 will be closed or taken over by commercial banks by 1992. By being limited so heavily to mortgage-lending activities, life may be difficult, if not impossible, for many S&Ls. Commenting on the S&L debacle, House Banking Committee Chairman Henry Gonzalex (D-Tex.) said, "They've taken a lot of dead horses and stretched them into one big horse that's just as dead and stinks even more."[3]

Summary of New Thrift Regulations

The new law is technically called the Financial Institutions Reform, Recovery, and Enforcement Act of 1989 (FIRREA). Under FIRREA, the regulatory structure of the S&Ls becomes similar to that of commercial banks. The law establishes the following:

1. *Office of Thrift Institution (OTS).* OTS is an arm of the Treasury Department functioning like the Treasury's Office of the Comptroller of the currency that charters and regulates commercial banks. It replaces the Federal Home Loan Bank Board. A new board, the Federal Housing Finance Board (FHB) oversees mortgage lending by regional Federal Home Loan Banks.
2. *Federal Home Loan Mortgage Corporation* (Freddie Mac). Freddie Mac retains its name and functions and has been given a new $2.5 billion line of credit with the U.S. Treasury and a new board of directors of 18 members. Thirteen are elected by the stockholders and 5 are appointed by the president of the United States.
3. *Federal Deposit Insurance Corporation* (FDIC). The FDIC remains the same, but now supervises and controls three new agencies:
   a. Resolution Trust Corporation (RTC) manages disposition of bankrupt savings and loans and disposes of their assets.
   b. Resolutions Funding Corporation (RFC) will sell $30 billion in bonds to finance the bailout in 1990 and 1991.
   c. Deposit Insurance Fund (DIF), new name for the federal deposit insurance system, includes two funds: the Bank Insurance Fund (BIF), which covers the insurance on commercial banks and savings banks previously handled by the FDIC; and the Savings Association Insurance Fund, which replaces the defunct FSLIC and puts the savings and loan insurance under the FDIC.

[3] *Wall Street Journal,* August 28, 1989, 12A.

COMMERCIAL BANKS

Commercial banks are private enterprises organized under federal or state charters for the benefit of their stockholders. They receive funds from time deposits and demand deposits. The funds from time deposits of commercial banks are invested in corporate bonds, state and municipal securities, consumer installment loans, business loans, purchases of federal securities, and mortgages.

For many years, commercial banks were large lenders in the commercial mortgage market but played a relatively small role in the residential mortgage market. In 1986 Citicorp, the banking giant, changed all that, and in 1988 wrote $14.8 billion in home mortgages. Citicorp's program is called Mortgage Power, and it is aided by a group of 3,000 real estate brokers, lawyers, insurance agents, and mortgage bankers in 37 states whose number is growing; by 1992, Citicorp hopes to obtain 10 percent of the nation's residential mortgage market.

The Citicorp program has been mirrored by other lenders, such as Prudential Insurance Company, Chase Manhattan Corporation, and many other large lenders. It works as follows:

1. A buyer goes to a broker in the program, makes application, and pays the broker about .5 percent of the loan as a fee (some brokers do not charge this fee).

2. Within 15 days, the mortgage application (with 20 percent down) is either accepted or rejected.

3. Citicorp does not require buyers to buy third-party mortgage insurance; Citicorp self-insures the mortgage.

Critics of the program contend that the .5 percent fee paid to the broker is tantamount to a kickback and that the broker is receiving a commission from the seller and therefore should not be entitled to the additional .5 percent fee. This is strongly denied by Citicorp, which states:

1. The fee is a matter between the broker and the buyer, and it expedites the sale of the property for the seller.

2. The buyer has to sign a form indicating he or she knows of the existence of the fee before making the loan application. Furthermore, brokers are not required to charge a fee.

3. Prior to 1986, it (Citicorp) requested and received approval of the program from HUD. HUD gave Citicorp its opinion that, under the 1974 Real Estate Practices Act, brokers are prohibited from receiving a fee from *lenders,* not from home buyers.

Kenneth Rosen, director of the real estate program at the University of California at Berkeley, states, "In five years, 15 large players will have 50 percent of the market."[4]

LIFE INSURANCE COMPANIES

Life insurance companies have, over the past decade, gradually withdrawn from the one- to four-family mortgage market. While doing this, they have increased their farm mortgage, commercial mortgage, and industrial mortgage portfolios.

The reason is simple. The yields on farm, commercial, and industrial mortgages are greater than on one- to four-family dwellings. In the farm lending area, insurance companies use a variable-rate mortgage. In commercial and industrial loans, they often "participate." That is, in addition to the market rate of interest on their mortgages, they often share in a percentage of rental income, capital appreciation, or both.

Like commercial banks, some life insurance companies are returning to the residential mortgage market.

MUTUAL SAVINGS BANKS

Mutual savings banks are the oldest type of savings institution in the United States. They have no stockholders; their objective is the mutual benefit of depositors. Historically, these institutions were formed for the purpose of encouraging savings to help relieve the distress of the poor. The greatest number is concentrated in the Middle Atlantic and New England states, with Massachusetts having the most, followed by New York. All earnings after payment of operating expenses, taxes, and setting aside of necessary reserves for the protection of depositors are distributed to the depositors in the form of interest. They tend to invest more heavily in government underwritten mortgages than do either the savings and loan associations or life insurance companies.

OTHER SOURCES OF FUNDS

There are basically six other sources of funds for mortgage loans, not including those that will be discussed later under secondary mortgage markets. These sources are the Farmers Home Administration, the Farm Credit System, credit unions, Real Estate Investment Trusts, mortgage companies, and pension funds.

Farmers Home Administration

The **Farmers Home Administration** (FmHA) is an arm of the Department of Agriculture. It administers direct rural housing loans, insured loans,

[4] *Wall Street Journal,* November 3, 1988, B1.

and grants. To qualify for a loan, a rural family must show it has been unable to obtain credit from private sources. The real property used for security must be in an area with a population of not more than 10,000, except in special circumstances where the population can be as high as 20,000 persons.

In 1972, the Rural Development Act created a Farmers Home Loan Guaranty Program for residential, commercial, and industrial property loans originated by private lenders. This enabled private mortgage credit to supplant direct loans by the Farmers Home Administration in several situations.

Most of the loans are insured and sold to private lenders. Many of the loans are subsidized with interest ranging from 1 percent (depending on ability to pay) to 9 percent. Any losses as a result of the subsidies are paid from general tax revenues.

FmHA insured loans may be for up to 100 percent of the appraised value. These low-income loans must be refinanced if the financial status of the family improves beyond the maximum income set for the number of family members.

By January 1990, the debt of the FmHA exceeded $24 billion. In 1988, it was forced to write off $1.8 billion on delinquent loans, and experts suggest that by 1993 it will be forced to declare another $8.7 billion in farm loans uncollectable. Some have even predicted a federal bailout similar to the savings and loan bailout will become necessary.

The critical situation at FmHA was caused by a series of farm and rural problems that occurred during the 1980s. These problems included

1. The collapse of agricultural land values. Between 1981 and 1986, farm value per acre fell 50 percent.

2. Crop surpluses coupled with an emphasis on export markets caused a drop in commodity prices.

3. Widespread drought resulted in failed crops and significant loss of farm income.

4. Farm foreclosures reverberated through rural communities. Rural businesses failed at a record rate, and there was significant migration from rural to urban areas.

The net result is that FmHA held foreclosed property whose value was significantly less than the remaining balance of mortgage loans issued. These problems also affected the Farm Credit System.

Farm Credit System

The Agricultural Credit Act of 1987 was signed into law in January 1988. The new law mandated the merger of the Federal Land Bank and the Federal Intermediate Credit Bank by July 6, 1988, and six months later added the Production Credit Association (a lender of short-term credit to farmers) to form the Farm Credit System. To obtain real estate mortgages, borrowers must purchase stock in the Farm Credit System amounting to a minimum of $1,000, or 2 percent of the loan, whichever is less. The stock is transferable if the loan is assumed during the life of the loan; when the borrower makes the final payment on the mortgage, the loan is redeemed at the same price the borrower or his or her assignee paid for it.

The 1987 act also provides for the establishment of the Farm Credit Insurance Corporation. Its function is to provide insurance to help protect the value of the association stock during the life of the loan.

Credit Unions

A **credit union** is a cooperative financial institution designed to make loans to its members for any reasonable purpose. Credit unions began in Germany and were introduced into the United States in 1909.

With the deregulation of financial institutions, credit unions have begun moving into the mortgage market in addition to the consumer loan market, where they have traditionally functioned. The main reason for this movement is that savings in credit unions have far outpaced the traditional demand for consumer loans.

Thirty percent of the mortgages originated by credit unions have a 15-year maturity. To serve as a conduit to the secondary market, the Credit Union National Association Mortgage Corporation was created in 1979. CUNA Mortgage Corporation purchases mortgages from individual credit unions, packages them, and sells them to the Federal Home Loan Mortgage Corporation, the Federal National Mortgage Association, the Government National Mortgage Association, and private investors. In turn, it receives a servicing fee. However, many of the more sophisticated credit unions sell the mortgages directly and retain the servicing fees.

Real Estate Investment Trust

In Chapter 16, the real estate investment trust will be discussed as an investment vehicle. Here, it is discussed as a source of funds for residential, commercial, and industrial funds.

Frequently, the REIT (or Reit) will handle the whole package from the land loan to the long-term loan. There various loans take the following forms:

First Mortgage Land Loans. These are loans to a builder-developer on land on which the builder-developer intends to build.

First Mortgage Development Loans. These funds are used to finance site improvements, such as installation of roads, clearing and leveling of land, and installation of utilities.

First Mortgage Construction Loans. As a group, the largest investment by REITs is in first mortgage construction loans. They are short-term mortgages with maturities between one and three years.

First Mortgage Long-Term Loans. The first mortgage long-term loan is used to pay off the construction loan. The typical REIT long-term loan has a maturity somewhere between 15 and 30 years and is made on apartments or commercial buildings.

First Mortgage and Short- and Intermediate-Term Loans. These are loans made on completed properties with maturities of less than ten years. Typically, they are interest-only loans; that is, no payment of principal is required. The purpose of these loans is to permit builder-developers to attempt to find other loans at lower rates in the interim.

Junior Mortgages. REITs hold a limited amount of junior mortgages. Typically, they are wraparound mortgages issued in connection with refinancing a completed structure.

Mortgage Companies

A **mortgage company,** according to the constitution of the Mortgage Bankers Association of America, is "any person, firm or corporation . . . engaged in the business of lending money on the security of improved real estate in the United States. . . ."

Approximately 2 percent of the total mortgage indebtedness in the country is held by mortgage companies. They are limited by the amount of their own available investment capital as a direct source of funds. Their major function is as intermediaries between the borrower and secondary mortgage market. Mortgage bankers perform three functions.

1. *Loan origination.* Working with real estate brokers and agents, they obtain referrals of buyers who apply for a mortgage loan.
2. *Underwriting.* They evaluate the mortgage loan application. The guidelines described in Chapter 13 (see Exhibit 13-1) are used to determine a borrower's ability to repay the loan.
3. *Servicing.* They pool mortgage loans sold in the secondary market to specific investors such as insurance companies or pension funds.

Other pools of mortgages are sold to Fannie Mae (FNMA) or Freddie Mac (FHLMC), both of which are discussed in the section on the secondary mortgage market.

After selling the pooled mortgages, the mortgage broker provides servicing. Servicing involves collecting the mortgage payment and forwarding the funds, minus a service fee, to the investor.

In the event of default, the servicing agent works with the lender to collect the delinquent borrower's payment. In a foreclosure, the servicing agent represents the interests of the mortgage investor.

Pension Funds

Traditionally, **pension funds** have had relatively little to do with real estate. Currently, less than $10 billion is invested in real estate, with about

$6 billion in mortgages. Although these figures are staggering, they amount to only about 2 percent of their assets.

Prior to December 29, 1980, retirement plan trusts were taxed on income from debt-financed real estate investments; for example, when the trust bought an apartment house with a mortgage held by a financial institution. It was taxed because the IRS considered it unrelated business income and therefore fully taxable.

On December 29, 1980, President Carter signed a bill exempting pension trusts from income tax. The law, however, still provides that the tax exemption does *not* apply if

1. The purchase price is not fixed or determined on the date of purchase.
2. The purchase price of debt repayment is time or dependent on future profits or revenues.
3. The property is leased back to the seller or related partners.
4. The seller provides a nonrecourse debt that bears either interest significantly below market rates or is subordinated to other debt on the property.

SECONDARY MORTGAGE MARKET

The **secondary mortgage market** is a market for the purchase of existing mortgages to provide more liquidity for mortgages. The concept arose out of the success of the Federal Reserve System in providing liquidity for certain types of paper held by commercial banks. For example, a small-town commercial bank that is a member of the Federal Reserve System may discount (or sell) some of its notes to the federal reserve bank in its district. Suppose a commercial bank holds an acceptable note for $30,000 with interest at 14 percent and it wants to discount the paper with the Federal Reserve at the Reserve's discount rate of 13 percent. This means that, for practical purposes, the bank can receive $30,000 for the note, pay the Federal Reserve 13 percent interest, earn 14 percent net, and then lend the $30,000 at whatever rate is obtainable.

The purpose of the secondary mortgage market is to provide a similar mechanism. For example, if there is a secondary market, then conceivably a financial institution might lend out $50,000 on a mortgage then sell the mortgage on the secondary market. The financial institution will then presumably have $50,000 more cash in hand with which to be able to make a new mortgage loan.

National Housing Act of 1934 and the Secondary Mortgage Market

The National Housing Act of 1934 established the Federal Housing Administration to provide for the establishment of privately owned mortgage associations to operate a secondary mortgage market nationally. However, there was no attempt under the 1934 act to form such associations.

In 1935, the Reconstruction Finance Corporation began buying some mortgages on urban commercial properties, but it exerceised no direct influence on the residential mortgage market.

In 1938, legislation was enacted to provide for a government-sponsored secondary mortgage market for residential mortgages. In that year, the RFC provided the necessary capital for the Federal National Mortgage Association, which was to operate as a secondary market. For ten years, the **Federal National Mortgage Association (Fannie Mae)** did relatively little buying of mortgages. In 1950, it was transferred from the jurisdiction of the Reconstruction Finance Corporation to the Housing and Home Finance Agency, which had been created in 1942.

Housing Act of 1954 and FNMA

Because FNMA was a wholly owned government corporation borrowing money from the Treasury and because FNMA often acted as a primary source of funds rather than as a true secondary market, Congress rechartered FNMA under the act of 1954. On November 1, 1954, FNMA began a new operation. It was rechartered as an agency of the Housing and Home Finance Agency. The HHFA administrator is the chairman of the board of directors of FNMA with the power to appoint the other four directors. Under the 1954 act, FNMA was to become divorced from government ownership and become *privately* owned.

The Private Fannie Mae

In May 1968, Fannie Mae was established as a privately owned corporation rather than a combination government/private corporation as it had been. The $142 million of its stock held by the Treasury was retired; and the common stockholders, who accounted for $139 million of the agency's capital (as of May 1968), had the sole equity interest in the portfolio of mortgages valued at $5.5 billion. The restructured Fannie Mae is run by a 15-member board of directors. Ten members of the board are to be elected by the stockholders; and five, representing real estate, mortgage banking, and home building, are appointed by HUD.

In 1970, FNMA was authorized to buy conventional mortgages as well as FHA and VA mortgages.

In Chapter 13 it was pointed out that FNMA, the nation's largest supplier of mortgage credit, has tightened its standards. The reason for this action was that FNMA discovered that when they compared foreclosures with purchases by loan-to-value ratio, loans with down payments of 10 to 19 percent were three times riskier. In short, the loans in that range had three times as many foreclosures as loans with 20 percent or higher down payments. Additionally, loans with down payments of less than 10 percent were five times riskier.

As a result, FNMA issued eight guidelines that are being typically viewed by mortgage lenders as the industry standard.

1. The required amount of income a borrower needs to qualify for mortgage loans with low down payments is increased. A loan for sale to FNMA with less than a 10 percent down payment will not be purchased unless the borrower's monthly housing expenses are less than 25 percent of gross monthly income and housing expenses plus installment debt do not exceed 33 percent of gross monthly income.
2. Purchases of adjustable-rate mortgages with graduated payment features are discontinued.
3. Adjustable-rate mortgages that do not include a cap, or ceiling, on how high interest rates can rise will not be purchased.
4. Limits are placed on contributions paid by any interested party to the transaction other than the home buyer (for example, the seller, builder, real estate agent, or some other party) equal to 3 percent of the sales price or appraised value, whichever is less, on fixed-rate loans with less than 10 percent down. No contributions will be permitted on behalf of the home buyer on adjustable-rate mortgages with less than 10 percent down. Buydowns are not permitted on adjustable-rate mortgages regardless of the size of the down payment. When the home buyer makes a down payment of 10 percent or more on a fixed-rate loan, contributions will be limited to 6 percent. Contributions include all financing costs, such as loan fees and buydowns, and other costs related to the transaction normally paid by the home buyer.
5. If a borrower is aided by a co-buyer who contributes to the down payment, the co-borrower must take title and occupy the property if the down payment is less than 10 percent of the loan amount. If the down payment amounts to 10 percent or more, the co-borrower must be an immediate family member.
6. A home buyer must make a minimum 5 percent cash down payment in addition to funds received as a gift toward purchase of a house.
7. FNMA will not purchase from an investor any second home loans that include scheduled, or the potential for, negative amortization.
8. FNMA will not purchase refinanced mortgages that include scheduled, or the potential for, negative amortization.

As a result of this tightening of standards by FNMA, and the subsequent acceptance of these lending standards by the entire lending industry, a number of home buyers have increasing difficulty in qualifying for loans.

Government National Mortgage Association

In 1968, when FNMA became privately owned, the **Government National Mortgage Association (Ginnie Mae)** was created to take over some of

FNMA's functions. Ginnie Mae holds the old, and still existing, Reconstruction Finance Corporation paper. It is to underwrite special-assistance loans, such as those on low-income housing projects, and operate liquidation and management functions.

As part of its special-assistance function, GNMA is involved in low-cost housing and hence the so-called **tandem plan.** For example, if a low-cost housing development is sponsored by a nonprofit corporation and interest rates rise, financial institutions will not lend except at market rates. Thus, Ginnie Mae insures a commitment to the lender or seller of the loan at a fixed price or par, then it sells it to FNMA at the prevailing market price and absorbs the loss. For example, suppose the project costs $1 million and GNMA pays the seller $1 million. If rates have risen and the $1 million is discounted to $950,000, then GNMA sells the loan to FNMA for $950,000 and absorbs the $50,000 loss, which usually shows up in the federal deficit.

Federal Home Loan Mortgage Corporation

The **Federal Home Loan Mortgage Corporation (Freddie Mac)** was formed in 1970. This secondary market for conventional loans was sought after primarily by savings and loan associations and was an arm of the Federal Home Loan Bank Board whose chief officers were three members of the Bank Board. It is now under control of the Resolution Trust Corporation.

It was authorized to hold, deal, or sell mortgages or part interest in loans. In short, it could do for conventional mortgages everything that FNMA has been doing for FHA and VA loans.

Selling Mortgages to Freddie Mac. Mortgages are sold by Freddie Mac the same way they are sold to FNMA. Most of its dealings are with savings and loan associations and it buys mostly mortgages originated by the associations.

Freddie Mac and Second Mortgages. According to information from Freddie Mac, second mortgages issued rose from $10 billion in 1978 to $75 billion in 1985. Consequently, it entered the secondary market in 1986 to purchase these mortgages along with FNMA who had been purchasing them for some time.

There are a number of strict rules applying to these purchases, however. The total amount of borrower's mortgage debt service plus hazard insurance premiums, real property taxes, installment debt with ten or more payments, mortgage insurance premiums, homeowner association dues and condominium fees, and alimony and child support payments cannot exceed 36 percent of gross monthly income.

The second mortgages purchased by Freddie Mac must be at a fixed rate and amortized over terms ranging from 5 to 15 years.

After purchasing the loans, Freddie Mac pools the second mortgages and sells securities backed by the Resolution Trust Corporation.

Sources of Secondary Market Funds

Basically, funds for mortgage purchases come from paybacks on existing mortgages and from borrowed money backed by existing mortgages.

FNMA. Because FNMA is said to be a private corporation "with a public purpose," the secretary of the Treasury has authority to buy up to $2.25 billion of FNMA obligations at any one time. However, this "backstop" has never been used. Money is raised by the sale of debentures, usually of intermediate term, one to seven years, which are issued in minimum amounts of $10,000.

Short-term notes. These are discounted notes (that is, sold at a price lower than face value to reflect current interest rates) with fixed rates and maturities up to 360 days. They are sold in minimum amounts of $50,000.

Master notes. These notes have fluctuating rates tied to the rate on 91-day U.S. Treasury bills and are adjusted weekly. The rates paid to investors move up and down with the Treasury bill rate.

Residential financing debentures. These securities are six-month or one-year debentures. They are issued monthly and are priced daily at interest rates publicly announced by Fannie Mae through a nationwide group of securities dealers and dealer banks.

Mortgage-backed securities. This security is by far the largest security device in money volume sold by FNMA. Its characteristics are

1. MBSs are backed by pools of new mortgages or seasoned FHA/VA loans. To meet investor objectives, the backing may be either single-family or multifamily loans; 15- or 30-year fixed-rate level payment loans; single-family or multifamily equity loans; variable-rate loans; or adjustable-rate loans.

2. Unlike GNMA securities, which are government backed, the FNMA security is guaranteed by the Federal National Mortgage Association to provide timely payment of scheduled principal and interest each month. The mortgages in the pool must meet the standards set by FNMA, and the lenders must meet FNMA's financial and operating standards. Investors receive one check monthly regardless of the number of Fannie Mae MBSs owned and regardless of whether FNMA received payment on all the underlying mortgages.

Liquidity of FNMA securities. All FNMA securities are highly liquid. There are two reasons for this: (1) Fannie Mae debt trades in the world's largest secondary market, the U.S. Treasury and federal agency debt market, and (2) Fannie Mae debt instruments have been given special status as legal investments. This special status allows commercial banks to deal in, underwrite, and purchase the securities for their own accounts without limitation. FNMA securities are also legal instruments for surplus and reserve funds of Federal Home Loan Banks.

GNMA. Basically, GNMA raises funds by selling a variety of securities all of which are fully guaranteed by the U.S. government and bear the full faith and credit of the federal government. In addition, all the various types are backed by an underlying pool of mortgages as security. The funds raised are, of course, used to purchase additional mortgages. These securities are

Straight pass-through security. Monthly payments of principal and interest are paid to the investor from payments actually collected on the pooled loans in an amount proportionate to the investor's share in the pool.

Modified pass-through security. Investors are paid monthly principal installment at a fixed rate of interest on unpaid mortgage principal balances. Both principal and interest payments must be made whether collected or not by the issuer.

Bond-type security. A specified rate of interest is paid to the investor semiannually. The principal is returned at the end of the term.

Resolution Trust Corporation. Originally, $100 million in capital was subscribed to by the 12 district Federal Home Loan Banks. Additional funds were raised by the sale of Freddie Mac certificates. Effective August 14, 1989, the principal and interest are now guaranteed by the Resolution Trust Corporation and backed by mortgages. Interest is paid on the amount outstanding whether or not collected. The principal passes through as collected. If the mortgage is delinquent, the principal is paid as collected. If there is a loss of principal due to a foreclosure, such loss is not passed through to the investor, but paid by Freddie Mac.

Federal Agriculture Mortgage Corporation. Established in 1988, the **Federal Agriculture Mortgage Corporation (Farmer Mac)** is referred to by the financial press as "the new kid on the block." Farmer Mac pools and sells investors' mortgage-backed farm securities on the secondary market with payment of principal and interest guaranteed by a federally chartered agency. It is an entity of the Farm Credit System, but is separately run. Farmer Mac is backed by a $1.5 billion line of credit from the U.S. Treasury.

Private Insurance Companies. There are two major private mortgage companies: Mortgage Investment Corporation of Milwaukee (MGIC) and P.M.I. Mortgage Insurance Co. Although both are primarily mortgage insurors, both have purchased mortgages on the secondary market. Basically, their funds are obtained on a line of credit from major commercial banks. They borrow on the line of credit; with the money, they buy mortgages, and with the paybacks from the mortgages, they pay back the commercial banks.

GLOSSARY

Commercial banks Full-service banking institutions organized under federal or state charters

Credit union A cooperative type of financial institution designed to make loans to its members for any reasonable purpose

Deflation Increase in the supply of goods and services relative to the money supply

Discount point The percentage discount lenders require for mortgages issued below market interest rates—one point equals 1 percent; one-time charge used to adjust the yield to what market conditions demand

Discount rate The rate of interest a bank must pay when it borrows from its federal reserve bank

Disintermediation Direct investments by the public rather than placing funds in a financial institution

Fannie Mae See Federal National Mortgage Association

Farmers Home Administration An organization authorized to make direct loans, insured loans, and grants to farmers

Farmer Mac See Federal Agriculture Mortgage Corporation

Federal Agriculture Mortgage Corporation (Farmer Mac) Pools and sells investors' mortgage-backed farm securities on the secondary market with payment of principal and interest guaranteed by a federally chartered agency

Federal Home Loan Mortgage Corporation (Freddie Mac) An agency that purchases Veterans Administration guaranteed loans, conventional loans, and FHA-insured mortgages

Federal National Mortgage Association (Fannie Mae) A privately owned, government-regulated corporation that buys and sells mortgages in the secondary mortgage market

Fractional reserve system A legal prohibition against banks operating in this country lending 100 percent of their deposits

Freddie Mac See Federal Home Loan Mortgage Corporation

Ginnie Mae See Government National Mortgage Association

Government National Mortgage Association (Ginnie Mae) A government-owned corporation that buys and sells mortgages on the secondary mortgage market to support low-income housing programs

Inflation A persistent rise in prices, which means the dollar purchases less and less

Interest rate The price paid for the use of money

Moral suasion Jawbone policy; in an inflationary period, the federal reserve banks sometimes try to discourage banks from extending undue amounts of credit for speculative purposes that are inconsistent with the maintenance of sound credit conditions

Mortgage company Any person, firm, or corporation engaged in the business of lending money on the security of improved real estate

Mutual savings banks Banks whose objectives are for the mutual benefit of depositors and therefore all earnings after payment of operating expenses, taxes, and setting aside of necessary reserves for the protection of depositors are distributed to the depositors in the form of interest

Pension funds Monies from retirement funds as a source of mortgage money

Reintermediation With declining interest rates, households increase their savings through deposits with financial institutions

Reserve requirements The amount of funds banks have on deposit which the Federal Reserve prohibits them from lending

Restrictive open market policy The sale of bonds by the Federal Reserve to banks to reduce the supply of loanable funds

Savings and loan associations Federal or state chartered thrift institutions who historically have been leaders in residential mortgage financing

Secondary mortgage market A market for the purchase of existing mortgages with the idea of providing more liquidity for mortgages

Selective controls Acts authorized from time to time by Congress that provide specific terms under which credit may be used

Tandem plan A secondary mortgage market plan that combines operations of GNMA and FNMA for sponsors of nonprofit housing projects

QUESTIONS FOR REVIEW

1. Discuss the present actions available to the Federal Reserve Board to raise or lower interest rates.
2. Why have life insurance companies switched in the past decade from home mortgage lending to farm, commercial, and industrial loans, and why are some now moving back to the residential mortgage market?

3. What is the secondary mortgage market?
4. Explain GNMA's tandem plan.
5. Discuss mortgage-backed securities.
6. What is the difference between GNMA's straight pass-through security and its modified pass-through security?
7. Explain Citicorp's Mortgage Power program. Does a real estate broker have a conflict of interest when using the program?
8. Describe the three functions of mortgage bankers.

PROBLEMS AND ACTIVITIES

1. Current TV ads point out that your house may have increased in value, consequently a second mortgage may be available to you. Assume you purchased a home ten years ago for $30,000 with a 90 percent loan. Currently, the balance due is $25,000. Today's appraised value is $45,000 and first mortgages are available with 10 percent down. What is the maximum amount you can borrow on a second mortgage?
2. You have an option on a parcel of land for $300,000 on which you wish to build a motel for $3 million. You approach a REIT for funds. What possible forms of financing are available to you from it?

15

TAX FACTORS IN REAL ESTATE

KEY TERMS

Adjusted basis
Basis
Boot
Depreciation
Fixing up expenses
Initial payment
Installment sale
Passive losses
Straight-line depreciation
Tax-free exchanges

As part of the Omnibus Budget Reconciliation Act, approximately 200 amendments to the Internal Revenue Code were made by the Revenue Act of 1987. The 1987 tax bill modified the personal mortgage interest deduction and restored installment sale income reporting for nondealers in real estate.

Corrections to the Tax Reform Act of 1986, long given up for dead, were presented to the taxpayer in the wee hours of October 22, 1988, as TAMRA, the Technical and Miscellaneous Revenue Act of 1988. The significant provisions of these bills affecting real estate are discussed in this chapter.

RECENT LEGISLATION AFFECTING REAL ESTATE

Although it is illegal to evade taxation, tax avoidance is a perfectly legitimate means of minimizing the tax on income and profits that must be paid to the federal government. In an attempt to encourage certain types of personal or business investment, Congress permits the postponement and oft-times permanent deferral of payment of income taxes.

For example, in an effort to encourage rehabilitation of existing real estate and construction of new housing units, factories, and office buildings, Congress passed the Economic Recovery Tax Act of 1981. The act established the Accelerated Cost Recovery System (ACRS), which replaced existing methods of depreciating real property and permitted real property to be depreciated over a 15-year-period. The ACRS rules simplified depreciation reporting and added significant incentives for real estate investment. Additionally, the 1981 law provided liberal tax credits for those who rehabilitated qualified older properties.

The tax provisions of the Deficit Reduction Act of 1984 modified ACRS rules, increasing the depreciation life of real property from 15 to 18 years. More importantly, perhaps, the holding period necessary to realize long-term capital gains was reduced to six months from one year.

Further changes in tax laws affecting real estate were passed in both 1985 and 1986. On October 11, 1985, PL 99-121 established new minimum and imputed interest rate rules for seller-financed sales of real property. In the spring of 1986, ACRS depreciation was further extended; this time from an 18- to a 19-year depreciable life.

In 1985, a call was issued by the Reagan administration for a revision of the federal tax code. It was to be fair and to result in tax simplification. In late 1986, Congress enacted the Tax Reform Act of 1986, whose provisions were to be phased in beginning in January 1987. As far as tax simplification was concerned, the revision of the code encompassed over 3000 pages, and prior to its signing was already being dubbed by accountants as the "Accountants' Full Employment Act of 1986."

The continual modification of income tax laws is not likely to abate. A student of real estate is by necessity a student of taxation and its effect on real estate values and profits. However, real estate continues to represent the best means to earn income that can be protected from taxation.

Before proceeding, one note of caution is necessary. Due to the enormity of changes in the tax code under the 1986 act, and after TAMRA, IRS regulations regarding specific rules have yet to be written. No doubt it will be several years before all the dust has settled. Changes, clarifications, and technical corrections will abound, and the authors advise users to proceed with caution and with counsel from their accountants and attorneys.

MAJOR CHANGES AFFECTING REAL ESTATE UNDER TAX ACTS OF 1986, 1987, AND 1988

Individual Tax Rates

Prior to passage of the 1986 act, individual tax rates ranged from 11 to 50 percent in 14 brackets. The 1987 "phase in" sets three personal income tax rates as shown in Table 15-1.

Table 15-1 Rate Table, Tax Reform Act of 1986

RATE (PERCENT)	INDIVIDUAL INCOME	JOINT RETURN INCOME
15	to $17,850	to $ 29,750
28	to 43,150	to 71,900
33	to 89,560	to 149,250
28*	on excess	on excess

*An additional 5% surtax is imposed to phase out personal exemptions.

Mortgage Interest Deductions

When enacting the tax laws, Congress usually justifies its actions as tax reform (1986) or tax simplification (1988). Before judging whether reform or simplification has been achieved, let's quickly review the mortgage interest deduction.

Prior to the Tax Reform Act of 1986, interest paid for mortgages on real estate had been tax deductible. There were no limits in the dollar amount deducted, the size or number of mortgages held, or the number of personal residences owned. All mortgage interest paid was tax deductible.

Although the interest cost for mortgages continued to be deductible under the Tax Reform Act of 1986, the new law did impose some limitations. Interest expense was still deductible for first and second home mortgages provided the total amount of the mortgage loans did not exceed the homes' original cost plus improvements. When the total mortgage loans were greater than the sum of the home's original cost plus improvements, interest expense was deductible *only* if the excess mortgage had been used for educational tuition or medical expenses.

For example, if the original cost of a home in 1977 was $75,000, additions costing $25,000 were completed in 1981 and 1982, and the current market value was $200,000, then:

1. An 80 percent mortgage loan was $160,000.
2. No tax was payable due to having a mortgage greater than cost.
3. Mortgage interest expense, for purposes of determining taxable income, was deductible for the first $100,000 (cost plus improvements) in mortgages unless the excess mortgage ($60,000) was used for tuition or medical expenses.

The limitation was that the Tax Reform Act provided for a phasing out of interest deductions on consumer loans on such things as credit cards, cars, or boats. Prior to the passage of the act, or as soon as it became evident that interest on consumer loans would no longer be deductible, borrowers learned that this provision could be circumvented by taking out a loan (second mortgage) against home equity to buy a car, for example, and deducting the interest on the second mortgage. Hence, the excess mortgage interest deduction was limited to educational tuition and medical expense loans.

The Technical and Miscellaneous Revenue Act (TAMRA) of 1988 redefined mortgage debt for tax purposes. A mortgage (one or more) used to construct, remodel, or buy a primary or second residence is called "acquisition of debt." Individuals are now limited to deducting interest expense for their acquisition debt.

Acquisition debt may not exceed $1 million and is not limited to the home's fair market value. As the mortgage is paid off, however, acquisition debt declines and is defined as the "remaining or unpaid mortgage balance." Acquisition debt may not be increased by refinancing the mortgage.

Other debt, for instance for which the first or second home is security, is defined as a "home equity loan." Interest expense on home equity loans is deductible up to the lesser of (1) $100,000 or (2) fair market value of the home, less acquisition debt.

Together, acquisition debt and home equity loans may not exceed $1.1 million. Interest expense on acquisition debt greater than $1 million and home equity debt greater than $100,000 are not tax deductible.

We cannot say why the mortgage interest deduction applies to second homes. We could conjecture that it is either because Congress has an abiding concern for those who own ski condos and lake cottages, or because representatives and senators need to maintain second residences in Washington.

Long-Term Capital Gains

Prior to the 1986 act, investment property held for six months or more was entitled to preferential tax rates if the property was sold for a gain. These preferential rates have been incorporated in the tax code since 1924.

As far as the Tax Reform Act of 1986 was concerned, it didn't matter if property was held for one day, six months, or ten years. If it was sold for a profit, it had to be taxed at the taxpayer's individual tax rate (see Table 15-1). However, separate statutory language was contained in the revised code that made it easier for lawmakers to reinstate a preferential rate for capital gains in the future.

Long-Term Capital Losses

The taxman taketh, but never giveth! If an individual suffers a long-term capital loss, the law remains the same: a long-term capital loss is a loss on property held for six months or more.

Offsetting Gains and Losses

Prior to the Tax Reform Act of 1986, $2 of long-term capital loss could be used to offset $1 of ordinary income. Under the 1986 law, long-term capital losses reduced, dollar for dollar, any long-term capital gains. When long-term capital losses exceeded long-term capital gains, up to $3,000 of the loss could be used to reduce taxable income by the same amount.

Losses in excess of $3,000 could be used to reduce taxable income in the future. Carry-forwards could continue until all excess long-term losses had been used.

Installment Sales Method of Reporting Gains

When real property is sold on the installment plan, the profit is proportioned; thus, the tax on the profit can be deferred by spreading out payments over the installment period. **Initial payments** means payments made or received in cash or property other than purchase money obligations during the taxable year in which the sale is made. This includes all payments, not just down payments.

For example, suppose you sold a property for $100,000 with a $10,000 down payment and an adjusted basis of $60,000. The tax on the profit of $40,000 ($100,000 – $60,000) can be deferred by means of an **installment sale.** Consider the above example with three annual payments of $30,000 (interest is ignored for illustrative purposes):

Down Payment			Taxable Gain	
Year 1	$ 10,000	down	taxable gain is	$ 4,000
Year 2	$ 30,000		taxable gain is	$12,000
Year 3	$ 30,000		taxable gain is	$12,000
Year 4	$ 30,000		taxable gain is	$12,000
Total payments	$100,000		Total profit	$40,000

In other words, as payments are received, a proportion of each payment is profit. In the preceding example, since 40 percent of the total sales price is profit, 40 percent of each payment received is reported as taxable gain.

Generally, the installment method of reporting gain may be utilized on sales of property used in a trade or business or rental income property sold for $5 million or less. Additionally, gain on the sale of residential property may be reported using the installment method. When deferred payments under the installment method exceed $5 million, an interest charge is imposed on the tax that is deferred. The interest charge applies to that part of the installment obligation that is unpaid at year-end.

The preceding rules under the installment method of reporting taxable gains apply to *nondealers* of real property. *Dealers* are people who

1. regularly sell or otherwise dispose of real property on the installment plan, or,
2. dispose of real property held by them for sale to customers in the ordinary course of their trade or business.

The Revenue Act of 1987 prohibits dealers' use of the installment method for sales of real property with three exceptions:

1. Property used in the trade or business of farming.
2. Sale of residential lots.
3. Time share ownership or rights to use residential real property for less than six weeks per year.

If the dealer elects the installment method of reporting for one of the three exceptions, the dealer must pay interest on the installment payment received. Interest is paid for the time from the date of sale to the date the installment is paid.

The repeal of the installment method for dealers applies to sales after December 31, 1987. The new rules do not affect installment sales occurring before March 31, 1986.

Depreciation on Real Estate Investments

An allowance for the wearing out of real property used in a trade or business or of real estate held for production of income is permitted by law. This allowance is called depreciation. Depreciation of property used for personal purposes is not permitted.

In essence, then, **depreciation** is a systematic and rational apportionment of the cost of fixed assets, not including natural resources. Buildings are included, but land is *not* included in the category of assets that can be depreciated. Furthermore, when determining depreciation of improvements on a parcel of real property, the 1986 act dictates the useful life of the improvements. Such improvements can be divided into two parts: (1) residential rental property and (2) nonresidential rental property. In the former, property must be written off in 27.5 years; in the latter, it must be written off in 31.5 years.

Basis and Adjusted Basis. Depreciation, therefore, can be written off in either 27.5 years or 31.5 years depending on the use of the property. For this to be done properly, it is necessary to have an understanding of the concepts of *basis* and *adjusted basis*.

Basis. **Basis** is the amount against which depreciation is deducted. Generally, the original basis is the cost of the property. However, in a number of situations, it is the fair market value of the property at the time it is placed in service. For example, if a home is converted into rental use, it is the fair market value as of the date of the change, or the cost plus improvements or additions since the date of the change minus changes in the basis since the acquisition of the property (for example, any casualty losses that might have been claimed by the taxpayer since the date of acquisition).

Adjusted basis. Generally, the **adjusted basis** is the basis minus any depreciation taken in prior years. For example, suppose a rental property is owned on which the basis is $100,000, and depreciation of $5,000 has been taken. It is sold for $110,000. The amount on which the tax is owed is $110,000 – $95,000 or $15,000.

Straight-Line Depreciation. Although there are a number of methods of depreciating real property improvements, the 1986 act specifically stated that the property must be written off using **straight-line depreciation.** Using this method, an equal amount of the cost is allocated to each time period during the 27.5 years (for residential income property) or 31.5

years (for nonresidential property). As dictated by law, the "remaining economic life" of the property is either the 27.5 years or the 31.5 years.

Suppose you own a rental/residential property valued at $275,000 (improvements only). The simple method of calculating straight-line depreciation is

$$\text{Depreciation} = \frac{\text{Cost (improvements, not including land)}}{27.5}$$

$$\frac{\$275{,}000}{27.5} = \$10{,}000 \text{ depreciation per year}$$

What difference does it make? The $10,000 is relevant because it is "written off" against income and increases an investor's cash flow while at the same time reducing that individual's tax liability. For example, tax savings from depreciation are equal to the depreciation expense multiplied by the investor's tax rate. In this example, depreciation shelters, or reduces, taxable income by $10,000, resulting in tax savings (taxes not paid) of $2,800.

Tax Benefit Limitation

The 1986 act contained a provision regarding "passive losses" from rental income property. Under the act, a taxpayer cannot use losses from real estate limited partnerships in which the taxpayer does not actively and materially participate to offset income from other sources. Such **passive losses** can be used *only* to offset income from similar passive investments.

For example, if the taxpayer owns a limited partnership interest in two rental properties and one shows a loss of $10,000 and the other a gain of $10,000, the loss may be offset against the gain. However, if the taxpayer has two such rental properties and one shows a loss of $20,000 and the other a gain of $10,000, the taxpayer can offset the gain against the $20,000 loss, but *cannot* use the remaining $10,000 passive loss and offset it against salary income. Excess passive losses may, however, be carried forward indefinitely to offset future passive income.

Under a special provision of the Tax Reform Act, as much as $25,000 of passive losses on rental real estate can be used each year by persons who *actively* participate in real estate activity and whose adjusted gross income is less than $100,000. To qualify to offset the $25,000 loss against other income, the investor must own, as a general partner, at least 10 percent of the property. The $25,000 allowable passive loss is reduced by 50 percent of the amount by which adjusted gross income exceeds $100,000. If, for example, there is an adjusted gross income of $125,000, the taxpayer can deduct *only* a $12,500 loss instead of the $25,000.

The rules regarding passive losses were to be phased in over four years beginning January 1, 1987. During the phase-in period, instead of 100 percent of excess passive losses being disallowed, the following percentages of excess passive losses were to be allowed:

1987–65%
1988–40
1989–20
1990–10
1991– 0

The active participation standard requires "active participation" in both the year in which the passive loss arises and the year in which the deduction is taken. Limited partners may be active participants; however, the IRS has yet to write the applicable guidelines.

Rehabilitation Tax Credits

To encourage retrofitting or rehabilitation of residential and nonresidential structures, the Tax Reform Act of 1986 continued to provide significant tax credits to redevelopers. Tax credits earned may be used to directly offset up to $25,000 of income taxes owed.

The 1986 law provided a 20 percent credit for certified historic structures and a 10 percent credit for rehabilitation of buildings first placed in service before 1936. This tax credit is reduced by 50 percent of the amount by which adjusted gross income (AGI) exceeds $200,000. The credit is completely phased out when AGI reaches $250,000. The basis of the property is reduced by the full amount of the credit.

The 1986 Tax Reform Act reduced both the credit for rehabilitation and the number of investors who could use the credit. The result was that the number of historic preservation projects dropped from 1,932 in 1987 to 1,092 in 1988, a decline of 43 percent. The decline in private investment in historic rehabilitation for the same period was $214 million.[1]

Low-Income Housing Tax Credits

To provide an incentive to construct or rehabilitate low-income housing, tax credits may be claimed by owners of qualified residential rental real estate. To be eligible for the credit, the property must meet the following criteria:

1. Tenant's rent cannot exceed 30 percent of tenant's income.
2. Forty percent of the units must be occupied by persons with incomes of 60 percent or less of the area median income, or 20 percent of the units must be occupied by individuals with 50 percent or less of the area median income.

[1]National Council for Economic Development, *Economic Developments,* March 1, 1989.

If the property meets the preceding criteria, tax credits earned depend on whether the project is federally subsidized or not. A 9 percent annual credit is available for non–federally subsidized projects while a 4 percent credit applies to federally subsidized new construction or rehabilitated property.

Failure to comply with these requirements for 15 years will result in recapture of the credits. The basis of the property, for purposes of depreciation, is not reduced by the tax credits. The low-income tax credit expired at the end of 1989.

Refinancing a Mortgage to Defer Taxes

A mortgage is a handy device to defer taxes if capital appreciation has occurred. Suppose *A* purchases a small apartment house a number of years ago for $100,000 and depreciated as much as possible. The apartment house has appreciated in value to $150,000. During the period in which *A* held the property, the mortgage was dutifully paid off. The depreciation has brought the adjusted basis down to $25,000. If *A* sells now, a taxable gain of $125,000 ($150,000 – $25,000 adjusted basis = $125,000 taxable gain) would be realized.

It would be logical to refinance the building, say at 60 percent of $150,000 appreciated current value, or $90,000 cash in hand. True, *A* would be paying interest on $90,000, but this is deductible, subject to the interest limitations imposed by the Tax Reform Act of 1986. Depending on *A's* income tax bracket, the *effective* interest payment could be as low as 5 percent. *A* could then spend the $90,000; or better still, invest it in a second income-producing property against which a "fast write-off" could be taken, resulting in some tax-free income. Therefore, *A* should not sell, but should refinance. (For tax limitations on refinancing using mortgages or home equity, refer to the earlier discussion of mortgage interest deductions.)

Reporting Requirement

There is a part of the Tax Reform Act of 1986 that directly affects the actions of real estate brokers. The code specifically provides that people responsible for closing real estate sales must file reports of the transactions with the Internal Revenue Service. If there is no such person, then it is the responsibility of the mortgage lender. When a lender is not involved, first the seller's broker, then the buyer's broker, is responsible for reporting to the IRS. Those required to file this report may not separately charge for preparing and distributing the required Form 1099-S. Some savings and loan and escrow companies charge $10 to $60 for this service.

The underlying reason for this reporting requirement is to make certain that those realizing profits on the sale of their properties pay the taxes due. Additionally, the reports provide a means of cross-checking the reporting of interest income when seller financing is provided.

RESIDENTIAL PROPERTY

In general, in any business, profits are taxed. In real estate, taxes on income or profits are often deferred. Ultimately, the taxes are paid; the inevitable day is simply put off, perhaps indefinitely. For example, the tax on any profit made on the sale of a residence is deferred if the seller, within 24 months of the sale of the property, buys another home or builds a new home at the same price or at a higher price than the home just sold.

How many times may a homeowner defer the tax? The answer is that tax deferment may occur any number of times *provided that* (1) not more than one transaction be made per 18-month period, and (2) the new residence not be purchased and resold before the older home is sold.

For instance, *A* buys a home in 1981 for $40,000 and sells it in 1990 for $85,000. Within a year, *A* buys another home for $95,000. The $45,000 profit earned from the 1981 purchase, if reinvested in the new home, is not taxable at the present time, but deferred to a later date. The cost of the new home is figured not at $95,000, the purchase price, but at $50,000 ($95,000−$45,000). In short, the profit is figured in determining what is called the *basis* of the new home.

Adjustments in the Basis

In determining the gain, or profit, on which the homeowner may postpone paying taxes, basically three things may change the basis or the original cost of the existing home: (1) cost of improvements added by the owner to the property, (2) "fixing up" expenses, and (3) selling expenses.

Cost of improvements means improvements of a substantial and permanent nature; for example, adding a new porch or garage as distinguished from repairing a light fixture.

Fixing up expenses are those that assist the sale of the home. To qualify under this category, the expenses must have been for work performed during a 90-day period immediately prior to the sale, and must have been paid for on or before 30 days after the sale. These expenses would include such things as redecorating and repainting.

Selling expenses include such things as brokerage commissions and legal fees. For example, suppose *A* purchases a home for $55,000 and later sells it for $65,000. Assume further that a porch was added for $3,000; fixing up expenses were $800; and selling expenses totaled $3,500. For tax purposes, the adjusted basis for the home would be calculated as $55,000 + $3,000 + $800 + $3,500, or $62,300; consequently, the gain would be $2,700 ($65,000 – $62,300, or $2,700).

Tax Advantages of Personal Residential Ownership

There are several major tax advantages in residential ownership: First, the real property tax is a deduction from ordinary income on one's personal income tax return, thus reducing the tax to be paid.

Second, as previously stated, interest paid on a mortgage is also deductible on personal income tax returns. In times of high interest rates, this deduction actually reduces the effective rate of interest paid on the loan. (See Chapter 20, Table 20-1, and the previous section in this chapter on refinancing a mortgage.)

Third, for homeowners age 55 or older there is a onetime exclusion of up to $125,000 on the gain from the sale of the taxpayer's principal residence. To qualify, the seller must have lived in the principal residence three out of the five years before sale. For homeowners who become incapable of providing self-care and thereafter move to a state-licensed facility or nursing home, the residence requirement is one year out of the five years preceding the sale of the home.

Rental of Second or Vacation Homes

Although expenses such as interest, taxes, and casualty losses on vacation homes are deductible whether a vacation home is rented or not, the 1976 Internal Revenue Act placed limits on depreciation and maintenance expense. The general rules remain in force and are as follows:

1. If the home is rented for less than 15 days during the year, the income is treated as a "wash" transaction. In short, the rent is not treated as income and expenses attributable to the rent are not deductible. All allowable normal ownership costs, however, may be deducted as usual.

2. If a taxpayer uses a vaction home for personal purposes up to the greater of 14 days or 10 percent of the days the home is rented during the year, depreciation and maintenance may be deducted. However, the amount of other allowable business deductions (depreciation and maintenance costs) cannot exceed the excess of rental income minus other allowable prorated expenses (mortgage interest, property taxes, etc.).

3. To determine the amount of expenses attributable to rental income, multiply the rental days by total expenses normally deducted by homeowners and divide by total days used. For example, the owner uses the home 10 days and rents it 100 days, and the mortgage interest and property taxes are $2,000. Then:

$$\frac{\text{Days rented} \times \text{Deductible expenses}}{\text{Total days used}} = \text{Expenses attributable to rental income}$$

$$\frac{100 \times \$2{,}000}{110} = \frac{\$200{,}000}{110} = \$1{,}818$$

If gross rental income were $30 per day or $3,000, the maximum allowable deduction for depreciation and maintenance costs would be:

$$\text{Rental income} - \begin{matrix}\text{Prorated normal}\\ \text{expenses attributable}\\ \text{to rental income}\end{matrix} = \begin{matrix}\text{Maximum allowable rental}\\ \text{business deductions}\end{matrix}$$

$$\$3{,}000 - \$1{,}818 = \$1{,}182$$

In other words, the owner of a vacation home is allowed to deduct, for purposes of determining taxable income, all costs normally deducted by homeowners. These costs must be apportioned, however, between rental usage and personal usage. Additionally, the vacation homeowner may deduct, pro rata, that part of depreciation and maintenance costs attributable to rental. This amount is limited to the difference between rental income and the prorated costs of home ownership normally allowable and deducted by homeowners.

TAX-FREE EXCHANGES

When properties are exchanged, they are often **tax-free exchanges.** This is one of the most misunderstood problems in real estate. In reality, there is no such thing as a tax-free exchange; it is a tax deferment. If the taxpayer exchanges a capital asset held for investment purposes for a capital asset held for like purposes and the asset is a piece of real property, the taxable gain on the exchange is deferred until the sale of the parcel being acquired.

Mortgages in Exchange

The problem in a so-called tax-free exchange may be somewhat complicated when there is a mortgage against the property. The general rule is that the amount of the mortgage debt is treated as the equivalent of cash. However, if the owner either assumes a mortgage or takes possession, subject to a mortgage on the property received in the exchange, the mortgage will not affect the owner's tax position.

To illustrate the situation, suppose *A* owns a property now valued at $75,000 with an adjusted basis of $50,000; *A* trades for a building with *B* valued at $175,000, on which there is a $100,000 mortgage. The basis of the new building will be $150,000:

Old property (adjusted) basis	$ 50,000
Plus mortgage assumed by *A*	100,000
Less mortgage assumed by *B*	0
Basis of the new building	$150,000

At this point, there is no taxable gain against *A*.

For the other party, *B*, assume *B* has an adjusted basis of $155,000 on the $175,000 building that was traded with *A*:

Price of property received from *A*	$ 75,000
Plus mortgage assumed by *A*	100,000
Total consideration	$175,000
Minus adjusted basis of the building transferred to *A*	$155,000
Plus mortgage assumed by *B*	0
Taxable gain	$ 20,000

Remember, the value of *A*'s property minus the value of *B*'s building always equals the sum of the mortgage assumed plus "boot" or the trade would not have been made. In other words, the price or value of the property acquired is equal to the sum of the mortgage assumed plus boot given plus the value of property traded minus any mortgage assumed by the other party.

The Effect of "Boot"

In an exchange, money is often paid to one of the parties "to boot." **Boot** may be either cash or "unlike" property. Consequently, the recognized gain is figured as actual cash plus the fair market value of the "unlike" property received.

For example, *A* has a building with a fair market value of $100,000. *A* trades for *B*'s building with a fair market value of $50,000 and an adjusted basis of $35,000. *A* receives $25,000 cash and a note and mortgage of $25,000 from *B*. The $100,000 building has an adjusted basis of $30,000. Using the following formula:

Fair market value of new asset	$50,000	
Less adjusted basis of old asset	30,000	
	20,000	
Plus cash received (boot)	25,000	
Plus note and mortgage received (boot)	25,000	
Realized gain		$70,000
Recognized gain, or boot:		
Net cash received	$25,000	
Note and mortgage	25,000	
Recognized gain for tax purposes		50,000
Tax deferral on exchange of like assets		$20,000

Adjusted basis of new asset:	
Fair market value of new asset	$50,000
Less realized gain	70,000
	−20,000
Plus recognized gain	50,000
Adjusted basis of new asset	$30,000

The tax on $20,000 of the realized gain is postponed; any additional taxable gain will be based on the sale of the new asset. The new asset takes the basis of the old one, $30,000. If the new asset is subsequently sold, say, for $190,000 in cash, then the tax would be computed on $190,000 – $30,000, or $160,000.

B's position is somewhat different because property has been acquired without any recognized or realized gain. Therefore, the basis in *B*'s old property is carried over to the new property.

Fair market value of new asset		$100,000
Less cash paid	$25,000	
Note and mortgage given	25,000	
Note and mortgage assumed	0	
Basis in old asset	35,000	
Adjusted basis in new asset		85,000
Realized gain		$ 15,000

Because *B* did not receive cash or "unlike" property (note and mortgage), no gain is recognized for tax purposes. The basis in the new property is $85,000.

TAXES AND LEASES

If a landlord-tenant relationship has been created, the landlord reports rental income and deducts expenses, real property taxes, and depreciation. The tenant deducts rent as an expense if it is commercial or business property. Although this is straightforward, special situations often arise that require different handling in lease situations. Some of these are given below.

Lessee's Improvements

Suppose an owner of vacant land rents it to a tenant who agrees to build on it. The land is valued at $25,000, and the tenant agrees to build a $100,000 gas station. It is further agreed that, at the end of the lease term, the landlord is to receive the land and the building. Assume at the end of the lease term the land is worth $30,000 and the building $25,000. The landlord sells it for $55,000. The basis is the $25,000 cost of the land, and tax is figured as a long-term capital gain, $55,000 – $25,000 (cost), or $30,000 taxable gain.

Had the landlord built the $100,000 gas station, he or she would have had to charge more rent as the rent minus depreciation would have been taxable as ordinary income. In some circumstances, the lessor may be better off if the tenant builds the improvements, in this example, a gas station.

Bonus Paid by Lessee

Frequently a tenant pays a bonus to obtain a favorable lease. This amount is reportable as ordinary income when received by the landlord. However, it is *not* immediately deductible by the tenant, who must write it off during the life of the lease.

Security Deposits

Technically, the landlord should deposit a security deposit paid by a tenant in a special account and use it only to cover costs as outlined in the written agreement. However, legally or illegally, depending on the state, lessors in practice frequently use security deposits either as working capital or as income.

As far as the Internal Revenue Service is concerned, if the security deposit is actually held as a deposit, it is not taxable. But as long as it is held as a deposit the lessee *cannot* deduct this amount as an expense. However, if a deposit is to be applied as payment of rent for the last month or year of the lease, it is advance rent and must be reported as income when received.

GLOSSARY

Adjusted basis The basis minus any depreciation taken in prior years

Basis The amount against which depreciation is deducted

Boot Cash or "unlike" property

Depreciation A general term covering loss of value from any cause; a systematic and rational apportionment of the cost of fixed assets not including natural resources; an allowance for the wearing out of real property used in a trade or business or of real estate held for production of income

Fixing up expenses Costs involved in assisting the sale of an older home

Initial payments Payments other than purchase money obligations made or received in cash or property during the taxable year in which the sale is made

Installment sale A sale in which taxes are deferred until a later date

Passive losses Defined by the IRS as losses attributable to passive activities that can be used only to offset income from similar passive investments; often applies to limited partnerships, but also can include rental real estate

Straight-line depreciation Depreciation of a constant annual percent of building value

Tax-free exchange Trading like properties in order to defer taxes

QUESTIONS FOR REVIEW

1. Discuss the loss limitations imposed by the 1986 Tax Reform Act.
2. Explain the straight-line method of depreciation.
3. What is the general rule for deferring the tax on a gain resulting from the sale of a residential property?
4. What are the restrictions on the number of times an individual may defer the tax on a gain in the sale of residential property?
5. What is a tax-free exchange and how is it used to defer income taxes?

PROBLEMS AND ACTIVITIES

1. You have a residence you acquired in 1983 for $35,000. You sell it for $65,000 on July 1, 1992. Meantime, you install a new furnace for $1,200. Your brokerage costs were $3,600, other costs of the sale were $450, and within 90 days of the sale you had the house painted for $800.
   a. Assume you move into an apartment after the sale. On how much of the $65,000 will you be taxed?
   b. Will the tax be on ordinary income?
   c. If there is a tax, what is the rate?
   d. Assume you buy a home for $85,000 ten months after the sale. On how much of the $65,000 will you be taxed?
2. You buy an apartment on July 1, 1982, for $600,000. You sell it on July 1, 1991, for $800,000. During the period of ownership, you depreciated the property using the straight-line method. What is the adjusted basis at the time of sale? How much of the gain will be taxed as ordinary income?

3. Your home mortgage was originally $115,000 for 15 years with an 11 percent rate of interest. Using Appendix C or Decision Assistant Term Loan amortization, answer the following questions. Assume the first payment is in January.
   a. How much is the monthly payment?
   b. What is the total interest paid the second year of the loan?

16

REAL ESTATE INVESTMENTS

KEY TERMS

Annuity
Break-even point
Cash flow
Cash on cash
Compound interest
Debt coverage ratio
Discount rate
Equity dividend rate
Free and clear rate of return
Future value
Internal rate of return
Leverage
Limited partnership
Liquidity risk
Loan-to-value ratio
Market risk
Mortgage loan constant
Occupancy ratio
Operating ratio
Opportunity cost
Present value
REITs
Reversion
Risk of business failure
Tax flow
Tax savings
Tax shelter
Vacancy ratio
Validation

Different people give different reasons for investing in real estate. Some say they need tax shelters. Some say they want an income or cash flow; others want a hedge against inflation. In the final analysis, however, all wish to maximize personal wealth. Because no one is able to indicate with certainty which investment opportunity is good for a particular individual, the most we can do here is suggest tools for making intelligent decisions.

WHY INVEST IN REAL ESTATE

There are numerous reasons for investing in real estate. Real estate investments provide the following advantages:

1. The protection of asset purchasing power through appreciation in value.
2. The ability to increase profits through leverage, or the use of borrowed money.
3. The tax sheltering of income through depreciation of buildings.
4. Optimum cash flow after taxes.

5. Opportunities for management control.
6. The pride of ownership.

These advantages are discussed in the following sections.

Inflation

Inflation can be thought of as a persistent rise in prices, which means that a dollar purchases less and less each year during periods of inflation.

The results of inflation on the individual can be devastating. Inflation favors debtors at the expense of creditors and fixed-income receivers. If you lend a person $1,000 today to be paid back a year from now, and if during the year prices have doubled, you will be paid back in *real purchasing power* only about one-half as much as you lent the person. For example, U.S. government savings bonds bought for $75 in 1973 were cashed at $100 in 1983. But the dollars in 1983 bought far less than $75 did in 1973. During this ten-year period, the average rate of inflation for all consumer prices was 8.5 percent, and the rate reached the double digits during four of the years.

What has this to do with real estate investment? Simply that all things *do not* inflate at the same rate. There is general inflation and specific inflation. *General inflation* is reflected in the Consumer Price Index, while *specific inflation* is reflected in a particular commodity, such as real estate. According to one source:

> There is no doubt that the *purchase price* of housing has risen relative to other prices in recent years. Between 1978 and 1988, the price of a single-family home of a given quality increased at about 8.3 percent annual rate, as compared with a 5.5 percent annual rate in overall consumer prices (as measured by the deflation for personal-consumption expenditures).[1]

Because real estate prices in general rise at a rate faster than the Consumer Price Index, persons holding real estate continue to gain as a result of inflation.

Inflation varies not only by the type of commodity but also by physical location of that commodity. Not only may the cost to construct identical properties vary in different parts of the country, but the rate of inflation may range from +30 percent to −6 percent depending on whether the property is located in Westchester County, New York, or Dallas, Texas.

Table 16-1 compares construction costs, property taxes, annual rental, and change in construction costs for an identical 2,000-square-foot home with three bedrooms, family room, dining room, two bathrooms, and a two-car garage in the ten most populous U.S. cities.

---

[1]Randall Pozdena and William Burke, "Housing: Sacred Cow" (San Francisco: Federal Reserve Bank, November 28, 1980), 2 (Updated for price changes since 1980 by authors).

Table 16-1 Housing Cost Comparison

CITY (by population)	1987 PRICE	PERCENT CHANGE FROM 1986	ANNUAL TAXES	ANNUAL RENTAL
New York[1]	$304,000	28.1	$3,918	$1,433
Los Angeles[2]	297,500	25.8	3,719	2,067
Chicago	133,700	13.0	1,670	1,150
Houston	86,300	(1.2)	1,480	625
Philadelphia	151,333	11.9	1,600	983
Detroit[3]	128,667	8.6	2,618	1,000
San Diego[4]	253,000	15.0	3,033	2,000
Dallas	117,667	(5.9)	1,289	850
San Antonio	81,500	0.9	1,251	600
Phoenix	101,500	3.7	646	800

[1]Westchester County, N.Y.

[2]Long Beach area of Los Angeles County.

[3]Wayne County suburbs.

[4]Main Line with suburbs.

SOURCE: Expansion Management, 1989 Expansion Guide *(Washington D.C.: New Hope Communications, 1989).*

Leverage

One of the advantages, and sometimes one of the disadvantages, of a real estate investment is leverage. **Leverage** is using borrowed money to increase gains. The assumption is that the borrower can earn more on the borrowed money than the cost of the borrowed money. For example, if *A* borrows at 12 percent and then earns 14 percent, leverage is being used positively. This can, of course, work in reverse. If *A* borrows at 12 percent but earns only 10 percent for a loss of 2 percent, disaster is being courted and leverage is negative.

How Leverage Works. Leverage works in the following manner. Suppose an individual has $50,000 to invest in real estate. Several alternatives are open. One alternative is simply to buy an income-producing property for $50,000. Assume the individual can earn 12 percent on the investment; then that individual's income is $6,000.

Suppose the individual can borrow an additional $50,000 at 11 percent and purchase a $100,000 property. Assume further that 12 percent can be made on the total $100,000 investment:

Borrow	$50,000	Earn on	$100,000
At 11 percent	.11	At 12 percent	.12
Cost	$ 5,500		$ 12,000

Effect of leverage

Earned on $100,000 (12 percent)	$12,000
Cost of borrowing $50,000 (11 percent)	5,500
Net earnings	$ 6,500

$$\text{Ratio of earnings to equity} = \frac{\$\ 6{,}500}{\$50{,}000} = 13 \text{ percent}$$

The example above is borrowing on a one-to-one ratio, or $50,000 equity to $50,000 borrowed.

Suppose the borrowing is done on a one-to-two ratio:

Borrow	$100,000	Earn on	$150,000
At 11 percent	.11	At 12 percent	.12
Cost	$ 11,000		$ 18,000

Effect of leverage

Earned on $150,000 (12 percent)	$18,000
Cost of borrowing $100,000 (11 percent)	11,000
Net earnings	$ 7,000

$$\text{Ratio of earnings to equity} = \frac{\$\ 7{,}000}{\$50{,}000} = 14 \text{ percent}$$

As previously suggested, this can work in reverse. Suppose instead of 12 percent, the net earnings are only 7 percent:

Borrow	$50,000	Earn on	$100,000
At 11 percent	.11	At 7 percent	.07
Cost	$ 5,500		$ 7,000

Effect of reverse leverage

Earned on $100,000 (7 percent)	$7,000
Cost of borrowing $50,000 (11 percent)	5,500
Net earnings	$1,500

$$\text{Ratio of earnings to equity} = \frac{\$\ 1{,}500}{\$50{,}000} = 3 \text{ percent}$$

Thus, the investor would have been better off having invested the $50,000 without leverage even though it would have earned only 7 percent. Earnings would total $3,500 ($50,000 × .07 = $3,500) as opposed to $1,500.

Leverage and Equity Growth. Capital appreciation goes to the equity investor. For example, suppose you have the following choices in making a $200,000 investment:

	(1) All cash	(2) A 90 percent loan
Purchase price	$200,000	$200,000
Equity	$200,000	$ 20,000

Assume an increase in value of 5 percent per year for five years:

Property value	$250,000	$250,000
Increased equity	$ 50,000	$ 50,000

$$\frac{\$\ 50{,}000}{\$200{,}000} = 25 \text{ percent} \qquad \frac{\$50{,}000}{\$20{,}000} = 250 \text{ percent}$$

$$\frac{\text{Equity growth}}{\text{Original investment}} = \text{Percent increase in equity}$$

Tax Shelters

Income from real estate is tax sheltered because the Internal Revenue Service permits depreciation expense to be deducted from revenue in determining taxable income for income tax purposes. This is particularly advantageous when one considers that real estate does not normally depreciate, but appreciates in value. Nevertheless, when a noncash expense is used to reduce taxable income, taxes payable are less and the income from the property is said to be "sheltered or protected" from taxation, hence the term **tax shelter**.

The **tax savings** from depreciation may be calculated by multiplying the amount of depreciation by the investor's tax rate. Under the Tax Reform Act of 1986, marginal tax rates are 15, 28, and 33 percent. The following illustration demonstrates these concepts:

Net income before tax and depreciation expense	$10,000	$10,000
Depreciation expense	—0—	8,000
Taxable income	$10,000	$ 2,000
Tax rate (28 percent)	.28	.28
Taxes payable	$ 2,800	$ 560

The difference between $2,800 and $560 taxes payable ($2,240) represents the tax savings from depreciation expense, thus:

Depreciation expense	$8,000
Tax rate (28 percent)	.28
Tax savings	$2,240

The tax savings results from sheltering $8,000 of rental income from taxation.

Cash Flow

Some real estate investors seek optimal cash returns from their investment (usually in the form of rent). **Cash flow** after tax from a real estate investment is generally greater than from purchasing stocks or bonds. Additionally, the investor has the advantage of long-term price appreciation, particularly during periods of inflation.

Investment Management Control

Some individuals prefer real estate investment because of the opportunity for direct control over building operations. They prefer to make their own decisions regarding rents charged, repairs made, and capital improvements undertaken. In turn, they do not like depending on unknown corporate managers located thousands of miles away. Responsibility for profit and a successful investment depends on them alone. For these individuals, investing in real estate can be a good choice.

Pride of Ownership

Real estate is a tangible asset. Investors can touch the building, see it, and drive by and know that it is theirs. If it is well-maintained, there is satisfaction that comes from knowing it is theirs. This is pride of ownership. Not often are stock certificates framed and hung on the wall or pointed out to friends and family.

REAL ESTATE INVESTMENT RISKS

Every investment by its very nature has a certain amount of risk—some more than others. One of the risks of most investments is the *purchasing power risk.* Essentially the previous discussion on inflation concerned itself with this risk. In short, in an inflationary period the yield on an investment may be wiped out by a loss of real purchasing power. As a matter of fact, inflation, combined with income taxes, may even cause a loss. Because construction costs, land values, and real estate over a period of time appreciate more rapidly than consumer prices, real estate is not typically subject to the purchasing power risk. Risks that apply to real estate are discussed in the sections that follow.

Market Risk

Market risk arises from fluctuations in the market price of investments over time. Price fluctuation may occur for many reasons and the individual investor has no control over any of them.

During periods of general real estate price appreciation, specific properties by class or geographic region may be falling in value. For example, from 1984 to 1990, overbuilding of office buildings in some metropolitan areas resulted in price declines and sales below the cost of construction. The closing of iron mines in northeast Minnesota and the resultant loss of jobs led to high foreclosure levels and sharply reduced prices for residential real estate in that region. Similarly, depressed agricultural conditions triggered drops in farmland prices of as much as 50 percent from 1980 to 1988. All this took place during a period of continued price appreciation and moderate inflation.

Real estate is made up of many submarkets, each with its own characteristics. Before investing in any real estate, it is essential that investors have a knowledge of current market conditions in the locality where they are buying (see Table 16-1).

Interest Rate Risk

This risk of loss was historically thought to apply to fixed income investments such as bonds and preferred stock, *not real estate.* Experience during the recent recession has demonstrated that even residential real estate is subject to a loss of value when there is rapid escalation of interest rates.

When a home has a given value at a point in time, that value is associated with the prevailing level of mortgage interest rates, say 8 percent. If interest rates rapidly increase to 14 percent, the cost of the home increases to potential buyers because the mortgage interest, and hence the principal and interest payment, increases.

The consequence of this change is that buyers withdraw from the marketplace when they cannot afford the home with a higher interest rate. This is the reason new home construction and sales of existing homes decline during periods of rising interest rates.

In order to retain the previous level of marketability and attract buyers to the marketplace, sellers have two choices: (1) to provide financing at a below-the-market rate of interest, thereby making the home affordable; or (2) to lower the price sufficiently to offset the buyer's higher mortgage interest costs.

As you can readily deduce, a rise in interest rates will cause the value of income-producing, as well as residential, property to decline.

Earning Power or Business Failure Risk

The **risk of business failure** either through poor management or the vagaries of the marketplace is as valid in real estate investment as in any other form of business enterprise. Poor management in real estate investment is often demonstrated by failure to adequately analyze the investment opportunity. In connection with new construction, feasibility studies limit business risk; for existing property, thoroughly prepared market and investment analysis, coupled with a management plan, limit the likelihood of failure.

Liquidity Risk

Liquidity risk is the risk of losing money as the result of a need to convert an asset into cash quickly. The more liquid the asset, the less sacrifice on conversion into cash. Obviously, cash is the most liquid of all assets. Real estate is among the least liquid of assets. Thus, it is necessary to sacrifice liquidity in a real estate investment to gain its numerous benefits.

INVESTMENT ANALYSIS

There are a number of steps for analyzing a proposed real estate investment. The first is to validate a schedule of income (rents) and operating expenses, generally provided by the seller to the real estate broker or licensee, and then to investigate the vacancy, break-even occupancy, operating, debt coverage, and loan-to-value ratios; cash flow and tax flow; profitability measures; revisions; and time value of money.

The statement of operating income and expenses may be analyzed based on the current represented performance or based on the property's projected performance in the future with new ownership. The former provides the basis for negotiating a purchase price, while the latter analysis reveals future expected profitability.

Validation

Validation of both the rent schedule and operating expenses, the essential "first step," is simply the process of confirming the accuracy and reliability of the information provided by the seller. It is important to note that often the financial data are unaudited, and there is a tendency to overstate revenues and understate expenses.

Validation of rents is accomplished by determining, through competitive analysis, if the existing rental schedule is high, low, or competitive with rents charged in comparable buildings of similar age, condition, and amenities. At this time it is also important to note the general level of vacancies and the number of new competitive buildings being constructed. The market for retail space, office buildings, and apartments is highly competitive and subject to cycles of over-/underbuilding.

Validation of operating expenses is accomplished by checking with utility companies and property tax assessors' offices, and by obtaining competitive bids for insurance and professional property management.

The most common errors relate to underestimating rental vacancy; failure to provide for property and resident manager costs; and ignoring the cost of replacing refrigerators, stoves, air conditioning, and drapes. Extreme caution must be exercised to ensure that all expenses are included, and that those included are not understated. Small errors have large effects. The value of real estate is a multiple of its income. Therefore, a $1,000 error in estimating revenue or expense may have an $8,000 to $12,000 effect upon price and/or value.

Income and expense validation also requires personal knowledge of the market. Assistance in estimating operating costs is provided by the Institute of Real Estate Management of the NATIONAL ASSOCIATION OF REALTORS® through annual publication of operating cost data for various regions of the United States. Exhibit 16-1 presents data that will be used to illustrate various analytical tools employed by real estate investors.

Vacancy Ratio

Based on historical experience, current local market conditions, or normal vacancy rates for the type of property being analyzed, the **vacancy ratio** is a measure of the expected loss of income due to tenant turnover and competitive supply/demand pressures. Vacancy is normal for all types of rental property, and profitability is overstated when vacancy is presented as zero (100 percent occupancy).

The vacancy ratio, rather than being calculated, is determined from analysis of the property, its competition, and the market. It is expressed as a percentage of potential gross income. In the absence of better information, a 5 percent vacancy ratio is presumed to be standard.

Exhibit 16-1 Statement of Revenue, Expenses, and Cash Flow

Potential Gross Income	$19,200	
Less: Vacancy allowance (5%)	960	
Effective Gross Income		$18,240
Expenses		
Real property taxes	$ 2,000	
Insurance	500	
Utilities	1,000	
Maintenance and replacement	1,000	
Professional management	1,150	
Miscellaneous	1,000	6,650
Net Operating Income		$11,590
Mortgage principal ($750) and interest ($4,000)		4,750
Cash Flow Before Taxes		$ 6,840

NOTE: Total cash payments = $6,650 expense + $4,750 principal and interest = $11,400.

Break-Even Occupancy Ratio

The maximum vacancy rate is simply the difference between 100 percent occupancy and the **break-even point**, or the percentage occupancy at which income will equal expenses. Put another way, when the property income goes below break-even, the owner must come up with out-of-pocket payments for debt service. It is particularly important when a second mortgage is being used for financing the investment.

For example, using the date from Exhibit 16-1:

Potential gross income (no allowance for vacancy	$19,200
Less expenses (including debt service of payment of interest and principal	11,400
Cash flow	$ 7,800

The total costs for the investor are $11,400. Potential gross income is $19,200. The break-even **occupancy ratio** is

$$\frac{\text{Cash expenses}}{\text{Potential gross income}} = \frac{\$11{,}400}{\$19{,}200} = \text{59.4 percent break-even occupancy ratio}$$

Then the maximum vacancy rate is 40.6 percent (100 − 59.4).

Assume the same situation except there is a second mortgage requiring an annual payment of principal and interest of $2,500, to be added to the expenses.

$$\frac{\$11{,}400 + \$2{,}500}{\$19{,}200} = \frac{\$13{,}900}{\$19{,}200} = \text{72.4 percent break-even occupancy ratio}$$

Then the maximum vacancy rate is 27.6 percent (100 − 72.4).

Calculation of the break-even occupancy ratio permits an investor to evaluate the extent of the investment risk or the likelihood of encountering negative cash flows.

Operating Ratio

The **operating ratio** measures the relationship of total operating costs to potential gross income. Unless the property is unique in some respect, operating costs generally fall within a narrowly defined percentage of gross potential or scheduled income. In other words, similar properties located in the same geographic market have similar utility, property tax, maintenance, and insurance expenses. When the calculated operating ratio falls outside these limits, it is a signal that rents and/or expenses are over- or understated and re-analysis and revalidation of the numbers is in order. The operating ratio is calculated thus:

$$\frac{\text{Operating expenses}}{\text{Potential gross income}} = \frac{\$\ 6{,}650}{\$19{,}200} = \text{34.6 percent operating ratio}$$

Debt Coverage Ratio

Lenders may specify a minimum **debt coverage ratio** when accepting or evaluating an application for a mortgage loan. The ratio is calculated as follows:

$$\text{Debt coverage ratio} = \frac{\text{Net operating income}}{\text{Annual debt service}}$$

Simply stated, the lender and investor are interested in knowing if there is sufficient operating income to meet mortgage principal and interest payments and provide a margin of safety. The minimum ratio is often expressed as 1.25, or income must be 125 percent of the annual debt service. At lower levels, risk of default increases substantially for the investor and lender.

Knowing both net operating income and the lender's (mortgage investor's) minimum debt coverage ratio permits the investor to determine the maximum amount that may be allocated for mortgage payments while still meeting the qualifications for a mortgage loan. For example, when net operating income is $50,000 and the debt coverage ratio is 1.25, the maximum debt service is $40,000 calculated as follows:

$$\frac{\text{Net operating income}}{\text{Debt coverage ratio}} = \frac{\$50{,}000}{1.25} = \$40{,}000 \text{ maximum annual debt service}$$

Loan-to-Value Ratio

Lenders also set limits on the maximum mortgage loan as a percentage of a property's purchase price. For commercial/investment real estate, the typical loan-to-value ratio is 70 to 80 percent. The **loan-to-value ratio** is calculated as follows:

$$\frac{\text{Mortgage loan}}{\text{Purchase price}} = \text{Loan-to-value ratio}$$

The LVR is also a measure of leverage and represents an investment parameter with regard to investor equity. When the LVR is 75 percent, the equity investment ratio is 25 percent of the purchase price.

Cash Flow and Tax Flow

Cash flow, or the cash left to the investor after all operating expenses, interest, and payments of principal have been made, may be measured on a before- or after-tax basis. A typical cash flow before tax situation was previously illustrated in Exhibit 16-1.

The **tax flow** is the amount of taxable income on which income taxes are paid. The formula to determine taxable income (tax flow) is:

Cash flow before taxes	$ 6,840
Plus: Principal payments	750
Less: Depreciation (assumed to be $7,000)	(7,000)
Taxable income (tax flow)	$ 590

Payments of mortgage principal are included in determining taxable income because they reduce mortgage debt and build investor equity in the property. As discussed, depreciation varies depending on the method used.

Cash flow after tax is calculated by deducting any income tax payable from cash flow before tax, as follows:

Cash flow before tax		$6,840
Less taxes payable		
Taxable income	$590	
X tax rate (28 percent)	.28	(165)
Cash flow after tax		$6,675

For some properties, taxable income may, in fact, be negative; that is, from a tax viewpoint, the property is operated at a loss. This situation most often arises because of depreciation deductions. To illustrate, if we assume that depreciation in the prior example was $9,000, the following situation would exist:

Cash flow before taxes	$ 6,840
Plus principal payments	750
Less depreciation	(9,000)
Taxable income (loss)	$(1,410)

Cash flow after tax would be greater than cash flow before tax because of the tax savings resulting from the tax loss:

Cash flow before tax		$6,840
Plus tax savings[2]		
Taxable loss	$1,410	
X tax rate (28 percent)	.28	395
Cash flow after tax		$7,235

Measure of Profitability

Although any ratio may be used to compare various real estate investment alternatives, the most simply understood and calculated are rates of return.

[2]The tax savings here is calculated under the assumption that investor has adjusted gross income of less than $100,000 and therefore may deduct up to $25,000 of passive losses from other income, per the Tax Reform Act of 1986.

These ratios are based on comparing various measures of income with either the purchase price of the property or the investor's equity.

Equity in this case includes the down payment plus discount points, legal fees, prepaid interest, and closing costs. All these costs are cash payments made in connection with acquiring investment real estate. The names of the ratios are not as important as the method by which they are calculated.

Free and Clear Rate of Return. This measure of profitability, **free and clear rate of return,** is calculated without consideration for financing, annual debt service, depreciation, and income taxes. Other measures of the rate of return are affected by the preceding factors and do not clearly present the operating profitability of the investment. The ratio is calculated as follows:

$$\frac{\text{Net operating income}}{\text{Purchase price}} = \text{Free and clear rate of return}$$

Broker's Equity Rate of Return. This profitability measure is also called the **cash on cash** rate of return or **equity dividend rate.** The ratio does not include the tax effects of depreciation, taxes payable, or tax savings. The ratio ignores taxes because after-tax measures of profitability require knowledge of a specific investor's tax bracket. When brokers inform each other of investment opportunities for sale, they do so without reference to the tax circumstances of an investor, which, at the time, are unknown. The ratio is calculated thus:

$$\frac{\text{Cash flow after debt service and before taxes}}{\text{Equity investment}} = \text{Broker's equity rate of return} = \text{Cash on cash rate of return}$$

$$= \text{Equity dividend rate}$$

More Rates of Return. Additional measures of profitability may be calculated to estimate equity rates of return. For each measure of income, there is an equivalent profitability ratio as follows:

1. Cash flow after taxes.
2. Cash flow after taxes plus equity growth from loan amortization.
3. Cash flow after taxes plus equity growth plus appreciation.

By dividing each of the preceding measures of income by investor equity, a ratio of profitability or rate of return is calculated. They may all be used to compare different real estate investment opportunities.

Payback Period. Although considered unsophisticated, the payback period is used by many investors to screen large numbers of properties. Simply stated, this ratio determines the number of years it will take for an investor to recover the initial investment. The shorter the payback, the greater the profitability. The payback period may be calculated as follows:

$$\frac{\text{Initial cash (equity) investment}}{\text{Cash flow after taxes}} = \text{Payback period in years}$$

Reversion

Previously discussed measures of profitability have not explicitly considered the receipt of cash on resale of the real estate investment. The lump sum received on resale of the property, or the **reversion,** includes recovery of the initial down payment, payments reducing the mortgage, and any increase in purchase price due to appreciation, less selling costs. Additionally, any profit from resale requires payment of taxes at the rate required for capital gains.

To appropriately determine the after tax cash flow from resale, the following computations must be made:

Sale price
Less selling costs
Less mortgage loan balance
= cash received before taxes

To determine the cash available to investors, it is also necessary to calculate the taxable gain on resale and taxes payable as follows:

Sale price
Less selling costs
Less adjusted basis[3]
= taxable gain on resale
× investor's marginal tax rate (28%)[4]
= tax on gain on resale

Lastly, the reversion is calculated as follows:

Cash received before taxes
Less tax on gain on resale
= reversion, after tax cash flow

Time Value of Money

Thus far, we have examined cash flow generated from operations and resale of a real estate investment. What has not been considered is the timing, or when these cash flows are to be received.

---

[3]Original cost less accumulated depreciation.

[4]The maximum tax rate under the Tax Reform Act of 1986 is 28 percent regardless of whether income is a capital gain or ordinary income. High income individuals lose the benefit of the initial 15 percent tax bracket and pay a surtax of 5 percent, thereby creating a third marginal tax bracket of 33 percent.

Before considering the effects of timing on the profitability of a real estate investment, three concepts should be kept foremost in mind.

1. *There are two types of cash flow.* (1) Cash flow may be a regular periodic payment with receipt of an equal amount of money in each time period, generally each year. This type of cash flow, because of its periodic and regular occurrence, is called an **annuity** payment. An example would be receipt of $2,000 per year for ten years. (2) Cash received that is unequal in amount and not received regularly or periodically, such as cash on resale of real estate, is called a reversion or lump-sum payment. An example would be $25,000 to be received ten years from now; $5,000 to be received in four years and $6,000 to be received in ten years are also lump-sum cash flows.

2. *The analyst must know or estimate the investor's rate of return,* when evaluating the timing (receipt) of cash flow from a real estate investment. This is the highest rate of interest the investor may earn from an alternative investment. This rate of return is also referred to as the investor's **opportunity cost, discount rate,** or desired rate of return and is used in analyzing the value of all future cash flows.

3. *Sooner is better than later and more is better than less.* These words provide the foundation for a concept of finance called compound interest, which is further defined in the next section. It is from this concept that six financial analytical factors of investment analysis are derived. Variously referred to as present value, discounted cash flow, time value of money, or capitalization, these concepts provide the basis for theoretically better investment analysis and presumably better decisions.

   The essential idea is that rational investors would rather have $1,000 today than $1,000 three years from today. In other words, the value of $1,000 three years from now is less than $1,000 today. Similarly, that same investor would rather earn interest on an investment at a 10 percent than a 4 percent rate.

Financial Functions. Each of the financial functions and their respective formulas are presented in Appendix C. These tables conveniently provide the numerical factors necessary for answering the commonly asked questions of investment analysis.

The remainder of this section discusses the basic use of the tables and the financial questions that may be asked and answered. For discussion purposes, the 10% Annual Compound Interest Table from Apppendix C is used (and illustrated as Exhibit 16-2).

Question 1: What is the value in the future, of $1 invested today for n years at i interest rate?

Answer: Investment × compound interest factor (column 1) adjacent to the number of years (1–30) for the interest rate specified.

Assuming a 25-year investment earning 10 percent interest, \$1 will grow to \$10.83 or \$1,000 will grow to \$10,834.71. The concept of **compound interest** is that each year interest is earned on the amount invested *and* nterest is earned on the interest earned in prior years. **Future value** (FV) is calculated thus:

FV = Investment × compound interest factor for $n = 25$, $i = 10$ percent
FV = \$1,000 × 10.83471
FV = \$10,834.71

Question 2: What is the value in the future, of \$1 invested each year for n years at i interest rate?

Answer: Annual investment × compound annuity interest factor (column 2) adjacent to the number of years (1–30) for the interest rate specified.

Assuming a 25-year investment earning 10 percent interest, \$1 invested each year plus compound interest will accumulate to \$98.35. For an IRA investment of \$2,000 per year for 25 years earning 10 percent interest, the total future value will be:

FV = Annual investment × compound annuity interest factor for $n = 25$, $i = 10$ percent
FV = \$2,000 × 98.347059
FV = \$196,694.11

Question 3: What is the value today of \$1 to be received in n years in the future when the opportunity cost is i interest rate?

Answer: Amount to be received × present value factor (column 4) adjacent to the number of years (1–30) for the interest rate specified.

If we assume waiting five years to receive \$1 and have the alternative (opportunity cost) of investing money at 10 percent interest, the value today (present value) of \$1 in five years is \$.620921.

PV = Amount to be received (reversion) × present value factor
PV = \$1 × .620921
PV = \$.620921

In the language of compound interest (Question 1), what is the future value of \$.620921 invested for five years at 10 percent interest?

Exhibit 16-2 10% Annual Compound Interest Table

Years	1 AMOUNT OF 1 AT COMPOUND INTEREST $S^n = (1+i)^n$	2 ACCUMULATION OF 1 PER PERIOD $S_{\overline{n}\vert} = \frac{S^n - 1}{i}$	3 SINKING FUND FACTOR $\frac{1}{S_{\overline{n}\vert}} = \frac{i}{S^n - 1}$	4 PRES. VALUE REVERSION OF 1 $V^n = \frac{1}{S^n}$	5 PRESENT VALUE ORD. ANNUITY 1 PER PERIOD $a_{\overline{n}\vert} = \frac{1 - V^n}{i}$	6 INSTALLMENT TO AMORTIZE 1 $\frac{1}{a_{\overline{n}\vert}} = \frac{i}{1 - V^n}$	Years
1	1.100 000	1.000 000	1.000 000	0.909 090	0.909 091	1.100 000	1
2	1.210 000	2.100 000	0.476 190	0.826 446	1.735 537	0.576 190	2
3	1.331 000	3.310 000	0.302 114	0.751 314	2.486 852	0.402 115	3
4	1.464 100	4.641 000	0.215 470	0.683 013	3.169 865	0.315 471	4
5	1.610 510	6.105 100	0.163 797	0.620 921	3.790 787	0.263 797	5
6	1.771 561	7.715 610	0.129 607	0.564 473	4.355 261	0.229 607	6
7	1.948 717	9.487 171	0.105 405	0.513 158	4.868 419	0.205 405	7
8	2.143 588	11.435 888	0.087 444	0.466 507	5.334 926	0.187 444	8
9	2.357 947	13.579 476	0.073 640	0.424 097	5.759 024	0.173 641	9
10	2.593 742	15.937 424	0.062 745	0.385 543	6.144 567	0.162 745	10
11	2.853 116	18.531 167	0.053 963	0.350 493	6.495 061	0.153 963	11
12	3.138 428	21.384 283	0.046 763	0.318 630	6.813 692	0.146 763	12
13	3.452 271	24.522 712	0.040 778	0.289 664	7.103 356	0.140 779	13
14	3.797 498	27.974 983	0.035 746	0.263 331	7.366 687	0.135 746	14
15	4.177 248	31.772 481	0.031 473	0.239 392	7.606 080	0.131 474	15
16	4.594 972	35.949 729	0.027 816	0.217 629	7.823 709	0.127 817	16
17	5.054 470	40.544 702	0.024 664	0.197 844	8.021 553	0.124 664	17
18	5.559 917	45.599 173	0.021 930	0.179 858	8.201 412	0.121 930	18
19	6.115 909	51.159 090	0.019 546	0.163 507	8.364 920	0.119 547	19
20	6.727 499	57.274 999	0.017 459	0.148 643	8.513 564	0.117 460	20
21	7.400 249	64.002 499	0.015 624	0.135 130	8.648 694	0.115 624	21
22	8.140 274	71.402 749	0.014 005	0.122 845	8.771 540	0.114 005	22
23	8.954 302	79.543 024	0.012 571	0.111 678	8.883 218	0.112 572	23
24	9.849 732	88.497 326	0.011 299	0.101 525	8.984 744	0.111 300	24
25	10.834 705	98.347 059	0.010 168	0.092 295	9.077 040	0.110 168	25
26	11.918 176	109.181 765	0.009 159	0.083 905	9.160 945	0.109 159	26
27	13.109 994	121.099 941	0.008 257	0.076 277	9.237 223	0.108 258	27
28	14.420 993	134.209 935	0.007 451	0.069 343	9.306 567	0.107 451	28
29	15.863 092	148.630 929	0.006 728	0.063 039	9.369 606	0.106 728	29
30	17.449 402	164.494 022	0.006 079	0.057 308	9.426 914	0.106 079	30

FV = Investment × compound interest factor for $n = 5$, $i = 10$ percent
FV = \$.620921 × 1.610510
FV = \$.9999994, say \$1

In other words, an investor should be indifferent between the choices of (1) receiving \$.620921 today and investing at 10 percent interest for five years to grow to \$1, or (2) waiting five years to receive \$1 when available, alternative investments earn interest at 10 percent. The present value factors in column 4 are used to evaluate the present worth of reversions to be received n years in the future.

Question 4: What is the value today of receiving \$1 each year, for n years, when the opportunity cost is i interest rate?

Answer: Amount to be received each year × Present Value Factor of an Annuity (column 5) adjacent to the number of years (1–30) for the interest rate specified.

Assuming \$1 will be received each year for $n =$ five years and the investor has the alternative of investing money at $i = 10$ percent interest, the value today (present value) of the annuity is \$3.790787.

PV = Amount to be received each year × present value factor of an annuity for $n = 5$, $i = 10$ percent
PV = \$1 × 3.790787
PV = \$3.790787

In other words, \$3.79 invested today at 10 percent will permit the investor to withdraw \$1 at the end of each year, for five years. At the end of five years, the entire \$3.79 and accumulated interest will have been withdrawn. Present Value Annuity Factors (column 4) allow the real estate investment analyst to value level, periodic cash flow from operations.

Question 5: How much must be paid each year, for n years, to repay \$1, when the cost of borrowing is i interest rate?

Answer: Amount borrowed × loan constant (column 6) adjacent to the number of years (1–30) for the interest rate specified.

Assuming \$1 is borrowed at 10 percent interest and will be repaid over 30 years, the annual payment is \$.106079 per year.

More realistically, if \$50,000 were borrowed at 10 percent interest repayable over 30 years, the annual payment would be:

Annual principal and interest payment = Amount borrowed × loan constant for $n = 30$, $i = 10$ percent
Annual PI payment = \$50,000 × .106079
Annual payment = \$5,303.95

The monthly payment may be estimated by dividing the annual payment by 12. The monthly payment is only an estimate and actually overstates the payment required. A financial calculator, or monthly amortization/loan constant tables, must be used to obtain a more precise monthly payment.

Real estate investors use a **mortgage loan constant** (column 6) to estimate the impact on cash flow of various mortgage financing alternatives. Remember that since "sooner is better than later and more is better than less," the reverse is true when borrowing and repaying loans. To increase cash flow, real estate investors seek lower interest rates (less is better than more) and longer repayment periods (later is better than sooner). Careful examination of loan constant tables reveals that lower interest rates and longer repayment periods result in lower mortgage or loan constant factors.

Question 6: How much must be invested each year at i interest rate to accumulate \$1 n years in the future?

Answer: Desired future value × sinking fund factor (column 3) adjacent to the number of years (1–30) for the interest rate specified.

Assuming that \$1 must be available to pay a note due in ten years and that money may be invested to earn 10 percent interest, the annual required investment is \$.062745, as follows:

More realistically, if \$50,000 were borrowed at 10 percent interest repayable over 30 years, the annual payment would be:

Annual investment = Desired factor value × sinking fund factor for $n = 10$, $i = 10$ percent
Annual investment = \$1 × .062745
Annual investment = \$.062745

Although the sinking fund factor is one of the six financial functions, it is rarely used by real estate investors in analyzing a particular property. Hence we have included it last among those financial questions to be considered.

Present Value of Future Cash Flow. Remember, there are two types of cash flows from a real estate investment. One is a series of equal, periodic cash flows from operations. The **present value** of an annuity cash flow may be determined by using the present value factor of an annuity (Appendix C, column 5).

The other cash flow is either a single lump sum or series of unequal payments. In either case the present values of cash flows which are not annuities are determined by using present value factors (Appendix C, column 4).

The sum of the present values of cash flows, given an investor's opportunity cost or desired rate of return, represents the value, in today's dollars, of the investment to the investor. When comparing the present value of future cash flow with the required equity investment, three different situations may arise.

1. When the present value of future cash flow is greater than the required equity investment, the rate of return on equity is greater than the discount rate. This is also a positive net present value.

2. When the present value of future cash flow is less than the required equity investment, the rate of return on equity is less than the discount rate. This is also a negative net present value.

3. When the present value of future cash flow equals the equity investment, the rate of return on equity is equal to the discount rate. In this situation, the rate of return is also known as the internal rate of return (IRR). In this case the net present value is zero.

Net Present Value (NPV). Is an initial investment of $20,000 a good investment if a cash flow of $5,276 per year for five years is earned? The investment should be made if the initial investment is less than the present value of cash flows. Thus:

$$\text{Initial investment} < \text{Present value of cash flow}$$

or

$$\text{Present value of cash flow} - \text{Initial investment} = \text{Positive net present value}$$

The reverse is also true; that is, when the initial investment is greater than the present value of cash flows, the investment should be rejected. Thus:

$$\text{Initial investment} > \text{Present value of cash flow}$$

or

$$\text{Initial investment} - \text{Present value of cash flow} = \text{Negative net present value}$$

Whether an investment should be accepted or rejected depends on the investor's expected rate of return, discount rate, or opportunity cost. If the selected rate is 9 percent, then:

PV of cash flow = Annual cash flow × Present value factor of annuity ($n = 5$, $i = 9\%$)
PV of cash flow = \$5,276 × 3.889651
PV of cash flow = \$20,522

The present value of the cash flow is \$20,522, which is greater than the initial investment of \$20,000. Several true statements may now be made.

1. There is a *positive* net present value of \$522 (\$20,522 − \$20,000).
2. The actual rate of return is greater than the discount rate of 9 percent.
3. If the investment criteria were to make all investments yielding more than 9 percent, this investment meets that criteria.

Conversely, if the investment criteria were to make only investments yielding 11 percent or more, 11 percent should be used as the discount rate or opportunity cost. Thus:

PV of cash flow = Annual cash flow × Present value factor of annuity ($n = 5$, $i = 11\%$)
PV of cash flow = \$5,276 × 3.695897
PV of cash flow = \$19,500

The present value of the cash flow is \$19,500, which is less than the initial investment of \$20,000. Therefore:

1. There is a *negative* net present value of \$500 (\$19,500 − \$20,000).
2. The actual rate of return is less than 11 percent.
3. The investment should be rejected.

Internal Rate of Return (IRR). In many investment analyses, it is not sufficient to know whether the net present value is positive or negative. Instead, the investor wants to know the expected rate of return.

The **internal rate of return** is the interest or discount rate that causes the present value of future cash flows to equal the initial investment. In other words, the IRR is the rate that results in a net present value equal to zero and represents the investor's expected rate of return.

From the previous example, what discount rate will result in a present value equal to the initial investment? Using the tables in Appendix C to determine the appropriate discount rate is a matter of trial, error, and interpolation. The solution for our example:

Initial investment = PV of cash flow = Annual cash flow × Present value factor of annuity ($n = 5$, $i = 10\%$)
\$20,000 = PV of cash flow = \$5,276 × 3.790787
\$20,000 = \$20,000, IRR = 10%

When the IRR is not a whole number such as 10 or 11 percent, the analyst must calculate where the IRR actually lies between 10 and 11 percent. This process can be simplified by using a computer and the Decision Assistant NPV and IRR software accompanying this book.

REAL ESTATE LIMITED PARTNERSHIPS

Real estate **limited partnerships** consist of a general partner and limited partners who are the equity investors. The operations of the partnership can take many forms. For example, a real estate broker or licensee may form a limited partnership with contributions ranging from $100, for the purpose of buying and holding a piece of land for future resale. Generally, the agreement incorporates a stipulation that the general partner will share any capital appreciation with the limited partners.

Sometimes the limited partnership occurs when a builder-developer is involved. The builder-developer acts as the general partner, agreeing to sell the land to the partnership, build at a predetermined price, and manage the property. The agreement provides for sharing of profits, losses, and cash flow. There is also provision for the sharing of any capital appreciation when the property is resold. The percentage of the capital appreciation may be on a fifty-fifty basis after the limited partners have received the return of their equity investment.

Regulation of Limited Partnerships

The offerings to limited partners have been ruled as security offerings and subject to federal and state regulations. Unless the offering is "private," it must be registered under the Securities Act of 1933. Although never statutorily defined, a private offering has been presumed to be a sale to fewer than 25 persons. It should be noted, however, that even a private offering does not exempt the seller from the fraud provisions of the act. There must be a full disclosure to proposed investors of all facts, circumstances, and risks involved in the investment. Furthermore, state laws have recently been tightened, which may affect the offering of limited partnership shares.

Risk and Advantages of Limited Partnerships

As in any investment, there are risks in the limited partnership:

1. Rents may be lower than projected and operating expenses may be higher. This is an earning power or management risk.
2. A partnership interest is not readily salable; consequently, there is a high degree of liquidity risk.
3. The unpredictable risk that a future Congress may reduce or even repeal liberal depreciation was realized with the passage of the Tax Reform Act of 1986.

Some of the advantages of the limited partnerships are:

1. Small investors may engage in real estate investment when they otherwise have insufficient funds.
2. A limited partner's risk is limited to the amount of money invested.
3. Although individuals share in sound real estate investments, they rely on the general partner to handle day-to-day management.

Tax Reform and Limited Partnerships

Until the Tax Reform Act of 1986, the limited partnership was one of the more popular forms of real estate investment, particularly for the small investor. The popularity of limited partnerships was enhanced by the tax code, which permitted liberal depreciation. Highly leveraged, these investments also incurred substantial interest expense, which, when combined with depreciation charges, resulted in significant tax losses. Each limited partner's pro rata share of the tax loss was used to reduce other taxable income. The result was tax savings that increased the cash flow of the investment.

Many limited partnership investments were therefore tax motivated. In fact, for many limited partnerships, the only cash flow generated was in the form of tax savings; in other words, cash retained from not paying taxes on other income.

The Tax Reform Act of 1986 substantially altered the tax benefits derived from real estate investments. The changes include the following:

1. The depreciation period was increased, thereby reducing the amount of income sheltered by depreciation.
2. The limited partners' ability to tax shelter other income was eliminated.
3. The tax savings from depreciation was reduced and the after-tax cost of mortgage interest was increased by reducing the marginal tax rate from 50 to 33 percent.

The net effect of these changes was to reduce the desirability of the limited partnership as an investment. The number and size of limited parnterships decreased dramatically. Limited partnerships after 1986 were structured to maintain a balance between depreciation and interest expense to avoid tax losses.

A review of a traditional $15,000,000 limited partnership offering is presented at the end of this chapter as a case study for discussion.

A Limited Partnership or a Corporation?

Not only is the Securities and Exchange Commission interested in the limited partnership, but the Internal Revenue Service also looks over the shoulder of the investors. Unless the agreement is properly drawn, the IRS will construe the limited partnership as a corporation. The Internal Revenue Code and its regulations provide that a partnership shall be classified as an association taxable as a corporation if its major characteristics more closely resemble those of a corporation than those of any other type of business organization.

There are six tests of a corporation:

1. Is it an association?
2. Is there an intention to do business for a profit?
3. Does it have continuity of life?
4. Is management centralized?
5. Does it have free transferability of interests?
6. Is the liability for the organization debts limited to the organization's property?

Because the first two are common to all business organizations, they are excluded. There must exist *more* than two of the remaining four characteristics for the limited partnership to be ruled a corporation. Regarding number 3, under the Uniform Partnership Act the general partner can dissolve the partnership at anytime. Or, in the alternative, the partnership agreement contains a terminal date. As to centralization of management, most limited partnerships have that. As to free transferability of interests, properly drawn agreements contain a clause requiring permission of the general partner or other partners before an investment can be transferred. Since the IRS regulations state that this interferes with free transferability, this test is eliminated. As to liability for the organization debts being limited to the organization's property: since the general partner has unlimited liability for the partnership debts, this point is eliminated.

This leaves only three which fit into the corporate category. Remember that the agreement can be more loosely drawn and even permit free transfers, for example, without losing the advantage of the limited partnership.

GENERAL PARTNERSHIPS

A general partnership consists of all general partners. The use of this investment vehicle is expected to grow as long as a special provision of the Tax Reform Act of 1986 remains in place. This special provision of the act allows the deduction of $25,000 of passive losses from rental real estate against other income. This provision, permitting the tax shelter of $25,000 of other income, will generate up to $8,250 ($25,000 × .33 marginal tax rate) of tax savings for individual investors who meet the following criteria:

1. Adjusted gross income is less than $100,000.
2. Ownership interest is 10 percent or more.
3. Partner actively and materially participates in the management of the investment.

When adjusted gross income exceeds $100,000, 50 percent of the excess is used to reduce the allowable $25,000 loss. With an adjusted gross income of $150,000, the loss is completely phased out.

For individuals or general partners who invest in low-income housing or earn rehabilitation credits, the $25,000 passive loss allowance will be phased out between $200,000 and $250,000 of adjusted gross income.

REAL ESTATE INVESTMENT TRUSTS

The real estate investment trust, or **REITs** as it is called, was set up by Congress in 1960, effective January 1, 1961. The intention of Congress was to give average people an opportunity for tax-sheltered investment. In essence the trust is not taxed first as a corporation but is treated as a conduit with respect to income distributed to the beneficiaries of the trust.

Very few trusts were organized until 1968 when stock was sold in quantity by over 200 REITs that commercial banks and insurance companies began to sponsor.

Requirements

To qualify as a real estate investment trust, the following tests must be met:

1. A REIT must be managed by one or more trustees.
2. A REIT beneficial ownership must be evidenced by transferable shares of beneficial interest.
3. A REIT would (expect for certain provisions of the Internal Revenue Code) be taxable as a domestic corporation.
4. A REIT must not hold property primarily for sale to customers in the ordinary course of its trade or business.
5. The REIT shares must be held by 100 or more beneficial owners.
6. The REIT must elect to be treated as a real estate investment trust.
7. At least 90 percent of the REITs' gross income must be derived from dividends, interest, rents on real property, or gains from the sale of real estate securities.
8. Seventy-five percent of gross income from a REIT must be derived from rents from real property, interest on mortgages, or interests in real property.
9. Less than 30 percent of the REITs' gross income may be from the sale or other disposition of stock or securities held for less than six months and real property held for less than four years.

Traditionally, REITs have had an infinite life and liquidation of investments was by means of investors selling their shares. REIT performance throughout the 1970s and early 1980s was generally poor. Investor disinterest resulted from poor earnings on mortgage investments and shares whose price did not reflect the appreciation of equity investments.

In the mid-1980s REITs generated investor interest since real estate limited partnerships came under scrutiny as abusive tax shelters. REITs also benefited from the Tax Reform Act of 1986. Many who would otherwise invest in limited partnerships will invest in REIT shares. These factors, coupled with creation of a fourth type of trust, the finite-life specified property REIT, have helped REITs regain their competitive position as a real estate investment.

Types of Trusts

There are four types of real estate investment trusts. They are:

1. *Equity trusts:* Invest in equity interests in real property in return for rental income. An example of this would be an equity investment in an apartment house.
2. *Mortgage trusts:* Invest in real property mortgages in return for interest income.
3. *Combination trusts:* Invest in a mix of some equity investment and some mortgage investment; the most popular type of REITs.
4. *Finite-life specified property trusts:* Properties to be purchased are specified in advance and the investment is closed end meaning no additional shares will be sold. The investment is unleveraged with debt accounting for 0 to 20 percent of the total investment. The life of the investment, 5 to 15 years, is specified in advance and all property will be sold at the end of that time with equity distributed to investors.

GLOSSARY

Annuity Payment or receipt of a series of equal amounts each period such as $100 monthy, semiannually, or annually

Break-even point See occupancy ratio

Cash flow The cash left to the investor after all operating expenses, interest, and payment on the principal are paid

Cash on cash A measure of profitability; also known as equity dividend and broker's equity; calculated cash flow after debt service and before taxes divided by equity investment

Compound interest Each year interest is earned on the amount invested; also interest earned on interest received in prior years

Debt coverage ratio Relationship between net operating income and annual debt service; minimum ratio specified by lender when evacuating a mortgage loan application

Discount rate See opportunity cost

Equity dividend rate See cash on cash

Free and clear rate of return Measure of profitability without consideration for financing, annual debt service, depreciation and income taxes; calculated by dividing net opertating income by purchase price

Future value The value in the future of an investment today; a series of investments earning a specified interest rate for a specific period of time

Internal rate of return The discount rate that results when the present value of future cash flow is equal to the initial investment

Leverage Using borrowed money to increase gains

Limited partnership A partnership consisting of a general partner (who manages) and equity partners whose liability is limited to the amount of equity they have invested

Liquidity risk The risk of losing money as the result of a need to quickly convert an asset into cash

Loan-to-value ratio The amount of the mortgage loan divided by the purchase price

Market risk Risk arising from fluctuations in market price of investments over time

Mortgage loan constant One of the six functions of finance derived from concept of compound interest; when amortization period and interest rate specified, the mortgage loan constant times amount borrowed equal the required periodic payment of principal and interest

Occupancy ratio Used to describe total rental occupancy required for an investor to break even; projected cash expenses divided by potential gross income

Operating ratio The relationship ot total operating costs to potential gross income

Opportunity cost The highest rate of interest that may be earned from a known alternative investment; also may be investor's cut off or desired rate of return

Present value The value in today's dollars of a future cash receipt or series of cash payments to be received at specified times given a specified discount rate, opportunity cost, or desired rate of return

REITs (Real Estate Investment Trusts) Corporations authorized to invest in real estate with exemption from federal corporate taxes that may be passed on to the shareholders

Reversion When *B* conveys to *A* for life and on *A*'s death to *B* and his or her heirs, the interest conveyed is said to be a reversionary interest; also that amount to be received in the future when the asset is sold or a lease is terminated

Risk of business failure Applies to real estate as in any other form of business enterprise. Management plans, feasibility studies, and thoroughly prepared market and investment analysis limit the likelihood of failure

Tax flow The amount of income on which taxes are paid from a real estate investment

Tax savings Deductions from revenue resulting in less tax-table income; calculated by multiplying expenses, depreciation, and taxable loss times tax rate

Tax shelter A taxable loss that may be used to reduce taxable income earned from other sources

Vacancy ratio A measure of expected loss of income due to tenancy turnover and competitive supply-demand pressures

Validation Confirming the accuracy and reliability of revenue and expense information provided by the seller of rental real estate

QUESTIONS FOR REVIEW

1. Why is a break-even occupancy ratio a handy guideline in deciding on how much of a second mortgage you can afford on an income-producing property?
2. Give an example of how leverage may work both for and against you.
3. When the investor's opportunity cost is 12 percent, what is the value of
   a. $17,000 to be received in 5 years?
   b. $4,500 per year for 14 years?
4. When a mortgage is for 30 years at 10 percent interest and the amount borrowed is $50,000, what is
   a. the annual principal and interest payment?
   b. the balance of the mortgage after 12 payments?
5. When figuring tax flow, why are payments on principal separated from interest payments?
6. Why are investors sometimes willing to pay a higher rate of interest in order to negotiate for a lower loan constant?

7. If the IRS rules that a limited partnership is a corporation, what would most certainly cause this ruling?
8. Explain the organization of the REIT.

PROBLEMS AND ACTIVITIES

1. Given the following validated information, determine (a) through (f) below:

Vacancy allowance	5 percent
Operating expenses	$21,000
Gross scheduled income	$54,000
Principal payments	$ 2,100
Interest payments	$15,000
Annual depreciation	$11,000
Marginal tax rate	33 percent

   a. Cash flow before taxes.
   b. Taxable income.
   c. Cash flow after tax.
   d. Break-even occupancy ratio.
   e. Operating ratio,.
   f. Debt coverage ratio.

2. Given the following information, what is the after-tax cash flow from resale of the property?

   Purchase price is $125,000. Depreciation expense has been $5,000 per year for six years. Selling price is $175,000. Brokerage costs are $10,500 and closing costs are $3,500. The investor's marginal tax rate is 33 percent and the original mortgage loan was $100,000. At the time of closing, the mortgage loan balance was $90,000.

3. Read and be able to discuss the following review of a $15 million limited partnership offering. Give particular emphasis to the tax benefits in light of current tax law.

GRIFFIN REAL ESTATE[5] FUND V

Griffin Securities Corporation
8200 Humboldt Avenue South
Minneapolis, Minnesota 55431

Offering Size: $15,000,000
Minimum Investment: $5,000
Retirement plans—$1,000

The Griffin Companies, which were organized in 1969, are engaged in all phases of real estate including brokerage, investment counselling, man-

[5]Reprinted with the permission of Brennan Reports, Inc., publisher of *Brennan Reports*, a monthly publication, devoted to analysis and discussion of tax shelter investment and tax planning. Further information regarding *Brennan Reports* may be obtained by writing Brennan Reports, Inc., Valley Forge Office Colony, Suite 200, P.O. Box 882, Valley Forge, PA 19482.

agement, and development. During the ten-year period from January 1, 1975, to December 31, 1984, Griffin has sponsored a total of 26 real estate programs—22 private placements and four public offerings.

These partnerships have acquired 40 properties (for over $162,700,000). Properties have been residential except for one commercial property. Griffin manages more than 5,300 apartment units located in Arizona, Arkansas, Colorado, Georgia, Florida, Indiana, Iowa, Minnesota, North Carolina, Oklahoma, South Carolina, South Dakota, Tennessee, and Wisconsin.

Structure. After payment of the front-end selling and organizational expenses, approximately 88% of investors' capital will be available for operations. Property acquisition fees (which include all costs of acquiring properties) are limited to 15% of the offering proceeds—including no more than 12% to Griffin.

The general partners have committed to purchase at least $100,000 of limited partnership interests on the same terms as other limited partners (except that no commissions will be paid). Profits and losses will be divided 99% to the limited partners and 1% to the general partner. Cashflow from operations will be paid 95% to the limited partners and 5% to the general partner.

Proceeds from sales or refinancing will be distributed to the limited partners until they have a complete return of the original investment (less prior cash distributions) plus a cumulative 6 percent per annum return thereon. Additional sales or refinancing proceeds (after payment of subordinated real estate commissions to Griffin) will be apportioned 85% to the limited partners and 15% to the general partner.

Other compensation to the general partner or affiliates is listed in the prospectus and should be reviewed by interested investors. All fees are reasonable and competitive.

Appraisals will be obtained on all properties acquired. The appraised value must equal the property purchase price plus acquisition fees.

Tax. Accelerated depreciation will be used on apartment properties acquired by the partnership. Therefore, some tax preferences during the early years can be expected.

The tax losses are not specified in the offering materials, but investors joining the prior public program (Griffin IV) in the early months of its formation had a first year write-off approximating 15% to 16% of their investment. After the first year, the annual write-off (again as a percentage of the original investment) approximates 20% to 25% per year. This is an attractive write-off particularly in view of the cash distributions that are expected to commence almost immediately!

Certain tax problems are outlined in the offering materials, but none of them appear to have the potential for a material impact.

Past Performance. Since none of the four publicly offered partnerships have sold any of their properties to date, no determination of overall results can be achieved. However, a review of cash distributions indicates that, in addition to attractive deductions spread over a period of years, cashflow to investors generally reaches 4% to 5% annually. Combining tax savings with cashflow, investors in the prior public programs are receiving about a 15% return annually.

Eight private placements (whose properties were specifiedc at the time of sale) have completed the cycle from acquisition to operations and ultimate sale. The after-tax, average annual yield and internal rate of return for these various partnerships over their respective holding periods are illustrated in Table I below.

Both methods of calculating returns are based on a 50% marginal tax rate. Yields have obviously been consistently attractive. To gain a perspective of absolute dollar returns, Table II was prepared to indicate the sales proceeds from property dispositions distributed to the limited partners. Some of the partnerships' properties were sold for cash and notes—the notes were considered part of the sales proceeds in Table II (at their face value).

■ TABLE I

Partnership Name	Years Property Held	After-Tax Internal Rate of Return	After-Tax Average Annual Yield
Calhoun Terrace, Ltd.	5.2	22.0%	22.2%
Hillsboro Court, Ltd.	6.8	26.4%	33.3%
Crown Ridge	4.8	19.0%	24.5%
Edina Park	6.8	33.0%	33.9%
Concord Estates	8.1	25.6%	47.1%
Park Ridge Apts.	3.8	33.7%	31.4%
Manor Royal	4.0	18.4%	14.9%
West Virginian	9.6	22.7%	61.3%
Overall Average	6.1	25.1%	33.6%

■ TABLE II

Partnership Name	Acquisition Date	Date of Sale	Sales Proceeds to Limited Partners per $10,000 Investment
Calhoun Terrace	12-30-71	2-28-77	$ 20,263
Hillsboro Court	6-01-72	3-01-79	63,732
Crown Ridge	12-16-74	9-21-79	49,785
Edina Park	12-01-72	10-31-79	52,483
Concord Estates	7-01-72	7-31-80	97,853
Park Ridge Apts.	12-16-76	10-01-80	53,174
Manor Royal	10-04-78	9-30-82	31,856
West Virginian	7-19-73	2-10-83	187,138

4. The following questions will familiarize the reader with the six functions of finance presented in Appendix C. These problems may also be solved using Decision Assistant.

a. What is the value, in the future, of $7,232 invested today for 9 years, earning 10% interest compounded semi-annually?
b. What is the value, in the future, of $4,000 invested each year for 30 years at 9% interest compounded annually?
c. What is the value today of $15,000 to be received in 10 years in the future, when the opportunity cost is 11% annually?
d. What is the value today of receiving $1,500 each month for 15 years, when the opportunity cost is 11% compounded monthly?
e. How much must be paid each month for 30 years to repay $65,000 when the cost of borrowing is 9% compounded monthly?
f. How much must be invested each year for 44 years at 10% interest annually to accumulate $1,000,000?

5. Given the following alternatives, which is the superior investment? Using Appendix C or Decision Assistant Net Present Value Analysis and a discount rate of 9 percent, which investment has the greater net present value?

	A	B
Initial investment	$20,000	$35,000
Cash flow year 1	8,000	13,000
2	7,000	12,000
3	7,500	12,500
4	9,000	15,000

6. Given the information in Problem 5 and using Decision Assistant IRR Analysis, calculate the internal rate of return for each investment. Based on the IRR, which alternative is the better investment?

7. Using Decision Assistant Real Estate Investment Analysis and the following information, analyze this real estate investment opportunity:

Price: $188,000 (building $165,000, land $23,000)
8- 1 BR units renting for $350.00 each
Expected vacancy and credit loss—5%
Mortgage: $145,000, 11% interest, 25 years
Down Payment: $43,000
Depreciation: 27.5 years—straight line method
Income Tax Rate: 28%
Annual Growth—Income 3%
Annual Growth—Expenses 3%
Annual Growth—Building Value 2%
Operating Expenses

Real Estate Property Taxes	$7,040
Insurance	$ 500
Utilities	$2,325
Maintenance and replacement	$1,880
Professional management	6%
Miscellaneous	$ 780

17

REAL PROPERTY MANAGEMENT

KEY TERMS

Asset management
Certified Housing Manager (CHM)
CERTIFIED PROPERTY MANAGER® (CPM)
Commercial property
Concession
Management agreement
Office plan
Property plan
Public housing
Retail property
Risk management
Space merchandising
Transcript

The broad scope and complexity of property management becomes apparent when the functions of the real property manager are considered. The real property manager plans, organizes, coordinates, controls, directs, supervises, communicates, and implements the activities associated with real property operations. When property is entrusted to the professional manager, the owners expect the manager to operate the property in a cost-effective manner, which maximizes profits. To this end, the management specialist must often employ a greater combination of skills than in most other areas of the real estate business.

To help meet the need for qualified property management specialists, the Institute of Real Estate Management (IREM) of the NATIONAL ASSOCIATION OF REALTORS® provides specialized instruction leading to professional certification. The **CERTIFIED PROPERTY MANAGER® (CPM)** designation may be earned from the institute. IREM reports that CPMs manage $1 trillion of the nation's real estate, comprising 12.6 million residential units and 8.2 billion square feet of office and commercial space.

Over $65 billion of our national income consists of rental income from real estate. Thirty-seven percent of the nation's housing stock is renter-occupied. The median rent paid is $364 and represents 30 percent of the renter's income. The median income of renters is $14,460 and 63 percent of the rented units have single or double occupancy.[1] Indirectly, rental properties furnish an additional portion of our national income in ex-

[1]*American Housing Survey of the United States, 1985* (Washington, D.C.: U.S. Department of Commerce and U.S. Department of Housing and Urban Development, December 1988).

penditures for maintenance and wages. Also, property taxes and fees for utility services are paid by property owners to municipal governments for use in operations.

BACKGROUND OF REAL PROPERTY MANAGEMENT

Although of comparatively recent origin, the management of real property has assumed a tremendous role in the real estate business. Property managers must have a vast background in real estate and business to do the job properly. They must be able to sell and to negotiate, must have a knowledge of advertising, and must possess a wealth of information concerning the fundamentals of engineering. Property managers must, in addition, be practical economists, with the ability to forecast the value of rental space and to convert these forecasts into leases affording the greatest return to the owner.

Development of Management

The field of real property management has developed as a result of numerous factors. The initial demand for management specialists was an outgrowth of the Great Depression of the 1930s.

Beginning with the stock market crash of 1929, banks and other financial institutions were soon engaged in massive mortgage foreclosures. By 1934, a substantial portion of previously mortgaged real estate was held by lending institutions. At first, members of the bank staff were appointed to take care of these properties. However, the banks soon discovered that the successful management of property was beyond the scope of their expertise, and local brokerage firms were requested to supply the needed property management skills.

A second reason for the increased interest in property management was the result of the growth in absentee ownership. Absentee ownership by corporations, or groups of investors forming syndicates, was a consequence of real estate investment advantages: specifically, as a hedge against inflation, the tax advantage of depreciation, and capital gains treatment of profits upon resale.

Typically, investors cannot, and do not, desire to be burdened with management problems. Consequently, the responsibilities of management are assigned to specialists who are capable of operating the property efficiently, thus increasing owner profits.

The demand for professional property managers was also a product of increasing urbanization. In order to maximize owner profits, the ability to understand and integrate knowledge of economic conditions, population trends, and city growth with rental pricing decisions is necessary. Effective property management also calls for extensive knowledge of the landlord's and tenant's legal, social, and economic relationships. These modern management skills are most often outside the scope of property owners, who increasingly must rely upon the advice and skills of the professional property manager.

Is Management Justified?

The question often arises in the minds of some as to the justification of the management process. This is the same question that frequently arises in connection with the function of the middleman in the field of marketing. Many people feel that the existence of the middleman is not justified; and, by the same token, they feel that the existence of the professional real property manager is not justified. Critics are reminded of the axiom that "you can get rid of the middleman, but you cannot get rid of the functions the middleman performs." It is felt that this is equally true concerning the professional manager. In most cases, however, the manager is able to operate more efficiently than the individual owner.

In other words, the professional property manager does a great deal more than collect the rent. With years of experience and training through the Institute of Real Estate Management, the manager has specialized knowledge that permits:

1. Effective advertising.
2. Pricing and selling of rental space.
3. Selection of desirable, creditworthy tenants.
4. Prompt attention to tenant complaints.
5. Maintenance of performance records.
6. Advising owners regarding required renovation or remodeling due to changing market conditions.

Additionally, the property manager is able to buy maintenance supplies and obtain repair services more quickly and in larger quantities than most owners. Thus, by taking advantage of quantity discounts, the manager can reduce operating and maintenance costs, and pass these savings on to the owner.

Often overlooked and rarely considered as part of the service rendered by property managers is risk management. The most carefully planned real estate investment may become a financial disaster. The standard solution is to "buy insurance." **Risk management** is the process of control applied to property when unforeseen loss poses a potential monetary risk. To illustrate, the failure to adequately assess the liability and risk of real estate ownership resulted in the California courts finding the owner liable when a tenant slipped in the bathtub, fell through the shower door, and was severely cut. Although the landlord had purchased the building years after it was built, the courts ruled that the landlord should have known the shower doors were not made of tempered glass and should have replaced them.

The problem of drugs is causing many communities to consider ordinances and legislation to fine apartment owners for having a "disorderly house." Some police departments have actually filed criminal charges against property owners for aiding and abetting drug dealers. Licensing is being proposed, and suggestions have been made to seize the property as well as require landlords to pay for police raids. Professional management works with local drug enforcement units and informs them of illegal activities. Leases must be amended to make it easier to evict persons suspected and/or convicted of drug dealing. Tenant selection procedures and screening must be tightened. As the courts find landlords responsible for tenant safety, the property manager becomes instrumental in protecting the property and the owners' investment. Property managers minimize risk by regular inspection for bypassed fuses, stored flammables, dangerous animals, and compliance with fire, health, and building codes. Tenant rules, established by the property manager, require tenants to report unsafe conditions and make requests for repairs in writing. Further, tenants should be advised that insurance for the building does not cover their personal property.

Property managers also stay currently informed. For example, in 1981, the Minnesota State Legislature passed the Minnesota Plain Language Contract Act, which went into effect in July 1983. This law required that "every consumer contract shall be written in a clear and coherent manner using words with common and everyday meanings and shall be appropriately divided and captioned by its various sections." The failure to comply with this legislation gives tenants the right to sue and seek damages or reformation of their leases. Alternatively, the attorney general's office can bring action and seek a penalty of up to $25,000. How many independent property owners were alert when Maine announced the availability of grants up to $12,500 to apartment building owners installing new solar domestic hot water systems? The state also funded the addition of insulation and the installation of storm doors and windows with grants equal to 20 percent of their cost up to $400 per unit. Staying abreast of changing laws is only part of the service rendered by professional property managers.

Management is a highly specialized field and more often than not buildings can be operated more effectively by a manager than by the individual owner. Efficient operation appears to be the keystone of management justification.

The efficiency of the professional manager may be demonstrated by the Institute of Real Estate Management's annual listings that show net vacancy rates. Although the rates are averages, they show that professionally managed apartment buildings do have vacancy rates that are lower than the national average.

Scope of Management

Residential Buildings. To a limited degree, management maintains, rents, and accounts for the operation of single-family units. Management's major function in the residential field is concerned with operation of apartment buildings. More and more investors in multifamily housing look to the property manager for tenant selection and retention. When coupled with proper maintenance and adjustment to a changing rental housing environment, the property's value is preserved and a fair profit may be earned.

Since enactment of the Housing Act of 1949, there has been a substantial increase in the number of **public housing** units in the United States. These public housing units employ property managers. Presently the Department of Housing and Urban Development requires all Public Housing Managers (PHM) and assistant PHMs to be professionally trained and demonstate their competence by passing the **Certified Housing Manager (CHM)** exam. With the increasing unaffordability of housing, a larger share of total construction will likely be public housing. Whether due to absentee investor ownership, condominium construction or conversion, or expanded public housing, the need for competent, professional property managers is expected to increase during the 1990s.

Although many apartments were converted to condominiums and cooperatives during the latter half of the 1970s, the need for professional management remained unchanged.

Condominiums and Townhomes. The management of condominiums and townhouses is a relatively new field and a new opportunity for professional managers. Instead of working for and reporting to an individual investor, condominium-townhome property managers work with homeowner associations and their boards of directors. A board of directors is elected by the condominium-townhome owners and charged with the responsibility of managing and maintaining the commonly owned property. Wise boards of directors hire professional management to give guidance and carry out their directives.

Basically, condominiums and townhomes are divided into two types whose managers function somewhat differently: (1) the permanent-resident condominium and (2) the recreational property.

In the residential or townhome condominium, the management problems are not too unlike those of the ordinary apartment house except that the manager collects no rent. Payments are made by the owner to the financial institution holding the loan. However, there are assessments collected that are included as costs in the operating budget. These generally are:

1. Real estate taxes, if not included in the owner's monthly payments, and a share of taxes on common spaces.
2. Fire insurance, if not included in owner's monthly payments.
3. A share in the cost of grounds maintenance.
4. Comprehensive liability insurance.
5. Planned capital improvements.

In the recreational condominium, the manager determines the time during which the owner desires to rent the condominium. It may then be rented daily, weekly, or monthly, with maid service provided much like a motel. A fee is deducted from the rents, additional expenses are paid, and the balance is remitted to the owner. Otherwise, the manager operates in the same manner as the manager of a residential condominium or townhomes.

Commercial Property. **Commercial property** is primarily retail property and office buildings. It is in these categories that we find one of the most active aspects of property management.

Retail property. Generally, one- and two-story buildings are considered **retail property.** The ground floor is usually occupied by retail establishments; the second story is devoted to office space.

Typically, the retail-office type of property is an outgrowth of the so-called taxpayers, which were first built during the waning years of the Depression. Although this property has always been important to managers of real property, it is felt that it will become increasingly less important with the present trend toward controlled shopping centers and other types of shopping centers being constructed in suburban areas.

Office buildings. Although some office buildings have their ground floors devoted to retail space and many retail properties have their second stories devoted to office space, the *office building* is distinguished by the fact that it has many stories, it is generally located in downtown business districts, and its primary purpose is the rental of space for office use.

Some of the larger office buildings are operated under the supervision of the owner who, besides having a building manager, may also have a legal staff to prepare leases and handle other pertinent legal details. There remain, however, a large segment of existing office buildings operated by management concerns.

Industrial Property. When office buildings in the larger cities are in the downtown sections, they are usually surrounded by an industrial section. Although many of the larger industrial establishments are operated by their owners, most of the smaller establishments are rented and provide a fertile field for the property manager who specializes in lease negotiations.

These industrial properties are often storage buildings, warehouses, and so called loft buildings tenanted by manufacturers engaged in light industry. For the most part, those real estate concerns engaged in industrial sales of this type also specialize in the rental of these properties.

Asset Management

The newest aspect of property management, **asset management,** evolved from the corporate takeover binge in the latter part of the 1980s. Corporate raiders bid up the stock of some corporations, like Dole Pineapple and Northwest Airlines, to double the prevailing market price. Why? Because among other things, the real estate assets of these corporations, carried on the books at historical cost, were worth more than the value of the company at current stock prices. The takeover could be financed by selling Dole's Hawaiian land or Northwest's property in downtown Tokyo. In short, these corporations did not manage their real estate assets in the stockholders' best interest; hence, the stock was undervalued.

Asset management involves evaluating corporate real estate assets, negotiating leases, disposing of excess land through sale or development, and acquiring, by construction, purchase, or lease. The purpose is to minimize cost, maximize returns on real estate, and otherwise manage the 30 to 50 percent of a corporation's assets tied up in real estate.

Beyond corporate asset management, state, county, and local governments are discovering that their real estate assets are manageable investments. Government entities must inventory their real estate assets, make optimal use of their property, and plan for real estate acquisition, rental, and sale. Because few government agencies recognize real estate as more than incidental to providing public services, they would benefit from professional management.

PROPERTY MANAGEMENT OPERATIONS

The Office Plan

A broker entering the property management field should prepare a budget or financial plan of future operations, known as the **office plan.** In its simplest form, a budget is an estimate of future receipts and disbursements. An estimate of receipts may be based on a survey of prospective business, and disbursements may be based on operating requirements of the anticipated volume of business.

The office plan should be tempered with good judgment. Although the forecasted business profit may be nominal or show a slight loss, consideration should be given to the amount of other business generated by providing property management services.

Obtaining Management Business

Although most of the smaller real estate concerns are engaged in management either as a convenience to an old client or with the hope of increasing their income from sales, the firm with a complete management department must be active in obtaining management business. In order for the management firm to employ its resources to the highest degree of efficiency, it is necessary to obtain a large volume of management business.

Owners of property—whether an individual, a syndicate, or a corporation—are the main sources of business for the management firm. A careful and complete list of these owners must be maintained and kept current. A daily list of transfers of ownership should be obtained from the recorder's office and new owners contacted. This can be done by approaching the new owner directly or by direct mail solicitation. Each transfer of ownership involves a possible source of new business. In large cities, these lists can often be purchased from abstract companies. In the City of New York, for example, a list of 5,000 properties can be purchased for as little as $100 and includes monthly supplements.

Contacts should be made with attorneys, especially those who handle large estates and whose main source of income is from real estate. Most savings banks in the larger cities have real estate departments. The managers of these departments should be contacted to obtain future management business. The chain stores, too, have real estate departments and are a good potential source of business.

Many of the investments held by insurance companies are in real property. For the most part, employees of a company manage the larger rental projects that their company owns; however, in many instances, when the company owns smaller properties, it is more economical for it to hire an outside management firm. Therefore, the company should be contacted and shown how the job of property management can be done more efficiently by employing the service of a management firm.

Another method of building a management portfolio is to approach owners of vacant properties. The owner is asked to turn over the management of the property if a good lessee is found.

In existing buildings, listings for rentals must be obtained. In general, they are obtained either by advertising or by direct solictation from the owners.

When new multiple-unit residential properties are being constructed, the job of renting the apartments is generally let out on bid. The active renting agent will seek out the owner or builder early to obtain the necessary information for bidding on the job. It is suggested that concerns interested in securing this renting business obtain information from the city building department as to permits issued for this type of construction. Thus, if practicable, the owner can be approached even before construction has begun.

One word of warning here: a definite agreement should be reached between the renting agent and the owner as to the payment for advertising, the number of lines of advertising, and the media to be used.

Time is an important element. The bid is often given at a flat rate, so much for renting all of the units; therefore, the faster the units are rented, the greater the profit. Needless to say, this rental arrangment often leads to a permanent owner-management relationship.

Rent Schedules

In the preparation of the budget for operating a property, the management firm needs to think in terms of rental schedules for new buildings.

These schedules are prepared prior to the construction of the building and often prior to the commencement of construction. The object of the rent schedule is to secure a fair return on the investment in the building.

To do so, the following items must be considered:

1. The cost of construction of the completed building.
2. The value of the land.
3. The cost of taxes and insurance incurred during the construction.
4. The interest cost during construction.
5. Promotion costs, unless they have already been included in the cost of the building.

The total of these items equals the investment from which a return must be received. However, the income to be received on the property can never be estimated as being more than that of like accommodations in a like location.

Essentially, the person establishing the rental schedule for a property must compare physical characteristics, location, services, and amenities with rental rates for competing properties. The rule of thumb, that one in every five rental prospects should become a tenant, is often used to indicate whether established rents are too high or low. If more than one in five rent, rents are too low. If less than one in five rent, rents may be considered to be too high.

Concessions

A **concession** is a special service rendered by an owner to a tenant to create a difference between the named rent and the real rent paid or to be paid by a tenant. For example, in order to get a tenant into a building, the landlord may pay the cost of moving expenses. If the moving expenses are $360 and the rent to be paid by the tenant is $300 per month, then the effect of paying for the moving expenses is to reduce the rent $30 per month. Often a concession is given by offering the first month's rent free to a tenant. The purpose is actually to induce prospective tenants to rent a property without reducing the rental figure. Thus, if market conditions warrant the raising of the rent, the owner can do this without changing the rent schedule by merely refusing to offer concessions to new incoming tenants. It is important for the management firm to remember the problem of concessions should be ironed out with the owner when the firm takes over the management of the building.

The Individual Property Plan

A **property plan** should be prepared by the management office for each property managed. In an older building, the basis is, of course, previous experience with that building. In a new building, the income is estimated after determining the estimated income of the property based on present pricing policies. The expenses will, for the most part, be based on experience with similar buildings.

The expenses fall into three categories: operating expenses, maintenance expenses, and fixed charges. The operating expenses include electricity, heating, air conditioning, elevators, cleaning supplies, administrative expenses, and repairs and the labor associated with these services. The maintenance expenses include tenant alterations, tenant decorating, and general repairs. The fixed charges include insurance, real property taxes, and depreciation on building and equipment.

In an older building, leases must be examined for dates of expiration and current rentals. Assuming a lease is near expiration, a determination of future rental income must be made in terms of a possible new lease. Should the period of the new lease be long or short? Should the rents for new leases be higher or lower? Owners naturally desire to maximize profits.

Maximization of rents, hence profits, for apartment buildings is most directly affected by rental prices and vacancy rates for competitive units. Profit maximization when renting commercial space is more directly affected by the position of the business cycle. For example, if there is a depression or threat of business contraction, the manager might be wise to suggest a short-term lease with rent commensurate with business conditions; because with improving business conditions, a new lease for a longer term may be written with a higher rent. In a period of business expansion, the lease may be written for a longer period.

A complete plan must include estimated disbursements, together with an allowance for the customary 10 percent deduction from income for vacancies and repairs—5 percent for vacancies and 5 percent for repairs.

One suggestion for advance planning is to have the manager prepare an annual budget, including therein such large items as annual taxes and insurance. The estimates are based on past experience or experience with similar properties. Also included in the budget are large items such as anticipated major repairs. The annual budget is divided by 12 to create the monthly budget. Automatically, then, reserves are included for the large tax items and repair items. A rigid comparison is made with the monthly items as actual operating expenses are incurred. An analysis is made of any deviation from the norm. For example, if a gas or electric bill is unusually high, a check is made to determine the reason. From such investigation, leakages or other problems may be found. The building of reserves into the budget generally avoids feast-or-famine situations. This is satisfactory to the owner because it provides a steady flow of income unaffected by major outlays for taxes and repairs.

Alternate Plans

The astute property manager will, when feasible, prepare an alternate budget for the owner. This must be prepared with a great deal of care. The purpose is to point out to the owner the possible increase in income as a result of improving the property. The current gross income of the building may not be as high as it could be if improvements were made. The life of the building may, for example, be lengthened with certain improvements, or modernization might increase net income. The estimates of the cost of improvements are accurately computed together with estimated increases in income as a result of these improvements. In general, the costs of improvements should be recovered through rentals within five years. Any final decision must lie with the owner, but this service, accurately computed, will be helpful to the owner and ultimately tend to build the reputation of the management firm.

Merchandising of Space

As in all other types of selling, in **space merchandising** prospective tenants must be qualified according to their *needs* and shown vacancies in terms of those needs. Too many places should never be shown at one time, for this may only confuse the prospects. It should, of course, be made clear to the tenants that all applications will be investigated prior to their acceptance. In any event, no concession should be promised other than those specifically agreed on by the landlord. Those salespeople of the firm who in their eagerness to rent space do promise any other concessions should be immediately discouraged from such practice. It is at this point that bad tenant relations often start.

Selecting Residential Tenants. One of the criteria for selecting a tenant for residential property is capacity to pay. For the average tenant, capacity to pay depends largely on income from employment. This suggests that the prudent property manager will investigate the source of the prospective tenant's income. Not only should the manager be interested in the source of the income, but more so in the type of employment. The best risks generally are those tenants whose employers are least affected by any downward swings in the business cycle. For example, the earnings of carpenters or bricklayers are generally high during periods of prosperity; but during a depression or sometimes even during a slight recession, their earnings are likely to be reduced or, what is even more likely, they will be unemployed. On the other hand, earnings of a governmental or institutional employee do not rise as rapidly during periods of prosperity; neither do they fall as much in a depression. In other words, in terms of future earnings, a governmental or institutional employee might make a better tenant than would an employee in a trade or firm.

Selection of tenants should also be based on compatibility with existing occupants. For example, an elderly widow may not be at home in an apartment occupied by swinging singles with an active social life. Similarly, to permit families with children to rent in a building where most tenants are childless is likely to prove disruptive and may create rapid turnover.

Discrimination and Fair Housing. In selecting tenants, the property manager must act in compliance with the Fair Housing Act of 1968 and the Fair Housing Amendment Act of 1988. The 1968 act prohibits discrimination in housing because of sex, race, color, religion, marital status, or national origin. The 1988 act extends protection to persons with a handicap. For all protected classes, even suggesting they might not be "comfortable" in your building is a discriminatory act. The Fair Housing Amendment Act further provides that with some limitations, a handicapped person can require a landlord or owners association to permit reasonable modification of the premises. The Department of Housing and Urban Development (HUD) rules define premises as the interior and exterior portions of the dwelling unit. The modifications are at the expense of the handicapped person. The property manager may require the handicapped renter to restore the interior of the unit, but not the common areas, at the end of the tenancy. An interest-bearing escrow deposit to cover the cost of restoration may also be required along with a description of the work to be performed.

In addition, landlords and owners cannot refuse to make reasonable modification of rules to give handicapped persons equal opportunity to use and enjoy the dwelling unit. Two examples are "no pets" rules and "first come, first served" parking assignments. Seeing-eye dogs must be permitted in spite of "no pets" rules. Handicapped persons needing a particular parking space are excepted from the "first come, first served" policy.

These rules apply to dwellings first occupied after March 13, 1991. Buildings with three or fewer units are not covered by the provisions of the 1988 act.

Selecting Commercial Tenants. It goes almost without saying that the financially strong, long-established commercial firms and the various governmental agencies make the best-paying tenants. Unfortunately, however, there are not enough financially sound firms to go around. It is incumbent on the renting agent, therefore, to select commercial tenants with care. For example, if a newly formed, financially weak corporation leases a commercial property, the manager should try to obtain the signature of one of the corporate owners as an individual on the lease. The owner signs this as surety for the payment of the rent. If practicable, it is sometimes helpful to obtain the signature of a third party as a guarantor. In this way, the property manager is able to overcome the limited liability feature of the corporate entity, at least insofar as the corporate owners are personally responsible financially.

Compatibility is also an important criterion when selecting commercial tenants. For example, one property owner incurred the loss of several prime tenants when an insurance office was established in a medical building. Similarly, to permit a massage parlor or topless bar to locate adjacent to a bath boutique or elegant dress shop is likely to have an adverse effect on tenant business. This may be particularly significant if the property owner is receiving a portion of the rent as a percentage of volume.

Commercial Space Renting. The renting of commercial space presents many different aspects from the renting of residential space. The main thing, however, is to supply the needs of the prospect. A person seeking a loft for light manufacturing should not be shown a property suitable for heavy industry. On the other hand, where loft space is listed, prospects who would be interested in loft space should be contacted, not prospects who are interested in heavy industrial space. Analyze the property; then attempt to find those prospects who are best suited for the property.

One important method of obtaining future management business is to keep, insofar as possible, a complete record of existing leases and their termination dates. Obtain the dates of expiration of store leases. The merchants who have to vacate their space are prospects for other suitable space, and the space being vacated is a source of listings that can be sold to still other prospects.

Chain stores constitute a source that is often overlooked by firms engaged in renting commercial space in larger cities. In most large cities, there are many types of chains comprising numerous small units, such as dry cleaning establishments and food shops. These chains are constantly looking for new locations. Most chain stores have real estate managers who are only too willing to supply the broker with a precise list of their requirements: the number of locations needed, the floor space required, the most desirable locations in the city, and any other pertinent details the broker requests. Their requirements should always be kept in mind and kept up to date by frequent contact with their real estate departments. Supply their needs, and a deal is assured.

Credit Standing

Prior to selecting any tenant, the property manager should obtain a credit report on the prospective tenant. The credit report will, of course, reflect on the tenant's capacity to pay. The report should show whether the prospect has any notes, chattel mortgages, judgments, or other debts outstanding, together with life insurance purchases or any time payments that mut be made.

In the final analysis, the property manager should carefully consider the following factors when evaluating the credit rating of all residential or commercial tenants:

1. Their ability to pay.
2. Their character.
3. Their paying habits. (This will show proof of their intent to pay.)
4. Their identification.

5. The security. (An attempt should be made to see if the tenant has any collateral—especially a commercial tenant.)

Tenant and Owner Relations

The manager acts, to a large degree, as a buffer between owner and tenant. Part of the manager's job is to make sure that both parties receive just and equitable treatment. Among other things, one might say the role of the manager is akin to that of the diplomat. The manager must strive constantly to maintain the goodwill of the tenant toward the client. In essence, then, there is a constant public relations job to be done.

Tenant Relations. All complaints concerning the property will be directed toward the property manager. These complaints must be investigated and given proper attention. It is relatively easy for the slipshod manager to brush complaints aside, either by ignoring them completely or by making a flat statement that they will be corrected. At the beginning of the relationship with the tenant, an understanding must be reached between the manager and the tenant. This understanding should result in a mutual acceptance of what will or what will not be done for the tenant by the management firm. Once this understanding has been reached, the tenant will know that certain things are not obtained merely for the asking. The key to effective management is successful communication.

Good tenants are a valuable asset to the management. If communication is practiced, a good relationship will be established and maintained and the manager need not fear more than the normal number of vacancies. In addition, with good tenant relationships the property will be well advertised to the friends and acquaintances of the tenants, and this is the best type of advertising a firm can have.

Owner Relations. The owner is the property manager's client, and the avoidance of misunderstanding begins with a clear, written contract defining the respective rights and duties of owner and agent. The second step toward a good owner-manager relationship is in the monthly statement of receipts and disbursements. The owner knows or should know what to expect in terms of income from the investment. An accurate monthly statement that meets the owner's expectations will keep the relationship on an even keel. However, all too frequently the owner's expectations, as a result of an unusual expense, may not be met. When this occurs, a reasonable and logical explanation of the failure to live up to the owner's expectations becomes important. Preferably, this should be done by personal contact with the owner or, if personal contact is not feasible, then a detailed letter of explanation must accompany the monthly receipt and disbursement statement. Under no circumstances should any extraordinary expense be paid without proper explanation. In the final analysis, a good owner-manager relationship depends fundamentally on the honesty and efficiency of the property manager. Most property owners, being businesspeople, can readily recognize these attributes and know whether their expectations will be met.

Collections

The cornerstone of the success of any management organization is that it must be prompt in collecting the rent. Rent must never by permitted to remain in arrears. It is, therefore, necessary for the property manager to send due bills to tenants in advance of the due date. If payment is not immediately forthcoming, a letter reminding the tenant of the delinquency is in order. The letter should be carefully worded to avoid the possibility of antagonizing the tenant. If payment still is not made, a more strongly worded letter follows, and then a notice that legal action will be taken to collect the rent. If, then, the rent is not promptly paid, the legal action is begun. The time allowance for payment of delinquent rent varies from state to state; however, the time allotted the delinquent tenant for the payment is generally from three to five days. If the debt is not paid within the allotted time, the tenant is evicted, and a judgment is entered against the tenant for the amount of overdue rent.

Tact on the part of the manager is the key to all collections. The manager must be firm with the tenants without arousing antagonism. Each person in the management firm should be constantly kept aware that the goodwill of the firm must be built up, and this can be done tactfully even while enforcing a firm collection policy.

Accounts and Records

The management contract calls for a monthly statement of "receipts, expenses, and charges," and the management is to remit receipts less disbursements. Each month a complete statement must be remitted to the owner. How then are these records to be kept? An accounts receivable ledger is the basis of the management accounting system. Each page contains the name of the tenant, a description of the space, a brief statement of the lease terms, and a debit column that consists of the total rent and any other charges the tenant might incur. A credit column and a debit balance column are shown. Basically, the record shows the amount billed and collected each month, and any balance remaining due at the end of the month.

The information from the tenant's accounts receivable ledger is posted to a master sheet called a **transcript.** The transcript is divided into columns, containing (1) the apartment number, (2) the number of rooms, (3) the expiration date of the lease, (4) charges for the current month, (5) debit balance carried over from the previous month, (6) total debits less credits, and (7) an ending balance.

The transcript is submitted to the owner together with a summary receipt and disbursement statement. From this, the operating expenses are deducted, leaving the net operating receipts. To the net operating receipts is added other income, such as receipts from vending machines and laundry equipment. Other disbursements are deducted from this figure, leaving a balance of net receipts remitted. The gross figures for the operating expenses are substantiated by a Statement of Operating Expenses Paid, which shows in detail the expenses paid. For example, the receipts and disbursements statement may contain such an item as Repairs and Maintenance, $300.

Records are, of course, kept for all expenses in connection with a property. Invoices are recorded in the proper records of account, and all payments should be made by check.

As previously stated, no money of the client should be commingled with any money of the manager. It is permissible, however, to place all of the clients' money in a single, special account.

Management Agreement

The **management agreement,** like any other contract, defines the rights and obligations of the contracting parties. The agreement creates an exclusive agency in the named agent and is binding on the heirs and assigns of both the owner and the agent. Briefly, the agent agrees to manage the premises, to investigate prospective tenants, to place and supervise tenants, to insure the property in accordance with the owner's instructions, and to render monthly statements of receipts and disbursements.

The agent is generally given the authority to advertise and make leases, collect rents, make all repairs, and contract for services. However, a limitation on the amount the agent can spend for repairs is usually included. Any sums over the specified amount may be disbursed with the owner's consent.

One of the most important clauses in the contract, from the agent's viewpoint, is that the agent has the right to hire and to fire all labor employees used to maintain the premises. These employees, according to the terms of the contract, are deemed employees of the owner. One general rule of law is that the act of the agent is construed as being the act of the principal. Therefore, the management firm includes a clause to protect itself from any negligent acts of persons whom they employ.

An indemnity clause is also generally inserted in the contract whereby the owner agrees to indemnify the agent in the event of any lawsuits arising from the management of the premises and from liability from injuries suffered by an employee. The owner also agrees to carry and pay the premiums for compensation insurance.

The contract, of course, details the method of payment and the rates of compensation of the agent for management, renting of the space, supervising of services and repairs, and the sale of the premises by the agent.

Compensation

The property manager usually receives a percentage of the gross income from the building with a minimum amount per month. In some areas, these commissions are paid on a sliding scale; for example, 6 percent on the first $100,000 of gross income, 3 percent on the second $100,000, and so forth.

In addition to the commission on the gross income from the property, the manager receives a commission on the renting space. This, too, is generally on a sliding scale and based on the type of lease. In most parts of the nation, local and state boards of realtors have established the fees. For example, in Colorado, the fee on a month-to-month tenancy is half the first month's rent, and on leases the commission is 5 to 6 percent of the face value of the lease but not less than half of the first month's rent; however, in no case can the commission be greater than the commission would have been had there been a sale of the fee.

GLOSSARY

Asset management Describes the property management function applied to corporate real estate assets; in addition to leasing, purchasing, selling, and maintaining corporate real estate, includes maximizing profit from investment in real estate

Certified Housing Manager (CHM) Property managers who have been professionally trained and who have demonstrated their competence by passing the CHM exam

CERTIFIED PROPERTY MANAGER® (CPM) Property managers meeting the training and experience requirements of the Institute of Real Estate Management of the NATIONAL ASSOCIATION OF REALTORS®

Commercial property Real property used for stores, restaurants, shopping centers, office buildings, hotels, and motels; retail property and office buildings

Concession A special service rendered by an owner to a tenant for the purpose of creating a difference between the named rent and the real rent paid or to be paid by the tenant

Management agreement A contract that defines the rights and obligations of the contracting parties, the owner, and the manager of the property

Office plan The plan a person engaged in property management prepares as an estimate of future receipts and disbursements

Property plan A plan that includes income and expenses for each property managed by a professional property manager

Public housing Housing provided by local, state, or federal government initiative at below cost, through rent, subsidy, purchase price, or mortgage interest rates

Retail property One- or two-story buildings with retail establishments on the first floor and office space on the second floor

Risk management The process of control applied to property when unforeseen loss poses a potential monetary risk

Space merchandising Selling rental space by qualifying prospective tenants according to their needs

Transcript The information from the tenant's accounts receivable ledger that is posted to a master sheet (the transcript)

QUESTIONS FOR REVIEW

1. Discuss in detail the scope of management.
2. Explain the importance of determining the needs of a prospect before attempting to merchandise space.
3. What should be done to obtain greater security for an owner when a newly formed corporation or financially weak firm seeks to lease a property?
4. What is a transcript?
5. Discuss in detail the typical owner-management contract.

PROBLEMS AND ACTIVITIES

1. You have listed in your office a number of retail properties rented on a flat rental basis. You have determined from your reading and study that a downswing in the business cycle is anticipated. The leases on these retail properties are about to terminate. Prepare and substantiate suggestions you might give your principal with regard to renewing these leases.
2. You are suddenly deluged with listings of retail rental properties. They range in size from the small "hole in the wall" to large spaces suitable for supermarkets. Prepare a list of prospects for these spaces. How would you contact the prospects?

PART FIVE

PROPERTY VALUATION

18

RESIDENTIAL APPRAISING

KEY TERMS

Appraisal
Cost
Cost approach
Curable/incurable obsolescence
Demand
Effective age
External obsolescence
Functional obsolescence
Gross rent multiplier
Highest and best use
Income approach
Market value
Physical deterioration
Price
Principle of anticipation
Principle of conformity
Principle of contribution
Reconciliation of value
Sales comparison approach
Scarcity
Substitution principle
Transferability
Unit-in-place or segregated cost method
Utility
Value

The need for accurate appraisals is critical to financial institutions that make, insure, or invest in mortgage loans. Appraisals of real property also provide the basis for compensating owners of condemned property, settling property disputes in divorce cases, and determining taxes payable in the settlement of estates and inheritances. Although there are numerous rules, theories, and computations related to appraisal, the actual quality of an appraisal is significantly influenced by the experience and judgment of the appraiser in applying state-of-the-art analytical techniques. There is a growing need for qualified real estate appraisers.

THE PROBLEM OF VALUE

An **appraisal** is an attempt to obtain a just and fair opinion or estimate of the value of a parcel of real property. One of the basic problems is to determine just what the word *value* means. William Stanley Miller, onetime president of the New York State Tax Commission, described over 50 types of value and then admitted the list was by no means exhaustive.

The problem of determining just what value is was pointed up in Florida where the state law requires all county assessors to assess at "full cash value." The governor of the state declared that a lack of a definition of full value had handicapped efforts to enforce the full value law. The governor said: "It is different from full value, and it is not 100 percent of market value. But I cannot say just what it is."

A few days later, a state legislator warned that assessors had better be careful to take "speculative value" into account when they were assessing at full cash value. The state comptroller then issued a statement saying that the time element would prevent any new definition of full cash value being applied to the property tax assessments. The comptroller wasn't altogether certain any new definition of full cash value could be arrived at. The comptroller also said that the Florida Supreme Court had indicated that full cash value meant the market value and the supreme court of another state subsequently held that market value was actually full cash value.[1]

It can readily be seen that the problem of determining value is rather clouded and complex. Value is nebulous, whatever it is, and it has been said that "value is in the eye of the beholder." In the final analysis, a person attempting to determine value may reach a conclusion depending on one's reasons for making the attempt. Remember value is a noun and, invariably, one will find this noun preceded by an adjective; for example, market value, capitalized value, intrinsic value, fair value, cash value, book value, nuisance value, liquidation value, potential value, *ad infinitum.*

Economic Concept of Value

To the economist **value** is the power of commanding commodities in exchange. This was expressed by Adam Smith in his *Wealth of Nations* when he observed that "the word 'value' has two different meanings, and sometimes expresses the utility of some particular object and sometimes the power of purchasing other goods which possession of that object conveys." The latter concept implies economic or exchange value.

This concept might be expressed as the rate at which commodities exchange for other commodities. Historically, barter was the usual mode of exchange. Today, the exchange usually is indirect; that is, one commodity is sold for money, and the money is used to pay for something else.

It should be clear that value is not necessarily determined by usefulness, utility, or importance. For example, water is most useful and its value is great, but in most parts of the world the power of water to command commodities in exchange is low. Thus, in the economic sense the value of water is low. Another example is iron, which is more useful than gold, but expressed in terms of value and in terms of exchange, gold commands a far greater amount of money.

Value and Price

If value can be thought of as power to command commodities in exchange, it must be distinguished from price. **Price** expresses an estimate of value in

[1]The Massachusetts Supreme Court has held that "fair" cash value and "market" value mean the same thing. In Massachusetts, assessments are made at "fair" cash value.

terms of accepted medium of exchange. If an individual says that a house sold for less than its value, the individual is talking about price.

One of the problems concerning the measurement of value is that one must think of the exchange power of goods in terms of money, which really means market value. Since the purchasing power of money constantly fluctuates, market value constantly fluctuates. During a depression, dollars in hand can purchase more goods than during an inflation. Thus, in a depression it pays an individual to move out of commodities into cash, and in a period of inflation to move from cash into commodities. This means that as the purchasing power of the dollar increases (as prices tumble), an individual holding cash can purchase more units of goods than possible before. The opposite is true in inflationary periods; then it is better to buy a washing machine, because, as prices rise, the price of the washing machine will also rise (even on the secondhand market). What has all this to do with value? The point is that while prices are changing, the *value* of a good *may* remain the same. Assume, for example, that *A* owns a new washing machine priced at $200. Assume further that suddenly goods are inflated so the same machine is now priced on the market at $400. This means that the purchasing power of the dollar has halved. As far as value or the power of a good to command other goods is concerned, the value of *A*'s washing machine has remained the same, though dollars have halved. By selling the washing machine for which a price of $200 was paid, the owner can now get $400 and thus command $400 worth of other goods at current prices. Therefore, the owner is able to obtain as many units as could be obtained before the inflation. Individuals holding money during this period are able to buy only half as many units of goods.

Cost

Cost is historical and is a measure of things that happened in the past. For example, if a person's house cost $40,000 five years ago, its value today could conceivably be only $20,000, or it could be $80,000 if inflation were serious enough. In speaking of cost, the person is thinking of the past and expenditures that have been made in the past. What makes value? People's thinking makes value, particularly when dealing with real estate. The important things are human needs and human desires. Humans need shelter, and they desire things other than just shelter. The social, economic, and political forces bear greatly on value within a specific area, and these forces are ultimately controlled or influenced by people.

The Elements of Value

An appraiser must recognize the existence of four primary elements that influence value: (1) physical elements, (2) economic elements, (3) social elements, and (4) legal elements. Many of these are discussed in detail later in the chapter. However, the following should be noted to point up their interrelationship and interaction in reaching some decision as to value.

Physical Elements. This concerns factors that can create, condition, or destroy value. For example, in determining the value of land the appraiser must consider location, size, shape, area, frontage, topsoil, drainage, contour, topography, accessibility, utilities, roads, climate, and even the beautiful or ugly view. In improvements, the appraiser must consider material, workmanship, and wear and tear on the property (physical depreciation).

Economic Elements. Here one must consider actual or potential income of the property, the earning power of the community, prevailing rates of interest, mortgage markets and federal participation in the mortgage market, national, state, and local business conditions.

Social Elements. Here one deals with neighborhoods, population trends, marriage rates, traffic hazards, dead-end streets, urban renewal, noise, civic attitudes, and even architectural design.

Legal Elements. Legal elements can also create, condition, and destroy values. Here one's concern is with zoning, deed restrictions, city planning or lack of city planning, condition of title, and even legislation that might restrict or change the character of the land. For example, a planned expressway might have a definite effect on value in that particular area.

CHARACTERISTICS OF VALUE

The characteristics of value are, in a sense, related to the above elements of value. They can, however, be discussed separately with the idea of making the concept of value more meaningful. These value characteristics include utility, scarcity, demand, and transferability.

Utility

Utility is defined as the power of a good to render a service or fill a need. Under this definition a common nail has utility, but it must be at the right place at the right time to have value. Furthermore, nails must be relatively scarce. Thus, air has utility; it is in the right place and at the right time, but it has no market value because it is not scarce. Often the characteristics that make up value must be in useful combination.

Scarcity

Scarcity is a relative term related to supply and demand. If a product has utility, is relatively scarce, and has the other characteristics of value, then its market price is likely to be high.

Demand

Demand can be defined in economic terms as the desire for a good or service backed by the ability to pay for the product. This is what the economist calls effective demand in order to emphasize the difference between wants and economic demand.

Transferability

Although **transferability** is a legal concept, it is essential to market value. A good may have all the other value characteristics, but if no one has the ability or right to transfer the good to another, it is without market value.

In many cases transferability is thought of as related to mobility, but in real property, for example, it need not be. An item may have utility, be scarce, and be in demand, but may have no market value because it cannot be transferred.

BASIC PRINCIPLES OF VALUE

There are a number of principles of value, but only a few will be mentioned. The principles discussed here are useful to the appraiser because they help in reaching an opinion of value.

Substitution Principle

The **substitution principle** states that when several similar or commensurate commodities, goods, or services are available, the one with the lowest price will attract the greatest demand and widest distribution.[2] Restated, due to competition, similar things sell for similar prices.

When considering the value of a home, the cost to construct a comparable substitute is an indication of value. The reasoning holds that a thing cannot be worth more than the cost of its replacement. Its value cannot be higher than the cost necessary to replace it, provided the substitution can be conveniently made. For example, a seller may wish to sell a home for $100,500. A new home, similarly constructed, including more conveniences, and only a few hundred feet away is priced at $102,000. The effect of the substitution principle will lower the asking price of the first home.

Principle of Conformity

The **principle of conformity** affirms that the maximum value of real property is realized when a property's quality, age, lot size, use, and other characteristics are reasonably similar to other properties in the area. In

[2]American Institute of Real Estate Appraisers, *Appraising Residential Properties* (Chicago: AIREA, 1988), 43.

other words, the maximum value of real property is found where there is a reasonable degree of homogeneity with all the standards of the area. In short, a lot must be developed in much the same way as the adjacent neighborhood. Thus, mixing land uses leads to lower values.

Principle of Anticipation

The **principle of anticipation** holds that the perception of value may be a function of the expectation of anticipated future benefits. In this sense, real property is divided into two broad categories: (1) income property (here, value may be the anticipated present value of a future stream of income flows); (2) single-family homes (here, a value judgment may be formed on the basis of the prospective future benefits of ownership). In short, value at a given time is the present value of all real and intangible future benefits.

Principle of Highest and Best Use

Highest and best use, for purposes of appraisal, is defined as "the reasonable, probable, and legal use of vacant land or improved property, which is physically possible, appropriately supported, financially feasible, and that results in the highest value. The four criteria the highest and best use must meet are legal permissibility, physical possibility, financial feasibility, and maximum profitability"[3]

Highest and best use is applicable to both residential and income property appraisals and must be determined prior to proceeding to actually analyze and value a property. Highest and best use is a significant factor in determining fair market value. As early as 1894, the U.S. Supreme Court decided:

> The value of the property results from the use to which it is put and varies with the profitableness of that use, the present and prospective, actual and anticipated. There is no pecuniary value aside from that which results from such use—the amount and profitable character of such use determines the value.

Consequently, an appraiser must always consider whether the present use of a property is its highest and best use (HBU). In determining highest and best use, consideration must be given to assemblage with adjoining parcels under single ownership, as well as uses different from the present use of the site. The principles, concepts, and methodologies of real estate appraisal do not exist in isolation but in combination. It is the appraiser's tack to select the valuation approach consistent with the principles and theories of value that apply to the specific appraisal assignment.

---

[3]American Institute of Real Estate Appraisers, *The Dictionary of Real Estate Appraisal,* 2d ed. (Chicago: AIREA, 1989), 149.

The factors of production are land, labor, and capital. Briefly, in order for there to be production, labor must be paid, a payment must be made for the use of capital, and a payment must be made for the use of the land. Both labor and capital are relatively mobile. Land is fixed; therefore, labor and capital must be both profitable and paid first, and the residual is paid to the land. If the land is not put to its highest and best use, then that amount left over for the land decreases; and, consequently, the value of the land also decreases because its net earnings are decreasing.

In practice, a problem might arise because of the inability to obtain comparable sales of vacant land in appraising a property in a downtown metropolitan area; hence, the value of land "as though vacant" cannot be determined by market comparison. Consequently, appraisers have developed the "land residual technique," discussed in Chapter 19, to meet this challenge. The land residual technique is consistent with the economist's allocation of profits to the factors of production.

Another example of the interdependence of the factors of production and HBU occurs when property is arbitrarily divided either by condemnation or donation. Suppose a profitable farm is valued at $100,000 and the farm is completely dependent on irrigation in order to produce any crops. Further suppose that only a few acres are condemned or donated to charity, but these acres control the water supply. As a result, the rest of the land will soon return to desert.

What is the value of the few acres controlling the water? What is the value of the land that will once again grow cactus? What is the HBU of this property?

Valued independently, the water may have minimal value without the land. Similarly, the land, valued independently, may have only nominal value without the water. Neither may be valued without consideration for the interrelatedness of the parts, an important consideration in properly defining an appraisal assignment and highest and best use.

The Principle of Contribution. The **principle of contribution** is also referred to as the "principle of diminishing returns." When analyzing component property parts, this principle requires the appraiser to recognize that the value of a particular component is determined by its contribution to value of the whole.

This principle relates to the over- and underimprovement of a property and "balance" for the entire property with its highest and best use. An example of overimprovement, imbalance, and the law of diminishing returns might be the installation of a swimming pool worth $20,000 in the rear yard of a $60,000 home located in a neighborhood of $55,000 to $65,000 homes. The property would be out-of-balance with the surrounding homes, overimproved, and the contribution to value would be significantly less than $20,000.

FUNDAMENTAL CONSIDERATIONS IN REAL ESTATE APPRAISALS

Ultimately, an appraisal is based on sound judgment, which implies a need for factual data supporting the judgment. Some judgment aids are discussed below.

Population Trends

The population of a city or town increases in importance according to the purpose for which an appraisal is made. The home buyer looks on a house as a place to live and the city in which the property is located as a place to work. Therefore, the buyer is not too much interested in population trends. The prime interest of the home buyer lies in today's worth of the building. A slightly different situation exists with an appraisal being made for a prospective investor. True, the investor is interested in present worth of the house under consideration, but the investor is also interested in anything that might affect the value of the property over a long period of time. The prime interest of the investor lies in the value of the property as security for a loan, the loan generally being repayable over a number of years.

Why, then, is the investor interested in population trends? The answer lies in supply and demand. The investor will recognize immediately that if the population trend of a city is down and has been going down for some time, there is a good possibility of housing being thrown on the market with a consequent depression of real property values and a corresponding impairment of investor's security. On the other hand, if the population trend is upward, then lending institutions might be more easily persuaded to lend money on the property. The lender feels that eventually the demand for houses will be high and will command a high resale price should resale become necessary.

General Neighborhood Characteristics

General neighborhood characteristics help the appraiser form an opinion as to the value of the property. The neighborhood has a tremendous influence on value. Certain trends within a neighborhood should be taken not only as danger signals with regard to future value, but must also be taken into consideration in terms of present value.

For example, suppose an otherwise fashionable district is changing into a rooming-house district. This would indicate that any further changes in that direction might conceivably affect the value of the property for residential purposes. How does one determine whether the area is becoming a rooming-house district? The answer is by a close inspection of the neighborhood—not by driving past, but by walking through the area and making careful observations.

Changes in a district can be found by making inquiries of people living in the area. If it is changing from residential into business, note the number of new businesses, new storefronts, and so forth.

The type of residential district may be noted from any new construction in the neighborhood. Determine whether or not the neighborhood has been kept up. For example, a dirty, unkept aura about a neighborhood is an indication of a downward trend.

One rule of thumb often helpful in appraising is that when the houses in a particular neighborhood are over 25 years old, that neighborhood is probably in for a period of decline.

Fire and Police Protection. The level of fire and police protection becomes important in the appraisal of property located in suburban areas. The lack of adequate police and fire protection will undoubtedly affect the market value of the property because of a natural tendency of people to shy away from a location without these essentials. Another consideration, although a minor one, is that insurance rates in places lacking fire and police protection are generally high.

Distances to Services. The distances to schools, stores, transportation, churches, etc., are important to the overall appraisal picture in the same manner as fire and police protection. A lack of proximity to these services will reflect on the market value of the property.

Authorized Public Improvements. In making an appraisal, it is important to be aware of any authorized public improvements. For example, there may not be a school in the area in which the building is located; therefore, this may previously have been taken as detrimental to the property. If, however, it is determined that a school has been authorized, this may offset previous determinations with regard to a lack of schools within a reasonable distance from the building being appraised.

The same may be true when current police and fire protection is considered inadequate, but improved protection has been authorized by the town council. The place to find out whether public improvements have been authorized is at the city or town offices.

Marketability. The degree of marketability of the property will have a direct effect on its sale price and, hence, affect the appraisal. If, for example, the property is located in an undesirable neighborhood, the marketablity of the property would have a tendency to be depressed. The question of marketability becomes even more important if the client is a lending institution because, again, the lender looks on the property as security for a long-term loan. A property that is difficult to sell is a hazard, and it is the duty of the appraiser to make clear to the client any hazardous conditions that exist.

In a marketability study, an analysis is made of risks affecting how long it will take to rent, lease, or sell a property, given current market conditions. A market study also considers historical and present levels of supply and demand.

Building Description

The problems identified when preparing the building description lead to more accurate understanding concerning the value of the property. Three important questions are, in part, answered here: (1) the question of physical deterioration or depreciation, (2) the value of any extra features, and (3) the cost of any exterior or interior repairs that must be taken into consideration before any final value can be assigned to the building. Keeping in mind that an attempt is being made to determine depreciated replacement or replacement cost of the property, one can then see these factors by finding replacement cost, subtracting the depreciation and the value of repairs, adding the value of extra features, and adding the value of the land.

The value to be assigned to such extra features as a fireplace or a garage should not be too difficult to obtain from contractors specializing in this work. The cost of interior repairs or exterior repairs may easily be determined in the same way.

Here, too, one should note the workmanship and construction of the building because of the influence this factor will have on determining the rate of depreciation.

Site Evaluation

One of the first things an appraiser does when visiting a property is to attempt to evaluate the site to determine whether the land is realizing its highest and best use. That is, an evaluation is made to determine the highest and best possible utilization of that site in terms of producing the maximum future return to the owner. The evaluation of the site in terms of income production is perhaps of more value when income-producing property is being appraised, but it nevertheless does have some importance in residential appraising.

The major importance of site evaluation when appraising residential property is in determining the existence of **external obsolescence** or the loss in value to a property due to the impairment of economic value; that is, due to a change in the character of a neighborhood. The evaluation of the site thus lays the groundwork for placing a market value on the land.

Market Value

The most important basis of valuation, as far as the practicing appraiser is concerned, is **market value.** When the purpose of the appraisal is to determine a different value concept (e.g., historical value of Lyndon B. Johnson's birthplace in Johnson City, Texas), the appraiser must treat it as a special case and proceed accordingly.

What then is market value? One of the best definitions is:

> The highest price in terms of money which a property will bring in a competitive and open market under all conditions requisite to a fair sale, the buyer and seller, each acting prudently, knowledgeably and assuming the price is not affected by undue stimulus.[4]

The above definition of market value is quoted on the last page of the standard FHLMC and FNMA Residential Appraisal Report. Among other things, it suggests:

> Implicit in this definition is the consummation of a sale at a specified date and the passing of title from seller to buyer under conditions whereby: (1) the buyer and seller are typically motivated; (2) both parties are well informed or well advised, and each acting in what he considers his own best interest; (3) a reasonable time is allowed for exposure in the open market; (4) payment is made in cash or its equivalent; (5) financing, if any, is on terms generally available in the community at the specified date and typical for the property type in its locale. . . .

The concept of market value evolves as legal decisions are rendered, laws are passed, and market conditions vary. As of this writing, the current economic definition of market value is as follows:

> The most probable price, as of a specified date, in cash, or in terms equivalent to cash, or in other precisely revealed terms for which the specified property rights should sell after reasonable exposure in a competitive market under all conditions requisite to a fair sale, with the buyer and seller each acting prudently, knowledgeably, and for self-interest, assuming that neither is under undue duress.[5]

APPROACHES TO RESIDENTIAL VALUE

There are three common approaches to appraising single-family residential real property: the cost approach, the sales comparison approach, and the income approach. These three approaches are also used in evaluating income properties in Chapter 19.

Cost Approach

In the **cost approach** to value, the cost to construct an existing building and the value of that building are analyzed. Buyers gauge the value of an existing structure by comparing it with the cost of a newly constructed building without functional obsolescence.

The cost approach requires the appraiser to estimate the cost to construct or replace the existing structure as of the date of the appraisal, less

[4]Byrl N. Boyce, ed., *Real Estate Appraisal Terminology* (Cambridge, Mass.: Ballinger Publishing, 1975), 137.

[5]*The Dictionary of Real Estate Appraisal,* 192.

depreciation, and add the value of the land "as though vacant" to provide a value indication. There are three basic steps to the cost approach to value:

1. Determine the cost to replace or reproduce the existing structure.
2. Determine the value of the land as though vacant and based on its highest and best use.
3. Determine the amount of depreciation resulting from physical, functional, and external obsolescence.

Determining Costs. Although a number of methods of cost determination are available, only the two most commonly used methods will be discussed here.

Comparative-unit method. The first step in the comparative-unit method is to determine the cost new per square foot of a comparable house. The square footage of the subject house is measured. The two figures are multiplied to obtain the cost to replace.

For example, assume a house with 1,200 square feet and a cost of $60 per square foot.

1,200 sq. ft × $60 = $72,000 cost to replace

The cost of additional features not found in the standard $60 per square foot house may be added to this figure, for example, a built-in range and oven costing $650, or a fireplace costing $3,000. In this case, the cost would be:

	1,200 sq. ft. × $60	$ 72,000
	Range	650
	Fireplace	3,000
	Cost to replace	$ 75,650
Add:	450 sq. ft. garage @ $30/sq. ft.	13,500
	Landscaping:	
	5,737 sq. ft. @ $.90/sq. ft.	5,163
	Total improvements	94,313
	Land	22,500
		116,813
	Total	$117,000

Depreciation, which will be discussed later, has not been included in this example.

Unit-in-place method. The **unit-in-place** or **segregated cost method** uses basic units of measurement such as square feet, linear or cubic feet, number of doors, plumbing drains, etc., to estimate total construction cost new. These costs may be derived from valuation services such as Marshall and Swift Valuation Service of Los Angeles, California.

For example, a partial list might appear as follows:

Excavation:	13,248 cu. ft. @ $.225	$2,981
Brick facing:	200 sq. ft. × 7.5 bricks per ft. @ $82 ($820 per 1,000 bricks)	1,230
Plumbing:	6 fixtures @ $975	5,850
	3 drains @ $370	1,110
	(2 bathrooms)	
Electrical:	1,200 sq. ft. @ $1.33	1,596
Framing:	1,200 sq. ft. @ $5.13	6,156

The total of all costs so estimated is the estimated cost new from which accrued depreciation is deducted.

Depreciation. Depreciation is the loss of value from any cause. Depreciation may result from physical deterioration, functional obsolescence, or external obsolescence. Physical deterioration and functional obsolescence can be further divided into their curable and incurable components. External obsolescence cannot be corrected.

Physical deterioration. **Physical deterioration** is the decay and natural wear and tear on a building. Dry rot sets in, the roof sags, the paint cracks and peels, plaster falls from the walls, and termites weaken the structure. All of these and many more contribute to physical deterioration. Such signs of wear and tear must be looked for and carefully noted by the appraiser.

Although all the elements listed above are existent or inherent in the property, the owner of the property does have a certain amount of control over physical deterioration.

Physical deterioration that can be readily observed and measured is *curable.* For example, on observation the curable items might be:

Replace roof	$3,400
Paint exterior	1,200
Replace kitchen floor covering	400
Total curable physical deterioration	$5,000

To determine whether an observed condition is curable or not, the appraiser should compare the cost to cure with the value added. When the value added is greater than the cost to cure, it is prudent to repair the deficiency; hence, the deficiency is considered curable.

Incurable items of physical deterioration are items that, in the opinion of the appraiser, are uneconomical to cure. Generally, they are thought of as normal wear and tear to the "bone structure"; for example, the foundation begins to sag.

Measuring incurable physical deterioration is highly subjective. Appraisers generally use either the "economic age-life method" or "physical age-life method" to estimate incurable physical deterioration.

The economic age-life method requires the appraiser to estimate the useful life of the observed condition, say roofing shingles, and the **effective**

age, or the amount used up, of the roof. The ratio of these two estimates is multiplied by the reproduction or replacement cost of the item.

$$\frac{\text{Effective age}}{\text{Useful life}} \times \begin{array}{c}\text{Replacement or}\\ \text{reproduction cost of}\\ \text{roof shingles}\end{array} = \begin{array}{c}\text{Physical incurable}\\ \text{deterioration}\end{array}$$

$$\frac{7 \text{ years}}{20 \text{ years}} \times \$3{,}150 = \$1{,}102.50$$

This method is also applied to other short-lived housing components such as interior and exterior painting, plumbing, fixtures, floor coverings, and mechanical equipment such as heating, air-conditioning, water heaters and softeners. The sum of all estimates of incurable physical deterioration is deducted from the previously determined cost to construct or replace.

As an alternative, incurable physical deterioration may be estimated using the physical age-life method. This method requires the appraiser to assume that a building deteriorates at a constant annual rate over the life of the building. For example, if the life of a building or component is expected to be 80 years, deterioration is expected to occur at the rate of 1.25 percent per year ($^{100}/_{80} = 1.25$). The annual rate of depreciation times the cost to construct times the age of the component or entire building yields an estimate of incurable physical deterioration. This amount is then deducted from the cost to construct along with the cost to cure the curable physical deterioration.

Either method may be applied to estimate incurable physical deterioration for both short- and long-lived building components. The physical age-life method may, however, be applied to the entire structure without distinguishing between short and long component lives. In any event, both the cost of curable and incurable deterioration are deducted from the cost to replace or reproduce to arrive at a cost which reflects all physical deterioration.

Functional obsolescence. **Functional obsolescence** is an impairment of desirability and usefulness brought about by changes in design, art, process, and the like, which make a property less desirable. It is distinguished from physical deterioration in that the owner has little or no control over this type of reduction of value, for example, over any radical changes in the architectural design of buildings. Nevertheless, the value of the building is reduced because of them unless the defects are corrected through modernization. A house may be physically sound, but the kitchen and bathroom fixtures may be old-fashioned. The fact that the fixtures are outmoded lessens the desirability of the property, and therefore reduces its value.

Curable items of functional obsolescence are measured by the cost of removing the functionally obsolete items, where possible. For example, modernizing a bathroom. Note that it is assumed that physically the bathroom has *not* deteriorated so that it is *not* included under an item of physical deterioration. Assume that the cost to modernize the bathroom would be $1,800. In this case curable functional obsolescence equals $1,800.

Incurable functional obsolescence is a loss in value due to a deficiency that cannot be economically corrected. A poor floor plan, inadequate basement, or high ceilings are examples of incurable functional obsolescence, which is generally measured in either one of two ways:

1. *Rental loss per month.* A comparable home with a proper floor plan is renting for an additional $15 per month. This figure is then multiplied by a gross monthly income multiplier (detailed later in this chapter under Income Approach). For instance, if the gross monthly multiplier is 100, then $1,500 (100 × $15) is the incurable functional obsolescence.

2. *Sales resistance loss.* The appraiser forms an opinion, which is highly subjective, of a percentage of cost to replace new, as the loss. Assume a poor floor plan. The cost to replace is $75,000. The appraiser determines (subjectively) that sales resistance is 10 percent; then $7,500 ($75,000 × .10) is the incurable functional obsolescence.

External obsolescence. This is the impairment of desirability or useful life of property arising from external forces. Although the property owner may limit to a large degree both physical depreciation and functional obsolescence, external obsolescence cannot be controlled. External obsolescence has to do with changes in the neighborhood and is probably the greatest cause of loss in value of real property. It is an *external* factor that causes loss of value. This is usually a result of deterioration of the neighborhood causing it to lose character; or it may be that changes inconsistent with the use of residential property occur in the neighborhood. For example, a factory may be erected or an expressway may be constructed with resultant traffic noise. All of these things make up external obsolescence with its consequent loss of value to homes.

Because economic obsolescence arises from conditions outside the building over which the owner has no control, it is always assumed to be incurable. For example, since the British-French Concorde has been permitted to land at Kennedy Airport, there has been a loss in value of the real property in the proximate area of the flight pattern.

External obsolescence can be measured by rental loss. Assume that rental loss is $15 per month and the gross monthly income multiplier is 100. The total loss to the entire property—land and buildings—would be $1,500 (100 × $15) incurable external obsolescence.

In this case, the loss of value is determined by the ratio of the building to the total property value. The argument is that the land value has already been determined and, consequently, already been lowered because of external obsolescence.

Assume in this case, you have found the following:

Cost to replace building	$75,000
Land value	15,000
Total cost to replace new	$90,000

The land represents a 1 to 5 ratio. In short, land is 20 percent of the building. Of the $1,500 loss, 80 percent or $1,200 ($1,500 × .80) is attributable to the building.

When adequate data are available, it is preferable to measure external obsolescence comparing sales of similar properties. This may be done by comparing the prices received for similar properties, some of which are subject to the negative external influence and some which are free from that condition.

Land Value. Using the cost approach, land value is added to the depreciated cost of improvements. Although there are various procedures for estimating land value, the most common employs comparable sales of vacant land whose highest and best use is the same as for the subject property.

Each land sale is compared to the subject land and its sale price is adjusted up or down depending on whether the characteristic being analyzed is better or worse than the subject land.

For example, presume that the subject property measures 70 by 140 feet and a comparable lot measures 80 by 140 feet. In this instance, the appraiser may determine that were the comparable lot equal in size to the subject, the comparable lot would sell for 8 percent less. As a result, the comparable lot's sales price is adjusted downward 8 percent. In this manner each comparable property is analyzed for differences between it and the subject land, and the sales price is adjusted correspondingly to reflect the impact on price.

The analysis typically includes adjustments for differences in size, location, topography, access, and price changes that would have taken place between the date of appraisal and the date of sale of the comparable property. This adjustment is called a time adjustment. For example, were the comparable property sold six months prior to the date of appraisal, and land prices are known to have increased 6 percent in the past year, the time-price adjustment would be plus 3 percent.

Analytical Tools. When adjusting comparable sales of land or home to reflect the value of the subject property, it is sometimes helpful to use a scatter diagram or simple linear regression models. These tools help the appraiser visualize the relationship between price and one other variable such as lot size or square feet of living area.

For example, from Table 18-1, to estimate land value the appraiser selected lot sales that are comparable in all respects to the subject except price and size. A scatter diagram has been prepared (Exhibit 18-1) for the sample sales in Table 18-1.

Table 18-1 Comparable Land Sales

	PRICE	SQ. FT./LOT	PRICE/SQ. FT.
	$10,500	7,500	$1.40
	12,000	8,000	1.50
	11,250	8,250	1.36
	12,000	8,750	1.37
	10,750	9,000	1.19
	13,250	9,500	1.39
	12,000	9,500	1.26
	13,000	9,750	1.33
	15,500	10,000	1.55
	11,000	10,000	1.10
	13,250	10,500	1.26
	12,250	10,500	1.17
Average	$12,229	9,271	$1.32

The average price is $1.32 per square foot. What is the value of a lot with 11,000 square feet? Is it $1.32 × 11,000 = $14,520? Using the scatter diagram, what value would you place on the 11,000 square-foot lot—$13,000?

The use of linear regression can mathematically describe the relationship between price and lot size or some other variable by solving the following equation:

$$y = a + bx$$

where y = estimated value of subject, a = constant dollar amount, b = variation in price per square foot, and x = square feet.

Solving this type of problem is simplified using computer programs that require only that sample data, in this case, price and square feet for each lot, be entered. Using the Decision Assistant that accompanies this book, the solution is as follows:

y	=	a	+	b	(x)
Value	=	$5,034.78	+	$ .776	(sq. feet)
Value	=	$5,034.78	+	$ .776	(11,000)
Value	=	$5,034.78	+	$8,536	
Value	=	$13,571			

Sales Comparison Approach

Of the three approaches in residential appraisal, the most often used is **the sales comparison approach.** The objective is to obtain comparable sales of comparable properties.

The sales prices of comparable properties vary because the real estate market is imperfect. For example, to determine the value of a listed share

■ **Exhibit 18-1 Scatter Diagram**

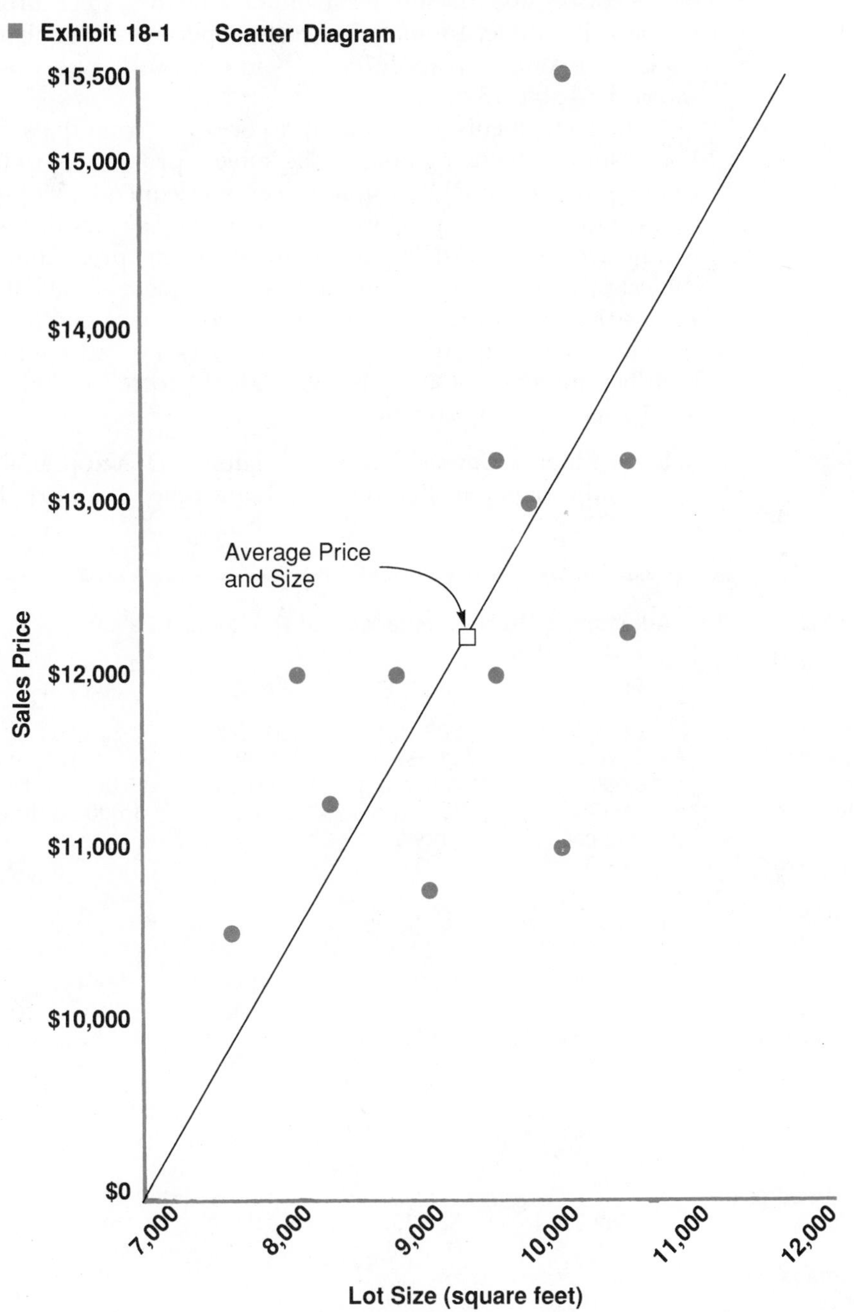

of corporate stock is simple: a phone call to a stock broker can easily establish the value. In analyzing real property, sales adjustments must be made to account for all differences in the property being compared, as shown in Table 18-2.

The adjustments are made up to or down from the subject property. For example, the living area of the subject property is 1,666 square feet. Comparable #1 has 1,456 square feet; consequently, its price is adjusted upward to the subject property by 11 percent. Sale 2 with 1,753 square feet is adjusted downward 4 percent to make the price comparable to the subject property on a square-foot basis. The logic is that Sale 2, were it the same size home as the subject property, would have sold for 4 percent less.

How many adjustments are made? It varies and appraisers must use their best judgment. On the FHLMC/FNMA form (see Exhibit 18-2), there are 18 separate adjustments.

Sales or Finance Concessions. The latest FNMA appraisal form contains a new adjustment in determining value called "sales or financing con-

Table 18-2 Adjustment Grid—Comparison of Residential Sales*

ADJUSTMENT FACTORS	SALE 1	SALE 2	SALE 3	SALE 4	SUBJECT PROPERTY
Sale price	$71,000	$80,000	$69,000	$77,000	?
Sale date	5/90	11/90	11/90	1/91	3/91
Lot size	15,000 sq. ft.	12,000 sq. ft.	11,000 sq. ft.	15,000 sq. ft.	15,000 sq. ft.
Living area	1,456 sq. ft.	1,753 sq. ft.	1,510 sq. ft.	1,600 sq. ft.	1,666 sq. ft.
Garage	2-car	none	1-car	2-car	2-car
Bedrooms	3	3	3	3	3
PRICE ADJUSTMENT					
Time*	+5%	+2%	+2%	+1%	
Lot size	–	+5%	+6%	–	
Living area	+11%	−4%	+8%	+3%	
Garage	–	+5%	+2%	–	
Bedrooms	–	–	–	–	
Total Adjustments	+16%	+8%	+18%	+4%	
Adjusted sales price	$82,360	$86,400	$81,420	$80,080	
Average adjusted price	$79,875				
Range	$80,080	$86,400			

*The assumption is made that the date of appraisal is March 1991, and analysis of the local market reveals that residential property prices are rising at the rate of 6 percent per year.

■ Exhibit 18-2 Uniform Residential Appraisal Report

Valuation Section **UNIFORM RESIDENTIAL APPRAISAL REPORT** File No.

Purpose of Appraisal is to estimate Market Value as defined in the Certification & Statement of Limiting Conditions.

COST APPROACH

BUILDING SKETCH (SHOW GROSS LIVING AREA ABOVE GRADE)
If for Freddie Mac or Fannie Mae, show only square foot calculations and cost approach comments in this space.

ESTIMATED REPRODUCTION COST-NEW-OF IMPROVEMENTS:
Dwelling ______ Sq. Ft. @ $ ______ = $ ______
______ Sq. Ft. @ $ ______ = ______
Extras ______ = ______
= ______
Special Energy Efficient Items ______ = ______
Porches, Patios, etc. ______ = ______
Garage/Carport ______ Sq. Ft. @ $ ______ = ______
Total Estimated Cost New ...... = $ ______
Less — Physical | Functional | External
Depreciation ______ = $ ______
Depreciated Value of Improvements ...... = $ ______
Site Imp. "as is" (driveway, landscaping, etc.) = $ ______
ESTIMATED SITE VALUE ...... = $ ______
(If leasehold, show only leasehold value.)
INDICATED VALUE BY COST APPROACH ...... = $ ______

(Not Required by Freddie Mac and Fannie Mae)
Does property conform to applicable HUD/VA property standards? ☐ Yes ☐ No
If No, explain: ______

Construction Warranty ☐ Yes ☐ No
Name of Warranty Program ______
Warranty Coverage Expires ______

SALES COMPARISON ANALYSIS

The undersigned has recited three recent sales of properties most similar and proximate to subject and has considered these in the market analysis. The description includes a dollar adjustment, reflecting market reaction to those items of significant variation between the subject and comparable properties. If a significant item in the comparable property is superior to, or more favorable than, the subject property, a minus (–) adjustment is made, thus reducing the indicated value of subject; if a significant item in the comparable is inferior to, or less favorable than, the subject property, a plus (+) adjustment is made, thus increasing the indicated value of the subject.

ITEM	SUBJECT	COMPARABLE NO. 1		COMPARABLE NO. 2		COMPARABLE NO. 3	
Address							
Proximity to Subject							
Sales Price	$		$		$		$
Price/Gross Liv. Area	$ ☐	$ ☐		$ ☐		$ ☐	
Data Source							
VALUE ADJUSTMENTS	DESCRIPTION	DESCRIPTION	+ (–) $ Adjustment	DESCRIPTION	+ (–) $ Adjustment	DESCRIPTION	+ (–) $ Adjustment
Sales or Financing Concessions							
Date of Sale/Time							
Location							
Site/View							
Design and Appeal							
Quality of Construction							
Age							
Condition							
Above Grade Room Count	Total | Bdrms | Baths	Total | Bdrms | Baths		Total | Bdrms | Baths		Total | Bdrms | Baths	
Gross Living Area	Sq. Ft.	Sq. Ft.		Sq. Ft.		Sq. Ft.	
Basement & Finished Rooms Below Grade							
Functional Utility							
Heating/Cooling							
Garage/Carport							
Porches, Patio, Pools, etc.							
Special Energy Efficient Items							
Fireplace(s)							
Other (e.g. kitchen equip., remodeling)							
Net Adj. (total)		☐ + ☐ –	$	☐ + ☐ –	$	☐ + ☐ –	$
Indicated Value of Subject			$		$		$

Comments on Sales Comparison: ______

RECONCILIATION

INDICATED VALUE BY SALES COMPARISON APPROACH ...... $ ______
INDICATED VALUE BY INCOME APPROACH (If Applicable) Estimated Market Rent $ ______ /Mo. x Gross Rent Multiplier ______ = $ ______
This appraisal is made ☐ "as is" ☐ subject to the repairs, alterations, inspections or conditions listed below ☐ completion per plans and specifications.
Comments and Conditions of Appraisal: ______

Final Reconciliation: ______

This appraisal is based upon the above requirements, the certification, contingent and limiting conditions, and Market Value definition that are stated in
☐ FmHA, HUD &/or VA instructions.
☐ Freddie Mac Form 439 (Rev. 7/86)/Fannie Mae Form 1004B (Rev. 7/86) filed with client ______ 19___ ☐ attached.
I (WE) ESTIMATE THE MARKET VALUE, AS DEFINED, OF THE SUBJECT PROPERTY AS OF ______ 19___ **to be $** ______
I (We) certify: that to the best of my (our) knowledge and belief the facts and data used herein are true and correct; that I (we) personally inspected the subject property, both inside and out, and have made an exterior inspection of all comparable sales cited in this report; and that I (we) have no undisclosed interest, present or prospective therein.

Appraiser(s) SIGNATURE ______ Review Appraiser SIGNATURE ______ ☐ Did ☐ Did Not
NAME ______ (if applicable) NAME ______ Inspect Property

Freddie Mac Form 70 10/86 12Ch. Forms and Worms Inc.,® 315 Whitney Ave., New Haven, CT 06511 1(800) 243-4545 Fannie Mae Form 1004 10/86

■ Exhibit 18-2 (continued)

Property Description & Analysis **UNIFORM RESIDENTIAL APPRAISAL REPORT** **File No.**

SUBJECT

Property Address		Census Tract	LENDER DISCRETIONARY USE
City	County	State	Zip Code
Legal Description			Sale Price $
Owner/Occupant		Map Reference	Date
Sale Price $	Date of Sale	PROPERTY RIGHTS APPRAISED	Mortgage Amount $
Loan charges/concessions to be paid by seller $		☐ Fee Simple	Mortgage Type
R.E. Taxes $	Tax Year	HOA $/Mo.	☐ Leasehold	Discount Points and Other Concessions
Lender/Client		☐ Condominium (HUD/VA)	Paid by Seller $
		☐ De Minimis PUD	Source

NEIGHBORHOOD

LOCATION	☐ Urban	☐ Suburban	☐ Rural
BUILT UP	☐ Over 75%	☐ 25-75%	☐ Under 25%
GROWTH RATE	☐ Rapid	☐ Stable	☐ Slow
PROPERTY VALUES	☐ Increasing	☐ Stable	☐ Declining
DEMAND/SUPPLY	☐ Shortage	☐ In Balance	☐ Over Supply
MARKETING TIME	☐ Under 3 Mos.	☐ 3-6 Mos.	☐ Over 6 Mos.

PRESENT LAND USE %	LAND USE CHANGE	PREDOMINANT OCCUPANCY	SINGLE FAMILY HOUSING PRICE $ (000) AGE (yrs)
Single Family ___	Not Likely ☐		
2-4 Family ___	Likely ☐	Owner ☐	
Multi-family ___	In process ☐	Tenant ☐	Low
Commercial ___	To:	Vacant (0-5%) ☐	High
Industrial ___		Vacant (over 5%) ☐	Predominant
Vacant ___			

NEIGHBORHOOD ANALYSIS	Good	Avg.	Fair	Poor
Employment Stability	☐	☐	☐	☐
Convenience to Employment	☐	☐	☐	☐
Convenience to Shopping	☐	☐	☐	☐
Convenience to Schools	☐	☐	☐	☐
Adequacy of Public Transportation	☐	☐	☐	☐
Recreation Facilities	☐	☐	☐	☐
Adequacy of Utilities	☐	☐	☐	☐
Property Compatibility	☐	☐	☐	☐
Protection from Detrimental Cond.	☐	☐	☐	☐
Police & Fire Protection	☐	☐	☐	☐
General Appearance of Properties	☐	☐	☐	☐
Appeal to Market	☐	☐	☐	☐

Note: Race or the racial composition of the neighborhood are not considered reliable appraisal factors.

COMMENTS: ______

SITE

Dimensions		Topography
Site Area	Corner Lot	Size
Zoning Classification	Zoning Compliance	Shape
HIGHEST & BEST USE: Present Use	Other Use	Drainage

UTILITIES	Public	Other	SITE IMPROVEMENTS	Type	Public	Private	
Electricity	☐		Street		☐	☐	View
Gas	☐		Curb/Gutter		☐	☐	Landscaping
Water	☐		Sidewalk		☐	☐	Driveway
Sanitary Sewer	☐		Street Lights		☐	☐	Apparent Easements
Storm Sewer	☐		Alley		☐	☐	FEMA Flood Hazard Yes* ___ No ___
							FEMA* Map/Zone

COMMENTS (Apparent adverse easements, encroachments, special assessments, slide areas, etc.): ______

IMPROVEMENTS

GENERAL DESCRIPTION	EXTERIOR DESCRIPTION	FOUNDATION	BASEMENT	INSULATION
Units	Foundation	Slab	Area Sq. Ft.	Roof ☐
Stories	Exterior Walls	Crawl Space	% Finished	Ceiling ☐
Type (Det./Att.)	Roof Surface	Basement	Ceiling	Walls ☐
Design (Style)	Gutters & Dwnspts.	Sump Pump	Walls	Floor ☐
Existing	Window Type	Dampness	Floor	None ☐
Proposed	Storm Sash	Settlement	Outside Entry	Adequacy ☐
Under Construction	Screens	Infestation		Energy Efficient Items:
Age (Yrs.)	Manufactured House			
Effective Age (Yrs.)				

ROOM LIST

ROOMS	Foyer	Living	Dining	Kitchen	Den	Family Rm.	Rec. Rm.	Bedrooms	# Baths	Laundry	Other	Area Sq. Ft.
Basement												
Level 1												
Level 2												

Finished area **above** grade contains: Rooms; Bedroom(s); Bath(s); Square Feet of Gross Living Area

INTERIOR

SURFACES Materials/Condition	HEATING	KITCHEN EQUIP.	ATTIC
Floors	Type	Refrigerator ☐	None ☐
Walls	Fuel	Range/Oven ☐	Stairs ☐
Trim/Finish	Condition	Disposal ☐	Drop Stair ☐
Bath Floor	Adequacy	Dishwasher ☐	Scuttle ☐
Bath Wainscot	COOLING	Fan/Hood ☐	Floor ☐
Doors	Central	Compactor ☐	Heated ☐
	Other	Washer/Dryer ☐	Finished ☐
	Condition	Microwave ☐	
Fireplace(s) #	Adequacy	Intercom ☐	

IMPROVEMENT ANALYSIS	Good	Avg.	Fair	Poor
Quality of Construction	☐	☐	☐	☐
Condition of Improvements	☐	☐	☐	☐
Room Sizes/Layout	☐	☐	☐	☐
Closets and Storage	☐	☐	☐	☐
Energy Efficiency	☐	☐	☐	☐
Plumbing-Adequacy & Condition	☐	☐	☐	☐
Electrical-Adequacy & Condition	☐	☐	☐	☐
Kitchen Cabinets-Adequacy & Cond.	☐	☐	☐	☐
Compatibility to Neighborhood	☐	☐	☐	☐
Appeal & Marketability	☐	☐	☐	☐
Estimated Remaining Economic Life				Yrs.
Estimated Remaining Physical Life				Yrs.

AUTOS

CAR STORAGE:	Garage ☐	Attached ☐	Adequate ☐	House Entry ☐
No. Cars ___	Carport ☐	Detached ☐	Inadequate ☐	Outside Entry ☐
Condition	None ☐	Built-In ☐	Electric Door ☐	Basement Entry ☐

COMMENTS

Additional features: ______

Depreciation (Physical, functional and external inadequacies, repairs needed, modernization, etc.): ______

General market conditions and prevalence and impact in subject/market area regarding loan discounts, interest buydowns and concessions: ______

Freddie Mac Form 70 10/86 12Ch. AO Forms and Worms Inc.,® 315 Whitney Ave., New Haven, CT 06511 1(800) 243-4545 Item #111710 Fannie Mae Form 1004 10/86 cessions." This includes monetary value of concessions such as builder or seller price discounts, financing charges or benefits (e.g., loan points included in the sales price and "buy-down" of the mortgage interest rate by the builder), and gifts of merchandise such as a free automobile. All of these must be reported for the subject property and comparables and the value adjusted accordingly.

In other words, a property may no longer be appraised without giving consideration to the terms of financing on value. Comparables with financing below the prevailing rate of interest should have their sales prices adjusted downward, or those with financing above the prevailing interest rate should have their values adjusted upward.

Present value techniques (refer to Chapter 17 and the Decision Assistant) need to be utilized to equalize price differences that result from differences in the rate and length of financing. There is little doubt of the need for financing adjustments. There are, however, some questions which must be answered with regard to selection of the appropriate discount rate. The authors suggest either the current market rate of interest or average market rate of interest for conventional mortgage loans for the preceding year.

Verification. Each comparable sale selected to provide an indication of value should be verified. The property must be inspected and the sales price and financing confirmed. Verification may be done by talking to the sales agent, or by examining the tax assessor's property appraisal card and filed certificates of real estate value. Verification helps the appraiser obtain the most accurate appraisal possible.

Income Approach (Gross Rent Multiplier)

In the **income approach,** using the gross rent multiplier, a value is determined as a multiple of gross monthly rent (see Table 18-3). Monthly rent for comparable sales of comparable properties is obtained. The rent is divided into the sale price to obtain the **gross rent multiplier.** For example, a residence sells for $80,000 and it is rented for $575 per month. The multiplier is 139 ($80,000/575 = 139).

Table 18-3 Gross Rent Multiplier—Comparable Sales

SALE	SELLING PRICE		RENT		MULTIPLIER
1	$80,000	÷	$575	=	139.1
2	90,000	÷	650	=	138.5
3	84,000	÷	600	=	140.0
4	70,000	÷	475	=	147.4

Again, the appraiser determines which property is most comparable; see, for example, Sale 2 in Table 18-3. The assumption is that the property being appraised could rent for \$675 per month. Then \$675 × 138.5 = \$93,487 (approximate) value of property being appraised.

Although useful, the gross monthly multiplier contains some serious defects and must be used with care. Some limitations are:

1. Gross income rather than net income is used. No accounting for operating or maintenance costs is included.
2. The multiplier assumes uniformity of the various properties in their operating ratios. There is an implied assumption that all real property taxes, heating costs, etc., are the same.
3. No importance is placed on the remaining economic life of the properties. Some have a longer remaining economic life than others. It is assumed here that all the properties examined are the same.
4. Currently, when "modest" homes are selling at prices from \$60,000 to \$80,000, the multiplier may have a certain amount of usefulness. However, when many homes are selling at prices between \$100,000 and \$150,000, the use of the multiplier can be seriously challenged. Furthermore, when rents are obtained, they appear to have little or no relationship to value.

Reconciliation of Value

Assume the appraiser has used the three approaches and arrived at the following:

Cost	\$92,000
Market	89,500
Income	85,750

The question is, which of the three figures is correct? Depending on the time period and local conditions, more weight may be given to one approach over the others. The appraiser must form an opinion of value after carefully considering each approach. This is known as **reconciliation of value.**

THE APPRAISAL PLANT

The practicing appraiser maintains what is commonly called a plant, handy records and references to assist in daily operations. It may be extensive or simple, for example, a card index of recent sales kept by plat or census tracts, economic and current business information, and maps and updated construction cost data. Typical sources of information are presented in Table 18-4.

Table 18-4 Sources of Information

Cost information	1. Construction cost manuals a. *Boeckh's Building Valuation Manual* (residential and commercial) b. *Marshall & Swift Valuation Manual* c. *Dodge Building Cost Calculation* 2. Local builders 3. Financial institutions (especially savings and loan associations for residential properties)
Comparable sales (land and buildings)	1. Recorder of deeds 2. Tax assessor 3. Multiple listing services 4. Real estate brokers 5. Financial institutions
Income	1. Multiple listing services 2. Real estate brokers 3. Financial institutions 4. Real estate investors
General information (e.g., population, income, household size, jobs, etc.)	1. Census bureau 2. Sales management magazine 3. Environmental Protection Agency 4. Chamber of Commerce 5. Bureaus of business research (state universities) 6. State employment services

CURRENT DEVELOPMENTS IN RESIDENTIAL APPRAISING

Like all fields of real estate, real estate appraisal changes in response to societal changes. In 1980, financing adjustments for sales comparisons were unheard of. By 1990, financing adjustments were standard. Real estate appraisal is responding to its role in the savings and loan crisis and in the areas of required licensing and environmental hazards.

R-41c and Uniform Standards of Professional Appraisal Practices

The failure of numerous savings and loan banks with an estimated bailout cost of $350 billion is partially attributable to faulty real estate appraisals. A congressional report issued in September 1986 detailed the appraisal deficiencies:

1. Significant appraisal deficiencies were found in 25 percent of federally insured thrifts. Collateral for mortgage loans was overvalued by $3 billion.
2. After the failure of Continental Illinois Bank and Trust, reappraisal of its 21 largest properties gave a value of $184 million for a portfolio originally valued at $518 million.
3. Forty percent of the Veterans Administration loan guarantee losses in 1985 were caused by inaccurate or dishonest appraisals.

In light of these problems, the Federal Home Loan Bank Board (FHLBB) issued Memorandum R-41c, which sets minimum standards that may be used to evaluate compliance in obtaining proper appraisals for mortgage loans. In 1986, to preclude federal regulation, nine national appraisal organizations developed the Uniform Standards of Professional Appraisal Practices. Memorandum R-41c is presented as Exhibit 18-3.

■ Exhibit 18-3 Federal Home Loan Bank Board Memorandum R-41c

APPRAISAL MANAGEMENT

Appraisals serve as an important basis in the decision processes involved in the underwriting of secured credit transactions as well as investment decisions involving interest in real property. Management must ensure that all appraisals utilized in these decisions:

1. Are based upon the following definition of market value:
   The most probable price which a property should bring in a competitive and open market under all conditions requisite to a fair sale, the buyer and seller, each acting prudently, knowledgeably and assuming the price is not affected by undue stimulus. Implicit in this definition is the consummation of a sale as of a specified date and the passing of title from seller to buyer under conditions whereby:

   a. buyer and seller are typically motivated;
   b. both parties are well informed or well advised, and each acting in what he considers his own best interest;
   c. a reasonable time is allowed for exposure in the open market;
   d. payment is made in terms of cash in U.S. dollars or in terms of financial arrangements comparable thereto; and
   e. The price represents the normal consideration for the property sold unaffected by special or creative financing or sales concessions granted by anyone associated with the sale.

2. Correctly employ all recognized appraisal methods and techniques that are necessary to produce a credible analysis, opinion, or conclusion.

Exhibit 18-3 (continued)

Exclusion or omission of any recognized method for cause must be fully justified.

3. Consider, analyze and disclose in reasonable detail:

   a. Any current agreement of sale, option, or listing of the property being appraised.
   b. Any prior sales of the property being appraised that occurred within the following time periods:

      (1) one year preceding the date when the appraisal was prepared for one to four family residential property, and
      (2) three years preceding the date when the appraisal was prepared for all other property types.

   c. A sales history of the comparables, if the subject property is located in a speculative market, which has experienced dramatic price fluctuations relative to regional norms, covering the speculative time period involving the comparable sales.

4. Contain the following information where an analysis, opinion or conclusion of a proposed project, improvement or change in use is involved: (i) plans, specifications, or other documentation in sufficient detail to identify the scope and character of the proposed improvements; (ii) evidence indicating the probable time of completion of the proposed improvements; (iii) clear and appropriate evidence supporting development costs, anticipated rent levels or per unit sales levels, occupancy projections, and the anticipated competition at the time of completion; and (iv) all value changes projected to occur from the conception of a project to its completion and/or stabilized occupancy should be set forth in sufficient detail so that the continuum of present value estimates over the life of the credit arrangement or investment can be reconciled with the values reported in the appraisal. Included as documentation should be an explanation of how discount and capitalization rates used in generating the present value estimates were deduced. In addition to the above requirements, whenever value is estimated as of completion and/or stabilized occupancy, the appraisal must contain the following information:

   a. The date or dates when the value estimate or estimates apply.
   b. Factual data supporting the reasonableness of all conditions and assumptions impacting each value conclusion cited in the appraisal. Such information must be presented in sufficient detail and directly linked to current market information so that the appraiser's logic, reasoning, judgment and analysis indicate to a third-party reader the reasonableness of the value or values reported.
   c. An explanation of the appraisal techniques selected and the data used to arrive at the final value estimate(s).

■ Exhibit 18-3 (continued)

d. A fully documented and supported highest and best use analysis and conclusion which coincides with the date(s) of the value estimate(s).

e. A definitive statement as to whether the value estimate reflects the worth of the property at stabilized occupancy and whether the appraiser considered and included the effect of income and expenses during the projected absorption period in developing a value estimate as of the date of completion.

5. Accurately reflect the impact upon value of any changes in plans and specifications from those utilized in an appraiser's analysis of a proposed project, improvement or change in use.

   In all instances where an institution utilizes an appraisal based upon preliminary plans and specifications in a loan or investment decision, it shall take appropriate steps, prior to the disbursement of any funds, to ensure the validity of the appraisal, relative to the decision, has not been negated. Further, whenever significant changes in plans and specifications occur after a loan or investment decision has been made, the institution's management shall take appropriate steps to ensure its financial position is appropriately protected. Typically, such steps will involve either having the original appraiser recertify his value estimate after examining the final plans and specifications for the project or a new appraisal will be obtained based on the final plans and specifications.

   For the purposes of this paragraph, significant changes in plans and specifications are defined as those which directly affect the value of the property, e.g., changes in the scope, character or timing of the proposed improvements.

6. Contain a properly documented and supported estimate of the highest and best use of the property appraised, which is consistent with the definition of market value cited in this memorandum. Such estimate must consider the effect on use and value of the following factors: existing land use regulations, reasonably probable modifications of such land use regulations, economic demand, the physical adaptability of the property, neighborhood trends, and the optimal usage of the property. In addition, the appraisal must consider the effect on the property being appraised of anticipated public or private improvements, located on or off the site, to the extent that market actions reflect such anticipated improvements as of the appraisal date.

   In all appraisals, including those involving proposed construction, development or changes in use, the appraiser must specifically address and consider in his analysis the anticipated economic feasibility, as well as cite all significant market data utilized in developing his/her conclusions. Such analyses must be presented in sufficient detail to support the appraiser's forecast of the probable success and the conclusion of highest and best use of the project.

   In all instances where the appraiser relies on feasibility/marketability studies prepared by a third party to support his estimate of the highest and best use, he must:

■ **Exhibit 18-3 (continued)**

a. Attest that such study has been thoroughly examined and that he fully concurs with its findings and conclusions, and;
b. Specifically identify both the study examined as well as set forth within the body of the appraisal, a summary of the significant data analyses and conclusions presented in the study. Such summary must be presented in sufficient detail, so that further reference to the study is unnecessary by a third-party reader of the appraisal, and;
c. Have available for future examination by users of the appraisal, complete copy of the feasibility/marketability study prepared by the third party.

7. Report the market value to a single purchaser as of the date of completion for all properties, wherein a portion of the overall real property rights or physical asset would typically be sold to its ultimate users over some future time period. Valuations involving such properties must fully reflect all appropriate deductions and discounts as well as the anticipated cash flows to be derived from the disposition of the asset over time. Appropriate deductions and discounts are considered to be those which reflect all expenses associated with the disposition of the realty, as of the date of completion, as well as the cost of capital and entrepreneurial profit.
8. For properties under construction, conversion or proposed, report the market value of the subject property as of the date of completion, excepting those properties described in paragraph 15 immediately above, where anticipated market conditions indicate stabilized occupancy is not likely as of the date of completion. Such valuations shall fully reflect the impact upon the "as if completed value" or all pertinent operating expenses as well as the anticipated pattern of income during the absorption period. In addition, the value estimate must reflect the impact of rental and other concessions, including the costs associated with preparing the improvement for occupancy by tenants.
9. Contain a summary of actual income and expenses experienced by the subject property where it is an existing income or revenue producing property. In addition, all such appraisals must contain a complete reconciliation of all deviations projected by the appraiser in his forecast of future financial performance from those historically realized by the property.
10. Report the "as is" value of the subject property as of the date when either the appraisal was prepared or when the property was last inspected. The date of the "as is" value estimate should be sufficiently current to reduce the likelihood of material changes in the actual market conditions from those upon which the loan or investment decision were predicated. In addition to any other value estimates contained in an appraisal, the "as is" value must be reported.
11. Consider and report the effect on value, if any, of the terms and conditions of any agreement establishing a fractional interest or estate, where the objective of the report is to estimate the value of such fractional

■ **Exhibit 18-3 (continued)**

interest or estate. All such appraisals must clearly demonstrate that the value of any fractional part or estate has been evaluated by an analysis of appropriate market data. Such analyses must recognize that it is generally considered inappropriate to arrive at either the value of the whole or its parts by simply summing the fractional interests or subdividing the value of the whole into proportional parts.

All analyses involving fractional interests or estates, where the combined value of all interests or estates is not reported, must definitively establish with market evidence whether the terms and conditions of the agreement creating the estates or fractional interests reflects market rates and terms.

In addition to the above requirements, all analyses involving fractional interests or estates must disclose whether the final value estimate of such fractional interests or estates included non-realty components, i.e., tenant or borrower's credit quality, other non-realty contractual arrangements, etc. Further, whenever such value estimate includes non-realty components, the value assignable to them must be specifically disclosed in the appraisal.

All appraisals, where there is a clear indication that the subject property is encumbered by a lease instrument or legal limitations upon its operation [e.g., when inspection reveals occupancy of the property by tenants or the property is subject to rent control statutes], must consider and report the impact of the terms of the lease or such legal limitations upon the value of the estate being appraised.

Appraisal Content

Prior to the approval of a loan or investment transaction, each appraisal accepted by an institution must be prepared in writing and contain sufficient information to enable the persons who receive or rely on the report to understand it properly. Appraisals which fail to set forth, in a clear and accurate manner, the analytical process followed by the appraiser, in a fashion that will not be misleading to the persons who receive or rely on the report, will be considered unacceptable.

The content of each appraisal accepted by an institution shall follow generally accepted and established appraisal practices, as reflected in the standards of the nationally recognized professional appraisal organizations and as noted in the body of this memorandum.

Specifically, each appraisal must:

1. Be totally self-contained so that when read by any third party, the appraiser's logic, reasoning, judgment and analysis in arriving at a final conclusion indicate to the reader the reasonableness of the market value reported.
2. Identify via a legal description the real estate being appraised.
3. Identify the property rights being appraised.
4. Describe all salient features of the property being appraised.
5. State that the purpose of the appraisal is to estimate market value as defined in this memorandum.

Exhibit 18-3 (concluded)

6. Set forth the effective date of the value conclusion(s) and the date of the report.
7. Set forth all relevant data and the analytical process followed by the appraiser in arriving at the highest and best use conclusion.
8. Set forth the appraisal procedures followed, the data considered, and the reasoning that supports the analyses, opinions, and conclusions arrived at by the appraiser. The analytical process followed by the appraiser must be presented so that:

   a. It includes a complete explanation of all comparable data adjustments utilized in the analysis together with appropriate market support for each adjustment, and;
   b. It contains descriptive information for all comparable data presented with sufficient detail to demonstrate the transactions were conducted under the terms and conditions of the definition of value being estimated or have been adjusted to meet such conditions; have a highest and best use equivalent to the best use of the subject property, and; are physically and economically comparable to the subject property.

9. Set forth all assumptions and limiting conditions that affect the analyses, opinions, and conclusions in the report; however, such assumptions and limiting conditions must not result in either a non-market value estimate or one so limited in scope that the final product will not represent a complete appraisal. A summary of all such assumptions and limiting conditions must be presented in one physical location within the appraisal.

Licensing and Certification

An outgrowth of the savings and loan crisis has been enactment of state laws providing for licensing or certification of appraisers. In February 1989, Wyoming became the third state to pass certification legislation. By June 1989, five more states had enacted licensure laws; by November 1989, 26 states had appraisal licensing laws.

The same pattern has been followed in each jurisdiction. A certification or licensing board is established along with two or more classes of licenses, their qualifications, and standards. Applicants must meet minimum education, experience, and testing requirements. Exhibit 18-4 presents the new licensing requirements for eight states.

Hazardous Substances

There is an increasing need for appraisers to be aware of environmental hazards that may have an impact on property values. The cost of making the property safe from radon, asbestos, or chemical contaminants may in some cases exceed the value of the real estate.

Exhibit 18-4 Appraiser Licensing or Certification Standards

STATE	BOARD OF CERTIFICATION	LICENSE	EDUCATION	EXPERIENCE	EXAM	REAL ESTATE SALES OR BROKERS LICS.	CONTINUING EDUCATION
Delaware (mandatory)	yes	Residential general	All requirements to be set by Board.				
Iowa	yes		All requirements to be set by Board.				
Minnesota	no	Level I: Residential Appraiser	75 class hours	none	yes	no	15 class hours each year
		Level II: Appraiser	165 class hours	2 years	yes	no	
Nevada (mandatory)	—	Residential Appraiser	60 class hours	2 years of past 5 as intern	yes	no	20 class hours every 2 years
	—	General Appraiser	120 class hours	3 years of past 5 as intern	yes	no	
North Carolina (mandatory)	no	State Licensed Appraiser	90 class hours	none	yes	no	
		State Certified Appraiser	180 class hours	2 years in past 5			
Texas (voluntary)	—	Residential Appraiser	80 class hours or college degree	2 years of past 5	yes	yes	none
		General Appraiser	150 class hours or college degree	3 years of past 5	yes	yes	none
Washington (voluntary)	no	Residential Appraiser Nonresidential Appraiser	As determined by Department of Licensing.				
Wyoming (voluntary)	yes	Appraisal Trainee	30 class hours	none	no		
		Residential Appraiser	60 class hours + 15 hours of Stds. of Practice	2 years	yes		60 class hours every 3 years
		General Appraiser	120 class hours + 15 hours of Stds. of Practice	2 years	yes		

GLOSSARY

Appraisal An attempt to obtain a just and fair evaluation of a parcel of real property

Cost A measure of things that happened in the past

Cost approach An approach whereby the cost to construct an existing building and the value of that building are analyzed

Curable/incurable obsolescence Curable if cost of improvement is less than loss of value from obsolete item; incurable if loss of value cannot be economically corrected

Demand The desire for a good or service backed by the ability to pay

Effective age The amount of an improvement considered by an appraiser to be "used up"

External obsolescence An impairment of desirability or useful life of property arising from external forces

Functional obsolescence An impairment of desirability and usefulness brought about by changes in design, art, process, etc.

Gross rent multiplier Relationship of ratio between sale price or value and gross monthly rent

Highest and best use The reasonable and probable use that supports the highest present value as defined as of the date of the appraisal

Income approach An attempt to determine property value by capitalizing its income

Market value The highest monetary price a property will bring in a competitive and open market under all conditions requisite to a fair sale: the buyer and seller, each acting prudently, knowledgeably, and assuming the price is not affected by undue stimulus

Physical deterioration Decay and natural wear and tear on a building

Price An individual estimate of value in terms of the accepted medium of exchange

Principle of anticipation Value may be a function of the present value of anticipated future returns

Principle of conformity The maximum value of real property found where there is a reasonable degree of homogeneity with all the standards of the area

Principle of contribution The value of a particular component determined by its contribution to value of the whole (also referred to as the principle of diminishing returns)

Reconciliation of value Process by which an appraiser gives consideration to indications of value derived from applying market, cost, and income approaches to value to arrive at final determination of value

Sales comparison approach A comparison of the property being appraised to similar properties that have been sold recently in the area

Scarcity One of the characteristics of value

Substitution principle A thing cannot be worth more than the cost of replacement

Transferability The ability or right to transfer a property

Unit-in-place method The use of basic units of measurement such as square feet, linear or cubic feet, number of doors or plumbing drains, etc., to estimate total construction cost new

Utility The power of a good to render a service or fill a need

Value The utility of a particular object; the power of purchasing other goods which possession of an object conveys

---

QUESTIONS FOR REVIEW

1. Define appraisal.
2. What is the economist's concept of value?
3. Distinguish between value and price.
4. How can value remain the same while prices change?
5. How are neighborhood characteristics determined?
6. How is it possible that proximity to schools can affect the value of a parcel of real property in a certain neighborhood?
7. What are the three approaches to appraising?
8. You are given two similar buildings to appraise. One is 4 years old and the other 25 years old. In attempting to arrive at an estimate of value, which approach would be most appropriate to use in each case?
9. Explain what is meant by the cost approach in residential appraising.
10. Explain the three factors that cause depreciation.
11. Why should one be aware of changes in a district?
12. Show how you would determine value by the sales comparison approach.
13. What are the criticisms of using a gross monthly multiplier in the income approach in obtaining an estimate of value?

PROBLEMS AND ACTIVITIES

1. Each of the following statements represents either (1) physical depreciation or deterioration, (2) functional obsolescence, or (3) external de-

preciation or obsolescence. Indicate the type of depreciation represented and comment.

a. Shingles on the roof are curled and rotted from the weather.
b. A residential property is next to a factory built in the neighborhood because of a lack of proper zoning regulations.
c. The property is an old house in a neighborhood crowded with rooming houses.
d. The property is a waterfront warehouse; the floor has a slant because the piles supporting it are rotting away.
e. A home contains old-fashioned bathroom fixtures and wainscoting on the kitchen walls.
f. A California-type (Spanish) bungalow is located in a neighborhood predominantly containing ranch-style homes.

2. Section 1027 (i) of the FHA *Underwriting Manual* lists the following sources of error in valuing property. Comment on each showing how it is true.

a. Misconception of the objective and purpose for which the valuation is made.
b. Lack of judgment and experience.
c. Haste and carelessness.
d. Inadequate data or data of poor quality.
e. Incorrect interpretation of data.
f. Incorrect method of valuation.
g. Faulty application of correct method.
h. Influence on valuator.

3. Two years ago you appraised a home with an effective age of six years, and you depreciated it at 12 percent. You are now called upon to appraise the same house. You obtain new cost figures, new comparable sales figures, and depreciate it at 16 percent, having determined the effective age from your old files. Can you justify this? Why or why not?

4. The subject property has 2,000 square feet of living space. Using sales data provided, estimate the value of the property based on:

a. average value per square foot.
b. judgment after preparing a scatter diagram, and
c. using the Decision Assistant Bivariate Linear Regression Model. (*Note:* The independent variable is square feet.)

Comparable Data

PRICE	SQ. FT.	PRICE	SQ. FT.
$ 97,000	1,942	$111,910	1,805
111,800	2,150	116,580	2,010
89,925	1,635	95,880	1,880
88,004	1,796	103,950	1,925
111,000	1,850	72,000	1,600

19

APPRAISING INCOME PROPERTY

KEY TERMS

Band of investments technique	**Equity residual technique**
Building residual technique	**Land residual technique**
Capitalization rate	**Mortgage residual technique**
Comparable sales	**Probable stable net operating income**
Contract rent	**Recapture**
Direct capitalization	**Replacement reserves**
Economic rent	**Residual techniques**
Effective gross income multiplier (EGIM)	**Summation method**

The appraisal of real estate involves three fundamental approaches to value: *market, cost,* and *income.* Depending on the type of property being appraised, the weight assigned to the methods varies. For example, the greatest emphasis is placed on the market approach to value in appraising residential property. The cost approach is most useful for valuing unique or special purpose buildings. The greatest reliance is placed on the income approach to value when appraising income-producing investments. This chapter will emphasize the determination of value based on a property's current and future expected income.

OWNER'S STATEMENT

Initially, the appraiser will receive the owner's statement of income and expense for the subject property. In all probability, this statement will contain inaccuracies, omissions, and understatements as well as items that should be excluded altogether.

The appraiser's first responsibility is to "reconstruct" this information to provide an estimate of **probable stable net operating income.** Net Operating Income describes a particular number and is not to be changed. For purposes of discussing the validation of revenue and expenses and reconstruction of the operating statement, assume the appraiser is given the operating statement shown in Exhibit 19-1.

Exhibit 19-1 Owner's Income Statement

Gross Annual Income		$34,158
Expenses		
Real property taxes	$4,747	
Personal property taxes	97	
Insurance	424	
Management	1,279	
Utilities	2,439	
Repairs and maintenance	2,466	
Legal	264	
Trash removal	237	
Supplies	83	
Advertising	93	
Extermination services	91	
Automobile	207	
Miscellaneous	38	
Total Expenses		12,465
Net Income Without Reserve for Expenses		$21,693

Gross Income

Gross income is also referred to as gross potential income or gross scheduled income and may be defined as the maximum income the property may generate under conditions of full occupancy with rents at the prevailing market level as of the date of the appraisal.

The appraiser observes the owner's gross annual rent (income) was $34,158. This is the contract rent. **Contract rent** is the rent collected either by written or oral lease. This differs from **economic rent,** which is the fair market rent at the time of appraisal. The need to appraise at the economic rent can be seen by means of an exaggerated illustration. Suppose you own a building on which the fair market rent could net you $20,000 a year. However, you have a friend you wish to help, so you rent the property at a rate which nets you $5,000 per year. Obviously, it is absurd to appraise the property at the contract rent of $5,000 per year: it must be appraised at the economic rent, or $20,000 per year.

Similarly, the present property owner may have permitted rents to fall below the prevailing market rents in order to minimize turnover and losses from vacancies. Nevertheless, a property should be appraised based on market level rents with provision for normal vacancy and collection losses. In this example, the appraiser found, from a comparison of similar apartment rents, that the economic rent was $38,700.

Vacancy and Collection Losses

The present owner reports no vacancy or collection losses and, in fact, may have had none. Regardless, the appraiser points out that normal management seeking market level economic rents will experience some losses from normal turnover of tenants and "skips," who fail to pay rent or must be evicted. Vacancy and collection losses may vary from 2 percent in a tight rental housing market to as high as 10 to 12 percent in periods of severe overbuilding. The tendency is to use a "normalized" amount of 4 to 6 percent to estimate rental losses. The exact amount should be based on local conditions.

Other Income

There may be income that is not reported on an owner's financial statements. The appraiser should estimate the potential income from garage rents, vending machines, and coin-operated washers and dryers, as well as entertainment centers in larger apartment complexes.

In this example, the appraiser observed pay washers and dryers in the building. On questioning, the owner revealed that income from the laundry appliances came to $1,192. The owner stoutly argued that this was none of the Internal Revenue Service's business. The appraiser noted that perhaps this was so, but it was indeed the appraiser's business.

Gross Operating Income

Gross operating income includes all potential income from operation of the property after deducting estimated vacancy and collection losses.

Operating Expenses

Operating expenses include all the necessary expenditures to maintain the property and permit operation at a level which will continue to produce the gross operating income previously estimated. The appraiser is responsible for ensuring that all costs necessary for building operation are included and the independent estimates or verification of each cost has been obtained.

Although any cost may be omitted or understated in order to increase net operating income, expenses typically omitted are management fees and reserves for replacement.

Management Fees. Professional management companies generally charge a percentage of gross operating income for their services. Fees may vary from 3 to 6 percent depending on the size of the property. This is an appropriate charge whether management services are provided by the owner or an outside firm. Services provided include tenant qualification, rent collections, unlawful detainer actions, accounting services, and provision for repairs and maintenance.

Resident manager fees provide for on-site showing of apartments and minor repairs, and may include rent collection. Costs vary from providing a free apartment in smaller buildings to including salaries and taxes for a full-time staff in the largest rental complexes.

The costs of management are often excluded by owners in determining net operating income. They argue that there is no cost because they provide management services for themselves. This is conceptually incorrect. The measure of net operating income is a profit returned to potential buyers for their ownership of the building were it free and clear of all debt. It is a measure of the return on capital invested and represents compensation for the risks of ownership.

Should owners provide management services for themselves, they deserve to be compensated for their effort at the same level as professional and/or resident managers. Self-provided management services do not increase profitability returns on invested capital or value of the property.

Reverve for Replacement. In any income property there are items that need to be replaced periodically. In an apartment, short-lived assets such as curtains, carpets, garbage disposals, bathroom fans, stoves, refrigerators, window air-conditioners, and furniture (if furnished) wear out quickly. The average life or replacement period for these items is approximately seven years.

Consequently, the expense of replacing these items is a hidden cost of a building's operation. The knowledgeable appraiser estimates the cost of replacement, the remaining useful life, and provides an annual charge against operations to reflect the replacement cost of these items at the end of their useful life. For example, to calculate the cost for **replacement reserves:**

$$\frac{\text{Replacement cost}}{\text{Remaining useful life}} = \frac{\$13{,}314}{7\text{ years}} = \begin{matrix}\$1{,}902\text{ annual}\\ \text{replacement reserve}\end{matrix}$$

Other Expenses

The following changes in the owner's expense statement were also made for the reasons stated.

The management service included minor repairs, lawn care and snow removal, and showing and renting the apartments. For these services, a two-bedroom apartment was furnished to the manager. Because rent for other units was raised to levels of economic rent, the appraiser also raised this cost to $1,800 per year.

Because of unusual maintenance (much painting) the previous year, the appraiser felt this figure should be reduced to $855 in the year of the appraisement. And because the legal services for $264 as shown by the owner seemed high, the appraiser reduced this amount to $200.

The $207 for use of the owner's automobile charged by the owner against the property was deleted by the appraiser.

No allowance was made for replacement reserves by the owner. By itemizing each item (such as refrigerators, carpets, stoves, etc.) and calculating their cost of replacement and remaining economic life, reserves were calculated on a straight-line basis and the total reserves cost was determined to be $1,902.

The appraiser then prepared a reconstructed income and expense statement as shown in Exhibit 19-2.

DIRECT CAPITALIZATION

Once having determined probable stable net operating income, the appraiser wishes to convert the future expected income stream into value. To do so the appraiser employs a discounting process. The question to be answered is What is the present worth of a future income stream for a fee simple estate?

The **direct capitalization** formula is

$$\text{Value} = \frac{\text{Net operating income}}{\text{Capitalization rate}}$$

Net operating income was determined by reconstructing the owner's income statement and was found to be $24,948. Determination of the appropriate **capitalization rate** is considerably more difficult.

Exhibit 19-2 Reconstructed Owner's Expense Statement

Potential Gross Income		$38,700
Less 5% vacancy and collection loss		1,935
Effective Gross Income		36,765
Other income (washers and dryers)		1,192
Gross Operating Income		37,957
Expenses		
Real estate taxes	$ 4,750	
Personal property taxes	97	
Insurance	424	
Management	1,800	
Utilities	2,439	
Repairs and maintenance	855	
Legal	200	
Trash removal	237	
Supplies	83	
Advertising	93	
Extermination services	91	
Miscellaneous	38	
Total	11,107	
Replacement Reserves	1,902	
Total Expense		13,009
Net Operating Income		$24,948

First, it is necessary to recognize that at any given time there are multiple rates of interest. Each rate, whether for mortgage loans, certificates of deposit, savings accounts, or car loans, represents the price of capital or the rental the investor (lender) expects to receive for the use of his or her money. These rates of interest do not include an amount for recapture or return of the initial capital investment.

Suppose the appropriate capitalization rate for real estate investments is 11 percent. Given this information and annual net operating income of $24,948, what is the value of the income stream?

Using the direct capitalization formula, the value would be $226,800.

$$\text{Value} = \frac{\text{Net operating income}}{\text{Capitalization rate}} = \frac{\$24{,}948}{.11} = \$226{,}800$$

Why would an individual not pay more than $226,800 for an income stream of $24,948? In the selection of the capitalization rate, it is presumed that if the property cannot be purchased to yield an 11 percent return, there is an alternative real estate investment which will. Therefore, the opportunity cost or capitalization rate is 11 percent.

CAPITALIZATION RATE

One of the most important and, likewise, one of the most difficult problems facing the income property appraiser is the selection of the proper rate of return (interest rate or discount rate). An error of even 1 percent in either direction can result in a serious miscalculation of value. In the problem given above, for example, the interest or discount rate was 11 percent and the net income as $24,948. Therefore, the top price of the asset was determined to be $226,800. Suppose the appraiser erroneously selected 10 percent as the interest rate. Then:

$$V = \frac{\$24{,}948}{.10}$$

$$V = \$249{,}480$$

In the problem above, the lowering of the interest rate by 1 percent resulted in an increase in value of $22,680, or an error of 10 percent. A *lowering* of the interest or discount rate, then, will *raise* the estimated value of the property, in this case from $226,800 to $249,480.

Suppose the error in the selection of the interest or discount rate was 1 percent in the other direction—12 percent was chosen instead of 11 percent. Then:

$$V = \frac{\$24{,}948}{.12}$$

$$V = \$207{,}900$$

Thus it can be seen, if the interest rate was *raised* incorrectly, the estimated value of the property would be *lowered.*

How, then, does one determine the capitalization rate?

Summation Method

The **summation method** is an explict recognition that an investor's capital should realize some return because of the various risks undertaken by the investor. Although it may be used to illustrate the components of the capitalization rate, it is not recommended as a means of determining a capitalization rate. The components of the capitalization rate include:

1. The *safe rate:* the rate usually paid by savings banks or on long-term government bonds.
2. The *rate for risk:* the amount to be paid to the investor for any risk of loss investor is taking.
3. The *rate for nonliquidity:* the rate given to the investor because of the nonliquidity of real estate.
4. *The rate for burden of management:* the rate given to compensate the investor for the cost of managing the investment. This is a different fee from the fee paid for managing the property.

The summary of these factors equals the capitalization or discount rate:

Safe rate	7 percent
Rate for risk	1
Rate for nonliquidity	1
Rate for burden of management	1
Discount rate	10 percent

The discussion above has dealt with the rate of return *on* capital or discount rate. In any investment there must be both a return *on* capital and a return *of* capital.

A capitalization rate is determined which includes the discount rate plus an allowance for **recapture** of the initial investment. To understand the basis for recapture, depreciation must be considered.

Depreciation

The depreciation affecting investment property is the same as the depreciation affecting residential properties; namely, physical deterioration, functional obsolescence, and external obsolescence. The combination of these three factors converted into a percentage constitutes the annual rate of depreciation. Basically, these rates are determined by the type of building and by the quality of the construction of the building. For example, an apartment of good construction may have a useful life of 50 years, and the normal rate of straight-line depreciation would be 2 percent per year. However, functional and external obsolescence may add to that figure. In the final analysis, the rate of depreciation is determined by the type of construction, the condition of the building, and the factors that create the functional and external obsolescence.

Since the land itself does not usually depreciate, what is done with the figure that has been determined as the rate of depreciation for the building? In income appraising, the rate of depreciation is added to the discount rate, the rate that is applied to income applicable to the improvements to determine the final worth of the improvements. The depreciation rate is added to the discount rate to provide for recapture of capital.

To repeat, every investor must think of two things. First, a return *of* the capital, and secondly, a return *on* the capital. For example, if one deposits $10,000 in a savings and loan association that pays a dividend rate of 5 percent, one certainly should be able to anticipate $500 per year return *on* the capital and the return *of* the $10,000 capital on demand.

It is basically no different with a real estate investment. *But* because improvements on real property depreciate and land does not, the capitalization rate applied on the improvements is generally greater than the land capitalization rate.

In direct capitalization, no explict attempt is made to determine the recapture rate. Both "return on" and "recovery of" capital are present when the overall capitalization rate is derived from similar properties recently sold in the market.

SELECTING THE CAPITALIZATION RATE

There are three principal means of deriving an overall capitalization rate and each will be briefly discussed in turn. These techniques are (1) band of investments, (2) comparable sales, and (3) gross income multipliers.[1]

Band of Investments Technique, Mortgage and Equity Components

In the **band of investments technique,** interest rates are weighted by their relative importance to total property value. The underlying assumption is that these rates can be determined from the investments market.

The return on the equity interest in a property must be sufficiently high to compensate the investor for the risks and illiquidity of a real estate investment. This means the return on equity is equal to or higher than

[1]One additional technique for deriving the overall capitalization rate is the debt service coverage formula.

alternative equity investment with similar perceived risks. If this were not the case, capital would be attracted to the alternative investment rather than real estate.

The rate for mortgages is the ratio of the annual payment for principal and interest to the initial principal amount of the mortgage debt. This rate is called the mortgage constant (also known as the Installment to Amortize in Appendix C, column 6). The mortgage constant provides for payment of both principal and interest. The rate for mortgages is *not* the interest rate stated in the mortgage.

Because of variation in risk, particularly the risk of loss, the highest rates of return go to equity, then second mortgages; the lowest risk and return applies to first mortgages. For example, suppose equity holders expect to receive a 12 percent return on their investment; the second mortgagee, 10 percent with a 10-year amortization period; and the first mortgagee, 9 percent with a 25-year loan amortization.

The annual constant for the second mortgage is 15.86 percent, and for the first mortgage, 10.07 percent (see Appendix C, column 6). By further assuming that equity represents 20 percent of property value and the second and first mortgages 10 and 70 percent, respectively, the capitalization rate may be calculated to be 11.04 percent as shown in Table 19-1.

Comparable Sales

As the name implies, the overall capitalization rate may be derived from analysis of **comparable sales.** In fact, this technique is preferred when there is adequate information on income, financing, and price of similar properties.

Deriving the capitalization rate from similar sales is computationally simple: net operating income is divided by the price. This simplicity, however, is deceiving. The appraiser must be sure that:

1. Net operating income has been calculated in the same way for each property. For example, has the reserve for replacement been included in each case?

Table 19-1 Capitalization Rate Under Band of Investments Technique

PROPERTY INTEREST	PERCENT OF TOTAL PROPERTY VALUE		INTEREST	WEIGHTED INTEREST
Equity (highest risk)	20	×	12.00%	2.40%
Second mortgage (intermediate risk)	10	×	15.86%	1.59%
First mortgage (lowest risk)	70	×	10.07%	7.05%
			Capitalization rate	11.04%

2. Owner financing or assumption of preexisting mortgages with below-market interest rates has not biased the price paid.
3. Adjustments have been made for any differences between comparables and the subject property that would affect the capitalization rate; for example, holding periods, tax benefits, appreciation, and market conditions at the time of sale or appraisal.

When caution has been observed and the appraiser is sure all factors affecting comparable capitalization rates have been accounted for, this approach will yield a market-derived indication of the capitalization rate and will provide a reliable estimate of the value of income.

Effective Gross Income Multipliers

To derive the overall capitalization rate from the **effective gross income multipler (EGIM),** the appraiser must obtain information regarding sales price, potential gross income, and vacancy/collection losses from comparable sales. From this information, the EGIM may be calculated as follows:

$$\frac{\text{Sales price}}{\text{Potential gross income} - \text{vacancy/collection losses}} = \text{Effective gross income multiplier}$$

Additionally, the appraiser must know the operating expense ratio for similar properties in the area. This information may be obtained from surveys such as the *Annual Income/Expense Analysis* published by the Institute of Real Estate Management. The operating expense ratio is derived by dividing operating expenses by effective gross income.

The EGIM technique is most often used when specific operating costs for comparable properties are unavailable. Information on operating costs for various types of buildings, including apartments, office buildings, and condominiums, in over 100 metropolitan areas may be obtained from the Institute of Real Estate Management.[2] Once obtained, the operating expense ratio may be combined with the effective gross income multiplier to determine the overall capitalization rate, as follows:

$$\frac{\text{Operating expense ratio}}{\text{EGIM}} = \text{Overall capitalization rate}$$

RESIDUAL TECHNIQUES

Residual techniques are a variation of the direct capitalization approach to value. In essence, they provide a means for valuing a component part of

[2]Institute of Real Estate Management of the NATIONAL ASSOCIATION OF REALTORS®, 430 North Michigan Avenue, Chicago, IL 60611-4087.

real estate when the value of the other component is known. The four techniques are (1) the building residual technique, (2) the land residual technique, (3) the equity residual technique, and (4) the mortgage residual technique.

Building Residual Technique

In the **building residual technique,** a value is assigned to the land, and a fair rate of return is attributed to it. This sum is deducted from the total net income and the balance is capitalized to determine the value of the building. The land value is then added to the value of the building to give a final determination of value.

To apply the building residual technique, the appraiser must know the value of the land and the net operating income as well as capitalization rates for land and buildings.

Assume the appraiser who reconstructed the income statement at the beginning of the chapter determines by a market data analysis that the land is worth $45,000, the land capitalization rate is 9 percent, and the building capitalization rate is 12 percent. The net operating income of $24,948 is to be "split" between the land and the building. The value of the land and building may be determined as shown below.

Net operating income	$ 24,948
Earned by the land ($45,000 × .09)	(4,050)
Building income	$ 20,898
Value of the building ($20,898 ÷ .12)	$174,150
Land value	45,000
Estimated property value	$219,150

Land Residual Technique

The **land residual technique** is the reverse of that employed in the building residual method. Rather than allocate income to the land and the residual to the building, this approach to value requires the appraiser to allocate income to the building and the residual to the land.

This technique is used when the appraiser is unable to obtain comparative data on the value of land. For example, in many downtown areas there have been no recent sales of vacant land; hence, no means of ascertaining value via comparable sales. If this be the case and the land value is unknown, the value of the structure must be estimated by determining the cost to build a new or proposed building. Note that the land residual technique is not suited to use with older buildings whose cost to reproduce new is substantially greater than the existing structure's contribution to total value. For example, assume the cost to reproduce a new building is $168,000, net operating income is $24,948, and the land and building capitalization rates are 9 and 12 percent, respectively. Value may be estimated as follows:

Net operating income	$ 24,948
Earned by the building ($168,000 × .12)	(20,160)
Land income	$ 4,788
Value of the land ($4,788 ÷ .09)	$ 53,200
Building value	168,000
Estimated property value	$221,200

Equity Residual Technique

The **equity residual technique** is useful when appraising an equity interest in a property subject to an existing mortgage. The appraiser must know the amount of the mortgage, its interest rate, and amortization period in order to determine the mortgage constant. In lieu of the mortgage constant, the annual principal and interest payment are sufficient. Given an equity capitalization rate of 13 percent, a $145,000 mortgage for 25 years with 10 percent interest, and a mortgage constant of .10905, the property value may be estimated as follows:

Net operating income	$ 24,948
Mortgage ($145,000 × .10905)	(15,812)
Equity income	$ 9,136
Value of the equity ($9,136 ÷ .13)	$ 70,277
Mortgage	145,000
Estimated property value	$215,277

Mortgage Residual Technique

The **mortgage residual technique** is the reverse of the equity residual approach to value. In this case, the amount of equity (down payment) and the income (rate of return) necessary to attract equity (13 percent) are known. The question, given knowledge of the mortgage constant (.10905) required by lenders, is how much debt may be acquired with the income available for debt service? When the mortgage debt is added, equity property value may be estimated as follows:

Net operating income	$ 24,948
Equity income ($50,000 × .13)	(6,500)
Income for debt service	$ 18,448
Mortgage ($18,448 ÷ .10905)	$169,170
Equity	50,000
Estimated property value	$219,170

Appraising Leasehold Interests

There are two parties in a lease, the lessor and the lessee. The lessor is entitled to rent during the term of the lease and to the reversion at the expiration of the term. The lessee is entitled to possession and to the profits from the property. The landlord's interest is called the leased fee. The tenant's interest is called the leasehold interest or leasehold estate.

Mathematically, the value of the leased fee is determined by determining the present value of the income stream plus the value of the reversion. For example, assume a 21-year lease at a net income to the lessor of $10,000 per annum with 10 years remaining on the lease. The present value of the reversion is assumed to be $100,000. The lessor dies and the appraiser is called upon to appraise the value of the leased fee for inheritance purposes. The capitalization rate is determined to be 10 percent. Then:

Value of leased fee = Present value of income stream + present value of reversion
V = $10,000 × 6.144 (PV of $1 per period—Appendix C) + $100,000 due in 10 years × .385 (PV of Reversion of 1—Appendix C)
V of leased fee = $99,940 (or approximately $100,000)

The above example deals with the value of the lessor's interest (the leased fee). It could be that the tenant may have a valuable and appraisable interest in the lease. Suppose the contract rent and economic rent are unequal. Recall that the *contract rent* is the amount paid under the terms of the lease and the *economic rent* is the fair market rent. Assuming that the tenant is paying $10,000 per annum contract rent with ten years remaining on the lease, the rate is 10 percent. Assume that the economic rent for similar properties is $15,000 per annum. The leasehold interest, or leasehold estate, has a $5,000 bonanza ($15,000 – $10,000 = $5,000) for ten years. What is the value of the leasehold estate? It is the present worth of the $5,000 per year savings. Thus:

V = $5,000 for 10 years at 10% × 6.144 (Appendix C)
V = $30,144

Of course, as the lease nears the end of the term, the value decreases.

APPRAISAL REPORTS

Appraisal reports generally consist of two types:

1. *Form reports,* such as the FHLMC/FNMA form, are used mainly by savings and loan associations and mutual savings banks. Other lending institutions employ similar forms of their own construction. Form reports follow the appraisal process quite logically evaluating
   a. Neighborhood.
   b. Site.
   c. Improvements.
   d. Interior finish and equipment.
   e. Property rating.
   f. Cost approach.
   g. Market analysis.
   h. Income approach (if applicable).

   Most important, too, is the Certification and Statement of Limitating Conditions.
2. *Narrative reports* are usually prepared by members of professional societies (named in the next section) for more expensive properties, those involved in condemnation proceedings, and—increasingly—properties involved in divorce proceedings.

   The narrative report recommended by the American Institute of Real Estate Appraisers consists of four basic sections:
   a. Introductory material.
   b. Descriptive information.
   c. Analytical processes.
   d. Judgment matters and conclusions.

   Exhibit 19-3 presents an outline for a narrative appraisal report. The assumptions and limiting conditions are the same as those in the residential appraisal (see Exhibit 18-2).

APPRAISAL SOCIETIES

Regardless of state licensing requirements, persons interested in genuine professionalism take training and education courses through various trade organizations such as:

The American Institute of Real Estate Appraisal
The Society of Real Estate Appraisers
The International Right of Way Association
The American Society of Farm Managers and Rural Appraisers
The National Association of Independent Fee Appraisers
The National Association of Assessing Officers
The American Society of Appraisers (in addition to real estate appraisals, some members appraise personal property, such as antiques, gems, etc.)

Training and experience qualifications can be rigorous—e.g., the MAI designation (Member of the American Institute of Real Estate Appraisal).

■ Exhibit 19-3 Table of Contents for a Complete Narrative Report

1. Letter of Transmittal
2. Summary of Important Data and Conclusions

A. *Introduction to the Report*

3. Purpose of the Appraisal
4. Definition of Value Concepts Used
5. Identification of the Property
6. Picture of the Property
7. Property Rights Appraised
8. Assumptions and Limiting Conditions
9. Qualifications of the Appraiser

B. *Pertinent Data*

10. City Description
    a. Historic (age of city, reasons for founding)
    b. Geographic (land forms, rivers, climate, water)
    c. Political (form of government, tax rates, planning, zoning)
    d. Social (population-age, composition, income, growth)
    e. Economic (employment, stability of economic activity, sources of income, diversity, wage rates, manufacturing)
11. Neighborhood Analysis
    a. Relation to Direction of City Growth
    b. Physical and Social Attractiveness
    c. Adequacy of Social, Civic, Commercial Centers
    d. Adequacy of Transportation and Rates
    e. Utilities and Services, Rates, Adequacy
    f. Level of Taxes and Assessments
    g. Number and Characteristics of Population
    h. Property Values and Trends in Values
    i. Protection Against Inharmonious Uses
    j. Maps of Area, Transportation, Major Traffic Arteries
12. Property Analysis
    a. The Site
        i. Size and Shape
        ii. Topography
        iii. Soil and Subsoil
        iv. Utilities
        v. Landscaping
        vi. Other Improvements
        vii. Plot Plan
    b. Buildings
        i. Use and Construction History
        ii. Construction Details
        iii. Floor Plans
        iv. Visual Analysis, Visual Appeal
        v. Mechanical Equipment
        vi. Condition Analysis
        vii. Classification for Use
        viii. Photographs

Exhibit 19-3 (concluded)

- c. Use Analysis
  - i. Zoning
  - ii. Deed Restrictions
  - iii. Assessed Value, Tax Rates, Tax Bills, Land and Buildings
  - iv. Highest and Best Use Conclusions

13. Data Analysis
  - a. Land Value
    - i. Comparable Sales
    - ii. Probable Value If Unimproved
    - iii. Probable Value of Land Improvements
    - iv. Value Estimate of Land
  - b. Cost Analysis
    - i. Sizes—Square feet or Cubic feet
    - ii. Cost Factors
    - iii. Cost Estimate—Land and Buildings
    - iv. Accrued Depreciation
  - c. Income Analysis
    - i. Gross Income
    - ii. Vacancy and Credit Loss
    - iii. Operating Expenses
    - iv. Reserves for Replacements
    - v. Allowances for Depreciation
    - vi. Fixed Expenses
    - vii. Net Income
    - viii. Capitalization Rate
    - ix. Capitalization Method, Value Estimate
  - d. Sales Comparisons
    - i. Relation to Subject Property
    - ii. Terms and Conditions of Comparable Sales
    - iii. Supply of and Demand for Comparable Properties
    - iv. Comparison with Subject Property
    - v. Conditions of the Sales Markets
    - vi. Value Estimate

14. Value Estimate Correlations
  - a. Correlation
    - i. Evaluation of the Data
    - ii. Consideration of the Typical Buyer and the Purpose of the Appraisal
  - b. Summary and Conclusion
    - i. Summary of Pertinent Data
    - ii. Review of Various Value Estimates
    - iii. Conclusion

Exhibits

A. Maps of the City and Area—Population Centers, Use, Occupancy
B. Economic Data Tables
C. Area Photographs
D. Leases and Other Pertinent Legal Items

GLOSSARY

Band of investments technique A method of selecting a capitalization rate by using the weighted average interest rates for first and second mortgages and equity

Building residual technique An appraisal technique in which a value is assigned to land and a fair rate of return attributed to it

Capitalization rate The sum of rates providing for a return on capital and a return of capital; the discount rate plus an allowance for recapture

Comparable sales Comparative analysis used to derive the capitalization rate

Contract rent Rents collected under a written or oral lease

Direct capitalization Process of determining value through dividing net operating income by the capitalization rate

Economic rent Fair market rent that would be realized at the date of appraisal

Effective gross income multiplier (EGIM) Derived from similar recent sales by dividing the sales price by potential gross income minus vacancy/collection losses to estimate property value

Equity residual technique An appraisal technique useful when appraising an equity interest in a property subject to an existing mortgage

Land residual technique An appraisal technique in which income is allocated to the land and the residual to the building

Mortgage residual technique An appraisal technique that is the reverse of the equity residual approach to value

Probable stable net income A revised income and expense statement prepared by an appraiser from an owner's income and expense statement

Recapture Recovery of initial investment

Replacement reserves Annual cost of replacing short-lived building assets such as carpets, drapes, furniture, garbage disposals, window air-conditioning units, etc.

Residual techniques Variation of direct capitalization approach to value; means of valuing one component of real estate, such as land and building or equity mortgage when the other component is known

Summation method Determining a capitalization rate by setting up component parts

QUESTIONS FOR REVIEW

1. How is net income figured in appraising income property?
2. In appraising income property, what is the relationship between income and the value of the property?
3. What is meant by the capitalization process?
4. Distinguish between the discount rate and the capitalization rate.
5. Why is the recapture rate added to the discount rate?
6. What may raise the rate of functional obsolescence?
7. How does an appraiser select the capitalization rate?
8. If one is unable to determine the comparative value of the land, how is the residual return process employed?

PROBLEMS AND ACTIVITIES

1. Using the income approach, determine the value of the following property:

Estimated annual gross income	$42,000
Vacancy loss 2.5 percent	?
Adjusted gross income	?
Other income (washing machines, etc.)	3,200
Effective gross income	?
Expenses	16,300
Net income before capital recapture	?

First mortgages are obtainable at 70 percent of value at a rate of 10 percent. Second mortgages are obtainable at 10 percent of value at a rate of 11 percent. Equity is at 20 percent of value and demands a 14 percent return. The value of the land and improvements (landscaping, etc.) is $170,300.

2. Some years ago, Stephen Smith rented a vacant lot to the Acme Oil Company, Inc. The lease was made for a term of 25 years at a rental that netted Smith $4,800 per year. Under the terms of the lease, the Acme Oil Company built a gasoline station and installed all the necessary equipment. The lease provides that Acme can remove both the station and equipment at the expiration of the lease if they desire to do so.

   Smith dies at the end of 9 years, and the executor of his estate finds it necessary to have Smith's interest appraised for purposes of settling the estate.

   You find that the land is now worth $60,000 and feel certain that it will be worth the same at the end of the term provided in the lease.

There is a good market for leased properties of this kind on a 9 percent net return.

Prepare an appraisal for the executor of the estate.

3. You are requested to estimate the market value of a 25-suite apartment house (including janitor suite) from data supplied based upon a comparison of the subject property with similar apartment houses. All the suites are three rooms. You visit the property, have an opportunity to talk with several tenants, inspect 5 suites, talk with the janitor, measure the building, and form an opinion as to cost, depreciation, and condition.

   The land is 50 feet by 100 feet, and by comparison you find it to be worth $30 per square foot. You estimate that a 10 percent return is appropriate for land and 13 percent for buildings.

   You then figure typical units as follows:

   Gross income—$100 per room per month
   Vacancy and credit loss—5 percent
   Taxes—actual expense $3,260 (checked at courthouse)
   Insurance—calculated at 1 percent of effective gross income
   Management—5 percent of effective gross income
   Heating—$22 per room per year
   Electric and gas—$27 per suite (tenants are metered; this is for halls, laundry, and dryers)
   Water—$45 per suite per year
   Janitor—$3,600 per year plus one suite
   Supplies, hauling, miscellaneous—$25 per month
   Decoration—two-thirds of one months rent
   Maintenance and repairs—one-half of one months rent
   Stoves, furnished—$600 each, 12-year life
   Refrigerators, furnished—$620 each, 12-year life
   Payments on first mortgage—$2,400 per month at 12 percent

   Prepare an income and expense statement based on the information given above. Analyze it and provide an indication of value by using the building residual land.

PART SIX

Property Ownership

20

HOME OWNERSHIP

KEY TERMS

Closing
Cooperative
Cooperator
Declaration
Economic obsolescence
Equal Credit Opportunity Act
Fair Credit Reporting Act
Interest rate risk
Master deed
Mobile home
Prefabricated homes
Red-lining
Site-built single-family home
Time-sharing

A large portion of the nation's $10 trillion in assets is in the hands of America's 57 million homeowners. They own most of the nation's housing, valued at $2.7 trillion, which represents 27 percent of total wealth in the United States.

Historically, the concept of "free men and women" related to the ownership of land. Dreams of land and a home inspired great migrations, revolutions, and portions of our Bill of Rights. A house—separate, secure, comfortable, occupied by family—is a way of life and part of the American dream.

A survey by *Professional Builder* magazine in 1985 revealed that when fulfilling their dream of home ownership, homebuyers looked first for lots of storage space. Exhibit 20-1 presents the changing character of the American home. Since 1978, new homes have become bigger and have more amenities.

The American life-style, and consequently the character of housing, however, is undergoing dramatic change. More and more families of the future will live in condominiums or cooperative housing; some buyers will purchase their homes while leasing the land beneath; others will have 75 percent ownership in their homes, while investors own the balance. Many people will not be able to afford to purchase a home, and those fortunate enough to be buyers will own smaller homes. These changes, and many others, essentially result from increased costs of land, material, labor, and borrowing.

Whatever the future holds, there is one thing which remains certain: there is no other place in the world where homes are as comfortable and convenient as they are here in the United States.

Exhibit 20-1 Selected Characteristics of Newly Completed Housing Units

		1978	1984	1985	1986	1987	1988
Single-Family	Median square feet	1655	1605	1605	1660	1755	1815
	Average square feet	1755	1708	1785	1825	1905	1995
Percent with:	Central air	58	71	70	69	71	75
	More than 2 baths	25	28	29	33	39	42
	4 bedrooms or more	24	18	18	20	23	26
	1 fireplace or more	64	59	59	62	62	65
	Gas heating fuel	37	45	44	47	52	54
	Garage: 2+ cars	62	56	55	60	65	66
Multifamily	Median square feet	863	871	882	876	620	935
	Average square feet	902	914	922	911	980	990
Percent with:	Air conditioning	79	89	88	88	86	84
	2 baths or more	20	35	37	36	39	41
	2 bedrooms	49	54	54	53	54	55
	3 or more bedrooms	9	9	7	7	7	8

SOURCE: Bureau of the Census.

HOUSING TRENDS

Uncertain economic conditions, changing values, high energy costs, and near record interest rates are a few of the factors affecting housing and home ownership. Most serious, perhaps, is how some of these elements have combined to push housing costs to record highs.

Affordability

Although the goal of many, custom or site-built single-family homes are systematically being priced out of reach. Increasing environmental concerns, higher materials costs, and spiraling land values have increased the median sales price of site-built homes over 380 percent since 1970.

Adding to higher single-family home costs are mortgage interest rates of 9 to 11 percent. Purchase of a median price site-built home requires approximately $20,000 cash for down payment and closing costs. Excluding taxes, insurance, and maintenance costs, the payment for principal and interest can be expected to range between $575 to $680 per month.

Additionally, many new mortgages have a variable interest rate feature that significantly increases homeowner risk of default due to future increased principal and interest payments. The combined effect of increased home prices and higher mortgage interest rates has pushed housing costs up 320 percent since 1970.

Furthermore, lenders generally require that borrowers meet safe loan guidelines. To qualify for the necessary mortgage loan on an average site-built home requires an annual income of approximately $27,000 to $33,000. As home prices increase, down payment, principal and interest payments, taxes, insurance, and maintenance costs increase proportionately.

In other words, at a time when median family income is $33,600 per year, the average family can barely afford to buy the average home. In 1970 *median income* was 159 percent of the income necessary to purchase a median price home. In 1989, a $33,600 median income represents 124 percent of the income needed to buy a median price home. First-time home buyers under age 30 with incomes up to $32,000 are most adversely affected. In short, when costs increase faster than income, affordability declines. Exhibit 20-2 graphically demonstrates the dilemma of housing costs and affordability.

The affordability crisis is not evenly distributed throughout the United States. As of the first quarter of 1989, a significant number of metropolitan areas had existing median home prices above $100,000 (see Exhibit 20-3). In these communities, affordability is a tremendous problem and contributes to the plight of the homeless.

The magnitude of the problem is demonstrated when we consider the plight of renter households in the 25- to 34-year-old group. In 1986, of the 11.1 million households in this group only 11.5 percent or 1.3 million had the cash to make a down payment on a typical starter home. Reducing the down payment from 20 to 10 percent and lowering interest rates 1.5 percentage points would allow another 670,000 in the 25- to 34-year-old age group to purchase starter homes.[1]

Environmental Impact

Adding to the cost spiral is increasing concern with the environmental and aesthetic impact of housing. Greenbelts, preservation of unique geographic features, environmental impact studies, restrictions on wells and septic systems, although desirable, add to the cost of subdividing and developing areas for new residential construction.

Less desirable are the exclusionary zoning tactics that result in *de facto* segregation. Moratoriums on building permits, high building cost covenants, and lack of "acceptable" sites for inexpensive housing push total housing costs higher for all economic classes.

---

[1]Twin Cities Housing Council, "New Housing Update" (August, 1989).

Exhibit 20-2 Changes in Housing Costs, Income, and Affordability, 1970–1988

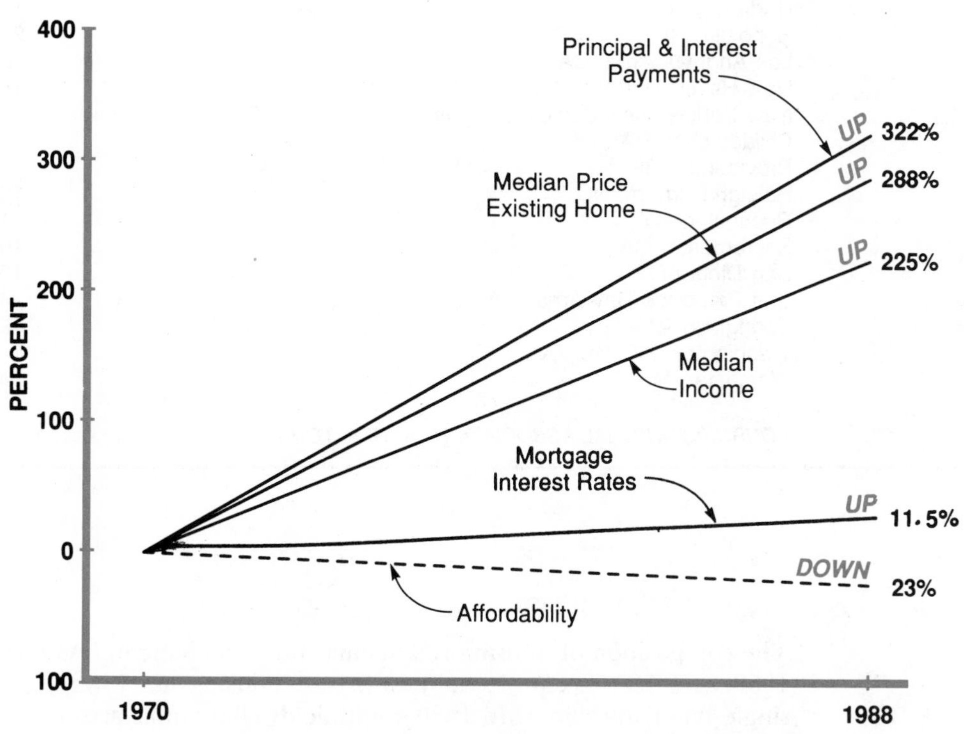

SOURCE: Prepared by the authors from data obtained from the NATIONAL ASSOCIATION OF REALTORS®, U.S. Department of Commerce, and Federal Home Loan Bank Board.

Inclusionary Zoning

Planning boards withhold zoning or development approval to force construction of low- or moderate-cost housing. Opponents of this argue that more affordable units could be produced by the private sector if greater density were permitted. Additionally, any cost savings produced for the buyers of lower cost housing is an indirect tax and results in higher cost for the nonsubsidized housing units. Inclusionary zoning was discussed in detail in Chapter 2.

Exhibit 20-3 Metropolitan Areas—Median Home Prices Greater Than $100,000, First Quarter 1989

Albany/Schenectady/Troy, NY	$102,100
Orange County, CA	237,800
Boston, MA	117,000
Hartford, CT	165,500
Honolulu, HI	245,000
Los Angeles Area, CA	201,000
New Haven/Meridian, CT	166,700
New York/N. New Jersey, Long Island, NY, NJ, CT	179,700
Philadelphia, PA	104,700
Providence, RI	128,800
Raleigh/Durham, NC	102,000
Rochester, NY	116,100
Sacramento, CA	100,300
San Diego, CA	163,900
San Francisco Bay Area, CA	243,900
Springfield, MA	124,400
Washington, DC/MD/VA	143,700
Worcester, MA	146,800

SOURCE: NATIONAL ASSOCIATION OF REALTORS®.

Housing Composition

The composition of housing is dynamic and ever changing. As recently as 1959, over 70 percent of total new private housing starts were traditional single-family dwellings. In 1980, multiple dwelling units accounted for 31 percent of new housing units constructed. By 1982, in response to the affordability crisis, 26 percent of new single-family homes were prefabricated or mobile homes, commonly called manufactured housing. In 1987, 27 percent of multifamily housing starts were condominiums.

Housing economists predict that by 2005, 50 percent of the U.S. population will live in multifamily units of some type. In comparison, approximately 90 percent of the world's population lives in some form of multifamily housing.

Similarly, homes continue to change in size in response to changing family size, increased divorce rates, and cost. From large Victorian homes of the 1900s, housing size decreased to a median of 900 square feet in 1950. Since 1950, the average size increased to 1,995 square feet.

Interestingly enough, experts forecast an end to the affordability problem as the baby boom generation ages. As baby boomers wish to sell their starter homes and move to larger, more expensive homes, it is expected that the "baby bust" generation, born between 1966 and 1976, will have a surplus of smaller properties from which to choose. However, as the baby boomers reach retirement age beginning in 2011, there will be a surplus of larger homes and a shortage of housing for the elderly. Technology, population, age, and general economic conditions interact to affect housing composition.

Government Participation

The continued position of the federal government in housing is uncertain. Government support for housing programs will continue, but reduced federal budget proposals for the Department of Housing and Urban Development indicate a reduced role for government in housing.

State and municipal governments, however, are playing expanded roles in providing financial assistance for home buyers. In the late 1970s, cities began to sell tax-free municipal mortgage bonds. Monies received are used to provide home mortgages at a below market rate of interest. The future of these programs is also uncertain. A summary of state housing finance programs was presented in Chapter 13.

Housing Trust Funds

In response to the decline of federal housing programs, states and municipalities have created housing trust funds to help provide housing for low- to moderate-income families.

Monies have been variously provided by real estate transfer taxes, broker interest-bearing trust accounts for deposits of less than $5,000, general tax revenues, and developer profits from the sales of moderate-priced housing. In the latter case, developers were granted permission to construct additional housing units in exchange for agreeing to construct and maintain moderate-priced housing for ten years.

Trust funds nationwide raised more than $300 million in 1987 and built or rehabilitated 8,000 housing units. In the absence of necessary federal housing programs, the role of housing trust funds can be expected to grow.

RENTING VERSUS BUYING

Should you rent or buy a home? Although the decision is personal, consideration should be given to family finances, size, and preferences. There are advantages and disadvantages to renting or buying that should also be considered before making such an important decision.

Reasons for Renting

Availability of Services. A maximum of service with a minimum of responsibility is an attractive feature of renting. Where else but in a rental complex will the average person have use of a private swimming pool, tennis courts, clubhouse, and party room? In the largest and most modern facilities, there may even be a golf course, lake, security guards, and a social director to assure tenants' well-being. In short, amenities available in varying degrees to renters are, most often, too costly for homeowners.

Maximum Flexibility. For individuals expecting frequent job transfers, for those whose housing needs are uncertain, and for those who need time to learn more about different residential areas in an unfamiliar city, renting permits easier and more frequent moves. In the event of illness, loss of employment, or an addition to the family, a smaller or larger unit may be obtained quickly.

The lease or rental agreement may be negotiated for a three- to twelve-month period. To meet individual needs for flexibility, some landlords are willing to accept tenants on a month-to-month basis.

Minimum Responsibility. When renting, you can take a weekend trip, travel, and vacation with the assurance that the grass will be mowed and the furnace tended. Real estate taxes, insurance, major and minor repairs, responsibilities normally assumed by homeowners, are all taken care of by the landlord. Tenant responsibility extends to paying the rent, taking reasonable care of the apartment interior, and fulfilling the rental agreement.

Financial Advantages. Perhaps the most important reason for renting is financial. For example, those who have limited resources can rent without making a major cash outlay. Generally a damage deposit plus the first month's rent is all that is required.

Some potential homeowners find rental attractive because low-cost rent permits savings that will enable them to buy a home later. Also, a renter incurs no risk of loss from home investment and has no commitment for home mortgage payments.

Disadvantages of Renting

The landlord is not obligated to tenants beyond the term of the lease. It is always possible that the rent may be raised or the lease may not be renewed. Rental units are also located in close proximity to one another and renters are not permitted to remodel apartments to their needs or tastes. For these reasons, significant to many, rental lacks the security and privacy associated with home ownership.

Another major drawback to renting is loss of the financial advantages of home ownership. These and other reasons for owning a home are discussed in the following section.

Reasons for Buying

Many of the benefits from home ownership accrue to the community in which the homeowner resides. They may be thought of as advantages to society as a whole and generally account for local and federal government encouragement and subsidy of home ownership. Other benefits of home ownership are personal in nature.

Community Benefits from Home Ownership. When a new homeowner receives the first real estate property tax bill, local government services for schools, roads, and police protection are often questioned. Persons paying for services are more concerned about the quality of those services and how family, home, and community are affected.

A strong sense of civic responsibility is one of the results of home ownership. The homeowner's civic participation appears to be greater than the nonhomeowner's. In other words, the degree to which an individual actually engages in the organized activities of the community in terms of membership, attendance at functions that affect the community, contributions, and willingness to hold office seems to correlate with home investment.

Home ownership in standard housing areas of a community increases the general health of the community, reduces the number of crimes, and reduces the costs to the community for various kinds of welfare assistance. For example, areas where homes are owner-occupied are better maintained and landscaped and have cleaner streets than areas where renter-occupied properties predominate.

Personal Advantages. In addition to the community benefits from home ownership mentioned above, there are personal reasons for owning a home. Although such reasons as peace of mind, pride of ownership, and improved credit standing might be included, the basic reasons for owning a home are that it provides individual or family *security* and represents a form of forced *savings.*

Security. Owning a home gives a person a certain feeling of security and independence. When a home has been paid for, wide fluctuations of the business cycle will usually find members of the homeowner's family with a "roof over their heads." Even in a period of full employment and rising prices, the homeowner is more secure than the renter. If prices rise, the value of the home will rise accordingly.

It is a deep feeling of satisfaction to members of a family to know that if one parent dies, the remaining spouse and children are provided with a home. To encroach on the domain of the philosopher, the "future" of most people lies in their children; and in a sense home ownership protects the children and thus protects their future.

Savings. The purchase of a home with its attendant obligations is a form of forced savings. The average person encounters difficulty in establishing a concrete and systematic savings program. A person who must meet various payments, such as principal, interest, and taxes, at fixed times must learn to set aside money to meet these obligations. The house often constitutes the major or only savings of medium- to low-income groups.

Disadvantages of Home Ownership

Maintenance Responsibilities. To be responsible for repair and maintenance is sometimes regarded as a disadvantage of home ownership. It has been estimated that maintenance will run about 1.5 percent of the cost of the house per year. For example, if a house costs $70,000, it is estimated that the cost of maintenance will be about $90 monthly. This is the average cost; in some years, the cost will be considerably higher than in other years.

Interest Rate Risk. Until recently **interest rate risk** was confined to investors in government and corporate bonds. In short, the value of a bond declines when interest rates increase. The value of a home similarly declines when interest rates and financing costs increase more rapidly than personal income. This occurred during 1979–1981. When mortgage interest rates increased from 9 percent to 15 or 16 percent in a short period of time, many people could not afford the increase in mortgage payments. Some home sellers, in order to make their homes marketable and affordable, had to reduce the selling price to below their cost.

Another form of interest risk is associated with the renegotiable, adjustable interest rate mortgages, which were discussed in Chapter 13. That is, if interest rates increase substantially at the time of mortgage renegotiation, homeowners could be faced with principal and interest payments that require great personal sacrifice.

Lack of Flexibility. The purchase of a home commits a person to monthly mortgage payments for a period of 25 to 30 years. Fixed payments for principal, interest, taxes, and insurance are not easily reduced in the event of illness or loss of employment. Further, it is not always possible to sell a home quickly if moving is necessary, without lowering the price significantly. This type of inflexibility is known as *liquidity risk.*

Price Volatility. Until 1980, housing prices in the United States moved in only one direction—up. In the latter 1980s, with reduced inflation and an uneven economic recovery has come housing markets with rampant price inflation, on the one hand, and declines in housing prices, on the other. In 1988, median housing prices in Orange County, California, increased by 32 percent, while in Oklahoma City median housing prices dropped 10 percent. So depending on where a person lives, local economic conditions, and the direction of housing prices, residential housing may be a poor or good investment.

Renting has the distinct advantage of allowing a person to acquire a temporary residence with a minimal cash outlay. However, home ownership has certain financial advantages that will more than compensate a family for making a home investment. Specifically, real estate property taxes and mortgage interest paid are tax deductible when determining the amount of personal income taxes owed. Futhermore, the value of single-family homes has traditionally increased at a rate greater than increases in the Consumer Price Index.

An Illustration

Raymond Elmer has offered Nettie and Will Wright the opportunity of buying his home for $81,500 or renting it for $750 per month. If the Wrights purchase Elmer's property, they must make a down payment of $16,500 and pay closing costs of $2,400. Mr. Elmer has arranged for the Wrights to obtain a mortgage at their local bank. The mortgage is for $65,000 at a 10 percent rate of interest, amortized over 30 years. Other costs important to the Wrights' decision are included in Exhibit 20-4.

Exhibit 20-4 Monthly Out-or-Pocket Expenses

Home Purchase

Mortgage payment (principal and interest)	$570
Property taxes	86
Homeowners insurance	31
Maintenance and repairs (average 1.5% of home cost per year)	102
Electrical service	60
Heat	80
Water	21
Total monthly out-of-pocket costs	$950

Home Rental

Rent	$750
Electric service	60
Heat	80
Water	21
Subtotal	911
Less: Interest income from savings not invested in home ($18,900 at 7% per year net of tax)	110
Total monthly out-of-pocket costs	$801

Out-Of-Pocket Costs. When considering only monthly out-of-pocket costs, the advantage, in this case, is decidedly in favor of renting. In this example, the average monthly cash advantage in favor of renting is $149 per month.

Tax Implications. Mrs. Wright, after comparing the monthly costs of buying and renting, felt that the tax implications of ownership should be taken into account. Exhibit 20-5 shows Mrs. Wright's analysis based on the Tax Reform Act of 1986.

When the tax deductibility of mortgage interest and real estate property taxes is considered, savings in income taxes paid is approximately $94 per month. After consideration of the tax implications of home ownership, the Wrights have found there is a $55 cash, out-of-pocket disadvantage to renting Mr. Elmer's home.

Actual cash savings from tax deduction of mortgage interest and property taxes will vary with the amount of interest and property taxes paid, as well as with the tax bracket of a particular family. Table 20-1 illustrates the impact of a family's tax bracket on the after-tax cost of mortgage interest.

Savings. Amortization of a mortgage loan has a built-in savings feature; that is, as monthly payments are made, part goes for loan interest and part goes to repayment of the loan principal. In our example, the Wrights can expect to reduce their loan balance, or save, $361 durng their first year of ownership. Table 20-2 illustrates both the amounts saved and the cumulative saving, also known as repayment or amortization of principal, at five-year intervals.

Exhibit 20-5 Tax Implications for Out-of-Pocket Home Ownership Costs

Wrights' 1991 taxable income		$29,500	
Estimated 1991 tax rate*		× .15	
1991 tax liability			$4,425
Wrights' 1991 taxable income		$29,500	
Less			
Mortgage interest paid	$6,484		
Property taxes paid	1,032	7,516	
Wrights' adjusted income		21,984	
Estimated 1991 tax rate*		× .15	
1991 revised tax liability			3,298
Cash savings on income tax paid			$1,127

*Estimates based on Tax Reform Act of 1986.

Table 20-1 After-Tax Cost of Interest on a Mortgage

TAX BRACKET	NET COST				
	At 8%	At 9%	At 10%	At 11%	At 12%
15%	6.80	7.65	8.50	9.35	10.20
28%	5.76	6.48	7.20	7.92	8.64
33%	5.34	6.00	6.67	7.34	8.00

SOURCE: Prepared by Thomera Raye Karvel.

Inflation. The precise effects of inflation over a 30-year period are difficult to predict. Generally, the value of homes has been increasing at a rate *greater* than prices for other products and services, or the Consumer Price Index. The Wrights' summary of their findings, including the effect of inflation, is shown in Exhibit 20-6.

When the noncash elements have been considered, the financial advantages of home ownership are substantial. The Wrights are quite willing to make a down payment and pay closing costs totaling $18,900 in order to realize the benefits of home ownership.

READY TO BUY?

Three rules of thumb are often used by lending institutions and government agencies to qualify a potential buyer for the necessary mortgage loan.

Table 20-2 Annual and Cumulative Saving for a $65,000, 10%, 30-Year Loan

END OF YEAR	ANNUAL SAVING	CUMULATIVE SAVING
1	361	361
5	538	2,227
10	886	5,892
15	1,457	11,921
20	2,398	21,842
25	3,945	38,164
30	6,490	65,000

SOURCE: Prepared by Ryan Marie Karvel.

Exhibit 20-6 Summary of Annual Ownership Costs

	RENT	BUY	DIFFERENCE
Out-of-pocket costs	$9,612	$11,400	$ (1,788)
Less: Tax saving	-0-	(1,127)	1,127
Net cash outlay	$9,612	10,273	(661)
Less: Loan amortization*		(361)	361
Inflationary gain at 5%		(4,075)	4,075
Net nonrecoverable expenditures	$9,612	$(5,837)	
Difference in favor of buying			$3,775

*May be recovered when the home is sold. Holding all other factors constant, there would be no advantage to buying if rents were to fall below $486 per month. Similarly, were appreciation to be less than .4 percent per year, there would be no cost savings from home ownership. Additionally, to recover the initial closing costs, broker's commission, and closing costs at the time of sale, the Wrights must live in their new home for approximately two years.

Use of these guides presupposes that the buyer has the necessary cash resources to make the down payment and pay closing costs.

The first guide states that the purchase price of the home should not exceed two-and-one-half times the annual family income. An exception may be granted to this restriction in the event the buyer has a substantial down payment and does not violate the second and third rules of thumb.

The second guide for "qualifying" a buyer limits housing expense to 28 percent of monthly income. Monthly housing expense includes the principal and interest payments on the mortgage loan as well as the average cost for insurance and property taxes. Last, lenders expect the total monthly installment payments, including monthly housing expense, not to exceed 36 percent of monthly income.

Table 20-3 applies these rules of thumb to estimating maximum home purchase price and monthly housing and installment expenditures. The table should be used only as a guide. Deviation, however, from the indicated amounts will require justification to the lender if the home loan is to be approved.

The lender's mortgage committee will also conduct further investigation to determine a loan applicant's personal integrity, responsibility, and honesty. Prior credit history, as evidenced by a credit report, is an important factor in the lender's final decision.

Other factors that influence a buyer's eligibility for a loan include net worth, personal expenses, stability of employment, and career potential. In short, to qualify for a mortgage loan requires a rigorous examination of the applicant's credit, character, and capacity.

Table 20-3 Buyer's Guide to Loan Qualification

ANNUAL INCOME	TWO-AND-ONE-HALF TIMES ANNUAL INCOME EQUALS MAXIMUM HOME PRICE	TWENTY-EIGHT PERCENT OF MONTHLY INCOME EQUALS MAXIMUM MONTHLY HOUSING EXPENDITURES	EIGHT PERCENT OF MONTHLY INCOME EQUALS MAXIMUM MONTHLY INSTALLMENT EXPENDITURES
$ 20,000	$ 50,000	$ 467	$133
25,000	62,500	583	167
30,000	75,000	700	200
40,000	90,000	933	267
50,000	125,000	1,167	333
75,000	187,500	1,750	500
100,000	250,000	2,333	667

To promote fairness, minimize discrimination, and generally provide comsumer protection in home financing, Congress passed the Truth-in-Lending and Real Estate Settlement Procedures acts. Both are detailed in Chapter 22. There are three additional acts that provide protection for consumers seeking home financing.

The Equal Credit Opportunity Act

The **Equal Credit Opportunity Act,** whose procedures are outlined by Regulation B of the Federal Reserve Board, seeks to prevent discrimination by lenders on the basis of sex or marital status.

A potential lender can ask only whether the loan applicant is married, unmarried, or separated. Specifically, lenders are prohibited from inquiring into birth-control practices or child-bearing intentions of the applicants. Combined salaries of both husband and wife must be considered in determining family income.

Furthermore, loan applicants cannot be denied credit because of race, color, religion, or age, or because all or part of the applicant's income is derived from any public assistance program or alimony. If credit is denied, the reasons must be disclosed on request.

The Fair Credit Reporting Act

When an applicant applies for a loan, a credit report is made by a credit reporting agency. In addition to investigating prompt payment of bills, judgments, and the like, agencies are likely to conduct interviews with neighbors regarding the applicant's life-style and character.

Prior to passage of the **Fair Credit Reporting Act,** credit could be denied as the result of vicious slander by a neighbor. Many, many times credit was denied becauce of an error concerning a common name. For example, Mary Smith might apply for credit, and the reporting agency might find a judgment against the wrong Mary Smith; and credit would be denied on that basis.

Previously, there was no way the report could be examined and the error of the reporting agency rectified. Now, under the Fair Credit Reporting Act, the applicant is entitled to a summary of the report, showing the nature, substance, and sources of the information in the report. If corrections are to be made and the agency refuses to make the corrections, the agency may be sued for "unlimited punitive damages."

Legislation Against Red-Lining

Red-lining is the practice by financial institutions of not making loans in "high-risk" neighborhoods. The term derives from the practice of lenders crossing out certain areas on a map with a red pencil. Lenders stoutly deny this practice.

Consequently, Congress and some states have legislated against this practice.[2] The federal government requires disclosure by lenders of mortgage loans by ZIP code numbers. The purpose is to enable depositors and possibly local government to withdraw funds in "no loan" areas.

Down Payment

For many families, the question is not whether a down payment is large or small. More often it is: Do we have enough cash resources to make a down payment and pay closing costs? Having the necessary cash for down payment and closing costs is as important a consideration in determining the ability to buy as the rules of thumb previously discussed.

The amount of the down payment required varies widely and typically depends on the type of mortgage financing obtained. Commercial banks and savings and loan institutions, which make conventional loans, often require the purchaser to make a down payment equal to 20 to 25 percent of the purchase price of the home. Down payments required to obtain VA or FHA loans may vary from 0 to 10 percent of the property's cost. Seller-financed sales and municipal or state mortgage loans may necessitate down payments ranging from 0 to 33 percent.

When buying a home, the buyer often requires cash for other expenses. For example, there may be moving and redecorating costs. Also, some reserve should be put aside to pay for minor repairs that will no doubt be necessary.

---

[2]California, Illinois, and Massachusetts.

When determining cash resources, consideration should be given to these sources.

1. Cash in checking and savings accounts.
2. Cash, net of broker commissions, from the sale of the present home.
3. Sale of stocks and bonds.
4. Cash value of life insurance policies.
5. Loans or gifts from parents or relatives.
6. Early withdrawal from company profit-sharing plans.

Closing Costs

Advertisements for a home might read: "10 Percent Down Plus Closing Costs," or "No Down Payment Plus Closing Costs." *Closing costs* are expenses for services received. They are paid by the purchaser at the **closing** (the time at which title is transferred and the purchase and sale are completed). Closing costs are discussed in detail in Chapter 22.

BASIC HOME SELECTION CONSIDERATIONS

Several factors must be given important consideration in the selection of a home. It is believed that a knowledge of these factors is important, not only to the prospective homeowner, but to the practicing broker who desires to make the sale. By stressing these things in presenting a property, the broker can show the prospect that the home being shown fits the prospect's needs.

Trend in the Neighborhood

With the growth of a city or even a fairly small town, there are created neighborhoods or districts. Neighborhoods are in a constant state of change. More often than not, the change is from a higher to a lower level of use. A declining level of use results in economic obsolescence.

Economic obsolescence is the impairment of desirability or usefulness of property brought about by economic and environmental changes of a neighborhood. In all probability, houses decline in value more from economic obsolescence than from any other cause. It becomes obvious, then, that one of the prime considerations in the selection of a home is the trend of the neighborhood.

In general, older sections of a city begin their decline soon after newer sections begin to make a strong appeal to home buyers. A prospective home purchaser should look for a neighborhood containing a high percentage of owner-occupied homes. Neighborhoods with owner-occupied homes, as distinguished from tenant-occupied homes, tend to be relatively stable in value. Further, it is wise to look for a neighborhood that contains well-planned and well-located homes of the same physical characteristics.

Some studies have indicated that changes in the physical characteristics of a neighborhood alone will not cause people to move. Apparently people will move more readily if the social characteristics of the neighbors become different from their own, even if they like their homes.

Site

In selecting the site, whether it be a vacant lot or an already built home, great care must be taken to avoid such things as a site located in the prevailing wind carrying noxious odors from factories and railroads.

When the site is located near water, it should be determined whether rivers will flood or if the nearby area will become swampy. Communities and counties that have investigated the existence and severity of flood hazards have this information available at the local planning and zoning office. Residents may also obtain flood insurance if the county has complied with the requirements of the National Flood Insurance Act. Additionally, the soil should be tested to determine whether the quality of the soil is such that it will bear the weight of the house. Often piles must be driven into the ground, thus adding materially to the cost of the house.

In the final analysis, the site should afford privacy, and, if possible, a pleasant view together with enough space for family recreation.

Utilities

Utilities generally means the existence of electricity, telephone, water, and sewage disposal. They are an important consideration when selecting a building site. Of course, when a house is already erected, the presence or absence of these things is obvious. Still, this factor is an especially important consideration when selecting a building lot.

Without water or sewage disposal, there will be the necessity of digging a well and the construction of septic tanks which will add substantially to the real cost of the lot.

Care must be exercised when purchasing an existing home with a private well and septic system. The water should be tested to ensure that it meets state health standards and is safe to drink. Similarly, the septic system should be checked for conformity with local health standards, adequate size, and operating condition.

Family Needs

Probably the most important consideration in the selection of a home is family needs. A home should be geared to the needs of the individual family. A good house design or plan should incorporate within it rooms and areas designed to accommodate these needs. When examining a house, it is wise to ask three major questions:

1. *Does the house have the necessary "housework space"?* Examine the building in terms of kitchen space, laundry (where is it?), housecleaning (that is, storage space for housecleaning tools), maintenance space (that is, basement workshop), and possible space for domestic help, if that is a consideration of the family.
2. *Does the house have the necessary and properly laid-out space to fulfill the needs of family group life?* Does it have the proper dining space (that is, a separate dining roon, living room-dining room, or part of the kitchen)? Is the living room large enough? Does it have a space for recreation (that is, basement game room)? Does it have the requisite space for small children's activities, if that is a factor? Is there a playroom? If not, will the living room fulfill this need?
3. *Does the house have the necessary space to fulfill the needs for family private life?* Are the bedrooms adequate, in terms of numbers and size? Is there sufficient space for proper clothes storage? Are there a sufficient number of baths? In addition, it might be considered whether the house has a study area. If there is to be entertaining of overnight guests, the question might be raised as to the size and type of guest accommodations.

Convenience

Convenience means convenience of the location for the family unit. What may be convenient for one family may not be convenient for another. One family may need a home located near schools; another may not be interested in location with regard to schools. In selecting a house, however, the family must consider its location in terms of convenience to the various members of the household.

Exterior Appearance

Exterior appearance is an important consideration in home selection. Architectural styles and designs vary with climate, customs, location, and economic conditions at the time the homes were built. The person contemplating purchasing an older home should consider whether the exterior appearance of the home conforms with the neighborhood. Also considered should be the question of whether the established landscaping is in harmony with the exterior appearance of the home.

In a study done for the U.S. Savings and Loan League by the research and design firm of Raymond Loewy/William Snaith, Inc., the motivations toward homes and housing were examined. Information was gleaned from 2,514 respondents in various age and socioeconomic strata. Among the many things examined was the rating of comparative importance of housing appeals shown in Table 20-4.

Table 20-4 Comparative Importance of Housing Appeals

	EXTREMELY IMPORTANT	VERY IMPORTANT	SOMEWHAT IMPORTANT	NOT TOO IMPORTANT
Good workmanship	61.7%	35.7%	2.1%	.6%
Builder's reputation	53.2	36.2	7.3	3.2
Good neighborhood	50.5	43.5	5.1	.9
Interior styling	27.1	43.9	21.7	7.2
Established community	26.1	43.5	21.3	9.1
Nationally branded materials	25.8	42.0	22.1	10.1
Landscaping	17.0	45.3	28.3	9.4

TYPES OF HOMES

Single-Family Site-Built Homes

Basically, there are two ways to acquire a **site-built single-family home.** The first is to buy a lot and build on it; and the second, acquire an already existing home. Each approach has its particular advantages, precautions, and disadvantages.

Buy a Lot and Build. If this method is decided on, care must be taken not to incorporate any objectionable features in the building that might injure the resale value. Much of the future value depends on the plan of the home; therefore, in planning a home, the home builder should either (1) obtain an architect's plans, or (2) make use of plan services. In the first case, an architect will prepare plans in conformity with the individual's ideas, the cost of construction, and the site. After the preliminary sketches have been agreed upon, the architect will then prepare working drawings.

There are many plan services throughout the country that furnish complete working drawings and specifications for homes for a relatively nominal fee. An important thing to remember here is that if any changes are to be made in the plans obtained from a plan service, these changes should be made by a competent person. There may be in this method the danger that the plans selected will not fit the site, but the greatest danger in using this method is in the selection of a competent contractor.

Regardless of the source of plans, care must be taken to find a contractor who is both a reliable worker and reliable financially. If either of these requisites is lacking, the contractor is apt to skimp on materials.

Although generalizations may be overstatements of fact, building contractors tend to understate the total costs involved in building a new home.

Caution should be exercised when accepting the contractor's bid. Costs typically overlooked or not planned for are new draperies, landscaping, appliances, and other amenities that make a house a home.

Buy an Already Erected Home. This method of acquiring a home has certain advantages over buying a lot and building. First, the purchaser will know to a certain degree what is being received for the price. Second, homes of this type are usually in developments where the character of the neighborhood has been created to conform with the homes in them. In short, the neighborhood is generally a new one, and the purchaser need not worry for some time about economic obsolescence. Third, when the home to be purchased is in a development, the house can usually be purchased for less than if the individual had the home constructed from plans. Developers, because they are building a number of homes at one time, usually can effect savings that are passed on to the purchasers.

When an already erected home is being purchased, it should be examined carefully to determine whether the builder skimped on material. For example, (1) Is the concrete work in the foundation crude? (2) Is the cutting and fitting of corner bracings, bridgings, and similar items expertly done? (3) Are the nails the right type and size? (4) Are there hammer marks, unset nails, or crushed edges on the trim and millwork? (5) Do the doors stick because of poor fitting? (6) Are holes and other imperfections in the woodwork puttied? (7) Is the house wired for adequate power? (8) Are there sufficient outlets in each room?

Many older homes are excellent buys and can be purchased with the idea of making them over into comfortable modern living quarters. The great danger in purchasing an older home to remodel is the trend in the neighborhood. This cannot be too strongly emphasized. All properties are interdependent; that is, their value tends to be either raised or lowered as a result of the value of adjacent properties. For example, it is possible to overimprove, in which case the sale value of the property is decreased by the less desirable character of the neighborhood. Thus, one might spend $10,000 on modernization and discover that it enhances the value of the house only $6,000. On the other hand, an expenditure of $6,000 might enhance the value of the property by $10,000.

Residential Construction Terminology. Appendix D presents illustrations of residential construction using common terminology of the trade. For the home buyer, broker, appraiser, or lender, a basic familiarity with residential construction and the terms used by those in the business will promote better communication and understanding, as well as facilitate judgment of the quality of both new and existing homes.

Appendix D illustrates the proper layout of a building excavation, using batter boards, mason's line, and a plumb bob. Common errors typical of poor footings and sloppy construction are contrasted with a proper footing designed to support the home, complete with drain tile, all of which should be placed below the frost level.

Good quality construction designed for safety, durability, and comfort includes a vapor barrier of polyurethane on the exterior basement walls, sealed soffits, and firestops between stud walls. With a growing emphasis on preventing winter heat loss, small features such as insulation or cement grout between the first floor sill plate and basement walls have become increasingly important.

An example of a foolish cost saving is elimination of cross bridging between floor joists. Cross bridging, although time-consuming to install, helps prevent twisting of joists and floor sag and eliminates shifting, thereby preserving interor finished walls and generally extending the useful life of a home.

Common roof types are also important to students of real estate; for instance, homes have hips, cripples, and ridges. See Appendix D for a further understanding of this brief discussion of basic home design and construction terminology.

Prefabricated Homes

Prefabricated homes are also known as modular, manufactured, or panelized housing. Unlike mobile homes, prefabricated homes are only partially prebuilt in a factory. The extent of prefabrication varies widely from one manufacturer to another. Some companies sell only building components, precut and ready for erection on a prepared foundation by a conventional construction crew. Others prebuild wall units, ceiling and roof trusses, and wooden foundations. A crane is used to put these panelized units in place.

Prefabricated home manufacturers have standardized their construction techniques by using unskilled labor and assembly-line techniques. Additional cost savings are realized from the purchase of building materials in bulk quantities. Some companies claim that on-site erection, on a preexisting foundation or a panelized wood foundation, may be completed in one day. Within five days the home's exterior is finished; plumbing, heating, and electrical work are roughed in; and sheetrock has been hung. The shortened construction time further reduces prefabricated home costs.

Although prefabricated housing may offer significant cost savings, there are precautions that should be taken to protect against common problems and an unsatisfactory result. For example, before making a deposit and signing a purchase agreement all plans and specifications should be reviewed by the local building department to ensure compliance with building codes. Also, a banker should review the proposed home to see if it is acceptable collateral for a mortgage loan, and a surveyor should evaluate the site to see if the topography is suitable for the type of home being built. Finally, it is important that the contractor be familiar with prefabricated home construction. Financing manufactured housing is identical to financing any conventional single-family residence.

Mobile Homes

The fastest growing segment of the single-family housing industry is the **mobile home.** At the time of this writing, about a quarter million mobile homes are being built and sold annually. This type of residence accounts for about 25 percent of the single-family residences being built each year. More important perhaps, mobile homes account for about 96 percent of *all* the single-family homes costing less than $30,000.

With the increased popularity of the mobile home, the design has changed. In 1961, 98 percent of all mobile homes were 10 feet wide by 50 or 60 feet long. Today most of the units are 14 feet wide and 60 to 75 feet long. The prices range from $15,000 to $40,000, with an average cost of $20,000.

The industry believes its greatest growth will come from development of mobile home condominiums. The Manufactured Housing Institute reported over 80 such developments in 1979–1980. Located primarily in the southern states, the condo units are produced in two sections that are mounted on a permanent foundation and bolted together. The average cost, including land, is $40,000, and the units are virtually indistinguishable from other types of construction.

Accompanying this departure from the traditional mobile park is the development of a full-fledged housing manufacturing industry. This is signaled by the increasing popularity of the double-wide, modular, or sectional home. The "double-wide" consists of two sections joined at the center to resemble a small conventional site-built home with approximately 1,400 square feet of living space and up to four bedrooms.

Community Housing

Community housing is a broad term applied to condominiums, townhouses, and cooperative dwelling units. Groups of units are referred to as community associations (CAs). Regardless of type, residents of community associations own their individual unit and share ownership of common areas. Owners elect other owners to provide a system of governance, dispute resolution, and management of commonly owned facilities.

In 1988, the Community Associations Institute reported that 12.1 percent of U.S. residents, or about 30 million people, live in over 12 million condominiums, townhomes, or cooperative housing units. On average, these dwelling complexes contain 95 housing units. The amenities and percentage of CAs having them are reported in Table 20-5.

Citing the need for affordable, energy efficient housing, effective land use, escalating construction costs, and smaller sized households, urban

■ **Table 20-5 Condominiums, Townhomes, and Cooperatives**

	AMENITIES PERCENTAGE
Swimming pool	69
Clubhouse/community room	46
Tennis courts	41
Playground	28
Park/nature area	20
Exercise facility	17
Lake	16
Marina	4
Golf course	4
Restaurant	4

SOURCE: Community Associations Institute, Community Associations Factbook, *1988.*

economists predict that by the year 2000 over half of the U.S. population will live in some type of condominium unit. In bold type, promotional literature claims all the advantages of apartment living and home ownership. Thus, it seems appropriate that this alternate form of housing be examined in considerable detail.

Condominiums

Briefly, the *condominium* is an ownership in fee simple by an individual of a single unit in a multi-unit structure, coupled with ownership of an undivided interest in the land and other elements of the structure held in common with other unit owners of the building. The fee simple ownership of the single unit generally applies to the airspace between the walls and between the floors and ceilings. If the walls are for the support of the building or are in common with another unit, they belong in the category called "common elements." Generally, the common elements consist of the land beneath the buildings, yards, service installations, and community entrances and exits. In the final analysis, a person owns the unit in fee and is a co-owner with others in the common elements.

Rights and Obligations. There are three main documents creating rights and obligations of the co-owners: the declaration, the map (or area plot plan), and the conveyance.

Declaration. The **declaration** defines the rights and obligations of the co-owners and the rules and regulations under which the condominium must operate. The declaration is also called the "enabling declaration" or **master deed.**

Generally, the contents of the declaration consists of 20 parts:

1. Legal description of the land upon which the condominium sits.

2. Definition and description of the condominium unit, usually according to state statute. For example, Colorado defines a condominium unit as an individual airspace unit together with interest in the common elements appurtenant to such unit.

3. A description of the common elements. State legislation recognizes certain elements as common elements. If there is a desire to make one of these elements not a common element or to add to the list of common elements, a statement to that effect must be made in the declaration. For example, common elements under Colorado statutes and most states are

   a. The land on which a building or buildings are located.
   b. The foundations, columns, girders, beams, supports, main walls, roofs, halls, corridors, lobbies, stairs, stairways, fire escapes, entrances, and exits of such building or buildings.
   c. The basements, yards, gardens, parking areas, and storage spaces.
   d. The premises for the lodging of custodians or persons in charge of the property.
   e. Installations of central services, such as power, light, gas, hot and cold water, heating, refrigeration, central air-conditioning, and incinerating.
   f. The elevators, tanks, pumps, motors, fans, compressors, ducts, and, in general, all apparatus and installations existing for common use.
   g. Such community and commercial facilities as may be provided for in the declaration.
   h. All other parts of the property necessary or convenient to its existence, maintenance, and safety, or normally in common use.

4. A description of the limited common elements. Colorado statute defines limited common elements as those common elements designated in the declaration as reserved for the use by fewer than all the owners of the individual airspace units.

5. Provision for reciprocal easements.

6. Provision for the administration of the property by an association or cooperative of owners.

7. Provision for assessments to establish a fund for the payment of common expenses. Common expenses covered by the assessment should include at least taxes, insurance, water, heat, recreational facilities, repairs, and service.

8. Method of collection for the common fund.

9. Remedies and procedure for collection of assessments.

10. Imposition of lien to insure collection of funds.
11. Provision for procedure or the enforcement of the lien.
12. Provision for insurance covering both common areas and individual units.
    a. How insurance for common units is to be paid.
    b. How insurance for individual units is to be paid.
    c. Requirements of insurance by unit owners.
13. Provision for rights of individual owner in respect to interior surfaces of the unit.
14. Provision restricting the use to which a condominium may be put.
15. Provision restricting partition by condominium units. For example, the Colorado statute governs such provision: "If such declaration . . . restricts partition of the common elements, the rules or laws known as the rule against perpetuities and the rule prohibiting unlawful restraints on alienation shall not be applied to defeat or limit any such provision."
16. Provision against animals, or certain types of animals.
17. Provision describing how common facilities are to be used.
18. Provision for relative rights and obligations of the co-owners in case of destruction, either partial or total.
19. Provision limiting individual owners from subleasing units. The limitation is usually that approval of the sublessee by the condominium management, or co-owners, or other designated group must first be made. This allows control as to the type of people living in the condominium. For example, Windsor Gardens permits families only where the head of the household is over 50.
20. Provision for amendment procedure to the declaration.

In some declarations, not all the provisions listed above will be used. In other declarations, additional and different provisions may be used. The use of these provisions is for the benefit of the entire condominium.

A set of bylaws to govern operation of the building might be used in place of some provision in the declaration. The bylaws need not be recorded and will constitute an agreement binding upon the unit owners.

Map. The map is necessary to describe a condominium unit in a form complying to adequate legal description. It must describe the unit both horizontally and vertically. It is a means to describe an individual unit, and when filed, units can be sold by such descriptions as registered on the map.

Basically, there are three methods for making a map:

1. Subdivision plat: Use of a three-dimension drawing of the entire building, which allows for both vertical and horizontal description.
2. Apartment survey: Describing the apartments as being all of that airspace or area on the land upon which the building or buildings are located which lies between two horizontal planes, the lower of which has an elevation of . . . feet, the upper of which has an elevation of . . . feet, and the vertical lines of which are bounded and described.
3. A system which is a variation of metes and bounds.

Conveyance. The same forms of conveyance can be used for condominiums as are used for any other type of real property interest. Basically, the form will be the same except for certain required provisions, and it must meet required rules of formality in order to be legal. The conveyances will probably cover:

1. Description of airspace that is to be subject of ownership.
2. Description of areas that are to be subject of exclusive right to use and occupancy.
3. Rights to use other common elements or common facilities.
4. Exception of the other airspaces and undivided interest.
5. Reserve to the grantor the right to convey similar interests to other parties.
6. Right to additional construction or improvement of common elements by grantor.
7. Right to reserve space for construction.
8. Any other provisions deemed necessary.

Financing the Condominium. The major breakthrough in financing came in September 1963, when the National Housing Act, Section 234, went into effect. This act enabled the FHA to insure mortgages on condominiums and gave a strong impetus to the movement in condominium ownership.

Probably the most important lenders in the condominium field are the savings and loan associations, national banks, insurance companies, and mortgage bankers. Generally, most of the different loan institutions impose, or have imposed on them, regulations restricting loans. General restrictions regarding the condominium loans are

1. Owner must have 100 percent title to unit; title must be a fee simple.
2. Owner must be able to pay own taxes, or may have to make monthly payments to a tax reserve.

3. Insurance requirements are usually very important in the case of condominiums.
4. A first lien is generally required.

Condominiums may have higher interest rates than single-unit structures because there may be some additional risks and costs associated with condominium loans, which are not associated with regular home loans. One of the most prevalent risks in condominium loans is that of the quality of management operating the condominium. Under a home loan, the lender has recourse if the owner lets the house deteriorate; and the lender may have recourse against the owner of an individual unit in a condominium if the owner lets the unit itself deteriorate. But the lender usually does not have any control over the management, who may let the common elements fall into a state of waste, impairing the lender's security. If a lender must foreclose and take over a condominium unit, expenses would be higher than in taking over a house of equal price because the lender must continue to pay expenses for common elements that are not present in a home. Furthermore, there is a moral obligation to keep up the unit because it may create a detriment to the rest of the condominium if not kept up. Servicing loans for a condominium are generally higher than for a home of equal price. Appraisals and inspections will generally be more costly than for a home because the entire condominium must be appraised as well as the individual unit. Also statutes and regulations governing condominiums and loans require extra legal and engineering services that are not required with regular home loans.

Precautions of Condominium Living. Condominium living, some unhappy owners have found, is not for everyone. Reasonable caution exercised before buying will enable prospective purchasers to avoid many common complaints.

Understanding of individual needs and family desires is important if the transition to condominium living is to be made smoothly. Some families are not temperamentally suited to the loss of privacy and the shared life-style of condominium living. Condominium owners may be free of doing yard work and maintenance; however, they are not free of the responsibility or expense of ownership.

Costs for maintenance, improvements, and services are paid for by individual unit owners in the form of monthly assessments. The level of assessments is determined by the owners' association and their operating budget. The assessment is an important cost, may be prohibitive, and must be carefully considered before buying. Additionally, it must be remembered that payment of this fee is not voluntary.

Condominium owners are legally bound by the declaration and bylaws of the owners' association, as previously discussed. These determine voting rights and management of common areas, as well as the level of assessment.

The owners' association is a quasi-governmental unit with all the attendant problems and benefits.

Unscrupulous developers have been known to take advantage of unsuspecting buyers by charging exorbitant fees for use of leased swimming pools, rental of parking space, and ground rents for land on which the project is built. In many cases, the condominium owners merely lease these facilities and have no ownership interest. To avoid extra payments for parking, recreational facilities, and ground leases, owners should ask to see any leases associated with the development and determine what is owned or rented.

Condominium management is another area subject to abuse. Management tie-in with project developers and long-term management agreements should be avoided. The owners' association should retain the right to set management fees and terminate the relationship if service is unsatisfactory. The condominium owner may be free of being physically responsible for maintenance but does have responsibility for the cost of these services. Similarly, each condominium owner is individually and jointly responsible for the success of the shared-living arrangement.

Time-sharing ownership is an extension of the condominium concept of joint ownership of common facilities and fee simple ownership of airspace. The new dimension is *time.* In short, each unit of a recreational facility is divided into occupancy periods. Purchasers acquire the right to occupy a unit for a specific time period each year.

Typically units are divided into 25 two-week periods, with two weeks each year set aside for repairs and renovation. Price for the right to a two-week recreational occupancy varies with the time of the year purchased. For example, two weeks on the beaches of Florida in January will bring a much better price than two weeks in July.

The ownership agreement should be carefully examined prior to purchase of a time-sharing unit. It will explain obligations for maintenance costs, fees, priorities, and procedures for use. Particularly important is the treatment of co-owners in the event that one or more individuals fail to meet the financial obligations of purchase.

Cooperatives. Condominium owners enjoy fee simple ownership of the airspace that their home occupies. Members of a **cooperative** own shares of stock in a nonprofit housing corporation. Stock ownership carries with it the right to occupy a particular housing unit.

The corporation owns the land, building, and recreational facilities and leases apartments to shareholders. This form of a lease is called a *proprietary lease* because each tenant is also a co-owner of the property. Each leaseholder agrees to pay a pro rata share of the corporation's mortgage, management and maintenance costs, property taxes, and other operating expenses.

To acquire interest in a cooperative housing project, stock is purchased from the corporation or another shareholder (tenant). The larger and more attractive the apartment, the more stock must be purchased or the higher the price per share will be. Unlike condominiums, buying stock in a cooperative housing corporation must be approved by the co-op owners' association. The owners' association also has the right to approve sublessees who may wish to rent the apartment of a shareholder.

Cooperator-shareholders (or simply referred to as **cooperators**) not only share ownership of their building but also share a common responsibility for the debts of the corporation. Legally it is the corporation which is liable for mortgage payments and other expenses associated with property ownership. Each shareholder, however, pays a pro rata share of these expenses. When one leaseholder fails to pay expenses, this burden must be carried by the other co-owners. Because of joint ownership and financial responsibility, the courts have upheld the cooperative's right to accept or reject potential purchasers and sublessees.

For example, shareholders of an exclusive New York cooperative, for reasons that were never stated publicly, rejected Richard Nixon's application to purchase shares of stock and occupy an apartment in their building. In fact, the owners' association may terminate the lease of a shareholder if that shareholder physically damages the apartment or becomes a nuisance. The owners' association must, however, return the cost of the individual's shares of stock.

Similar to the condominium, the rules, regulations, and operating procedures of the cooperative are established through bylaws and restrictive covenants. Shareholders elect a board of directors to hire professional building managers, establish further rules necessary for use of common facilities, and otherwise represent all shareholder interests.

GLOSSARY

Closing The time at which title is transferred and the purchase and sale are completed

Cooperative Stock ownership in a cooperative housing unit

Cooperator A shareholder in cooperative housing project

Declaration A writing that defines the rights and obligations of co-owners and the rules and regulations under which a condominium must operate

Economic obsolescence The impairment of desirability or usefulness of property brought about by economic and environmental changes in a neighborhood

Equal Credit Opportunity Act Regulation B of the Federal Reserve Board prohibiting discrimination in lending on the basis of sex or marital status

Fair Credit Reporting Act The law giving an individual the right to a summary of his or her credit report from a credit reporting agency

Interest rate risk The risk of a decline in home values when interest rates rise more rapidly than personal income

Master deed Synonymous with the "declaration" in condominium ownership

Mobile home Includes single- or double-wide, or sectional units and is the fastest growing segment in the single-family housing industry

Prefabricated homes Houses partially prebuilt in a factory

Red-lining The practice by financial institutions of not making loans in high-risk neighborhoods

Site-built single-family homes Housing built on a particular site

Time-sharing A condominium is divided into occupancy periods, and purchasers acquire the right to occupy a unit for a specific time period each year

QUESTIONS FOR REVIEW

1. What single design element is most often sought after by home buyers?
2. What generalization can be drawn with regard to the relationship between income and housing expense?
3. List and explain three reasons for owning a house.
4. Discuss two advantages and two disadvantages of home ownership.
5. The following statement appeared in the *New York Times* in an article entitled "Equity v. Mortgage"—"Another question to be considered is that of inflation. Money tied up in the home's equity is subject to the same inflationary reactions as funds that are immobile in life insurance accounts." Point out and explain the fallacy.
6. What are some of the guarantees borrowers enjoy because of the passage of the Equal Credit Opportunity Act? the Fair Credit Reporting Act?
7. What are the types of homes that may be acquired?
8. Why might the interest rates be higher for financing a condominium than for a single-family residence?
9. Explain how the maintenance of common spaces is handled in condominiums.
10. How does cooperative housing differ from condominium ownership?

PROBLEMS AND ACTIVITIES

1. Frank and May Smith rent an apartment for $350 per month. Some of their friends are trying to get them to buy a home to obtain tax advantages.

   a. What are the advantages of home ownership?
   b. The Smiths both hate yard work, but they do want the tax advantages. What should they do?

2. Eloise and David Shaw would like to buy a home for $65,000. They have two children. David earns $24,000 annually, and Eloise is not employed. They have $10,000 in cash and could assume two mortgages totaling $55,000: a first mortgage with monthly payments of $450 (including principal, interest, insurance, and taxes), and a second mortgage of $200. Can they afford this home? Why, or why not?

3. The Johnsons are trying to decide whether it is financially advisable to buy a home instead of renting. The home that meets their needs costs $122,750; for an equivalent property, rent is $1,100.

   To purchase the home, a down payment of $25,000 is required, and closing costs are expected to be $3,600. A mortgage for $97,750 is available for 10.5 percent amortized for 30 years.

   Other costs important to the Johnsons' decision are: property tax, $1,800; homeowners insurance, $540; maintenance and repairs, an average 1.5 percent of the home's price per year. In addition, electrical, water, sewer, and heating costs are expected to be $240 per month.

   The Johnsons average tax rate is 21 percent. Taxable income is expected to be $57,000 per year. Residential property is expected to appreciate at the rate of 2 percent per year. The savings rate is 7 percent.

   Using Decision Assistant or following the example in Exhibits 20-4, 20-5, and 20-6, determine whether it is financially advantageous to rent or buy.

   a. How many years must the Johnsons live in their home to recover closing costs and resale brokers commissions.
   b. Answer question 3a assuming appreciation will average 8 percent per year.

21

SEARCH, EXAMINATION OF TITLE, AND TITLE INSURANCE

KEY TERMS

Abstract of title
Acknowledgment
ATA mortgagee's policy
Authentication of acknowledgment
Chain of title
Flag
***Lis pendens* index**
Livery of seizin
Mortgagee's title policy
Opinion of title
Owner's title policy
Purchaser's policy
Recording acts
Title insurance
Torrens Law

The average person in the real estate industry may never be called on to prepare an abstract of title. However, everyone connected with the real estate industry must have some knowledge of the technical aspects of the title search. The broker, for example, must be able to obtain legal descriptions where necessary; appraisers must be able to search records for comparable sales data; owners of mineral lands must be able to obtain data on ownership of mineral and oil rights. The list is endless.

In short, title searching and its ramifications can be considered the capstone of the more technical aspects of the real estate industry.

OBJECT OF THE TITLE SEARCH

There are numerous instances in real property transactions when a title search is needed. The scope of a search varies according to the purpose for which the search is made.

When a contract for the sale of real property is executed, the purchaser will want an abstract of title, or a title insurance policy.[1] The **abstract of title** is a condensed history of the title to land. It consists of a summary of the operative parts of all instruments of conveyance affecting the land, or the title or any interest therein, together with a statement of all liens, charges, and encumbrances thereon, or liabilities to which the land may be

[1]In some states where title insurance is used exclusively, the purchaser will never see an abstract of title although the title companies may have one for their own use.

subject, and of which it is in any way material for the purchaser to be apprised (given notice of).

In the usual transaction, the abstract of title will be ordered either at the request of a buyer or of a seller according to the terms of the sales contract. The purpose of the search will be to determine if there are any flaws in the title. A *flaw* is an apparent gap or break in the chain of title (the history of the previous ownership of the property). In addition, the purpose of the search is to disclose any possible cloud on title (an outstanding claim or encumbrance) that, if valid, would affect or impair the owner's title. For example, a mortgage or judgment or even an imperfect description of the property might be a cloud on a title. In a real sense, the cloud does not reach the merits of the title, but will tend to obscure it.

When prospective mortgagees order a search made, they have a different purpose in mind than a purchaser has. Their main object in making the search is to determine, first, whether or not the person making the application for the loan actually owns the property; and second, whether or not any liens exist against the property that might be superior to their lien. A bank must make certain that no mortgages are outstanding against the property under consideration as security. The bank's main object in ordering a search is to determine its position relative to other possible lienors in the event that the loan is granted.

A mortgagee and the holder of a mechanic's lien always have a title search made prior to a foreclosure action. They, too, are interested in the possibility of prior existing rights against property defaulted. They are interested in any liens that might exist against the property; for to properly complete their foreclosure action, it is necessary to bring into the action any parties having interests in the property. This must be done even though the interests of the parties may be inferior to their own. Not to bring in all parties having interests would be to render the foreclosure action defective.

For example, a mortgage foreclosure action is initiated that involves property on which there exists a mechanic's lien. The mechanic's lien is inferior to the mortgage because it was placed against the property after the inception of the mortgage. The mortgagee brings a foreclosure action against the property in the amount of $20,000, and the property brings $40,000 at the foreclosure sale. The overplus of $20,000 is paid to the mortgagor. The lienor's rights would be severed if it were not for the fact that the law requires that all parties having interests in the property be notified. In our hypothesis this notification was not made. Thus, the mortgagee's purpose in making a search is to identify many parties having interests in the property in order that proper notice might be given them.

Chain of Title

Although an abstract of title is a history of all the instruments affecting a particular parcel of land, a **chain of title** is a part of that history. The chain of title shows the ownership of the property over a period of time, depending on the length of the search. It can be run back to the original title. Thus, it may show that *A* received the property as a grant from the King of England in prerevolutionary days; *A* then conveyed to *B*, *B* to *C*, and so forth until the present date.

Recording Acts

The **recording acts,** which are similar in all the states, are statutes of registration and provide generally for the recording of every instrument in writing by which any estate or interest in land is created, transferred, mortgaged, or assigned, or by which the title to land may be affected either in law or in equity.[2]

The purpose of the recording acts, which exist in substantially the same form in all of the states, is to give notice to anyone concerned with a title about the status of that title. By virtue of the recording acts, persons can be prevented from selling the same land twice. Notice can be *actual* notice of the fact that *A* owns a certain parcel of real property. The notice may be actual because *A* has informed *B* of *A*'s ownership of the property; therefore, it may be said that *B* has actual notice of the ownership of the property.

The recording acts, however, are designed to go a step farther in the giving of notice. They are designed to give notice to the world of the fact that *A* owns a certain parcel. This concept of "notice to the world" is figurative, for not many people actually *know* the status of property in a certain locale. This notice to the world is called "constructive notice." However, in order for there to be constructive notice concerning a particular parcel of property, it is necessary to comply with the recording statutes.

Basically, the recording acts state that conveyances may be recorded in the office of the county clerk, county recorder, or county registrar depending upon the particular state involved. Conveyances in this sense generally mean:

> (written instruments by which) any estate or interest in real property is created, transferred, mortgaged or assigned, or by which the title to any real property may be affected, including an instrument in execution of a power, although the power be one of revocation only, and an instrument postponing or subordinating a mortgage lien; except a will, a lease for a term not exceeding three years, an executory contract for the sale or purchase of lands, and an instrument containing a power to convey real property as the agent or the attorney for the owner of such property.[3]

The recording, then, is the entry in detail upon the proper records of the clerk of the county in which the property is located of a written

---

[2]Some acts use the term *filing*. Generally, filing and recording are synonymous.

[3]New York Real Property Law, Sec. 290-3. The laws of the several states are substantially the same.

instrument meeting certain qualifications. The recording may be done by copying or by photography. Most counties now use photography. After the instrument has been reproduced, it is indexed so that it may be easily found. In most states, the recording acts provide that separate sets of indexes be made for the various types of instruments; for example, one for conveyances, one for mortgages, and so forth.

Each set of indexes consists of two indexes, one for each party to the instrument. When a deed is presented to the clerk to be recorded, it is indexed in a grantor index and at the same time in a grantee index. A mortgage is indexed in a mortgagee index and in a mortgagor index.

These sets of indexes are lists that are kept in alphabetical and chronological order. They are generally alphabetized according to the last and first names. For example, the name of a present property owner is Frank Johnson and someone desires to determine from whom he had received the property. The basic assumption then is that Frank Johnson is the grantee of somebody. The question is Of whom? The searcher will proceed to the grantee index marked "J," which indicates that those grantees whose last names begin with "J" will be found there. The first page in the index will contain a list of those persons whose last names begin with the letter "J" and whose first names begin with the letter "A." Thus, the first name in the list might be Jamison, Abe; followed by Jones, Alice; Jurgens, Arthur; and so forth. To find Frank Johnson, then, the searcher would turn to the page where the last names begin with the letter "J" and the first names with the letter "F." The exact procedure is discussed in detail later in the chapter.

In some counties where conveyances are relatively infrequent, indexes are prepared by last name only. In some states, however, where there are many conveyances, the indexes are broken down to a finer degree. For example, in the County of Suffolk, State of New York, the conveyances are indexed alphabetically both by beginning letters of the last and first names and also by townships. There is a grantor and grantee index in which lands in the town of Brookhaven are indexed. This index is alphabetized according to first letters of the last and first names.

As previously mentioned, the indexes are kept in alphabetical and chronological order. It can now be recognized that the names are not listed in strict alphabetical order, but only by the beginning letters of the first and last names. The real reason for this is that the entries are made in the indexes as the instruments are received for the purpose of recording. Assume that the recorder starts with a blank page in the index. On September 1 a deed comes into the office to be recorded. This deed is analyzed and is entered on line 1 of the index according to the beginning letters of the last and first names. On September 2 another deed is to be recorded in which the beginning letter of the first and last name is the same as the instrument recorded on September 1. The second instrument is entered on line 2 of the index, even though from a strict alphabetical point of view it comes ahead of the September 1 instrument.

Acknowledgments. The county clerk, recorder, or some other designated person is required to record and index certain instruments as provided by the statute. This person is not required, however, to record these instruments until they have been properly acknowledged. An **acknowledgment** is a formal declaration made before some public officer, usually a notary public, by a person who has signed a deed, mortgage, or other instrument stating that the instrument is her or his act and deed. The instrument to be recorded is usually signed in the presence of a notary or other public officer with the acknowledgment attached substantially in the form illustrated in Exhibit 21-1.

Authentication of Acknowledgment. Although the county clerk may not record an instrument unless it has been properly acknowledged, the clerk may sometimes not record an instrument even when it has been acknowledged. Most states require that if the acknowledgment is made in a state other than the one in which the property described in the instrument is located, an **authentication of acknowledgment** must be attached. In other words, the county clerk in *Y* county of state *B* needs proof that the notary before whom an acknowledgment was made in county *X* of state *A* actually was a notary.

This proof is furnished by the clerk of the county where the notary or other public officer who took the acknowledgment resides or has filed. The proof consists of a certificate commonly called a **flag.** When a notary receives the commission or warrant, a signature card is required in the

Exhibit 21-1 An Acknowledgment

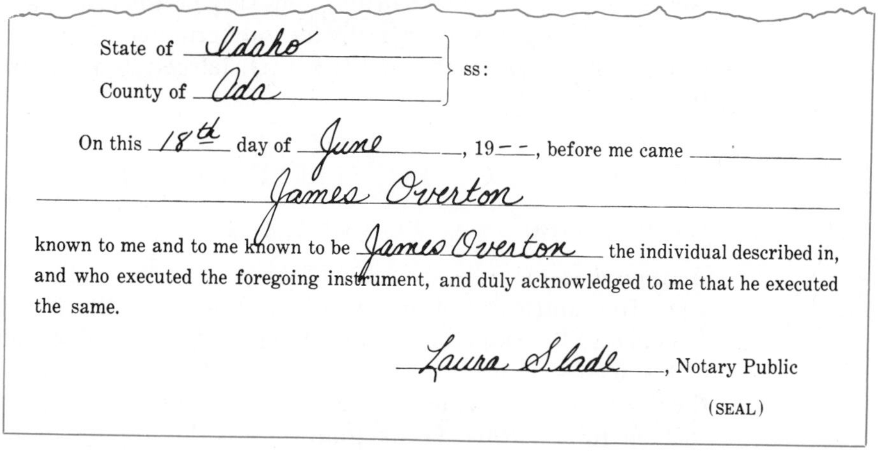

State of *Idaho* }
County of *Ada* } ss:

On this *18th* day of *June*, 19– –, before me came *James Overton*

known to me and to me known to be *James Overton* the individual described in, and who executed the foregoing instrument, and duly acknowledged to me that he executed the same.

Laura Slade, Notary Public

(SEAL)

office of the county clerk of each county in the state in which the notary desires to act as a notary. The cards contain the name of the notary, the expiration date of the commission, the notary's residence, and other pertinent information. When a flag or certificate is desired, the county clerk checks the file of signed cards to determine if the person named is a commissioned notary. If a card is located for the person named, it is certified that the person is actually a notary. The certificate is attached to the instrument to be recorded, and with the certificate the instrument will be accepted for recording.

In some states, notably New York, a certificate is required between counties. Thus, if an acknowledgment is taken in Queens County before a Queens County notary who has not filed in Suffolk County, the clerk of the County of Suffolk will refuse to record the instrument unless a certificate is attached.

Time of Recording. When an instrument is presented to the county clerk to be recorded, the date and time are stamped on the instrument together with the book and page where it is recorded. In law, the general rule is that an instrument is considered to be recorded when it is delivered to the clerk.

Subsequent Purchasers. In most states, the statutes provide that a conveyance that is not recorded is void against subsequent purchasers in good faith. For example, *A* executes and delivers a deed to *B* on July 1. *A* then executes and delivers a deed to *C* dated July 2. If *C* is a bona fide purchaser and records the instrument before *B*, then the conveyance will be deemed to have been made to *C*.

But, if *C* had actual notice of the transaction between *A* and *B*, *C* would not have made the purchase in "good faith." Hence, even though *C*'s deed was recorded prior to *B*'s deed, *B* would have defensible title to the property.

Recording Fees. The recording fees vary between the various states and counties. Generally speaking, the fee is determined by the number of pages of the instrument to be recorded. It is charged at a rate of so much per page.

MECHANICS OF THE TITLE SEARCH

Grantor-Grantee System of Indexing

Assume that a search is to be made to determine whether Frank Johnson owns free and clear of any encumbrances Lot 1 Block 3 of the map of Greenacres Development Company. Frank Johnson makes available a copy of his deed so that his title can be traced. (Ordinarily a search begins with the deed showing title in the present owner.) Assuming that his deed shows that on July 1, 1964, Frank Johnson was the grantee of John Huff, the following procedure would be followed in making a title search.

Running the Chain of Title. The first step in the process is to run the chain of title in order to find the ownership of the property for a number of years past. John Huff conveyed the property to Frank Johnson and, hence, must have been a grantee himself. Since he conveyed title on July 1, he must have received title sometime before July 1, 1964. The searcher examines the grantee index beginning in the "H" index at the *end* of the list of names of persons whose first names begin with "J" and that were recorded on July 1, 1964. Thus, the researcher proceeds backward, searching from the last entry on July 1 back to June 30, June 29, and as far back as necessary. Suppose that Huff received the property on June 25. The page in the index might appear something like that shown in Exhibit 21-2.

In tracing the conveyances of title to Huff, the searcher looks first at the date column, reasoning that the conveyance to Huff must have been made prior to July 1. Thus, the searcher begins with the conveyance from Sam Corelle to Jan Hanson and works back up the list of grantees until coming to the conveyance from Frances P. Kelly to John Huff dated June 25. Part of the entry reads "Liber (book) 360, page 14." This notation indicates the location of the recorded deed. The searcher finds Liber 360 and turns to page 14 to check the photostat of the deed from Kelly to Huff against the property description on the deed being searched. The reason for this check is that the conveyance quite conceivably may be an entirely different parcel from the one being searched. If the property in Liber 360 on page 14 turns out to be different from the one being traced, the searcher continues the search, examining each deed in the name of John Huff until finding a property conveyed to Huff that answers the correct description.

Assume that the deed from Kelly to Huff in Liber 360, page 14, checks with the property that is being searched. After having determined that, the next step is to ascertain if it is a quitclaim, bargain and sale, full covenant

Exhibit 21-2 Portion of Page From Grantee Index

	GRANTEE	GRANTOR	DATE	LIBER	PAGE
1.	Hendrickson, Joan	Schmidt, Lincoln	June 24	348	99
2.	Hartley, Joseph	Weiner, Maureen	June 24	348	187
3.	Hundson, Juanita	Felice, John	June 25	359	52
4.	*Huff, John*	Kelly, Frances P.	June 25	360	14
5.	Heathcliff, James	Schneider, Dorothy	June 26	362	89
6.	Hobart, Jane	Leavandowsky, Frank	June 27	366	673
7.	Hester, Junior	Karakas, William	June 28	370	19
8.	Hooten, Joseph	Kyer, Carla	June 29	372	345
9.	Herd, Jean	Steiner, Holly	June 30	377	65
10.	Hanson, Jan	Corelle, Sam	July 1	379	90

and warranty, or other type of deed. The searcher then examines the deed to determine if internal revenue stamps are affixed (on deeds after April 1, 1932, to January 1, 1968), whether or not the deed was acknowledged, the date of acknowledgment, the date of recording, and the date of execution. The deed is then read to determine whether or not it contains any restrictive covenants, easements, or any other unusual features that might introduce a flaw in the title. Notations of all these items are made so that they might later be incorporated into the abstract of title. Assume Frances P. Kelly transferred the deed to the property to John Huff on June 7, 1964. The notations made might appear like this:

	warranty deed (Liber 360, p.14)
Frances P. Kelly	dated June 4, 1964
to	ack. June 4, 1964
John Huff	recorded June 25, 1964
	revenue stamps $2.20

Conveys premises at head of search.[4]

The next step in the chain of title is to determine the source from which Frances P. Kelly obtained the property. Although Frances P. Kelly was the grantor to John Huff, she, herself, was the grantee of someone. Thus, the grantee index will be examined to determine Kelly's grantor. The searching process is repeated until the chain of title has been run back to the date of the beginning of the search.

Checking the Grantors. After having completed the chain of title, the next step is to check the grantors. The question to be answered is Did any of the grantors in the chain of title convey the same property twice? It is known that Frank Johnson recorded a deed to the property from John Huff on July 1, 1964. It is also known that John Huff received the property from Frances P. Kelly on June 25, 1964. What happened between June 25 and July 1 during the ownership of Huff? Conceivably, Huff may have made a conveyance to someone other than Johnson in the interim. To determine this, the searcher must check the grantor index. The grantor index is set up in almost the same manner as the grantee index except that the grantee and grantor columns are reversed. The searcher looks now for John Huff as grantor between the date he recorded the property he received from Frances P. Kelly and the date he conveyed the property to Frank Johnson.

If John Huff is a builder or real estate operator, there may be a number of conveyances between those dates. Each one of those conveyances must be examined and the description checked against the premises being searched. Somewhere, the index will list John Huff as grantor

---

[4]The premises mentioned in the example refer to the property being searched, which is fully described at the beginning of the completed abstract.

and Frank Johnson as grantee together with the liber and page number of the deed. If Huff did not convey the property to any other grantee, Johnson may be assumed to have good title as far as ownership is concerned. The same process is repeated with each person named in the chain of title for that period of time during which the person owned the property.

In community property states or where dower or homestead still exists, it is important that one check for husband and wife relationships. Where real property is sold under these circumstances, the signature of the wife must be on the deed.

Mortgages. When all of the persons in the chain have been "grantored," the next step in the search is to examine the mortgagor index to check whether or not any of these persons in the chain of title have had a mortgage on the property and whether these mortgages are still in force. Beginning with the last person in the chain of title (Frank Johnson), and checking backwards, a search for mortgages is made against each person in the chain during that period of time during which the property was held.

Assume that James R. Skinner owned the property being searched from August 1, 1942, to September 22, 1948. By checking the mortgagor index, it is determined that he made a mortgage to the First National Bank of Patchogue, New York, recorded November 15, 1942. The entry in the index appears as shown in Exhibit 21-3.

A notation is made of this entry, and Liber 89 of mortgages, page 365, is checked. If the mortgage remains unpaid, a copy of the mortgage will appear on page 365 and that is all. Assume, however, that the mortgage has been satisfied. In this case there will be a notation on the margin of the recorded mortgage in this manner: "Sat. Liber 2010, page 34."

Liber 2010, page 34, will then be examined to determine whether the satisfaction was made properly. A notation is made of the findings for later incorporation into the abstract of title.

If the mortgage has been assigned by the bank, a notation will appear on the margin of the copy of the mortgage to this effect: "Assignment Liber 2389, page 56."

The assignment will then be examined to determine its validity and the ownership of the mortgage.

Exhibit 21-3 Entry in Mortgagor Index

MORTGAGOR	MORTGAGEE	DATE	LIBER	PAGE
James R. Skinner	The First National Bank of Patchogue	Nov. 15	89	365

Lis pendens. In Chapter 12 it was explained that the *lis pendens* is a notice of pendency of action. Whenever a legal action is begun concerning a particular parcel of property, the notice of pendency of action is filed in the office of the clerk of the county in which the property is located. This ***lis pendens* index** is set up alphabetically according to plaintiffs and defendants. The index is examined for all people in the chain of title as possible defendants.

Each time a lawsuit is filed, the case is assigned a file number by the county clerk. An envelope or a folder with the file number is set up by the clerk; and all papers containing that suit, including any record of disposition made, are filed therein.

The *lis pendens* index, in addition to containing the names of plaintiffs and defendants, contains the date of the filing of the *lis pendens* and a column for file numbers. If someone in the chain of title has been sued, that person's name will appear in the index as a defendant. The file number of the action is also recorded. The searcher upon discovering this will examine the file to determine the disposition of the suit.

Judgments. When a judgment is entered, it becomes a lien on the real property of the judgment debtor within the jurisdiction of that court. The length of the lien varies among the several states. If the judgment remains a lien against the property for ten years (as it is in many states), then it becomes necessary to search back for ten years. In other words, those persons who had title to the property under consideration for the past ten years may have had a judgment lien against the property that followed the property to the date of the search. The judgments are entered alphabetically on the judgment rolls in the county clerk's office in the county in which the property is located.

Minor Liens. A search is made for the so-called minor liens. Each type of lien has a separate index that must be examined. Included among these are mechanic's liens, criminal surety bonds, federal tax, building loan agreements, and warrants. In addition, it is customary to search for financing statements of sale on the assumption that one might be filed affecting the real property in some manner.

In several states when a person is the recipient of public welfare, the recipient enters into a written agreement with the Commissioner of Public Welfare. This agreement becomes a lien on the property to the extent of the amount of money received from the commissioner as public assistance. In those areas a search must be made for that type of instrument in addition to the minor liens.

Tax Search. Taxes on real property are due and payable at a stated time each year; and when the date of the search is made after this time, and before the time fixed for the sale of lands for delinquent taxes, a search must be made to ascertain the fact of payment or nonpayment. In the final analysis, this means that as a practical matter tax rolls are always searched.

The tax rolls are generally located in the county treasurer's office in the county in which the property is located, or in the tax assessor's office in the city in which the property is located. Usually, the tax rolls are indexed according to property description.

City Taxes. In most sections of the country, there is no way to determine from an examination of the county records if city taxes have been paid. As protection, therefore, the buyer will often require that the seller sign a statement certifying that there are no city taxes due on the property.

Surrogate or Probate Court Records. Very often when the searcher is running a chain of title, there will be a break in the chain, or the searcher may run across an administrator's or executor's deed in the chain. In either of these situations, it becomes necessary to examine the records of the surrogate or probate court.

In the first instance, suppose one finds a deed conveyed by Mary Reynolds. On searching the grantee records for Mary Reynolds, the searcher finds no deed conveyed to her. The probate court records will be searched for the death of a Reynolds to determine finally whether the deceased "Reynolds" is the husband of Mary. If one is found, the files of the probate court are examined to determine whether Mary Reynolds was actually entitled to the property and therefore entitled to execute a deed herself, as grantor, to someone else as grantee.

In those states where there is a state inheritance tax, it also becomes necessary to determine whether the tax was paid. Or, if the value of the property was low enough to be exempted from tax, there should be a tax waiver in the files of the probate court to indicate that the tax had been waived. If there is no record of the tax payment, the tax department must be queried to determine whether or not any tax is due. If there is none due, a tax waiver is obtained from the state department.

The files of the surrogate or probate court are also to be examined when there is an administrator's or executor's deed in the chain of title to determine whether the property was distributed to the proper persons.

Dower. In Chapter 6, *dower rights* were described as the rights a wife has in her husband's estate at his death. In those states where common-law dower rights still exist, the wife must join the husband on a deed in order to transfer real property effectively. If the wife does not execute the deed, at the death of her husband she may have an interest in the property, although it may long since have been in the possession of another person under a deed executed by the husband.

Microfilm System of Indexing

In some counties where there has been a great deal of real estate activity, recording has taken the form of a microfiche—a microfilm system of indexing—to save space.

The procedure is basically the same as outlined above. The indexes are entered on microfiche and refer to a microfilm number instead of a book. An appraiser searching for a comparable sale will be referred to the microfilm of a deed. If the appraiser needs to "pull" the deed, a copy can be ordered, which will be made full size by the recorder or county clerk.

Use of the Computer

In most of the urban centers of the nation, the title searching process has been computerized. For example, information as to where a plat has been filed and all of the instruments, deeds, mortgages, etc., pertaining to that lot have been entered into a computer and any or all of these instruments can and are duplicated at will.

In addition to "pulling" the records by lot and block number, the instruments are available by street number. In counties where instruments have been computerized, rural areas within those counties can be searched when a legal description of the property is available.

Important, too, is the fact that title companies have these instruments in their computers. For example, a title company situated many miles from the county recorder's office can duplicate recorded instruments using the title company's data base. Since many of the title companies have branches nationwide, it is possible for a title company located in state *A* to obtain instruments in state *B* for a particular parcel of property in that state.

Thus, you can readily see that modern technology has made the process of title searching much easier.

Preparation of the Abstract of Title

During the search, the searcher makes notes concerning all of the transactions regarding the property. After the search has been completed, the searcher organizes the notes into the form of an abstract or brief history of the property.

The abstract also contains a certification and exceptions, substantially as follows:

> This is to certify that I have searched the records in the office of the clerk of the County of Suffolk, State of New York, for deeds, mortgages, judgments and any other liens that might affect the premises at the head of the search and find nothing; except what any records of the federal courts might show and any other exception that might be made.

EXAMINATION OF TITLE AND TITLE INSURANCE

Although the real estate broker plays no direct part in the examination of title, the broker should be aware of what the title examiner is doing. Examinations of titles, because of the highly technical nature of real property law, are generally made by an attorney or an examiner of title employed by a title insurance company. If a broker gives an opinion of title, it is tantamount to practicing law without a license.

The question is, then, What takes place when the title is examined? An attorney who is to pass upon the title is given a state of facts on which to base an opinion. This state of facts is presented to the attorney by the abstract of title. Technically, too, the attorney is not presumed or supposed to extend the investigations beyond what is directly or inferentially disclosed by the abstract of title. Where links in the chain of title are missing, the examiner must make inquiries regarding these missing links, but the existence of unrecorded evidence or of equities not apparent or fairly deducible does not properly come within the province of the examiner.

However, some examiners of title feel that they should go beyond what is technically required of them. In many cases, the examiner feels it is necessary to inquire into the present possession of the property. The feeling is that, although the purchaser of the land under examination is protected by the records, it should be determined that the actual state of title corresponds with what appears of record. For example, the record may show *A* as the owner, but actual inspection of the premises may show *B* in possession of the premises; and from actual inspection and inquiry concerning the premises, it may be shown that *B* is the true owner of the property under examination.

Certain types of easements that do not appear in the record may be shown by actual inspection of the property, easements by implication, for example. This is the reason why so many lending institutions and title companies require a survey in addition to the abstract of title. The thought is that the survey will reveal easements and encroachments that the record does not reveal.

Opinion of Title

The **opinion of title** is contained in the "certification of title," which is annexed to the abstract as outlined above. In essence, this certification of title is based on the assumption of title in a particular person at a certain date, and the examiner certifies the title from examination of the records from that date. This raises the question as to how far back a title search should be made. To some degree this depends on the purpose for which the search is being made. Most examiners feel reasonably certain in searching back 40 years. This figure seems appropriate because of various statutes of limitations that have been passed in the several states prohibiting actions after the passage of certain specified lengths of time. Some states have statutes defining the length of time of the search for specific purposes. For example, when one registers a title under a Torrens proceeding (discussed later in this chapter), some states require that an abstract of title be filed going back 40 years. Some states require that an abstract be filed with a map of the subdivision and that the abstract go back 20 years.

When a title is being certified, the examiner looks for defects in the title. If any are found, steps are taken to remedy them. However, if the client is willing to accept the title with the defects, they are listed as exceptions to the title.

Title Insurance

Historically, abstracts of title were, and in many suburban areas still are, made by attorneys. With the advent of abstract companies, abstracts of title were prepared by them, and the abstracts were examined for legal defalcations by attorneys. In many ways both the abstract companies and the certifications of title by attorneys are imperfect and open to objection. An attorney, for example, may make an honest mistake against which the owner of a real property has no recourse. The honest mistake may be due to a forged deed or any number of other types of false statements that are impossible to detect. If an attorney makes a negligent mistake or if an abstract company is guilty of negligence, the property owner may be indemnified. However, although the property owner may have recourse against an attorney who is negligent, it does not necessarily mean that the property owner may be compensated for the loss. To provide this protection, **title insurance** is available.

When a title policy enters the picture, the homeowner will be compensated not only if the company is negligent, but for any of the unknown defects in title, subject to any exceptions in the title policy, for which an attorney is not ordinarily liable.

In short, when a title policy is issued, the title to the property is guaranteed. Upon the payment of a flat fee as the premium, the policy insures for any undisclosed defects in the title, subject to any exceptions in the title policy. As far as an owner is concerned, the policy should be for the full value of the property; however, the situation is a little different as far as mortgagee is concerned as will be seen later.

Owner's Title Policy. Like any other contract of insurance, the **owner's title policy** contains the names of the parties and a consideration, which in this case is the premium paid for the policy. The maximum loss for which the company may be liable is stated in the policy as being so many dollars as follows:

> . . . which the Insured may sustain by reason of any defect in the Insured's title to all of the estate or interest in the premises specified and hereinafter described or by reason of liens or encumbrances charging the same at the date of the policy, saving and excepting, and this policy does not insure against loss or damage by reason of any estate or interest, defect, lien, encumbrance or objection hereinafter set forth in the written or printed exceptions contained in this policy.

This is followed by Schedule A, which describes the estate or interest covered by the policy and then describes the property that is insured by the policy.

Schedule B in the owner's title policy contains exceptions, substantially as follows:

> This policy does not insure against:
>
> 1. Any state of facts an accurate survey and inspection would show; the existence of roads, easements or ways not established of record, or existence of public roads; water locations; water rights, mining rights; exceptions and reservations in United States patents.
> 2. Rights or claims of persons in possession or claiming to be in possession, not shown of record; rights claimed under instruments of which no notice is of record but of which the Insured has notice; material or labor liens of which no notice is of record.
> 3. Matters relating to special assessments and special levies, if any, preceding the same becoming fixed and shown as a lien; taxes not yet payable; matters relating to vacating, opening or other changing of streets or highways preceding the final termination of the same.
> 4. Regulations and restrictions imposed by building and zoning ordinances or by a planning authority; any governmental action based on the claim that any part of the insured premises is within or under navigable waters.

The policy, of course, contains certain conditions. Ordinarily a policy reserves the right of the company to defend suits. It contains several other conditions that must be met for payment to be made; for example, when there has been a final determination in a court of competent jurisdiction under which the insured may be dispossessed. The policy also contains a statement that the policy is not assignable.

Purchaser's Policy. The **purchaser's policy** insures the interest of the purchaser of real property. The main distinction between the owner's policy and the purchaser's policy is that in the former case the owner's title itself is insured, while in the latter case the title of the seller is insured. By means of this, the purchaser knows that the title being delivered is free and clear from all encumbrances. This policy is most common in those states where the purchaser is responsible for having the title search made. The owner's policy is most common in those states where it is the responsibility of the owner to furnish the purchaser with either an abstract of title or a title insurance policy.

Mortgagee's Title Policy. The **mortgagee's title policy** insures the interest of the mortgagee in the property under consideration. It covers any loss of the mortgagee arising from a defect in the mortgagor's title or by reason of any lien or encumbrance impairing the security of the mortgage with the exceptions basically outlined in the discussion of the owner's title policy.

The mortgagee's policy is used most often by banks to insure the security for the loan. It is paid for by the mortgagor; and in general when a title company has already issued a policy to the mortgagor, the fee is very reasonable. Unlike the owner's policy, the morgtgagee's policy is assignable by the lender.

ATA Policy. The Amerian Title Association Loan Policy, which is an additional coverage policy, goes a step farther in its coverage in that it includes the exceptions enumerated above. For example, the **ATA mortgagee's policy** states, among other things, that the insured shall be insured for ". . . any statutory lien for labor or material . . . which now have gained or hereafter may gain priority over the lien upon said land of said mortgage."

This clause gives a measure of security otherwise not available in those states following the Pennsylvania System of mechanic's liens, as outlined in Chapter 12. Under the Pennsylvania System, a mechanic's lien filed within the statutory period relates back to the date of the completion of the contract or the last delivery of materials to the job. Thus, under the ATA mortgagee's policy, a mortgagee is assured of protection even if a mechanic's lien is filed after the mortgage has been recorded.

The title companies protect themselves from the possibility of a later lien being filed by a rather tight inspection system. A representative of the company visits the property to be insured and examines it for any recent improvements that have been made upon the property. They look also for any materials or tools that might have been recently delivered to the land, and for any excavation work or grading done on the land.

The title policies of the various states have minor variations, but they are essentially uniform.

TITLE REGISTRATION

Background of Title Support

From very early times, it has been the custom and the law of every civilized nation to establish rules of evidence in support of land titles. During the Roman Empire, deeds were required to be in writing and to be executed formally in the presence of numerous witnesses. In feudal England, title was transferred by **livery of seizin.** The livery of seizin was superseded by the written conveyance, which is employed in all enlightened nations of the world today.

The requirement that conveyances of real property be in writing was an advance toward securing a degree of proof in support of titles. However, it was soon recognized that even though conveyances were in writing, something was lacking.

To provide what was thought to be a final remedy for removing uncertainty, various recording laws were enacted. They impose on the recipient of a conveyance the duty to make the transaction a matter of public record. By these recording laws, certain legal effect is given to all records publicly filed. The first secures ownership of a bona fide instrument first filed. Second, priority of liens among creditors was secured where land was made the basis of credit. Secret titles and secret liens were no longer recognized. Creditors recognized for the first tme that land afforded them the safest security for their claims. Sales of real property were stimulated.

Thus, at present, publicity concerning titles to land prevails, and the laws charge all persons with notice of that which the public record reveals. With the frequent changes of ownership of land and the passage of time, the title to land grows more and more complex. With this increasing complexity, purchasers and prospective lenders demand a careful examination of the records. Such examinations involve the expenditure of time and money and the ever-increasing possibility of error. To meet the needs of the times, systems of title registration have been developed and are employed at present in 12 states and a number of foreign countries.[5] These systems of title registrations, which are fundamentally the same, originated with the Australian law known as the Torrens Law, which is described below.

Torrens Law

In 1857, Sir Robert Torrens, a British businessman, worked out a system of title registration that was first adopted in South Australia in 1858. **Torrens Law,** where it has been adopted, ensures that any landowner who has been issued a Torrens certificate of title shall in law conclusively be presumed to be the owner of the land described in the certificate. Although the Torrens system varies somewhat in the states where it has been adopted, the procedure remains basically the same. One should be aware of the great distinction between the deed and the Torrens title. Under the system of recording deeds, the deed is always open to contest and is thus an object of possible future controversy. A deed is not conclusive evidence of title. Under the recording system, a deed is registered; but under the Torrens system, the *title* to real property is registered, and this is the great distinction. In the remaining sections of this chapter, detailed attention is given to a number of aspects of the Torrens system.

Procedure for Registering Title. In the states where the Torrens system has been adopted, the procedure for registering title varies, but only to a minor degree. Basically the procedure is the same:

1. The owner of the property must seek to have the title registered. The owner does this by petition under oath in a court designated for that purpose.

---

[5]California, Colorado, Hawaii, Illinois, Massachusetts, Minnesota, New York, North Carolina, Ohio, Oregon, Virginia, and Washington.

2. The application or petition usually contains the name, age, residence, and domestic condition of the applicant (that is, whether or not the applicant is married, divorced, widowed, and so forth). The land is described and the nature of the interest of the owner is mentioned; for example, "The estate interest or right claimed by the petitioner in the property the title to which is sought to be registered is as follows: fee simple absolute."
3. If the land is occupied by anyone other than the petitioner, his or her name and address and interest in the property are mentioned.
4. A statement is made of the liens against the land, if any, together with the names and addresses of the lienors.
5. The names and addresses of any persons (including any corporation) having or claiming any interest in or lien upon the property, or any part thereof, the title to which is sought to be registered, and whether or not any of them are minors or otherwise incompetent are included in the petition to register title.
6. The application is addressed to the court having the proper jurisdiction in the county in which the land is located and power is given to that court to inquire into the condition of the title and to make all necessary orders, judgments, and decrees, including removal of clouds on title, establishing and declaring of the title or interest against all persons known or unknown, and declaring the order of preference of all liens and encumbrances.
7. As soon as the application has been filed, an order is entered referring the application to one of the examiners of title appointed by the registrar of title (usually the county clerk). The examiner then examines into the title and the truth of the facts recited in the petition. Examiner is given the full power to administer oaths and to examine witnesses, and may, if necessary, apply to the court for directions. After the examination, the examiner reports to the court the findings and conclusions from the examination.
8. The court may then either (1) reject the application in toto, (2) defer entering a decree until such future time as may be deemed according to the justice in the case, or (3) enter an order that the registrar issue a certificate of title to the petitioner or to such other person as may be entitled to a certificate of title.

Conveyances and Liens After Registration. For there to be any force and effect of future dealings after the title to the land has been registered, it is necessary that all instruments pass through the registrar's office and be noted on the registered land. For example, if a registered owner wishes to convey the land, the owner makes out a deed and transfers the deed together with the certificate of title. The deed and the certificate of title are filed with the registrar. The registrar cancels the old certificate of title and makes out a new one to the grantee. Each certificate issued contains a statement of all liens and the order of their priority.

Insurance Fund. The question arises as to what will happen in the event of error in these somewhat complicated proceedings. In some states, indemnity for errors or fraud is provided for by requiring that the registrar of title, as well as the examiner of title, execute indemnity bonds in favor of the people of the state. In addition to this, all states require the establishment of an indemnity fund. In some states a small fraction of the value of the property is charged at the time the land is registered, while in others a portion of the fees collected is set aside. For example, assume the enactment of a registration system where a $50 fee is established for the cost of registering the title. Thus, after the completion of the action, there exists $50 in the indemnity fund. The second action increases the fund to $100, and so on.

Arguments for the Torrens System. The proponents of the Torrens system feel that both the owners of property and the public will be benefited by the system.

The owner benefits because:

1. The title, after having been registered, is safe beyond question.
2. The title can be exhibited easily and accurately and without charge to any prospective purchaser or to any person to whom application for credit is being made.
3. No abstracts or examinations of title are necessary after title is registered, thus eliminating that expense.
4. There is no loss of sales through delay in securing abstracts or from frequent and technical objections of examining attorneys.

The public at large benefits because

1. A prospective mortgagee can learn within a few minutes the nature of the security; and a loan can be closed within a few hours after application, thus speeding up commercial transactions.
2. A prospective buyer can, at no expense and in a few moments, ascertain from the registrar of title the status of the title of the property that prospect desires to purchase.
3. A judgment creditor can ascertain easily and without expense whether or not the judgment debtor has lands subject to execution.
4. Unskilled abstractors and conveyancers cannot bungle transactions leading to later doubts of the status of title.

Arguments Against the Torrens System. The opponents of the Torrens system offer a number of arguments; chiefly,

1. In many states, the indemnity funds are applicable only in the county in which previous fees have created the fund. For example, the funds paid to the registrar in Suffolk County, New York, do not provide an indemnity for property registered in New York County. Thus, the opponents of the Torrens system say that it would be almost useless to bring valuable property under the provisions of the law.
2. Some opponents of the Torrens system argue that the cost of title registration is much greater than the cost of title insurance, even after due allowance is made for the cost of the survey (which, in most instances, must be filed with the petition in a registration proceeding and, in many instances, is a prerequisite for obtaining title insurance). In addition, the registration proceeding takes time and is sometimes exceedingly complex.
3. Although memorials (notations) are made on the certificate of title of the mortgages, liens, etc., they are only warnings; and the original instruments creating these memorials must be carefully and methodically examined as to nature and extent of such interest.
4. Property once registered cannot be removed from the system except by permission of the court.
5. It may deprive a person of property without due process of law and thus be repugnant to the constitution. This argument is based on the fact that notice is published naming the parties to the action. Some parties having an interest in the property may not have been named in the publication of the notice because their names might have been overlooked in preparing the abstract. It is argued that such an omission does, in a very real way, deprive them of their property without due process of law.

GLOSSARY

Abstract of title A condensed history of the title of land

Acknowledgment A formal declaration made before some public officer, usually a notary public, by a person who as signed a deed, mortgage, or other instrument, stating that the instrument is that person's genuine and voluntary act or deed

ATA mortgagee's policy American Title Association Loan Policy, which covers exceptions enumerated in other policies

Authentication of acknowledgment Certification by the county clerk of the authority and validity of a notary public

Chain of title A part of an abstract of title that shows the ownership of the property over a period of time, depending on the length of the search

Flag A certificate of proof that a person is a commissioned notary

***Lis pendens* index** An index located in the county clerk's office containing the names of plaintiffs and defendants, the date of the filing of the *lis pendens,* and a column for file numbers

Livery of seizin Historically, a means of conveying an interest in real property by the symbolic delivery to the grantee of a piece of turf or twig from the property to be transferred

Mortgagee's title policy A title insurance policy which insures the interest of the mortgagee in the property under consideration

Opinion of title An opinion based on the assumption of title in a particular person at a certain date and contained in the certification of title annexed to the abstract; the examiner's certification of the title from an examination of the records from that date

Owner's title policy See purchaser's title policy

Purchaser's policy Policy insuring the interest of the purchaser of real property

Purchaser's title policy A title insurance policy insuring the interest of the purchaser of real property

Recording acts Statutes of registration which provide generally for the recording (filing) of every instrument in writing by which any estate or interest in land is created, transferred, mortgaged, or assigned, or by which the title to land may be affected in law or in equity

Title insurance Insurance issued by a title insurance company insuring against any defects in an owner's title to real property

Torrens Law A system whereby title to real property is registered

QUESTIONS FOR REVIEW

1. Why should an appraiser have a working knowledge of title searching?
2. Melinda Davis has a signed contract for the sale of her real property. You, the buyer, have an abstract brought up to date and deliver it to your attorney. Your attorney discovers a recorded lease with four years to go. What would your attorney advise?
3. What is the purpose of the recording acts?
4. Why must a title company have an abstract?

5. In addition to a title insurance policy, most financial institutions will insist on a survey. Why?
6. What are the advantages of a title insurance policy over an abstract?
7. Briefly explain the Torrens system.

PROBLEMS AND ACTIVITIES

1. Obtain a list of rates from your local title company and compare them with fees charged either by a local title company or a local attorney.
2. Select a lot or other piece of property in your county and prepare an abstract going back ten years. Use the materials located in the county clerk's office or the county recorder's office.
3. You are the lending officer of a savings and loan association. The local title company notifies you that the property on which you are prepared to lend money had a mechanic's lien filed against it in 1989, on which no action has been taken. What are your alternatives with regard to the loan?

22

TITLE CLOSING OR SETTLEMENT

KEY TERMS

Assumption statement
Bill of sale
Certificate of occupancy
Counter proposal
Real Estate Settlement Procedures Act
Reduction certificate
Survey
Title closing
Title search
Truth in Lending Act

The **title closing,** or settlement as it is often called, marks the completion of a transaction. The transaction has proceeded from contract to delivery of the deed. At the closing the necessary documents change hands, computations are made to determine amounts due all the parties connected with that transaction, and the necessary monies are paid to the parties involved. Most closings move along without a hitch, yet some present problems that cause much difficulty.

A broker's error or uncertainty may cause the collapse of a title closing in the Southern, Western, and Midwestern states where brokers are responsible for real estate transactions. However, even in those states where title is closed by attorneys, knowledgeable brokers can often avoid losing a hard-earned commission.

CLOSING METHODS

At the closing of title, one of two things will happen:

1. A deed may be delivered in escrow. Escrow, as defined in Chapter 7, is

> A scroll, writing, or deed delivered by the grantor into the hands of a third person to be held by the latter until the happening of a contingency or the performance of a condition and then delivered by the third person to the grantee.

2. A deed may be delivered to the purchaser, the more common procedure.

Delivery of Deed

In the latter situation, the deed is actually delivered, and a mortgage is taken by a bank or other lending institution to cover part of the purchase price of the property. This is the consummation of the terms of the ordinary contract for the sale of real property. At the closing, the deed is executed and delivered by the seller to the purchaser; the mortgage is executed and delivered by the purchaser (mortgagor) to the lending institution (the mortgagee); and the funds are paid over to the seller.

Assume the purchaser is a builder or developer buying a $1 million piece of land on which to build an apartment complex. The lender is a life insurance company. The builder-developer has paid $25,000 as earnest money with an additional $225,000 due on closing.

At the closing, both the seller and the purchaser will be present, together with their respective attorneys and the attorney for the insurance company. The closing will take place either at the office of one of the attorneys or at the insurance company office. If a real estate broker is involved, the broker will also be present at the closing in order to collect the commission from the seller.

On arriving at the closing, the attorneys will make a note of the persons present at the closing. If a broker is handling the closing, the broker, too, should make a notation of the persons present at the closing. This is an important record to make in the event any later question arises; for if there is any dispute, the names of the witnesses are available for consultation.

After this has been completed, the attorney for the seller delivers a prepared deed to the attorney for the purchaser who examines it for proper description and so forth. The attorney representing the insurance company will also examine the deed. The title policy will be examined by the attorney for the purchaser and the attorney for the insurance company.

A mortgage, or a note and mortgage, is usually prepared by the attorney for the insurance company and is examined by the attorney for the purchaser for description, prepayment clauses, or any other pertinent details. This, together with the note, is then signed by the purchaser. The insurance company representative gives a check, in the amount of $750,000 in this case, payable to the purchaser. The purchaser endorses the check and delivers it to the seller together with the $225,000 due to the seller, and purchaser receives from the seller a properly executed deed, which is then promptly recorded by the attorney for the purchaser. The attorney for the insurance company records the mortgage.

At the same time, adjustments are made for commissions, taxes, and so on.

If the property to be transferred is a home valued at, say, $70,000, and the mortgage financing is done through a savings and loan association, then the Real Estate Settlement Procedures Act of 1975 must be strictly complied with. This is detailed later in the chapter.

Closing Through Escrow

There are several ways that the term *closing through escrow,* or *settling the escrow,* is used.

Suppose real property is to be sold on contract or a contract for deed, as outlined in Chapter 7. A formal contract for the sale of property is drawn, defining the rights of the parties, the amount to be paid on closing, and the interest to be paid. A deed is prepared and executed by the seller, and an abstract or title insurance is generally obtained by the seller. The abstract or insurance may be obtained by the purchaser, however, depending on local custom. In those states where it is the custom for the seller to deliver the abstract or title insurance policy (which will have been spelled out in the contract of sale) and where title insurance is a relatively new device, most sellers who have received abstracts of title themselves will deliver an abstract rather than a title policy. When the purchaser desires a title policy in these states, arrangements might be made with the seller for a title policy, with an agreement, if necessary, to pay any additional costs.

The purchaser pays the down payment to the seller. The signed deed, the insurance policies, and the contract are then delivered to an escrow agent. The escrow agent is often a real estate broker or a bank's escrow department. The escrow agents charge a small fee in return for which they collect the monthly payments and deliver the sums collected to the seller.

A carefully drawn list of instructions that defines the duties of the escrow agent is included in addition to the instruments listed above. These instructions are signed by both the purchaser and the seller.

When a deed is delivered in escrow, title is transferred to the grantee only on performance of the conditions of the contract. Usually, however, the purchaser, by terms of the agreement, is entitled to the possession of the property, and the grantor retains the right to foreclose in the event of default upon the part of the purchaser.

Escrow, or closing through escrow, is used in a different sense, particularly in California, Colorado, Idaho, Minnesota, and Nevada.

Assume a real estate broker has brought together a buyer and a seller and a contract for the sale of real property is drawn. The transaction is then placed in escrow or "an escrow is opened"—as it is said. The contract, earnest money, and a list of instructions are given to a licensed and bonded escrow agent (the agent may be an escrow department of a title company, financial institution, or an independent escrow company).

The escrow agent holds the earnest money in a special account, orders a title policy, receives the money from the lenders, accumulates all the documents, and effects the transaction alone. All communications are handled through the real estate broker to the escrow agent.

Instruments are recorded, monies paid out, and title is passed. The transaction is then "out of escrow."

These are the specific ways title is closed, or settled. However, there are numerous details that must be examined from the point of view of both the seller and the purchaser.

THE CLOSING FROM THE SELLER'S VIEWPOINT

Taxes and Liens

The seller will be required to bring to the closing the latest tax receipts that have been received from the treasurer of the county in which the property is located. The receipts indicate that the real property taxes have been paid. Although the purchaser will know either from the abstract of title or from the title policy whether or not the seller has paid the taxes, it is quite conceivable an error might have been made by the tax collector's office, and the receipts will indicate that the seller has truly paid the taxes. If the seller has paid the taxes in advance, an apportionment, which is explained later in the chapter, will be made with the seller receiving credit for that part of the taxes that have been paid in advance.

Great care must be taken by the person closing title to determine the tax regulations of the locale in which the property is situated. In some localities, although tax bills are not presented to the taxpayer until the middle of the year, they nevertheless become a lien against the property from the first of the year. In these places, it is customary to prorate the taxes on the basis of the previous year's tax bill.

The seller knows, or should know, before appearing at the closing, whether or not there are any liens against the property. These must be taken care of prior to the closing; otherwise the deal cannot be consummated. If, for example, there is a judgment against seller in the amount of $500, then the seller will appear at the closing with the satisfaction piece. The satisfaction piece, together with the recording fee, will be delivered to the attorney for the purchaser; or if a bank is involved, to the attorney for the bank who will record the satisfaction piece at the same time the mortgage is recorded.

The seller must, at this time, be prepared to remove any other liens or clouds on the title. If there is a preexisting mortgage, for example, either the seller must appear with the satisfaction of mortgage indicating the mortgage has been paid, or the seller must notify the mortgagee who will then appear at the closing with a properly executed satisfaction that will be delivered to the seller on receiving payment at the closing.

Possibility of Reduction Certificate or Assumption Statement

If the contract for the sale of the property calls for a statement of the amount due on existing mortgages that are being "assumed" or taken "subject to" by the purchaser, then the seller must obtain and bring to the closing the mortgagee's **reduction certificate** filled out as shown in Chapter 11. The certificate shows the amount of the unpaid principal, the interest thereon, the rate of interest, and the date of maturity of the mortgage.

In some states an **assumption statement** is used instead of a reduction certificate. The statement is obtained from the lending institution holding the mortgage which is to be assumed. Basically, it contains the same information as the reduction certificate.

Insurance Policies

At this point the subject of insurance becomes of paramount importance to the purchaser or to the mortgagee. The seller, therefore, brings the insurance policies to the closing so that if a question arises about the amount of apportionment to be made, a ready answer as to the amount of premium paid will be available. In some instances, the purchaser will want to accept the existing policies. The seller should obtain a letter from the insurance company in which the insurance company agrees to the transfer of the policies to the purchaser. In this case, the policies themselves are assigned to the purchaser.

Leases

If the purchaser is buying investment property and there are tenants in the property, it is incumbent on the seller to deliver the original leases to the new purchaser, together with a prepared schedule of rents being paid by the tenants. Any tenant's deposits are turned over to the purchaser who gives a receipt and indemnifies the seller from any subsequent claim of the tenants.

Bill of Sale

When personal property is involved in the deal, the seller should appear at the closing with a **bill of sale** covering it. Whereas the deed conveys title to the real property, the bill of sale conveys title to personal property.

The bill of sale names the parties to the transaction together with the statement that the seller conveys title to the chattels contained in a schedule, which is made a part of the instrument. This is followed by the covenant whereby the seller warrants to defend the sale of the goods and chattels. A schedule of the items sold is then prepared and attached to the bill of sale and made a part of it. The instrument is executed by the seller and an acknowledgment is usually made.

Sometimes a statement is contained in the bill of sale to the effect that it was made to induce the purchaser to purchase the chattels. This statement provides easy proof of the necessary elements of fraud should the seller's title to the chattels later prove defective. Technically, it shows there was an intent on the part of the seller to defraud.

Internal Revenue Stamps

Until January 1, 1968, a provision of the Internal Revenue Code provided that a stamp tax amounting to 55 cents for every $500 or part thereof over $99 be placed on deeds in the form of a stamp. Now the states have legislation providing for a nominal tax on deeds based on the selling price. The purpose of both of these taxes was to enable county assessors to determine actual selling prices for tax purposes and to aid appraisers in ascertaining selling prices to determine comparative market values of homes under appraisement.

THE CLOSING FROM THE PURCHASER'S VIEWPOINT

Title Search

Whether the abstract of title or title insurance is to be furnished by seller or purchaser, a **title search** must be made. This is done substantially as outlined in Chapter 21.

In those states where the broker, rather than an attorney, customarily closes title, the broker must not render a judgment or an opinion concerning the validity of the title as shown by the abstract. To do this would encroach on the province of the attorney and in all cases is a violation of the broker's licensing law.

The attorney will examine the title report and pass upon any encumbrances of liens that are shown therein. It is at this point that the title may be rejected on the grounds that it is not "good and marketable," as called for in the contract. It may be that the contract for the sale of the property called for the title to be an "insurable title." If there are encumbrances that cannot be cleared within a reasonable time, the title will be rejected. The deposit will be returned to the purchaser and, in some instances, the seller may be liable to the purchaser for out-of-pocket expenses and also to the broker for commissions due.

Survey

Generally, a **survey** is required by lending institutions before they will lend money on a particular parcel of property. The survey determines things that are not of record, for example, encroachments. The eaves of a roof overlapping the property of a neighbor, or a building on an adjoining property wrongly built upon the land that is the subject of the transaction are examples of encroachments.

The survey may also show a zoning violation that would be of interest to a lending institution. For example, a municipality passes a zoning ordinance stating in effect that no building shall be built less than 15 feet from either side of the property line. A survey will show the relation of the building to the property line. If the building has been built after the ordinance was passed and is less than 15 feet from either line, this is a clear violation of the ordinance, and a lending institution may refuse the loan.

Examination of Existing Leases

If the building is an income property and there are existing leases at the time of the sale, the attorney for the purchaser must examine the leases in detail. The leases are examined in conjunction with statements made by the seller in the contract. For example, the purchaser wishes to purchase a parcel of property, demolish the existing building, and construct a parking lot on the land. In the contract for the sale of the property, there should be a statement about the length of existing leases and the amounts of rent received from each of the tenants. It is quite possible the termination date of the leases might have been misrepresented in the contract, in which case it might be impossible for the new purchaser to proceed with the demolition of the building at that time.

If the property is being purchased for income purposes, the attorney will examine the leases to see whether or not the income is as represented by the contract.

In addition, the brokers, when obtaining listings of this type, attempt to ascertain the income from rents as accurately as possible, and in those areas having rent control to determine whether or not the rents are at ceiling or above.

If there are leases in conjunction with a closing, the mere examination of the lease in and of itself is not enough. The purchaser must be protected from the possibility that the rents have been paid to the seller in advance. Therefore, to protect the purchaser, the attorney for the purchaser should insist that the seller make an affidavit to the effect that no rents have been paid in advance by the tenants to the seller.

Corporate Franchise Taxes

If there are unpaid state corporate franchise taxes in the chain of title, they should be cleared at the time of the closing. Some states and the federal government place a tax on a corporation for the privilege of doing business. This tax is not based on income, but must be paid regardless of whether or not any business is actually done by the corporation. The franchise tax is not customarily apportioned, but is paid by the seller unless there is a special agreement to the contrary.

Certificate of Occupancy

In some instances, especially when a new building is being purchased, a **certificate of occupancy** is one of the items required to be delivered by the seller to the purchaser. Many municipalities have enacted ordinances requiring that certain standards be met, especially with regard to plumbing and electrical wiring. When a building is constructed, it is inspected to determine whether or not these standards have been met; if they have been met, a certificate of occupancy attesting to the fact is delivered to the builder. This certificate should be obtained from the seller at the closing when it is necessary.

Violations of Municipal Departments

Any violations of municipal departments must be removed by the seller at the time of the closing. For example, there may be a fire violation against the premises. If the seller has not removed the violation at the time of closing of title, it is customary to deposit in escrow a sum sufficient to clear the violation. The seller is then given a certain time after the closing to remove the violations. In the event that the violations are not removed by the time stated in the escrow instructions, then the purchaser may proceed to remove the violations. The seller authorizes the escrow agent to apply the deposit against any cost of removing the violations and further agrees that if there is deficiency, the difference will be paid. If there is any balance in escrow after the violations have been removed, it is paid to the seller.

Apportionments

At the closing, certain charges must be apportioned between the parties. The items commonly apportioned are taxes, water and electric charges, gas, rents, certain services that have been paid in advance like burglary protection, and sometimes even the value of growing crops.

The problem of apportionment reduces to a problem of simple arithmetic. The main difficulties that arise are, first, the local customs with regard to apportionment must be determined; and, second, these customs must be followed to the letter.

For example, in some parts of the country, apportionments are made to the day prior to closing; in others, the closing is to and including the day of closing. An outline for handling the charges is shown in Exhibit 22-1.

THE CLOSING FROM THE VIEWPOINT OF A MORTGAGE LENDER

The flowchart shown as Exhibit 22-2 summarizes a title closing from the viewpoint of a mortgage lender. It should be pointed out that not all of the steps are necessary in some closings; for example, where a mortgage is assumed or where the sale is on a contract for deed.

ADJOURNMENT OF CLOSING (SETTLEMENT)

Unless the contract for the sale of the property states that "time is of the essence," the closing may, if necessary, be adjourned for a reasonable time. Occasionally, for example, a bank has not yet completed the processing of a loan, or the abstractor has not yet completed the title search. In such instances, the closing will be adjourned until a later date.

When attorneys are handling the closing, this is done by a written stipulation between the attorney for the seller and the attorney for the buyer. In those states where the closing is handled by brokers, a **counter**

Exhibit 22-1 Computing Backward or Forward from the Date of Closing

KIND OF ITEM	ENCOUNTERED	DEBIT TO	WHY?	CREDIT TO	WHY?	FIGURE
Interest accumulated	Usual	Seller	He rid himself of a debt.	Buyer	He will pay cash later.	Back
Interest paid in advance	Unusual	Buyer	He gets the right to use the house free of interest payments.	Seller	He sold a right in addition to the house.	Forward
Insurance premium paid in advance	Usual	Buyer	He bought something besides a house.	Seller	He sold the future effectiveness of a policy.	Forward
Insurance premium which is in arrears	Unusual	Seller	He rid himself of an accounts payable.	Buyer	He will pay out cash later.	Back
Rent paid in advance	Usual	Seller	The tenant made a part of the last month's rent payment for the benefit of the buyer.	Buyer	The right to use this house will be denied him for the rent period.	Forward
Rent in arrears	Unusual	Buyer	He bought an accounts receivable in addition to a house.	Seller	He sold one of his accounts receivable.	Back
Taxes paid in advance	Often	Buyer	He bought the right to live in a house without paying taxes.	Seller	He sold a house *plus* the right to live there without paying rent for rest of tax period.	Forward
Taxes in arrears	Often	Seller	He rid himself of an accounts payable.	Buyer	He will pay this money out later.	Back

SOURCE: C. Glenn Lewis, "The Broker's Three Primary Legal Instruments," *(mimeo). By special permission of the author.*

Exhibit 22-2 Title Closing From Mortgage Lender's Viewpoint

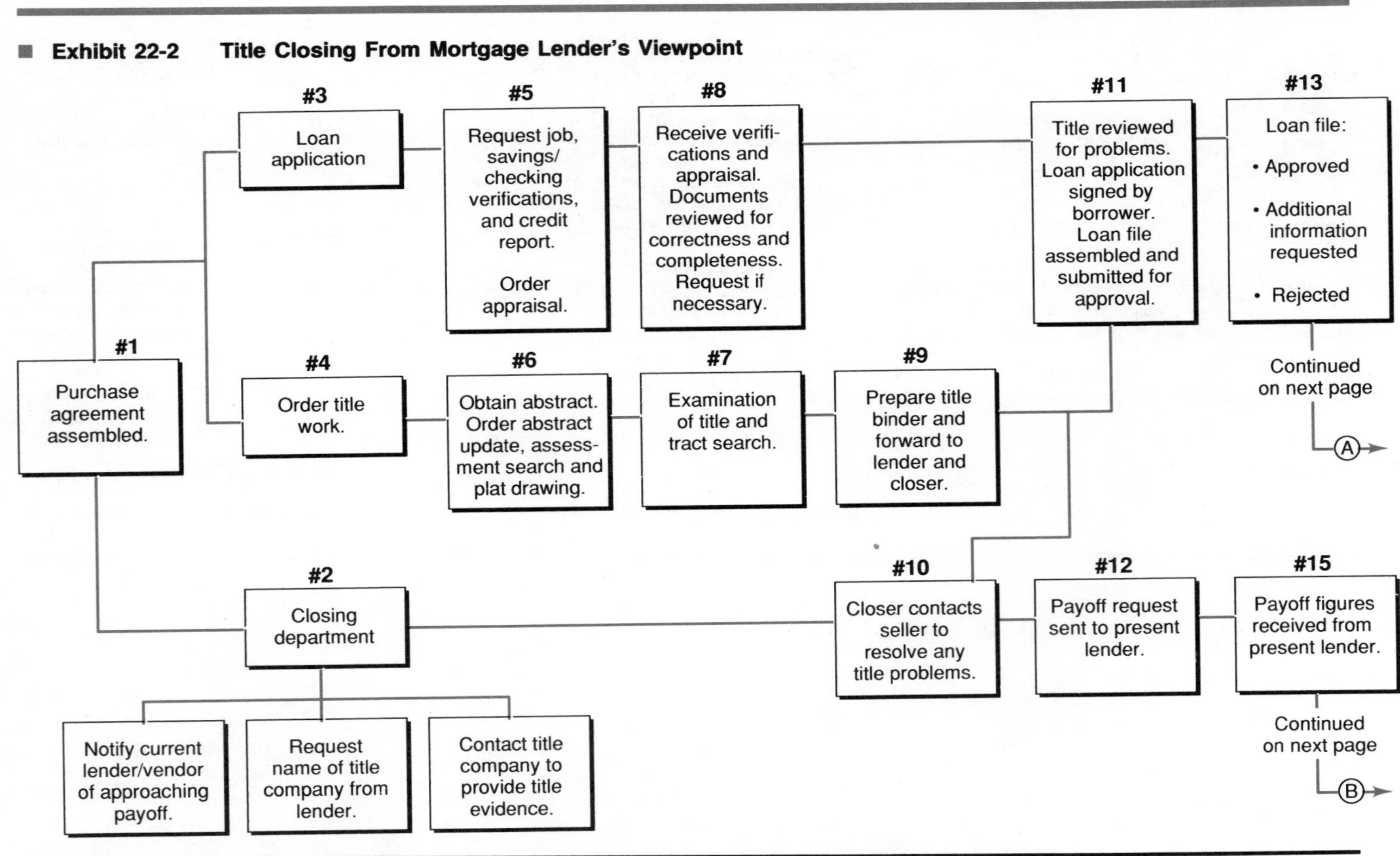

Exhibit 22-2 (continued)

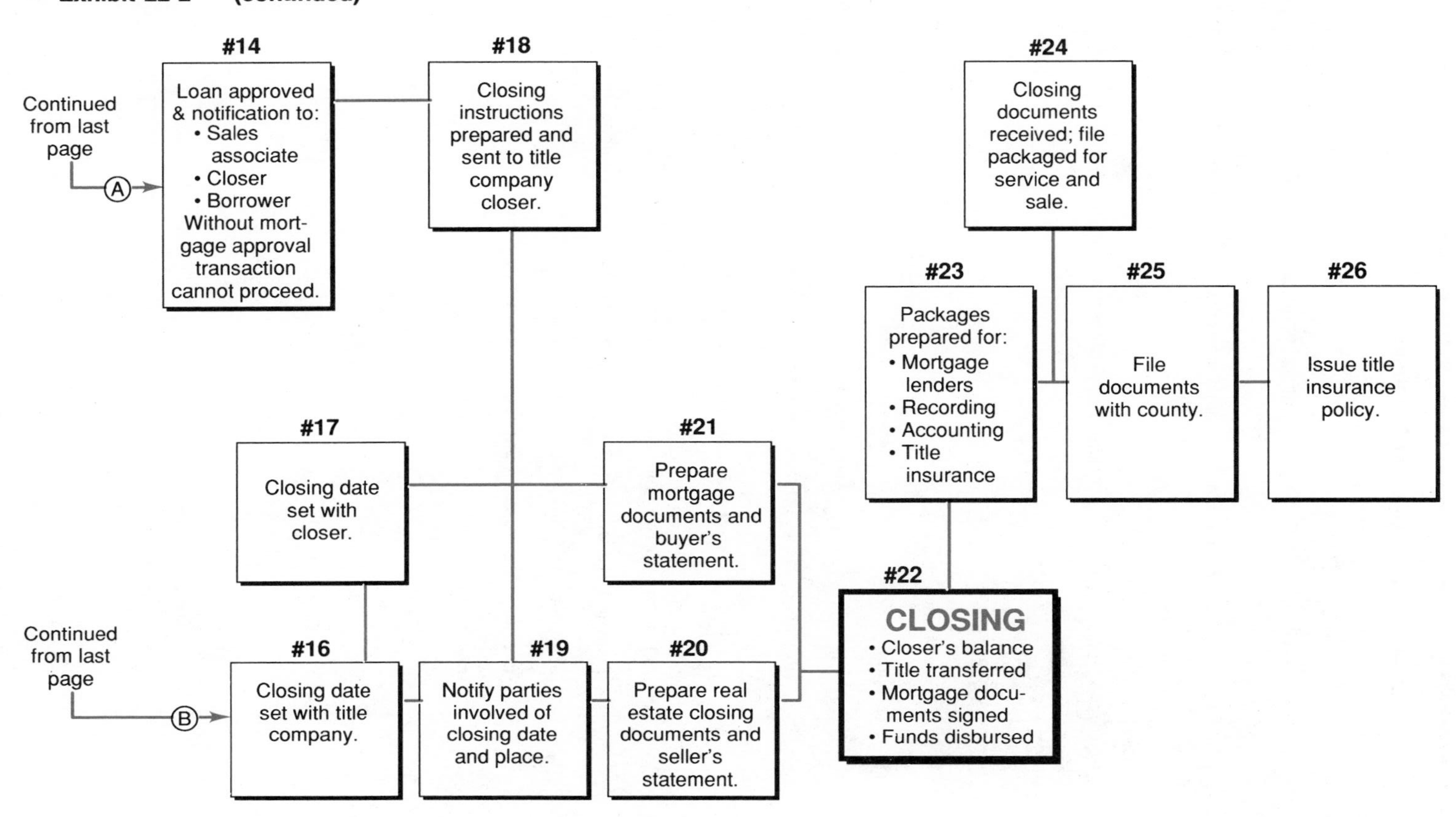

SOURCE: Edina Realty, Inc.

Exhibit 22-3 Counter Proposal

COUNTER PROPOSAL

Regarding the proposed contract for the purchase of property described as:

[the legal description]

situated in the City of , County of ,
State of , dated 19 ,
between as Owner(s)
and as Purchaser(s).

The undersigned Owner(s) accepts said proposed contract, subject to the following amendments:

(extend the date of closing to)

All other terms and conditions remain the same. If this Counter Proposal is accepted by Purchaser(s), as evidenced by Purchaser(s)' signature(s) hereon, on or before 19 , the said proposed contract, as amended hereby, shall become a contract between the parties.

____
Owner(s)

The foregoing Counter Proposal is accepted this day of , 19 .

____
Purchaser(s)

proposal is signed by both the owner and purchaser of the property in a form similar to Exhibit 22-3.

The document in Exhibit 22-3 is also used in the strict sense of the words *counter proposal.* For example, a buyer, through a broker, enters into a receipt and agreement to purchase as outlined in Chapter 7. Assume the listing is for $60,000, and the buyer offers $53,000. The broker transmits the offer to the seller who counters with $55,000 (written on the form after the words, "subject to the following amendments"). If the buyer then signs the counter proposal, the purchase price of the property is $55,000.

REAL ESTATE SETTLEMENT PROCEDURES ACT

The **Real Estate Settlement Procedures Act,** first passed in 1974 and amended in 1975, established a uniform procedure for closing loans on one- to four-family residential dwellings.

Congress found (in 1974) that consumers needed protection from "... unnecessarily high settlement charges caused by certain abusive practices that have developed in some areas of the country."

The *only* legal sanctions provided by the Real Estate Settlement Procedures Act involve

1. *Kickbacks.* The law prohibits anyone from giving or taking a fee, kickback, or anything of value under an agreement that business will be referred to a specific person or organization. For example, attorneys often received a "referral fee" (really a kickback) from title companies for placing title insurance.

   In addition, the aggrieved party can collect three times the amount of the kickback.

2. *Title insurance.* A seller may not require, as a condition of sale, that the buyer purchase title insurance from a particular company. A violation of this provision also provides a penalty in the amount of three times the cost of the policy.

3. *Reserve accounts.* Under the Real Estate Settlement Procedures Act, the maximum amount a lender can require a borrower to put in a reserve account cannot exceed the sum of (1) an amount that would have been sufficient to pay taxes, insurance premiums, or other charges that would have been paid under normal lending practices, and ending on the due date of the first full monthly installment payment; plus (2) an additional amount not in excess of one-sixth (2 months) of the estimated total amount of taxes, insurance premiums, and other charges to be paid on the dates indicated above during any 12-month period to follow.

For example, assume the settlement date is April 30, and the due date for taxes is December 1 for the calendar year. The due date of the first mortgage loan installment is June 1, and the yearly taxes are $720. The reserve for (1) is $360 or the amount of taxes between December 1 of the previous year and June 1 ($60 per month × 6 months = $360). Reserves under (2) *can be* up to two months advance payments times $60, or $120. Thus, the total *maximum* tax reserves on the April 30 settlement date can be $360 + $120 = $480.

The same procedure is used for insurance premiums and other charges. The reason, of course, is to prevent lenders from collecting *excessive* reserves.

Who Must Comply

All federally regulated lenders must comply with the act. This means financial institutions supervised by the Federal Reserve Board, Federal Home Loan Bank Board, Federal Deposit Insurance Corporation, Veterans Administration, and other government-backed or government-assisted lenders. Under consideration by regulators is the need for real estate brokers who advertise financing to comply with RESPA.

What Loans Are Exempt

Because the act is designed to protect homeowners, commercial loans are exempt. Furthermore, assumptions, loans to finance the purchase of property for resale (construction loans), home improvement loans, and loans on property in excess of 25 acres are exempt.

Lender Requirements

Under the act, the borrower applying for a loan must be given

1. A HUD information booklet explaining the settlement proceedings.
2. A "good faith" estimate of the closing costs (or the lender has three business days to give the good faith estimate to the person applying for the loan).

An example of the good faith closing costs estimate form is shown as Exhibit 22-4.

All of the items are self-explanatory, with the possible exception of the loan origination fee. As defined in the HUD booklet, "This fee covers the lender's administrative costs. Often expressed as a percentage of the loan, the fee will vary among lenders and from locality to locality." This is patently incorrect—a perfect example of bureaucratic naivete. Although the origination fee is often expressed as a percentage of the loan, it has absolutely nothing to do with administrative costs. A 2 percent charge on a $40,000 loan is $800; a 2 percent charge on a $30,000 loan is $600. The cost of the paperwork is exactly the same in either case. Lenders simply charge what the traffic will bear.

For example, assume a buyer agrees to buy a condominium for a total purchase price of $65,000. (If the property were a home, the calculations

Exhibit 22-4 Estimated Closing Costs Form

FEDERAL SAVINGS

444 17th Street
Denver, Colorado 80202
303/573-7283

ESTIMATED CLOSING COSTS

The following are estimates of the amount of costs for certain services which Borrowers are likely to purchase in connection with the settlement on the purchase of real property.

These estimated amounts reflect charges experienced in the locality, but may be substantially different from the actual costs you will incur.

This is not a loan commitment.

ESTIMATED CLOSING COSTS BASED ON A LOAN AMOUNT OF $ 58,500.00.
RATE 12 TERM 360 RATIO 90

NO. ON UNIFORM SETTLEMENT STATEMENT		
801	LOAN ORIGINATION FEE	1,462.50
804	CREDIT REPORT	20.00
805	INSPECTION (APPRAISAL) FEE	85.00
806	PRIVATE MTG. INS.	-
	APPLICATION REVIEW FEE	-
807	ASSUMPTION FEE	
808	COMMITMENT FEE ____ %	-
901	INTEREST ____ days	-
902	PRIVATE MTG. INS. PREMIUM	-
903	MORTGAGEES HAZARD INSURANCE PREMIUM*	248.00
1001	INSURANCE RESERVE	-
1002	PRIVATE MTG. INS. RESERVE **	-
1102	ABSTRACT OR TITLE SEARCH	-
1103	TITLE EXAMINATION	-
1107	ATTORNEYS CERTIFICATE OF TITLE	25.00
1108	TITLE INSURANCE-LENDER'S COVERAGE	138.00
1111	TAX SERVICE	15.00
1201	RECORDING FEES	10.00
1203	DOCUMENTARY FEE	5.00
1301	SURVEY	35.00
___	TAX CERTIFICATE	5.00
___	FHA INSURANCE RESERVE	
___	OTHER	

APPROXIMATE LOAN PAYMENT

P&I =	601.75
TAX =	106.00
INS =	22.00
MTG INS =	
TOTAL =	729.75

APPROXIMATE SETTLEMENT AMOUNT:

A. PURCHASE PRICE	65,000.00
B. REPAIRS AND IMPROVEMENTS	
C. TOTAL CLOSING COSTS	2,148.50
D. PREPAID ESCROWS	
E. TOTAL	67,148.50
F. AMT. THIS LOAN	58,500.00
G. OTHER FINANCING	
H. DEPOSIT TO DATE	1,000.00
I. CLOSING COSTS PAID BY SELLER	
J. CASH REQUIRED FOR CLOSING	7,648.50

* Hazard insurance is required. You may purchase insurance from any person or organization you choose.
** Mortgage insurance, if required, is paid from the interest charged.

An attorneys certificate of title will be provided to the lender at an estimated cost of $ 25.00,

by (name) ____________________

(address) ____________________ (phone) ____________________.
This provider has a business relationship with Midland Federal Savings.

THIS FORM DOES NOT COVER ALL ITEMS YOU WILL BE REQUIRED TO PAY IN CASH AT SETTLEMENT, FOR EXAMPLE, DEPOSIT IN ESCROW FOR REAL ESTATE TAXES. YOU MAY WISH TO INQUIRE AS TO THE AMOUNT OF SUCH OTHER ITEMS.

Date: ____________________

____________________ BORROWER ____________________ LOAN COUNSELOR

____________________ BORROWER

SOURCE: Midland Federal Savings, Denver, Colorado

would be the same, except for homeowners dues.) The closing is to be on June 29, and a loan was applied for on April 27. The first document given to the buyer is a good faith estimate of the closing costs on a $58,500 loan being applied for.

TRUTH IN LENDING

Although the Real Estate Settlement Procedures Act does *not* provide for **truth in lending,** Regulation Z does. Under the law, the terms and conditions of the loan must be declared in writing to the borrower. The disclosures consist of

1. The total finance charges.
2. The date finance charges begin.
3. The number of payments.
4. The due dates of payments.
5. The prepayment penalties.
6. The total of all payments.
7. The annual percentage rate (APR).
   The APR is most important. It is the total annual cost of credit. It includes interest, discount points, and other fees, such as application fees, inspection fees, closing fees, any loan discount fees, prepaid interest, prepaid mortgage insurance premiums (MIP) on FHA loans, and also prepaid mortgage insurance premiums on conventional loans.

The APR is *not* the interest rate. It is a combination of the interest rate plus the other charges outlined above and is designed to reveal to the borrower the true cost. Assume, for example, $10,000 is borrowed for a year at an interest rate of 12 percent plus two points as an origination fee. At the end of the year, $11,200 is paid back. The effective rate is not 12 percent because the borrower had the use of only $9,800 for the year due to the origination fee of two points. The borrower paid $1,400 for the use of $9,800 ($11,200 – $9,800 = $1,400). Thus, an effective rate of 14.29 percent ($1,400 ÷ $9,800 = .1429) was paid. This, rounded off to the nearest quarter percent, is 14.25 percent.

The above has been reduced to the following formula:

$$\frac{\text{Total finance charges}}{\text{Amount financed}} = \text{Factor} \times 100 = \frac{\text{Interest factor}}{\$100}$$

The Federal Reserve tables (see Table 22-1) are used to obtain the APR. For example, assume the finance charges on a $20,000 loan are $3,500, the contract rate is 15 percent, and the number of monthly payments is 24 (with adjustable rate mortgages which were discussed in Chapter 13, this is

Table 22-1 Sample Page from Table for Computing Annual Percentage Rate

Number	Annual Percentage Rate of															
Payments	14.00%	14.25%	14.50%	14.75%	15.00%	15.25%	15.50%	15.75%	16.00%	16.25%	16.50%	16.75%	17.00%	17.25%	17.50%	17.75%
	(Finance Charge per $100 of Amount Financed)															
1	1.17	1.19	1.21	1.23	1.25	1.27	1.29	1.31	1.33	1.35	1.37	1.40	1.42	1.44	1.46	1.48
2	1.75	1.78	1.82	1.85	1.88	1.91	1.94	1.97	2.00	2.04	2.07	2.10	2.13	2.16	2.19	2.22
3	2.34	2.38	2.43	2.47	2.51	2.55	2.59	2.64	2.68	2.72	2.76	2.80	2.85	2.89	2.93	2.97
4	2.93	2.99	3.04	3.09	3.14	3.20	3.25	3.30	3.36	3.41	3.46	3.51	3.57	3.62	3.67	3.73
5	3.53	3.59	3.65	3.72	3.78	3.84	3.91	3.97	4.04	4.10	4.16	4.23	4.29	4.35	4.42	4.48
6	4.12	4.20	4.27	4.35	4.42	4.49	4.57	4.64	4.72	4.79	4.87	4.94	5.02	5.09	5.17	5.24
7	4.72	4.81	4.89	4.98	5.06	5.15	5.23	5.32	5.40	5.49	5.58	5.66	5.75	5.83	5.92	6.00
8	5.32	5.42	5.51	5.61	5.71	5.80	5.90	6.00	6.09	6.19	6.29	6.38	6.48	6.58	6.67	6.77
9	5.92	6.03	6.14	6.25	6.35	6.46	6.57	6.68	6.78	6.89	7.00	7.11	7.22	7.32	7.43	7.54
10	6.53	6.65	6.77	6.88	7.00	7.12	7.24	7.36	7.48	7.60	7.72	7.84	7.96	8.08	8.19	8.31
11	7.14	7.27	7.40	7.53	7.66	7.79	7.92	8.05	8.18	8.31	8.44	8.57	8.70	8.83	8.96	9.09
12	7.74	7.89	8.03	8.17	8.31	8.45	8.59	8.74	8.88	9.02	9.16	9.30	9.45	9.59	9.73	9.87
13	8.36	8.51	8.66	8.81	8.97	9.12	9.27	9.43	9.58	9.73	9.89	10.04	10.20	10.35	10.50	10.66
14	8.97	9.13	9.30	9.46	9.63	9.79	9.96	10.12	10.29	10.45	10.62	10.78	10.95	11.11	11.28	11.45
15	9.59	9.76	9.94	10.11	10.29	10.47	10.64	10.82	11.00	11.17	11.35	11.53	11.71	11.88	12.06	12.24
16	10.20	10.39	10.58	10.77	10.95	11.14	11.33	11.52	11.71	11.90	12.09	12.28	12.46	12.65	12.84	13.03
17	10.82	11.02	11.22	11.42	11.62	11.82	12.02	12.22	12.42	12.62	12.83	13.03	13.23	13.43	13.63	13.83
18	11.45	11.66	11.87	12.08	12.29	12.50	12.72	12.93	13.14	13.35	13.57	13.78	13.99	14.21	14.42	14.64
19	12.07	12.30	12.52	12.74	12.97	13.19	13.41	13.64	13.86	14.09	14.31	14.54	14.76	14.99	15.22	15.44
20	12.70	12.93	13.17	13.41	13.64	13.88	14.11	14.35	14.59	14.82	15.06	15.30	15.54	15.77	16.01	16.25
21	13.33	13.58	13.82	14.07	14.32	14.57	14.82	15.06	15.31	15.56	15.81	16.06	16.31	16.56	16.81	17.07
22	13.96	14.22	14.48	14.74	15.00	15.26	15.52	15.78	16.04	16.30	16.57	16.83	17.09	17.36	17.62	17.88
23	14.59	14.87	15.14	15.41	15.68	15.96	16.23	16.50	16.78	17.05	17.32	17.60	17.88	18.15	18.43	18.70
→ 24	15.23	15.51	15.80	16.08	16.37	16.65	16.94	17.22	17.51	17.80	18.09	18.37	18.66	18.95	19.24	19.53
25	15.87	16.17	16.46	16.76	17.06	17.35	17.65	17.95	18.25	18.55	18.85	19.15	19.45	19.75	20.05	20.36

SOURCE: Board of Governors of the Federal Reserve System, Exhibit b, "Truth in Lending—Consumer Credit Cost Disclosure."

not unique—the tables are designed for many more months than this, of course). Then, the solution is

$$\frac{\$3{,}500}{\$20{,}000} = .1750 \times 100 = \$17.50$$

Follow the left-hand column of Table 22-1 to the line for 24 months. Read across until you find the nearest number to $17.50—in this case, $17.51. Reading up the column shows an annual percentage rate of 16 percent.

As a result of the Monetary Control Act of 1980, the disclosure of the annual percentage rate is deemed accurate if the rate is within a tolerance not greater than one-eighth of 1 percent more or less than the actual rate, or rounded to the nearest one-fourth of 1 percent.

An example of a Notice to Customer statement, which is required by HUD, is shown in Exhibit 22-5.

THE SETTLEMENT (OR CLOSING)

At the settlement, a HUD settlement statement is prepared, the items prorated, and the broker and seller paid as shown in Exhibit 22-6.

BROKERS' RESPONSIBILITIES

It is the broker's responsibility when handling the closing of title to see that the transaction is consummated with a high degree of smoothness and that all parties leave with the feeling they have been fairly treated.

What else can the broker do with respect to smoothly closing a title?

1. Prepare accurately and thoroughly a closing statement for both the buyer and the seller and be able to explain in detail the figures on the statements to the satisfaction of all parties to the transaction.
2. Advise the seller to bring the deed from seller's grantor to the closing in the event the purchaser's attorney is present at the closing and desires to inspect it in terms of property description.
3. Advise the seller to bring tax receipts, receipts for assessments, and water charges, if any, to avoid any possible discussion in this regard.
4. Transfer insurance policies to the purchaser. If the purchaser is going to obtain insurance from another company, the broker should obtain the agent's name and telephone number from the buyer prior to the closing so the agent can be telephoned the moment the deed is delivered in order to make certain the house in the hands of the purchaser is covered. Although this may not be the broker's duty, it is one of those things that causes a feeling among purchasers that the broker is acting fairly and honestly.

■ Exhibit 22-5 Federal Savings Notice to Customer Form

NOTICE TO CUSTOMER
REQUIRED BY FEDERAL LAW
FEDERAL RESERVE REGULATION Z

MIDLAND
FEDERAL SAVINGS

REAL PROPERTY TRANSACTION – PURCHASE LOAN
SECURED BY FIRST LIEN ON A DWELLING

The FINANCE CHARGE on this transaction will begin to accrue on June 29, 19__

The AMOUNT OF THE LOAN in this transaction is .... $ 58,500.00

Less the PREPAID FINANCE CHARGE on this transaction which includes:

1. Loan Fee 2½%	$ 1,462.50	9. FHA Insurance Premium	$ 292.00
2. Agent's Fee	$	10.	$
3. Loan Discounts	$	11.	$
4. MGIC Appraisal Review Fee	$	**ASSUMPTIONS ONLY**	
5. IMIC Appraisal Review Fee	$	1. Assumption Fee	$
6. Construction Interest (Estimate)	$	2. Mtgee's title policy	
7. Tax Service	$ 15.00	endorsement fee	$
8. Interest to Date – 7/1/19	$ 35.16 Est.		
		TOTAL	$ 1,804.66 Est.

Equals the AMOUNT FINANCED in this transaction .... $ 56,695.34 Est.

This amount includes the following charges which are EXCLUDABLE from the FINANCE CHARGE in this transaction:

1. Title Insurance Premium	$ 138.00 Est.	7. Documentary Fee	$ 5.00 Est.
2. Inspection Fee	$ 85.00	8. Buyer's Recording Fees	$ 10.00 Est.
3. Credit Report	$ 20.00	9. Survey	$ 135.00 Est.
4. Tax Reserve	$ 212.00 Est.	10. Tax Certificate	$ 5.00 Est.
5. Insurance Reserve	$ -0- Est.	11. Abstracting	$
6. Initial Hazard Insurance Premium	$ 248.00 Est.	12. Attorney Opinion	25.00 Est.
		NET PROCEEDS	$ 55,812.34 Est.

The ANNUAL PERCENTAGE RATE on this transaction is 12 %.

Payments for principal and interest on this transaction shall be 360 monthly installments of $ 601.75 beginning on the first day of August (approx.) 19__ and due on the first day of each month thereafter.

This institution's security interest in this transaction is a Deed of Trust and Assignment of Rent on property located at 1234 Greenbriar Blvd., Anytown, Your State also specifically described in the documents furnished for this loan. The documents executed in connection with this transaction cover all after-acquired property and also stand as security for future advances, the terms for which are described in the documents.

Describe late payment formula, if any, in accordance with Section 226.8 (b)(4).

- Conv. (X) Five percent of the principal and interest included in any monthly installment not received 15 days after the installment is due.
- Conv. ( ) One-sixth of one percent of the outstanding loan balance at time of delinquency.
- Conv. ( ) The holder may charge a late payment penalty up to____% of any monthly installment not received within 15 days after the installment is due.
- VA ( ) Four percent of the total monthly payment at the time of delinquency.
- FHA ( ) Two percent of the total monthly payment at the time of delinquency.
- Other ( )

Describe prepayment formula, if any, in accordance with Section 226.8 (b)(6).

- Conv. (X) There is no prepayment penalty except during the first five years, when a prepayment penalty is due equal to____% of any amount in excess of twenty percent of the original loan balance prepaid during any loan year for the first three years, and three percent of any amount in excess of twenty percent of the original loan balance for the fourth and fifth loan years.
- Conv. ( ) An amount equal to six months interest on the amount prepaid after deducting twenty percent of the original loan amount.
- VA-FHA ( ) Not Applicable
- Other ( )

MISCELLANEOUS DISCLOSURES, OR EXPLANATIONS, IF ANY.

- VA-FHA ( ) the loan documents contain an acceleration clause in the event of default.
- Conv. (X) the loan documents contain acceleration clauses in the event of default or unauthorized transfer of the property.
- Other ( )

INSURANCE

PROPERTY INSURANCE

Property insurance may be obtained by borrower through any person of his choice, provided however, the creditor reserves the right to refuse, for reasonable cause, to accept an insurer offered by the borrower. If borrower desires property insurance to be obtained from or through Midland Federal Savings & Loan Association, the cost will be $ 248.00 est. for the 1st year term of the initial policy.

OTHER INSURANCE

Credit life, accident, health or loss of income insurance is not required to obtain this loan. No charge is made for such insurance and no insurance is provided.

Midland Federal Savings & Loan Association.

By /S/ Louise O. A. Nesbit

Title Loan Department

Date May 31, 19__

I hereby acknowledge receipt of the disclosures made in this notice.

Customer /S/ JOHN A. KINDER

Customer /S/ MARGE W. KINDER

Date ____

Exhibit 22-6 HUD Settlement Statement Form

A. U.S. DEPARTMENT OF HOUSING AND URBAN DEVELOPMENT
SETTLEMENT STATEMENT

Midland Federal Savings and Loan Association

B. TYPE OF LOAN

1. ☐ FHA 2. ☐ FMHA 3. ☐ CONV. UNINS.
4. ☐ VA 5. XX CONV. INS.

6. FILE NUMBER:

7. LOAN NUMBER: 21-774104-7

8. MORT. INS. CASE NO.: 091467

C. NOTE: This form is furnished to give you a statement of actual settlement costs. Amounts paid to and by the settlement agent are shown. Items marked "(p.o.c.)" were paid outside the closing; they are shown here for informational purposes and are not included in the totals.

D. NAME OF BORROWER:	E. NAME OF SELLER:	F. NAME OF LENDER:
JOHN A. KINDER and MARGE W. KINDER	WILSON, Clayton 1234 Greenbriar Blvd. Anytown, Your State	MIDLAND FEDERAL SAVINGS & LOAN

G. PROPERTY LOCATION:	H. SETTLEMENT AGENT:	I. SETTLEMENT DATE:
1234 Greenbriar Blvd.	Transamerica Title Insurance Col PLACE OF SETTLEMENT: 1300 Canyon Blvd., Anytown, Your State	June 29, 19__

J. SUMMARY OF BORROWER'S TRANSACTION:		K. SUMMARY OF SELLER'S TRANSACTION:	
100. **GROSS AMOUNT DUE FROM BORROWER**		400. **GROSS AMOUNT DUE TO SELLER**	
101. Contract sales price	65,000.00	401. Contract sales price	65,000.00
102. Personal property		402. Personal property	
103. Settlement charges to borrower (line 1400)	2,215.66	403.	
104.		404.	
105.		405.	
Adjustments for items paid by seller in advance		Adjustments for items paid by seller in advance	
106. City/town taxes to		406. City/town taxes to	
107. County taxes to		407. County taxes to	
108. Assessments to		408. Assessments to	
109. Homeowners dues 6/29/-- - 7/1/--	4.67	409. Homeowners dues 6/29/-- - 7/1/--	4.67
110.		410.	
111.		411.	
112.		412.	
120. **GROSS AMOUNT DUE FROM BORROWER**	67,220.33	420. **GROSS AMOUNT DUE TO SELLER**	65,004.67
200. **AMOUNTS PAID BY OR IN BEHALF OF BORROWER**		500. **REDUCTIONS IN AMOUNT DUE TO SELLER**	
201. Deposit or earnest money	1,000.00	501. Excess deposit (see Instructions)	
202. Principal amount of new loan(s)	58,500.00	502. Settlement charges to seller (line 1400)	4,673.00
203. Existing loan(s) taken subject to		503. Existing loan(s) taken subject to	
204.		504. Payoff of first mortgage loan	
205.		505. Payoff of second mortgage loan	
206.		506.	
207.		507.	
208.		508.	
209.		509.	
Adjustments for items unpaid by seller		Adjustments for items unpaid by seller	
210. City/town taxes to		510. City/town taxes to	
211. County taxes 1/1/-- to 6/29/--	312.95	511. County taxes 1/1/-- to 6/29/--	312.95
212. Assessments to		512. Assessments to	
213.		513.	
214.		514.	
215.		515.	
216.		516.	
217.		517.	
218.		518.	
219.		519.	
220. **TOTAL PAID BY/FOR BORROWER**	59,812.95	520. **TOTAL REDUCTION AMOUNT DUE SELLER**	4,985.95
300. **CASH AT SETTLEMENT FROM OR TO BORROWER**		600. **CASH AT SETTLEMENT TO OR FROM SELLER**	
301. Gross amount due from borrower (line 120)	67,220.33	601. Gross amount due to seller (line 420)	65,004.67
302. Less amounts paid by/for borrower (line 220)	(59,812.95	602. Less reduction amount due seller (line 520)	(4,985.95)
303. **CASH (X FROM) (☐ TO) BORROWER**	7,407.38	603. **CASH (X TO) (☐ FROM) SELLER**	60,018.72

Exhibit 22-6 (concluded)

L. SETTLEMENT CHARGES		PAID FROM BORROWER'S FUNDS AT SETTLEMENT	PAID FROM SELLER'S FUNDS AT SETTLEMENT
700.	TOTAL SALES/BROKER'S COMMISSION based on price $65,000.00 @ 7 % = 4,550.00		
	Division of commission (line 700) as follows:		
701.	$ to		
702.	$ to		
703.	Commission paid at Settlement		4,550.00
704.			
800.	ITEMS PAYABLE IN CONNECTION WITH LOAN		
801.	Loan Origination Fee 2½ %	1,462.50	
802.	Loan Discount %		
803.	Appraisal Fee to		
804.	Credit Report to Midland Federal Savings & Loan	20.00	
805.	Lender's Inspection Fee	85.00	
806.	Mortgage Insurance Application Fee to		
807.	Assumption Fee		
808.			
809.			
810.			
811.			
900.	ITEMS REQUIRED BY LENDER TO BE PAID IN ADVANCE		
901.	Interest from 6/29/-- to 7/1/-- @ $ 17.58 /day	35.16	
902.	Mortgage Insurance Premium for 12 mo. to FHA	292.00	
903.	Hazard Insurance Premium for yrs. to		
904.	yrs. to		
905.			
1000.	RESERVES DEPOSITED WITH LENDER FOR		
1001.	Hazard insurance mo. @ $ /mo.		
1002.	Mortgage insurance mo. @ $ /mo.		
1003.	City property taxes mo. @ $ /mo.		
1004.	County property taxes 2 mo. @ $106.00 /mo.	212.00	
1005.	Annual assessments mo. @ $ /mo.		
1006.	mo. @ $ /mo.		
1007.	mo. @ $ /mo.		
1008.	mo. @ $ /mo.		
1100.	TITLE CHARGES		
1101.	Settlement or closing fee to		
1102.	Abstract or title search to		
1103.	Title examination to Caplan and Earnest	25.00	
1104.	Title insurance binder to		
1105.	Document preparation to Ron Brotzman	15.00	
1106.	~~Notary fees~~ to Document preparation to Caplan & Earnest		15.00
1107.	Attorney's fees to		
	(includes above items No.:)		
1108.	Title insurance to Transamerica Title	30.00	108.00
	(includes above items No.:)		
1109.	Lender's coverage $ 58,500.00		
1110.	Owner's coverage $ 65,000.00		
1111.	TA Tax Service	15.00	
1112.	Tax Certificate	5.00	
1113.			
1200.	GOVERNMENT RECORDING AND TRANSFER CHARGES		
1201.	Recording fees: Deed $ 2.00 ; Mortgage $ 10.00 ; Releases $	12.00	
1202.	City/county tax/stamps: Deed $; Mortgage $		
1203.	State tax/stamps: Deed $; Mortgage $		
1204.	Your State Documentary Fee	5.00	
1205.	Warranty Deed	2.00	
1300.	ADDITIONAL SETTLEMENT CHARGES		
1301.	Survey to	NC	
1302.	Pest inspection to		
1303.			
1304.			
1305.			
1400.	TOTAL SETTLEMENT CHARGES *(enter on lines 103 and 502, Sections J and K)*	2,215.66	4,673.00

The Undersigned Acknowledges Receipt of This Settlement Statement and Agrees to the Correctness Thereof.

/S/ JOHN A. KINDER
/S/ MARGE W. KINDER
Buyer

/S/ CLAYTON WILSON
Seller

5. Advise the seller, when necessary, to have any satisfactions of judgment or mechanic's liens prepared by an attorney and to bring them to the closing in order to have these removed as exceptions in the title.
6. Advise the seller, if there are any leases, to bring to the closing a letter of introduction for the buyer to the tenants and the keys to the building. Also suggest that the seller have an affidavit prepared showing that rents have not been prepaid.
7. Advise the seller to have an attorney prepare a bill of sale covering any personal property included in the transaction.
8. Advise the seller, if the seller is acting as "attorney," to bring the necessary power of attorney to the closing in the event the attorney for the buyer desires to examine it. This should be done even though the power of attorney may be recorded.

The above list is by no means complete, but will give the broker an idea of some of the things necessary to bring a transaction to a smooth ending. It is suggested that the broker prepare a checklist, prepared in accordance with local custom, as to what must be done in order to close a transaction. A copy of this can be inserted in the "deal" envelope to ensure that everything has been done that could be done to create a feeling of confidence in the people with whom the broker is dealing.

TITLE CLOSING AND THE TAX REFORM ACT OF 1986

Because Congress believed many taxpayers failed to include profits from the sale of commercial and residential properties as income on their income tax returns, a special provision was included in the Tax Reform Act of 1986. This provision requires the closing agents (attorneys, real estate brokers, escrow agents, title companies, or anyone else who closes title) to submit a Form 1099-B to the IRS showing the gross proceeds received by the seller as the result of the transaction.

GLOSSARY

Assumption statement A statement issued by a lender when a mortgage is assumed showing the unpaid principal, interest, rate of interest, and date of maturity of the mortgage

Bill of sale An instrument that conveys title to personal property

Certificate of occupancy A statement issued by the building inspector stating that the building code and/or zoning regulations have been complied with

Counter proposal A written stipulation between seller and buyer to extend closing date

Real Estate Settlement Procedures Act A congressional act establishing a uniform procedure for closing loans on one- to four-family residential dwellings

Reduction certificate An instrument executed by a mortgagee stating the balance due on a mortgage

Survey A measurement of the boundaries of real property by a surveyor

Title closing The event marking the completion of a real estate transaction

Title search The preparation of an abstract of title

Truth in Lending Act An act to encourage competition among financial institutions by informing consumers of the cost of credit and permitting consumers to compare various credit terms available

QUESTIONS FOR REVIEW

1. Under what circumstances, if any, would a purchaser be justified in requesting a bill of sale at a closing?
2. Why does the seller ordinarily bring the insurance policies to a closing (settlement)?
3. Why is it advisable for all purchasers of real property to have a survey made?
4. What is the main purpose of the Real Estate Settlement Procedures Act?
5. What types of loans are exempt from the Real Estate Settlement Procedures Act?

PROBLEMS AND ACTIVITIES

1. *A* is selling an investment property to *B*. In the contract of sale, *A* lists gross rental from the property at $24,000 per year. What, if anything, should *B* require from *A* at the title closing pertaining to the tenants?
2. Buyer agrees to purchase a parcel of property from Seller through a broker. The First National Bank of Folkstown has agreed to finance part of the transaction, namely $20,000, on a total price of $32,000, buyer to furnish the difference in cash. Seller agrees to furnish an abstract of title. At the closing, the broker, the buyer, the seller, and the cashier of the bank appear. Without attempting to apportion any of the

charges involved, draw a simple flowchart indicating how and what instruments pass hands, how much money passes from hand to hand, and in what manner.

3. Prepare a closing statement for both the purchaser and the seller under the circumstances stated below. Is a RESPA settlement needed here? Why or why not?

   A agrees to purchase Meadowbrook from *B*. The purchase price is $72,000, $8,000 cash paid on the signing of contract. *A* agrees to take the property "subject to" a $20,000 mortgage and pay the balance in cash. The taxes are $638 per year payable semiannually, January 1 and July 1. The interest on the mortgage is at 12.5 percent, payable quarterly, the last payment having been made to but not including July 1. The insurance premium is $327 for three years and was purchased on March 1, 1989. The title policy cost $215. The attorney for the seller charged a $185 fee, and the attorney for the purchaser charged a $172 fee. There is a recording fee of $5. Title is to close on August 18, 1989.

23

REAL PROPERTY INSURANCE

KEY TERMS

Adjusted value or inflation guard endorsement
Co-insurance
Consequential losses
Flood insurance
Home warranty contract
Insurable interest
Insurance policy
Liability insurance
Premium
Pro rata liability clause
Replacement value
Subrogation clause

The broad subject of real property insurance has a definite place in the study of real estate and real estate principles because the real estate practitioner often engages in the insurance business. A more important reason, perhaps, is that an individual dealing with any property must, of necessity, become involved with a certain amount of risk. Over some risks, the individual has little or no control. However, property owners should be aware of those risks involving possible loss for which insurance protection is available. Some risks of loss are presented in Exhibit 23-1.

Exhibit 23-1 Risks of Loss

Glass Breakage
Collision
Contamination
Electrical Disturbances
Dishonesty
Employee Negligence
Explosion
Falling Objects
Fire
Construction Hazards
*Intentional Destruction
*Shortages
Condition of the Premises
Negligence
Lightning
Removal
Vehicles
Aircraft
Theft
Freezing
*Obsolescence
Civil Authority
*Riots, Civil Disorders
Rupture, Puncture of Vessel
Smoke, Smudge
Collapse
Vandalism, Malicious Mischief
*War
Water Damage (flood, ground water, sprinkler leakage)
Weight of Ice and Snow
Windstorm or Hail
Operations on the Premises
Contract

*Uninsurable risks.

FUNDAMENTAL PRINCIPLES

Insurance Defined

Insurance can be defined in many ways. *Legally,* insurance is a contractual arrangement whereby one party transfers a risk to another party. Legal scholars would further require that the second party (the insurer) also pool the risk with other similar risks so that all insureds share in the cost of losses that do occur.

Economists describe insurance as a device by means of which the risk of an uncertain large loss (an accident or a fire) is exchanged for a certain small loss—the premium. *Mathematically,* insurance is defined as a mechanism by which risk is transferred from one party to another party, and through which overall risk is reduced by the application of the law of large numbers.

Individuals cannot know what the future holds—accidents, poor health, etc.—so they face great uncertainty. Through the purchase of insurance, they can reduce uncertainty by transferring the economic consequences of risk. They may still suffer losses, but the insurance policy will indemnify them for those losses.

An insurance company is willing to accept risks because the law of large numbers allows the insurer to accurately predict losses. As the number of pooled risks increases, the power to predict increases mathematically. It is true that the insurer does not know *who* will have a loss next year, but the insurer can statistically estimate the number and cost of losses that will occur.

One interesting assumption that underlies the law of large numbers is *independence.* Risks must be independent of one another. This is significant in real property insurance because it limits the number of policies an insurance company sells in a given geographic area. For example, an insurer is reluctant to sell homeowners insurance only in communities on the Gulf Coast because a single hurricane could result in hundreds of claims.

Insurable Interest

Given the previous description of insurance, an **insurance policy** can then be described as a contract whereby the insured pays the insurance company a **premium,** and the insurance company promises to pay the insured for any loss that might occur, providing it is a covered loss.

The term *covered loss* actually means many things. It, of course, means the property suffering a loss is covered under the policy. It also means the property was damaged or destroyed by a cause of loss (fire, flood, etc.) that is covered. Finally, covered loss also means the policyholder has an insurable interest in the loss.

Insurable interest exists when a policyholder has a legally enforceable economic interest in the thing insured; in other words, the policyholder must be able to demonstrate that he or she would lose economically if a loss occurred. The interest of the insured may be legal or equitable, but the insured does not have to have legal or equitable title in the property. The insured must, however, in some way be actually interested in the subject matter of the insurance at the time of loss.

The legal concept of insurable interest has not always existed. In the early days of ocean marine insurance a speculator could purchase insurance on an ocean-going vessel, even if the speculator had no connection with the ship or its cargo. In effect, such policies were a form of gambling since the policyholder might purchase a policy in the hope of a disaster at sea. Such policies imposed a moral hazard on society, and thus arose the concept of insurable interest.

Due to this concept of insurable interest, it can be said that insurance and gambling are not the same thing—contrary to the opinion of some. In *gambling* the risk is created by the contract, whereas in *insurance* the risk exists independent of the contract.

HOMEOWNERS INSURANCE

Like any insurance policy, the homeowners policy is designed to indemnify the policyholder. Although most people correctly assume *indemnify* means "restoring the value of the loss," they often do not consider the implications. *Indemnification* also means "you shall not profit from a loss," and insurance contracts scrupulously ensure this through many provisions in their policies.

Parties

The insurance policy is a contract; and, like any other contract, it contains the names of the parties. This is important because the contract does not follow the property; it is a contract with a particular person—a contract to indemnify that particular person in the event of a loss. Thus, it becomes obvious this is the real reason for the care that must be exercised by the broker or attorney to transfer the insurance or to have a new policy issued to the purchaser on title closing. Because, having transferred the property, a seller no longer has an insurable interest in the property and also because this is a "personal contract," a new policy must be made between the company and the new owner as the parties to the contract.

It will be recalled in the discussion of mortgages it was stated that one of the common clauses of the mortgage is the insurance clause stating that insurance will be carried by the mortgagor for the benefit of the mortgagee. Therefore, when such a situation exists, the mortgagee is named as one of the parties to the insurance contract, and the amount of the loss to the extent of the interest of the mortgagee in the property will be paid to the mortgagee. Any loss over and above the interest of the mortgagee will be paid to the owner or mortgagor.

Consideration

In any contract, parties must provide consideration. In insurance, the consideration assumes some unique properties. The consideration that a policyholder must give is twofold. First, the *premium payments* made to the insurance company are consideration. The amount of the policy, and the consideration is given as so much per $100 of the policy's coverage. It should be remembered that the face value of the policy merely measures the insurance company's maximum liability, and not necessarily its actual liability on any particular loss, except in those states that have valued policy laws.

The second consideration, and this is often overlooked, is *compliance with contract conditions.* Each contract has a Conditions section, which details obligations and responsibilities to which the policyholder must adhere (for instance, reporting losses in a timely manner, or notifying the insurer when there is a substantial change in the nature of the risk). In effect, this means that paying premiums is not enough: if policy conditions have not *also* been met, the insurance company can deny coverage.

The insurance company's consideration is its promise to indemnify the policyholder in the event of a covered loss. The promissory nature of the insurer's consideration explains, in large part, why insurance companies are subject to regulation.

Description of the Property

The description of the property is an important part of the insurance contract. The description is given in a form that is attached to the policy and describes not only what is insured but also the location of the insured property. Because insurance rates vary with the location and the use of the premises, various forms are employed to cover different situations. For example, if the property insured is a private home, the form will specifically state that the coverage is for a private dwelling. If a manufacturing concern is being covered, the form will describe the building, machinery, stock, etc., because the various items mentioned may carry different rates of insurance.

The form, therefore, is a device to aid brokers and agents. Through its use, brokers and agents have a ready instrument to cover all situations without the necessity on their part of drawing up the contract, using their own language, which would more often than not prove inadequate and a source of later trouble. Thus, the many types of coverage are readily available in various insurance forms; i.e., dwelling house forms, apartment forms, mercantile forms, and forms for churches, garages, and so on.

Extent of Protection

Homeowners insurance is a package policy in that it provides coverage for property, coverage for losses arising from legal liability (that is, of the homeowner), coverage for extra expenses, and coverage for the medical expenses of others injured on the policyholder's premises or due to the policyholder's actions.

Today's homeowners policy is one of a series of policies made available through the Homeowners 76 Program. This program, instituted in the mid-1970s and significantly amended in the 1980s, is an attempt by the insurance industry to simplify and broaden homeowners insurance.

Under this program, the consumer has a choice of four policies—HO1, HO2, HO3, and HO4. HO1 is referred to as the Basic Form; it covers property for losses due to a limited number of perils (causes of loss). HO2, the Broad Form, covers property for losses due to a larger number of perils. HO3, the Special Form, offers the broadest coverage. With only a few exceptions, it covers for losses due to any peril. Exhibit 23-2 summarizes the coverage differences of the three policies.

HO4, the Contents Form, is identical to the coverage provided in HO2 except that it does not cover losses to the dwelling. HO4 is frequently referred to as renters insurance.

Liability coverage under all four forms is the same. Essentially, a homeowner and any resident family members are protected if they are found to be legally liable for property damage or bodily injuries arising from the premises (for example, a visitor falls and is injured due to icy steps) or arising from the actions of the homeowner (for instance, in felling a tree, the homeowner inadvertently damages a neighbor's house).

Medical expense coverage provides limited medical and funeral expense coverage for anyone injured or killed due to the premises or actions of the homeowner. This is a form of health insurance, not liability insurance, so fault is not at issue. The extra expense coverage provides monies for extra living expenses, if the dwelling is temporarily uninhabitable after a loss.

The amount of coverage provided in the property section is based on the insured value of the home. "Other structures" are given coverage equal to 10 percent of the insured value of the home (this amount may be raised), personal property is granted coverage equal to 50 percent of the insured value of the home (this may be raised or lowered), and extra living expenses coverage is equal to 20 percent of the insured value of the structure.

As an example, if a home were insured for $80,000, the homeowner would also have the following coverages:

1. $8,000 for other structures (a detached garage).
2. $40,000 for personal property (furniture, clothes).
3. $16,000 for extra living expenses.

Typically, the minimum limit for liability coverage will be $25,000 per person per occurrence. The medical expense coverage is usually limited to $500 per person per occurrence.

■ **Exhibit 23-2 Comparison of Insured Perils Under Various Homeowners Policies**

PERILS INSURED AGAINST	BASIC COVERAGE (HO1)	BROAD COVERAGE (HO2)	SPECIAL COVERAGE (HO3)
Fire	X	X	X
Lightning	X	X	X
Windstorm or hail	X	X	X
Removal	X	X	X
Explosion	X	X	X
Riot, civil commotion	X	X	X
Vehicle (not owned or operated by occupant of premises)	X	X	X
Vehicle (owned or operated by occupant	X	X	X
Aircraft	X	X	X
Smoke from faulty operation of heating or cooking unit	X	X	X
Smoke from other than agricultural or industrial operations	X	X	X
Vandalism and malicious mischief	X	X	X
Theft	X	X	X
Sudden and accidental tearing asunder, cracking, burning, or bulging of steam or hot water heating systems		X	X
Falling objects		X	X
Weight of ice, snow, or sleet		X	X
Collapse of building(s) or parts		X	X
Accidental leakage from plumbing, heating, or air-conditioning systems or domestic appliances		X	X
Glass breakage	X	X	X
Sudden and accidental tearing asunder, cracking, burning, or bulging of appliances for heating water		X	X
Freezing of plumbing, heating, or air-conditioning systems		X	X
Sudden and accidental damage to electrical appliances		X	X
All risks of physical loss to the building(s)			X

Coverage is also limited to the extent of the deductible provisions of the policy, normally $50. The deductible provision requires the homeowner to bear the first $50 of loss per occurrence.

The homeowners policy is extremely important insofar as giving full protection to both the owner of property and any mortgagees. Most lending institutions throughout the country require that the mortgagor procure complete insurance coverage in order to guarantee full protection to the security for the loan.

An important distinction between basic or broad coverage (HO1 or HO2) and special "all risks" coverage (HO3) should be noted. To recover any loss under a basic or broad coverage policy, the policyholder must prove the loss was caused by one of the risks listed. If loss is incurred when insured by a special or all risks policy, the burden of proof lies with the insurance company. In other words, the insurance company must demonstrate that the cause of loss was excluded from coverage. Additionally, HO3 provides protection for fixed property only. Homeowners insurance, HO5, is the same as HO3, except that it extends all risk coverage to both the building and contents.

COMMERCIAL INSURANCE

Business Property Insurance

Insurance for businesses, in some respects, can parallel the homeowners program. Small businesses can purchase a package policy, the business owners policy. It contains property and liability coverages that offer options similar to the homeowners series.

Larger businesses, by design or by necessity, tend to purchase separate property and liability coverages. For instance, a typical large business might purchase a commercial property coverage policy to cover buildings and contents. The perils covered closely follow the perils detailed in Exhibit 23-2.

Steam Boiler Insurance

Steam boiler insurance is the common name given to boiler and machinery insurance, often called power plant insurance. In essence, it is insurance against explosion or breakdown of boilers, engines, machinery, and electrical apparatus, such as motors and generators. The policy includes not only an agreement by the company to pay for loss of the insured's property damaged by an accident, the extra cost of repairing the property as expeditiously as possible, bodily injury, and loss to another person's property, but also for indirect losses if provided for by endorsements. The endorsements cover use and occupancy; that is, a certain sum per day for total suspension of business and a pro rata sum for partial suspension of business. In addition, consequential damages may be covered by an endorsement; that is, damage to property other than the insured object. By endorsement, "outage" may also be covered; that is, a sum per hour for each hour the object named in the schedule is out of service.

One interesting facet of the boiler and machinery policy is inspection service. Approximately 30 to 40 percent of the premium goes toward inspections and loss-control services provided by the insurer. The quality of these services (from reputable insurers) is highly valued by property managers.

Sprinkler Leakage Insurance

Most modern industrial buildings are equipped with automatic sprinkler systems for protection from fire. With the installation of a sprinkler system, the fire insurance rates are lowered. However, with the installation of the system, it is necessary to obtain sprinkler leakage insurance.

The policy covers damage from three causes: leakage, accidental discharge, and accidents to the tank that furnishes water to the system. In general, any damages to stock, furniture, and fixtures are covered under the policy. It follows that the rates are different, depending on the type of merchandise that is most likely to be found in stock in the particular property insured.

Glass Insurance

In this policy, a schedule is attached listing all the glass to be covered under the terms of the insurance. The company promises to pay for any damage to glass, excluding coverage from damage by fire. The rates are determined by the size, cost, kind and use, location, type of occupancy, and territory in which the glass is located. The policy usually has a $50 deductible provision.

Consequential Insurance

This insurance insures the policyholder against losses from a fire other than the direct loss to the property of the insured. It is important for the real estate broker to be aware of this type of insurance because the damages resulting from these **consequential losses** may oftentimes be greater than the loss suffered from the damage by fire to the property itself. The important forms of loss to remember are rent, leasehold, and demolition insurance.

Rent Insurance. This insurance covers the loss of future rents or rental value of the premises. This is similar to an endorsement to a fire policy and protects the insured from the loss of rents or rental value if the property is made untenantable by fire or other physical damage. The time during which payments are made is limited by the policy; but in no case is the insured entitled to more than the net income that would have been received had the property not been damaged.

Leasehold Insurance. This insurance covers loss of the leasehold value. In other words, it protects a tenant when property has been leased with a use (economic rent) value greater than the contract (rent) value in the lease. The use value may be greater because of the tenant's having made a profitable lease, improvement in business conditions, or improvement in the building or neighborhood; or because the tenant sublet the premises for more than the contract price. The loss falls on the tenant in this case, either as a result of the termination of the lease or as a result of the loss of use of the premises during the period of repair in the event the lease is not terminated.

Demolition Insurance. By the demolition endorsement to the homeowners policy, the company assumes liability for any increased cost of repair to the building if such increase is due to legal requirements regulating modes of construction. This provision or coverage also provides for payment of demolition costs, if necessary.

Commercial Liability Insurance

Most businesses use the commercial general liability (CGL) policy as the anchor coverage for liability protection. This policy is designed to offer comprehensive coverage so that the business does not have to purchase individual policies covering various risks. Typically, a survey of exposures is made by the insurance company. Through this survey, the insurer is able to determine the specific nature of the coverage a company will require.

Generally the CGL policy provides coverage for liability losses arising from the premises, from activities, and from the products that are under the control of the company. One current controversy swirls around CGL's coverage for pollution liability. The CGL is not intended to cover pollution losses that occur over time (long-term seepage of waste or sewage into groundwater, for instance). However, some courts have chosen to interpret the CGL as providing such coverage. Since liability for pollution has become a serious and complex aspect of real estate transactions, this coverage uncertainty will continue to be an important issue.

There are many types of **liability insurance,** but the basic purpose of all the various liability policies is to protect the insured from any acts of negligence that may have been committed against the public. For there to be negligence, the insured must have acted without exercising reasonable care. For example, a landlord may fail to repair carpeting on the stairs of an apartment building after having been notified that it is defective. Someone falls as a result of the defective carpeting and is injured. The landlord is sued—the allegations being that the injury was caused by reason of the negligence of the landlord and that the injured person was in no way contributorily negligent. Similarly, a homeowner may be held liable for injury caused by failure to remove ice from porch steps.

Without insurance to cover these situations, the owner of the property may suffer the loss of the property. Hence, the property owner must be covered for any number of situations, some of which will be discussed below. In general, the types of liability insurance carried by property owners cover bodily injury, property damage, and medical payments to others, as well as associated court costs. For the homeowner, this protection is incorporated in the homeowners policy.

For some businesses the CGL may be inappropriate or inadequate. Some other liability policies that may fit specific business needs would include the following specific coverages.

Owners, Landlords, and Tenants Liability Policy. This policy covers liability arising from ownership, maintenance, or use of the premises described in the policy. *Use,* in this case, is interpreted as meaning, among other things, pickups and deliveries, installation, servicing, or removal. The policy also covers injury resulting from uninstalled equipment and abandoned or unusual materials.

The policy covers the premises and accidents that occur away from the premises in connection with the insured's business.

"Fall down" cases are covered by this policy. For example, the floor of a bank is wet after a rainstorm, the bank has failed to wipe the floor, and a customer falls and is injured.

In general, the policy does not cover accidents resulting from defective elevators or hoists of any kind without an extra premium being paid for that protection; and it does not cover any situation that should be covered by workers compensation insurance, products liability insurance, or a contractors policy.

Elevator Liability Policy. This is a special policy designed to give protection for the specific exemption in the owners', landlords', and tenants' liability policy. This insurance specifically covers liability for ownership, maintenance, or use of elevators, hoists, shafts, and so forth. As a practical matter, the amount of this policy should be higher than on any other type of liability policy purchased in connection with real property. The reason is that the more serious accidents and, consequently, the greater damages in terms of money loss to owners usually result from accidents of this nature.

A genuine accomplishment resulting from this type of insurance is that even in cities where the city elevator inspection is poor, the owners of buildings with elevators are subject to frequent inspection by insurance inspectors, with consequent increase in the safety of this equipment.

Water Damage Liability Policy. This policy is designed to cover damage to commercial and private properties resulting from water escaping from proper receptacles and conduits. Thus, any leakage from plumbing systems, heating systems, air-conditioning systems, or refrigerating systems may be covered. Rain or snow entering through broken skylight or defective roof and causing damage to the premises and water entering through an open door and causing damage are covered by this policy. If a water tank on a roof collapses, with consequent damages, this also is covered by a water damage policy.

Like most policies, the water damage liability policy contains some exceptions. Among them are damages from sprinkler systems, floods, rising tides, and blocked sewers. It also does not cover seepage through the floors of the basement or the building walls.

SPECIAL CONTRACT PROVISIONS

Co-insurance

Co-insurance is a provision of commercial property insurance contracts that encourages an owner to purchase more insurance relative to the value of the property than might otherwise be purchased. Co-insurance is no longer found in homeowners insurance contracts, though there is a co-insurancelike provision when replacement cost coverage is purchased (see the following section). In such a case, the provision determines whether actual cash value or replacement cost will be the basis of settlement. The following discussion, then, pertains to commercial insurance coverages only.

The co-insurance clause states, in effect, that the company shall be liable in the event of loss only in the proportion that the amount of insurance bears to the insurance required. The purpose of the co-insurance clause is to adjust the rates equitably between the various policyholders. The fact is that in most fires there is not total loss. Thus, if one were to insure property for far less than its real worth and there were a fire, without the co-insurance clause the insured would be able to collect the full amount without paying much in the way of a premium. This would be unfair to the person whose property was insured in the proper amount and who had been paying a higher premium.

The most common co-insurance clause is the "80 percent clause," although there may be a 70 percent or 90 percent clause. Under this clause, it would not be economical for a person to carry either too little or too much insurance. The question then becomes How much is enough? Someone once remarked that anything that made sense could be reduced to a formula, and so it is with co-insurance. The co-insurance clause states:

> This company shall not be liable for a greater proportion of any loss or damage to the property described herein than the sum hereby insured bears to 80 percent of the actual cash value of said property at the time such loss shall happen, nor for more than the proportion which this policy bears to the total insurance thereon.

Converting this statement into a formula,

$$\frac{\text{Amount carried}}{\text{Amount should carry}} \times \text{Actual loss} = \text{Recovery}$$

Assume the actual cash value of a building is $60,000 and an 80 percent clause is in effect; assume further that *A* carries insurance in the amount of $48,000, and there is a loss in the amount of $15,000. Will *A* be able to collect the full $15,000? Applying the formula given above we get this result:

$$\frac{\text{Amount carried} = \$48{,}000}{\text{Amount should carry} \; (.80 \times \$60{,}000 = \$48{,}000} \times \$15{,}000 \text{ (loss)} = \$15{,}000$$

Assume the same situation as above, except *A* carries $60,000 in insurance instead of $48,000. Apply the following formula:

$$\frac{\$60{,}000}{\$48{,}000} \times \$15{,}000 = \$18{,}750 \text{ (recovery)}$$

Will this mean the insured will be able to collect $18,750 when there has been a $15,000 loss? The answer is obviously no. No one makes a profit from a loss; therefore, the insured, *A*, will collect only the $15,000 loss. The inference from this is that *A* is carrying more insurance than should be carried and is wasting money on the extra $12,000 worth of insurance.

Assume the same situation exists, except *A* is carrying only $30,000 in insurance. Then:

$$\frac{\$30{,}000}{\$48{,}000} \times \$15{,}000 = \$9{,}375$$

In this situation, the insured did not carry the amount that was required, and so with the 80 percent clause was able to collect only $9,375 for the $15,000 loss.

The important thing, as far as the business owner and the broker are concerned, is to be aware of the amount that is required and to carry no less. Extreme care must be taken, however, in periods of rising prices to ascertain the proper amount to carry; otherwise, the insured may discover an insufficient amount of insurance is being carried.

However, an **adjusted value** or **inflation guard endorsement** to the business owners policy may be obtained which provides that the limits of liability applying to a dwelling shall be adjusted on each policy anniversary date. The adjustment shall be by the percentage change, during the past 12 months, in construction costs in the area in which the home is located.

As a final passing comment, it should be noted that in some recent commercial property policies the co-insurance provision is optional. Property owners still have an incentive, however, to select this option since it adds valuable additional coverages.

Cash Value and Replacement Cost

The policy states that the company "does insure to the extent of the actual cash value at the time of the loss." There may, however, be complete destruction of a building and there may not necessarily be a payment to the insured of the full face value of the policy. Recall again that the face value of the policy defines the maximum. In the final analysis, this means that the company will usually pay the **replacement value** of the property. Thus, cash value in the clause above is construed to mean reproduction cost less depreciation. In all homeowners policies, personal property is insured for its "actual cash value" or "depreciated value."

For an additional premium, a policyholder may obtain an endorsement that changes the loss payable to replacement cost for equivalent materials and workmanship. This endorsement also amends the co-insurance clause: "actual cash value" is changed to read "replacement costs without deduction for depreciation."

Arbitration

The standard policy contains a provision for arbitration in the event the contracting parties cannot agree to the extent of the loss. Ordinarily when a loss occurs, the insured obtains estimates of the cost of replacing the loss and any differences are amicably adjusted between the insured and the adjuster for the insurance company. However, in some instances where the parties cannot agree to the extent of the loss, the policy provides that each of the parties may select an appraiser to estimate the damage. Between them they select an umpire, and the findings of the appraisers are submitted to the umpire for consideration. If the parties cannot agree on the umpire, then the judge of a court of record may be asked by either party to select an umpire. The award arrived at is considered to be the actual cash value of the property at the time of the loss, and this then is the amount that is paid to the insured for the loss.

Pro Rata Liability

In addition to the clauses above, the homeowners policy contains the statement:

> This company shall not be liable for a greater portion of any loss than the amount hereby insured against shall bear to the whole insurance covering the property against the peril involved, whether collectible or not.

This clause is inserted to provide for the situation in which the insured may have placed insurance with several companies. This is done particularly when large policies are involved. For example, assume one policy is placed with company *A* in the amount of $30,000, and a second policy is placed with company *B* in the amount of $10,000, totaling $40,000. Under these circumstances, if a loss occurs, company *A* is liable to the extent of three-quarters of the loss under the **pro rata liability clause,** and company *B* will be liable for one-quarter of the loss.

Cancellation

The policy contains a clause stating:

> This policy may be canceled at anytime at the request of the insured, in which case, this company shall, upon demand and surrender of this policy, refund the excess of paid premium above the customary short rates for the expired time.

The important thing to be remembered about this clause is that on cancellation by the insured, the "short rates" are applicable to the policy for the period of time it was in effect. This means a higher premium rate than a strict mathematically prorated amount for the period covered by the policy. It should be remembered that in order for the policy to be canceled, there must be actual notice given to the company. This notice may be either oral or written.

Subrogation

The insurance contract contains this clause:

> This company may require from the insured an assigment of all right of recovery against any party for loss to the extent that payment therefor is made by this company.

Although the insured may collect from the company even though the loss is due to the insured's own negligence, the **subrogation clause** is added to enable the company to collect any sums it may have paid out to the insured as a result of the negligence of third persons. For example, suppose a house is situated near a farm and the farmer on the adjoining premises burns weeds at the edge of the farm in such a negligent manner that the house of the insured catches fire and is destroyed. The insurance company pays the insured and from the insured may, if it desires, have any rights assigned to it that the insured might have had against the farmer for negligence. The company may then bring an action against the farmer for negligence for the amount it has paid out to the insured.

TENANTS AND CONDOMINIUM INSURANCE

Apartment dwellers and renters of cooperative housing may protect their personal property against loss by purchasing a broad coverage (HO4) tenants policy. A tenants policy does not cover the structure, but rather the property owner or cooperative corporation insures the building separately. Improvements made to a cooperative apartment must also be insured in the corporation's policy.

Condominium owners may also purchase broad coverage to protect personal property against loss, to protect against liability losses, medical expenses, and so on. This policy is known as HO6. A condominium policy also covers additions and improvements made to the condominium unit. A condominium's common areas and building structure are insured by a policy purchased by the owners association.

FLOOD INSURANCE

The U.S. Water Resources Council has estimated that without measures to regulate construction in flood hazard areas the cost in federal flood disaster relief will reach $5 billion annually by the year 2020. At the council's recommendation, Congress passed the Flood Disaster Protection Act of 1973, which implemented the National Flood Insurance Program. The program has two major objectives:

1. To provide flood insurance at reasonable cost.
2. To promote community regulation of flood area construction.

Through the joint efforts of private insurance companies and the Department of Housing and Urban Development, every homeowner who lives in a qualified community may purchase **flood insurance** at rates below expected losses. Community enactment of precise regulations controlling flood plain construction and enactment of flood control measures to reduce future damage are the criteria for qualification for the flood insurance program.

Flood insurance is required for most mortgage loans made in areas prone to flooding. To determine if a property is located in a "special flood hazard area," maps prepared by the National Flood Insurance Program should be reviewed.[1]

HOME WARRANTY CONTRACTS

More and more state courts are holding builders liable for defects in home building. As one writer put it, the law has evolved to the incongruous state where

> It offers greater protection to the purchaser of a seventy-nine-cent dog leash than it does to the purchaser of a $40,000 home. If the dog leash is defective, the purchaser can get his money back and he may be able to recover damages if he loses his dog because of the defective leash. If the purchaser of the house is required to replace the heating unit two months after the purchase, he probably has no recourse against the seller. Quality

[1]To obtain maps for your area, write to the National Flood Insurance Program, P.O. Box 34294, Bethesda, MD 20034.

is generally at the risk of the buyer of real property, absent an express warranty or fraud.[2]

This old rule is changing. In a leading case the builder-vendor was held liable on an implied warranty for damages resulting from water seeping into the basement of the house. The court said, "Where a person holds himself out as specially qualified to perform work of a particular character there is an implied warranty that the work shall be done in a reasonably good and workmanlike manner and that the completed product or structure shall be reasonably fit for its intended purpose" (*Waggoner v. Midwestern Development, Inc.*, 154 NW2d 803 [S.D. 1967]).

Furthermore, in at least one state lenders have been held liable for defective housing. "As a result of a decision in *Connor v. Great Western Federal Savings and Loan Association* 447 P2d 609 [Cal. 1968]), a new trail . . . has been blazed. The law may no longer allow lending institutions to slither into a sanctuary after having unleashed and sponsored an irresponsible developer."[3]

Offered as a service to clients by the listing or selling agent, a **home warranty contract** provides protection against the mechanical failure of basic home systems and appliances. If any major system or appliance breaks down or fails during the period of coverage, it is replaced or repaired.

Home warranty contracts are an innovation that reflects the growing professionalism of full service real estate brokers. Contrary to popular belief, brokers or their agents do not earn a fee or commission for each contract purchased and they do not represent the company that provides HWC protection.

The typical HWC provides coverage for the primary heat source, accessible duct work, plumbing fixtures, interior plumbing system, water heater and softener, internal electrical system, and built-in appliances such as oven, range, garbage disposal, compactor, dishwasher, garage-door opener, and central vacuum. The contract will also carry a $200 deductible clause per occurence.

Coverage is strictly limited. No protection is provided for building code violations or home improvement work. Also excluded are equipment failures due to power failure or outside perils such as lightning, fire, wind, hail, freezing, etc., or other conditions which should be covered through homeowners insurance. Further contract exclusions include roofs, walls, foundations, basements, septic systems, window air-conditioners, clothes washers and dryers, refrigerators, and microwave and electronic ovens.

---

[2]Haskell, "The Case for an Implied Warranty of Quality in the Sales of Real Property," *Georgetown Law Journal* 53 (1965), 633; quoted by William Schwartz, "Defective Housing: The Fall of Caveat Emptor," *Journal of American Trial Lawyers Association* 33 (1970), 122.

[3]Schwartz, "Defective Housing," 138.

Sellers' contracts are for the duration of the listing agreement up to six months. An HWC assures potential buyers that the covered mechanical systems and appliances will be in working order as of the date of purchase. Cautious buyers may wish to acquire HWC coverage for one to two years after the date of closing.

From the seller's viewpoint, an HWC is riskless protection that may facilitate the sale of their property. Uniquely, an HWC is not paid for until the time of closing. If the home does not sell, there is no charge for the protection provided.

Although individual companies have developed home warranty programs for existing homes, the most significant effort has been by the National Association of Home Builders. Voluntarily, the NAHB established the National Home Warranty Insurance Program for new housing. This program is presently operated by the Home Owners Warranty Corporation (HOW).

The HOW contract is available from approved builders. An approved contractor, when beginning new home construction, will enroll the home in the HOW plan and pay a contract fee. The contractor builds the home to meet local and federal building codes. Three times during construction, HOW inspects the home to ensure compliance with these standards.

> Under this program, a 10-year warranty covers every new home sold by a participating member, and protection passes to successive owners. The NAHB program requires that the builder cover all defects due to faulty workmanship, as well as major construction defects and defects in plumbing, electrical, and heating systems, exclusive of the defects in those portions of the mechanical systems covered by manufacturers warranty. From the third to the tenth year, the insurance company will cover major construction defects. In addition, the insurance company will underwrite the builder's performance during the first two years and make good any arbitration awards where the builder fails to honor commitments to buyers.[4]

No longer may home sellers, or their representatives, assume an attitude of *caveat emptor*—"Let the Buyer Beware." This is the age of *caveat venditor*—"Let the Seller Beware."

GLOSSARY

Adjusted value or inflation guard endorsement An endorsement in a homeowners insurance policy whereby the limits of liability are adjusted on each policy anniversary date by the percentage change dur-

[4]Donald W. Hackett, and John R. Darling, "A Comparison of Consumer and Realtor Attitudes Regarding Consumer Issues Affecting the Housing Industry," *AREUEA Journal* (Fall 1976), 97.

ing the past twelve months in construction costs in the area where the home is located.

Co-insurance The clause in a homeowners policy stating that the company shall be liable in the event of loss only in proportion that the amount of insurance bears to the insurance required

Consequential losses Insurance against losses from a fire other than the direct loss of the property involved

Flood insurance Insurance against flooding required by some mortgage lenders

Home warranty contract Insurance coverage providing protection against the mechanical failure of basic home systems and appliances

Insurable interest A relationship existing between the insured and the event insured against so that the happening of the event will cause the insured some injury or loss

Insurance policy A contract whereby the insured pays the insurance company a premium, and the company agrees to pay the insured for any loss that might be suffered to property, provided the loss actually occurs

Liability insurance Insurance that protects the insured from any acts of negligence insured may have committed against the public

Premium The consideration for an insurance policy

Pro rata liability clause If a homeowners insurance policy is placed with more than one company, each company agrees to pay a pro rata share of losses

Replacement value Reproduction cost less depreciation

Subrogation clause A clause in an insurance policy enables the insurance company to collect any sums that may have been paid to the insured as a result of the negligence of third persons

QUESTIONS FOR REVIEW

1. What is meant by insurable interest?
2. Why do many lending institutions require evidence of complete insurance coverage at the time of closing?
3. Explain the difference between rent insurance and leasehold insurance.
4. What is the 80 percent co-insurance clause in a business owners policy?
5. What is the best way to take inflation into account when insuring your home?

6. Explain the term *cash value* as it is found in a homeowners insurance policy.

PROBLEMS AND ACTIVITIES

1. A mortgagee has a mortgage in the amount of $30,000 on a parcel of real property. The building is valued at $75,000 and the land is valued at $25,000. How much fire insurance does the mortgagor have to carry in order to satisfy the mortgagee? Assume there is an 80 percent co-insurance clause in the policy.

2. *A* owns a building valued at $50,000 without the land. There is an 80 percent co-insurance clause in the insurance contract. *A* insures the property with company *X* for $10,000 and with company *B* for $20,000. The building burns and damages the property to the extent of $30,000. What is the liability of each company?

3. Mildred Martin has a building with an appraised value of $100,000. A fire causes damage of $25,000. She has one policy of $25,000 with company *A*, one of $35,000 with company *B*, another $35,000 with company *C*, and one of $5,000 with company *D*. How much is each company liable for?

4. Summarize homeowners insurance HO1 through HO6.

PART SEVEN

Real Estate Brokerage

24

BROKERAGE

KEY TERMS

Actual agency
Agency coupled with an interest
Agent
Automatic renewal clause
Co-brokerage
Exclusive agency
Exclusive right to sell
Fair Housing Act of 1988
Fiduciary concept
General agent
Listing contract
Multiple listing service
Net listing
Open listing
Ostensible agency
Principal
Procuring cause
Ratification
Real estate broker
Special agent
Universal agent

In the business sense, a **real estate broker** is a person or corporation engaged primarily in the marketing of one or more of the various rights in real property. The broker's basic function is that of a negotiator, and success or failure lies in the broker's ability to bring together a buyer and a seller who are "ready, willing, and able."

In the legal sense, a real estate broker is defined as:

> any person, association, partnership, or corporation, who for a compensation or valuable consideration sells or offers for sale; buys or offers to buy, or negotiates the purchase or sale or exchange of real estate, or who leases or offers to lease or rents or offers to rent, any real estate or the improvements thereon for others.

Primarily, the practicing broker's business consists of selling or leasing property or space in a building, placing a mortgage or collecting rents, or performing other services for a certain percentage of the money value of the transaction.

The broker operates under a contract of employment. In many states this contract of employment does not need to be in writing or in any particular form. However, in 15 states the employment contract must be in writing. The contract under which the broker operates, whether it be oral or in writing, is known as a **listing contract.** These listing contracts give the broker the right to sell or lease the property and to classify and file descriptions of the property. Because the broker works under a contract of employment for either the buyer or the seller (or sometimes both by consent of the parties), the broker is governed by the law of agency.

THE AGENT AND AGENCY

An **agent** is one who acts for another known as the **principal** in dealing with third persons on behalf of the principal. A contract of agency is established in an agreement between the parties, or it may be created by appointment. The agency right is most often expressly granted by the principal in written or oral form, but sometimes an agency is created by the implied act or acts of the principal. Literally, the term *agent* is of broader scope than the term *broker.* A person is an agent or a broker depending on the extent of the authority possessed. For example, when a real estate broker is given the authority to enter into a written contract on behalf of the principal, the broker is a true agent; when this authority is absent, the broker is a broker only in the legal sense.

There are three parties involved in every contract the agent negotiates: the principal (the seller in real estate), the agent (the broker), and the buyer.

Purpose of an Agency

Generally, an agency can be established for any lawful purpose. This means merely that the objects of the agency may not be contrary to public policy or criminal in nature.

Who May Be a Principal or an Agent

Anyone who is legally competent to enter into a contract may be a principal or an agent. A person capable of acting in one's own behalf is capable of acting for another if proper authority has been given. A capable person may also appoint another capable person to act in her or his stead.

This normally excludes the insane and minors. Most of the states having real estate licensing laws specifically exclude minors from holding a real estate broker's license.

Kinds of Agents

Sometimes agents have been classified as ostensible and actual. An **ostensible agency** occurs when the authority for the agency arises from the fact that a third person has relied on the express or implied representations of the principal to the effect that the relationship existed. The **actual agency** relationship is one in which the authority to act has been delegated by the principal. Another method of classification of agents is in terms of the business to be transacted by them as general, special, or universal.

A **general agent** is authorized by the principal to transact all affairs in connection with a particular kind of business or trade, or to transact all business at a certain place.

A **special agent** is authorized by the principal to transact a business affair or to do a special act. In real estate, for example, when a broker is authorized to purchase a particular house, the broker is designated as the special agent of the principal.

The **universal agent** is authorized to do all acts that can be lawfully delegated to a representative.

Termination of an Agency

Ordinarily the agency is terminated when the purpose for which the agent/principal relationship was established has been completed, but it may be terminated at any time by the principal. The agency may also be terminated by the death or insanity of either party or by bankruptcy of the principal. In the latter instance, the agency is said to have been terminated by "operation of law." Destruction of the subject matter of the agency will also terminate the relationship. For example, if a house is listed with a broker for sale and the house is destroyed by fire, then the principal and agent relationship is terminated.

There is one exception to the general rule that an agency may be terminated by the principal at any time; that is, when it is an **agency coupled with an interest.** In order for the agency to be coupled with an interest, the agent must have an interest in the authority that has been granted or an interest in the subject matter of the agency. In the first instance, the agent has an interest in the authority when a consideration has been given for the right to exercise authority granted to the agent. In the second instance, an agent has a property interest in the subject matter with which the agent is dealing.

As far as real property is concerned, to be coupled with an interest, the agency must in some way concern the land itself and not merely the proceeds from the sale of the property. Division of the proceeds with the owner does not give the selling agent an interest in the land sold, and a commission on the sale does not make the agent's authority irrevocable.[1]

Consider the following example in which the agency is coupled with an interest because there is an interest in the authority when money is borrowed to purchase real property.

A approaches *B*, a real estate broker engaged in management, and tells *B* of a desire to purchase an office building. *A* asks *B* to lend the money on a mortgage on the premises. *B* is willing to lend the money to *A* provided *B* has a right to manage the building. *B*'s real purpose in managing the building is to obtain additional security for the loan. Assume *A* agrees to allow *B* to manage the property. Sometime later, *A* attempts to dismiss *B* as

[1] *W. M. Martin & Son v. Lamkin,* 188 Ill. App. 431 (1914).

the management agent of the building. In these situations, the courts generally hold the agency of *B* cannot be terminated at the will of *A* because *B*'s agency is of such a nature as to be coupled with an interest. *B* has, in effect, an interest in the authority.

Broker's Protection Against Termination

Although it is the general rule that an agency may be terminated at any time, there are a number of exceptions to the rule that have particular application to real estate brokers. The most obvious situation in which the agency cannot be terminated at the will of the owner occurs when the broker has procured a purchaser and the owner then states that the agency is terminated. In this case, the broker is entitled to a commission. If no time for the duration of the agency is included in the broker's contract of employment and the broker is negotiating with a prospect, the owner [principal] cannot terminate the agency and finish the transaction without paying the broker.

For example, an exclusive real estate agency contract specifies the duration of the contract. On the basis of this agreement, the broker spends money advertising and showing the property; the owner then terminates the contract before the expiration of the time called for in the contract. In a case of this nature, the owner may be liable to the broker for the money and time spent seeking a purchaser for the property.

Broker's Duties as Agent

Just as the principal has certain obligations to the agent, the agent has certain obligations to the principal.

Loyalty. Foremost among these obligations is loyalty. The broker must be loyal to the principal. Given a position of trust and confidence, the broker is not permitted to make a secret profit as a result of this position of trust. The broker cannot secretly purchase, either directly or indirectly, a property the broker has listed or attempt to make a secret profit therefrom. For example, *A* lists a property with a broker for $70,000. The broker later states that there is an offer for $60,000, and *A* accepts the offer. At the closing, *A* transfers a deed to a woman and later discovers that the woman is the wife of the broker and is using her maiden name. *A*, meanwhile, has paid the broker $3,600 in commissions. *A* may recover the $10,000 and the commission paid. In New York State, *A* is entitled to recover the commission that has been paid, and, in case of deception, is entitled to recover four times the amount of the commission paid.

Accounting for Money and Property. A real estate broker handling funds or property belonging to a principal must account for the money or property on demand from the principal. In some states, the broker is required by law to submit a closing statement to the interested parties in a sales transaction. This, in effect, requires an accounting in writing by the broker of the funds handled. In other states, the principal can force the accounting by order of the courts.

The theory behind this is that when receiving money or property for a client, a broker is placed in the position of a trustee. Thus, the broker becomes liable not only under the brokerage laws of the states but, in the event of breach of trust, may become liable under the penal laws of the states as well. As trustee, the broker holds the money for the benefit of a client and must exercise care with any funds so held. The broker must not, under any circumstances, commingle any personal funds with money held for the client. It is a universal provision of the brokerage license laws that the mere commingling of a broker's own funds with money held on behalf of a client is a basis for the revocation or suspension of the broker's license. To avoid this situation, the broker, on entering business, should immediately open a special bank account, and this special account should be reserved exclusively as a depository for the funds belonging to clients.

Attention to Delegation of Authority. The agent is selected by the principal because the principal places trust and confidence in the agent alone. A broker may, however, delegate ministerial or mechanical duties involving the agency to another. In order to avoid complications of this nature, most of the broker's contracts of employment contain a statement substantially to this effect:

> You may, if desired, secure the cooperation of any broker, or group of brokers, in procuring a sale of said property.

In the absence of a statement of this nature, the broker takes the risk of refusal on the part of the owner to consent to such employment when employing a subagent. However, the owner may consent either expressly or by implication. If the owner keeps silent, the broker's employment of a subagent will be construed by the courts to be an implication of consent on the part of the owner.

A broker is generally held liable for the acts of a subagent employed to handle the sale of a property. For example, a property is listed with a broker at $1,500 per acre. The broker hires another broker, *X*, to help transact the deal. *X*, the subagent, receives a $2,000 per acre offer but reports only an offer of $1,500 per acre to the broker. The owner accepts the offer, and the property is deeded over to a person conspiring with the subagent. The subagent later sells the property to the original offeror. The owner may sue the broker under these circumstances, and the broker will be held personally liable for the actions of the subagent even though the broker had no actual knowledge of the deceptive phase of the transaction.

Obedience to Instructions. When a property is listed with a broker, the listing contains instructions to the broker that must be obeyed. In addition, the owner may impose limitations on the broker by special instructions, which the broker is also bound to obey. Brokers who deviate from the instructions given by the principal may find themselves liable to their principal for damages resulting from such deviations.

Avoidance of Negligence. The general rule of agency regarding negligence is applicable to brokers. The agent is bound to exercise the same skill as other brokers operating in the same capacity. If negligent in the pursuance of duties, the agent is liable for any resulting loss that might be sustained by the principal.

Fiduciary Responsibility. It is commonly stated that the agent acts in a **fiduciary** (founded in trust or confidence) capacity with the principal. At all times, then, the broker must be completely honest with the principal. The broker must reveal to the principal all information and all material facts concerning a transaction. For instance, if the broker knows that the purchaser is acting for someone else, that fact must be revealed to the principal. This is known as the **fiduciary concept**.

Service to One Party. It is commonly believed that no person may serve two masters, and so it is with regard to real estate brokers. No broker may ordinarily serve both parties to a transaction because the interests of the buyer and the seller are diametrically opposed. The seller wants the highest price possible for the property, and the purchaser wants to buy it at the lowest price possible. The broker obviously cannot serve both the seller of the property and the prospective buyer equally well in this regard.

A broker may serve the interests of both parties when obtaining the consent of both the buyer and the seller. The consent should be obtained in writing from both parties and should be kept in the broker's files. In some states, the real estate license laws specifically require that this consent be obtained in writing and filed "in the deal envelope." In these states, the law further declares that the state real estate board may, at any time, demand a written consent. In the absence of such written consent, a broker's license may be revoked.

True Representation of the Facts. A broker must not make any statements misrepresenting material facts. If the broker misrepresents the facts, the commission may not only be lost, but the broker will be liable to the purchaser for resulting damages. For example, a parcel of property described as having a frontage of 100 feet is listed with a broker. The broker brings the prospect to see the property, which is bordered on one side by a hedge. The broker assumes the property line begins with the hedge. The purchaser asks the broker if the property includes the hedge, and the broker answers in the affirmative. On the basis of this statement, the property is purchased. Later it is discovered that the property line is actually about 14 feet inside the hedge. The purchaser sues the broker and collects damages as a result of this misrepresentation even though it was not deliberate on the broker's part.

Perceptible Statements. The broker is not ordinarily liable for extraordinary and extravagant statements made in the course of selling a parcel of property. The attitude of the courts is that a buyer, as a reasonable person, should not believe such statements implicitly, and therefore cannot hold the seller to them should they prove false. For example, if a broker takes a prospect to a piece of property and says that the property has the "best view in the world," the purchaser cannot later bring an action against the broker claiming the property actually did not contain the "best view in the world." The purchaser either knew or should have known that the broker was making an obviously extravagant statement about the property.

Recent Developments. In the past few years, brokers have been faced with increased litigation from both sellers and buyers, and in all probability this will increase in the future.

In the early 1980s there was an increase in so-called new and creative financing. For the most part this consisted of a buyer assuming a mortgage (taking over an existing one) and a seller taking back a note and second mortgage calling for a balloon payment. For example, assume the selling price of a home is $100,000 with an existing mortgage of $60,000. Typically, the buyer would obtain an $80,000 mortgage through a thrift institution and pay the seller $20,000 in cash. However, in many cases the buyer is unable to qualify for a loan and a deal is entered into whereby the buyer assumes the $60,000 existing mortgage, pays the seller $10,000 in cash, and the seller than takes back a note and mortgage in the amount of $30,000, the entire transaction totaling the $100,000 purchase price. The problem is that the $30,000 second mortgage is, in many cases, due and payable at the end of five years.

The argument put forth for this "creativeness" is basically twofold: (1) that the house will rise in value, and (2) that in five years the buyer will qualify for a new loan, thereby paying off the seller. Unhappily for the sellers, the value of the property often does not rise and the buyer is unable to obtain a new loan.

This arrangement results in some peculiar litigation. For instance:

1. Alleging fraud and negligence, buyers sometimes sue brokers claiming that they had been assured by the broker that new financing would be available.

2. Sellers sue brokers when a buyer fails to pay the seller the lump-sum second mortgage; and, in the meantime, the seller has purchased a new home calling for a lump-sum payment. The seller loses the new home because of failure to make the payment and has to foreclose on the old home because the payment was not made by buyer. Seller alleges that the broker failed to protect his or her interests.

It is suggested that brokers who become involved in creative financing deals be certain to advise both parties to consult an attorney and also obtain a signed statement from both parties stating that this advice was given to them by the broker.

Acting for an Undisclosed Principal

Very often real estate brokers are called upon to negotiate for a principal without disclosing that person's identity. The broker has two alternatives: (1) to proceed as if buying the property for himself or herself or (2) to state that he or she is acting for a principal who prefers to remain anonymous.

In either situation, the agent can sue or be sued on any contract the agent executes. By the same token, the principal can either sue or be sued on any contract that has been executed by the agent. If the agent states that he or she is working for a principal, it may be clearly indicated in the contract that the agent assumes no personal liability under the contract.

Ratification

Agents are generally authorized to do a specific act, and the agents are bound to obey the instructions given them by the principal. However, if the agent performs an authorized act, this act may be ratified by the principal. **Ratification** is

> the express or implied adoption and confirmation by one person of an act or contract performed or entered into on his behalf by another who at the time assumed to act as his agent in doing or making the contract, without the authority to do so.[2]

For there to be a ratification, the person acting must have done the act as the agent and not as an individual. In addition, the person ratifying must have full knowledge of all of the material facts or have sufficient facts to enable that person to choose to assume full responsibility for the act.

It should be especially noted that the principal cannot ratify part of the transaction and disaffirm the remainder of the transaction. If the principal seeks to ratify the act of the agent, the entire act must be ratified. Principal is then bound by the entire act of the agent in the same manner as if the agent had been given the authority to carry out the act.

Honest Mistakes

The broker cannot be held liable for an honest mistake unless it can be shown that the honest mistake was the result of gross negligence. For example, a seller tells a broker that the size of the property is 160 acres and shows the broker a survey showing the property to be 160 acres. After

[2]Corpus Juris, Sec. 77.

having acquired a purchaser, it is shown that the property is only 150 acres actually. The broker cannot be held liable in a situation of this type; the mistake was an honest one.

Errors and Omissions

Recent court decisions have held real estate brokers liable for errors and omissions—even honest mistakes. Underlying this is the fact that real estate brokerage is becoming more complex, and the broker is called upon to answer more complex questions. Tax questions are an example. Because brokers are becoming more professional, buyers rely more on their advice. Consequently, courts have held brokers liable for improper advice, as in malpractice. To protect themselves, brokers rely more on errors and omissions insurance.

The penalty for fraudulent representations made by a broker is serious. For example, a broker subdivides a parcel of property and represents to prospective purchasers that arrangements have been made for water and sewage disposal. The prospect purchases the property, then discovers that no such arrangements have been made, nor was there any attempt on the part of the broker to arrange for water and sewage disposal for the subdivision. In a case of this kind, not only is the broker liable for damages to the purchaser for fraud, but broker's license will be revoked either on grounds of misrepresentation or on the grounds that broker proved to be untrustworthy.

THE REAL ESTATE BROKER AND FAIR HOUSING LEGISLATION

In 1988, Congress passed the Fair Housing Act of 1988, which will affect real estate brokers and agents for decades to come. To understand this act, it is necessary to review previous fair housing laws.

Fair Housing Act of 1968

"Fair housing" can be broadly thought of as encompassing two federal laws designed to ensure equal treatment of minorities by real estate brokers and owners.

The first of these laws was enacted in 1866 shortly after the Civil War (the Civil Rights Act of 1866). The 1866 act prohibited *owners* of property from discriminating in the sale or rental of real or personal property to anyone on racial grounds. For all practical purposes, the 1866 act had little effect until 1968.

In 1968, Title VIII of the Civil Rights Act was passed by Congress and enacted into law. Also in that year, Mr. Jones, a black man, won a case he had instituted in 1965 against the Mayer Company because the Mayer

Company had refused to sell him a home solely because he was black.[3] The U.S. Supreme Court in this decision reaffirmed the 1866 act by holding that the statute covers racial discrimination in private transactions and that the act was constitutional under the Thirteenth Amendment to the Constitution. More importantly, perhaps, the Jones decision drastically affected the Civil Rights Act of 1968, as will be pointed out shortly.

The 1968 act came about mainly because "blockbusting" and "steering" had reached scandalous proportions. *Blockbusting* consists of using scare tactics to force owner sale of homes at below market prices. For example, an individual purchases one home on a block and installs a minority family in the house. The word is then passed that others are contemplating the sale of their homes to minorities. Panic is created. At this point, the individual, usually through a straw man, will make an offer to people in the entire neighborhood at prices substantially below market value. The homes are purchased, and the "blockbuster" then sells the homes to minorities at inflated prices.

Steering occurs when prospective home buyers are channeled to a particular neighborhood for one of two reasons: (1) to start a blockbust or (2) to maintain a homogeneous neighborhood (for example, a black will be taken to a strictly black area and a white shown properties in a strictly white area).

As a result of these activities and an increasing awareness of civil rights, the 1968 act was passed. Among other things, this act provides that real estate brokers acting in behalf of principals must consider all real property as open for sale, lease, and mortgage to all legally competent persons. In short, discrimination because of sex, race, color, religion, or national origin in real estate transactions is prohibited. To enforce the act, complaints must be made to the Fair Housing section of a HUD office within 180 days of the alleged infraction.

There are three important exemptions given *owners* under the 1968 Civil Rights Act:

1. A sale or lease is arranged without the aid of a real estate agent.
2. A sale or lease is arranged without the aid of discriminating advertising.
3. Fewer than three houses or fewer than four apartment units (one of which is owner-occupied) are owned by the seller.

However, as previously noted, the Jones case was decided immediately after the passage of the 1968 act and the 1866 act was reaffirmed. The net effect of the Jones case was that it immediately voided the three exemptions to the 1968 act noted above, *but* with an important distinction:

---

[3]*Jones v. Alfred H. Mayer Co.*, 392 U.S. 409 (1968).

that the 1968 act is enforced by HUD, while the individual seeking redress under the Civil Rights Act of 1866 must bring an action personally against an owner.

The real estate broker should be familiar with all of the ramifications of fair housing law and should assume responsibility for seeing that it is complied with by all parties concerned.

Fair Housing Act of 1988

The **Fair Housing Act of 1988,** which became effective on March 12, 1989, is an amendment to the 1968 act. Basically it does two things: (1) it eliminates a ceiling of $1,000 imposed by the 1968 law for punitive damages, and (2) it adds the disabled and families with children to those protected from discrimination on the basis of sex, race, color, religion, or national origin.

Under the 1988 act, a broker facing a discrimination charge can choose to be heard before an administrative law judge or in a federal court. The administrative law judge is empowered to impose civil penalties ranging from $10,000 to $50,000. The judge can also assess actual damages and unlimited compensatory damages for the "humiliation" and "stigma" resulting from the discriminatory practice. The federal courts can impose higher punitive damages in addition to actual damages.

In addition, the act provides the plaintiffs with a government lawyer. The suit may also be brought before an officer in a state or locality with a fair housing law certified as "substantially equivalent" to the federal law. It extends protection to those discriminated against in rental property as well as property being offered for sale.

In the law's first ten weeks on the books, more than 1,000 complaints were filed, 40 percent of which involved the two new classes extended protection by the law: the handicapped and families with children.

BROKERS' EMPLOYMENT CONTRACTS

Many states provide that the contract of employment, or listing contract as it is commonly called, between the broker and client must be in writing.[4] In these states, a written agreement is a prerequisite to the collection of a commission. In other states, the contract of employment may be oral. Even in these states, however, it is desirable that employment contracts be in writing, especially those contracts containing an exclusive right or an exclusive agency agreement. The advantage of a written agreement is that it avoids later misunderstanding about the true contents of the listing and avoids misunderstanding about the rights of brokers under the contract of employment.

---

[4]Arizona, California, Florida, Idaho, Indiana, Iowa, Kentucky, Michigan, Montana, Nebraska, New Jersey, New Mexico, Ohio, Oregon, Texas, Utah, Washington, and Wisconsin.

A copy of the signed contract is kept by the broker. In some states, the brokerage laws require that the broker deliver a copy of the listing contract to the seller. At this point it would be a good idea to study the broker's employment contract form shown as Exhibit 24-1.

Points Covered

The ordinary real estate broker's listing contract contains the names and addresses of the seller and the broker, the selling price, and any encumbrances against the property. The contract describes the property and states the manner in which the property is to be conveyed. There is a statement setting forth the commission to be paid to the broker. (Commissions may be negotiated and range from flat fees for minimal service to between 2 and 7 percent of the selling price. It should be noted, however, that the commission is the seller's offer of compensation to the broker. An inadequate commission may result in receiving less than full service from an unmotivated broker.) The contract also lists the personal property that is included in the deal, such as shades, venetian blinds, and door screens, and a declaration by the seller that a bill of sale will be delivered to the buyer to cover the transfer of such personal property. If it is an exclusive contract, the instrument will contain an expiration date. In some states, such as Oregon, all listing contracts must have a definite expiration date.

Automatic Renewal Clauses

Most states have outlawed the inclusion of an **automatic renewal clause** in the listing contract. This clause can cause endless trouble between seller and broker, and furthermore, it is basically unfair to the seller. In contracts containing an automatic renewal clause, the contract includes an expiration date for the contract and states substantially as follows:

> After the date last mentioned, this contract will continue in force as a nonexclusive listing in every respect as above set forth until canceled by me in writing, or until the property is sold.

In states where the automatic renewal clause is prohibited, brokers should be certain it is not included in their contracts, because its inclusion in a broker's contract of employment may lead to loss of license.

TYPES OF EMPLOYMENT CONTRACTS

Open Listing

The **open listing** is a listing given by an owner to many brokers. In giving an open listing, the owner hopes one of the brokers will be able to produce a purchaser for the property. In the event broker *A* enters into negotiations with a prospect and obtains a signed binder, or contract, broker *A* is not

Exhibit 24-1 Real Estate Broker's Employment Contract Form

No. 674 © Rev. TL
Stevens-Ness L.P.Co.
Portland, Or. 97204

REAL ESTATE BROKER'S EMPLOYMENT CONTRACT

RESIDENCE PROPERTY

DESCRIPTION: ______________________________

(If said property is incorrectly described, owner hereby expressly authorizes broker subsequently to write in hereon or attach hereto, the correct legal description thereof.)

City of ______________, County of ______________, State of ______________; for better description see owner's title deed on record, now made a part hereof. For personal property, if any to be included in property offered for sale for price next mentioned, see below or see signed inventory, to be attached.

Selling price, free of encumbrances: $ ______________; Terms ______________

Is signed inventory attached as part hereof? Yes_____; No _____; to be attached as part hereof? Yes_____; No_____.

To ______________ (REAL ESTATE BROKER) ______________ (CITY) ______________ (STATE) ______________, 19_____ (DATE)

FOR VALUE RECEIVED, you hereby are employed to sell or exchange the property described hereon at the selling price and on the terms noted. You hereby are authorized to accept a deposit on the purchase price. You may, if desired, secure the cooperation of any other broker, or group of brokers, in procuring a sale of said property. In the event that you, or any other brokers cooperating with you, shall find a buyer ready and willing to enter into a deal for said price and terms, or such other terms and price as I may accept, or that during your employment you place me in contact with a buyer to or through whom at any time within 90 days after the termination of said employment I may sell or convey said property, I hereby agree to pay you in cash for your services a commission equal in amount to__________% of the above stated selling price. I agree to convey said real estate to the purchaser by a good and sufficient deed, to transfer and deliver said personal property, if any, by good and sufficient bill of sale and to furnish title insurance insuring marketable title to said real estate and good right to convey. I hereby warrant that the information shown hereon below is true, that I am the owner of said property, that my title thereto is a good and marketable title, that the same is free of encumbrances except as shown hereafter under "Financial Details" and except taxes levied on said property for the current tax year which are to be pro rated between the seller and buyer. In case of an exchange, I have no objection to your representing and accepting compensation from the other party to the exchange as well as myself. I hereby authorize you and your customers to enter any part of said property at any reasonable time to show same. Also, I authorize you, at any time, to fill in and complete all or any part of the "Informative Data" below, except financial details. The following items are to be left upon the premises as part of the property purchased: All irrigation, plumbing, ventilating, cooling and heating fixtures and equipment (including stoker and oil tanks but excluding fire place fixtures and equipment), water heaters, attached electric light and bath room fixtures, light bulbs and fluorescent lamps, venetian blinds, wall-to-wall carpeting, awnings, window and door screens, storm doors and windows, attached floor coverings, attached television antenna, all plants, shrubs and trees and all fixtures except ______________
The following personal property is also included as a part of the property to be offered for sale for said price: ______________

______________(or see signed inventory, if any, attached). This agreement expires at midnight on______________, 19_____, but I further allow you a reasonable time thereafter to close any deal on which earnest money is then deposited. In case of suit or action on this contract, I agree to pay such additional sum as the court, both trial and appellate, may adjudge reasonable as plaintiff's attorneys fees. It is further agreed that my signature affixed to the renewal clause below shall have the effect of renewing and extending your employment to a new date to be fixed by me on the same terms and all with the same effect as if the said new date had been fixed above as the expiration date of your employment.

*THIS LISTING IS AN EXCLUSIVE LISTING and you hereby are granted the absolute, sole and exclusive right to sell or exchange the said described property. In the event of any sale, by me or any other person, or of exchange or conveyance of said property, or any part thereof, during the term of your exclusive employment, or in case I withdraw the authority hereby given prior to said expiration date, I agree to pay you the said commission just the same as if a sale had actually been consummated by you.

I HEREBY CERTIFY THAT I HAVE READ AND RECEIVED A CARBON COPY OF THIS CONTRACT.

Accepted: ______________, 19_____ Owner ______________

Broker ______________ Owner ______________

Owner's Address ______________ City ______________ State ______________ Phone ______________

FOR VALUE RECEIVED, the above broker's employment hereby is renewed and extended to and including ______________, 19_____

Accepted: ______________, 19_____ Owner ______________

Broker ______________ Owner ______________

Exhibit 24-1 (continued)

FINANCIAL DETAILS

Selling price (free of encumbrances)

$ ____ Terms: ____

Payments include: Prin. ___ Int. ___ Taxes ___ Ins. ___
(Check items to be included in payments)

Interest on deferred payments ____ %

Fire ins. $ ____ Ann'l prem. $ ____

Taxes last fiscal year $ ____

F.H.A. commitment $ ____

ENCUMBRANCES — Payable

1st mtg. $ ____ Int. ____ % ____

2nd mtg. $ ____ Int. ____ % ____

Mtg. held by ____

Contr. bal. $ ____ Int. ____ % ____

Delinquent taxes $ ____

Municipal liens $ ____

	B	1F	2F	A	Comment
Living rm.					
Dining rm.					
Family rm.					
Kitchen					
Brkft. nk.					
Bedrms.					
Slpng. pch.					
Bath					
Den					
Party rm.					
Utility rm.					
Hallway					
Attic: Fin. Unfin.					

RESIDENCE PROPERTY INFORMATIVE DATA

Office
Listing No. ____

Address ____ Bet. ____ & ____ District ____

Lot ____ Block ____ Addition ____ Facing N ___ S ___ E ___ W ___

Dimension of lot ____ x ____ Dimension of house ____ x ____ No. rooms ____ No. stories ____ Attic ____

Owner has: Abstract ____ Title Insurance ____ Cert. of Title ____ Contract ____ Deed ____

Occupied by: Owner ____ Vacant ____ Renter ____ Renter's name ____ Tel. ____ Rent $ ____

Owner's name ____ Tel. ____

May we use pass key ____ Key at ____

Possession may be had ____

Type of house ____

Type of construction ____ Type of roof ____

Condition: roof ____ paint exterior ____ paint interior ____

Utilities: Electricity ____ Gas ____ Phone ____ Water ____ Garbage service ____

For details as to chattels included in sale: See employment contract ____ See signed inventory ____

FEATURES & FINISH	HEATING & COOLING	OUTSIDE	DISTANCE TO
Sink ____	House ____	Garage: Sgle. Dbl. ____	Bus ____
Dishwasher ____	____	Carport ____	Name of line ____
Disposal ____	____	Lawn ____	Grade School ____
L. trays ____	____	Garden ____	High School ____
Shower ____	____	Shrubbery ____	Pub. Park ____
Hdwd. floor ____	____	Sprinkler ____	Grocery store ____
Fir floor ____	____	____	MISCELLANEOUS
W/W Carpeting ____	Water ____	____	Sewer ____
Vinyl floors ____	____	STREETS	Cesspool ____ Sep. tank ____
Plaster ceil. ____	BASEMENT	Paved ____	Outdoor frplce. ____
Beam ceil. ____	Full ____ Part ____	Macadam ____	Walks ____
Rms. papered ____	Fin. ____ Unfin. ____	Graded ____	Weatherstripping ____
Rms. tinted ____	Floor Drain ____	Ungraded ____	Insulation: Ceil. ____ Wall ____
Enam. finish ____	____	Sidewalk ____	Blt. in Rng. ____ Oven ____
Nat. finish ____	____	Alley ____	Wired elect. stove ____

Remarks: ____

Listed by ____

Signs permitted ____

Inspected by ____

Will consider exchange for ____

BROKER'S COPY

* TO MAKE NON-EXCLUSIVE—Strike complete paragraph following asterisk (*) in Employment Contract and have owner initial deletion.

entitled to a commission if another broker has succeeded in obtaining a signed binder or contract prior to the completion of the transaction by broker *A*.

In many respects, an open listing is bad not only from the broker's viewpoint but also from the owner's viewpoint. Brokers are naturally reluctant to spend a great deal of money advertising a property when they know it may very well be all in vain; hence, owners who give open listings often receive no action on their properties.

Exclusive Agency

The **exclusive agency** gives a broker the right to sell a property exclusive of all other brokers. If broker *A* receives an exclusive agency, such broker is entitled to a commission from the owner even though the property is sold by broker *B*. However, in the exclusive agency, the owner may sell the property and not be liable for payment of a commission to the broker.

Exclusive Right to Sell

The **exclusive right to sell** differs from the exclusive agency only in one respect: the broker is entitled to receive a commission no matter who sells the property. When the exclusive right is given, although the owner sells the property, the broker is entitled to a commission from the owner. An exclusive right to sell listing contract is shown in Exhibit 24-2.

Although some brokers favor open listings and exclusive agency listings, most brokers favor the exclusive right. The problems facing the broker are similar to the problems facing the marketer of any other commodity. To market a commodity properly, the marketer must have confidence in being able to deliver the product to the purchaser. A real estate broker selling under an open listing cannot be sure of being able to deliver, for at any time another broker may tender the seller a bona fide offer. It is difficult for a broker to represent the client properly when the stock in trade is of a nebulous character.

Some of the advantages of the exclusive listing to the owner are that the broker holding exclusive sales rights can afford to spend time and money promoting a sale because the broker is assured of compensation when successful. By giving the listing close attention, the broker is likely to effect a sale at a better price; confidence placed in one broker helps to ensure action in the best interests of the owner; cooperation with other brokers is still possible; and an exclusive broker saves the owner time the owner would otherwise spend in talking with many agents and their prospects. The broker cannot in good conscience devote the same amount of time and energy to a client who has listed a property as an open listing as is possible with other clients with whom the broker has an exclusive listing. The

Exhibit 24-2 Exclusive Right to Sell Listing Contract

Edina Realty Inc.

EXCLUSIVE RIGHT TO SELL LISTING CONTRACT

DEFINITIONS

This Contract involves the property located at: ______ (property)
"I" means: ______
"You" means: EDINA REALTY, INC. (the real estate broker).

LISTING

I give you the exclusive right to sell the property for the price of $ ______. I will require the following terms: ______ ______. This contract starts ______, 19____ and ends at 11:59 p.m. on ______, 19____.
In exchange, you agree to list the property and try to sell it. You may place a "For Sale" sign and a lock box with keys on the property.
I understand you are a member of the Regional Multiple Listing Service (RMLS) and you will give information to RMLS concerning the property. I will keep you notified of relevant information important to the sale of the property. If you sell the property, you may notify RMLS and members of the area boards of REALTORS® of the price and terms of the sale. I understand that this Contract DOES NOT give you authority to rent or manage my property. I understand that mortgage financing services are usually paid for by the buyer; however, certain insured government loans may require the seller to pay a portion of the fees for the mortgage loan. I understand that I will not be required to pay the financing fees on any mortgage without giving my written consent.

MY DUTIES

I will cooperate with you in selling the property. I will promptly tell you about all inquiries I receive about the property. I agree to provide and pay for any inspections and reports if required by the city or state. I agree to provide homeowners association documents if required. I will provide the buyer an updated abstract of title, or owner's duplicate certificate of title and registered property abstract, or owner's title insurance policy to the property. I have the full legal right to sell the property. I will sign all closing documents (including a warranty deed or contract for deed) necessary to transfer to the Buyer marketable title (full and unquestioned ownership) to the property.

NOTICE: THE COMMISSION RATE FOR THE SALE, LEASE, RENTAL OR MANAGEMENT OF REAL PROPERTY SHALL BE DETERMINED BETWEEN EACH INDIVIDUAL REAL ESTATE BROKER AND ITS CLIENT.

YOUR COMMISSION

I will pay you as your commission ______% of the selling price if I sell or agree to sell the property before this contract ends. In addition, if before this contract ends you present a Buyer who is willing and able to buy the property at the price and terms required in this contract, but I refuse to sell, I will still pay you the same commission. I agree to pay your commission whether you, I, or another agent or broker sells the property. **I hereby permit you to share part of your commission with other real estate brokers, including brokers only representing the buyer.** I agree to pay your commission in full upon the happening of any of the following events: (1) The closing of the sale. (2) My refusal to close the sale, or (3) My refusal to sell at the price and terms required in this contract.

If within 180 days after the end of this contract, I sell or agree to sell the property to anyone who:
(1) During this contract made inquiry of me about the property and I did not tell you about the inquiry; or
(2) During this contract made an affirmative showing of interest in the property or was physically shown the property by you and whose name is on a written list you give me within 72 hours after the end of this contract.
Then I will still pay you your commission on the selling price, even if I sell the property without your assistance. I understand that I do not have to pay your commission if I sign another valid listing contract after the expiration of this Contract, under which I am obligated to pay a commission to another licensed real estate broker.
To secure the payment of your commission I hereby assign to you the proceeds from the sale of my property in an amount equal to the commission due you under this Contract. If either you or I bring an action for enforcement of this Agreement, the prevailing party in such action, whether or not such action proceeds to final judgement, shall be entitled to recover all costs and expenses including all reasonable attorneys' fees and court costs.

CLOSING SERVICES

As the Real Estate Broker you will be responsible for closing the sale of my property and will provide the closing services through Equity Title Services, Inc. I will pay a fee of $200.00 to Equity Title Services, Inc. at the time of closing for closing services incidental to the sale of my property.

NOTICE: THE REAL ESTATE BROKER, REAL ESTATE SALESPERSON, OR REAL ESTATE CLOSING AGENT HAS NOT AND, UNDER APPLICABLE STATE LAW, MAY NOT EXPRESS OPINIONS REGARDING THE LEGAL EFFECT OF THE CLOSING DOCUMENTS OR OF THE CLOSING ITSELF.

NOTICES AND NONDISCRIMINATION

As of this date I have not received notices from any municipality, government agency or homeowners association about the property that I have not told you about, and I agree to promptly tell you of any notices of that type that I receive. I understand that I may not refuse to sell, or discriminate in the terms, conditions or privileges of sale, to any person due to their race, color, creed, religion, national origin, sex, marital status, status with regard to public assistance, handicap, whether physical or mental or family status. I understand further that local ordinances may include other protective classes.

ACCEPTED BY: EDINA REALTY, INC.
Real Estate Company

By: ______
Sales Associate

Date signed: ______, 19____

ACCEPTED BY: ______
Owner

______
Owner

Address: ______

Phone: ______

Owner's Social Security #: ______

Social Security #: ______

Federal I.D. # (if corporation) ______

I/we would like relocation services. Yes____ No____

Date signed: ______, 19____

ER 201C (3/89)

WHITE, EDINA REALTY'S COPY; CANARY, OWNER'S COPY

SOURCE: *Edina Realty.*

broker seeking exclusive listings should point out these facts to clients. There are strong arguments in favor of the exclusive listing, and the client should be made aware of them so that the values of exclusive listing may be appreciated.

The main disadvantage of the exclusive listing to the owner is that no matter how capable the broker may be and no matter how hard that broker may work, his or her circle of contacts could not possibly include all of the buyers in a city.

Multiple Listings

A **multiple listing service** is a means by which the participating broker makes a blanket, unilateral offer of subagency to the other participating brokers and is a facility for the orderly correlation and dissemination of listing information among the participating brokers so that they may better serve their clients and the public.

In practice, a broker may elect, when entering business, to join a multiple listing service. For the privilege of joining an MLS, the broker pays a fee. These fees vary with the size of the city and the MLS. When obtaining a listing, the broker is bound by rules of the MLS to transmit the listing to the MLS after a stated period of time. Within the stated period, the broker may attempt to sell the property; but if the broker fails to sell the property within this period, the information is transmitted to the MLS who sends out information on the listing to all of the members. In this way, the seller has the advantage of all the members of the MLS attempting to sell the property. When the property is sold, the listing broker pays either a portion of the commission or a flat fee to the selling broker. If the listing broker makes the sale, she or he is entitled to the entire commission on the transaction.

On November 15, 1971, the multiple listing policy of NAR (then NAREB) was adopted by its board of directors.

The MLS policy represents NAR's firm determination that REALTOR® multiple listing services shall be organized and operated to serve the basic purpose for which they are established: "to make possible the orderly dissemination and correlation of listing information to its members so that REALTORS® may better serve the buying and selling public." The 14-point policy is as follows:

> A multiple listing service shall not enact or enforce any rule that restricts, limits, or interferes with the actions of its members in their relations with each other or in their REALTOR®/client relationship or in the conduct of their business including, but not limited to:

1. A multiple listing shall not "fix, control, recommend, suggest, or maintain commission rates or fees for services to be rendered by members."

2. A multiple listing service shall not "fix, control, recommend, suggest, or maintain any percentage division of commission or fees between cooperating members or non-members."
3. A multiple listing service shall not "require financial support of multiple listing service operations by any formula based on commission or sales prices."
4. A multiple listing service shall not "require or use any form which establishes or implies the existence of any contractual relationship between the multiple listing service and the client (buyer or seller)."
5. A multiple listing service shall not "make any rule relating to the posting or use of signs."
6. A multiple listing service shall not "make any rule prohibiting or discouraging cooperation with non-members."
7. A multiple listing service shall not "limit or interfere with the terms of the relationship between a member and his salesmen (Interpretations 16 and 17)."
8. A multiple listing service shall not "prohibit or discourage any members from political participation or activity."
9. A multiple listing service shall not "make any rule granting blanket consent to a selling member to negotiate directly with the seller (owner) (Interpretation 10)."
10. A multiple listing service shall not "make any rule regulating the advertising or promotion of any listings."
11. A multiple listing service shall not "prohibit or discourage a member from accepting a listing from a seller (owner) preferring to give 'office exclusive.' "
12. A multiple listing service shall not "adopt any rule denying a listing member from controlling the posting of 'sold signs.' "
13. A multiple listing service shall not "refuse any exclusive listing submitted by a member on the basis of the quality or price of the listing."
14. A multiple listing service shall not "adopt rules authorizing the modification or change of any listing without the express, written permission of the listing member."

Agency Disclosure Legislation

As the result of a Federal Trade Commission survey revealing that over 70 percent of the purchasers believed the agent showing them a house listed by *another* broker represented them, most states have enacted, or are contemplating enacting, disclosure legislation. The reason the legislation was necessary is that the lack of disclosure that an agent may in fact be a subagent of the listing broker has resulted in expensive and needless litigation throughout the country.

Among the states requiring disclosure in various forms are California, Hawaii, Minnesota, Pennsylvania, and New Jersey. These states were joined by Florida in 1988 and Idaho in 1989. Others are apt to follow suit. New Jersey requires a three-day cooling-off period after closing so that both parties may consult their attorneys. As one wag put it, "This requirement was sponsored by the New Jersey attorneys' early retirement fund!"

Broker-Buyer Contract

An extension of agency disclosure is the request by buyers to engage a broker to represent their interests in the purchase of a home. The buyer's broker may be paid by the buyer. Alternatively, the buyer's broker may share the commission of the listing broker just as when a co-op sale is completed. Permission for the sharing of commissions with a buyer's broker is given in the listing agreement (see Exhibit 24-2). An example of a broker-buyer contract is presented in Exhibit 24-3.

Net Listings

A **net listing** occurs when an owner lists a property with a broker and says in effect: "I want $40,000 for the property. Anything over that amount is your commission." When this is done, the listing may be made with the broker as an open listing, an exclusive right, or the exclusive agency listing.

The net listing is considered by most brokers to be bad business. Some states prohibit it under their license laws, and brokers run the risk of losing their licenses. Rule 6 of the Michigan Corporation and Securities Commission, for example, states:

> A broker shall not become a party to any net listing agreement for an owner or seller as a means of securing a real estate commission.

Even in those states where net listings are not specifically prohibited, the astute broker will avoid securing listings in this manner. They are a constant source of trouble for the broker and cause extremely poor public relations. No matter what commission is received under this listing, the broker is bound to be criticized by either the buyer or the seller, and more often by both.

COMMISSIONS

Employment

For a real estate broker to establish a claim for a commission, it must be shown that the broker was actually employed by the principal. In states

Exhibit 24-3 Broker-Buyer Contract Form

Edina Realty

BROKER-BUYER CONTRACT
NON-SPECIFIC PROPERTY
EXCLUSIVE AGREEMENT WITH BUYER

THIS AGREEMENT Made by and between **EDINA REALTY, INC.** hereinafter referred to as EDINA, and ____________________

____________________ hereinafter referred to as Buyer.

Buyer hereby retains EDINA for the purpose of locating property to purchase by

Buyer in the city of ____________________, County(ies of) ____________________

State of ____________________, in the nature of ____________________

____________________, for use as ____________________

____________________ under terms and conditions acceptable to Buyer.

If Buyer, or any other person acting for Buyer or in Buyer's behalf, purchases any property, during the term of this contract or within __________ days thereafter, which was first presented or submitted to Buyer by EDINA during the term of this contract, and the description of which was submitted to Buyer in writing, either personally or by mail posted prior to the termination date of this contract, Buyer agrees to pay to EDINA a fee of __________% of the purchase price.

If Buyer, or any other person acting for Buyer, or in Buyer's behalf, exercises or assigns an option to purchase any property, during the term of this contract or within __________ days thereafter, which property was first presented or submitted to Buyer by EDINA during the term of this contract, and the description of which has been submitted to Buyer in writing either in EDINA or by mail posted prior to the termination date of this contract, Buyer agrees to pay EDINA the sum of $ __________ fee and further agrees to pay __________% of the purchase price minus the amount previously paid to EDINA for obtaining said option.

In consideration of Buyer's agreement set forth above, EDINA agrees to use reasonable efforts to find the required property and to procure an accepted offer to purchase or option to purchase the required property and agrees that he/she will not accept a fee from the owner of said property unless such fee is disclosed to the Buyer in writing before any offer to purchase or option is executed.

In consideration for EDINA's agreement as set forth above, Buyer agrees to pay EDINA a retainer fee of $__________ which shall be subtracted from any fee due to EDINA should EDINA be successful in obtaining a satisfactory property, otherwise to be retained by EDINA for services rendered.

The following property has been submitted to Buyer and is excluded from this agreement ____________________

____

The term of this contract shall be from 12:01 AM, the __________ day of __________, 19 ______ to midnight the __________ day of __________ 19 ______.

Dated this __________ day of __________, 19______.

Receipt of a copy hereof is hereby acknowledged.

ACCEPTED **EDINA REALTY, INC.** BUYER ____________________

BY ____________________ BUYER ____________________
Sales Associate

OFFICE: ____________________ ADDRESS ____________________

APPROVAL BY SALES MANAGER: ____________________ TELEPHONE ____________________

ER Form 345 (8/85)

ORIGINAL TO CLOSING WITH CHECK; COPY 2 TO BUYER; COPY 3 TO SALES ASSOCIATE.

SOURCE: Edina Realty.

where the employment contract must be in writing, the broker must produce the written contract authorizing her or him to act as the agent for the seller. In those states where the contract is not in writing, a suit for a commission becomes a question of proof to be submitted to the jury. The broker testifies at the trial that she or he was employed by the seller. If there are no witnesses to corroborate this statement, the broker is apt to discover that the action has been lost.

Licensing

A second requisite in establishing a claim for a commission is that the broker must be licensed. In those states that require a license, if the broker is suing for a commission, the broker must allege in the complaint:

> that at all times hereinafter mentioned, the plaintiff was, and still is, legally engaged as a real estate broker duly licensed to carry on business under the laws of the state of. . . .

At the trial, the broker must prove such allegation. Licensing is proved by broker's submitting the license in evidence. Generally, in practice, a smaller pocket card, rather than the original, is admitted in evidence at the trial for this purpose.

Not only must the broker be licensed, but the broker must have been licensed at the time the service was rendered. The courts have also held that the broker renders the service when people "ready, willing, and able" are brought together or when there is a meeting of the minds between the seller and the purchaser.

For example, a person makes application for a broker's license and takes the examination on June 27. On June 30, the person produces a purchaser for a seller and the purchaser and seller enter into a contract for the sale of real property, title to close one month later on July 30. On July 15, the person receives a broker's license and proceeds to the closing on July 30. There arises a question here as to whether or not the broker is entitled to the commission on July 30. The broker is not entitled to the commission because the person was not duly licensed at the time the service was rendered; that is, when the two people who were "ready, willing, and able" were brought together.

Purchaser Ready, Willing, and Able

The broker must find a purchaser who is ready, willing, and able to purchase the property. *Ready and willing* means that the broker has produced a purchaser who is prepared to accept the terms offered by the owner and who has indicated a willingness to enter into a written contract with the owner. The best evidence of the readiness and willingness of the purchaser to purchase is a signed contract or receipt and agreement to purchase. However, the readiness and willingness of the purchaser can also be established when there is an oral agreement between the purchaser and the seller.

In the final analysis, when a contract or a receipt and agreement to purchase has been entered into by the parties, it is considered a contract for the sale of real property. Such a document signed by a prospect and drawn according to the terms of the listing contract establishes a meeting of the minds between the buyer and the seller.

Even though there is no written contract between the buyer and the seller, if the buyer has indicated a readiness, willingness, and ability, and the seller refuses to go through with the sale, the broker is entitled to a commission.

In addition to producing a purchaser who is ready and willing, the broker must produce a purchaser who is *able,* meaning that the purchaser must be financially able to go through with the transaction, or the seller is not liable to the broker for a commission. In the event of legal action, the broker has the burden of establishing proof of the financial ability of the prospect. The broker must show that the purchaser actually possesses, or has the ability to raise, the amount of cash necessary for the signing of the contract and the closing of title. When part of the purchase price is to be a purchase money mortgage, the broker need not show that the purchaser has sufficient cash or other assets to pay off the mortgage in order to win the suit.

Deferring or Waiving Commissions

A commission becomes due to the broker when the broker produces to the principal a party ready, willing, and able to purchase on the terms of sale authorized or accepted by the principal. However, in many brokerage offices, it is considered good policy to defer or waive the commission if the title to the property for some reason does not pass.

The contract for the sale of the property usually contains a clause stated substantially as given below:

> The parties agree that [the broker's name] brought about this sale and the seller agrees to pay the commission at the rates established or adopted by the Board of Real Estate Brokers in the locality where the property is situated.

If the broker wishes to waive or defer the commission, an additional statement is inserted in the contract.

> It is understood and agreed by the undersigned that the seller shall incur no obligation or liability for said brokerage commissions, except only when, as, if, and in the event title actually closes, at which time the said brokerage commissions shall become due and payable.

The contract is then initialed in the margin by the parties and by the salesperson. It is important that the salesperson initial the clause in order that the broker be relieved of liability to the salesperson if the title is not conveyed.

Procuring Cause

The broker must be the efficient or **procuring cause** of the sale to be entitled to a commission. For example, a broker has an open listing and brings a prospect to the property. The owner is not at home and the prospect states an unwillingness to buy, but the prospect later returns to the owner and concludes a private deal with the owner. The broker is entitled to the commission because the law would hold that the broker was the procuring or efficient cause of the sale.

It has been held that the broker is the procuring cause of the sale if his or her action indirectly procures a buyer. For example, a broker introduces a prospect to a seller. The prospect does not purchase the property, but the prospect's cousin does. In a case of this sort, the broker is entitled to the commission.

One device commonly employed by brokers to avoid possible trouble when owners are not at home and property is shown to prospects is to use a postal card. A sample card is shown in Exhibit 24-4.

At the very least, this device may prove a moral deterrent on the part of the seller from making a private sale to the prospect. It also indicates to the seller that the broker is working on the sale. Further, this card can be used as a legal weapon if a copy is made and a postal receipt is requested from the post office at the time of mailing. If the owner makes a private sale despite the card and the broker sues for a commission, the postal receipt will indicate the card was mailed. If the seller is served with a notice to produce the card at the trial and fails to do so, the copy may be offered as evidence without violating the "best evidence" rule.

Sales on Terms of Employer

The broker must bring about the sale on the terms that have been authorized by the client. If a broker brings an offer to the client for an amount less than that included in the listing contract, the broker is not entitled to a commission. However, if the seller accepts the offer, the sale is on the terms of the employer, and the broker is entitled to the commission.

If the owner lists a parcel of property with a broker at $50,000 and the broker finds a purchaser ready, willing, and able, the broker is entitled to a commission even if the seller refuses to sell at the price because broker has found a purchaser on the terms authorized by the seller. The salesperson may sue the broker for a share of the commission arguing that the broker can waive if broker wishes, but that this does not relieve the broker of the commission due the salesperson. The courts have agreed, and the broker is forced to pay the salesperson half of the amount due, although the broker has actually received no fee.

Exhibit 24-4 Postal Card Notice of Home Showing

May 10, 19--

Dear Owner

This is to inform you that we have this date shown your property at 2519 Eastbourne Ave. to John J. Marzetti

We regret that you were not at home at the time, and if anything further develops, we shall let you know immediately.

Sincerely yours,

Anne Stone

Anne Stone, Broker

Co-brokerage

Co-brokerage occurs when the broker, either by consent of the owner in writing or by implication, hires another broker to assist in the sale of the property. Generally, the listing broker agrees to pay the co-broker a portion of the commission in those cases in which the co-broker brings about the sale. More often than not, large investment properties are sold in this manner.

Factoring

An innovation in real estate brokerage is the factoring of real estate commissions. A *factor* is a corporation or an individual who buys accounts receivable at a discount, and, actually, a real estate commission is an account receivable due a broker at closing. Normally, the broker must wait between 30 and 90 days, or until the closing, to obtain this money.

This innovative program was developed by Donald J. Stewart, president of Realty Factors Ltd. of Central Islip, New York. Realty Factors is currently doing business in ten states and will doubtless expand further. The program works like this. A broker sells a residence for $100,000 with a commission due of $6,000, or 6 percent. Closing is set for 60 days hence. Realty Factors will buy 75 percent of the commission ($6,000 × .75 =

$4,500) at 90 cents on the dollar ($4,500 × .9 = $4,050). To ensure that the broker remains involved until the closing, the whole commission is not bought. The broker receives a check for $4,050 within 24 hours after Realty Factors receives copies of three instruments: a listing contract stating the commission, a signed contract of sale, and a mortgage commitment. When the transaction closes, Realty Factors receives $4,500, thus clearing $450 on the deal, and the broker receives $1,500, the remainder of the commission.

GLOSSARY

Actual agency A relationship in which the authority to act has been delegated by the principal

Agency coupled with an interest A situation in which the agent has an interest in the authority and/or in the subject matter of the agency

Agent One who acts for another—the principal—in dealing with third persons on behalf of the principal

Automatic renewal clause A clause in a lease that gives both landlord and tenant the right to notify the other that he or she does not wish to renew the lease

Co-brokerage The broker, either by consent of the owner in writing or by implication, hires another broker to assist in the sale of property

Exclusive agency The right given to a broker to sell a property exclusive of all other brokers

Exclusive right to sell An arrangement whereby the broker is entitled to receive a commission no matter who sells the property

Fair Housing Act of 1988 Eliminates $1000 ceiling and adds handicapped and families to the 1968 act

Fiduciary concept The idea that an agent must act in a fiduciary (founded in trust) capacity with the principal

General agent A person authorized by the principal to transact all of the principal's affairs in connection with a particular kind of business or trade, or to transact all of principal's business at a certain place

Listing contract The contract under which the real estate broker operates

Multiple listing service A means by which the participating broker makes a blanket, unilateral offer of subagency to the other participating brokers and is a facility for the orderly correlation and dissemination of listing information among the participating brokers so that they may better serve their clients and the public

Net listing A listing in which the seller establishes a minimum acceptable net price

Open listing A listing given by an owner to many brokers, hoping that one of them will be able to produce a purchaser for the property

Ostensible agency An agency which occurs when the authority for the agency arises from the fact that a third person has relied on the express or implied relationship of the master and servant

Principal The employer or constitutor of an agent; a person who gives authority to an agent or attorney to do some act for her or him

Procuring cause The broker's actions that bring about the sale of property even though the sale is made by the property owner

Ratification The approval by the principal of the unauthorized act of an agent

Real estate broker A person or corporation engaged primarily in the marketing of one of more of the various rights in real property

Special agent A person authorized by the principal to transact a business affair or to do a special act

Universal agent A person authorized to do all acts that can be lawfully delegated to a representative

QUESTIONS FOR REVIEW

1. Explain why an agent must account for money and what steps should be taken to assure this.
2. When may a broker act for both the buyer and the seller?
3. Discuss the advantages to a seller in giving the broker the exclusive right to sell.
4. What are the advantages to multiple listings?
5. List and explain four requisites to the broker's earning a commission.
6. Discuss the expression "ready, willing, and able."
7. What must a listing broker do to be certain the law of agency is not being violated when entering into a co-brokerage agreement?

PROBLEMS AND ACTIVITIES

1. Seller employed Broker to sell four lots on an open listing contract. Broker sold three of the lots to Frank Smith who informed his cousin that the fourth lot was still for sale. The cousin approached Seller directly and purchased the fourth lot. Broker then claimed Seller owed a commission on all four lots. Discuss.

2. In states where employment contracts must be in writing, many brokers feel that this is an unjust discrimination against brokers. Prepare a statement for a real estate board in which you argue that this law should be required in all states.

3. Jones hired Broker to sell a parcel of land. Shortly thereafter, Smith hired Broker to buy similar land. Broker then promptly brought Smith to Jones, and they entered into a contract that finally was consummated in a sale. Broker then charged Jones a full commission. Broker also charged Smith a full commission. Which one, if any, is liable to Broker for the commission?

4. Broker without any request from Sullivan, an owner of land, brought Sullivan an offer of $9,000. Sullivan told Broker the land was worth $10,000 whereupon Broker secured an offer from another person for $10,000, but Sullivan refused to sell. Broker sues Sullivan for a commission. Is Broker entitled to a commission? Why or why not?

25

OPERATING A REAL ESTATE OFFICE

KEY TERMS

Binder agreement
Blind advertisement
Canvassing
Code of Ethics
Continuing education
Corporation
Experience requirement
Franchising
Irrevocable consent
Listing file
Listing form
Listings
Open house
Partnership
Property brief
Proprietorship
Prospect card
Recovery fund
Sales kit
Stick
Unsolicited listings

Real estate brokerage is a fascinating and exciting business that provides the broker with independence, personal growth, and financial rewards commensurate with individual ability. In addition to personal satisfaction, brokers contribute to the development and improvement of their communities.

Once a location for the practice of real estate has been selected, the brokerage process begins with contacting homeowners to secure listing agreements. The process culminates in the sale of the homes and providing post-closing services to ensure buyer satisfaction. Before an individual becomes a broker, however, a thorough knowledge of real estate must be demonstrated by passing a sales license examination, working as a real estate salesperson, and passing a broker's license examination.

LICENSING REAL ESTATE BROKERS AND SALE PERSONNEL

Only a few states permit a novice to take the broker's license examination without prior experience. Most states require individuals to be employed as salespersons until they have sufficient experience to become brokers. The **experience requirement** ranges from one to five years.

In California, for example, a person must have two years of active real estate sales experience and complete 225 classroom hours of approved real estate education to qualify to take the broker's examination. Kentucky requires seven three-semester-hour units from a college or accredited school, as well as two years of active real estate sales experience, prior to taking the broker's examination.

The increasing complexity of real estate, coupled with growing consumer expectation of licensee competency, has led many states to incorporate **continuing education** (post-license) as part of their license law. Pre-license education requirements have also increased rapidly since 1970. Texas presently requires 630 classroom hours in general college courses, and Pennsylvania requires 240 classroom hours of real estate education before one is permitted to take the broker's license examination.

License requirements for brokers and sales personnel for the 50 states are summarized in Appendix B.

Typical License Laws

Although the license laws of the various states differ, all of them have a number of things in common. Basically, the purpose of all licensing laws is to protect the public from incompetent and unscrupulous brokers. Fundamentally, these laws are generally divided into several parts: the statutes, as enacted by state legislatures; the administrative orders, as promulgated by the body governing the licensing laws; and sometimes principles of the **Code of Ethics** of the NATIONAL ASSOCIATION OF REALTORS® are incorporated into these laws by administrative order.

The statutes of all states define *broker* in more or less the same manner:

> [A broker is] a person who, for compensation or promise thereof, sells or offers for sale, lists or offers to list, buys or offers to buy, negotiates or offers to negotiate, either directly or indirectly, the purchase, sale, exchange, lease, or the rental of real estate or any interest therein.

Some states include the sale of a business opportunity under the jurisdiction of the real estate broker. In these states, the law defines a business opportunity as a "business, an established business, a business opportunity, or goodwill of an established or existing business, or any interest therein."

Other states divorce the sale of business opportunities from the real estate broker so the seller of a business opportunity need have no license. In such states—for example, New York—when a seller of a business opportunity sells the real property along with the business opportunity, a real estate license is not required if it can be shown that the real estate was a part of the going concern.

All state statutes provide exceptions to the requirement of being licensed; for example, the Washington state law provides:

> This chapter shall not apply to (1) any person who purchases property and/or a business opportunity for his own account, or who, as the owner of

> the property, and/or a business opportunity, in any wise disposes of the same; nor (2) any duly authorized attorney in fact, or an attorney at law in the performance of his duties; nor (3) any receiver, trustee in bankruptcy, executor, administrator, guardian, or any person acting under the order of any court, or selling under a deed of trust; nor (4) any escrow agent.

The New York brokerage law specifically exempts attorneys at law who may, by virtue of this exemption, act as real estate brokers and receive commissions without being licensed. However, if they hire real estate sales personnel, they must become licensed.

The statutes usually provide further for examinations for brokers and sales personnel, and for penalties in the event there has been a violation of the law. Also, there are procedures in all of these laws for hearings on possible suspensions or revocations of licenses by the administrative bodies who enforce the laws, together with the right of appeal from a decision of the administrative body.

In addition to criminal penalties, some states provide for civil damages by a party aggrieved. For example, the New York law provides for damages in the amount of four times the commission when a broker is charged and subsequently convicted of defrauding a client.

The second part of the license laws typically consists of rules and regulations promulgated by the Real Estate Brokers Board, the Division of Licenses, or whatever the administrative body administering the license laws may be called. Until these rules and regulations have been declared void by a court of competent jurisdiction, they have the full effect of the law in the same manner as if they had been made a part of the statute by the state legislature.

These rules are more or less similar among the several states. They provide, among other things, that the real estate broker must not insert **blind advertisements** in any advertising media. This means that the name of the broker must be given or it must be clear that it is an advertisement submitted by a broker, rather than an advertisement placed by an individual.

License laws also generally provide that there shall be no automatic renewal clauses incorporated in listings. They provide that monies received by the broker on behalf of a client shall not be commingled with the broker's own monies and that the broker shall not purchase property he or she has listed on his or her own behalf, either directly or indirectly, without first making the broker's true position known to the client. Some rules provide that a broker shall not place a sign on a parcel of property without first obtaining the consent of the owner.

The Code of Ethics of the NATIONAL ASSOCIATION OF REALTORS® can be found in Appendix A. Every person interested in real estate and real estate transactions should be familiar not only with the code, but also should adhere completely to its tenets.

Uniform Real Estate Examinations

Because laws are designed to protect the public from incompentent brokers and salespersons, most states require proof of competency by examination. Examinations are currently becoming more standardized in an effort to raise the educational level required by brokers and sales personnel.

Successful candidates for licensing require a broad base of real estate knowledge as the following topical outline of exam content indicates.

1. Real Estate Law
   a. Conveyances
   b. Property descriptions
   c. Terminology, rules, regulations
   d. Fair housing
   e. Agency, contracts
   f. Real estate instruments
2. Real Estate Finance and Mathematics
   a. Money markets
   b. Truth-in-lending
   c. Income analysis and capitalization
   d. Appraising, valuation
   e. Depreciation and taxation
   f. Commissions
   g. Interest
   h. Closing statements and settlement procedures
3. Land Use Control
   a. Planning and zoning
   b. Building codes
   c. Site analysis
   d. Land development and environmental impact
4. Other
   a. Property management
   b. Ethics

The greatest emphasis on exams, 40 to 50 percent, is placed on real estate law. Real estate mathematics, including appraisal, account for an additional 25 to 30 percent of the exam content.

Ordinarily, the examination for the real estate salesperson is not as difficult as the examination for the real estate broker. The examination for the sales license usually requires one to three hours for completion, but for the broker's license, it often takes a full day.

Generally, 75 percent is a passing grade on these examinations, and if the applicant fails the examination, reapplication must be made and the examination must be retaken. Some states have prepared real estate primers or guides containing some of the information that will be asked of the applicant on an examination. In other states, it is necessary for the applicant to study general texts on real estate to acquire the necessary information to pass the examination.

In many states, the applicant for a broker's license must be recommended by several responsible property owners or citizens who certify that the applicant has a good reputation for honesty and fair dealing. The numbers and qualifications of the sponsors vary in different states. In those states where a broker must be licensed and can be licensed without passing a formal examination, this is one of the most important requisites to the granting of the license.

In most states, an applicant for a sales license must be sponsored. This sponsor is generally a broker or brokerage firm who has agreed to hire the salesperson in the event a license is obtained. In other states, salespeople, after having been employed, are granted temporary licenses enabling them to be gainfully employed until the time of the examination. In some areas, salespeople are referred to as sales associates or sales agents.

Brokers' Bonds and Recovery Funds

In states where the law makes no specific provision for money penalty or no provision for returning money fraudulently obtained, the licensee is required to post a bond; the amount varies generally from $1,000 to $2,500. This protects the customer because revocation of the broker's license will not compensate a defrauded individual, and in most instances brokers who engage in sharp practices have no tangible assets. The bond is especially desirable because it not only protects the broker's client, but also tends to ensure that the broker's duties will be faithfully performed.

In 1963, Arizona took what proved to be a leading step toward further protection of the public. A bill initiated and backed by the Arizona Association of Realtors was passed by the Arizona Legislature. In essence, the bill provided for a real estate **recovery fund** from which damages could be paid to persons "aggrieved" by acts of real estate brokers or salespersons and unable to collect damages from them. The fund was financed through the collection of additional fees from Arizona licensees. Since that time, over 30 states have adopted similar statutes. At this writing a number of other states have enacted or have bills of this nature pending before their legislatures.

Nonresident Brokers

Many states have entered into reciprocal agreements with neighboring states providing that if brokers are licensed in one state, they may be licensed in the neighboring state and practice there without actually residing there. This is done to require the nonresident broker to meet the same qualifications as the resident broker.

When state laws regulate nonresident brokers, they require an irrevocable consent to the service of process, which must be filed, generally with the secretary of state. An **irrevocable consent** is a written statement that (1) actions and suits at law may be started against such nonresident broker in any county of the state wherein a cause of action may arise, (2) service of summons in any such action may be served on a designated officer of the state real estate commission (or secretary of state) for and on behalf of such nonresident broker, and (3) such service shall be held sufficient to give the courts jurisdiction over such nonresident broker and the broker's sales personnel.

FORMS OF OWNERSHIP

When one has the requisite experience as a salesperson and has taken and passed the broker's examination, the next step is to open an office, which can be established as an individual proprietorship, a partnership, or a corporation.

Individual Proprietorship

The **proprietorship** has certain obvious advantages including those of ease of organization, absolute control, flexibility, ownership of all profits, and the intangible reward (sometimes called psychic income) that comes to the owner in the feeling of independence. On the other hand, the operations of the owner are limited to the extent of available capital and experience, and the success of the enterprise depends on continuous personal attention to the business.

The individual may operate under her or his own name, or may operate under an assumed or trade name. In the latter case, the proprietor gives the business a name and carries out operations under the assumed name.

When a person operates under an assumed name, the assumed name must be registered with a recording office, generally the office of the county clerk. This is done by filing a certificate of doing business under an assumed name. The certificate contains both the assumed name and the true name of the person filing. The proprietor will be addressed in legal papers as "Christine Roberts doing business under the name and style of Lake City Realty" or "Christine Roberts d/b/a Lake City Realty."

The purpose of requiring persons doing business under an assumed name to file the certificate of doing business under an assumed name is to prevent the individual from defrauding creditors. Whether or not an individual operates under an assumed name, the individual's liability to creditors is not reduced. All the individual's property, both the business property and all other property owned by the proprietor, is subject to the payment of the business debts.

If a real estate broker does business under an assumed name, the license must be taken out under the assumed name; and if the business name is changed, the board enforcing the licensing laws must be notified.

Partnership

A **partnership** is a legal relationship created by the voluntary association of two or more persons to carry on a business for profit as co-owners. The rights and duties of the partners toward each other and toward the public are regulated by a partnership agreement and by the state partnership laws. The agreement between the individuals comprising the partnership may be either oral or written. In most instances the agreement is written, and in most states the law requires that a certificate of doing business under a partnership name must be filed in the same manner as a certificate of doing business under an assumed name.

The partnership agreement is a contract, and any business that a person may lawfully operate may be conducted in the partnership form. The contract or articles of agreement between the partners set forth the capital and service that each of the partners is to contribute, the share of the profits and losses to which each may be entitled, and other details concerning their relationship and the operation of the business.

Advantages of the Partnership. The chief advantage of the partnership is that it permits the pooling of the capital, skill, experience, and business contacts of the co-owners, thereby increasing the scope of the business and enhancing its prestige. Freedom from federal taxation is regarded as another of the advantages of the partnership form of business enterprise. Although the individuals are taxed on their share of the income, the partnership entity as such is not taxed.

Disadvantages of the Partnership. Under the partnership laws of most states, there is a presumption that each partner has an equal voice in the operation of the partnership; that each of the partners is the agent of the other; and that, unless the partnership agreement provides otherwise, each partner is bound by the other when acting within the scope of the business. The laws of some states afford protection by providing that persons outside the firm who make certain types of contracts with a partner, such as a contract to sell all of the partnership assets of the film, must ascertain whether that partner has been authorized to so act by the other partners. A further major disadvantage is that the personal assets of each of the partners may be looked to by the creditors. In short, there is an unlimited liability feature.

The licensing laws of the majority of the states provide that when a partnership exists between two or more persons for the purpose of conducting a real estate business, all of the partners must be licensed as brokers. Thus, one partner cannot be a broker and the other partner a salesperson.

Corporation

First, a **corporation** is an instrument for the ownership and the management of a business enterprise. Second, it is a device whereby a person may invest a sum of money in the enterprise without becoming personally liable for its indebtedness beyond the amount invested. A characteristic peculiar to the corporation is its status as an artificial being or entity separate and apart from its stockholders, officers, or directors—to such a degree that it may sue or be sued by any one of them on the matter affecting the relationship between them.

A corporation comes into existence when a certificate of incorporation or charter, signed by three or more incorporators or prospective stockholders, is accepted for filing by the proper state authority, generally the secretary of state. Thereafter, it is authorized to hold property and conduct the business specified in its charter. In exchange for such property or money capital, it issues shares of stock to the stockholders. Such shares, representing stockholders' ownership interest in the corporation, are readily transferable.

Advantages of the Corporation. A major advantage of the corporate form of business enterprise is the limited liability feature, which is often the first thought of anyone or any small group of people considering a business enterprise. A corporation often is given a perpetual life, which is a further advantage of the corporate form of doing business.

Disadvantages of the Corporation. One disadvantage of the corporate form of business enterprise is the cost. This includes the cost of incorporating and often stock transfer taxes. In addition, the small corporation may encounter difficulty in obtaining credit, since the potential creditor knows that the stockholders cannot be proceeded against to satisfy a debt that is beyond the ability of the corporation to pay from its own assets. A creditor knows that an individual or partnership can be sued and a judgment may be obtained against their personal assets. As a practical matter, the prospective creditor of a corporation will often demand that the owners of the corporation sign a note pledging their personal assets in addition to the individual executing the note as an officer of the corporation. When this is done, the major advantage of the corporation is negated.

Another major disadvantage of the corporate form of business is the federal tax. The income of the corporation is taxed, and the amounts distributed to the stockholders are taxed again as personal income. This is often referred to as double taxation, which may be avoided through formation of a Subchapter S corporation. The Subchapter S corporation is taxed as a proprietorship or partnership. All income or losses flow through to be reported on the tax returns of individual shareholders. In other words, the Subchapter S corporation itself pays no income taxes.

When a corporation is formed to engage in the real estate business, most state laws require that at least one of the officers of the corporation be a licensed real estate broker. Some state laws require that only one of the officers be a licensed broker; the other owners may be only licensed real estate salespersons. In states having laws requiring only one of the officers of the corporation to be licensed and both of the incorporating parties to have brokers' licenses, one of them gives up the license while remaining an officer of the corporation. That party is given a sales license with the stipulation that if the individual desires to leave the corporation and practice as an individual, the broker's license will be restored.

SELECTING A LOCATION AND EQUIPPING AN OFFICE

The broker's office is one of the most important tools for creation of an effective, efficient, and profitable working environment. Properly selected and equipped, the office is a symbol of the firm's competency and professionalism.

Basically, the office should be easy to find, have a recognizable street address, and be located in proximity to the market the firm serves. The location and site should not detract from the company's image. The office building should be clean and have a businesslike appearance. If at all possible, an office in the broker's house should be avoided.

The office should be decorated in an attractive, comfortable manner that makes people at ease when they enter. The layout should include a reception area, conference room for sales meetings and closings, and a private broker's office. The sales staff may be housed in a large room with or without partitions or in individual offices. In any event, salespeople should have ready access to one another yet have facilities for privacy when needed. Last, adequate storage space is a necessity; and room for word processing, duplication, and computer equipment might be considered.

Capital Requirements

Too many potentially good brokers fall by the wayside for lack of sufficient capital. At the start of operations, the beginning broker should have a certain minimum amount of capital for furniture and other initial expenses. It is felt, too, that the new broker ought to have enough capital to cover estimated operating expenses and living expenses for at least six months. Unless the person embarking on a brokerage career has several commissions in sight, the question of ready capital must be given attention, otherwise the venture may result in tragic failure for the broker—and what is worse, for the broker's family.

Financial Control

In addition to maintaining records of receipts and disbursements from trust or escrow accounts, the beginning broker should establish a system of financial record keeping. Successful business operations depend not only on sales, but on control of operating costs and commissions.

Assistance in financial management may be obtained from local CPAs. Membership in the REALTORS® National Marketing Institute of the NATIONAL ASSOCIATION OF REALTORS® offers an opportunity for training in brokerage management. RNMI also compiles annual financial reports on brokerage operations that permit financial comparisons and provide a basis for implementing financial controls.

OBTAINING LISTINGS

Listings are the stock in trade of any broker. Without listings, the broker has nothing to sell. To have an initial inventory of listings, it is recommended that the new broker affiliate with the local Multiple Listing Service. The broker may then sell the listings of cooperating participants in MLS.

If the broker does not wish to participate in an MLS, individual brokers may be solicited to obtain permission to sell their listings. There is no limitation on the broker's right to develop bilateral cooperative relationships. Regardless of the opportunity to sell the listings of others, however, brokers should solicit and obtain their own listings.

Canvassing

There are several ways in which brokers canvass for listings. Many brokers habitually scan the classified sections of their local newspapers looking for advertisements placed by owners. Then they telephone the owners and try to persuade them to list the property with them. Some brokers write letters to these owners requesting the listing. However, this method generally produces poor results because it is human nature to follow the path of least resistance, and owners are reluctant to answer these letters.

Door-to-door **canvassing** can be an effective means of obtaining listings. Door-to-door canvassers, through repetitive contact, should establish a personal relationship with homeowners in the area they serve. Such a relationship may lead to information regarding the homeowner's friends who wish to move to the neighborhood and neighbors who are planning to move.

One effective device used by some brokers who canvass door to door is to have an attractive card printed that can be easily affixed to the doorknob when the owners are not at home (see Exhibit 25-1).

In some areas, financial institutions often have properties for sale. A letter to them requesting a list of their properties and permission to offer them for sale may result in a satisfactory number of listings.

Another good way of obtaining listings is by watching for For Sale and To Let signs in a neighborhood or on bulletin boards at grocery stores, churches, and clubs. Then the owner can be located and an attempt made to obtain authority to sell or lease the property.

■ **Exhibit 25-1 Broker's Door Card**

XYZ REALTY COMPANY

We called on you today to find out if you wish to sell your home. Our office has had several inquiries about homes in this neighborhood. If you are interested, please telephone 621-1234 and ask for Lucille Smith.

Lucille Smith

News items are frequently a source of leads to properties that might be for sale. Items often appear stating that certain owners are moving from the city. If such persons are property owners, they will probably want to sell or rent their homes immediately. Property often is sold when the the owner dies, and listings can be obtained by contracting the attorney acting for a decedent's estate.

Similarly, listings may be obtained by contacting individuals placing furniture for sale or garage sale ads. These are often the first steps taken by owners who are preparing to sell their homes. Owners contemplating moving may also have contacted a moving and storage company. Contact with their representatives may provide names from recent inquiries about moving costs and can be an excellent source of listings.

Other prospects for listings may be obtained from company personnel managers who are aware of employees being transferred into or out of town. Notices of impending divorces also are a source of potential sellers of homes. The expired MLS listings of competitors are also "fair game" in the quest for an inventory of homes to sell. In addition, don't overlook new home builders, out-of-town property owners identified on tax rolls, and notices of retirement, foreclosures, marriages and births as signs of changes in economic conditions that may result in the purchase or sale of real estate.

Advertising

Advertising is probably the least effective way of obtaining listings. Listings obtained by this method are mainly of co-brokerage listings. However, advertising for listings in newspapers is a method of presenting the firm name to the public and thus may have some value. In addition to newspaper advertising, letters to selected prospects may bring good results.

Personal Contacts

Business and social contacts are probably the most fertile source of listings. The broker who establishes a reputation for rendering service to the community, either through business relationships with the rest of the community or through memberships in service organizations, will never lack for listings.

Unsolicited Listings

Listings obtained from previous clients are a result of having rendered competent professional services. The number of **unsolicited listings** obtained is a direct reflection on the firm's reputation and the quality of the firm's service.

A reputation is built over many years. Some brokers report that as many as 50 percent of the homes they have to sell are listings from former clients, referrals from former clients, and social contacts gained through participation in community activities.

Promoting the Listing Service

Some people persist in attempting to sell their property without the services of the real estate broker. Often it is no easy matter to persuade people to allow the broker to handle the sale of the property; therefore, the broker must be prepared to sell this service to owners. The owner's confidence and respect must be won. Some of the arguments used to convince owners to list property with a broker are

1. Because the real estate broker has a knowledge of the current market and knows where favorable prospects may be found, he or she is in a much better position than the average owner to sell a property at a fair price.

2. Because the broker has no interest other than as an intermediary, negotiations will have a better chance of success than if two interested persons sat face to face across the same table.

3. The buyer may be timid about talking things over frankly with an owner, may dislike discussing personal finances, or may ask for terms that make the deal an impossibility.

4. The real estate broker knows how to advertise properties to the best advantage.

5. The owner of the property is inclined to be sensitive and may resent criticism. The interview with a prospect may end in an argument instead of a sale.
6. All prospects will be screened, unqualified buyers and "lookers" will be eliminated, and only bona fide purchasers will be shown the home.
7. If desired, all showings may be by appointment and at a time convenient for the seller.
8. The commissions charged by the broker are small compared with the advantages of having the sale in the hands of an expert.

Inspecting the Premises

While obtaining a listing or immediately after obtaining a listing, the property must be inspected. All listings should be personally inspected either by the broker or a designated salesperson. The broker must know the product before being able to sell it. The property should be inspected regardless of whether it was listed in the same office at some previous time. One broker, for example, had listed a rambling old house. The house was familiar because the broker had played in it as a child. But it had passed through many hands. The broker took a prospect out to see it and things went smoothly until they reached the second-floor bedrooms. The broker showed the prospect the first bedroom and then happily flung open the door of the second bedroom. To their utter amazement, they were greeted by the peeping of a thousand baby chicks the owner was brooding in the bedroom. Needless to say, the sale was lost. Had the property been inspected, the broker certainly would not have brought the prospect to see it.

When inspecting a property, one of the best procedures is to start with the listing form, filling in all of the blanks in detail. In addition to increasing the broker's knowledge of the product being sold, this will increase the confidence of the seller in the broker, because seller will be impressed with broker's thoroughness and knowledge.

The advantages of the property should be noted. They will be the strong selling points to be pointed out to the prospect when selling the property. Familiarity with the property enables it to be discussed intelligently and hence sold more quickly.

During the inspection, the broker may also note physical changes that are needed to effect an early sale and may suggest to the owner that these changes be made before the sale is attempted.

Setting the Price

One of the difficult problems that confronts the broker in obtaining listings is the establishment of a selling price. Owners have a tendency to overestimate the value of their homes, which is a distinct disadvantage to both the owner and the broker when a sale can result only from a modification of terms and after a considerable delay.

After a careful inspection and evaluation, the owner should be told what the broker thinks the property will bring at the prevailing market price. This should be done tactfully. Support an opinion of value with facts and figures comparing the seller's property with similar recently sold homes. If possible, prepare a written market data report reflecting the comparison of properties. An example of a competitive property report is presented in Exhibit 25-2.

It may be better to refuse the listing unless the owner will agree to a reasonable and fair price for the property. Many owners do not realize that a listing that is too high receives little attention. Frequently brokers resort to the bad practice of accepting a listing that is too high and merely filing it in the office. It is better practice to reject a listing that is unfairly priced by the owner. By doing this, the broker will actually perform a service for the owner and at the same time build a better reputation as a broker.

FINDING BUYERS

Although listings are important to a broker, their importance is relative to the strength of the housing market. From 1976 to 1979, homes sold as fast as they were available and therefore listings were the "name of the game." Since 1980, most housing markets have had excess listings and a shortage of qualified buyers. In a buyers' market, emphasis shifts to finding potential buyers who may choose among a multitude of homes offered by anxious sellers. Following are the principal means of contacting buyers.

Open House

An **open house** promotes the sale of a particular property and provides potential buyers an opportunity to tour the home without an appointment. Many families will take a Sunday drive to view a series of open houses staffed by sales associates ready to answer their questions. For these salespeople, an open house presents the opportunity to meet potential buyers of other properties.

The Stick

In offices with large sales forces, trouble sometimes arises concerning which sales associate is to handle a prospect who calls at the office. Many of the larger offices attempt to solve this problem using the **stick,** which is simply a board listing the names of the salespeople. The sales associate whose name is on the bottom of the list handles the first prospect entering the office and the associate's name is then placed at the top of the list. The

■ Exhibit 25-2 Competitive Property Report

Edina Realty

Competitive Property Report

DATE ☐ SOLD COMPARISONS ☐ PRESENT MARKET COMPARISONS

	SUBJECT PROPERTY	ADDRESS	ADDRESS	ADDRESS
	OWNER	OWNER	OWNER	OWNER

		CARPETING		CARPETING		CARPETING		CARPETING
STYLE								
NO. OF BEDROOMS								
SQUARE FOOTAGE								
TAXES (NOT INCLUDING SPECIALS)								
LOCATION								
LIVING ROOM	FIREPLACE ☐YES ☐NO	☐Y ☐N	FIREPLACE ☐YES ☐NO	☐Y ☐N	FIREPLACE ☐YES ☐NO	☐Y ☐N	FIREPLACE ☐YES ☐NO	☐Y ☐N
DINING ROOM		☐Y ☐N		☐Y ☐N		☐Y ☐N		☐Y ☐N
FAMILY ROOM	FIREPLACE ☐YES ☐NO	☐Y ☐N	FIREPLACE ☐YES ☐NO	☐Y ☐N	FIREPLACE ☐YES ☐NO	☐Y ☐N	FIREPLACE ☐YES ☐NO	☐Y ☐N
BEDROOMS		☐Y ☐N		☐Y ☐N		☐Y ☐N		☐Y ☐N
AMUSEMENT ROOM	FIREPLACE ☐YES ☐NO	☐Y ☐N	FIREPLACE ☐YES ☐NO	☐Y ☐N	FIREPLACE ☐YES ☐NO	☐Y ☐N	FIREPLACE ☐YES ☐NO	☐Y ☐N
BATHS								

INCLUSIONS				
MISC. FEATURES				
EXTERIOR				
GARAGE	☐SINGLE ☐DOUBLE	☐SINGLE ☐DOUBLE	☐SINGLE ☐DOUBLE	☐SINGLE ☐DOUBLE
UTILITIES	☐SEWER ☐WATER	☐SEWER ☐WATER	☐SEWER ☐WATER	☐SEWER ☐WATER

DAYS ON MARKET				
OFFERING PRICE				
SALE PRICE				
VARIANCE FROM COMPARABLE PROPERTY				
VALUE OF YOUR PROPERTY AS INDICATED BY COMPARABLE PROPERTY				

PREPARED BY:

E.R. 304H (6/86)

SOURCE: *Edina Realty.*

next associate's name in order falls into the bottom position and that person handles the next prospect. In this way, each sales associate gets a turn at the prospects as they come into the office.

Floor Time

Another method used by brokers is to assign customers for one day to one salesperson and the following day to another one who "takes the floor." Floor time involves having a sales associate available in the office to answer questions from potential buyers who call or walk in in response to an advertisement. Many brokers rotate floor time among their associates. Although floor time permits sales associates to talk with potential buyers, some salespeople do not like being tied to the office.

Employers

Every effort should be made to contact the personnel or human resources office of major employers in the area. The broker or sales associate should let these companies know that they would like to supply their employees and potential employees with information regarding housing in the community. Initial contact with potential buyers moving to the community may be made by sending them information on schools, churches, shopping, and available homes. In addition, an offer can be made to show them housing when they are visting the area.

Advertising

As with an open house, advertising a particular property does not often produce the prospect who ultimately buys the home. Real estate advertising, however, according to the Association of Classified Advertising Managers, motivates over 50 percent of home buyers to contact a real estate agent. Because of the importance of advertising in marketing real estate, it is discussed in greater detail in Chapter 26.

Friends and Neighbors

The more people who know that a sales associate is available to help a newcomer to the community find satisfactory housing, or a new home buyer find a home, the more potential buyers will be referred to him or her. The importance of social contacts cannot be overemphasized. Getting to know people and being ready to help them and their friends and family with their housing needs results in more sales, as well as more listings.

In order of importance, eleven criteria in buyer's and seller's selection of a brokerage firm are presented in Table 25-1.

Table 25-1 Buyer's and Seller's Criteria in Selecting a Broker

1. Friend's recommendation
2. Used agent before
3. Used broker before
4. Yard sign
5. Builder's recommendation
6. Newspaper ads
7. Saw agent firm name on listing
8. TV ads
9. Billboard ads
10. Radio ads
11. Yellow pages

SOURCE: Texas Real Estate Research Center Technical Report No. 456.

MARKETING TOOLS

Property Brief

The **property brief** is, in essence, an information folder concerning a particular property. It should contain a sketched map showing the relationship between the property and schools, shopping districts, and transportation. The sketched map may, for example, show the property, including dimensions of the lot, where it is located, and may bear notations: bus line one block, grammar school two blocks, shopping four blocks, with arrows indicating the direction of each from the house.

In addition, the brief should contain a photograph of the building, a diagram showing the floor plan, and a notation regarding the taxes and insurance rates on the building. If the property is income property, all the pertinent information concerning income and expenses should be included in the property brief, together with information about the balance of the mortgage due and the rate of amortization. (See Exhibit 25-3a on page 616 for a portion of a brief showing a lot for sale and Exhibit 25-3b on page 617 for a portion of a brief showing a house for sale.)

The property brief is a timesaver when it comes to selling the property. Many trips to the property can be eliminated by showing the prospect the brief prior to leaving the office.

Sales Kit

The **sales kit** is one of the most inexpensive, yet most effective, means that the broker has to help in the sale of real property. The kit provides answers to many of the questions that will be put to the broker by the prospect and often is what causes the prospect finally to make a decision regarding the purchase of the property.

Exhibit 25-3a A Portion of a Property Brief Showing a Lot for Sale

148'

134' 2 134'

148'

A SO: DOM: SD: $
L335384 E06MO 2 SYCAMORE RUN $76,900
Subu MONTGOMER Dis SYCAMOR
Bk Pg Par Zip45242 CoopER3 CLB
N ON MONTGOMERY RD LEFT ON PFEIFFER RD
R ON DEERFIELD JUST PAST ELBRECHT

Type RES LOT	Elem MAPLEDA	Rms Bed Bath	
Lot 149X134	HS SYCMAOR	Farm	
Acre 1	PrEL ALL STS	Bsmt	Gar
Zone RESID	PrHS MOE/MND	Heat	Cool
Elev FLAT	Deed OF REC	Inc$	$Acr
Wood PARTLY	Ease OFREC	Tob	Bld#
Gas NATURAL	Asse N/A	Till	Timb
Wat PUBLIC	Occ AT CLOS	Road	Fenc
Sew PUBLIC	STax N/A	Asu	

WOODED HALF ACRE LOT IN SYCAMORE RUN
IN THE HEART OF MONTGOMERY. JUST 10 LOTS
IN THE SUBDIVISION. UNDERGROUND UTILITIES
Firm SIBCY CLINE # SIBC02 P793-2121
Agent M. BECHTOLD/P. VADAS # 247642 P793-9155
All information herein is believed accurate but NOT guaranteed

SOURCE: Courtesy Sibcy Cline, Inc. REALTORS®.

The contents of the kit are varied and should be changed from time to time. A map of the city and a zoning map are essential. It is also wise to have tax rates, data on insurance rates, amortization tables, and a table showing the various rental amounts tenants pay annually or monthly and over what period. Newspaper clippings containing pertinent information about the city should be included; for example, whether the government is going to spend a large sum on a dam or atomic energy plant in the locale, or a large corporation is going to build a plant in the city. These data should be kept in the sales kit to show to prospects who are strangers to the city, or to prospects who are interested in purchasing investment properties or business opportunities in the city.

Reports of the local Chamber of Commerce on population trends and reports of bank deposits showing increases over a period of years are other items that might be included in the kit. All of these provide information that will assist the salesperson in making the sale. The zoning map, for example, may even prevent the salesperson from inadvertently offering a lot in a residential zone for sale as a business property.

Prospect Cards

Everyone who comes into the broker's office, as the result of an advertisement or for any other reason, is a potential customer. If the needs of the

■ **Exhibit 25-3b A Portion of a Property Brief Showing a House for Sale**

```
SEARCH V2.2-B  9-MAR-1990 11:40:03.89

..........Copyright  9-MAR-1990 11:40, MLS OF GREATER CINCINNATI,INC..........
A
S340338 E06ST  11561 STABLEWATCH C              LP$435,500
RM: 9   BD: 4  BATH:3-2    SUBU:SYMMES TW  DIS:SYCAMORE       VOL:E009
BK:       PG:      PAR:            ZIP:45249  COOP:ER3   YES  PAGE:257
 MONTGOMERY TO CALUMET WAY (CALUMET FARMS)
 TO RIGHT ON STABLEWATCH                                        DIM   LEV
AGE :1             LEV :2 STORY     CONS:BRICK           LIV:18X14  1
LOT :135X200       BSMT:FULL        FPL :1 STONE         DIN:14X14  1
ACRE:              FND :POURED      GAR :3 ATT,SID       KIT:24X13  1
ZONE:RESID         ROOF:ASPHALT     HEAT:GAS             FRM:22X20  1
ELEM:MAPLEDA       GAS :NATURAL     COOL:CEN AIR         STU:13X12  1
HIGH:SYCAMOR       WAT :PUBLIC      ASMT:NONE            MBD:31X13  2
PELE:AVAILAB       SEW :PUBLIC      HOA FEE$             BD2:13X12  2
PHIG:MOE/MND       EASE:OF REC      STAX$N/A             BD3:12X12  2
OCC :AT CLOS       ASU%:            $                    BD4:15X13  2
 FANTASTIC MASTER SUITE WITH SITTING AREA                BDR LEV1   NO
 PELLA WINDOWS/FRONT&REAR STAIRS/BEAUT. FR               BTH LEV1   Y
 WITH FLOOR TO VAULTED CEILING STONE WBFP
FIRM :SIBCY CLINE                  LO:SIBC02    PHONE:793-2121
AGENT:JUDY RECKER                FILE:241371    PHONE:793-2270
--All information herein is believed accurate but NOT guaranteed--
..............................................................................
```

SOURCE: Courtesy Sibcy Cline, Inc. REALTORS®.

customer cannot be satisfied with the listings the broker has at the moment, they might be satisfied at some future date. This suggests that the potential prospect should not be allowed to leave the broker's office without the broker's having first obtained some information from the prospect. Once having obtained this information, the broker ought to make a record of it on a prospect card. The **prospect card** contains the name, address, and telephone number of the prospect (see Exhibit 25-4). It also contains the price range in which the prospect is interested, and the amount of down payment available. The card might also be used to test the effectiveness of advertising by asking prospects why they decided to visit the office.

After having obtained the above information, the card should be filed; and when new listings are obtained that might satisfy the needs of the prospect, prospect should be notified personally, either by telephone or by mail.

Exhibit 25-4 Prospective Buyer Data Card

EDINA REALTY, INC., PROSPECTIVE BUYER DATA CARD

Name		Home Phone No.		Date		
Address		Zip		Bus. No. (His)		Bus. No. (Hers)
She Works (Occupation)		Address		No. Years		
He Works (Occupation)		Address		No. Years		
No. Children:	No. Boys	No. Girls	Ages	Now:	Own Home	Rent Home
Called on:				Action Taken		
Sign	Ad	Referral From				
Type Home Needed		No. Br's		No. Baths		Location Preferred
Price Range	Max PITI		Down-Payment			Preferred Financing
Special Requirements						
Follow-Up						

E.R. 402

SOURCE: Edina Realty.

Listing File

The contents of the **listing file** should be arranged in some definite and logical order—according to the various types of properties. For example, residential properties and industrial properties are separated. The file should be subdivided into sections. Some brokers do this by neighborhood and others by price classes.

Usually when inquiring about a property, the prospect is interested in location, type of house, and price. Although limited by a price range, a prospect will desire a particular type of house and will have a preference as to location. Thus, in addition to indexing listings by location and price, properties may also be indexed by type of house.

A systematic filing system is essential and will prove to be a great timesaver. The material should always be as complete as possible, and active and inactive listings should be separated. In many firms, these functions are performed by a computer.

FORMS AND RECORDS

Listing Forms

The real estate broker opening an office should obtain a number of forms and various employment contracts. The most important of these is the **listing form.** This contains all of the pertinent details of a property, such as its location, price, the amount of the mortgage, the number of bedrooms, baths, and so forth. Copies of these forms are made so that each salesperson has a copy from which to obtain this information prior to showing the property to a prospect.

Appointments to Show

Preparing sellers for what to expect is an important part of successfully representing their interests. Some brokers require their agents to discuss open houses, previewing, and procedures for setting and canceling appointments. Exhibit 25-5 itemizes appointment procedures. Its coverage of all contingencies ensures professionalism.

Earnest Money Receipt and Agreement to Purchase

In many states, the broker actually prepares the contract for sale, which is a combination receipt for the earnest money and a contract of sale. It contains a complete property description, a closing date and the type of deed to be transferred by the seller, a description of any personal property that is included in the transaction, and a statement that such personal property will be transferred by a bill of sale.

In the final analysis, it is an offer to be transmitted by the broker to the seller. However, it is more than that because it contains a time limit for the seller to accept the offer. Once the seller has accepted the offer, no other contract must be prepared. (See Exhibit 7-1 for an illustration of a purchase and sale agreement.)

Binder Agreements

In those states where the broker does not prepare an earnest money receipt and agreement to purchase, the broker should have a suitable **binder agreement** readily available that will comply with the Statute of Frauds. This simple form contains a place for a date and a brief description of the property. It also contains the terms of the sale and a place for the signatures of the parties. It contains, too, a statement that the parties agree as to the broker who brought about the sale and that the parties will enter into a more formal contract within a specified number of days.

After the binder has been signed by both parties, a copy is usually turned over to the attorney for the seller who prepares the contract for the sale of real property. Then a date for closing of title is set.

■ Exhibit 25-5 Appointment Procedures

Edina Realty INC

REALTORS®, MLS

INFORMATION TO THE SELLERS ABOUT SHOWING APPOINTMENTS

Dear Sellers,

Thank you for listing your property with Edina Realty. Your listing agent and the staff of Edina Realty are committed to making the sale proceed as quickly and as smoothly as possible.

The following are the procedures we use for the making of appointments with you to show your property to prospective buyers:

ALL APPOINTMENTS WITH YOU WILL COME FROM THE APPOINTMENT CENTER SECRETARIES . . .
Any Sales Associate from Edina Realty or any of the sales associates from a Multiple Listing Company, will call our Edina Realty Office to request an appointment to show your property (or to preview the property prior to actually showing your property to a prospective buyer.) The Appointment Center Secretaries should identify to you whether it is a preview or that the Sales Associate will be bringing prospects to the property.

ALL APPOINTMENTS WITH YOU WILL BE FOR A SPECIFIC TIME FRAME . . .
The Edina Realty Appointment Center Secretaries will call you and identify themselves as being from the Edina Realty Office Appointment Center. The Appointment Secretaries will ask your permission for a named Sales Associate from a specific company to bring a prospective buyer (or preview) your property during a time frame. The time frame may be as soon as minutes to as distant as the next day or two. The time frame for being at your property also allows for the Sales Associate to have some flexibility in arriving at the property. Thus it is not unexpected to have a request for a time frame of approximately 3-4:00, for example.

IF YOU CANNOT BE REACHED BY PHONE FOR THE APPOINTMENT . . .
In the event you cannot be reached by phone to establish the appointment, the Edina Realty Appointment Center Secretaries will call the requesting Sales Associate back and inform the Sales Associate of not being able to reach you to confirm the appointment. The requesting Sales Associate will then be given the lock box combination for your property and asked to ring the door bell before entering the home. The Appointment Center Secretaries will continue to try to reach you up to approximately one hour before the requested time frame of the showing.

IF YOU ARE PLANNING TO BE AWAY FOR AN EXTENDED PERIOD OF TIME . . .
So that Edina Realty Appointment Center Secretaries may serve you more efficiently, we would ask that you inform your listing agent of any extended periods when you will not be available to get permission for appointments. It is also suggested that you provide your listing agent with a phone number where you could be reached by the listing agent in the event he or she needs to present a purchase agreement to you by phone.

IF YOU HAVE ANY SPECIAL INSTRUCTIONS FOR SHOWINGS . . .
If you have any special instructions for Sales Associates showing your property, please inform your listing agent and he or she will see that the records for your property are noted about your special instructions. If someone in your home is ill, or the showing time is not possible, please tell the Appointment Center Secretary.

ALL SALES ASSOCIATES TRY TO BE PUNCTUAL, BUT . . .
All Sales Associates attempt to be punctual for their showing appointments, however, changes along their route can cause the Sales Associate to be earlier or later than expected. We hope that if this does happen to you, you will understand and be prepared.

SOMETIMES IT IS NECESSARY TO CANCEL A PREVIOUSLY MADE APPOINTMENT . . .
If in the event the Sales Associate having an appointment to show your property finds it necessary to cancel that appointment, the Edina Realty Appointment Center Secretaries will call you as soon as possible to advise you of the cancellation. (Cancellations may be caused by illness, car breakdown or the prospect is delayed. Sometimes it occurs that the prospect has made a decision to purchase a previously inspected property.) In the event the Appointment Center is closed for the day and the agent is unable to notify you, please accept their apologies in advance.

IF A STRANGER CALLS AT YOUR DOOR ASKING TO SEE YOUR HOME . . .
In rare instances, a stranger may see the for sale sign and stop at your door without a Sales Associate being with them, and ask if they could see your home. It is the suggestion of Edina Realty that you not allow any unexpected strangers to walk into your home. Ask them to call your listing agent for an appointment to see the home. Also ask the person for their name and phone number and call your listing agent to follow up with the stranger.

ALL REAL ESTATE SALES ASSOCIATES WILL IDENTIFY THEMSELVES . . .
All real estate Sales Associates have business cards and will identify themselves as being from Edina Realty or another real estate firm. If the business card is not offered to you, please do not hesitate to request one of the Sales Associate. If the agent does not leave a card when showing your home, please understand that they may have been distracted by the buyer and it was an oversight.

PREVIEWING BY A SALES ASSOCIATE . . .
A Sales Associate who is previewing your property, without a prospective buyer being along, is simply attempting to match the needs of prospective buyers they are working with at the time, with the amenities of your property. If they find a match to a particular prospect, they will call the Edina Realty Office and make another appointment to bring that prospect to your property.

SUDDENLY, AN UNEXPECTED SHOWING REQUEST BY A SALES ASSOCIATE . . .
Occasionally, a Sales Associate may drive by a property for sale and the prospect may urge the Sales Associate to stop and see if they can be shown the property like—NOW. Thus the Sales Associate may come to your door, introduce him/herself as not having an appointment, but a prospect is in the car and asks if they could see the property now. It is Edina Realty's suggestion that in situations like this, if the time is convenient to you, get the Sales Associate's business card, and allow him/her to bring the prospect through the property. If it is not convenient, ask the Sales Associate to call Edina Realty Appointment Center for another time to see the property.

YOUR LISTING AGENT WILL HAVE MORE SUGGESTIONS . . .
There are many other areas which are more specific to your property which your listing agent will review with you. Some of these areas are: the lights; special locks or security systems; what to do when prospects are being shown through the property; conversations with and questions from the prospect and what to do with children and pets during the showing. The listing agent can answer your questions or concerns.

A SOLD SIGN ON THE FOR SALE SIGN IS OUR GOAL . . .
You have selected the Edina Realty team and your listing agent to market your property. We will work toward getting that sold sign on your for sale sign as quickly and as smoothly as possible. We ask from you your patience and cooperation while we proceed to accomplish our goal.

THANK YOU FOR LISTING WITH EDINA REALTY . . .
ROGER ROVICK DAVID ROVICK
OWNERS

ER 230H 2/87

SOURCE: Edina Realty.

The binder, despite its simplicity, is a valid contract for the sale of real property provided that all its details have been completed, and provided there is nothing further for the parties to do but enter into the more formal contract as called for by the binder agreement.

RELATIONSHIP WITH SALES PERSONNEL

Hiring Sales Personnel

Every broker who hires sales personnel wants good salespeople. The problem is to determine whether or not a person is going to be good before hiring.

Successful real estate sales personnel have certain characteristics in common. Foremost is good health. They also are reasonably well dressed, have knowledge of local real estate and real estate law, and speak clearly in a manner that gains the respect and confidence of their clients. Additionally, individuals who are active in community affairs and are members of local clubs and fraternal groups have a circle of acquaintances that form a base for obtaining listings and sales prospects.

One major Western real estate broker believes that sports activists have the competitive drive necessary to be successful in real estate. Therefore, this broker hires individuals who have continued to participate in competitive sports. The broker's $300 million annual sales volume says that this can't be all wrong.

Kirkpatrick and Russ report the most common reasons for failure among salespersons.[1] The ten leading causes of failure in order of importance are

1. Lack of initiative.
2. Poor planning and organization.
3. Inadequate product knowledge.
4. Lack of enthusiasm.
5. Salesperson not customer-oriented.
6. Lack of proper training.
7. Inability to get along with buyers.
8. Lack of personal goals.
9. Inadequate knowledge of market.
10. Lack of knowledge of company.

Items 2, 3, 6, 9, and 10 may be compensated for with thorough company training. Causes of failure numbers 1, 4, 5, 7, and 8 are characteristics whose presence may be determined during the interviewing process. In a positive sense, brokers seek to recruit sales associates who are optimistic,

[1]Joseph F. Hair, Jr., Francis L. Notturno, and Frederick A. Russ, *Effective Selling* (Cincinnati: South-Western Publishing Co., 1991), 59.

enthusiastic, confident, sincere, and dependable and who have the drive to succeed and will use initiative and imagination to do so.

Compensation for Sales Personnel

The usual arrangement for compensating sales personnel is on a commission basis. A study by Richey and Fusilier at the University of Colorado revealed that 95 percent of the firms relied on straight commissions. Commissions and drawing accounts were used in 4 percent of the firms. The smaller firms were the most frequent users of straight commissions, while only 1 percent of the firms employing over 50 employees used straight commissions.

Compensating sales associates with commission payments based on successful sales of real estate would seem to provide all the incentive necessary. Nevertheless, many brokers report using bonuses to further motivate salespersons or reward outstanding performance.

A common bonus system is to increase the sales associate's share of commission as various levels of performance are attained. Beginning, for example, with a 50 percent share of commission for listing and selling a property, bonuses may be earned based on total commissions generated (Table 25-2).

A further extension of the commission plus bonus system of compensation is the "100 percent office." Some offices give 100 percent of future commissions to salespersons after a set minimum level of commissions has been earned.

Another version of the 100 percent office permits the sales associate to retain all commissions earned. The sales associates, in turn, pay the broker a monthly fee for office space, training, telephones, etc. The sales associates also pay their own advertising and promotion costs.

Because the rates of compensation vary considerably, the rates of commissions and any other duties of sales associates should be made clear to them when they are hired to avoid occasions for any future misunderstanding with the broker.

Table 25-2 Commission Schedule (Percentages)

EARNINGS ($)	LIST	SALE	MLS SALE YOUR LIST	YOUR SALE MLS LIST
0–12,500	25	25	25	50
12,500–25,000	30	30	30	60
25–50,000	35	35	30	70
50–75,000	37.5	37.5	35	75
75–100,000	40	40	35	75
Over 100,000	42.5	42.5	40	80

Agreement with Sales Personnel

Generally speaking, the sales personnel in most offices pay their own gas and oil expenses for their automobiles. Naturally, for income tax purposes, the salespersons take these expenses as deductions. However, in a few instances these deductions have been disallowed by the Internal Revenue Service because the salespeople had no written agreement with their brokers. The IRS contended, due to the lack of a written agreement, this expenditure was a gratuity to the salespersons. Its contention was upheld by the courts. It is, therefore, extremely important for salespersons to enter into a written agreement with their brokers. The agreement should state, among other things, that the salespeople are to pay for gas, oil, and maintenance of their automobiles. In this way, a deduction will be allowed for income tax purposes.

Furthermore, because oral instructions are often vague and forgotten, it is suggested that sales personnel will be more aware of what is expected of them if suggestions are in writing. A policy manual is, therefore, recommended to minimize misunderstandings.

Training

In essence, sales associates are independent businesses who maintain their affiliation and share their commissions with brokers in exchange for services received. One of the benefits of affiliation with a broker is sales training.

There are basically two types of sales training meetings. One is purely educational. These meetings may involve product training that exposes sales associates to new zoning or license laws, financing methods, or viewing new listings. Other educational sessions might present sales techniques, company policy, or mutual problem solving.

The other category of sales training is motivational or morale building. These meetings recognize superior performance, introduce sales contests, and create enthusiasm for the company and real estate in general. Effective use of training builds company loyalty, decreases turnover of sales associates, and builds sales productivity and profitability.

REAL ESTATE FRANCHISES

Problems in sales training, office management, and advertising have led to rapid growth in **franchising** the local realty broker. Providing professional management assistance has helped Century 21 Real Estate Corporation develop thousands of franchised-affiliated brokers.

The advantages offered local brokers are similar to those offered by any national fast food chain; namely, in exchange for a franchise fee and a percentage of gross sales, the broker receives

1. Recognition from association with national television advertising.
2. Brokerage management training.
3. Training for up to four weeks for sales associates at one of several schools located throughout the nation.
4. The right to purchase videotapes and educational materials for continued training of sales associates.
5. Assistance, through pre-planning, with local advertising.
6. A client referral service through affiliated brokers.

Although not yet available, some observers anticipate that national franchisors will provide homeowners a guaranteed sale when moving and assistance in financing another home. These services would be available only if a family sold and bought through affiliated brokers.

GLOSSARY

Binder agreement In the absence of an earnest money receipt and agreement to purchase, a valid contract for the sale of real property if all details are included

Blind advertisement An advertisement that does not contain the broker's name or some indication that it is not a private individual's ad

Canvassing Obtaining listings by phone or door-to-door contact

Code of Ethics Ethics promulgated by the NATIONAL ASSOCIATION OF REALTORS® under which REALTORS® operate

Continuing education A certain number of classroom hours required by the different states before becoming eligible for a license

Corporation An instrument for the ownership and the management of a business enterprise; an artificial being; an entity

Experience requirement One to five years training for a real estate agent to become a broker

Franchising A situation in which the local broker affiliates with a larger corporation to receive management assistance

Irrevocable consent A statement filed by nonresident brokers with the Secretary of State that a summons may be served on the Secretary of State to give the courts jurisdiction over the nonresident broker

Listing file A system of maintaining a record of all properties a firm is offering

Listing form A form containing all the pertinent details of a property, such as its location, price, the amount of the mortgage, the number of bedrooms and baths, etc.

Listings The right by prospective sellers given to real estate brokers to sell their property

Open house A selling device whereby the public is invited to inspect a furnished home

Partnership A legal relationship created voluntarily by two or more persons to carry on a business for profit

Property brief An information folder concerning a particular property

Proprietorship An individual form of business enterprise

Prospect cards Cards containing names, addresses, and telephone numbers for every potential customer who walks into a broker's office

Recovery fund A fund, established by law, in some states to enable persons aggrieved by acts of real estate brokers or salespersons to collect damages

Sales kit A broker's aid in selling real property, including map of city, zoning map, tax rates, data on insurance rates, amortization table, an area rent table, etc.

Stick A board listing the names of the salespersons in a broker's office

Unsolicited listings Listings obtained by a broker from previous clients

QUESTIONS FOR REVIEW

1. What is the purpose of the brokerage licensing laws?
2. What is the purpose of requiring brokers to be bonded in many states?
3. Compare the advantages and disadvantages of the partnership form of business enterprise to the corporate form of business enterprise.
4. Name and explain three ways of obtaining listings.
5. List and explain five advantages to an owner of having the sale of property handled through a brokerage office instead of attempting to sell it without a broker's services.
6. Why should a broker inspect a premises that has been listed or is about to be listed?
7. Why is setting a price on a property sometimes difficult, and what should be done if the owner persists in demanding an unreasonable price for the property?
8. Based on Table 25-1, describe a program for generating clients.
9. List and discuss the common causes of failure among salespersons.

10. Explain the advantages of having a written agreement with the salesperson.

PROBLEMS AND ACTIVITIES

1. The following is from Section 475.43 of the Florida Real Estate License Law:

> An option contract may sometimes amount only to an exclusive listing. This will occur where it is understood that the optionee has no intention of buying the property himself, but intends to sell it to someone else for a sum sufficient to net a compensation for his efforts. A contract of this character is frequently given as a means of expediting a brokerage transaction. Thus, the owner may live at a distance, and a quick sale may result. In this way the broker may bind the principal to sell, and the broker's authority to do so may be exhibited to the prospect. It does not change the essential relations of the parties and cannot be considered as a true option. . . .

   a. Why is it not a true option?
   b. Suggest another way of accomplishing the same thing.

26

ADVERTISING AND SELLING

KEY TERMS

Advertising media
Buying motives
Copy
Copy block
Emotional motives
Follow-up services
Goodwill advertisement
Institutional advertisement
Layout
Novelties
Open house
Rational motives
Release
Specific advertisement
White space

In the real estate business a broker, acting as an intermediary between buyers and sellers of homes, has a marketing problem. Although marketing is the heart of the brokerage operation, advertising introduces the home to potential buyers and prepares the way for the potential sale of the property. The main purpose of advertising is to gain the undivided attention of the prospect.

TARGETING THE MARKET

To meet the objective described above, real estate advertisers must target their messages to sharply designed consumer profiles. Successful advertising zeros in on narrowly segmented markets and directs customized messages personally to them. Emphasis is placed less on high readership and more on producing responses. Copy should be written to conform to the tastes and expectations of the target market. Narrowly segmented audiences have a built-in readiness to buy; therefore, the message should be personalized to them.

To properly introduce a parcel of real estate to the market, the broker must determine the market to be reached. In other words, the broker should be able to answer the following questions before attempting to write the ad:

1. What kind of property is this?
2. Who will purchase the property?
3. For whom is it a good buy?
4. What motivates the purchaser?

TYPES OF REAL ESTATE ADVERTISING

Real estate advertising generally falls into three broad categories: goodwill, institutional, and specific. All three types have definite purposes and are by their very nature limited in their scope and appeal.

Goodwill Advertisement

The so-called **goodwill advertisement** is sometimes referred to as general advertising. Its primary purpose is to present and keep the broker's name before the public. Its effectiveness in terms of specific result is difficult, if not impossible, to evaluate. For example, if an advertisement is inserted in a church benefit's program, it is generally done to present one's name to the public and not with the idea of promoting a specific piece of real estate. Any suburban broker will speak eloquently on the unproductiveness of this type of advertising, but it is just one of those things that *has* to be done by brokers in small communities.

Goodwill advertising may be a name card inserted in the classified columns of a newspaper, for example, GWENDOLYN BROWN—INVESTMENT PROPERTIES. Large companies do a lot of goodwill advertising, which, of course, benefits all those doing business under their umbrella. Exhibit 26-1 is an example of one of Sibcy Cline's handouts.

A card advertisement in a real estate trade journal circulated among investment property owners is an effective means of advertising for the broker interested in obtaining management properties. An insertion in a journal with wide circulation among brokers, operators, and landlords is not only a goodwill advertisement but a general invitation to operators to investigate your investment properties. It is also an invitation for a co-brokerage participation in your listings.

This advertising may work in a dual capacity; namely, promoting goodwill and promoting *immediate* productive results.

Institutional Advertisement

The **institutional advertisement** used in real estate is generally a joint advertisement by a board or group. Its primary purpose is to promote confidence in the board or group, or to promote confidence in a particular community.

An example of institutional advertising was employed by a Long Island real estate group to instill the idea of the value to the individual in owning a home. "If you rent," the advertisement read in part, "you will have nothing but a handful of rent receipts to show for your money at the end of 20 years."

It then went on to explain the price home that could be purchased and paid off at different mortgage rates instead of paying the equivalent amount in rent. This advertisement proved very effective in terms of sales among the group who ran the advertisement.

■ **Exhibit 26-1 An Example of Goodwill Advertising**

SOURCE: Courtesy Sibcy Cline, Inc. REALTORS®.

These advertisements have been criticized by some who say that the figure given as the mortgage payment does not take into account the maintenance, real property taxes, and insurance necessary to carry the building. On the other hand, this argument may be countered by the fact that at least part of the monthly payments on the property builds an equity in the property and is in the nature of forced savings, while the interest and the real property tax paid are deductible from the homeowner's income tax.

Specific Advertisement

The **specific advertisement** is written and designed to sell a particular parcel of property. In most cases, it is inserted in the classified columns of local newspapers. This advertising best illustrates the two functions of advertising: namely, introducing the product to the market and assisting the salesperson to contact prospects.

ADVERTISING MEDIA

Advertising media are the means by which an advertisement is presented to the public. The most common forms are newspapers, magazines and real estate journals, direct mail, radio and television, outdoor advertising, and novelties.

Newspapers

The most important advertising medium for the real estate broker is the newspaper. About 80 percent of the average broker's advertising budget is spent on this medium. One study revealed that between 30 and 45 percent of the actual number of contacts and subsequently produced sales come from newspaper ads.

Most classified advertising appears on Sundays, because brokers feel that this will result in more sales. However, research at the University of Arizona suggested that classified advertising on Sundays does not bring about the best results.[1] The purpose of the study was to measure the relative effectiveness of four different time periods during the week—Monday and Tuesday, Wednesday and Thursday, Friday and Saturday, and Sunday only. The results of the experiments suggest

> that weekdays rather than weekends afford greater response to classified advertisements on residential properties. . . . Moreover, the pattern of response shows that the early part of the week is superior to midweek, which, in turn, is superior to the weekend for producing inquiries in the advertised properties.

---

[1]As reported in *Realtor's Headlines* 38, no. 7 (February 1971).

It appears that the fewer advertisements run in the early part of the week have less competition for readership by prospective buyers than advertisements run on Sundays and the latter part of the week.

A study of media selection has indicated that national or even regional patterns do not exist for the most effective media.[2] The authors of the study tried to determine how Colorado home buyers select a particular real estate firm contrasted to similar findings in California and Connecticut. The results are summarized in Table 26-1.

The California 2 study in Table 26-1 applies only to *new* homes, which show a surprising 50 percent effectiveness from For Sale signs.

Fusilier and Richey concluded, among other things:

> The effect of local factors on the real estate market carries important implications for the broker's advertising program. The broker must accumulate accurate data as to the effectiveness of advertising according to the type of property offered. Advertising expenditures are too substantial to approach the problem haphazardly. (We found that the average firm spent approximately 20 percent of the total operating expenses, excluding commissions, for advertising.)
>
> Each broker must determine which advertising media is best for the specific types of property according to the characteristics of the market in his locality. Only by accumulating fairly extensive records on the responses received from his advertising program will the broker be able to make effective, and money-saving, decisions on advertising media.[3]

Magazines and Real Estate Journals

Every broker should be aware of the various trade journals and the groups by whom they are read. For example, many of the farm journals are excellent sources of farm sales, and the cost in some instances is not much greater than the cost of an advertisement in a local newspaper. Another

Table 26-1 Effectiveness of Advertising Media (Percentage)

MEDIA	COLO.	CONN.	CALIF. 1	CALIF. 2
For Sale signs	33.4	10	27.7	50
Newspaper ads	21.0	38	32.0	14
Referrals	19.1	26	30.0	16
Misc.	26.5	26	10.3	20

[2]H. L. Fusilier and Clyde W. Richey, *What Is Effective Residential Real Estate Advertising?* (Boulder: University of Colorado, Center for Real Estate and Land Use Studies, Business Research Division, January 1972).

[3]Fusilier and Richey, *What Is Effective Advertising?*, 11.

example is the trade journal circulated among people in the motel business. Many brokers having motels for sale find it profitable to advertise in these journals. It is read by people interested in motels, and, in addition, is employed by brokers all over the country with whom co-brokerage deals can very often be arranged.

Although strictly speaking a paper like the *Wall Street Journal* cannot be considered a trade journal, recognition should be given it in terms of advertising the higher-priced business and industrial properties. In addition, West Coast brokers have found it a profitable medium for the sale of high-priced ranch and farm properties.

Direct Mail

Direct mail, although an expensive form of advertising, has many uses for the real estate broker. This form of advertising is used to a large degree by country farm brokers who live near urban areas. Generally an advertisement is prepared and inserted in the classified column of a nearby city newspaper. The advertisement states that a free catalog or list of farm properties will be mailed by the broker on request. The listings can range from mimeographed material to a well-planned, well-printed catalog. Once having received requests for a catalog, the broker has a ready-made mailing list to which further listings can be sent. As with all mailing lists, care should be taken to prevent the list from becoming inactive. If a list brings only a few inquiries, the persons who fail to respond after several mailings should be weeded out. The names of any persons whose mail is returned for lack of forwarding address should also be eliminated.

Methods of Obtaining Lists. In addition to obtaining mailing lists as described above, one of the most effective, but sadly neglected, ways is by obtaining the names and addresses of prospects that call at the office. These names should be classified in terms of price and property interest. For example, a prospect calls at the office in answer to a newspaper advertisement for a $60,000 home but does not like the particular listing offered. The prospect's name and address should be obtained, and an attempt should be made to obtain a listing in the $60,000 bracket that might be satisfactory. As soon as this is done, a letter should be written informing the prospect of the new listing together with all pertinent details. After all, the secret of success in real estate is the matching of available listings with the wants and desires of the prospects.

Presumably the broker will have studied the advertisements of competitors and will know other local brokers who might have the listing the client desires. If this is true, then the thing to do is to contact the fellow broker and work out a co-brokerage deal. "Half a loaf is better than none."

Another method of obtaining a mailing list, especially for brokers in small towns, is to watch newspaper wedding announcements. A courteous letter should be sent to the newlyweds suggesting that in the event they desire a new home, you might be able to help them. Although this may not bring immediate results, it may pay off in the long run. Your name as a broker will be uppermost in their minds; and if they ever want a house in the future, they may come to you for help.

Various Uses for Direct Mail. Direct mail has other uses for the alert broker. It is used to a very large degree to invite co-brokerage. Usually a listing is run off on a copier and mailed to a number of brokers. The list of brokers is generally obtained from the classified section of the telephone directory. This method may be successfully used by brokers who do not participate in an MLS.

By far the largest users of direct mail are those brokers who sell industrial real estate. For example, if a broker decides that an industrial listing is suitable as a manufacturing plant for plumbing supplies, a brochure should be prepared describing the property and direct mail used as a means of contacting plumbing supply manufacturers. Generally, the list will be prepared from either a trade organization directory or *Thomas' Register,* a directory of manufacturers.

Radio and Television

Radio and television are often used effectively by real estate brokers. Most of the advertising is used to keep the broker's name before the public rather than to sell a specific property, although cable television has opened the opportunity of advertising specific properties on local access channels. In general, brokers successfully use station break announcements, one-minute announcements, or special features.

The one-minute announcements, which are also sold by stations, enable the advertiser to employ a commercial of about 125 words. They have been employed by some brokers to sell specific properties, but this usage has, for the most part, been limited to rural areas.

Outdoor Advertising

Outdoor or billboard advertising is generally an institutional advertisement in the real estate field. A local broker's board will pay the cost of advertising for the town or city with the purpose of building confidence in the city, or the board of brokers may advertise a Red Cross drive as a public service. Developers of country and summer homes often use billboard advertising. The billboards are strategically located along main arteries of travel leading toward the development. The billboards contain pictures of the development along with a statement of directions to the development.

Broadly speaking, the For Sale sign may be classified as outdoor advertising. With the results related to cost, this is probably the most effective type of advertising. It is suggested that when a property is sold, a Sold sign be placed over the For Sale sign. This is an effective public relations tool for the selling broker.

Novelties

Novelties, ranging from calendars to record books, have their place in the advertising of real estate. Some brokers employ them to promote goodwill after a sale has been made. A gift of a wallet with "Thanks—Tri-State Real Estate" inscribed on it will bring both the buyer and the seller into the office for aid in any of their future needs. It is important in employing novelties that they be in good taste.

PUBLICITY RELEASES

Successful publicity campaigns are possible because of that queer quirk of human nature that makes all of us want to be "in on the know."

Brokers have a specialized knowledge of which the public as a whole is unaware. A broker should not hide this talent, for modesty does not often become the broker. Therefore, the up-to-date broker will not hesitate sending articles concerning recent property transactions to newspapers.

A **release** is the information sent to the newspapers for publication. The word *release* should be written in the upper right-hand corner of the news story. If it is desirable to have the story published as soon as possible, the statement "for immediate release" should be written under the word *release*. If for some reason a delay in the release is necessary, the words "not to be released before January 5" should be typed under *release*. This is important especially if the story has been sent to a number of papers, and they are all to be given an equal chance at the feature.

Contents

The difficult problem involved in any press release is creating a story that will be newsworthy. It is a relatively simple matter to get publicity regarding a new development in a small community, but it is difficult to receive mention of an event so prosaic as the sale of a single house. Make the release newsworthy; the editor of a newspaper attempts to fill the paper with news, not with the mere mention of the broker's name. Try, for example, to find some historical event concerning the building that has been sold; or if it is a new property, perhaps the land was once a part of the farm belonging to a noted personage of the village; or perhaps some historic event of local interest occurred in the vicinity. Anything that will attract the eye of the editor who is receiving the release is important. Perhaps the seller might have an unusual reason for selling the property; if so, be sure to point out the unusual reason in the copy for the story.

Form

The form of the news release is extremely important. A release has more chance of publication if it is brief and to the point than if it is long and rambling. The lead paragraph is the important paragraph in any newspaper story. The first paragraph should contain the essence of the entire story so that if the editor desires, the rest of the release may be cut without losing the "meat" of the story. The broker's name should, of course, be included. The remainder of the release contains the details designed to complement the first paragraph.

GENERAL ADVERTISING RULES

Attract Attention

The advertisement must attract attention before it will be read; it must be eye-catching. However, a broker must use discretion in choosing eye-catching pictures so they will be in good taste. There must be a close kinship between the picture or illustration and the text of the ad.

Hold Attention

It is all very well for the broker to attract attention in advertising copy, but it is perhaps even more important to *hold* the attention of the reader. To hold attention and arouse the interest of the reader, the advertisement should

1. Be written in the present tense whenever possible to make the reader experience the act while reading the copy.
2. Use pictorial nouns and descriptive adjectives and create a picture in the reader's mind so he or she can identify with the story being told.
3. Use short, simple-sentence construction and adequate and careful punctuation.
4. Use a vigorous, flowing style.

Repetition

As a general rule most advertising is repetitious; however, real estate advertising is peculiar in this respect. If the same advertisement for the same house is repeated in the same form too many times, the reader will receive the impression that the house is difficult to sell and that there will eventually be a price reduction. In other words, repetition of the advertisement may defeat its purpose. One should try not to keep the same form more than twice running; i.e., the copy should be changed, broken up, and reworded, or new copy should be written to appeal to different buying motives.

Honesty

Is the advertisement honest? Every broker should raise the question before submitting an advertisement for publication. Dishonesty in advertising is not only ethically unsound, but it may prove to be an economic catastrophe. Real estate brokers have had a difficult time living down the dishonest and misleading advertisements written in the past by some of their colleagues. Nothing can cause the loss of a sale faster than a dishonest advertisement. It may bring people into the office filled with great expectations, but it will only cause them to leave filled with great apprehension.

A California study revealed something even more serious resulting from what prospects considered misleading advertising. In cases where the prospect *thought* the ad was misleading, 40 percent of the prospects absolutely eliminated the offending broker from any future transactions.

Buyer's Viewpoint

It is axiomatic in the marketing of any product that the advertising of the product must be approached from the viewpoint of the potential buyer. What the broker thinks regarding the property is of little importance. More corporations have failed in their selling campaigns because of management's sales egotism than from any other cause. An agent should not become so enthusiastic over the house that it is not seen through the eyes of the potential buyer. And the agent should not take the opposite view of looking at a house and saying, "I wouldn't pay a dollar for that shack." Nobody cares what you, as an individual, would do. That shack might look like a palace in the eyes of a buyer.

It should not be taken for granted that a buyer can see the merits in a house as well as the agent. Rather, the merits of the property should be made known in the advertisement and should be instilled in the buyer's mind even before he or she sees the building.

ADVERTISING APPEALS

Basically, advertising is designed to appeal to two broad classes of motives or reasons why people buy: emotional motives or rational motives, or more generally a combination of both.

Emotional Motives

Emotional motives are those that lead a person to react in a certain way in response to a specific set of stimuli without consciously bringing logical analysis of the situation into play. A photograph of a pretty girl in a bathing suit to advertise summer cottages, for instance, is a common advertising presentation of an emotional appeal. To choose the most effective emotional appeal for a specific purpose, one must exercise great care. There are many emotional appeals, the most common of which are discussed below.

Pride. One of the basic human needs is the need for shelter. It might be said then that any building that will keep us warm and dry should be sufficient to supply our housing needs. But this is not the case. Pride is one of our strongest emotions and makes us want something more than we actually require. The practicing real estate broker knows that almost as soon as a house is listed in an outstanding neighborhood, the house is sold, provided the price is right. If the broker has an "exclusive" on such a property, the neighborhood should be advertised. It appeals to the pride of the prospect to live in the best area that can be afforded. Use such words as *High Street Section* or *Roe Park* in the advertisement. This pinpoints the property in the mind of the reader and enables the prospect to imagine the delights and benefits of living in a so-called better neighborhood.

Emulation. Emulation may best be described as "keeping up with the Joneses." It is somewhat connected with pride. It seems to be human nature to want to conform to the actions of the leaders of the "crowd." In presenting an advertisement designed to appeal to the desire to emulate, the advertiser should stress modern up-to-date features. For example, nationally advertised kitchen fixtures should be emphasized in presenting a home, the implication being that this is the kind of kitchen the "Joneses have."

Comfort. People want a home instead of a shack in which to live because of their desire for comfort. People visualize themselves toasting their toes before a fireplace, their thoughts at peace with the world. If a listing has any of the features that might appeal to comfort, the broker should stress them. A fireplace, a new heating or air-conditioning system, or other things in a home that make living easier should be featured in the advertising.

Love for Children. Parental love is one of the strongest of all the human emotions. All people want their children to have the best. Many city dwellers believe the country is the best place to raise children. All people want their family to enjoy good health. The real estate broker should take a tip from this and advertise properties accordingly.

Most parents want their children to have good schooling and religious upbringing. A broker will then stress, when advertising a property, the nearness of schools along with the availability of churches and shopping centers.

It should be proved to the reader of the advertisement that the home being offered will make a child happier, healthier, and more capable. The broker who can do this has the house half sold.

Security. The desire for security is present in each of us. Most of the advertisements promoting the "family farm" play on the desire for security. The idea is that no matter what happens to the economy—inflation or depression—the owner of the farm can be self-sufficient. The headline of this type of advertising generally reads "Compact Security Farm" or "Ideal Retirement Farm." It is to fulfill this desire for security that one finds more and more city dwellers migrating to the country with ever-increasing opportunities for the broker who handles any agricultural properties.

Fear. Although advertisements instilling fear have no true place in real estate advertising, they have been used rather effectively in some parts of the country and are, therefore, important enough to bear mention here, if only to discourage their use.

Rational Motives

Rational motives are those motives for buying that involve conscious reasoning. The prime use of rational motives in real estate advertising is found in the promotion of investment properties. However, it should be remembered that the rational advertisement can also be employed in advertising residential properties. When effectively combined with emotional appeals, rational appeals can aid greatly in selling real estate. A discussion of some of the more common rational motives follows.

Economy. Business people or investors in property are vitally interested in the answer to one major question; namely, How much will this property earn? They are, therefore, interested in economy of purchase and economy in use. In an investment property, therefore, the amount of cash needed to close the deal should be advertised. Investors are interested in net returns on cash invested; they are not so interested in the purchase price of the property. Advertise the net return, or if you have the proper listing, use an eye-catching headline that would appeal to the investor, such as EIGHT TIMES RENT. This means there will be a return of 12.5 percent on the money invested and that the buyer's cash investment will be returned in eight years.

The idea of economy in use is employed both in advertising designed to promote investment properties and in advertising to sell residential properties. For example, when mentioning that a house is well insulated, the broker is trying to put forth the idea that insulation not only makes the house warmer but also reduces the cost of fuel.

Convenience. Convenience as a motive is often used in the sale of homes and in the rental of apartments and lofts or buildings to be used for factory purposes. An advertisement reading, "One Minute to School, One Minute to Churches, and Three Minutes to a Bus Stop," might be the deciding factor in the sale of a home.

Nearness to transportation can very well be a decisive factor in the rental of an apartment. The working members of a family want to live in a place where they can get to their jobs quickly. Transportation is also of vital importance to renters of lots and factory space. Factory help is easier to obtain if the loft is located near suitable transportation. Ease of transportation should be emphasized because experienced factory managers will shun property not located near suitable transportation.

Enhancement of Earnings. Enhancement of earnings is another rational appeal. If the property is an investment property, such as an apartment house, or if it is a business opportunity, like a grocery store, and if the present owner is not receiving as much in net returns as should be expected, then this should be pointed out in the advertisement. Perhaps a new landlord could get higher rentals with the installation of certain improvements, or perhaps the owner of the grocery store has been ill so that the earnings as shown on the books do not reflect the true potential of the business. In cases such as these the information as to the causes of the low earnings should be emphasized in the advertisement.

COPY AND LAYOUT FOR ADVERTISEMENTS

Copy consists primarily of plotting and writing the advertisement. A decision on the appeals to be used and the approach to be followed is made; then these are put into words. **Layout** refers to the form in which the final advertisement will appear.

Paragraphs

The paragraphs in an advertisement should be short and to the point. Each paragraph should be indented, not kept flush with the preceding paragraph. To make the advertisement more readable, it should be double-leaded between paragraphs: there should be more space between the paragraphs than between the lines within the paragraphs. The amount of space left between lines will depend on the type size, the legibility of the typeface, and the length of line used.

Copy Blocks

The **copy block** refers to the width of the copy. It should not be too wide in relation to type size. As a general rule, larger type sizes are used at the beginning of the advertisement and gradually drop to a smaller type size.

Subheads

Subheads or subheadlines are used to separate copy and to lend better appearance to the body of the advertisement.

Type Size

The type size should be as large as is consistent with the copy length. More important than type size is the question of whether the copy holds interest. If it does hold interest, then a smaller type size than is ordinarily indicated can be used.

White Space

White space, that part of the page not covered with copy, when used effectively, can catch the attention of the reader. The copywriter should not employ white space unnecessarily, however, for every unnecessary line of white space prevents the addition of copy that might be considerably more effective than white space.

Artwork

Because the real estate broker uses classified advertising more often than display advertising, artwork is not often used to illustrate an ad. However, when artwork is used, the broker should keep in mind that it is not used for decoration; it is used fundamentally to illustrate and substantiate the story that is being told in the advertisement.

Headlines

Headlines designed to attract attention seem to be the most difficult part of the advertisement to write. They must be eye-catching, have punch, and at the same time must not be too trite. The approach should be different, but not too different.

It should be noted that even a headline having punch and eye appeal will lose its effectiveness if it is too crowded. Use plenty of white space as a device for making the headline stand out.

Statistics of the National Bureau of Advertising show that the headline, or first ten words of the ad, often accounts for 50 to 75 percent of an ad's effectiveness.

Further, when headlines are used they should be fully explained in the body of the ad. The following headlines were taken from various newspapers and nowhere in the copy that followed were they further explained.

VALUE! (No explanation of why it was a value.)
SACRIFICE! (No explanation of why it was a sacrifice.)
YOU WON'T BELIEVE THIS! (Did not tell me why, so I didn't.)
FIRST COME—FIRST SOLD! (This is ridiculous!)
THE PRICE IS UNBELIEVABLE! (No price in this ad.)
RED HOT! (Why?)
GREAT LOCATION (Where?)
PRICED TO SELL (Aren't they all?)
REDUCED! (From what? To what?)
SELLER PAYS ALL (All what? Including cost of house?)
FREE BAHAMA CRUISE (Not one more word about the cruise.)
CHOICE NEIGHBORHOOD (Where?)
POOL! POOL! POOL! (Three pools?)
UNDER BUILDER'S PRICE (No price.)
DON'T READ THIS AD (This would stop almost everyone.)
X-RATED AD (Now, is this any kind of a headline?)
DESPERATE (Why?)
HARD TO FIND (Not explained. Does it mean property may not be found, or exceptional value?)

The advertisement in Exhibit 26-2 is an example of effective use of emotional and rational appeals, copy, and layout.

Completeness

Advertising, like anything else, if done at all, should be done properly. Too many brokers are penny-wise and pound-foolish in this regard. The broker should put into advertising copy whatever is necessary to help effect the sale. A nickel or a dime saved here and there by unintelligible abbreviations may very well lose a sale. Too little copy is often a mistake.

Above all, avoid words that waste money. Here is a list of phrases and words that ad writers should eliminate from their copy with suggestions for making the advertisement more complete.

> REASONABLE PRICE (From whose point of view? Tell the price.)
> ALL IMPROVEMENTS (For instance, what?)
> MODERN IMPROVEMENTS (Modern lighting, disposal, or just bath and running water?)
> NEWLY RENOVATED ("Renovated" is an objectionable word that almost suggests "fumigated.")
> MUST BE SEEN TO BE APPRECIATED (Probably true, but this is lazy. Make the reader want to see it.)
> CONVENIENT LOCATION (Convenient to what? Everything is convenient to something.)

■ Exhibit 26-2 Advertisement Using Emotional and Rational Appeals

a. Durability	SOLID BRICK HOME
b. Convenience	Convenient to Everything
	!We Dare You!
c. Economy of Purchase	We dare you to compare this home with any other in this price class in Coeur d'Alene. Check this list and see it for yourself.
d. Durability	1. All-brick ranch type.
e. Special Appeal	2. Beautifully landscaped.
f. Easier Housekeeping	3. Six rooms, all on one floor.
g. Love of Comfort	4. Log-burning fireplace.
h. Convenience	5. Three bedrooms.
i. Love of Luxury	6. Two modern tiled baths.
j. Love of Recreation	7. Finished recreation room in basement.
k. Economy in Use	8. Completely insulated.
l. Easy Credit	9. Check this price; not $75,000, not $65,000 but only $59,500, terms.

THREE ELEGANT ROOMS (Since when has elegance moved into three rooms?)
LEAVING TOWN SUDDENLY (Of course, it's none of the reader's business, but . . . ?)
VERY ATTRACTIVE (Name some of the attractions.)
UNUSUAL OPPORTUNITY (Tell something to prove it.)
NO REASONABLE OFFER REFUSED (The last resort of a despairing salesperson. Why admit despair?)
OWNER SAYS SELL! (Naturally. How else could you have gotten the listing?)
POSSESSION SOON (Say when or don't talk about it.)

When it comes to completeness in real estate advertising, be sure to include the price of the property. Marketing research has found that ads are 48 percent more effective when price is mentioned.

Compare the two advertisements in Exhibit 26-3, which advertise the same property. The advertisement by Mr. Willsey won first prize in a contest of the New York Realtors. The first line is eye-catching; there are no hackneyed phrases and abbreviations. The advertisement is complete and attractive.

Follow-up Card

It is good business practice for the real estate broker to use the follow-up card when running an advertisement. This type of card, printed on an

Exhibit 26-3 Examples of Good and Poor Advertising

THE MOST PRICELESS

thing in America today is privacy for family living. Situated on 100 × 120 lot on the crest of a hill and framed by 47 big white pines is this gorgeous 7-room brick and frame split-level home. Gas heat, attached garage. An appealing place for $87,500. Call 421-8701 today for appointment.

REALTOR
CARL A. WILLSEY
225 W. Church St., Elmira, N.Y.

Good

7-rm. brick & frame house, gas heat, att. gar. 100 × 120 lot. $87,500. Call 421-8701 for appt.

Poor

SOURCE: Carl A. Willsey, Elmira, New York. (Figures updated by authors.)

Exhibit 26-4 Sample Follow-Up Card

YES! Your Property Is Being Advertised

Here is A Copy of Some Current Advertising

You can rest assured that consistent advertising and recommendation of your Real Estate is being made at all times to consummate a quick, satisfactory sale.

ARNOLD REALTY CO.
Rita B. Arnold, Realtor—Phone 376-6676

ordinary postal card, is illustrated in Exhibit 26-4. It has a good psychological effect on the seller and indicates an interest in selling the property. In addition, there is a possibility of obtaining additional listings as a result of the satisfied client showing the card.

ADVERTISING LIMITATIONS

Real estate advertising prepares the way for the sale. In other words, the advertisement creates the contact between the broker and the potential buyer. It brings prospects into the broker's office; and, having done that, it has served its purpose. The rest depends on the quality of the product and the selling ability of the broker.

Here is a word of warning. The novice in real estate often expects too much from advertising. Advertising has a cumulative effect. Its favorable results tend to build up over a long period of time. It not only brings people into the office to purchase, but the constant presentation of one's name to the public may bring tangible results in the form of goodwill. In this sense, the goodwill lies in being known to the public.

SELLING RESIDENTIAL PROPERTY

Real estate is a fundamental commodity; people need it, and people want it. The novice should realize that psychologically people *want* to buy. To be able to buy something flatters the ego, and the very act of buying itself gives the purchaser a feeling of pleasure. The salesperson ought to realize that the purchaser contemplating the purchase of a home is in fact anticipating the pleasure of enjoyment in the owning of a home, and the person purchasing commercial property is anticipating the possibility of profits from the purchase.

At this point, the logical question might be: If people really want to buy, why is it so difficult to sell them something—especially real estate? It is ordinarily true that people are not ready buyers. Sales resistance by a prospect may be conscious or unconscious. Most buyers have only a limited amount of funds with which to make purchases. Doubts may be reinforced by conflicting claims that are making demands on these sums. The prospect may fear being sold something that is not needed or may be cautious because of a desire to make a good bargain. Many prospects do not want to be pushed into making a decision. The reasons for a resistance to buying are endless, and the attempts to sell real estate may increase the psychological effect of these deterrents to an even higher degree because for the average person the purchase of a parcel of real property is probably the largest investment made during a lifetime.

Knowledge of Buying Motives

Motives tend to explain *why* things are done or not done. **Buying motives** tend to explain *why* people buy.

These motives or desires of prospective purchasers are not too unlike the motives that are appealed to in advertising—economy in use, expectation of profit, comfort, love of children, pride of possession—to mention only a few. If a salesperson has a prospect who is interested in the purchase of a home because of love for children, the salesperson should know that this is one of the strongest motives for prospect's purchase of a home. As a result of the knowledge of this motive, when the salesperson comes to the street on which the property is located, those things that make the street safe for children are pointed out to the prospect. It is not a through street; there are signs warning drivers to slow down; the street has a jog in it that naturally slows down drivers. In making the prospect see, then, that this is the right kind of neighborhood for children, the salesperson has assisted the prospect in the satisfaction of the buying motive.

On the other hand, if the prospect is looking at a commercial property with the idea of making a profit from the property, the salesperson can go over the income and expense figures showing where the profit lies and how much will be earned from the property. That is what the prospect wants—expectation of profit is the buying motive. The salesperson should be frank and honest with the prospect, who will then respect the salesperson's judgment. By not trying to conceal anything from the prospect, the salesperson will gain the prospect's respect and confidence. By recognizing the buying motives of their potential purchasers, real estate brokers or salespeople can "help their prospects buy" instead of "selling" them. It is only when brokers help their prospects buy that they have really satisfied customers.

Knowledge of the Product

Although a broker must have a knowledge of the product being sold, many brokers are sadly lacking in really knowing anything about their listings. There is a saying among people in real estate that "a house well listed is half sold." In Chapter 25, much space was devoted to the listing of the home and the inspection of the home. This does not mean there is nothing beyond the mechanics of taking a listing. When a property is listed, the broker must be sure, first, that it is a salable listing; that is, that it is not listed at a price that is too high. Second, inspecting the listing must involve more than just the mechanics of going over the property. Inspecting the property means obtaining a thorough knowledge of the product that is going to be sold. Mental photographs of the property, both inside and out, are taken by the person inspecting the property.

The broker should know everything there is to know about the product, and especially the reason that the seller wants to sell.

Sources of Prospects

The sources of prospects are almost limitless. One important source may be the neighbors of the listing owner. After obtaining a listing, the broker might stop at the home of the next-door neighbors and tell them that the home has just been listed and that it is the broker's desire to bring compatible people into the neighborhood. The neighbors may suggest a friend who might be interested in the house or the neighbors might be interested in listing their own home for sale. The neighbors will realize that the broker is trying to serve them by informing them of what is happening. The entire block might be worked in this manner. The number of listings and prospects that can be found in this way will be surprising. It will, in effect, create a situation whereby everyone in the block will be thinking of prospects for the broker, if for no other reason than to bring one's own friends into the neighborhood.

Former Customers. Previous customers are always good prospects. Generally, a broker will find that one sale can be built into two by employing lists of previous clients.

Owners of Listed Properties. The broker knows or should know the reason why every person who has listed property desires to sell the property. Many want to sell because they desire to move to a new neighborhood. Some older people who have listed their homes for sale have done so because their families have grown to adulthood and left home. Perhaps they no longer have a need for a large home and want to move to a smaller one. They may be prospects for a sale.

Investors and Operators. Brokers who deal in investment properties should have a list of investors handy. This list can easily be compiled by the beginner from advertisements in newspapers and real estate journals. As a routine matter, all listings of investment properties that might be of interest to operators or investors should be submitted to them, preferably personally, although in large cities this might not prove to be practicable.

Recent Sellers. Recent sellers are a particularly rich source of prospects. The chances are that they are qualified, at least monetarily, as prospective purchasers. Current lists of sellers can be made from the real estate pages of newspapers or from the records in the county clerk's office. It is important to keep these lists up to date and to use them as rapidly as possible. This source of prospects is especially good in a rising market because the chances are that these sellers have made a profit from the sale of their previously held property and believe they can do it again, in which case they will be susceptible to sales overtures.

Open Houses. A number of sales result from the **open house.** Usually a well-furnished listing in a moderate price bracket is selected for the open house. An advertisement is run stating that the home will be open for inspection and giving the time and date. Generally, the open house is handled by two salespeople—one who is stationed at the front door, and another at the back door or in the kitchen. When prospects come in, they are treated as guests and shown the house. If the open house is run properly, the salespeople are able to obtain a list of prospects, not only for the house shown, but for other listings if the house shown does not happen to meet the needs and requirements of the prospects.

Tenants. Real estate brokers who operate management departments as well as selling departments become known to a great many people. At least once a month, the tenants call at the management office, and most of these tenants sincerely desire to own their own homes one day. Property managers, if doing the job well, are acquainted with the financial status of the tenants. Tenants often discuss their personal problems with the property manager, and the firm may have listings suitable for particular tenants who desire to own their own homes.

Often tenants will become prospects for investment or commercial properties. By promoting good public relations with the tenants, brokers will have a ready source of prospects.

Personal Contacts. There is no question but that successful brokers, especially in small towns, must sacrifice a certain amount of family life. Brokers must keep up contacts and should take part in civic affairs. Although these contacts are time-consuming, it is through them that brokers find many prospects.

The sources of prospects are infinite, and successful brokers are quick to recognize situations that lead to purchasers. Brokers should never forget, or let other people forget, that they are real estate brokers. As brokers, there are services to perform; therefore, they should become acquainted with as many people as possible. It is a good policy to try to inform at least four people a day that you are in real estate. It is surprising the number of additional prospects that can be developed from these new contacts.

Qualifying Prospects

The essence of qualifying prospects is to determine their needs and to match those needs with the listings in the office. It must first be determined, however, if prospects are real prospects, or if they are "shoppers." The latter should be quickly identified and no time wasted on them.

The obvious things to determine are names, addresses, the business in which they are engaged, whether they are married and have children, and the number of children in each family.

Do they have the money with which to purchase a home? The answer to this question is most difficult to obtain from a prospect.

Where would the prospect like to live? What church is preferred? These and many other questions of a personal nature are important to the broker in qualifying the prospect.

With the above information, the broker can proceed with the sale. The broker now has an idea of the neighborhood in which the prospect wishes to live, an idea of the price the prospect can afford to pay, and the size of the house the prospect needs. If there are children at home, it will have to be near a school or close to a school bus stop. From the qualifications of the prospect, the broker has partially determined the prospect's needs—unless the prospect has misrepresented facts.

The broker should have readily available the listings in the files that fit these requirements. They should be considered in terms of the *needs* of the prospect and which of the listings best fits the bill. They should be categorized in the best order possible. Perhaps the broker has learned from the prospect that a brick house is preferred to a frame house. After having thus analyzed the prospect's needs, the time has come for the broker actually to show the property. In this case, the broker should first show the brick house that best fits the prospect's needs in relation to the other factors.

Showing the Property

Prospects should be shown property under the most favorable circumstances. If the property is occupied, it would be well to make sure the present occupants are ready to receive visitors. If possible, the prospect and members of the family should be shown the property together; otherwise, several additional trips to the property may be necessary.

One important factor in making a sale is appearance. Not only is the appearance of the salesperson important, but also the appearance of the salesperson's car. It should be clean and uncluttered.

On the way to the property, the broker should refrain from discussing the property unless the prospect has asked specific questions in regard to the property itself. Presumably, the broker is completely prepared, having gained a thorough knowledge of the product (listing) that is being offered for sale. If the prospect should ask questions concerning the property, the broker is prepared to answer these questions in detail. If the prospect is a stranger to the city, the broker can talk about the city, the cultural advantages, the beautiful scenery, the good fishing nearby, and any other thing that will point up the city advantageously. If the prospect is familiar with the city, then the neighborhood in which the listing is located may be discussed. If the prospect has children, the broker can drive past the school to show its location in relation to the home that is about to be shown.

After arriving at the home to be shown, the broker should not park the car directly in front of the property. By parking a few doors away and letting the prospect walk to the house and up the front walk, the prospect is given the feel of the neighborhood—a feeling of belonging.

Once in the house, the broker or salesperson should talk very little. Too many sales are ruined by salespeople who talk themselves out of a sale. If the prospect asks questions, the salesperson should answer them thoroughly and intelligently.

If the prospect seems dissatisfied with the property, then the prospect should be shown another property that will perhaps be more satisfactory. If at all possible, the prospect should not be shown more than two or three homes at one time, or there will be too much possibility of confusion arising in the prospect's mind. The good salesperson will be able to sense the one property out of the three shown that appeals most to the prospect. This ability to sense the right property, and consequently, the one to concentrate on, is done not by some mystic sixth sense, but by getting the prospect to talk. Generally, a prospect will reveal likes or dislikes about a certain property. If the prospect indicates a desire to wait and think it over, the salesperson should be sure to follow up and give prospect a call as soon as possible after having had a chance to decide on a course of action.

Key Actions for Successful Selling

Dr. Charles L. Lapp, professor of marketing at the Washington (St. Louis) University School of Business, suggests six key actions for someone to become successful at real estate sales:[4]

1. Have the proper viewpoint toward selling. Consider yourself a professional . . . and sell like a professional. Also have the proper viewpoint toward your superiors. Selling is a real art and being an art, salespeople should perfect their persuasive know-how through more practice.

[4]*Realtor's Headlines* 39, no. 2 (January 1972).

2. Be organized to utilize your time and talents most effectively. Put some time on pre-call planning and specific pre-approach analysis to improve your face-to-face selling.
3. Conduct your sales interview professionally. Sell your product properly and then ask the person to buy. Improve each phase of your sales interview from approach through follow-up activities.
4. Use tested selling strategies such as eye control, hesitating, and questioning. The "yes, but" technique should be replaced by the "I know how you feel, others have felt the same way, and now our customers have found thus and thus," technique.
5. Follow some fine lines in your face-to-face selling such as being effectively persuasive and ineffectively high pressure; being effectively persistent and ineffectively a pest; and being effectively creative and ineffectively accused of trickery.
6. Set up a program of self-analysis and self-improvement. You might, during a six-week period, learn at least five selling points; set up a work pattern for more efficiently covering existing clients; make a pre-call analysis of prospects; and read one book on selling or real estate every six weeks.
7. Make it a point to professionalize your selling by practice . . . practice . . . and more practice.

Closing the Sale

Closing the sale is the logical conclusion of all that has gone before. The proper listing, the proper qualification of the prospect, the proper showing of the property are all concluded in the closing. It is difficult to determine when the psychological moment has arrived. Most buyers have a fearful moment before they are ready to sign the sales agreement. The broker might ask the prospect when it would be convenient to take possession of the property and thus prod the prospect into action. The broker should be calm and unafraid of the prospect's reaction to the gentle prodding.

The prospect may not be willing to offer the listed price. If a price lower than the listed price is offered, accept it and explain that you will communicate the offer to the seller. Try to obtain as large a down payment as possible, especially if the offer is less than the listed price. The larger the down payment, the easier it will be to convince the seller of the sincerity of the offer and the more difficult it will be for the buyer to back out of the deal. Too many transactions are lost after a contract has been signed because only a small deposit has been made.

When the time comes for the signing of the earnest money receipt and purchase agreement, explain the agreement in detail to prevent later discussion and misunderstanding. In those states in which the broker does not fill in the sales agreement, tell the purchaser that the binder will be delivered to the attorney for the seller who will draw the contract. Explain, too, that this formal contract can be read by the attorney for the purchaser and that the attorney will see that the transaction is carried through smoothly to completion.

The do's and don't's for a real estate closing are presented in Exhibit 26-5.

Follow-up Services

Future listings, sales, and success are dependent to a large degree on client satisfaction. A good broker does not end the client relationship after closing the sale. Post-closing follow-up ensures a smooth transition from the buyer's old residence to the new home. Service-conscious brokers may provide their customers with applications for checking accounts, credit cards, utility connections, etc.

The following is a suggested list of **follow-up services** brokers may provide their clients:

1. Process utility application and ensure hook-up.
2. Provide school transfer forms.
3. Process phone application and arrange installation.

Exhibit 26-5 Do's and Don't's of Closings

Do's

1. Maintain a friendly attitude at the close; avoid arguments by being friendly even though there will be minor disagreements.
2. Before closing, be sure that you have the necessary deposit receipts, pens, and forms.
3. Realize that begging for a sale looks bad and turns the prospect away.
4. Ask the prospect to approve the offer instead of asking the prospect to sign.
5. Make it possible for the prospect to reach an easy decision.
6. Close in a protected setting. Avoid interrupting phone calls or other distractions.
7. Treat each prospect as you would your listings. Direct the closing to the prospect's preferences.
8. Lead the prospect to think as an owner of the new home you show.

Don't's

1. Don't let the prospect know how much closing the sale means to you.
2. Don't apologize about the listed house or its price.
3. Don't make promises (written or oral) that you cannot fulfill.
4. Don't make the closing a formal ceremony that may scare the prospect.
5. Don't ask the prospect questions that can be answered with a no—that closes the door.
6. Don't make it difficult for the prospect to execute the closing quickly; once having decided, some prospects wish to expedite the formalities and make other plans.
7. Don't make it easier to reject the sale than to buy.

SOURCE: William M. Shenkel, Marketing Real Estate, *2d ed. (Englewood Cliffs, N.J.: Prentice-Hall, Inc., 1985), 215.*

4. Obtain post office change-of-address kit.
5. Provide local store charge account applications.
6. Process motor vehicle and drivers license applications.
7. Provide medical records transfer forms.
8. Secure garbage collection services.
9. Furnish local maps showing the location of churches, schools, and shopping.
10. Contact client on moving day (arrival day) to offer assistance and ensure that everything is progressing satisfactorily.

GLOSSARY

Advertising media The means by which an advertisement is presented to the public

Buying motives Reasons why people buy

Copy The plotting and writing of an advertisement

Copy block In advertising, the width of the copy

Emotional motives Those reasons that lead a person to react in a certain way in response to a specific set of stimuli without consciously bringing into play logical analysis of the situation

Follow-up services Assistance to new buyers with applications for checking accounts, utility hook-ups, etc.

Goodwill advertisement An advertisement with the primary purpose of presenting and keeping the broker's name before the public

Institutional advertisement A joint advertisement done by a board or group whose primary purpose is to promote confidence in the board or group, or to promote confidence in a particular community

Layout The form in which a final advertisement will appear

Novelties A form of advertising, e.g., calendars, record books, etc.

Open house A selling device whereby the public is invited to inspect a furnished home

Rational motives Those reasons for buying that involve a form of conscious reasoning

Release Information sent to newspapers for publication

Specific advertisement An advertisement written and designed to sell a particular property

White space Space not covered with copy in an advertisement

QUESTIONS FOR REVIEW

1. What are the two functions of real estate advertising?
2. How is outdoor advertising usually used by a real estate broker?
3. Why is it important that a publicity release be newsworthy?
4. Discuss the general rules of advertising.
5. Distinguish between rational and emotional motives in advertising and give three examples of each.
6. Why should the advertising of investment properties be of the rational type?
7. What is meant by the cumulative effect of advertising?
8. Why is knowledge of the listing (product) important in selling real estate?
9. What is meant by qualifying a prospect?
10. Why should the broker be interested in determining the needs of a prospect?
11. How does one help a prospect buy?
12. Why should a salesperson attempt to obtain as large a down payment as possible when closing a sale?

PROBLEMS AND ACTIVITIES

1. Listed below are several typical lines of copy from real estate ads. For each line of copy identify the market segment you feel the copy would be most likely to reach; identify the appeal that makes the copy effective; or rewrite the copy to make it more effective.
   a. $300 total closing costs with VA financing.
   b. If you're handy with tools, here's an older home you can have fun with.
   c. Economy plus luxury. An excellent buy at only $84,500.
   d. Five bedrooms. Close to schools and parks. Excellent home for a growing family.
   e. If you really want to get the maximum square footage for the money, you must see this two-story beauty.
   f. At the end of a dead-end street.
2. Following are some of the factors a broker should analyze in terms of the prospect's needs in qualifying a prospect for a particular property. Study the list, then add other factors that should be included.

a. What kind of construction does the prospect desire? (Brick, frame, other?)
b. One story or two story? (Maybe the prospect is ill and cannot, on doctor's orders, climb stairs.)
c. Can the husband drive? Can the wife drive? (Silly? But suppose the wife cannot drive, and they have to be near transportation.)
d. Children? (Boys, girls, ages?) (This is important because the prospect may want to be reasonably near schools or a school bus. It may also determine the number of rooms necessary.)
e. If the prospect rents, how much rent is being paid? (You are trying to get an idea of the amount of monthly payment the prospect can afford. This, of course, doesn't tell the whole story.)
f. Amount of maximum down payment available? (This is the question that can often make or break a deal.)
g. Church preference? (Prospect would probably prefer a location near this church.)
h. Any preferred location? (Prospect's friends might be located in one section of town and therefore this section may be most desirable.)

3. In selling real property, the prospect is apt to offer objections. Some will be serious and some can be ignored by the salesperson. Following are several common objections to buying. Examine them and offer counter-arguments or suggestions to overcome the objections.

   a. Prospect looks at a home, shakes his or her head sadly. "I like it," the prospect says, "but I'm afraid of business conditions. I think the market is going to drop. If I wait, I won't lose any money."
   b. "It's a good home," the prospect declares, "but the price is too high."
   c. "I rather like the property," the prospect says, "but I'd like to talk it over with a friend and see what she says about it."

APPENDICES

APPENDIX A

Code of Ethics and Standards of Practice

of the

NATIONAL ASSOCIATION OF REALTORS®

Where the word REALTOR® is used in this Code and Preamble, it shall be deemed to include REALTOR-ASSOCIATE®. Pronouns shall be considered to include REALTORS® and REALTOR-ASSOCIATE®s of both genders.

Preamble...

Under all is the land. Upon its wise utilization and widely allocated ownership depend the survival and growth of free institutions and of our civilization. The REALTOR® should recognize that the interests of the nation and its citizens require the highest and best use of the land and the widest distribution of land ownership. They require the creation of adequate housing, the building of functioning cities, the development of productive industries and farms, and the preservation of a healthful environment.

Such interests impose obligations beyond those of ordinary commerce. They impose grave social responsibility and a patriotic duty to which the REALTOR® should dedicate himself, and for which he should be diligent in preparing himself. The REALTOR®, therefore, is zealous to maintain and improve the standards of his calling and shares with his fellow REALTORS® a common responsibility for its integrity and honor. The term REALTOR® has come to connote competency, fairness, and high integrity resulting from adherence to a lofty ideal of moral conduct in business relations. No inducement of profit and no instruction from clients ever can justify departure from this ideal.

In the interpretation of this obligation, a REALTOR® can take no safer guide than that which has been handed down through the centuries, embodied in the Golden Rule, "Whatsoever ye would that men should do to you, do ye even so to them."

Accepting this standard as his own, every REALTOR® pledges himself to observe its spirit in all of his activities and to conduct his business in accordance with the tenets set forth below.

Articles 1 through 5 are aspirational and establish ideals the REALTOR® should strive to attain.

ARTICLE 1

The REALTOR® should keep himself informed on matters affecting real estate in his community, the state, and nation so that he may be able to contribute responsibly to public thinking on such matters.

ARTICLE 2

In justice to those who place their interests in his care, the REALTOR® should endeavor always to be informed regarding laws, proposed legislation, governmental regulations, public policies, and current market conditions in order to be in a position to advise his clients properly.

ARTICLE 3

The REALTOR® should endeavor to eliminate in his community any practices which could be damaging to the public or bring discredit to the real estate profession. The REALTOR® should assist the governmental agency charged with regulating the practices of brokers and salesmen in his state. (Amended 11/87)

ARTICLE 4

To prevent dissension and misunderstanding and to assure better service to the owner, the REALTOR® should urge the exclusive listing of property unless contrary to the best interest of the owner. (Amended 11/87)

ARTICLE 5

In the best interests of society, of his associates, and his own business, the REALTOR® should willingly share with other REALTORS® the lessons of his experience and study for the benefit of the public, and should be loyal to the Board of REALTORS® of his community and active in its work.

Articles 6 through 23 establish specific obligations. Failure to observe these requirements subjects the REALTOR® to disciplinary action.

ARTICLE 6

The REALTOR® shall seek no unfair advantage over other REALTORS® and shall conduct his business so as to avoid controversies with other REALTORS®. (Amended 11/87)

- **Standard of Practice 6-1**
  The REALTOR® shall not misrepresent the availability of access to show or inspect a listed property. (Cross-reference Article 22.) (Amended 11/87)

ARTICLE 7

In accepting employment as an agent, the REALTOR® pledges himself to protect and promote the interests of the client. This obligation of absolute fidelity to the client's interests is primary, but it does not relieve the REALTOR® of the obligation to treat fairly all parties to the transaction.

- **Standard of Practice 7-1**
  Unless precluded by law, government rule or regulation, or agreed otherwise in writing, the REALTOR® shall submit to the seller all offers until closing. Unless the REALTOR® and the seller agree otherwise, the REALTOR® shall not be obligated to continue to market the property after an offer has been accepted. Unless the subsequent offer is contingent upon the termination of an existing contract, the REALTOR® shall recommend that the seller obtain the advice of legal counsel prior to acceptance. (Cross-reference Article 17.) (Amended 5/87)

- **Standard of Practice 7-2**
  The REALTOR®, acting as listing broker, shall submit all offers to the seller as quickly as possible.

- **Standard of Practice 7-3**
  The REALTOR®, in attempting to secure a listing, shall not deliberately mislead the owner as to market value.

• Standard of Practice 7-4

(Refer to Standard of Practice 22-1, which also relates to Article 7, Code of Ethics.)

• Standard of Practice 7-5

(Refer to Standard of Practice 22-2, which also relates to Article 7, Code of Ethics.)

• Standard of Practice 7-6

The REALTOR®, when acting as a principal in a real estate transaction, cannot avoid his responsibilities under the Code of Ethics.

ARTICLE 8

The REALTOR® shall not accept compensation from more than one party, even if permitted by law, without the full knowledge of all parties to the transaction.

ARTICLE 9

The REALTOR® shall avoid exaggeration, misrepresentation, or concealment of pertinent facts relating to the property or the transaction. The REALTOR® shall not, however, be obligated to discover latent defects in the property or to advise on matters outside the scope of his real estate license. (Amended 11/86)

• Standard of Practice 9-1

The REALTOR® shall not be a party to the naming of a false consideration in any document, unless it be the naming of an obviously nominal consideration.

• Standard of Practice 9-2

(Refer to Standard of Practice 21-3, which also relates to Article 9, Code of Ethics.)

• Standard of Practice 9-3

(Refer to Standard of Practice 7-3, which also relates to Article 9, Code of Ethics.)

• Standard of Practice 9-4

The REALTOR® shall not offer a service described as "free of charge" when the rendering of a service is contingent on the obtaining of a benefit such as a listing or commission.

• Standard of Practice 9-5

The REALTOR® shall, with respect to the subagency of another REALTOR®, timely communicate any change of compensation for subagency services to the other REALTOR® prior to the time such REALTOR® produces a prospective buyer who has signed an offer to purchase the property for which the subagency has been offered through MLS or otherwise by the listing agency.

• Standard of Practice 9-6

REALTORS® shall disclose their REALTOR® status when seeking information from another REALTOR® concerning real property for which the other REALTOR® is an agent or subagent.

• Standard of Practice 9-7

The offering of premiums, prizes, merchandise discounts or other inducements to list or sell is not, in itself, unethical even if receipt of the benefit is contingent on listing or purchasing through the REALTOR® making the offer. However, the REALTOR® must exercise care and candor in any such advertising or other public or private representations so that any party interested in receiving or otherwise benefiting from the REALTOR®'s offer will have clear, thorough, advance understanding of all the terms and conditions of the offer. The offering of any inducements to do business is subject to the limitations and restrictions of state law and the ethical obligations established by Article 9, as interpreted by any applicable Standard of Practice. (Adopted 11/84)

• Standard of Practice 9-8

The REALTOR® shall be obligated to discover and disclose adverse factors reasonably apparent to someone with expertise in only those areas required by their real estate licensing authority. Article 9 does not impose upon the REALTOR® the obligation of expertise in other professional or technical disciplines. (Cross-reference Article 11.) (Amended 11/86)

ARTICLE 10

The REALTOR® shall not deny equal professional services to any person for reasons of race, color, religion, sex, handicap, familial status, or national origin. The REALTOR® shall not be party to any plan or agreement to discriminate against a person or persons on the basis of race, color, religion, sex, handicap, familial status, or national origin. (Amended 11/89)

ARTICLE 11

A REALTOR® is expected to provide a level of competent service in keeping with the standards of practice in those fields in which the REALTOR® customarily engages.

The REALTOR® shall not undertake to provide specialized professional services concerning a type of property or service that is outside his field of competence unless he engages the assistance of one who is competent on such types of property or service, or unless the facts are fully disclosed to the client. Any person engaged to provide such assistance shall be so identified to the client and his contribution to the assignment should be set forth.

The REALTOR® shall refer to the Standards of Practice of the National Association as to the degree of competence that a client has a right to expect the REALTOR® to possess, taking into consideration the complexity of the problem, the availability of expert assistance, and the opportunities for experience available to the REALTOR®.

• Standard of Practice 11-1

Whenever a REALTOR® submits an oral or written opinion of the value of real property for a fee, his opinion shall be supported by a memorandum in his file or an appraisal report, either of which shall include as a minimum the following:

1. Limiting conditions
2. Any existing or contemplated interest
3. Defined value
4. Date applicable
5. The estate appraised
6. A description of the property
7. The basis of the reasoning including applicable market data and/or capitalization computation

This report or memorandum shall be available to the Professional Standards Committee for a period of at least two years (beginning subsequent to final determination of the court if the appraisal is involved in litigation) to ensure compliance with Article 11 of the Code of Ethics of the NATIONAL ASSOCIATION OF REALTORS®.

• Standard of Practice 11-2

The REALTOR® shall not undertake to make an appraisal when his employment or fee is contingent upon the amount of appraisal.

- **Standard of Practice 11-3**

REALTORS® engaged in real estate securities and syndications transactions are engaged in an activity subject to regulations beyond those governing real estate transactions generally, and therefore have the affirmative obligation to be informed of applicable federal and state laws, and rules and regulations regarding these types of transactions.

ARTICLE 12

The REALTOR® shall not undertake to provide professional services concerning a property or its value where he has a present or contemplated interest unless such interest is specifically disclosed to all affected parties.

- **Standard of Practice 12-1**

(Refer to Standards of Practice 9-4 and 16-1, which also relate to Article 12, Code of Ethics.) (Amended 5/84)

ARTICLE 13

The REALTOR® shall not acquire an interest in or buy for himself, any member of his immediate family, his firm or any member thereof, or any entity in which he has a substantial ownership interest, property listed with him, without making the true position known to the listing owner. In selling property owned by himself, or in which he has any interest, the REALTOR® shall reveal the facts of his ownership or interest to the purchaser.

- **Standard of Practice 13-1**

For the protection of all parties, the disclosures required by Article 13 shall be in writing and provided by the REALTOR® prior to the signing of any contract. (Adopted 2/86)

ARTICLE 14

In the event of a controversy between REALTORS® associated with different firms, arising out of their relationship as REALTORS®, the REALTORS® shall submit the dispute to arbitration in accordance with the regulations of their Board or Boards rather than litigate the matter.

- **Standard of Practice 14-1**

The filing of litigation and refusal to withdraw from it by a REALTOR® in an arbitrable matter constitutes a refusal to arbitrate. (Adopted 2/86)

- **Standard of Practice 14-2**

The obligation to arbitrate mandated by Article 14 includes arbitration requests initiated by the REALTOR®'s client. (Adopted 5/87)

- **Standard of Practice 14-3**

Article 14 does not require a REALTOR® to arbitrate in those circumstances when all parties to the dispute advise the Board in writing that they choose not to arbitrate before the Board. (Adopted 5/88)

ARTICLE 15

If charged with unethical practice or asked to present evidence or to cooperate in any other way, in any disciplinary proceeding or investigation, the REALTOR® shall place all pertinent facts before the proper tribunal of the Member Board or affiliated institute, society, or council in which membership is held and shall take no action to disrupt or obstruct such processes. (Amended 11/89)

- **Standard of Practice 15-1**

The REALTOR® shall not be subject to disciplinary proceedings in more than one Board of REALTORS® with respect to alleged violations of the Code of Ethics relating to the same transaction.

- **Standard of Practice 15-2**

The REALTOR® shall not make any unauthorized disclosure or dissemination of the allegations, findings, or decision developed in connection with an ethics hearing or appeal. (Adopted 5/84)

- **Standard of Practice 15-3**

The REALTOR® shall not obstruct the Board's investigative or disciplinary proceedings by instituting or threatening to institute actions for libel, slander or defamation against any party to a professional standards proceeding or their witnesses. (Adopted 11/87)

- **Standard of Practice 15-4**

The REALTOR® shall not intentionally impede the Board's investigative or disciplinary proceedings by filing multiple ethics complaints based on the same event or transaction. (Adopted 11/88)

ARTICLE 16

When acting as agent, the REALTOR® shall not accept any commission, rebate, or profit on expenditures made for his principal-owner, without the principal's knowledge and consent.

- **Standard of Practice 16-1**

The REALTOR® shall not recommend or suggest to a client or a customer the use of services of another organization or business entity in which he has a direct interest without disclosing such interest at the time of the recommendation or suggestion. (Amended 5/88)

- **Standard of Practice 16-2**

When acting as an agent or subagent, the REALTOR® shall disclose to a client or customer if there is any financial benefit or fee the REALTOR® or the REALTOR®'s firm may receive as a direct result of having recommended real estate products or services (e.g., homeowner's insurance, warranty programs, mortgage financing, title insurance, etc.) other than real estate referral fees. (Adopted 5/88)

ARTICLE 17

The REALTOR® shall not engage in activities that constitute the unauthorized practice of law and shall recommend that legal counsel be obtained when the interest of any party to the transaction requires it.

ARTICLE 18

The REALTOR® shall keep in a special account in an appropriate financial institution, separated from his own funds, monies coming into his possession in trust for other persons, such as escrows, trust funds, clients' monies, and other like items.

ARTICLE 19

The REALTOR® shall be careful at all times to present a true picture in his advertising and representations to the public. The REALTOR® shall also ensure that his status as a broker or a REALTOR® is clearly identifiable in any such advertising. (Amended 11/86)

• Standard of Practice 19-1

The REALTOR® shall not submit or advertise property without authority, and in any offering, the price quoted shall not be other than that agreed upon with the owners.

• Standard of Practice 19-2

(Refer to Standard of Practice 9-4, which also relates to Article 19, Code of Ethics.)

• Standard of Practice 19-3

The REALTOR®, when advertising unlisted real property for sale in which he has an ownership interest, shall disclose his status as both an owner and as a REALTOR® or real estate licensee. (Adopted 5/85)

• Standard of Practice 19-4

The REALTOR® shall not advertise nor permit any person employed by or affiliated with him to advertise listed property without disclosing the name of the firm. (Adopted 11/86)

• Standard of Practice 19-5

Only the REALTOR®, as listing broker, may claim to have "sold" the property, even when the sale resulted through the cooperative efforts of another broker. However, after transactions have closed, the listing broker may not prohibit successful cooperating brokers from advertising their "cooperation," "participation," or "assistance" in the transaction, or from making similar representations.

Only the listing broker is entitled to use the term "sold" on signs, in advertisements, and in other public representations. (Amended 11/89)

ARTICLE 20

The REALTOR®, for the protection of all parties, shall see that financial obligations and commitments regarding real estate transactions are in writing, expressing the exact agreement of the parties. A copy of each agreement shall be furnished to each party upon his signing such agreement.

• Standard of Practice 20-1

At the time of signing or initialing, the REALTOR® shall furnish to the party a copy of any document signed or initialed. (Adopted 5/86)

• Standard of Practice 20-2

For the protection of all parties, the REALTOR® shall use reasonable care to ensure that documents pertaining to the purchase and sale of real estate are kept current through the use of written extensions or amendments. (Adopted 5/86)

ARTICLE 21

The REALTOR® shall not engage in any practice or take any action inconsistent with the agency of another REALTOR®.

• Standard of Practice 21-1

Signs giving notice of property for sale, rent, lease, or exchange shall not be placed on property without the consent of the owner.

• Standard of Practice 21-2

The REALTOR® obtaining information from a listing broker about a specific property shall not convey this information to, nor invite the cooperation of a third party broker without the consent of the listing broker.

• Standard of Practice 21-3

The REALTOR® shall not solicit a listing which is currently listed exclusively with another broker. However, if the listing broker, when asked by the REALTOR®, refuses to disclose the expiration date and nature of such listing; i.e., an exclusive right to sell, an exclusive agency, open listing, or other form of contractual agreement between the listing broker and his client, the REALTOR®, unless precluded by law, may contact the owner to secure such information and may discuss the terms upon which he might take a future listing or, alternatively, may take a listing to become effective upon expiration of any existing exclusive listing. (Amended 11/86)

• Standard of Practice 21-4

The REALTOR® shall not use information obtained by him from the listing broker, through offers to cooperate received through Multiple Listing Services or other sources authorized by the listing broker, for the purpose of creating a referral prospect to a third broker, or for creating a buyer prospect unless such use is authorized by the listing broker.

• Standard of Practice 21-5

The fact that a property has been listed exclusively with a REALTOR® shall not preclude or inhibit any other REALTOR® from soliciting such listing after its expiration.

• Standard of Practice 21-6

The fact that a property owner has retained a REALTOR® as his exclusive agent in respect of one or more past transactions creates no interest or agency which precludes or inhibits other REALTORS® from seeking such owner's future business.

• Standard of Practice 21-7

The REALTOR® shall be free to list property which is "open listed" at any time, but shall not knowingly obligate the seller to pay more than one commission except with the seller's knowledgeable consent. (Cross-reference Article 7.) (Amended 5/88)

• Standard of Practice 21-8

When a REALTOR® is contacted by an owner regarding the sale of property that is exclusively listed with another broker, and the REALTOR® has not directly or indirectly initiated the discussion, unless precluded by law, the REALTOR® may discuss the terms upon which he might take a future listing or, alternatively, may take a listing to become effective upon expiration of any existing exclusive listing. (Amended 11/86)

• Standard of Practice 21-9

In cooperative transactions a REALTOR® shall compensate the cooperating REALTOR® (principal broker) and shall not compensate nor offer to compensate, directly or indirectly, any of the sales licensees employed by or affiliated with another REALTOR® without the prior express knowledge and consent of the cooperating broker.

• Standard of Practice 21-10

Article 21 does not preclude REALTORS® from making general announcements to property owners describing their services and the terms of their availability even though some recipients may have exclusively listed their property for sale or lease with another REALTOR®. A general telephone canvass, general mailing or distribution addressed to all property owners in a given geographical area or in a given profession, business, club, or organization, or other classification or group is deemed "general" for purposes of this standard.

Article 21 is intended to recognize as unethical two basic types of solicitation:

First, telephone or personal solicitations of property owners who have been identified by a real estate sign, multiple listing compilation, or other information service as having exclusively listed their property with another REALTOR®; and

Second, mail or other forms of written solicitations of property owners whose properties are exclusively listed with another REALTOR® when such solicitations are not part of a general mailing but are directed specifically to property owners identified through compilations of current listings, "for sale" signs, or other sources of information required by Article 22 and Multiple Listing Service rules to be made available to other REALTORS® under offers of subagency or cooperation. (Adopted 11/83)

- **Standard of Practice 21-11**

The REALTOR®, prior to accepting a listing, has an affirmative obligation to make reasonable efforts to determine whether the property is subject to a current, valid exclusive listing agreement. (Adopted 11/83)

- **Standard of Practice 21-12**

The REALTOR®, acting as the agent of the buyer, shall disclose that relationship to the seller's agent at first contact. (Cross-reference Article 7.) (Adopted 5/88)

- **Standard of Practice 21-13**

On unlisted property, the REALTOR®, acting as the agent of a buyer, shall disclose that relationship to the seller at first contact. (Cross-reference Article 7.) (Adopted 5/88)

- **Standard of Practice 21-14**

The REALTOR®, acting as agent of the seller or as subagent of the listing broker, shall disclose that relationship to buyers as soon as practicable. (Adopted 5/88)

- **Standard of Practice 21-15**

Article 21 does not preclude a REALTOR® from contacting the client of another broker for the purpose of offering to provide, or entering into a contract to provide, a different type of real estate service unrelated to the type of service currently being provided (e.g., property management as opposed to brokerage). However, information received through a Multiple Listing Service or any other offer of cooperation may not be used to target the property owners to whom such offers to provide services are made. (Adopted 2/89)

- **Standard of Practice 21-16**

The REALTOR®, acting as subagent or buyer's agent, shall not use the terms of an offer to purchase to attempt to modify the listing broker's offer of compensation to subagents or buyer's agents nor make the submission of an executed offer to purchase contingent on the listing broker's agreement to modify the offer of compensation. (Adopted 2/89)

ARTICLE 22

In the sale of property which is exclusively listed with a REALTOR®, the REALTOR® shall utilize the services of other brokers upon mutually agreed upon terms when it is in the best interests of the client.

Negotiations concerning property which is listed exclusively shall be carried on with the listing broker, not with the owner, except with the consent of the listing broker.

- **Standard of Practice 22-1**

It is the obligation of the selling broker as subagent of the listing broker to disclose immediately all pertinent facts to the listing broker prior to as well as after the contract is executed.

- **Standard of Practice 22-2**

The REALTOR®, when submitting offers to the seller, shall present each in an objective and unbiased manner.

- **Standard of Practice 22-3**

The REALTOR® shall disclose the existence of an accepted offer to any broker seeking cooperation. (Adopted 5/86)

- **Standard of Practice 22-4**

The REALTOR®, acting as exclusive agent of the seller, establishes the terms and conditions of offers to cooperate. Unless expressly indicated in offers to cooperate made through MLS or otherwise, a cooperating broker may not assume that the offer of cooperation includes an offer of compensation. Entitlement to compensation in a cooperative transaction must be agreed upon between a listing and cooperating broker prior to the time an offer to purchase the property is produced. (Adopted 11/88)

ARTICLE 23

The REALTOR® shall not publicly disparage the business practice of a competitor nor volunteer an opinion of a competitor's transaction. If his opinion is sought and if the REALTOR® deems it appropriate to respond, such opinion shall be rendered with strict professional integrity and courtesy.

The Code of Ethics was adopted in 1913. Amended at the Annual Convention in 1924, 1928, 1950, 1951, 1952, 1955, 1956, 1961, 1962, 1974, 1982, 1986, 1987, and 1989.

EXPLANATORY NOTES (Revised 11/88)

The reader should be aware of the following policies which have been approved by the Board of Directors of the National Association:

In filing a charge of an alleged violation of the Code of Ethics by a REALTOR®, the charge shall read as an alleged violation of one or more Articles of the Code. A Standard of Practice may only be cited in support of the charge.

The Standards of Practice are not an integral part of the Code but rather serve to clarify the ethical obligations imposed by the various Articles. The Standards of Practice supplement, and do not substitute for, the Case Interpretations in *Interpretations of the Code of Ethics.*

Modifications to existing Standards of Practice and additional new Standards of Practice are approved from time to time. The reader is cautioned to ensure that the most recent publications are utilized.

Articles 1 through 5 are aspirational and establish ideals that a REALTOR® should strive to attain. Recognizing their subjective nature, these Articles shall not be used as the bases for charges of alleged unethical conduct or as the bases for disciplinary action.

Form No. 166-288-2 (11/89)

APPENDIX B

TABLE OF STATE REQUIREMENTS FOR BROKERS AND SALES PERSONNEL

Real estate exams are required in all states in order for a broker or salesperson to become licensed. They are made up in one of six ways:

1. American College Testing Program (ACT)
2. Educational Testing Service (ETS)
3. Staff- or commission-designated exams
4. University-designated exams
5. Assessment Systems, Inc. (ASI)
6. American Guidance Service (AGS)

Salespersons' exams consist of:

1. Real estate contracts .... (26%)
2. Tenancy .... (20%)
3. Real estate ownership .... (19%)
4. Real estate brokerage .... (20%)
5. Real estate valuation .... (15%)

Brokers' exams consist of:

1. Real estate instruments .... (30%)
2. Basic elements of real estate value, deeds, and contracts (20%)
3. Leases, property management, and real estate finance (20%)
4. Legal and governmental aspects of real estate .... (10%)
5. Arithmetic functions .... (20%)

The table on the following pages shows education and experience requirements and examination for brokers and salespersons in all 50 states.

STATE	EDUCATION REQUIREMENTS FOR SALESPERSON APPLICANTS	ADDITIONAL EDUCATION REQUIREMENTS FOR BROKER APPLICANTS	EXPERIENCE REQUIREMENTS FOR BROKER APPLICANTS	EXAM TYPE	REQUIRED CONTINUING EDUCATION
ALABAMA	45-hour course	225-hour course, or college major in RE	2 years as salesperson, full-time within last 3 years	ACT	None
ALASKA	None	None	2 years active as salesperson in past 4 years	ETS	None
ARIZONA	45 classroom hours pre-license + 6 hours within 90 days	90 classroom hours	3 years experience as salesperson within past 5 years	ASI	12 classroom hours per year
ARKANSAS	None to take exam; 30-hour course completed within 1 year from passing exam	30 classroom hours	2 years	ASI	None
CALIFORNIA	135 classroom hours, 45 pre-license + 90 within 18 months	225 classroom hours	2 years full-time experience	Staff	45 classroom hours every 4 years
COLORADO	72 classroom hours	48 classroom hours	2 years as duly licensed salesperson	ETS	None
CONNECTICUT	30 hours approved RE Principles and Practice course	60 classroom hours or 2 courses consisting of Appraisal 1, & related RE course	2 years experience as licensed RE salesperson	ETS	12 hours every 2 years or exam

DELAWARE	93 classroom hour course approved by Commission, or equivalent	90 classroom-hour course	5 years RE sales experience	ETS	15 classroom hours every 2 years
FLORIDA	63 classroom hours pre-license + 45 hours within 2 years	72 classroom hours + 60 hours within 2 years	12 months RE sales experience during preceding 5 years	Staff	14 classroom hours every 2 years
GEORGIA	60 in-class hours	60 in-class hours	3 years active salesperson	ACT	80 classroom hours first 2 years, then 6 hours every 2 years
HAWAII	40 classroom hours at accredited school or equivalent experience	46 classroom hours at accredited school or equivalent experience	2 years experience as RE salesperson or its equivalent	ETS	None
IDAHO	90 classroom hours or equivalent correspondence hours in designated RE course	90 hours classroom instruction	2 years as salesperson in state	ASI	None
ILLINOIS	30 classroom hours of instruction from approved RE school	90 hours of instruction from approved school or 4-year degree with minor in RE or license to practice law in state	1 year sales experience in past 3 years	ETS	None
INDIANA	40 classroom hours approved course	24 classroom hours of BA degree permits applicant to sit for exam	1 year sales experience	ASI	None

STATE	EDUCATION REQUIREMENTS FOR SALESPERSON APPLICANTS	ADDITIONAL EDUCATION REQUIREMENTS FOR BROKER APPLICANTS	EXPERIENCE REQUIREMENTS FOR BROKER APPLICANTS	EXAM TYPE	REQUIRED CONTINUING EDUCATION
IOWA	30 classroom-hour course	60 classroom hours	2 years experience	ACT	36 classroom hours per 3 years
KANSAS	30 classroom hours of instruction + 50 hours before first license renewal	24 additional classroom hours of instruction	2 years RE experience during 5-year period immediately preceding date of RE broker application	ASI	8 classroom hours every 2 years
KENTUCKY	96 classroom hours (6 university credit hours in real estate)	240 classroom hours	2 years RE sales experience (apprenticeship reduced to 1 year if applicant holds degree in RE	ASI	None
LOUISIANA	90 classroom hours of study or 15 university semester credits	60 classroom hours of study or 15 university semester credits	2 years as licensed RE salesperson before applying for RE broker license	ASI	15 classroom hours every 2 years
MAINE	30 classroom hours	129 classroom hours	3 year sales experience	Staff	12 classroom hours every 2 years
MARYLAND	45 clock hours of approved RE education or 3 semester hours	135 clock hours of approved RE education or 2 semester hours	3 years as licensed salesperson	ASI	12 classroom hours every 2 years

MASSACHU-SETTS	24 classroom hours	30 classroom hours	1 year as licensed salesperson	ASI	None
MICHIGAN	40 classroom hours if applicant fails first exam	90 classroom hours	3 years sales experience	ETS	6 classroom hours per year
MINNESOTA	90 classroom hours pre-license; 30 classroom hours within 1st year of licensure	30 classroom hours	2 years RE sales in state or state with similar qualifications	Staff	15 classroom hours every year
MISSISSIPPI	60 class hours	120 class hours—150 hours no experience	1 year experience as salesperson—waive with 30 class hours	ACT	None
MISSOURI	60 clock hours in Commission-approved school	80 additional clock hours in commission-approved school	1 year sales experience	ACT	12 classroom hours per year
MONTANA	60 classroom hours	60 classroom hours	2 years actively engaged as salesperson or equivalent experience as determined by Board	ETS	None
NEBRASKA	Minimum of 60 classroom hours	60 in-class hours + 2 years experience or 120 in-class hours in RE courses	2 years active licensed experience with 60 classroom hours of RE education	ACT	6 hours 1st 2-year period; then 12 hours every 2 years
NEVADA	90 classroom hours	270 hours designated RE + 600 hours in general college courses	2 years active licensed experience	ACT	20 classroom hours first 2 years; then 10 classroom hours every 2 years

STATE	EDUCATION REQUIREMENTS FOR SALESPERSON APPLICANTS	ADDITIONAL EDUCATION REQUIREMENTS FOR BROKER APPLICANTS	EXPERIENCE REQUIREMENTS FOR BROKER APPLICANTS	EXAM TYPE	REQUIRED CONTINUING EDUCATION
NEW HAMPSHIRE	None	None	1 year sales experience or 2,000 hours part-time	ETS	3 classroom hours per 2 years
NEW JERSEY	75 classroom hours	90 classroom hours RE instruction	2 years immediately before application	ASI	None
NEW MEXICO	60 classroom hours of accredited RE instruction	30 classroom hours of accredited course in RE plus 2 years as salesperson or 90 class hours	2 years sales experience or additional 60 class hours instruction	ACT	30 hours every 3 years
NEW YORK	45 classroom hours of approved RE instruction	Completion of approved 45-hour RE course	1 year active RE sales or 2 years equivalent experience	Staff	45 classroom hours
NORTH CAROLINA	30 classroom hours at approved RE school or equivalent experience	90 classroom hours at approved RE school	2 years sales experience	Staff	None
NORTH DAKOTA	30 classroom hours of RE education in first year of licensure	90 classroom hours	2 years sales experience or equivalent experience as determined by commission	ETS	24 classroom hours every 3 years
OHIO	60 classroom hours of RE education plus 60 hours within 2 years	180 classroom hours of RE education plus 2 years college	2 years experience	Staff	30 hours every 3 years after second 60 hours

OKLAHOMA	45 classroom hours	45 classroom hours	1 year sales experience	Staff	21 classroom hours every 3 years
OREGON	90 classroom hours RE instruction	60 clock hours in RE Principles, Law, and Finance	3 years sales experience within past 5 years	Staff	24 classroom hours every 2 years. After 3 renewals 12 hours every 2 years
PENNSYLVANIA	60 classroom hours in approved RE courses	240 classroom hours of RE courses approved by RE Commission	3 years sales experience or equivalent thereof	ETS	None
RHODE ISLAND	None	90 hours approved study at licensed schools	1 year sales experience	ETS	None
SOUTH CAROLINA	30 classroom hours + another 30 hours within first year of licensure	30 classroom hours	3 years sales experience or equivalent experience	College/Univ.	None
SOUTH DAKOTA	30 classroom hours	60 classroom hours	2 years sales experience	ETS	24 classroom hours every 2 years
TENNESSEE	60 class hours	60 class hours	3 years sales experience	ETS	Yes
TEXAS	180 classroom hours RE education plus 90 hours over first 3 years of licensure	630 classroom hours in general college courses	2 years sales experience in Texas during 36-month period immediately preceding filing application	Staff	None

STATE	EDUCATION REQUIREMENTS FOR SALESPERSON APPLICANTS	ADDITIONAL EDUCATION REQUIREMENTS FOR BROKER APPLICANTS	EXPERIENCE REQUIREMENTS FOR BROKER APPLICANTS	EXAM TYPE	REQUIRED CONTINUING EDUCATION
UTAH	90 classroom hours of RE Principles and Practices	120 classroom hours of RE study	3 years full-time active licensed experience or equivalent	ASI	12 classroom hours per year if inactive over 1 year
VERMONT	High school graduate—None	8 class hours	1 year sales experience	ETS	None
VIRGINIA	3 semester hours at accredited college or 45-classroom-hour course in approved proprietary school	180 classroom hours of RE education or 12 semester credit hours	36 of preceding 60 months full-time sales experience	ASI	None
WASHINGTON	30 clock hours RE education	90 clock hours RE education	2 years or equivalent experience in past 5 years	ACT	None
WEST VIRGINIA	90 classroom hours RE education	90 classroom hours RE education	2 years sales experience	Staff	None
WISCONSIN	45 classroom hours	40 classroom hours of education program approved by Examining Board	1 year sales experience	ACT	10 classroom hours every 2 years
WYOMING	30 classroom hours	30 classroom hours	2 years sales experience	ETS	60 class hours every 3 years

SOURCE: National Association of Real Estate License Law Officials, 1989 Digest of Real Estate License Laws in the United States and Canada, *Centerville, Utah.*

APPENDIX C

COMPOUND INTEREST TABLES

9% Monthly Compound Interest Table

EFFECTIVE RATE = ¾% BASE = 1.0075

MONTHS	1 AMOUNT OF 1 AT COMPOUND INTEREST $S^n = (1+i)^n$	2 ACCUMULATION OF 1 PER PERIOD $S_{\overline{n}\vert} = \frac{S^n - 1}{i}$	3 SINKING FUND FACTOR $1/S_{\overline{n}\vert} = \frac{i}{S^n - 1}$	4 PRES. VALUE OF REVERSION OF 1 $V^n = \frac{1}{S^n}$	5 PRESENT VALUE ORD. ANNUITY 1 PER PERIOD $a_{\overline{n}\vert} = \frac{1 - V^n}{i}$	6 INSTALLMENT TO AMORTIZE 1 (LOAN CONSTANT) $1/a_{\overline{n}\vert} = \frac{i}{1 - V^n}$	n MONTHS
1	1.007500	1.000000	1.000000	.992555	.992555	1.007500	1
2	1.015056	2.057000	.498132	.985167	1.977722	.505632	2
3	1.022669	3.022556	.330845	.977833	2.955556	.338345	3
4	1.030339	4.045225	.247205	.970554	3.926110	.254705	4
5	1.038066	5.075564	.197022	.963329	4.889439	.204522	5
6	1.045852	6.113631	.163568	.956158	5.845597	.171068	6
7	1.053696	7.159483	.139674	.949040	6.794637	.147174	7
8	1.061598	8.213179	.121755	.941975	7.736613	.129255	8
9	1.069560	9.274778	.107819	.934963	8.671576	.115319	9
10	1.077582	10.344339	.096671	.928003	9.599579	.104171	10
11	1.085664	11.421921	.087550	.921094	10.520674	.095050	11
YEARS							
1	1.093806	12.507586	.079951	.914238	11.434912	.087451	12
2	1.196413	26.188470	.038184	.835831	21.889146	.045684	24
3	1.308645	41.152716	.024299	.764148	31.446805	.031799	36
4	1.431405	57.520711	.017385	.698614	40.184781	.024885	48
5	1.565681	75.424136	.013258	.638699	48.173373	.020758	60
6	1.712552	95.007027	.010525	.583923	55.476848	.018025	72
7	1.873201	116.426928	.008589	.533845	62.153964	.016089	84
8	2.048921	139.856163	.007150	.488061	68.258438	.014650	96
9	2.241124	165.483222	.006042	.446204	73.839381	.013542	108
10	2.451357	193.514276	.005167	.407937	78.941692	.012667	120
11	2.681311	224.174837	.004460	.372951	83.606419	.011960	132
12	2.932836	257.711569	.003880	.340966	87.871091	.011380	144
13	3.207957	294.394278	.003396	.311724	91.770017	.010896	156
14	3.508885	334.518079	.002989	.284990	95.334563	.010489	168
15	3.838043	378.405768	.002642	.260549	98.593409	.010142	180

9% Monthly Compound Interest Table (continued)

EFFECTIVE RATE = ¾% BASE = 1.0075

YEARS	1 AMOUNT OF 1 AT COMPOUND INTEREST $S^n = (1+i)^n$	2 ACCUMULATION OF 1 PER PERIOD $S_{\overline{n}\rvert} = \frac{S^n - 1}{i}$	3 SINKING FUND FACTOR $1/S_{\overline{n}\rvert} = \frac{i}{S^n - 1}$	4 PRES. VALUE OF REVERSION OF 1 $V^n = \frac{1}{S^n}$	5 PRESENT VALUE ORD. ANNUITY 1 PER PERIOD $a_{\overline{n}\rvert} = \frac{1 - V^n}{i}$	6 INSTALLMENT TO AMORTIZE 1 (LOAN CONSTANT) $1/a_{\overline{n}\rvert} = \frac{i}{1 - V^n}$	n MONTHS
16	4.198078	426.410426	.002345	.238204	101.572769	.009845	192
17	4.591886	478.918251	.002088	.217775	104.296613	.009588	204
18	5.022637	536.351738	.001864	.199098	106.786855	.009364	216
19	5.493795	599.172746	.001668	.182023	109.063530	.009168	228
20	6.009151	667.886868	.001497	.166412	111.144953	.008997	240
21	6.572851	743.046850	.001345	.152140	113.047869	.008845	252
22	7.189430	825.257356	.001211	.139093	114.787589	.008711	264
23	7.863848	915.179775	.001092	.127164	116.378106	.008592	276
24	8.601531	1013.537537	.000986	.116258	117.832217	.008486	288
25	9.408414	1121.121935	.000891	.106287	119.161622	.008391	300
26	10.290988	1238.798492	.000807	.097172	120.377014	.008307	312
27	11.256354	1367.513922	.000731	.088838	121.488171	.008231	324
28	12.312278	1508.303747	.000662	.081219	122.504035	.008162	336
29	13.467254	1662.300628	.000601	.074254	123.432775	.008101	348
30	14.730576	1830.743479	.000546	.067886	124.281865	.008046	360
31	16.112405	2014.987432	.000496	.062063	125.058136	.007996	372
32	17.623860	2216.514738	.000451	.056741	125.767833	.007951	384
33	19.277100	2436.946695	.000410	.051875	126.416663	.007910	396
34	21.085425	2678.056691	.000373	.047426	127.009849	.007873	408
35	23.063383	2941.784467	.000339	.043358	127.552164	.007839	420
36	25.226887	3230.251727	.000309	.039640	128.047967	.007809	432
37	27.593344	3545.779207	.000282	.036240	128.501249	.007782	444
38	30.181790	3890.905340	.000257	.033132	128.915658	.007757	456
39	33.013050	4268.406685	.000234	.030291	129.294525	.007734	468
40	36.109901	4681.320260	.000213	.027693	129.640901	.007713	480
41	39.497259	5132.967977	.000194	.025318	129.957571	.007694	492
42	43.202375	5626.983364	.000177	.023146	130.247083	.007677	504
43	47.255056	6167.340803	.000162	.021161	130.511766	.007662	516
44	51.687906	6758.387497	.000147	.019346	130.753748	.007647	528
45	56.536588	7404.878447	.000135	.017687	130.974978	.007635	540
46	61.840110	8112.014707	.000123	.016170	131.177236	.007623	552
47	67.641139	8885.485227	.000112	.014783	131.362146	.007612	564
48	73.986344	9731.512616	.000102	.013516	131.531199	.007602	576
49	80.926774	10656.903210	.000093	.012356	131.685753	.007593	588
50	88.518263	11669.101820	.000085	.011297	131.827052	.007585	600

9% Quarterly Compound Interest Table

EFFECTIVE RATE = 2¼%   BASE = 1.0225

QUARTERS	1 AMOUNT OF 1 AT COMPOUND INTEREST $S^n = (1+i)^n$	2 ACCUMULATION OF 1 PER PERIOD $S_{\overline{n}\vert} = \frac{S^n - 1}{i}$	3 SINKING FUND FACTOR $1/S_{\overline{n}\vert} = \frac{i}{S^n - 1}$	4 PRES. VALUE OF REVERSION OF 1 $V^n = \frac{1}{S^n}$	5 PRESENT VALUE ORD. ANNUITY 1 PER PERIOD $a_{\overline{n}\vert} = \frac{1 - V^n}{i}$	6 INSTALLMENT TO AMORTIZE 1 (LOAN CONSTANT) $1/a_{\overline{n}\vert} = \frac{i}{1 - V^n}$	n QUARTERS
1	1.022500	1.000000	1.000000	.977995	.977995	1.022500	1
2	1.045506	2.022500	.494438	.956474	1.934470	.516938	2
3	1.069030	3.068006	.325945	.935427	2.869897	.348445	3
YEARS							
1	1.093083	4.137036	.241719	.914843	3.784740	.264219	4
2	1.194831	8.659162	.115485	.836938	7.247185	.137985	8
3	1.306050	13.602222	.073517	.765667	10.414779	.096017	12
4	1.427621	19.005398	.052617	.700466	13.312631	.075117	16
5	1.560509	24.911520	.040142	.640816	15.963712	.062642	20
6	1.705767	31.367403	.031880	.586247	18.389036	.054380	24
7	1.864545	38.424222	.026025	.536124	20.607828	.048525	28
8	2.038103	46.137912	.021674	.490652	22.637674	.044174	32
9	2.227816	54.569619	.018325	.448870	24.494666	.040825	36
10	2.435189	63.786176	.015677	.410646	26.193522	.038177	40
11	2.661864	73.860642	.013539	.375677	27.747710	.036039	44
12	2.909640	84.872872	.011782	.343685	29.169548	.034282	48
13	3.180479	96.910157	.010319	.314418	30.470307	.032819	52
14	3.476528	110.067912	.009085	.287643	31.660298	.031585	56
15	3.800135	124.450435	.008035	.263149	32.748953	.030535	60
16	4.153864	140.171731	.007134	.240740	33.744902	.029634	64
17	4.540519	157.356417	.006355	.220239	34.656039	.028855	68
18	4.963166	176.140711	.005677	.201484	35.489587	.028177	72
19	5.425154	196.673510	.005085	.184327	36.252153	.027585	76
20	5.930145	219.117569	.004564	.168630	36.949781	.027064	80
21	6.482143	243.650796	.004104	.154270	37.588001	.026604	84
22	7.085522	270.467657	.003697	.141133	38.171873	.026197	88
23	7.745066	299.780721	.003336	.129114	38.706024	.025836	92
24	8.466003	331.822342	.003014	.118119	39.194689	.025514	96
25	9.254046	366.846503	.002726	.108061	39.641741	.025226	100
26	10.115444	405.130829	.002468	.098859	40.050723	.024968	104
27	11.057023	446.978788	.002237	.090440	40.424877	.024737	108
28	12.086247	492.722093	.002030	.082739	40.767170	.024530	112
29	13.211275	542.723337	.001843	.075693	41.080315	.024343	116
30	14.441024	597.378863	.001674	.069247	41.366793	.024174	120

9% Quarterly Compound Interest Table (continued)

EFFECTIVE RATE = 2¼% BASE = 1.0225

YEARS	1 AMOUNT OF 1 AT COMPOUND INTEREST $S^n = (1+i)^n$	2 ACCUMULATION OF 1 PER PERIOD $S\overline{n\|} = \frac{S^n - 1}{i}$	3 SINKING FUND FACTOR $1/S\overline{n\|} = \frac{i}{S^n - 1}$	4 PRES. VALUE OF REVERSION OF 1 $V^n = \frac{1}{S^n}$	5 PRESENT VALUE ORD. ANNUITY 1 PER PERIOD $a\overline{n\|} = \frac{1 - V^n}{i}$	6 INSTALLMENT TO AMORTIZE 1 (LOAN CONSTANT) $1/a\overline{n\|} = \frac{i}{1 - V^n}$	n QUARTERS
31	15.785243	657.121907	.001522	.063350	41.628875	.024022	124
32	17.254586	722.426031	.001384	.057956	41.868640	.023884	128
33	18.860700	793.808880	.001260	.053020	42.087987	.023760	132
34	20.616316	871.836281	.001147	.048505	42.288655	.023647	136
35	22.535351	957.126733	.001045	.044375	42.472234	.023545	140
36	24.633017	1050.356302	.000952	.040596	42.640181	.023452	144
37	26.925940	1152.263989	.000868	.037139	42.793826	.023368	148
38	29.432296	1263.657582	.000791	.033976	42.934387	.023291	152
39	32.171951	1385.420060	.000722	.031083	43.062979	.023222	156
40	35.166623	1518.516594	.000659	.028436	43.180620	.023159	160
41	38.440049	1664.002195	.000601	.026015	43.288243	.023101	164
42	42.018177	1823.030078	.000549	.023799	43.386701	.023049	168
43	45.929368	1996.860804	.000501	.021773	43.476775	.023001	172
44	50.204626	2186.872272	.000457	.019918	43.559179	.022957	176
45	54.877839	2394.570637	.000418	.018222	43.634565	.022918	180
46	59.986051	2621.602256	.000381	.016671	43.703531	.022881	184
47	65.569751	2869.766731	.000348	.015251	43.766625	.022848	188
48	71.673202	3141.031179	.000318	.013952	43.824346	.022818	192
49	78.344781	3437.545822	.000291	.012764	43.877151	.022791	196
50	85.637373	3761.661032	.000266	.012677	43.925460	.022766	200
51	93.608784	4115.945962	.000243	.010683	43.969655	.022743	204
52	102.322200	4503.208907	.000222	.009773	44.010087	.022722	208
53	111.846690	4926.519573	.000203	.008941	44.047075	.022703	212
54	122.257752	5389.233400	.000186	.008179	44.080914	.022686	216
55	133.637909	5895.018169	.000170	.007483	44.111871	.022670	220
56	146.077369	6447.883062	.000155	.006846	44.140192	.022655	224
57	159.674735	7052.210453	.000142	.006263	44.166101	.022642	228
58	174.537790	7712.790645	.000130	.005729	44.189804	.022630	232
59	190.784346	8434.859831	.000119	.005242	44.211488	.022619	236
60	208.543186	9224.141613	.000108	.004795	44.231326	.022608	240

9% Semi-Annual Compound Interest Table

EFFECTIVE RATE = 4½% BASE = 1.045

HALF YEARS	1 AMOUNT OF 1 AT COMPOUND INTEREST $S^n = (1 + i)^n$	2 ACCUMULATION OF 1 PER PERIOD $S_{\overline{n}\rvert} = \frac{S^n - 1}{i}$	3 SINKING FUND FACTOR $1/S_{\overline{n}\rvert} = \frac{i}{S^n - 1}$	4 PRES. VALUE OF REVERSION OF 1 $V^n = \frac{1}{S^n}$	5 PRESENT VALUE ORD. ANNUITY 1 PER PERIOD $a_{\overline{n}\rvert} = \frac{1 - V^n}{i}$	6 INSTALLMENT TO AMORTIZE 1 (LOAN CONSTANT) $1/a_{\overline{n}\rvert} = \frac{i}{1 - V^n}$	n HALF YEARS
1	1.045000	1.000000	1.000000	.956938	.956938	1.045000	1
YEARS							
1	1.092025	2.045000	.488998	.915730	1.872668	.533998	2
2	1.192519	4.278191	.233744	.838561	3.587526	.278744	4
3	1.302260	6.716892	.148878	.767896	5.157872	.193878	6
4	1.422101	9.380014	.106610	.703185	6.595886	.151610	8
5	1.552969	12.288209	.081379	.643928	7.912718	.126379	10
6	1.695881	15.464032	.064666	.589664	9.118581	.109666	12
7	1.851945	18.932109	.052820	.539973	10.222825	.097820	14
8	2.022370	22.719337	.044015	.494469	11.234015	.089015	16
9	2.208479	26.855084	.037237	.452800	12.159992	.082237	18
10	2.411714	31.371423	.031876	.414643	13.007936	.076876	20
11	2.633652	36.303378	.027546	.379701	13.784425	.072546	22
12	2.876014	41.689196	.023987	.347703	14.495478	.068987	24
13	3.140679	47.570645	.021021	.318402	15.146611	.066021	26
14	3.429700	53.993333	.018521	.291571	15.742874	.063521	28
15	3.745318	61.007070	.016392	.267000	16.288889	.061392	30
16	4.089981	68.666245	.014563	.244500	16.788891	.059563	32
17	4.466362	77.030256	.012982	.223896	17.246758	.057982	34
18	4.877378	86.163966	.011606	.205028	17.666041	.056606	36
19	5.326219	96.138205	.010402	.187750	18.049990	.055402	38
20	5.816365	107.030323	.009343	.171929	18.401584	.054343	40
21	6.351615	118.924789	.008409	.157440	18.723550	.053409	42
22	6.936123	131.913842	.007581	.144173	19.018383	.052581	44
23	7.574420	146.098214	.006845	.132023	19.288371	.051845	46
24	8.271456	161.587902	.006189	.120898	19.535607	.051189	48
25	9.032636	178.503028	.005602	.110710	19.762008	.050602	50
26	9.863865	196.974769	.005077	.101380	19.969330	.050077	52
27	10.771587	217.146372	.004605	.092837	20.159181	.049605	54
28	11.762842	239.174267	.004181	.085013	20.333034	.049181	56
29	12.845318	263.229279	.003799	.077849	20.492236	.048799	58
30	14.027408	289.497954	.003454	.071289	20.638022	.048454	60
31	15.318280	318.184003	.003143	.065281	20.771523	.048143	62
32	16.727945	349.509886	.002861	.059780	20.893773	.047861	64
33	18.267334	383.718533	.002606	.054743	21.005722	.047606	66
34	19.948385	421.075231	.002375	.050129	21.108236	.047375	68
35	21.784136	461.869679	.002165	.045905	21.202112	.047165	70

9% Semi-Annual Compound Interest Table (continued)

EFFECTIVE RATE = 4½% BASE = 1.045

YEARS	1 AMOUNT OF 1 AT COMPOUND INTEREST $S^n = (1+i)^n$	2 ACCUMULATION OF 1 PER PERIOD $S\overline{n\rvert} = \frac{S^n - 1}{i}$	3 SINKING FUND FACTOR $1/S\overline{n\rvert} = \frac{i}{S^n - 1}$	4 PRES. VALUE OF REVERSION OF 1 $V^n = \frac{1}{S^n}$	5 PRESENT VALUE ORD. ANNUITY 1 PER PERIOD $a\overline{n\rvert} = \frac{1 - V^n}{i}$	6 INSTALLMENT TO AMORTIZE 1 (LOAN CONSTANT) $1/a\overline{n\rvert} = \frac{i}{1 - V^n}$	n HALF YEARS
36	23.788821	506.418237	.001975	.042037	21.288077	.046975	72
37	25.977987	555.066375	.001802	.038494	21.366797	.046802	74
38	28.368611	608.191358	.001644	.035250	21.438884	.046644	76
39	30.979233	666.205168	.001501	.032280	21.504896	.046501	78
40	33.830096	729.557698	.001371	.029559	21.565345	.046371	80
41	36.943311	798.740245	.001252	.027068	21.620700	.046252	82
42	40.343109	874.289317	.001144	.024787	21.671390	.046144	84
43	44.055586	956.790791	.001045	.022699	21.717809	.046045	86
44	48.109801	1046.884463	.000955	.020786	21.760316	.045955	88
45	52.537105	1145.269006	.000873	.019034	21.799241	.045873	90
46	57.371832	1252.707386	.000798	.017430	21.834885	.045798	92
47	62.651475	1370.032783	.000730	.015961	21.867526	.045730	94
48	68.416977	1498.155050	.000667	.016416	21.897417	.045667	96
49	74.713050	1638.067768	.000610	.013385	21.924788	.045610	98
50	81.588518	1790.855955	.000558	.012257	21.949853	.045558	100
51	89.096701	1957.704474	.000511	.011224	21.972805	.045511	102
52	97.295825	2139.907228	.000467	.010278	21.993824	.045467	104
53	106.249474	2338.877191	.000428	.009412	21.013071	.045428	106
54	116.027081	2556.157364	.000391	.008619	22.030696	.045391	108
55	126.704474	2793.432747	.000358	.007892	22.046836	.045358	110
56	138.364453	3052.543396	.000328	.007227	22.061616	.045328	112
57	151.097442	3335.498702	.000300	.006618	22.075150	.045300	114
58	165.002184	3644.492971	.000274	.006061	22.087544	.045274	116
59	180.186510	3981.922436	.000251	.005550	22.098893	.045251	118
60	196.768173	4350.403847	.000230	.005082	22.109286	.045230	120

9% Annual Compound Interest Table

EFFECTIVE RATE = 9% BASE = 1.09

YEARS	1 AMOUNT OF 1 AT COMPOUND INTEREST $S^n = (1+i)^n$	2 ACCUMULATION OF 1 PER PERIOD $S_{\overline{n}\rvert} = \frac{S^n - 1}{i}$	3 SINKING FUND FACTOR $1/S_{\overline{n}\rvert} = \frac{i}{S^n - 1}$	4 PRES. VALUE OF REVERSION OF 1 $V^n = \frac{1}{S^n}$	5 PRESENT VALUE ORD. ANNUITY 1 PER PERIOD $a_{\overline{n}\rvert} = \frac{1 - V^n}{i}$	6 INSTALLMENT TO AMORTIZE 1 (LOAN CONSTANT) $1/a_{\overline{n}\rvert} = \frac{i}{1 - V^n}$	n YEARS
1	1.090000	1.000000	1.000000	.917431	.917431	1.090000	1
2	1.188100	2.090000	.487469	.841680	1.759111	.568469	2
3	1.295029	3.278100	.305055	.772183	2.531295	.395055	3
4	1.411582	4.573129	.218669	.708425	3.239720	.308669	4
5	1.538624	5.984711	.167092	.649931	3.889651	.257092	5
6	1.667100	7.523335	.132920	.596267	4.485919	.222920	6
7	1.828039	9.200435	.108691	.547034	5.032953	.198691	7
8	1.992563	11.028474	.090674	.501866	5.534819	.180674	8
9	2.171893	13.021036	.076799	.460428	5.995247	.166799	9
10	2.367364	15.192930	.065820	.422411	6.417658	.155820	10
11	2.580426	17.560293	.056947	.387533	6.805191	.146947	11
12	2.812665	20.140720	.049651	.355535	7.160725	.139651	12
13	3.065805	22.953385	.043567	.326179	7.486904	.133567	13
14	3.341727	26.019189	.038433	.299246	7.786150	.128433	14
15	3.642482	29.360916	.034059	.274538	8.060688	.124059	15
16	3.970306	33.003399	.030300	.251870	8.312558	.120300	16
17	4.327633	36.973705	.027046	.231073	8.543631	.117046	17
18	4.717120	41.301338	.024212	.211994	8.755625	.114212	18
19	5.141661	46.018458	.021730	.194490	8.950115	.111730	19
20	5.604411	51.160120	.019546	.178431	9.128546	.109546	20
21	6.108808	56.764530	.017617	.163698	9.292244	.107617	21
22	6.658600	62.873338	.015905	.150182	9.442425	.105905	22
23	7.257874	69.531939	.014382	.137781	9.580207	.104382	23
24	7.911083	76.789813	.013023	.126405	9.706612	.103023	24
25	8.623081	84.700896	.011806	.115968	9.822580	.101806	25
26	9.399158	93.323977	.010715	.106393	9.928972	.100715	26
27	10.245082	102.723135	.009735	.097608	10.026580	.099735	27
28	11.167140	112.167140	.008852	.089548	10.116128	.098852	28
29	12.172182	124.135356	.008056	.082155	10.198283	.098056	29
30	13.267678	136.307539	.007336	.075371	10.273654	.097336	30
31	14.461770	149.575217	.006686	.069148	10.342802	.096686	31
32	15.763329	164.036987	.006096	.063438	10.406240	.096096	32
33	17.182028	179.800315	.005562	.058200	10.464441	.095562	33
34	18.728411	196.982344	.005077	.053395	10.517835	.095077	34
35	20.413968	215.710755	.004636	.048986	10.566821	.094636	35

9% Annual Compound Interest Table (continued)

EFFECTIVE RATE = 9% BASE = 1.09

YEARS	1 AMOUNT OF 1 AT COMPOUND INTEREST $S^n = (1+i)^n$	2 ACCUMULATION OF 1 PER PERIOD $S_{\overline{n}\vert} = \frac{S^n - 1}{i}$	3 SINKING FUND FACTOR $1/S_{\overline{n}\vert} = \frac{i}{S^n - 1}$	4 PRES. VALUE OF REVERSION OF 1 $V^n = \frac{1}{S^n}$	5 PRESENT VALUE ORD. ANNUITY 1 PER PERIOD $a_{\overline{n}\vert} = \frac{1 - V^n}{i}$	6 INSTALLMENT TO AMORTIZE 1 (LOAN CONSTANT) $1/a_{\overline{n}\vert} = \frac{i}{1 - V^n}$	n YEARS
36	22.251225	236.124723	.004235	.044941	10.611763	.094235	36
37	24.253835	258.375948	.003870	.041231	10.652993	.093870	37
38	26.436680	282.629783	.003538	.037826	10.690820	.093538	38
39	28.815982	309.066463	.003236	.034703	10.725523	.093236	39
40	31.409420	337.882445	.002960	.031838	10.757360	.092960	40
41	34.236268	369.291865	.002708	.029209	10.786569	.092708	41
42	37.317532	403.528133	.002478	.026797	10.813366	.092478	42
43	40.676110	440.845665	.002268	.024584	10.837951	.092268	43
44	44.336960	481.521775	.002077	.022555	10.860505	.092077	44
45	48.327286	525.858735	.001902	.020692	10.881197	.091902	45
46	52.676742	574.186021	.001742	.018984	10.900181	.091742	46
47	57.417649	626.862762	.001595	.017416	10.917597	.091595	47
48	62.585237	684.280411	.001461	.015978	10.933575	.091461	48
49	68.217908	746.865648	.001339	.014659	10.948234	.091339	49
50	74.357520	815.083556	.001227	.013449	10.961683	.091227	50
51	81.049697	889.441077	.001124	.012338	10.974021	.091124	51
52	88.344170	970.490773	.001030	.013319	10.985340	.091030	52
53	96.295145	1058.834943	.000944	.010385	10.995725	.090944	53
54	104.961708	1151.130088	.000866	.009527	11.005252	.090866	54
55	114.408262	1260.091796	.000794	.008741	11.013993	.090794	55
56	124.705005	1374.500057	.000728	.008019	11.022012	.090728	56
57	135.928456	1499.205063	.000667	.007357	11.029369	.090667	57
58	148.162017	1635.133518	.000612	.006749	11.036118	.090612	58
59	161.496598	1783.295535	.000561	.006192	11.042310	.090561	59
60	176.031292	1944.792133	.000514	.005681	11.047991	.090514	60

10% Monthly Compound Interest Table

EFFECTIVE RATE = 5/6% BASE = 1.00833333

MONTHS	1 AMOUNT OF 1 AT COMPOUND INTEREST $S^n = (1 + i)^n$	2 ACCUMULATION OF 1 PER PERIOD $S_{\overline{n}\rvert} = \frac{S^n - 1}{i}$	3 SINKING FUND FACTOR $1/S_{\overline{n}\rvert} = \frac{i}{S^n - 1}$	4 PRES. VALUE OF REVERSION OF 1 $V^n = \frac{1}{S^n}$	5 PRESENT VALUE ORD. ANNUITY 1 PER PERIOD $a_{\overline{n}\rvert} = \frac{1 - V^n}{i}$	6 INSTALLMENT TO AMORTIZE 1 (LOAN CONSTANT) $1/a_{\overline{n}\rvert} = \frac{i}{1 - V^n}$	n MONTHS
1	1.008333	1.000000	1.000000	.991735	.991735	1.008333	1
2	1.016736	2.008333	.497925	.983539	1.975274	.506258	2
3	1.025208	3.025069	.330570	.975410	2.950685	.338904	3
4	1.033752	4.050278	.246896	.967349	3.918035	.255229	4
5	1.042366	5.084030	.196694	.959355	4.877390	.205027	5
6	1.051053	6.126397	.163228	.951426	5.828817	.171561	6
7	1.059812	7.177450	.139325	.943563	6.772380	.147658	7
8	1.068643	8.237262	.121399	.935765	7.708146	.129732	8
9	1.077549	9.305906	.107458	.928031	8.636177	.115791	9
10	1.086528	10.383456	.096307	.920362	9.556540	.104640	10
11	1.095583	11.469984	.087184	.912755	10.469295	.095517	11
YEARS							
1	1.104713	12.565568	.079582	.905212	11.374508	.087915	12
2	1.220390	26.446915	.037811	.819409	21.670854	.046144	24
3	1.348181	41.781821	.023933	.741739	30.991235	.032267	36
4	1.489354	58.722491	.017029	.671432	39.428160	.025362	48
5	1.645308	77.437072	.012913	.607788	47.065369	.021247	60
6	1.817594	98.111313	.010192	.550177	53.978665	.018525	72
7	2.007920	120.950418	.008267	.498027	60.236667	.016601	84
8	2.218175	146.181075	.006840	.450820	65.901488	.015174	96
9	2.450447	174.053712	.005745	.408088	71.029355	.014078	108
10	2.707041	204.844978	.004881	.369406	75.671163	.013215	120
11	2.990504	238.860492	.004186	.334391	79.872985	.012519	132
12	3.303648	276.437875	.003617	.302695	83.676528	.011950	144
13	3.649584	317.950100	.003145	.274003	87.119542	.011478	156
14	4.031743	363.809198	.002748	.248031	90.236200	.011082	168
15	4.453919	414.470344	.002412	.224521	93.057438	.010746	180
16	4.920303	470.436373	.002125	.203239	95.611258	.010459	192
17	5.435523	532.262776	.001878	.183974	97.923008	.010212	204
18	6.004693	600.563212	.001665	.166536	100.015632	.009998	216
19	6.633463	676.015596	.001479	.150750	101.909902	.009812	228
20	7.328073	759.368830	.001316	.136461	103.624619	.009650	240
21	8.095418	851.450237	.001174	.123526	105.176801	.009507	252
22	8.943114	953.173772	.001049	.111817	106.581857	.009382	264
23	9.879575	1065.549089	.000938	.101218	107.853729	.009271	276
22	10.914096	1189.691570	.000840	.091624	109.005045	.009173	288
25	12.056944	1326.833392	.000753	.082939	110.047230	.009087	300

10% Monthly Compound Interest Table (continued)

EFFECTIVE RATE = 5/6% BASE = 1.00833333

YEARS	1 AMOUNT OF 1 AT COMPOUND INTEREST $S^n = (1+i)^n$	2 ACCUMULATION OF 1 PER PERIOD $S_{\overline{n}\rvert} = \frac{S^n - 1}{i}$	3 SINKING FUND FACTOR $1/S_{\overline{n}\rvert} = \frac{i}{S^n - 1}$	4 PRES. VALUE OF REVERSION OF 1 $V^n = \frac{1}{S^n}$	5 PRESENT VALUE ORD. ANNUITY 1 PER PERIOD $a_{\overline{n}\rvert} = \frac{1 - V^n}{i}$	6 INSTALLMENT TO AMORTIZE 1 (LOAN CONSTANT) $1/a_{\overline{n}\rvert} = \frac{i}{1 - V^n}$	n MONTHS
26	13.319464	1478.335753	.000676	.075078	110.990629	.009009	312
27	14.714186	1645.702391	.000607	.067961	111.844605	.008940	324
28	16.254954	1830.594505	.000546	.061519	112.617636	.008879	336
29	17.957060	2034.847238	.000491	.055688	113.317391	.008824	348
30	19.837399	2260.487900	.000442	.050409	113.950820	.008775	360
31	21.914633	2509.756088	.000398	.045631	114.524207	.008731	372
32	24.209382	2785.125915	.000359	.041306	115.043244	.008692	384
33	26.744421	3089.330559	.000323	.037390	115.513083	.008657	396
34	29.544911	3425.389403	.000291	.033846	115.938387	.008625	408
35	32.638649	3796.638004	.000263	.030638	116.323378	.008596	420
36	36.056343	4206.761180	.000237	.027734	116.671875	.008571	432
37	39.831913	4659.829611	.000214	.025105	116.987341	.008547	444
38	44.002835	5160.340233	.000193	.022725	117.272903	.008527	456
39	48.610506	5713.260852	.000175	.020571	117.531398	.008508	468
40	53.700662	6324.079483	.000158	.018621	117.765390	.008491	480
41	59.323823	6998.858807	.000142	.016856	117.977204	.008476	492
42	65.535802	7744.296352	.000129	.015258	118.168940	.008462	504
43	72.398257	8567.790939	.000116	.013812	118.342502	.008450	516
44	79.979301	9477.516170	.000105	.012503	118.499611	.008438	528
45	88.354179	10482.501530	.000095	.011318	118.641830	.008428	540
46	97.606016	11592.721980	.000086	.010245	118.770568	.008419	552
47	107.826641	12819.197020	.000078	.009274	118.887103	.008411	564
48	119.117499	14174.100030	.000070	.008395	118.992592	.008403	576
49	131.590658	15670.879080	.000063	.007599	119.088082	.008397	588
50	145.369919	17324.390450	.000057	.006879	119.174520	.008391	600

10% Quarterly Compound Interest Table

EFFECTIVE RATE = 2½% BASE = 1.025

	1 AMOUNT OF 1 AT COMPOUND INTEREST $S^n = (1+i)^n$	2 ACCUMULATION OF 1 PER PERIOD $S\overline{n\rvert} = \frac{S^n - 1}{i}$	3 SINKING FUND FACTOR $1/S\overline{n\rvert} = \frac{i}{S^n - 1}$	4 PRES. VALUE OF REVERSION OF 1 $V^n = \frac{1}{S^n}$	5 PRESENT VALUE ORD. ANNUITY 1 PER PERIOD $a\overline{n\rvert} = \frac{1 - V^n}{i}$	6 INSTALLMENT TO AMORTIZE 1 (LOAN CONSTANT) $1/a\overline{n\rvert} = \frac{i}{1 - V^n}$	n
QUARTERS							QUARTERS
1	1.025000	1.000000	1.000000	.975610	.975610	1.025000	1
2	1.050625	2.025000	.493827	.951814	1.927424	.518827	2
3	1.076891	3.075625	.325137	.928599	2.856024	.350137	3
YEARS							
1	1.103813	4.152516	.240818	.905951	3.761974	.265818	4
2	1.218403	8.736116	.114467	.820747	7.170137	.139467	8
3	1.344889	13.795553	.072487	.743556	10.257765	.097487	12
4	1.484506	19.380225	.051599	.673625	13.055003	.076599	16
5	1.638616	25.544658	.039147	.610271	15.589162	.064147	20
6	1.808726	32.349038	.030913	.552875	17.884986	.055913	24
7	1.996495	39.859801	.025088	.500878	19.964889	.050088	28
8	2.203757	48.150278	.020768	.453771	21.849178	.045768	32
9	2.432535	57.301413	.017452	.411094	23.556251	.042452	36
10	2.685064	67.402554	.014836	.372431	25.102775	.039836	40
11	2.963808	78.552323	.012730	.337404	26.503849	.037730	44
12	3.271490	90.859583	.011006	.305671	27.773154	.036006	48
13	3.611112	104.444494	.009574	.276923	28.923081	.034574	52
14	3.985992	119.439695	.008372	.250879	29.964858	.033372	56
15	4.399790	135.991590	.007353	.227284	30.908657	.032353	60
16	4.856545	154.261786	.006482	.205908	31.763692	.031482	64
17	5.360717	174.428664	.005733	.186542	32.538311	.030733	68
18	5.917228	196.689123	.005084	.168998	33.240078	.030084	72
19	6.531513	221.260505	.004520	.153104	33.875844	.029520	76
20	7.209568	248.382713	.004026	.138705	34.451817	.029026	80
21	7.958014	278.320556	.003593	.125659	34.973620	.028593	84
22	8.784158	311.366333	.003212	.113841	35.446348	.028212	88
23	9.696067	347.842688	.002875	.103135	35.874616	.027875	92
24	10.702644	388.105759	.002577	.093435	36.262606	.027577	96
25	11.813716	432.548655	.002312	.084647	36.614105	.027312	100
26	13.040132	481.605297	.002076	.076686	36.932546	.027076	104
27	14.393866	535.754651	.001867	.069474	37.221039	.026867	108
28	15.888135	595.525406	.001679	.062940	37.482398	.026679	112
29	17.537528	661.501135	.001512	.057021	37.719177	.026512	116
30	19.358150	734.325996	.001362	.051658	37.933687	.026362	120

10% Quarterly Compound Interest Table (continued)

EFFECTIVE RATE = 2½% BASE = 1.025

YEARS	1 AMOUNT OF 1 AT COMPOUND INTEREST $S^n = (1 + i)^n$	2 ACCUMU-LATION OF 1 PER PERIOD $S\overline{n\rvert} = \frac{S^n - 1}{i}$	3 SINKING FUND FACTOR $1/S\overline{n\rvert} = \frac{i}{S^n - 1}$	4 PRES. VALUE OF REVERSION OF 1 $V^n = \frac{1}{S^n}$	5 PRESENT VALUE ORD. ANNUITY 1 PER PERIOD $a\overline{n\rvert} = \frac{1 - V^n}{i}$	6 INSTALL-MENT TO AMORTIZE 1 (LOAN CONSTANT) $1/a\overline{n\rvert} = \frac{i}{1 - V^n}$	n QUARTERS
31	21.367775	814.711016	.001227	.046799	38.128022	.026227	124
32	23.586026	903.441037	.001107	.042398	38.304081	.026107	128
33	26.034559	1001.382378	.000999	.038410	38.463581	.025999	132
34	28.737282	1109.491294	.000901	.034798	38.608080	.025901	136
35	31.720583	1228.823308	.000814	.031525	38.738989	.025814	140
36	35.013588	1360.543523	.000735	.028560	38.857586	.025735	144
37	38.648450	1505.937994	.000664	.025874	38.965030	.025664	148
38	42.660657	1666.426286	.000600	.023441	39.062368	.025600	152
39	47.089383	1843.575332	.000542	.021236	39.150552	.025542	156
40	51.977868	2039.114732	.000490	.019239	39.230442	.025490	160
41	57.373841	2254.953642	.000443	.017430	39.302818	.025443	164
42	63.329985	2493.199414	.000401	.015790	39.368388	.025401	168
43	69.904454	2756.178168	.000363	.014305	39.427790	.025363	172
44	77.161438	3046.457506	.000328	.012960	39.481606	.025328	176
45	85.171790	3366.871582	.000297	.011741	39.530361	.025297	180
46	94.013719	3720.548769	.000269	.010637	39.574530	.025269	184
47	103.773555	4110.942208	.000243	.009636	39.614545	.025243	188
48	114.546588	4541.863516	.000220	.008730	39.650797	.025220	192
49	126.438000	5017.520012	.000199	.007909	39.683639	.025199	196
50	139.563895	5542.555784	.000180	.007165	39.713393	.025180	200
51	154.052426	6122.097036	.000163	.006491	39.740348	.025163	204
52	170.045054	6761.802144	.000148	.005881	39.764768	.025148	208
53	187.697922	7467.916888	.000134	.005328	39.786892	.025134	212
54	207.183386	8247.335444	.000121	.004827	39.806934	.025121	216
55	228.691692	9107.667692	.000110	.004373	39.825092	.025110	220
56	252.432838	10057.313520	.000099	.003961	39.841542	.025099	224
57	278.638621	11105.544820	.000090	.003589	39.856445	.025090	228
58	307.564901	12262.596050	.000082	.003251	39.869946	.025082	232
59	339.494103	13539.764110	.000074	.002946	39.882178	.025074	236
60	374.737967	14949.518680	.000067	.002669	39.893259	.025067	240

10% Semi-Annual Compound Interest Table

EFFECTIVE RATE = 5% BASE = 1.05

HALF YEARS	1 AMOUNT OF 1 AT COMPOUND INTEREST $S^n = (1+i)^n$	2 ACCUMULATION OF 1 PER PERIOD $S\overline{n\|} = \frac{S^n - 1}{i}$	3 SINKING FUND FACTOR $1/S\overline{n\|} = \frac{i}{S^n - 1}$	4 PRES. VALUE OF REVERSION OF 1 $V^n = \frac{1}{S^n}$	5 PRESENT VALUE ORD. ANNUITY 1 PER PERIOD $a\overline{n\|} = \frac{1 - V^n}{i}$	6 INSTALLMENT TO AMORTIZE 1 (LOAN CONSTANT) $1/a\overline{n\|} = \frac{i}{1 - V^n}$	n HALF YEARS
1	1.050000	1.000000	1.000000	.952381	.952381	1.050000	1
YEARS							
1	1.102500	2.050000	.487805	.907029	1.859410	.537805	2
2	1.215506	4.310125	.232012	.822702	3.545951	.282012	4
3	1.340096	6.801913	.147017	.746215	5.075692	.197017	6
4	1.477455	9.549109	.104722	.676839	6.463213	.154722	8
5	1.628895	12.577893	.079505	.613913	7.721735	.129505	10
6	1.795856	15.917127	.062825	.556837	8.863252	.112825	12
7	1.979932	19.598632	.051024	.505068	9.898641	.101024	14
8	2.182875	23.657492	.042270	.458112	10.837770	.092270	16
9	2.406619	28.132385	.035546	.415521	11.689587	.085546	18
10	2.653298	33.065954	.030243	.376889	12.462210	.080243	20
11	2.925261	38.505214	.025971	.341850	13.163003	.075971	22
12	3.225100	44.501999	.022471	.310068	13.798642	.072471	24
13	3.555673	51.113454	.019564	.281241	14.375185	.069564	26
14	3.920129	58.402583	.017123	.255094	14.898127	.067123	28
15	4.321942	66.438847	.015051	.231377	15.372451	.065051	30
16	4.764941	75.298829	.013280	.209866	15.802677	.063280	32
17	5.253348	85.066959	.011755	.190355	16.192904	.061755	34
18	5.791816	95.836323	.010434	.172657	16.546852	.060434	36
19	6.385477	107.709546	.009284	.156605	16.867893	.059284	38
20	7.039989	120.799774	.008278	.142046	17.159086	.058278	40
21	7.761588	135.231751	.007395	.128840	17.423208	.057395	42
22	8.557150	151.143005	.006616	.116861	17.662773	.056616	44
23	9.434258	168.685164	.005928	.105997	17.880066	.055928	46
24	10.401270	188.025393	.005318	.096142	18.077158	.055318	48
25	11.467400	209.347996	.004777	.087204	18.255925	.054777	50
26	12.642808	232.856165	.004294	.079096	18.418073	.054294	52
27	13.938696	258.773922	.003864	.071743	18.565146	.053864	54
28	15.367412	287.348249	.003480	.065073	18.698545	.053480	56
29	16.942572	318.851445	.003136	.059023	18.819542	.053136	58
30	18.679186	353.583718	.002828	.053536	18.929290	.052828	60
31	20.593802	391.876049	.002552	.048558	19.028834	.052552	62
32	22.704667	434.093344	.002304	.044044	19.119124	.052304	64
33	25.031896	480.637912	.002081	.039949	19.201019	.052081	66
34	27.597665	531.953298	.001880	.036235	19.275301	.051880	68
35	30.426426	588.528511	.001699	.032866	19.342677	.051699	70

10% Semi-Annual Compound Interest Table (continued)

EFFECTIVE RATE = 5% BASE = 1.05

YEARS	1 AMOUNT OF 1 AT COMPOUND INTEREST $S^n = (1+i)^n$	2 ACCUMULATION OF 1 PER PERIOD $S\overline{n}\rvert = \frac{S^n - 1}{i}$	3 SINKING FUND FACTOR $1/S\overline{n}\rvert = \frac{i}{S^n - 1}$	4 PRES. VALUE OF REVERSION OF 1 $V^n = \frac{1}{S^n}$	5 PRESENT VALUE ORD. ANNUITY 1 PER PERIOD $a\overline{n}\rvert = \frac{1 - V^n}{i}$	6 INSTALLMENT TO AMORTIZE 1 (LOAN CONSTANT) $1/a\overline{n}\rvert = \frac{i}{1 - V^n}$	n HALF YEARS
36	33.545134	650.902683	.001536	.029811	19.403788	.051536	72
37	36.983510	719.670208	.001390	.027039	19.459218	.051390	74
38	40.774320	795.486404	.001257	.024525	19.509495	.051257	76
39	44.953688	879.073761	.001138	.022245	19.555098	.051138	78
40	49.561441	971.228821	.001030	.020177	19.596460	.051030	80
41	54.641489	1072.829775	.000932	.018301	19.633978	.050932	82
42	60.242241	1184.844827	.000844	.016600	19.668007	.050844	84
43	66.417041	1308.341422	.000764	.015056	19.698873	.050764	86
44	73.224821	1444.496418	.000692	.013657	19.726869	.050692	88
45	80.730365	1594.607301	.000627	.012387	19.752262	.050627	90
46	89.005227	1760.104549	.000568	.011235	19.775294	.050568	92
47	98.128263	1942.565265	.000515	.010191	19.796185	.050515	94
48	108.186410	2143.728204	.000466	.009243	19.815134	.050466	96
49	119.275517	2365.510344	.000423	.008384	19.832321	.050423	98
50	131.501258	2610.025154	.000383	.007604	19.847910	.050383	100
51	144.980137	2879.602732	.000347	.006897	19.862050	.050347	102
52	159.840601	3176.812012	.000315	.006256	19.874875	.050315	104
53	176.224262	3504.485244	.000285	.005675	19.886508	.050285	106
54	194.287249	3865.744982	.000259	.005147	19.897060	.050259	108
55	214.201692	4264.033842	.000235	.004668	19.906630	.050235	110
56	236.157366	4703.147310	.000213	.004234	19.915311	.050213	112
57	260.363496	5187.269910	.000193	.003841	19.923184	.050193	114
58	287.050754	5721.015076	.000175	.003484	19.930326	.050175	116
59	316.473456	6309.469122	.000158	.003160	19.936804	.050158	118
60	348.911985	6958.239706	.000144	.002866	19.942679	.050144	120

10% Annual Compound Interest Table

EFFECTIVE RATE = 10% BASE = 1.10

YEARS	1 AMOUNT OF 1 AT COMPOUND INTEREST $S^n = (1 + i)^n$	2 ACCUMULATION OF 1 PER PERIOD $S\overline{n}| = \frac{S^n - 1}{i}$	3 SINKING FUND FACTOR $1/S\overline{n}| = \frac{i}{S^n - 1}$	4 PRES. VALUE OF REVERSION OF 1 $V^n = \frac{1}{S^n}$	5 PRESENT VALUE ORD. ANNUITY 1 PER PERIOD $a\overline{n}| = \frac{1 - V^n}{i}$	6 INSTALLMENT TO AMORTIZE 1 (LOAN CONSTANT) $1/a\overline{n}| = \frac{i}{1 - V^n}$	n YEARS
1	1.100000	1.000000	1.000000	.909091	.909091	1.000000	1
2	1.210000	2.100000	.476190	.826446	1.735537	.576190	2
3	1.331000	3.310000	.302115	.751315	2.486852	.042115	3
4	1.464100	4.641000	.215471	.683013	3.169865	.315471	4
5	1.610510	6.105100	.163797	.620921	3.790787	.263797	5
6	1.771561	7.715610	.129607	.564474	4.355261	.229607	6
7	1.948717	9.487171	.105405	.513158	4.868419	.205405	7
8	2.143589	11.435888	.087444	.466507	5.334926	.187444	8
9	2.357948	13.579477	.073641	.424098	5.759024	.173641	9
10	2.593742	15.937425	.062745	.385543	6.144567	.162745	10
11	2.853117	18.531167	.053963	.350494	6.495061	.153963	11
12	3.138428	21.384284	.046763	.318631	6.813692	.146763	12
13	3.452271	24.522712	.040779	.289664	7.103356	.140779	13
14	3.797498	27.974983	.035746	.263331	7.366687	.135746	14
15	4.177248	31.772482	.031474	.239392	7.606080	.131474	15
16	4.594973	35.949730	.027817	.217629	7.823709	.127817	16
17	5.054470	40.544703	.024664	.197845	8.021553	.124664	17
18	5.559917	45.599173	.021930	.179859	8.201412	.121930	18
19	6.115909	51.159090	.019547	.163508	8.364920	.119547	19
20	6.727500	57.274999	.017460	.148644	8.513564	.117460	20
21	7.400250	64.002499	.015624	.135131	8.648694	.115624	21
22	8.140275	71.402749	.014005	.122846	8.771540	.114005	22
23	8.954302	79.543024	.012572	.111678	8.883218	.112572	23
24	9.849733	88.497327	.011300	.101526	8.984744	.111300	24
25	10.834706	98.347059	.010168	.092296	9.077040	.110168	25
26	11.918177	109.181765	.009159	.083905	9.160945	.109159	26
27	13.109994	121.099942	.008258	.076278	9.237223	.108258	27
28	14.420994	134.209936	.007451	.069343	9.306567	.107451	28
29	15.863093	148.630930	.006728	.063039	9.369606	.106728	29
30	17.449402	164.494023	.006079	.057309	9.426914	.106079	30
31	19.194342	181.943425	.005496	.052099	9.479013	.105496	31
32	21.113777	201.137767	.004972	.047362	9.526376	.104972	32
33	23.225254	222.251544	.004499	.043057	9.569432	.104499	33
34	25.547670	245.476699	.004074	.039143	9.608575	.104074	34
35	28.102437	271.024368	.003690	.035584	9.644159	.103690	35

10% Annual Compound Interest Table (continued)

EFFECTIVE RATE = 10% BASE = 1.10

YEARS	1 AMOUNT OF 1 AT COMPOUND INTEREST $S^n = (1+i)^n$	2 ACCUMU-LATION OF 1 PER PERIOD $S\overline{n\rvert} = \frac{S^n - 1}{i}$	3 SINKING FUND FACTOR $1/S\overline{n\rvert} = \frac{i}{S^n - 1}$	4 PRES. VALUE OF REVERSION OF 1 $V^n = \frac{1}{S^n}$	5 PRESENT VALUE ORD. ANNUITY 1 PER PERIOD $a\overline{n\rvert} = \frac{1 - V^n}{i}$	6 INSTALL-MENT TO AMORTIZE 1 (LOAN CONSTANT) $1/a\overline{n\rvert} = \frac{i}{1 - V^n}$	n YEARS
36	30.912681	299.126805	.003343	.032349	9.676508	.103343	36
37	34.003949	330.039486	.003030	.029408	9.705917	.103030	37
38	37.404343	364.043434	.002747	.026735	9.732651	.102747	38
39	41.144778	401.447778	.002491	.024304	9.756956	.102491	39
40	45.259256	442.592556	.002259	.022095	9.779051	.102259	40
41	49.785181	487.851811	.002050	.020086	9.799137	.102050	41
42	54.763699	537.636992	.001860	.018260	9.817397	.101860	42
43	60.240069	592.400692	.001688	.016600	9.833998	.101688	43
44	66.264076	652.640761	.001532	.015091	9.849089	.101532	44
45	72.890484	718.904837	.001391	.013719	9.862808	.101391	45
46	80.179532	791.795321	.001263	.012472	9.875280	.101263	46
47	88.197485	871.974853	.001147	.011338	9.886618	.101147	47
48	97.017234	960.172338	.001041	.010307	9.896926	.101041	48
49	106.718957	1057.189572	.000946	.009370	9.906296	.100946	49
50	117.290853	1163.908529	.000859	.008519	9.914814	.100859	50
51	129.129938	1281.299382	.000780	.007744	9.922559	.100780	51
52	142.042932	1410.429320	.000709	.007040	9.929599	.100709	52
53	156.247225	1552.472252	.000644	.006400	9.935999	.100644	53
54	171.871948	1708.719477	.000585	.005818	9.941817	.100585	54
55	189.059142	1880.591425	.000532	.005289	9.947106	.100532	55
56	207.965057	2069.650567	.000483	.004809	9.951915	.100483	56
57	228.761562	2277.615624	.000439	.004371	9.956286	.100439	57
58	251.637719	2506.377186	.000399	.003974	9.960260	.100399	58
59	276.801490	2758.014905	.000363	.003613	9.963873	.100363	59
60	304.481640	3034.816395	.000330	.003284	9.967157	.100330	60

11% Monthly Compound Interest Table

EFFECTIVE RATE = 11/12% BASE = 1.00916667

MONTHS	1 AMOUNT OF 1 AT COMPOUND INTEREST $S^n = (1+i)^n$	2 ACCUMULATION OF 1 PER PERIOD $S_{\overline{n}\rceil} = \frac{S^n - 1}{i}$	3 SINKING FUND FACTOR $1/S_{\overline{n}\rceil} = \frac{i}{S^n - 1}$	4 PRES. VALUE OF REVERSION OF 1 $V^n = \frac{1}{S^n}$	5 PRESENT VALUE ORD. ANNUITY 1 PER PERIOD $a_{\overline{n}\rceil} = \frac{1 - V^n}{i}$	6 INSTALLMENT TO AMORTIZE 1 (LOAN CONSTANT) $1/a_{\overline{n}\rceil} = \frac{i}{1 - V^n}$	n MONTHS
1	1.009166	1.000000	1.000000	.990916	.990916	1.009166	1
2	1.018417	2.009166	.497718	.981915	1.972832	.506885	2
3	1.027752	3.027584	.330296	.972996	2.945828	.339463	3
4	1.037173	4.055336	.246588	.964158	3.909987	.255755	4
5	1.046681	5.092510	.196366	.955400	4.865387	.205533	5
6	1.056275	6.139192	.162887	.946722	5.812110	.172054	6
7	1.065958	7.195468	.138976	.938122	6.750233	.148143	7
8	1.075729	8.261426	.121044	.929601	7.679834	.130211	8
9	1.085590	9.337156	.107098	.921157	8.600992	.116265	9
10	1.095541	10.422746	.095943	.912790	9.513782	.105110	10
11	1.105584	11.518288	.086818	.904499	10.418281	.095985	11
YEARS							
1	1.115718	12.623873	.079214	.896283	11.314564	.088381	12
2	1.244828	26.708565	.037441	.803323	21.455618	.046607	24
3	1.388878	42.423123	.023572	.720005	30.544874	.032738	36
4	1.549598	59.956150	.016678	.645328	38.691421	.025845	48
5	1.728915	79.518079	.012575	.578397	45.993033	.021742	60
6	1.928983	101.343692	.009867	.518407	52.537346	.019034	72
7	2.152203	125.694939	.007955	.464640	58.402903	.017122	84
8	2.401254	152.864084	.006541	.416449	63.660103	.015708	96
9	2.679124	183.177212	.005459	.373256	68.372043	.014625	108
10	2.989149	216.998138	.004608	.334543	72.595274	.013775	120
11	3.335050	254.732784	.003925	.299845	76.380486	.013092	132
12	3.720978	296.834038	.033368	.268746	79.773108	.012535	144
13	4.151566	343.807201	.002908	.240872	82.813858	.012075	156
14	4.631980	396.216043	.002523	.215890	85.539231	.011690	168
15	5.167987	454.689576	.002199	.193498	87.981936	.011365	180
16	5.766021	519.929598	.001923	.173429	90.171292	.011090	192
17	6.433258	592.719119	.001687	.155442	92.133575	.010853	204
18	7.177707	673.931759	.001483	.139320	93.892336	.010650	216
19	8.008303	764.542231	.001307	.124870	95.468684	.010474	228
20	8.935015	865.638042	.001155	.111919	96.881538	.010321	240
21	9.968965	978.432542	.001022	.100311	98.147855	.010188	252
22	11.122562	1104.279491	.000905	.089907	99.282835	.010072	264
23	12.409651	1244.689302	.000803	.080582	100.300097	.009970	276
24	13.845682	1401.347173	.000713	.072224	101.211853	.009880	288
25	15.447888	1576.133312	.000634	.064733	102.029043	.009801	300

11% Monthly Compound Interest Table (continued)

EFFECTIVE RATE = 11/12% BASE = 1.00916667

YEARS	1 AMOUNT OF 1 AT COMPOUND INTEREST $S^n = (1+i)^n$	2 ACCUMULATION OF 1 PER PERIOD $S_{\overline{n}\rvert} = \frac{S^n - 1}{i}$	3 SINKING FUND FACTOR $1/S_{\overline{n}\rvert} = \frac{i}{S^n - 1}$	4 PRES. VALUE OF REVERSION OF 1 $V^n = \frac{1}{S^n}$	5 PRESENT VALUE ORD. ANNUITY 1 PER PERIOD $a_{\overline{n}\rvert} = \frac{1 - V^n}{i}$	6 INSTALLMENT TO AMORTIZE 1 (LOAN CONSTANT) $1/a_{\overline{n}\rvert} = \frac{i}{1 - V^n}$	n MONTHS
26	17.235500	1771.145496	.000564	.058019	102.761477	.009731	312
27	19.229972	1988.724266	.000502	.052002	103.417946	.009669	324
28	21.455242	2231.480999	.000448	.046608	104.066327	.009614	336
29	23.938018	2502.329255	.000399	.041774	104.533684	.009566	348
30	26.708097	2804.519759	.000356	.037441	105.006345	.009523	360
31	29.798727	3141.679397	.000318	.033558	105.429983	.009484	372
32	33.247002	3517.854756	.000284	.030077	105.809682	.009450	384
33	37.094306	3937.560686	.000253	.026958	106.150002	.009420	396
34	41.386816	4405.834502	.000226	.024162	106.455022	.009393	408
35	46.176050	4928.296419	.000202	.021656	106.728408	.009369	420
36	51.519489	5511.217017	.000181	.019410	106.973440	.009348	432
37	57.481264	6161.592513	.000162	.017396	107.193057	.009328	444
38	64.132930	6887.228705	.000145	.015592	107.389896	.009311	456
39	71.554318	7696.834666	.000129	.013975	107.566320	.009296	468
40	79.834500	8600.127295	.000116	.012525	107.724446	.009282	480
41	89.072856	9607.947896	.000104	.011226	107.866170	.009270	492
42	99.380263	10732.392330	.000093	.010062	107.993196	.009259	504
43	110.880431	11986.956140	.000083	.009018	108.107048	.009250	516
44	123.711386	13386.696640	.000074	.008083	108.209091	.009241	528
45	138.027124	14948.413480	.000066	.007244	108.300550	.009233	540
46	153.999462	16690.850360	.000059	.006493	108.382523	.009226	552
47	171.820100	18634.920020	.000053	.005820	108.455995	.009220	564
48	191.702923	20803.955170	.000048	.005216	108.521846	.009214	576
49	213.886562	23223.988540	.000043	.004675	108.580868	.009209	588
50	238.637266	25924.065330	.000038	.004190	108.633767	.009205	600

11% Quarterly Compound Interest Table

EFFECTIVE RATE = 2¼% BASE = 1.0275

QUARTERS	1 AMOUNT OF 1 AT COMPOUND INTEREST $S^n = (1+i)^n$	2 ACCUMULATION OF 1 PER PERIOD $S\overline{n\rvert} = \frac{S^n - 1}{i}$	3 SINKING FUND FACTOR $1/S\overline{n\rvert} = \frac{i}{S^n - 1}$	4 PRES. VALUE OF REVERSION OF 1 $V^n = \frac{1}{S^n}$	5 PRESENT VALUE ORD. ANNUITY 1 PER PERIOD $a\overline{n\rvert} = \frac{1 - V^n}{i}$	6 INSTALLMENT TO AMORTIZE 1 (LOAN CONSTANT) $1/a\overline{n\rvert} = \frac{i}{1 - V^n}$	n QUARTERS
1	1.027500	1.000000	1.000000	.973236	.973326	1.027500	1
2	1.055756	2.027500	.493218	.947188	1.920424	.520718	2
3	1.084790	3.083256	.324332	.921838	2.842262	.351832	3
YEARS							
1	1.114621	4.168046	.239921	.897166	3.739428	.267421	4
2	1.242381	8.813838	.113458	.804906	7.094314	.140958	8
3	1.384784	13.992137	.071469	.722134	10.104204	.098969	12
4	1.543509	19.763980	.050597	.647874	12.804573	.078097	16
5	1.720428	26.197398	.038172	.581251	15.227252	.065672	20
6	1.917626	33.368222	.029969	.521478	17.400797	.057469	24
7	2.137427	41.360975	.024177	.467852	19.350826	.051677	28
8	2.382421	50.269868	.019893	.419741	21.100326	.047393	32
9	2.655498	60.199910	.016611	.376577	22.669918	.044111	36
10	2.959874	71.268145	.014032	.337852	24.078101	.041532	40
11	3.299138	83.605035	.011961	.303109	25.341475	.039461	44
12	3.677290	97.355996	.010272	.271939	26.474931	.037772	48
13	4.098785	112.683108	.008874	.243975	27.491829	.036374	52
14	4.568593	129.767034	.007706	.218886	28.404155	.035206	56
15	5.092251	148.809141	.006720	.196377	29.222662	.034220	60
16	5.675932	170.033877	.005881	.176183	29.956999	.033381	64
17	6.326514	193.691420	.005163	.158065	30.615821	.032663	68
18	7.051667	220.060621	.004544	.141810	31.206893	.032044	72
19	7.859938	249.452292	.004009	.127227	31.737183	.031509	76
20	8.760854	282.212874	.003543	.114144	32.212941	.031043	80
21	9.765034	318.728514	.003137	.102406	32.639775	.030637	84
22	10.884315	359.429624	.002782	.091875	33.022715	.030282	88
23	12.131889	404.795946	.002470	.082427	33.366276	.029970	92
24	13.522461	455.362213	.002196	.073951	33.674508	.029696	96
25	15.072422	511.724449	.001954	.066346	33.951042	.029454	100
26	16.800042	574.546995	.001741	.059524	34.199140	.029241	104
27	18.725684	644.570341	.001551	.053403	34.421724	.029051	108
28	20.872046	722.619851	.001384	.047911	34.621419	.028884	112
29	23.264426	809.615495	.001235	.042984	34.800579	.028735	116
30	25.931024	906.582688	.001103	.038564	34.961315	.028603	120

11% Quarterly Compound Interest Table (continued)

EFFECTIVE RATE = 2¼% BASE = 1.0275

YEARS	1 AMOUNT OF 1 AT COMPOUND INTEREST $S^n = (1 + i)^n$	2 ACCUMU-LATION OF 1 PER PERIOD $S\overline{n\rvert} = \frac{S^n - 1}{i}$	3 SINKING FUND FACTOR $1/S\overline{n\rvert} = \frac{i}{S^n - 1}$	4 PRES. VALUE OF REVERSION OF 1 $V^n = \frac{1}{S^n}$	5 PRESENT VALUE ORD. ANNUITY 1 PER PERIOD $a\overline{n\rvert} = \frac{1 - V^n}{i}$	6 INSTALL-MENT TO AMORTIZE 1 (LOAN CONSTANT) $1/a\overline{n\rvert} = \frac{i}{1 - V^n}$	n QUARTERS
31	28.903271	1014.664383	.000986	.034598	35.105521	.028486	124
32	32.216200	1135.134539	.000881	.031040	35.234899	.028381	128
33	35.908861	1269.413135	.000788	.027848	35.350972	.028288	132
34	40.024780	1419.082912	.000705	.024985	35.455108	.028205	136
35	44.612471	1585.908029	.000631	.022415	35.548536	.028131	140
36	49.726008	1771.854850	.000564	.020110	35.632356	.028064	144
37	55.425666	1979.115130	.000505	.018042	35.707557	.028005	148
38	61.778626	2210.131845	.000452	.016187	35.775024	.027952	152
39	68.859770	2467.627986	.000405	.014522	35.835554	.027905	156
40	76.752563	2754.638659	.000363	.013029	35.889859	.027863	160
41	85.550039	3074.546857	.000325	.011689	35.938579	.027825	164
42	95.355892	3431.123335	.000291	.010487	35.982290	.027791	168
43	106.285704	3828.571058	.000261	.009409	36.021505	.027761	172
44	118.468305	4271.574742	.000234	.008441	36.056688	.027734	176
45	132.047292	4765.356065	.000210	.007573	36.088253	.027710	180
46	147.182719	5315.735225	.000188	.006794	36.116572	.027688	184
47	164.052987	5929.199538	.000169	.006096	36.141978	.027669	188
48	182.856947	6612.979902	.000151	.005469	36.164773	.027651	192
49	203.816241	7375.136033	.000136	.004906	36.185223	.027636	196
50	227.177915	8224.651458	.000122	.004402	36.203570	.027622	200
51	253.217334	9171.539411	.000109	.003949	36.220030	.027609	204
52	282.241424	10266.960850	.000098	.003543	36.234798	.027598	208
53	314.592291	11403.356030	.000088	.003179	36.248047	.027588	212
54	350.651256	12714.591110	.000079	.002852	36.259933	.027579	216
55	390.843344	14176.121600	.000071	.002559	36.270597	.027571	220
56	435.642300	15805.174560	.000063	.002295	36.280165	.027563	224
57	485.576169	17620.951610	.000057	.002059	36.288749	.027557	228
58	541.233522	19644.855330	.000051	.001848	36.296450	.027551	232
59	603.270389	21900.741430	.000046	.001658	36.303359	.027546	236
60	672.418001	24415.200040	.000041	.001487	36.309557	.027541	240

11% Semi-Annual Compound Interest Table

EFFECTIVE RATE = 5½% BASE = 1.055

HALF YEARS	1 AMOUNT OF 1 AT COMPOUND INTEREST $S^n = (1 + i)^n$	2 ACCUMULATION OF 1 PER PERIOD $S\overline{n\rceil} = \frac{S^n - 1}{i}$	3 SINKING FUND FACTOR $1/S\overline{n\rceil} = \frac{i}{S^n - 1}$	4 PRES. VALUE OF REVERSION OF 1 $V^n = \frac{1}{S^n}$	5 PRESENT VALUE ORD. ANNUITY 1 PER PERIOD $a\overline{n\rceil} = \frac{1 - V^n}{i}$	6 INSTALLMENT TO AMORTIZE 1 (LOAN CONSTANT) $1/a\overline{n\rceil} = \frac{i}{1 - V^n}$	n HALF YEARS
1	1.055000	1.000000	1.000000	.947867	.947867	1.055000	1
YEARS							
1	1.113025	2.055000	.486618	.898452	1.846320	.541618	2
2	1.238825	4.342266	.230294	.807217	3.505150	.285294	4
3	1.378843	6.888051	.145179	.725246	4.995530	.200179	6
4	1.534687	9.721573	.102864	.651599	6.334566	.157864	8
5	1.708144	12.875354	.077668	.585431	7.537626	.132668	10
6	1.901207	16.385591	.061029	.525982	8.618518	.116029	12
7	2.116091	20.292572	.049279	.472569	9.589648	.104279	14
8	2.355263	24.641140	.040583	.424581	10.462162	.095583	16
9	2.621466	29.481205	.033920	.381466	11.246074	.088920	18
10	2.917757	34.868318	.028679	.342729	11.950382	.083679	20
11	3.247537	40.864310	.024471	.307926	12.583170	.079471	22
12	3.614590	47.537998	.021036	.276657	13.151699	.076036	24
13	4.023129	54.965980	.018183	.248563	13.662495	.073193	26
14	4.477843	63.233510	.015814	.223322	14.121422	.070814	28
15	4.983951	72.435478	.013805	.200644	14.533745	.068805	30
16	5.547262	82.677498	.012095	.180269	14.904198	.067095	32
17	6.174242	94.077122	.010630	.161963	15.237033	.065630	34
18	6.872085	106.765189	.009366	.145516	15.536068	.064366	36
19	7.648803	120.887324	.008272	.130739	15.804738	.063272	38
20	8.513309	136.605614	.007320	.117463	16.046125	.062320	40
21	9.475526	154.100464	.006489	.105535	16.262999	.061489	42
22	10.546497	173.572669	.005761	.094818	16.457851	.060761	44
23	11.738515	195.245720	.005122	.085190	16.632915	.060122	46
24	13.065260	219.368367	.004559	.076539	16.790203	.059559	48
25	14.541961	246.217477	.004061	.068767	16.931518	.059061	50
26	16.185566	276.101207	.003622	.061783	17.058483	.058622	52
27	18.014940	309.362546	.003232	.055509	17.172555	.058232	54
28	20.051079	346.383248	.002887	.049873	17.275043	.057887	56
29	22.317352	387.588214	.002580	.044808	17.367124	.057580	58
30	24.839770	433.450372	.002307	.040258	17.449854	.057307	60
31	27.647286	484.496101	.002064	.036170	17.524183	.057064	62
32	30.772120	541.311272	.001847	.032497	18.590965	.056847	64
33	34.250139	604.547979	.001654	.029197	17.650964	.056654	66
34	38.121261	674.932014	.001482	.026232	17.704871	.056482	68
35	42.429916	753.271205	.001328	.023568	17.753304	.056328	70

11% Semi-Annual Compound Interest Table (continued)

EFFECTIVE RATE = 5½% BASE = 1.055

YEARS	1 AMOUNT OF 1 AT COMPOUND INTEREST $S^n = (1+i)^n$	2 ACCUMULATION OF 1 PER PERIOD $S\overline{n\rfloor} = \frac{S^n - 1}{i}$	3 SINKING FUND FACTOR $1/S\overline{n\rfloor} = \frac{i}{S^n - 1}$	4 PRES. VALUE OF REVERSION OF 1 $V^n = \frac{1}{S^n}$	5 PRESENT VALUE ORD. ANNUITY 1 PER PERIOD $a\overline{n\rfloor} = \frac{1 - V^n}{i}$	6 INSTALLMENT TO AMORTIZE 1 (LOAN CONSTANT) $1/a\overline{n\rfloor} = \frac{i}{1 - V^n}$	n HALF YEARS
36	47.225558	840.464683	.001190	.021175	17.796819	.056190	72
37	52.563226	937.513204	.001067	.019025	17.835914	.056067	74
38	58.504185	1045.530634	.000956	.017093	17.871040	.055956	76
39	65.116620	1165.756734	.000858	.015357	17.902599	.055858	78
40	72.476426	1299.571389	.000769	.013798	17.930953	.055769	80
41	80.668074	1448.510445	.000690	.012396	17.956428	.055690	82
42	89.785584	1614.283338	.000619	.011138	17.979316	.055619	84
43	99.933599	1798.792713	.000556	.010007	17.999879	.055556	86
44	111.228594	2004.156260	.000499	.008990	18.018355	.055499	88
45	123.800206	2232.731022	.000448	.008078	18.034954	.055448	90
46	137.792725	2487.140445	.000402	.007257	18.049868	.055402	92
47	153.366747	2770.304495	.000361	.006520	18.063267	.055361	94
48	170.701024	3085.473160	.000324	.005858	18.075306	.055324	96
49	189.994507	3436.263764	.000291	.005263	18.086122	.055291	98
50	211.468636	3826.702476	.000261	.004729	18.095839	.055261	100
51	235.369879	4261.270524	.000235	.004249	18.104570	.055235	102
52	261.972559	4744.955625	.000211	.003817	18.112415	.055211	104
53	291.582008	5283.309235	.000189	.003430	18.119462	.055189	106
54	324.538064	5882.510262	.000170	.003081	18.125795	.005170	108
55	361.218979	6549.435984	.000153	.002768	18.131484	.055153	110
56	402.045754	7291.740985	.000137	.002487	18.136595	.055137	112
57	447.486976	8117.945011	.000123	.002235	18.141187	.055123	114
58	498.064191	9037.530746	.000111	.002008	18.145313	.055111	116
59	554.357896	10061.052660	.000099	.001804	18.149020	.055099	118
60	617.014197	11200.258130	.000089	.001621	18.152351	.055089	120

11% Annual Compound Interest Table

EFFECTIVE RATE = 11% BASE = 1.11

YEARS	1 AMOUNT OF 1 AT COMPOUND INTEREST $S^n = (1+i)^n$	2 ACCUMULATION OF 1 PER PERIOD $S\overline{n}\rvert = \frac{S^n - 1}{i}$	3 SINKING FUND FACTOR $1/S\overline{n}\rvert = \frac{i}{S^n - 1}$	4 PRES. VALUE OF REVERSION OF 1 $V^n = \frac{1}{S^n}$	5 PRESENT VALUE ORD. ANNUITY 1 PER PERIOD $a\overline{n}\rvert = \frac{1 - V^n}{i}$	6 INSTALLMENT TO AMORTIZE 1 (LOAN CONSTANT) $1/a\overline{n}\rvert = \frac{i}{1 - V^n}$	n YEARS
1	1.110000	1.000000	1.000000	.900901	.900901	1.110000	1
2	1.232100	2.110000	.473934	.811622	1.712523	.583934	2
3	1.367631	3.342100	.299213	.731191	2.443715	.409213	3
4	1.518070	4.709731	.212326	.658731	3.102446	.322326	4
5	1.685058	6.227801	.160570	.593451	3.695897	.270570	5
6	1.870415	7.912860	.126377	.534641	4.230538	.236377	6
7	2.076160	9.783274	.102215	.481658	4.712196	.212215	7
8	2.304538	11.859434	.084321	.433926	5.146123	.194321	8
9	2.558037	14.163972	.070602	.390925	5.537048	.180602	9
10	2.839421	16.722009	.059801	.352184	5.889232	.169801	10
11	3.151757	19.561430	.051121	.317283	6.206515	.161121	11
12	3.498451	22.713187	.044027	.285841	6.492356	.154027	12
13	3.883280	26.211638	.038151	.257514	6.749870	.148151	13
14	4.310441	30.094918	.033228	.231995	6.981865	.143228	14
15	4.784589	34.405359	.029065	.209004	7.190870	.139065	15
16	5.310894	39.189948	.025517	.188292	7.379162	.135517	16
17	5.895093	44.500843	.022471	.169633	7.548794	.132471	17
18	6.543553	50.395936	.019843	.152822	7.701617	.129843	18
19	7.263344	56.939488	.017563	.137678	7.839294	.127563	19
20	8.062312	64.202832	.015576	.124034	7.963328	.125576	20
21	8.949166	72.265144	.013838	.111742	8.075070	.123838	21
22	9.933574	81.214310	.012313	.100669	8.175739	.122313	22
23	11.026267	91.147884	.010971	.090693	8.266432	.120971	23
24	12.239157	102.174151	.009787	.081705	8.348137	.119787	24
25	13.585464	114.413307	.008740	.073608	8.421745	.118740	25
26	15.079865	127.998771	.007813	.066314	8.488058	.117813	26
27	16.738650	143.078636	.006989	.059742	8.547800	.116989	27
28	18.579901	159.817286	.006257	.053822	8.601622	.116257	28
29	20.623691	178.397187	.005605	.048488	8.650110	.115605	29
30	22.892297	199.020878	.005025	.043683	8.693793	.115025	30
31	25.410449	221.913175	.004506	.039354	8.733146	.114506	31
32	28.205599	247.323624	.004043	.035454	8.768600	.114043	32
33	31.308214	275.529222	.003629	.031940	8.800541	.113629	33
34	34.752118	306.837437	.003259	.028775	8.829316	.113259	34
35	38.574851	341.589555	.002927	.025924	8.855240	.112927	35

11% Annual Compound Interest Table (continued)

EFFECTIVE RATE = 11% BASE = 1.11

YEARS	1 AMOUNT OF 1 AT COMPOUND INTEREST $S^n = (1 + i)^n$	2 ACCUMU- LATION OF 1 PER PERIOD $S\overline{n}\rvert = \frac{S^n - 1}{i}$	3 SINKING FUND FACTOR $1/S\overline{n}\rvert = \frac{i}{S^n - 1}$	4 PRES. VALUE OF REVERSION OF 1 $V^n = \frac{1}{S^n}$	5 PRESENT VALUE ORD. ANNUITY 1 PER PERIOD $a\overline{n}\rvert = \frac{1 - V^n}{i}$	6 INSTALL- MENT TO AMORTIZE 1 (LOAN CONSTANT) $1/a\overline{n}\rvert = \frac{i}{1 - V^n}$	n YEARS
36	42.818085	380.164406	.002630	.023355	8.878594	.112630	36
37	47.528074	422.982490	.002364	.021040	8.899635	.112364	37
38	52.756162	470.510564	.002125	.018955	8.918590	.112125	38
39	58.559340	523.266726	.001911	.017077	8.935666	.111911	39
40	65.000867	581.826066	.001719	.015384	8.951051	.111719	40
41	72.150963	646.826934	.001546	.013860	8.964911	.111546	41
42	80.087569	718.977896	.001391	.012486	8.977397	.111391	42
43	88.897201	799.065465	.001251	.011249	8.988646	.111251	43
44	98.675893	887.962666	.001126	.010134	8.998780	.111126	44
45	109.530242	986.638559	.001014	.009130	9.007910	.111014	45
46	121.578568	1096.168801	.000912	.008225	9.016135	.110912	46
47	134.952211	1217.747369	.000821	.007410	9.023545	.110821	47
48	149.796954	1352.699580	.000739	.006676	9.030221	.110739	48
49	166.274619	1502.496534	.000666	.006014	9.036235	.110666	49
50	184.564827	1668.771153	.000599	.005418	9.041653	.110599	50
51	204.866958	1853.335979	.000540	.004881	9.046534	.110540	51
52	227.402323	2058.202936	.000486	.004397	9.050932	.110486	52
53	252.416579	2285.605259	.000438	.003962	9.054894	.110438	53
54	280.182402	2538.021837	.000394	.003569	9.058463	.110394	54
55	311.002466	2818.204239	.000355	.003215	9.061678	.110355	55
56	345.212738	3129.206705	.000320	.002897	9.064575	.110320	56
57	383.186139	3474.419443	.000288	.002610	9.067185	.110288	57
58	425.336614	3857.605581	.000259	.002351	9.069536	.110259	58
59	472.123641	4282.942195	.000233	.002118	9.071654	.110233	59
60	524.057242	4755.065835	.000210	.001908	9.073562	.110210	60

APPENDIX D

RESIDENTIAL CONSTRUCTION BASIC DESIGN AND TERMINOLOGY

LOCATING BUILDING & EXCAVATION LINES

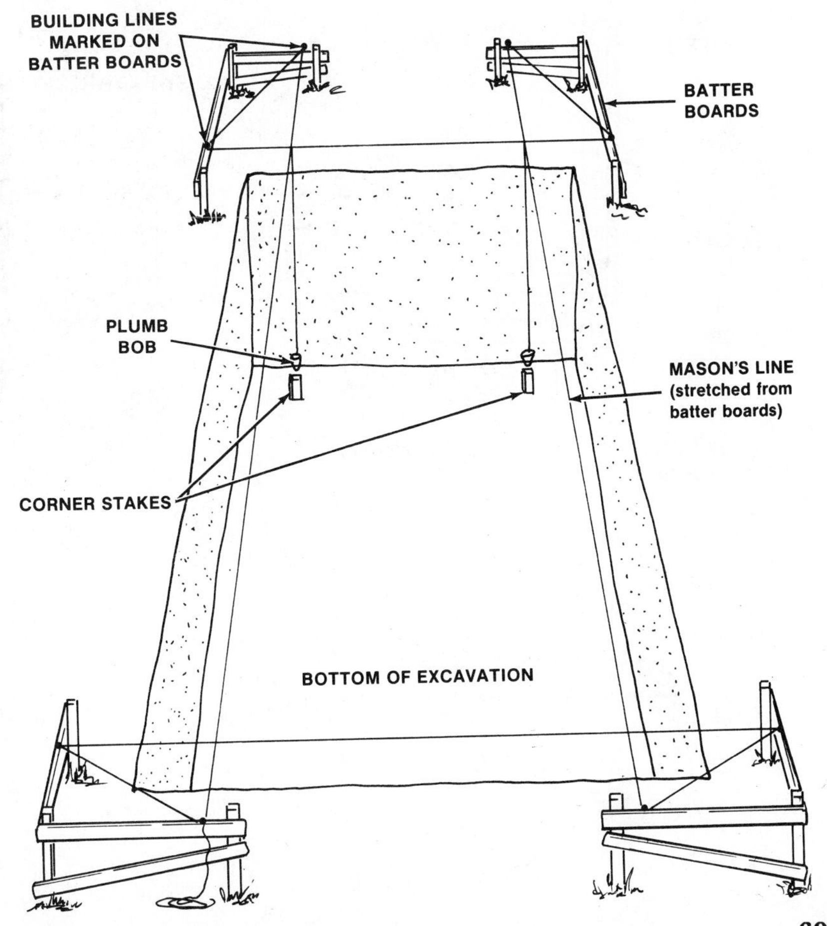

FRAMING COMPONENTS

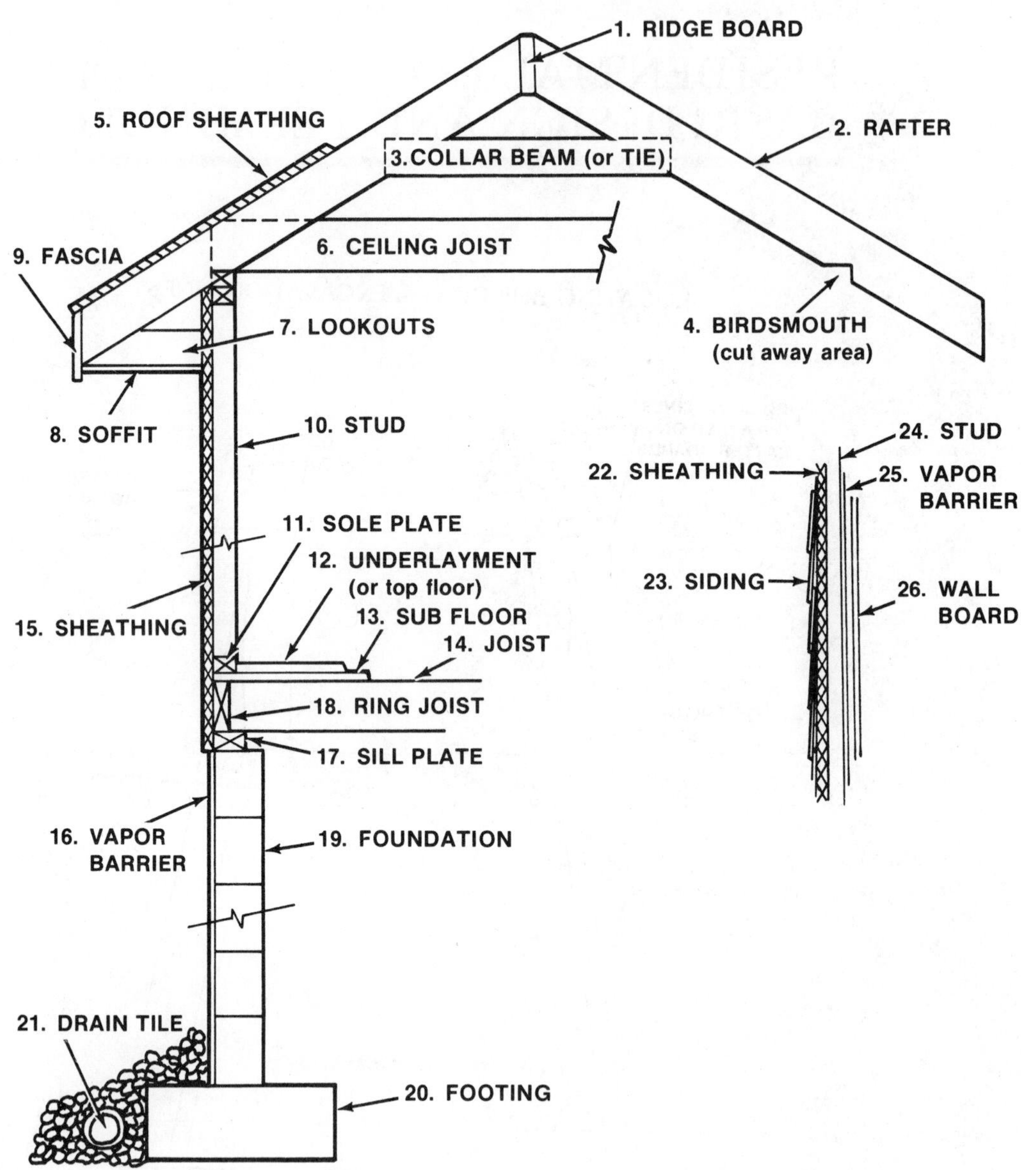

WALL AND COLUMN FOOTINGS

POOR FOOTINGS

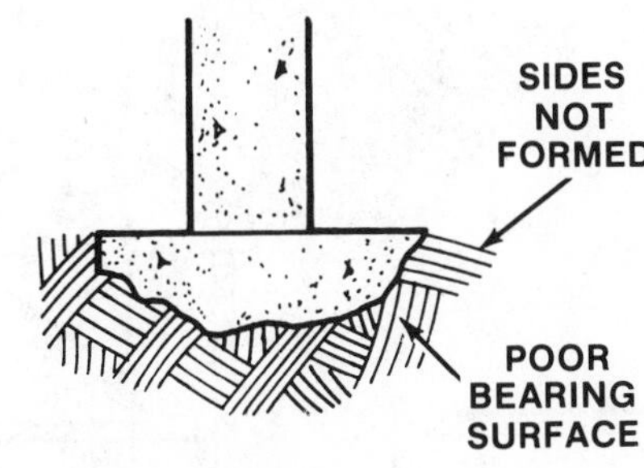

INSUFFICIENT SIZE AND THICKNESS

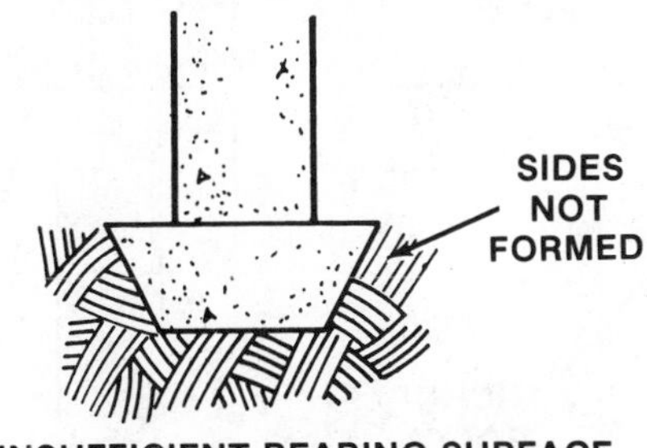

INSUFFICIENT BEARING SURFACE
POOR SHAPE

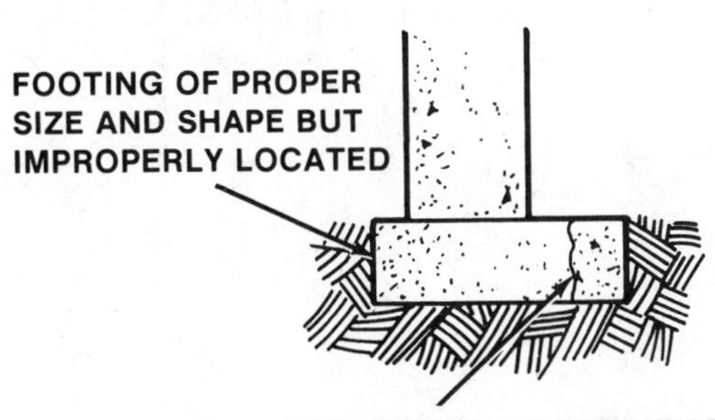

PROPER FOOTING

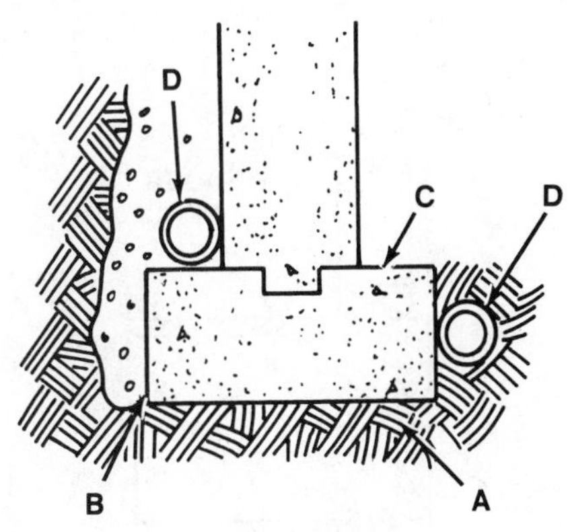

A. BOTTOM FLAT AND HORIZONTAL.

B. SIDES VERTICALLY FORMED.

C. PROPER WIDTH AND THICKNESS.

D. DRAIN TILE WHEN REQUIRED.

TYPES OF SILLS

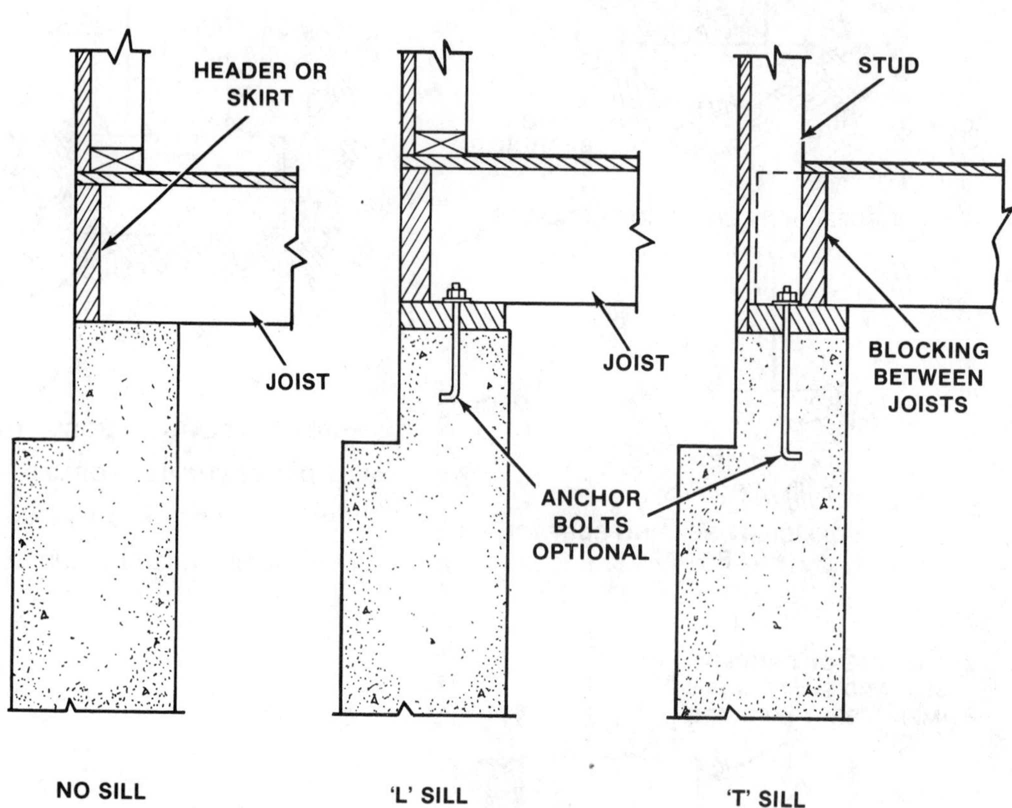

MODERN BRACED FRAMING

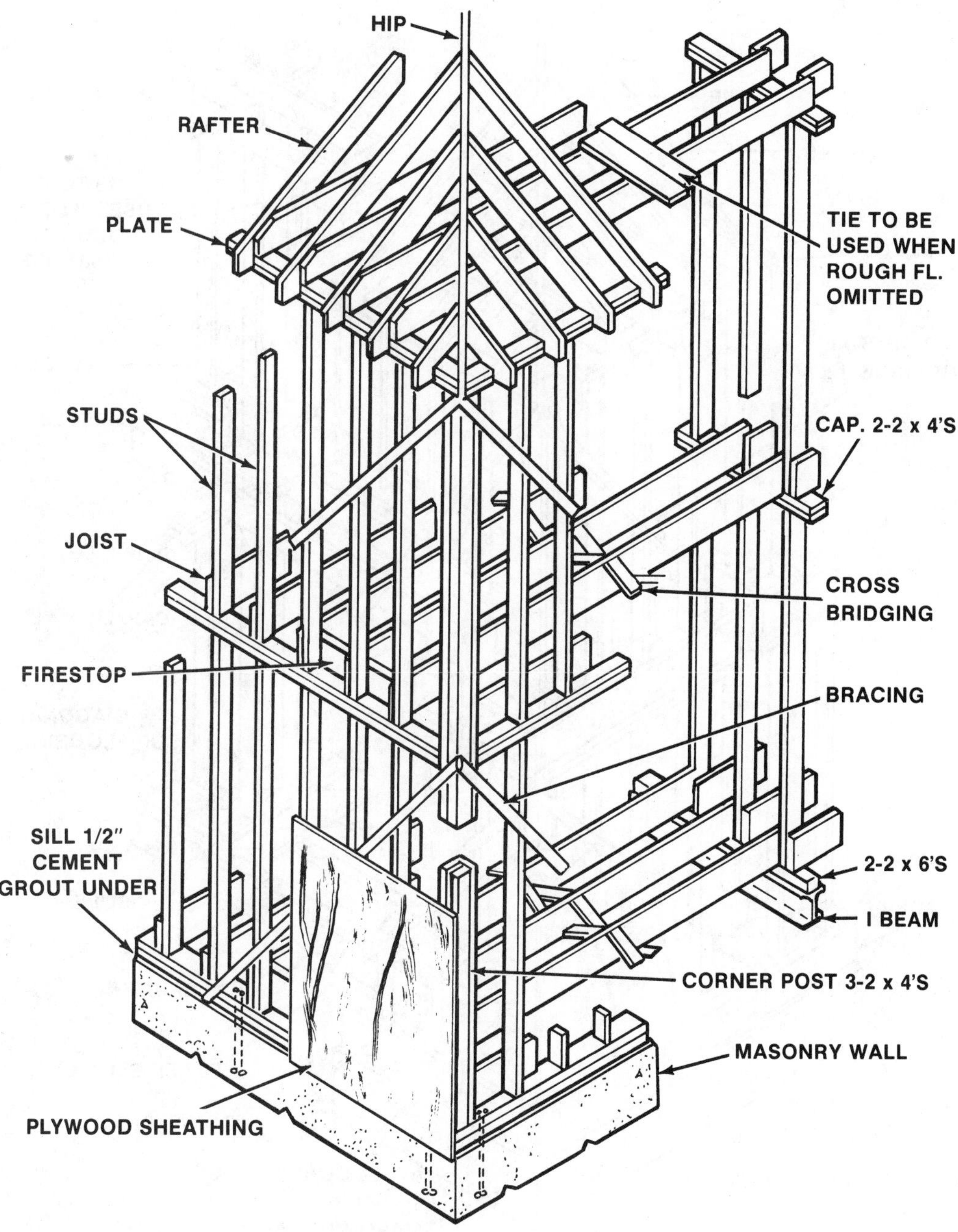

WESTERN OR PLATFORM FRAMING

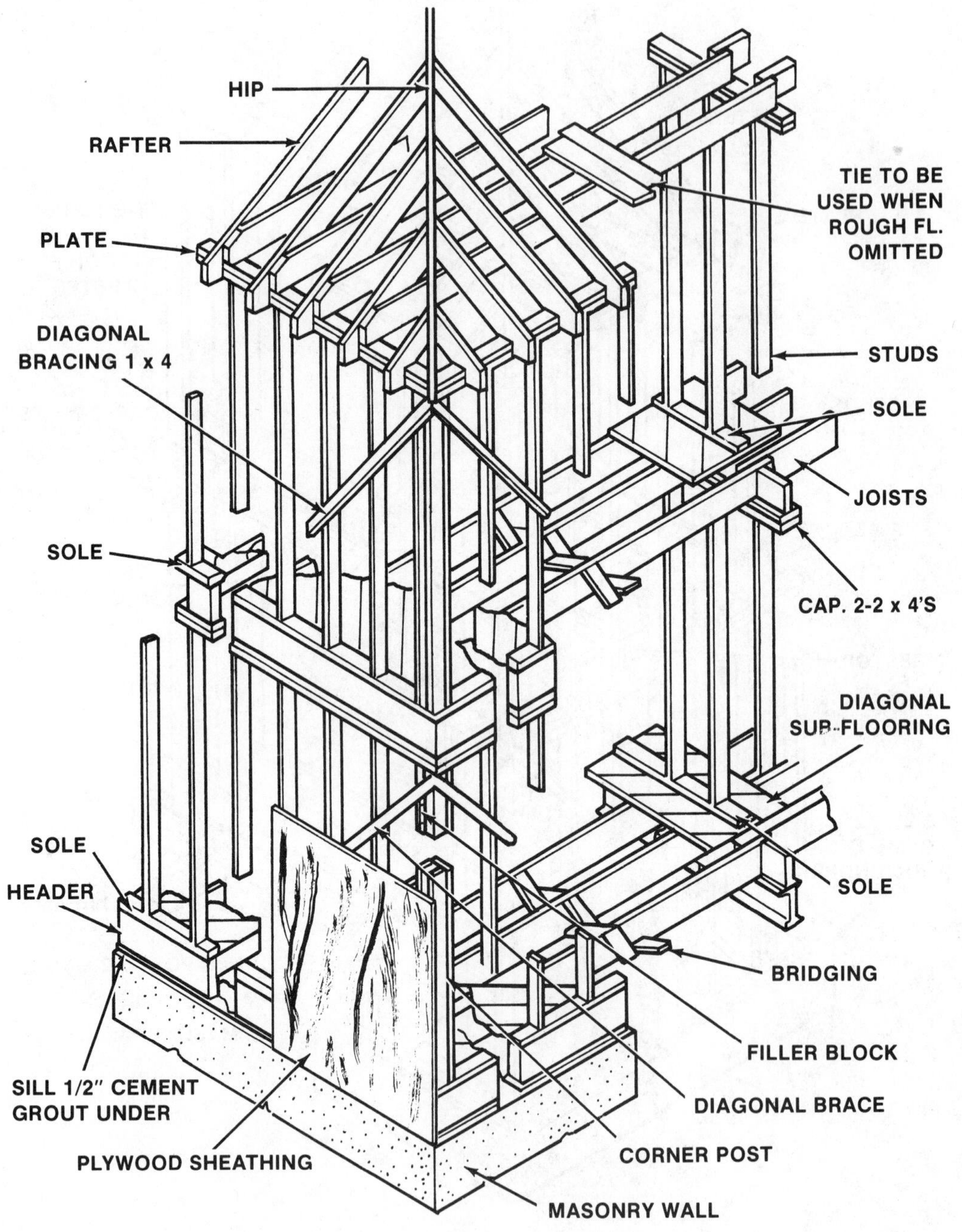

FRAMING FLOOR OPENINGS

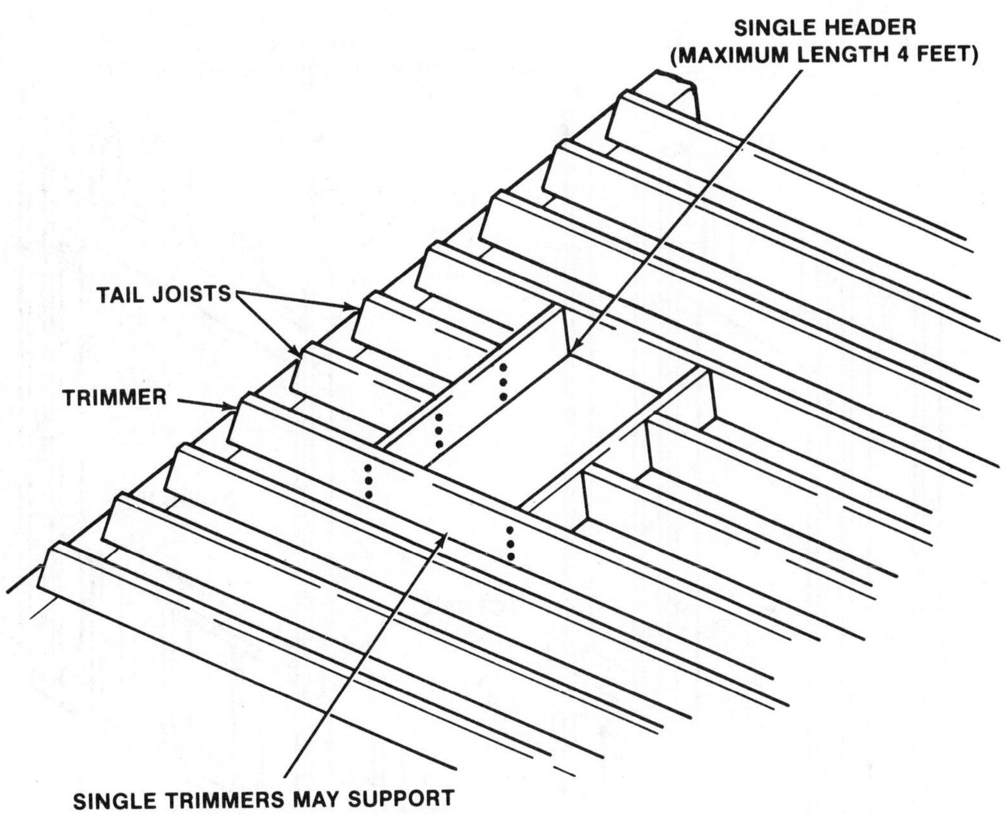

FRAMING WALL OPENINGS

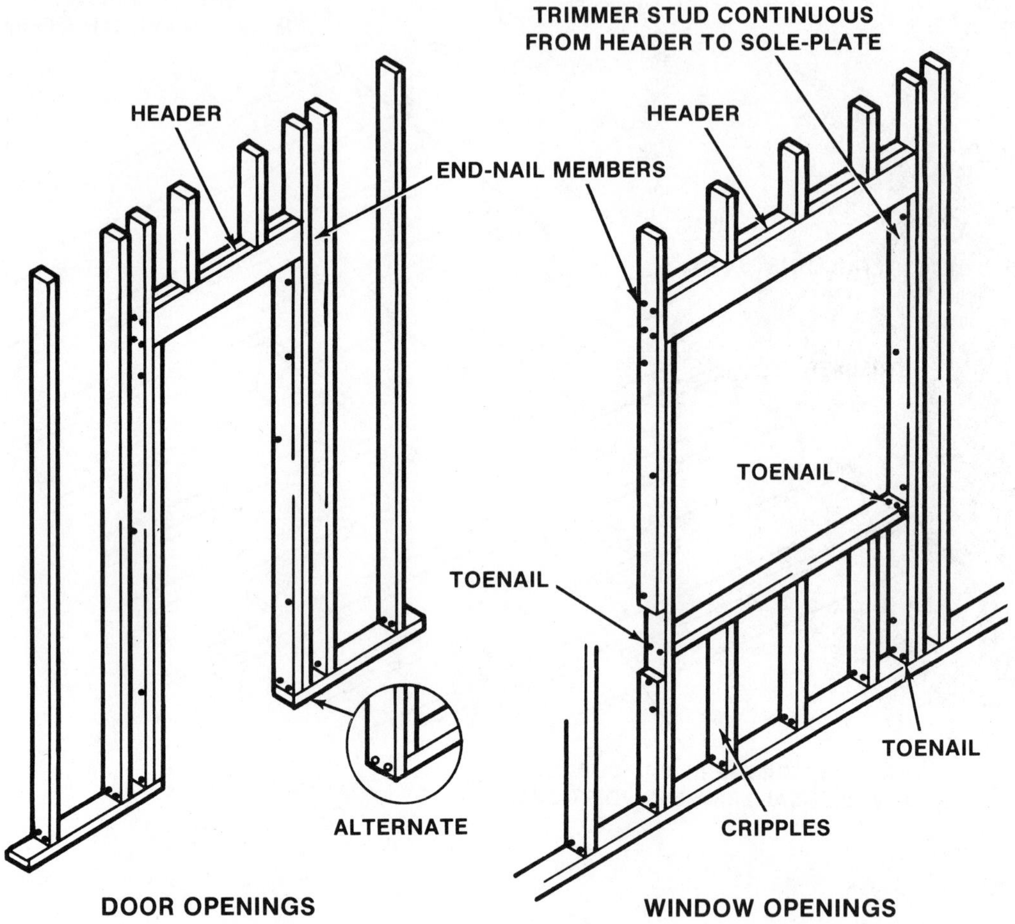

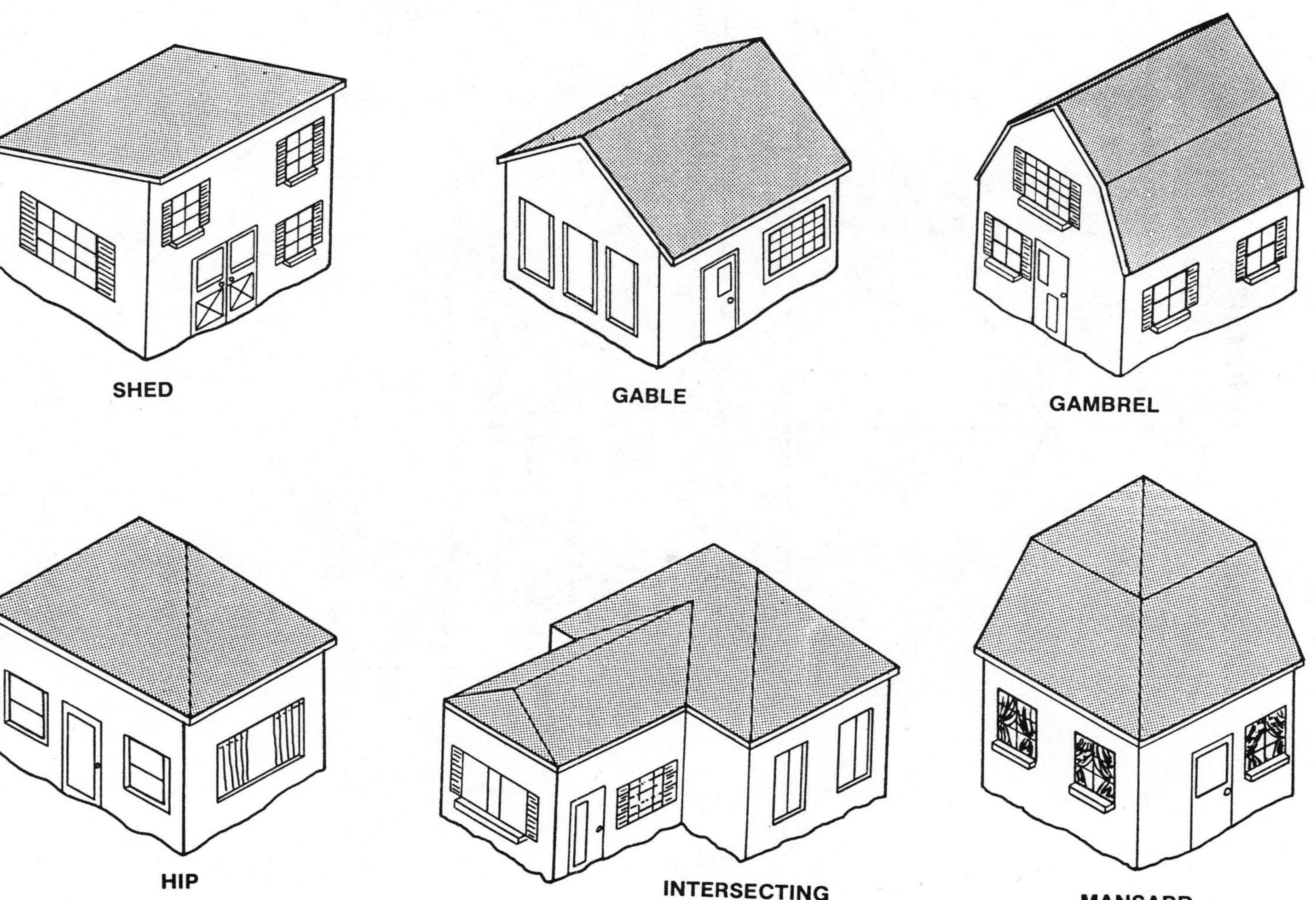
ROOF TYPES
SHED
GABLE
GAMBREL
HIP
INTERSECTING
MANSARD

ROOF FRAMING TERMS

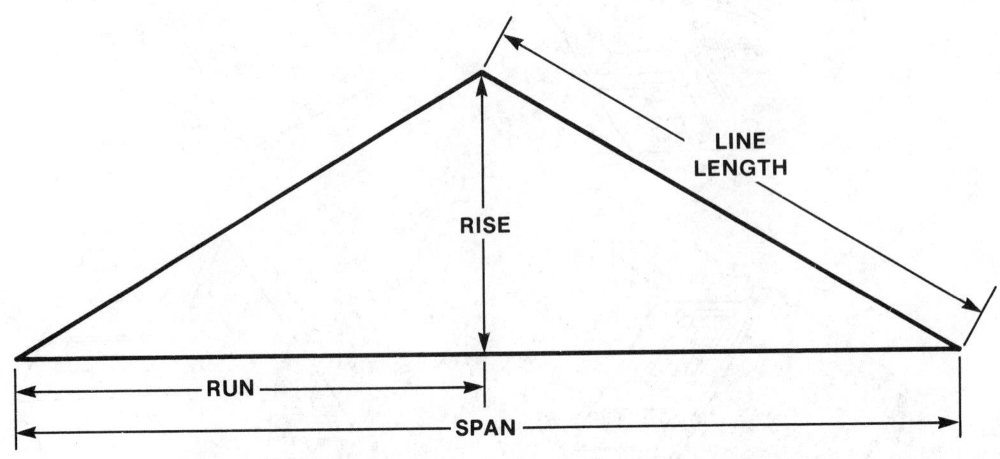

SPAN -- BUILDING WIDTH

RUN -- ONE-HALF SPAN

RISE -- DISTANCE RAFTER RISES ABOVE PLATE

LINE LENGTH -- LENGTH OF RAFTER (before shortening)

$$\text{PITCH} = \frac{\text{RISE}}{\text{SPAN}}$$

RAFTERS

COMMONS
VALLEY JACKS
VALLEY
TOP PLATE
RIDGE
HIP-JACKS
CRIPPLE
HIP-JACKS
HIPS

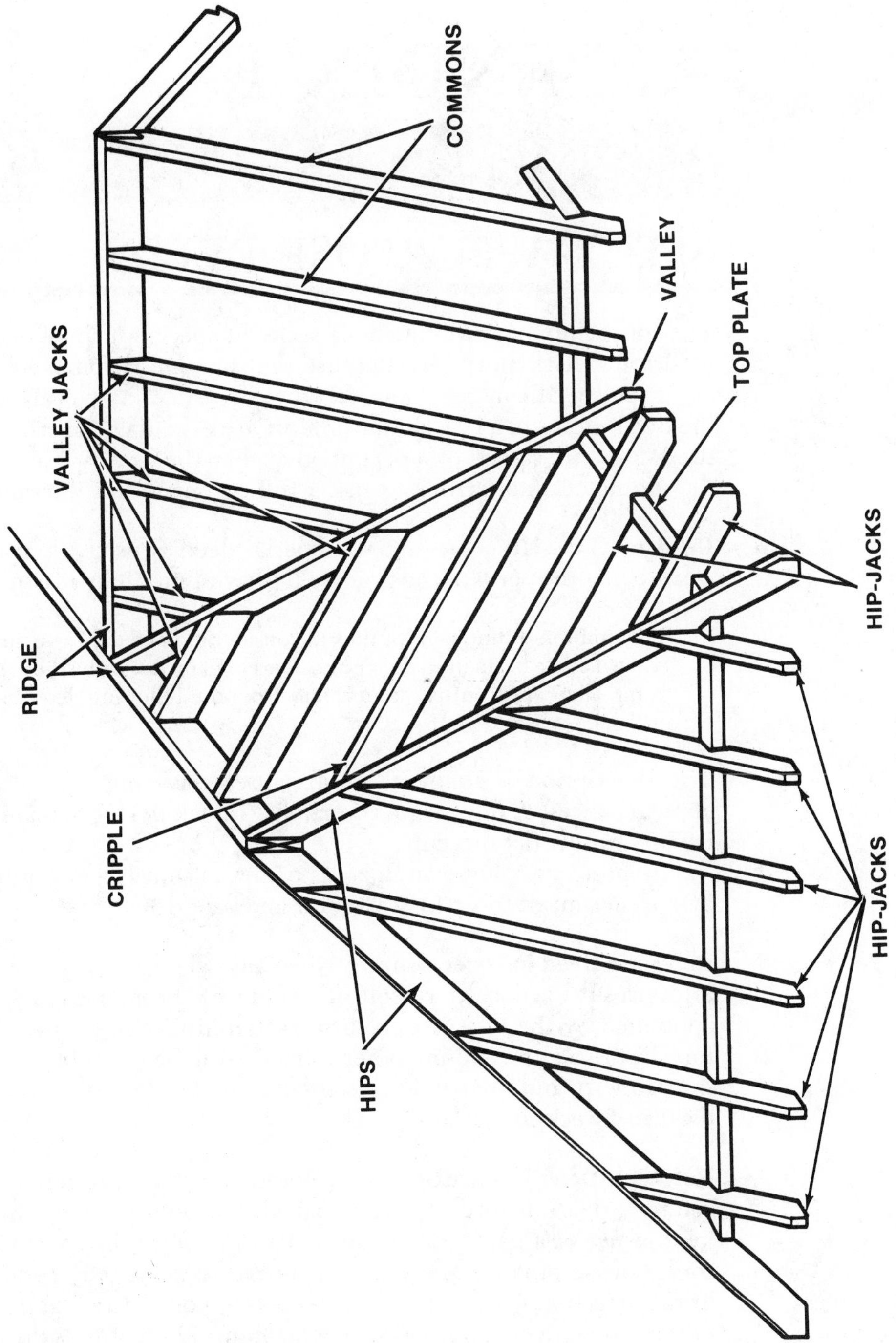

APPENDIX E

SPECIAL PURPOSE DEEDS

The following pages will discuss a series of special purpose deeds that are used for specific purposes. Because they are special purpose deeds, they are given specific names; however, they are in reality merely variations of the deeds described in Chapter 8. Most are essentially a form of quitclaim deed. Most are signed by a person other than the true owner; consequently the grantor cannot afford to risk a full covenant and warranty deed.

Deed of Gift. In some states, a special deed is used when the grantor conveys the property to the grantee by way of gift. The instrument states:

> The grantor [John Doe] for and in consideration of the Love and Affection which he bears unto the grantee herein named does by these presents, grant, alien and confirm unto [Mary Doe] the following described property situated in . . .

The description is followed by a clause conveying the hereditaments, appurtenances, reversion or reversions, remainder or remainders, rents, issues, and profits thereof.

In most states, however, it is customary to convey a gift property either by a quitclaim deed or by a bargain and sale deed.

Referee's Deed in Foreclosure. Normally, when a mortgagee commences a foreclosure action by reason of default of the mortgagor, a referee is appointed by the court to perform certain duties in connection with the foreclosure action. Among other things, it will be the referee's duty to sell the property and to give deed to the purchaser. This deed is the referee's deed in foreclosure.

Referee's Deed in Partition. A referee's deed in partition is much like a referee's deed in foreclosure. A partition action is usually brought by a joint owner of a parcel of real property to dissolve the concurrent ownership. For example, *A* and *B* own property as tenants in common, and *B* brings an action for partition. A referee is appointed and, at the conclusion of the action, the property is sold at auction with the funds divided according to the respective rights of *A* and *B*. The purchaser at the auction will receive a referee's deed in partition from the referee.

Guardian's Deed. The guardian's deed is used to convey an interest of a minor (infant) in real property. The deed cites the court order appointing the guardian, the application of the guardian to the court for permission to convey the property, the court order authorizing the sale of the property, the full consideration for the transaction, and this covenant:

> And the said party of the first part, as guardian, covenants with the party of the second part for and in behalf of the said infant that neither party of the first part, as guardian, nor the said infant has done or suffered anything whereby the said premises have been encumbered in any way whatsoever.

Committee's Deed. The committee's deed is similar to the guardian's deed. Mentally incapacitated persons and minors are unable to make a valid conveyance. When an insane person owns real property, a committee is appointed by the court and, after having obtained the requisite permission, may convey the real property.

Deed by Assignee for Benefit of Creditors. Often a person who becomes insolvent and does not choose to file a petition in bankruptcy will hold a meeting of creditors. It may be decided that the debtor will pay off the creditors as rapidly as possible. A trust agreement is drawn between the debtor and the creditors and, among other things, the instrument appoints a trustee for the benefit of the creditors. This trustee is often called an assignee for the benefit of the creditors. The trustee's job is to gather the assets of the debtor, convert them into cash, and distribute the cash to the creditors according to the terms of the agreement made by them. If the debtor has real property, it is conveyed to the assignee by deed of assignment. The assignee is then free to convey to a third party; this is done by the deed by assignee for the benefit of creditors. This deed recites the conveyance by the debtor to the assignee, and a statement that the assignee conveys

> all the right, title, and interest that the said [Debtor] had at or immediately before the execution and delivery of said deed of assignment to the party of the first part, and also the right, title, and interest that the party of the first part acquired in, under, and by virtue of said deed of assignment.

Deed of Surrender. The deed of surrender is used to merge an estate for life or years with either a reversionary or remainder interest. This can also be accomplished by means of a quitclaim deed in which the life tenant, for example, quitclaims to the remainderman.

Correction Deed. A correction deed, sometimes called a deed of confirmation, is used to correct an error in a deed. For example, if *A* conveys to *B* and there is an error in description; *A*, on request, will correct the error. This is usually done by means of a quitclaim deed containing a statement explaining the purpose of the instrument.

If the seller refuses to correct, for example, a description in a deed, a court order known as a reformation of an instrument can be obtained to correct the error.

Cession Deed. This is a form of quitclaim deed used to convey the street rights of an abutting owner to a municipality. The purpose of the conveyance is recited in the instrument.

Deed of Release. The deed of release is used to release the described premises from a dower interest, a reverter for a breach of condition subsequent, or a remainder interest. It is, however, used mostly in connection with mortgages as described in Chapter 9.

INDEX

C

D

E

M

N

O

P

Q

R

S

T

U

V